Jihad in the City

Tawhid was a militant Islamist group which implemented Islamic law at gunpoint in the Lebanese city of Tripoli during the 1980s. In retrospect, some have called it "the first ISIS-style Emirate." Drawing on 200 interviews with Islamist fighters and their mortal enemies, as well as on a trove of new archival material, Raphaël Lefèvre provides a comprehensive account of this Islamist group. He shows how they featured religious ideologues determined to turn Lebanon into an Islamic Republic, yet also included Tripolitan rebels of all stripes, neighbourhood strongmen with scores to settle, local subalterns seeking social revenge and profit-driven gangsters, who each tried to steer Tawhid's exercise of violence to their advantage. Providing a detailed understanding of the multifaceted processes through which Tawhid emerged in 1982, implemented its "Emirate" and suddenly collapsed in 1985, this is a story that shows how militant Islamist groups are impacted by their grand ideology as much as by local contexts – with crucial lessons for understanding social movements, rebel groups and terrorist organizations elsewhere.

Raphaël Lefèvre is a Senior Research Fellow in the Department of Politics and International Relations at the University of Oxford. He is the author of *Ashes of Hama: The Muslim Brotherhood in Syria* (2013). His PhD thesis was awarded the Best Dissertation Prize by the Syrian Studies Association as well as the Bill Gates Sr. Prize. He was previously a Research Fellow at the Carnegie Endowment for International Peace's office in Beirut, where he published on Middle Eastern politics and Islamist movements.

Jihad in the City

Militant Islam and Contentious Politics in Tripoli

Raphaël Lefèvre
University of Oxford

CAMBRIDGE
UNIVERSITY PRESS

University Printing House, Cambridge CB2 8BS, United Kingdom

One Liberty Plaza, 20th Floor, New York, NY 10006, USA

477 Williamstown Road, Port Melbourne, VIC 3207, Australia

314–321, 3rd Floor, Plot 3, Splendor Forum, Jasola District Centre, New Delhi – 110025, India

79 Anson Road, #06–04/06, Singapore 079906

Cambridge University Press is part of the University of Cambridge.

It furthers the University's mission by disseminating knowledge in the pursuit of education, learning, and research at the highest international levels of excellence.

www.cambridge.org
Information on this title: www.cambridge.org/9781108426268
DOI: 10.1017/9781108564816

© Raphaël Lefèvre 2021

This publication is in copyright. Subject to statutory exception and to the provisions of relevant collective licensing agreements, no reproduction of any part may take place without the written permission of Cambridge University Press.

First published 2021

A catalogue record for this publication is available from the British Library.

ISBN 978-1-108-42626-8 Hardback
ISBN 978-1-108-44498-9 Paperback

Cambridge University Press has no responsibility for the persistence or accuracy of URLs for external or third-party internet websites referred to in this publication and does not guarantee that any content on such websites is, or will remain, accurate or appropriate.

Contents

List of Maps	*page* viii
List of Figures	ix
List of Tables	x
Acknowledgments	xi
Glossary of Concepts	xv
Note on Transliteration	xviii
Maps	xix
Introduction	1
"Welcome to Allah Square"	1
How Local Space Impacts Conflictual Mobilizations	5
How Ideology Affects Social, Rebel and Terrorist Movements	16
Researching Space and Ideology in Tawhid	28
The Structure of the Book	33
1 Tales of a Rebel City	38
The Strength of Tripolitan Identity	40
Narratives of a Lost Glory	46
The Contentious Tripolitans	52
Political and Social Antagonisms	57
Tripoli's Global Sense of Place	64
The Failure of the Left	70
Tripoli's Islamists between Ideology and Local Identity	73
The Cultural Momentum of Islamism	80
Theorizing Back	84
2 Neighborhood Islamism	88
A Stronghold of Contention	90
The *Qabaday*, Champion of Mobilization	96
Marxism or Spatially Oriented Activism?	99
Ideology to Ally across Space and Class	105
A Fateful Rapprochement	110
Neighborhood Rivalries	115
A Slum War	122
Militant Islamism as a Protest Ideology	128
From the *Hara* to the *Umma*?	137

v

vi   Contents

Neighborhood Islamism	144
Theorizing Back	153

3 The Emergence of Tawhid — 156

The Islamic Group Gets Outclassed	157
The Growth of Sufi Jihadism	166
From One Protest Ideology to Another	170
Instrumental or Sincere Embrace of Khomeinism?	175
The Emir of Tripoli	182
The Syrian Hammer and the Israeli Anvil	187
Tawhid's Rise to Islamist Stardom	196
Theorizing Back	204

4 A Vernacular Islamist Ideology — 206

On the Radical Fringes of the Muslim Brotherhood	208
A Revolutionary Political Orientation	214
Making the Islamic Republic of Lebanon	218
Vernacular Islamism	225
Tawhid's Tripolitan Habitus	229
Theorizing Back	234

5 Social Jihad — 237

Tripoli's Subalterns	239
A Tale of Two Cities	245
Criminal Violence as Contentious Politics	251
Subaltern Islamism	262
Tawhid's Social Jihad	265
Overcoming Spatial Barriers	274
Becoming Emirs	277
A New Cultural and Social Order	281
Protest Masculinity	284
A Struggle for Tripolitan Identity	288
Taking on the Notability	294
From Karame Square to Allah Square	299
Theorizing Back	305

6 The Illusion of Religious Violence — 309

Tawhid's Ideological Entrepreneurs	311
Controlled Violence in Abu Samra	321
Bloody Wednesday in Mina	329
Holy War or Social Jihad?	335
Variation in Tawhid's Anti-Christian Acts	344
The Spread of Islamo-Gangsterism	351
Theorizing Back	362

7 The Geopolitics of Islamism — 366

Cross-Border Ties to Syria's Islamists	368
In the Shadow of Fatah	375
Tripoli, Epicenter of the Palestinian Civil War	381
Palestinian, Syrian and Lebanese Islamists	385
The Genesis of the Tawhid–Iran Relationship	390

Contents   vii

From Spatially Oriented to Ideologically Driven?   395
Behind the Ideological Alliance, a Marriage of Convenience   401
Theorizing Back   411

8 The Downfall of Tawhid   415
Syria Raises the Cost of Islamist Activism   417
The Spiral of Violence   424
A Battle between Islamism and Secularism?   428
The Role of Ideology in High-Risk Activism   432
The Activation of Local Identities and Solidarities   440
The Resilience of Spatially Oriented Activism   447
The Return of Neighborhood Islamism   451
Spatial Repression in Bab al-Tebbaneh   457
Theorizing Back   465

Conclusion   468
The Importance of Space in Contentious Politics   469
Ideology in Social, Rebel and Terrorist Movements   472

Bibliography of Essential Sources   476
Index   481

Maps

1 Map of Lebanon and Syria	*page* xix
2 Neighborhoods of Tripoli	xx
3 Main sites of Tripoli	xxi

Figures

I.1 Tawhid, an ideologically heterogeneous Islamist movement	*page* 27
2.1 The timing of the Popular Resistances's ideological shift	133
2.2 Neighborhood Islamism: ideology and localized concerns	152
3.1 Esmat Murad's shift from Maoism to Khomeinist Islamism	181
3.2 Violence between pro- and anti-Assad forces in Tripoli in 1982	194
4.1 Temporal variation in Tawhid's Khomeinist ideology	219
4.2 The sudden increase of violence in Tripoli in mid-1984	220
4.3 Soliciting external support, a strategic function of ideology	221
4.4 Tawhid's ideological production: eclectic and vernacular	226
5.1 Tripoli's Outlaws between criminal and political violence	258
5.2 Subaltern Islamism, or how Tawhid courted Tripoli's poor	266
6.1 The ideological entrepreneurs, influential actors in Tawhid	321
6.2 Spatial variation in Tawhid's violence against the Communists	333
6.3 Organizational variation in Tawhid's anti-leftist violence	344
6.4 Sudden increase in Tripoli's port activities in 1984–5	354
6.5 "Islamo-gangsterism": economic gains vs. ideological consistency	357

Tables

I.1 A localism-based typology of Islamist mobilization *page* 17
I.2 An ideologically heterogeneous Islamist movement 27
5.1 Social and spatial variation of Islamist mobilization
in Tripoli 266

Acknowledgments

Writing this book was a long and arduous process. It took me seven years, half a dozen different drafts and many headaches to reach the stage when I would finally be satisfied sending my manuscript out for publication. Unquestionably, my determination to give my best throughout this drawn-out process stemmed from my passion for Tripoli, its people and history. I did not expect to develop such a passion for Tripoli. In fact, my first trip there in 2012 resulted from chance. Frustrated by my inability to return to Damascus to conduct the doctoral research I had just started on Syrian history and politics, I set my eyes on this Lebanese city: it not only used to be the coastal hub of Greater Syria but, up until today, remains organically linked to the country and still "feels" Syrian – from its architecture and its food to the family relations and cultural references of many Tripolitans. This book, therefore, is as much the product of the passion I then developed for Tripoli itself as of my older love for Syria, where I briefly lived before the 2011 revolution and underwent experiences which shaped my subsequent life journey as well as my intellectual interests. Before acknowledging the specific individuals who proved key in the elaboration of this book, then, I wanted to highlight the significance of my stays in both Syria and Lebanon's Tripoli. My emotional connection to these two places has guided this book from beginning to end.

Because this book relies extensively on ethnography, interviews and archival research in Tripoli, I first wish to thank the people who, each in their own way, provided the type of essential support without which this book could not have seen the light of day. I am deeply grateful for the friendship and assistance of many Tripolitans and friends of Tripoli. This includes Mustafa Hajar for his help in locating archival sources; Ibrahim Chalhoub for his aid in setting up interviews; Hassan Mallat and Ibrahim Saleh for their trust and opening up their contact books; Mayez Adhami for giving me access to records of his newspaper, *al-Incha*; Tine Gade, Marie Kortam, Toufic Allouche and Adib N'ame for all introducing me to the city and helping me to set up a preliminary network of contacts;

xii   Acknowledgments

Roula Naboulsi for teaching me how to speak Lebanese and Tripolitan colloquial Arabic; and finally Ali El-Yessir, Joanne Boustani, Yahya Dandashi, Wissam Tayar, Yasmine Hajar, Ali Jam, Moustafa Asaad and Ali Harfouche for acting as local research assistants at various stages throughout my research.

In turn, my ability to conduct such extensive field research in Tripoli and, also, to take the time to reflect on my findings and to write this book, stems from the generous financial support I received from key institutions and from the sometimes crucial help of specific individuals. I would like to express my gratitude, in chronological order, to Cambridge University's King's College, the Project on Middle East Political Science run by Marc Lynch, the Gates Cambridge scholarship program, the Carnegie Middle East Centre in Beirut and especially Yezid Sayigh, Lina Khatib and Maha Yahya, Oxford's New College and in particular Elizabeth Frazer and Miles Young, Cambridge's Partnership for Conflict, Crime and Security Research run by Tristram Riley-Smith, the UK Economic and Social Research Council for funding my project on "Islamo-gangsterism" as well as the University of Oxford for providing its institutional home and, finally, Aarhus University's "The Other Islamists" project headed by Morten Valbjørn and Jeroen Gunning. I deeply thank all these institutions and individuals for their financial support throughout this project.

This book started off as a doctoral dissertation which I undertook in the Department of Politics and International Studies at the University of Cambridge between 2012 and 2016. I feel incredibly privileged having benefited from the unique combination of complete freedom and thorough guidance provided by my PhD supervisor, George Joffé, who encouraged me to do much fieldwork but also asked for updates and draft chapters regularly. Being a part of the community of Gates scholarship holders also allowed me to forge lasting friendships in Cambridge and I am grateful to my friends Vaibhav, Siddhartha and Danny. During this period, finally, my work benefited from the in-depth feedback on my doctoral dissertation by two scholars I respect and admire, Yezid Sayigh and Glen Rangwala, who acted as my PhD examiners in 2016 and have since then continued to support and encourage me. I look back to the years of my PhD as stimulating and formative but also fun – and I am grateful to all these individuals for having contributed to making it such a good experience.

Although this book takes my doctoral research as its backbone, the core literatures it addresses and the arguments it makes bear little resemblance to what my thesis looked like. After getting my PhD from Cambridge, I moved to Oxford University as the Rank-Manning Junior

Acknowledgments xiii

Research Fellow in Social Sciences at New College and then as Senior Research Fellow at the Department of Politics and International Relations, a period during which I was fortunate enough to focus exclusively on engaging with theory and on writing this book. Throughout the slow and sometimes confusing process of revision which took place in Oxford, I was lucky to count on the presence of my colleagues and friends Kevin Mazur and Stathis Kalyvas, who each in their own way provided the mentoring and guidance I needed. The shape which this book took also owes a lot to a manuscript workshop I organized in May 2018 in Oxford. There, the additional comments I received and the discussions which took place helped me to turn my very empirical PhD thesis into a book more grounded in political science. I am incredibly grateful to the scholars who kindly accepted my invitation, took time off to read my draft and actively participated in the event, including Salwa Ismail, Louise Fawcett, Kevin Mazur, Stathis Kalyvas, Jeroen Gunning, Neil Ketchley and Chris Pickvance.

Overall, from the early dissertation stage all the way to the final draft of this book, the manuscript has benefited from many pairs of eyes. Some have kindly taken the time to comment on individual chapters, and here I am indebted to extremely useful feedback, in addition to the participants to my manuscript workshop, by Anne Wolf, Jean Thomas, Hanna Baumann, Rory McCarthy, Stephanie Cronin, Jonathan Leader Maynard, Sidney Tarrow, Doug McAdam, Toby Matthiesen and Morten Valbjørn. Others have shown great generosity by commenting on the entire manuscript. In this respect, in addition to my PhD supervisor and my two examiners, I am grateful to Tine Gade, whose excellent research on Tripolitan politics and society I have long admired, Saleh al-Machnouk, whose intimate knowledge of Lebanon proved insightful, and Mikael Naghizadeh, whose in-depth familiarity with the broader scholarship on conflicts helped me sharpen the manuscript before I finally sent it out. I also wish to thank the two anonymous reviewers commissioned by Cambridge University Press, whose feedback on an earlier version was key in helping me improve the manuscript. Finally, as this process took much longer than initially anticipated, I would like to express my gratitude to Maria Marsh, Daniel Brown, Atifa Jiwa and the rest of the team at Cambridge University Press for being so effective but also so kind and patient with me.

Most importantly, I want to conclude by thanking those who have been close to me every step of the way and, by providing regular encouragements throughout this drawn-out process, have contributed more than they know to my ability to finish writing this book. They include several of the friends and colleagues mentioned above who, whether from

xiv   Acknowledgments

Tripoli, Beirut, Cambridge, Oxford or Aarhus, have accompanied me throughout this long journey. But here I would especially like to express my thanks to my family. My parents Maryline and Sylvain, my two brothers Amaury and Lancelot and my grandmother Jeannine have heard me complain about my book revisions for seven years. By consistently encouraging me to pursue my project until I reached some satisfaction, they gave me the confidence I needed. In addition, I owe to Anne Wolf much more than she knows. During all this time, she has not simply been a very patient partner dealing with my occasional mood swings and providing me crucial support but, as a scholar of Middle Eastern politics herself, has been a fantastic person with whom to brainstorm on a sometimes daily basis about the intricacies of Tripoli in the 1980s and their broader significance. My drive to write this book therefore owes as much to her active presence by my sides as it does to all the Tripolitans whose stories inspired me.

Glossary of Concepts

Champion of mobilization: informal leader with such a large and dedicated following in his community that he becomes uniquely placed to activate local solidarities and to channel them into activism, thus drawing community members to the protests and movements he joins.

Contentious Tripolitans: this critical mass of Tripolitans across time who mobilize to express primarily local grievances and are buoyed by the ideal of the defense of the city.

Cultural momentum of an ideology: the set of transformations in culture (e.g. religious practice, clothing style, social views, artistic genres) which either underpins or helps pave the way for the growth of a political ideology, making it more widely available in society.

Habitus of place: the set of local historical, cultural and political narratives specific to a place which become so internalized by local actors that it pushes them to interpret the world through partially local lenses, shaping some of their concerns, beliefs and behavior.

Ideological artifacts: works of art meant to indoctrinate society by projecting ideas visually.

Ideological entrepreneurs: these highly dedicated figures at the extreme of a movement's "spectrum of ideological commitment" who are not only motivated by ideology but also go to lengths to mold the nature of activism and of the broader environment around their worldviews, typically by seeking to spread their beliefs to society and to movement members and by lobbying its leaders to make decisions consistent with or, indeed driven by, ideology.

Ideological entrepreneurship: the mobilization of worldviews with the aim of translating ideology into action in order to mold movement behavior and society around these beliefs.

xvi   Glossary of Concepts

Islamo-gangsterism: the involvement by some Islamist movements in those criminal activities and networks which prioritize economic gain over ideological consistency.

Neighborhood Islamism: an Islamist mobilization so rooted in the neighborhood's fabric that it may be shaped by local solidarities, concerns and antagonisms more than by ideology.

Protest ideology: a corpus of symbols, discourse, practices and infrastructure associated with a specific ideology but which are embraced instrumentally to express dissent because of the contentious potential they are associated with, more than because of their intrinsic appeal.

Sites of transcendence: those sites whose location, shape and history have such salient meanings in society that they hold the potential to enhance mobilizations; both by politically transcending older cleavages to enable short-term but potentially transformative coalitions across class, space and ideology and by emotionally transcending activists who rally there.

Social jihad: involvement in a type of political violence which takes the form of militant Islamism but, at core, remains more shaped by preexisting social tensions than by ideology.

Spatial barriers: those features through which space can hinder broad-based collective action because of physical properties like distance or the built-in environment, but even more importantly because of the socially and symbolically consequential local rivalries, conflicting priorities and different traditions or identities of geographically proximate spaces.

Spatial repression: a calculated attempt by the target of contention to deactivate the resources provided by space for activists, whether through physical infrastructures of support or the social and symbolic local solidarities, identities and emotions that enable mobilization, aiming at turning a "safe space" for activism into a "repressed space" where it is made harder.

Spatially oriented movements: those social movements which are not just based in a space but also oriented toward it, engaging explicitly with local grievances and identities and striving to achieve some local social change – "the local" is what they are primarily about.

Spectrum of ideological commitment: the disaggregated analysis of the strength of commitment of the main factions and figures to their movement's professed ideology, with implications on whether they will try to steer the movement toward or away from ideology.

Glossary of Concepts

Stronghold of contention: a space characterized by its propensity to nurture frequent and sustained episodes of collective action across time.

Subaltern Islamism: the readiness and ability of some Islamist movements to court a subaltern base by providing the dominated sections of society with a conduit for their revolt against power structures and by ushering in a new social order in which they grow dominant.

Sufi jihadism: a politically revolutionary and socially conservative breed of Sufism whose millenarian religious prophecies can pave the way for the spread of militant Sufi movements.

Sunni Khomeinism: a current within Sunni Islamism which advocates for the embrace of the Iranian model; that is, supports the overthrow of secular regimes and their replacements by Islamic Republics featuring clerical guidance over politics and backs Iran's post-1979 anti-imperialist foreign policy and bid for regional leadership (e.g. Palestinian Islamic Jihad).

Tales of contention: narratives putting forward a history of shared struggles and associating a community with a glorified tradition of rebellion which, when revived, help movements signal rootedness, activate local identities and cast activism as a duty in line with local culture.

Vernacular ideology: the transmission of a grand beliefs system in the local language of the grievances, identities or cultural and historical narratives which are all specific to a place.

Vernacular Islamism: an Islamist discourse cast in and shaped by a local cultural backdrop.

Note on Transliteration

I have used an extremely simplified system of transliteration from the Arabic. I base my transliteration on the guidelines of the *International Journal of Middle East Studies*, for instance using the diacritic ' for the glottal stop *hamza* and ' for the consonant *ayn*. But, to facilitate reading, I have not transliterated the *ayn* when it features at the beginning of a word (e.g. I write Ali Eid instead of 'Ali 'Eid or Akkawi instead of 'Akkawi); I have foregone bars and dots above and below the letters and I have kept the spelling of words which have long been transliterated into English in a certain way and have therefore acquired wide recognition that way, even if their spelling is not fully accurate (e.g. Rashid Karame instead of Rashid Karami, Hezbollah instead of Hizbullah, or the Beqaa Valley instead of the Biq'a).

Maps

1 Map of Lebanon and Syria.

xx   Maps

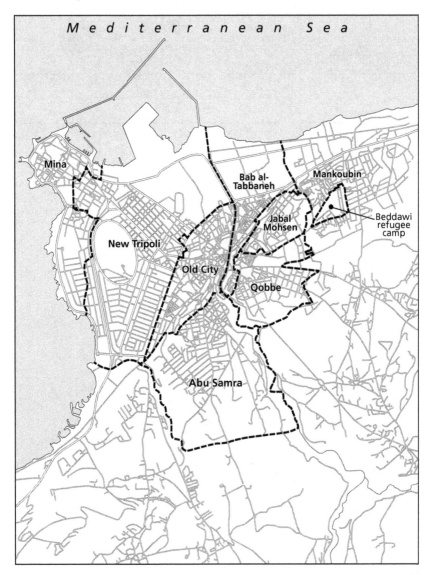

2 Neighborhoods of Tripoli.

Maps xxi

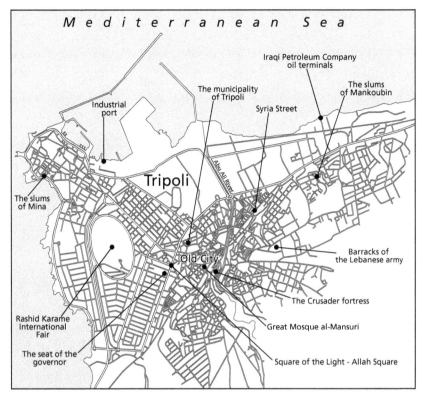

3 Main sites of Tripoli.

Introduction

"Welcome to Allah Square"

My first visit to Lebanon's northern city of Tripoli, in 2013, was memorable to say the least. I had come from Beirut to spend the day discovering this historical port of 500,000 inhabitants long reputed for the beauty of its old quarters, the quality of its food and the welcoming spirits of its residents. Yet, already during the journey, a passenger had vaguely warned me to "stay safe" and, upon disembarking the bus, I was unsettled by the sight of a giant black flag bearing Quranic inscriptions, which is often seen as a marker of militant Islamist ideology. The driver had dropped me off on Square of the Light, also known as Allah Square, Tripoli's most central roundabout which overlooks a massive three-dimensional metal structure of the word "God" (*Allah*) visible from afar, surrounded by high-rise black flags widely associated with groups like Al-Qaeda or ISIS. What made the whole setup even more intriguing was the large and austere marble stele on which the metal structure was installed, for it read: "Tripoli the fortress of the Muslims welcomes you" (*qal'at al-Muslimin Trablus turahhib bi-kum*).

Welcomed I did not especially feel, though, and a growing sense of panic even gripped me as, minutes later, I heard gunshots in the air and saw a crowd of hundreds of bearded men, some on mopeds and other carrying weapons, marching toward Allah Square. This, in theory, could have been a golden opportunity to do research and ask some of them questions for, after all, I was writing on Islamist movements in Syria and Lebanon back then. Not feeling very brave, however, I instead rushed toward a side alley, entered the nearest restaurant, ordered a sandwich and rapidly headed for the furthest table away from the street. The owner, who right away grasped my anxiety but did not visibly share it, soon brought my food and tried to reassure me: scenes like this happened regularly, these were just bands of youths who neither hailed from Tripoli nor represented its spirits and would soon return to their districts. The loud and agitated protesters soon passed the alley and continued on their

2   Introduction

way toward Allah Square, where they gathered and began chanting a mix of slogans to the glory of Islam, the Syrian revolution but, strangely enough, to Tripolitan pride too. I relaxed and wondered: who were these demonstrators supposedly "not from Tripoli," but who seemed to know their way around the city and engaged with local identity? And why did the owner characterize them as "bands of youths," when to me they looked more like militant Islamists?

The protesters, as my interlocutor had predicted, all dispersed barely an hour later. Tripoli's city center regained its calm and the rest of my visit went as planned. The old quarter, with its millennial mosques, narrow alleyways and Crusader castle, was indeed a true architectural jewel; the local food had exceeded my expectations and the Tripolitans I met that day were all incredibly kind and warm, visibly proud that a foreigner visited their city. On my way back to Beirut in the evening, then, I was confused but also increasingly curious and intrigued at the various facets Tripoli had offered me. I would go back dozens of times.

As I kept returning to Tripoli over the next seven years, for research stays of a few weeks and one consecutive stay of five months, what increasingly struck me was the flagrant disconnect between the seeming prevalence of Islamist mobilization and militancy in the city, something which pushed journalists to dub it an "Islamist stronghold" or a "powder keg of fundamentalism," and the sheer diversity lying behind the phenomenon of militant Islamism.

The story of Allah Square epitomized the need to investigate the whole spectrum of motivations which pushed parts of local society to embrace militant Islamism as an ideology. The massive metal structure of the word "Allah," the black flags of jihad and the stele associating Tripoli to a "fortress of Muslims" had been erected in 1983 by a militant Islamist group known as Tawhid (*Harakat al-Tawhid al-Islami* or Islamic Unification Movement). Tawhid had seemingly emerged out of nowhere in 1982; within the mere space of months mobilizing 2,000–3,000 members and many more sympathizers, taking military control of the city and implementing what it grandly called an "Islamic Emirate." In retrospect, some authors even characterized it as the "first ISIS-style Emirate"[1] because of the widespread sense that Tawhid had imposed Islamic law at gunpoint, ushered in a new social and cultural order in Tripoli and violently fought its ideological nemeses – from secular Sunni notables and leftist parties to the city's religious minorities and the Syrian

---

[1] Alastair Crooke, "If Syria and Iraq become fractured, so too will Tripoli and North Lebanon," *Huffington Post* (January 6, 2015).

regime whose army, back then, was occupying large swathes of Lebanese territory, including North Lebanon.

Most obviously, the rise of Allah on Tripoli's most central square reflected Tawhid's ideological supremacy. In fact, it had stemmed from the lobbying of a few dozen cadres within the movement who were especially ideologically driven and had long advocated for the erection of a symbol of divinity on the city's main roundabout which, until then, had for nearly three decades featured a statue of Abdel Hamid Karame, a prominent local notable. They argued that a symbol of divinity would not only conform more to Islam, which prohibits "idolatry," but that it would also indoctrinate Tripolitan society into Islamist ideology by anchoring into the local collective psyche the demand for "God's rule on Earth."

Yet, as I gradually became aware throughout my research, ideology was only part of the story. Allah Square, for many other members and sympathizers of Tawhid, had other types of connotation. While for some it symbolized Tripoli's identity as a rebel city and its resistance against a "secular" Syrian regime despised for its brutal repression of the Syrian opposition in nearby Homs and Hama and for its occupation of Northern Lebanon, for the many poor who were marginalized it reflected their dislike of Tripolitan notables, epitomized their overthrow of the traditional power structures and mirrored their conquest of the city. And this, in turn, also explained Tawhid's own success at recruiting and mobilizing so many. Far from homogeneously made up of hardened ideologues only, its members were committed to Islamism to various degrees and many had instrumentalized it; using ideology alternatively to channel tales of Tripolitan identity, protest against their conditions, prevail in preexisting neighborhood rivalries and social conflicts or get access to criminal networks and activities. In the shadow of Allah Square, Tawhid and the 1980s "Islamic Emirate" of Tripoli, then, lay ideology but also local solidarities, identities, grievances and myriad older antagonisms.

This book tells the fuller story of why and how Tawhid emerged in 1982, mobilized many Tripolitans into militant Islamism and was eventually defeated militarily in 1985. The story of these three years of Tripolitan history is gripping in itself. It features neighborhood strongmen and wealthy notables, staid traditional clerics in long robes and charismatic ideologues wearing the militant Afghan dress, a host of former Marxists turned Islamists as well as gangsters of all kinds; all competing with one another over the scenic setting of Tripoli's port and maze of alleyways, historic mosques and Crusader castle, posh districts and dangerous wastelands with, in the looming shadow, the imposing presence of Allah Square. And it is far from a purely local tale. These struggles in fact soon attracted attention from some of the major

4   Introduction

geopolitical players of the time, from Syrian President Hafez al-Assad and Palestinian leader Yasser Arafat all the way to Iran's Supreme Guide Ruhollah Khomeini, who each dispatched some of their best spies to infiltrate Tripoli and plot in the background. Conflict was at the heart of that story too and, from peaceful protests to scenes of urban unrest all the way to assassinations, bombings, military battles and even true massacres, Tripoli witnessed a tragically large panoply of incidents which killed 3,600 people. In truth, this three-year period was so significant that it changed the course of its history. More than thirty years later, indeed, the city is still reeling from it. The wounds that were opened have not fully healed, resentment for much of the bloodshed still simmers and, although many residents try hard to exorcise the old demons, they always seem on the verge of resurrection.

This story is therefore intrinsically fascinating in its own right and, because it has never been told comprehensively before, it fills important gaps in the scholarship on the Lebanese civil war (1975–90) as well as on some overlooked aspects of Lebanese/Syrian and wider Middle Eastern history and politics. But, crucially, delving deep into the way Tawhid recruited, operated and engaged in violence also allows me to make local, city- and neighborhood-specific details speak to wider debates in political science. I especially use this story to theorize back on two themes of concern to those more broadly interested in "contentious politics" – this spectrum of conflictual mobilizations which traditionally aim at the state and range from peaceful and violent protests all the way to terrorism and civil war – with insights for the study of social, rebel and terrorist movements, including Islamist ones.

First, this book shows how space affects the way movements mobilize. I claim that Tawhid's success in the 1980s at recruiting 2,000–3,000 members and many more sympathizers stemmed from its ability to root itself in local space – that is, in Tripoli's physical structure (e.g. streets and mosques) but, as importantly, in its social fabric (e.g. local solidarities, grievances and antagonisms) and its symbolic meaning (e.g. local narratives and identities). The fact that the movement had built Allah Square as a site which addressed grand Islamist ideology but also explicitly engaged with issues of Tripolitan identity and local conflicts showed how far it was ready to go in order to use space to recruit and mobilize. I therefore argue that space was utilized as a physical, social and symbolic resource and I then highlight how it shaped the movement's discourse and behavior, enhancing and restricting the prospect of mobilization. Through Tawhid's case, then, I illuminate the importance of space in spurring, hindering and in any case in significantly informing the nature of activism.

Second, this book addresses the role of ideology in social, rebel and terrorist movements. Rather than assuming that Tawhid's declaratory beliefs guided all of its members and leaders and as a result homogeneously drove its behavior, I show that the movement was in fact deeply heterogeneous and made up of some who were sincerely committed to its ideology while others instrumentalized it for a variety of reasons. This internal variation in ideological commitment and motivations is here again reflected in the rise of Allah Square, which came to hold different meanings depending on Tawhid factions. I thus argue that even the most outwardly ideological movements can feature a surprisingly great degree of heterogeneity and I point to the disproportionate influence which small groups of highly ideological cadres can then have on movement discourse and behavior. The story of Tawhid therefore demonstrates the importance of disaggregating ideological commitments and considering the effect this internal variation has on movement behavior.

Throughout this book I also address the scholarship on Islamism by analyzing the duality and sometimes the tension between Tawhid's embeddedness in local space and its loyalty to a much grander ideology. Islamism is often seen as a universalistic beliefs system advocating the unity of the worldwide community of Muslims irrespective of local solidarities and mandating the instauration of a religiously inspired political order, through violence in its militant version. But Tawhid's case suggests that this ideology may resonate in some places for very local reasons; with a space's traditions, identities, solidarities or antagonisms then impacting significantly the way such movements operate and pushing them toward a behavior unrelated to, and occasionally even in contradiction with, their Islamist beliefs. By exploring the duality of space and ideology in Tawhid, I suggest new ideal types to help grasp the interactions between Islamist movements, ideology and local contexts; in the process also stressing the importance of factoring in "the local" in studies of Islamism.

In sum, although this book provides an account of the "Islamic Emirate" of 1980s Tripoli, it also offers an in-depth look into how space and ideology respectively triggered and sometimes shaped the types of mobilizations Tawhid spearheaded in the city, with significant takeaways for all those interested in Islamist movements and in contentious politics at large. In the rest of this introduction I present in more detail the broader scholarships with which this book engages, my key concepts and contributions and the methods I employed.

How Local Space Impacts Conflictual Mobilizations

Tawhid was a militant Islamist movement which professed grand ideological goals, such as creating an Islamic Republic in Lebanon, struggling against Israel and the Syrian regime and even carrying out attacks on

6   Introduction

American soil. Yet it was also grounded in local space to a striking extent, its activities remaining tied to Tripoli's physical, social and symbolic structures.

Although, in theory, the movement had the potential to recruit in the Sunni Islamist constituencies growing elsewhere in Lebanon, its membership remained confined to Tripoli. And, remarkably, in this large city with a population that is 80.9 percent Sunni, it only attracted certain segments of Tripolitan Sunni society and became popular in some neighborhoods only. There, some may have been attracted by Tawhid's Islamist ideology. But many also seemed drawn by other factors, such as the great degree to which Tawhid's discourse was imbued in local narratives that glorified Tripoli's prestigious past and rebel mythology, or the movement's willingness to address grievances specific to the city and to some of its neighborhoods particularly, like its scathing criticism of the locally rooted power structures. In turn, the degree to which the movement grounded itself in space came to affect the way it mobilized and the nature of its activism. Instead of taking the struggle to its self-professed enemy in Beirut, the Christian-dominated Lebanese government, Tawhid became a spatially oriented movement vying for local resources and identities. It imposed its view of Tripoli as a "fortress of Muslims," despite the presence of religious minorities such as its 8.9 percent of Alawis and 10.2 percent of Christians, even going to lengths to transform the city's main roundabout into Allah Square. It also got drawn into locally rooted antagonisms unrelated to ideology, like a rivalry pitting two Tripolitan neighborhoods, Jabal Mohsen and Bab al-Tebbaneh, against each other, and the social tensions opposing wealthy New Tripoli to the impoverished districts of the Old City. And, finally, Tawhid's embeddedness in Tripoli's cross-border solidarities with Syria dragged it into a doomed struggle with the Assad regime. At times, therefore, it appeared as though local antagonisms, identities and solidarities drove it more than ideology. This demonstrates the importance of grasping how space affects conflictual mobilizations.

What is the role of local space – in other words, "the local," or a locality's physical structure, social fabric and symbolic meaning – in the basis and behavior of social, rebel and terrorist movements? Through which mechanisms can space constitute and shape activism?

Within the several subfields which make up the broader spectrum of contentious politics, the scholarship on social movements should in theory be best placed to answer these questions. It has risen to considerable prominence in political science and sociology in the past decades chiefly because of its success in countering the long-held view that contention, as "confrontational claim-making," resulted from the

How Local Space Impacts Conflictual Mobilizations 7

manipulation of "mad crowds" and arguing, instead, that it represented a rational way of conducting "politics by other means."

As a result, four broad paradigms have emerged from this rich scholarship in order to analyze the factors affecting mobilizations and to address the recurring mechanisms through which activists make claims – although, at first, none of them made much place for space. The "political process" approach strove to explain dynamics of contention in relation to the broader and typically national context by arguing that social movements are more likely to emerge when they perceive the existence of political opportunities to affect change; the "resource mobilization" track offered an organizational account centered on how social movements acquire resources and mobilize members in order to take political action; the "cultural turn" emphasized the subjective dimensions of mobilization by pointing to the role of collective action frames, emotions and identities; and finally the "networks perspective" pointed to the embeddedness of movement participants in a broader web of social ties and to how these resulting networks and solidarities can at times become channeled into activism.[2] Each of these traditions within social movement theory is empirically and conceptually rich and they all have insightful things to say

---

[2] For some of the best known examples of scholarly work drawn from (1) the "political process" approach, (2) the "resource mobilization" track, (3) the "cultural turn" and (4) the "networks" perspective, see: (1) William Gamson, *The strategy of social protest* (Belmont: Wadsworth Publishing, 1975), Charles Tilly, *From mobilization to revolution* (London: Longman Higher Education Press, 1978), Doug McAdam, *Political process and the development of Black insurgency, 1930–1970* (Chicago: Chicago University Press, 1982), Sidney Tarrow, *Democracy and disorder: protest and politics in Italy, 1965–1975* (Oxford, Clarendon Press, 1989), Sidney Tarrow, *Power in movement* (Cambridge: Cambridge University Press, 1998) or Donatella Della Porta, *Social movements, political violence and the state* (Cambridge: Cambridge University Press, 1995); (2) John McCarthy and Meyer Zald, "Resource mobilization and social movements: a partial theory" *American Journal of Sociology* (Vol. 82, No. 6, 1977), pp. 1212–41 and John McCarty and Mayer Zald, "The resource mobilization research program: progress, challenge and transformation" in Joseph Berger and Morris Zelditch Jr. (eds.), *New directions in contemporary sociological theory* (New York: Rowan and Littlefield Publishers, 2002); (3) David Snow and Robert Benford, "Ideology, frame resonance and participant mobilization" in Bert Klandermans, et al. (eds.), *From structure to action: comparing social movement research across cultures* (New York: JAI Press, 1988), James Jasper, "The emotions of protest: affective and reactive emotions in and around social movements" *Sociological Forum* (Vol. 13, No. 3, 1998), pp. 397–424; Jeff Goodwin, James Jasper and Francesco Polletta (eds.), *Passionate politics: emotions and social movements* (Chicago: Chicago University Press, 2000) or James Jasper, "Emotions and social movements: twenty years of theory and research" *Annual Review of Sociology* (Vol. 37, 2011), pp. 285–303; (4) Doug McAdam and Ronnelle Paulsen, "Specifying the relationship between social ties and activism" *American Journal of Sociology* (Vol. 99, No. 3, 1993), Mario Diani, "Social movements and social capital: a network perspective on movement outcomes" *Mobilization* (Vol. 2, No. 2, 1997), pp. 129–47 and Mario Diani and Doug McAdam (eds.), *Social movement analysis: the network perspective* (Oxford: Oxford University Press, 2002).

8   Introduction

about the way Tawhid mobilized in 1980s Tripoli. Yet none accounts for how space may constitute and shape activism; that is, for how movements can use a locality's physical layout but also preexisting solidarities, narratives, antagonisms and identities to recruit and operate as well as the ways in which, in turn, "the local" comes to affect sometimes significantly the terms on which mobilization occurs.

This is not to say that space, as such, has been entirely overlooked in social movement theories. In the early 2000s, in fact, academics called for the scholarship to follow the broader "spatial turn" which, already since the 1980s, had witnessed other disciplines of social science such as geography and history incorporating the study of the role of spatial dynamics in their analysis. As a result, a new research agenda emerged that took space as more than a backgrounder or a mere local reflection of larger trends, instead highlighting how contentious actors could view it as a resource. In particular, Roger Gould, in his groundbreaking study of the Parisian insurrection of 1870–1, found that rebels had recruited not on the basis of class but, rather, of neighborhood ties; Dingzin Zhao in a seminal article recounted how the leaders of the 1989 Beijing student movement had profited from the built-in structure of the local campus architecture to mobilize; William Sewell contended that activists from Tiananmen Square to the Lincoln Memorial exerted what he called "spatial agency" by using and changing the meaning of symbolic sites in order to energize the base; and finally Charles Tilly explained the importance for dissidents to take control of "safe spaces," which he defined as areas safe from enemy intervention where it is possible to meet, organize and act.[3] These contributions were crucial because they shed light on the importance of space as a resource for movements and participated in the rise of a broader research agenda centered on the spatiality of contention. But they rarely emphasized the specific mechanisms through which space could come to constitute, trigger, restrict and in any case shape mobilizations.

In parallel, the scholarship on social movements witnessed another development as academics originally from more spatially aware disciplines brought their insights to the field. This was particularly the case with

---

[3] See: Roger Gould, *Insurgent identities: class, community and protest in Paris from 1848 to the Commune* (Chicago: University of Chicago Press, 1995), Dingxin Zhao, "Ecologies of social movements: student mobilization during the 1989 prodemocracy movement in Beijing" *American Journal of Sociology* (Vol. 103, No. 6, 1998), pp. 1493–529, William Sewell Jr., "Space in contentious politics" in Ronald Aminzade et al. (eds.) *Silence and voice in the study of contentious politics* (Cambridge: Cambridge University Press, 2001), Charles Tilly, "Spaces of contention" *Mobilization: An International Quarterly* (Vol. 5, No. 2, 2000), pp. 135–59.

How Local Space Impacts Conflictual Mobilizations 9

geographers. Some of them, such as Byron Miller, Paul Routledge, Deborah Martin and Walter Nicholls were instrumental in showing the spatiality of some of the processes identified by the four schools of social movement theory. They called for more attention to be paid to how political and economic processes unfold in uneven ways and produce spatial variations in grievances, to the extent they may even give rise to "terrains of resistance" which become ripe for activism; they highlighted the benefits movements could gain from "place-framing" their social and political agenda against the backdrop of the concerns specific to some spaces; and finally they pointed to the role of space and proximity as a "relational incubator" that could help networks of contention to connect.[4]

The contributions of these geographers therefore played an important part in the growth of the research agenda centered on space and social movements. They can be credited with enriching our understanding of space as a resource in contention and with ushering new discussions, for instance on the way movements may spatially diffuse through "scale-shift." But their impact on the field of social movements has remained limited to a few scholars, something due to the fact that the discipline of geography has long been mired in a postmodern epistemological paradigm, which has limited the ability of geographers interested in certain localities to theorize on broader, more generalizable, processes and mechanisms. A few exceptions apart, then, the insights of geographers have tended to remain sidelined.

A similar dynamic has delayed the elaboration of fruitful discussions between the mainstream scholarship on social movements and urban sociologists. This is equally regrettable because the latter's work has long highlighted the local rootedness of contention. A pioneer in the field,

---

[4] See: Byron Miller, *Geography and social movements: comparing antinuclear activism in the Boston area* (Minneapolis: University of Minnesota Press, 2000), Deborah Martin and Byron Miller, "Space and contentious politics" *Mobilization: an International Quarterly* (Vol. 8, No. 2, 2003), pp. 143–56, Paul Routledge, *Terrains of resistance: nonviolent social movements and the contestation of place in India* (Westport: Praeger, 1993), Deborah Martin, "'Place-framing' as place-making: constituting a neighbourhood for organising and activism" *Annals of the Association of American Geographers* (Vol. 93, No. 3, 2003), pp. 730–50 and Walter Nicholls, "The urban question revisited: the importance of cities for social movements" *International Journal of Urban and Regional Research* (Vol. 32, No. 4, 2008), pp. 841–59. Other noteworthy works by geographers on contentious politics include: Helga Leitner, Eric Sheppard and Kristin Sziarto, "The spatialities of contentious politics" *Transactions of the Institute of British Geographers* (Vol. 33, No. 2, 2008) and Walter Nicholls, "Place, networks, space: theorising the geographies of social movements" *Transactions of the Institute of British Geographers* (Vol. 34, No. 1, 2008), pp. 78–93 and Walter Nicholls, Justin Beaumont and Byron Miller (eds.), *Spaces of contention: spatialities and social movements* (London: Ashgate, 2013).

10   Introduction

Henri Lefebvre, was in fact at the forefront of the "spatial turn" in social sciences and some of his insights remain invaluable forty years later. For instance, by arguing that space was a social product which reflected power relations, he emphasized the spatiality of politics and thus pointed to the role of space, here the city, not just as a container of social movements and a resource for them but also as a target of popular mobilizations. Writing in the wake of the 1968 protest movement, which shook major Western cities, he acknowledged that the demonstrators aimed at the state but also claimed that one of their key demands was the "right to the city," then more fully conceptualized by David Harvey as a collective claim to "some kind of shaping power" over the local processes taking place in cities. Manuel Castells took the logic further when he coined the concept of "urban social movements" to refer to those mobilizations which are not just based in but also oriented toward the city and strive to get more services, defend local identities and obtain autonomy.[5]

These insights could have helped shape the agenda on the spatiality of contention for they revealed how some movements were not just based in but also oriented toward space. But urban sociologists regret that, instead, their scholarship developed "in relative isolation from social movement theorizing generally,"[6] as one of them put it; something due to the fact that this literature, for all the insights it yielded, was long characterized by its structuralism and locked in side debates over terminology and the specificities of "the urban." As a result, its guiding ideas never powerfully entered mainstream social movement research, which continues to grapple with the question of how space constitutes and shapes contention.

Crucially, this question is relevant for social movement scholars, but also for those interested in the full spectrum of contentious politics – all the way to terrorism and civil wars. Much like social movements, in the

---

[5] See: Henri Lefebvre, *The production of space* (Cambridge, MA: Blackwell, 1991 [1974]), Henri Lefebvre, *Le droit à la ville: espace et politique* (Paris, Economica Anthropos, 2001 [1968]), David Harvey, "The right to the city" *International Journal of Urban and Regional Research* (Vol. 27, No. 4, 2003) and Manuel Castells, *The city and the grassroots: a cross-cultural theory of urban social movements* (Berkeley, University of California Press, 1983).

[6] Chris Pickvance, "From urban social movements to urban movements: a review and introduction to a symposium on urban movements" *International Journal of Urban and Regional Research* (Vol. 27, No. 1, 2003), p. 104. See also: Margit Mayer and Julie-Anne Boudreau, "Social movements in urban politics: trends in research and practice" in Peter John et al. (eds.), *The Oxford handbook of urban politics* (Oxford: Oxford University Press, 2012) and Walter Nicholls, "The urban question revisited: the importance of cities for social movements" *International Journal of Urban and Regional Research* (Vol. 32, No. 4, 2008), pp. 841–59.

How Local Space Impacts Conflictual Mobilizations 11

past decade these subfields of contentious politics have started to acknowledge the importance of space. While the transnational character of the 9/11 attacks and the growth of "lone wolf" actions initially cemented the assumption that political violence was becoming deterritorialized, it transpired in the 2010s that terrorist groups were in fact deeply embedded in certain spaces in particular, which then had to be investigated. Some scholars of terrorism thus called for the "subnational turn"[7] which is gaining traction in social science to be echoed in the field of terrorism studies and, consequently, a new generation of researchers has sought to assess where, below the level of the state, terrorist groups root themselves and why.[8] But, on the whole, this literature is still in its infancy.

For its part, the scholarship on civil wars was long more sensitive to space. Yet its view of space has mostly been associated with physical structure, for instance correlating the presence of resources, borders or rugged terrain to the likelihood that a conflict erupts. The rise of a new research agenda spearheaded by Stathis Kalyvas on the "micro-dynamics of civil war,"[9] in which he calls for the disaggregation of data at the subnational level, has the potential to enhance our understanding of how rebel groups can be grounded in, at times oriented toward, "the local." Yet, so far a full analysis of the ways in which local features can impact the make-up, objectives, tactics and trajectory of a rebellion has yet to emerge.

Like social movement studies, then, the two fields of political violence and civil wars have so far tended to view space as a physical resource for terrorist and rebel groups typically aiming at the state. There has been little consideration of how the social and symbolic aspects of space can

---

[7] Augustina Giraudy, Eduardo Moncada and Richard Snyder, *Inside countries: subnational research and comparative politics* (Cambridge, Cambridge University Press, 2019).

[8] See, for instance: Colin Flint, "Terrorism and counterterrorism: geographic research questions and agendas" *The Professional Geographer* (Vol. 52, No. 2, 2003), pp. 161–9, Michael Findley and Joseph Young, "Terrorism and civil war: a spatial and temporal approach to a conceptual problem" *Perspectives on Politics* (Vol. 10, No. 2, 2012), pp. 285–305, Gary LaFree et al., "Spatial and temporal patterns of terrorist attacks by ETA, 1970–2007" *Journal of Quantitative Criminology* (Vol. 28, No. 1, 2012), pp. 7–29 and Karim Bahgat and Richard Medina, "An overview of geographical perspectives and approaches in terrorism research" *Perspectives on Terrorism* (Vol. 7, No. 1, 2013), pp. 38–72.

[9] Stathis Kalyvas, "Promises and pitfalls of an emerging research program: the microdynamics of civil war," chapter 16 in Stathis Kalyvas, Ian Shapiro and Tarek Masoud, *Order, Conflict and violence* (Cambridge: Cambridge University Press, 2008). See also: Lars-Erik Cederman and Kristian Skrede Gleditsch, "Introduction to special issue on 'disaggregating civil wars'" *Journal of Conflict Resolution* (Vol. 53, No. 4, 2009), pp. 487–95.

12   Introduction

also be a resource and of the sometimes very local nature of contentious politics. The scholarship is still missing an account of how movements engage with local solidarities, narratives, antagonisms and identities in order to recruit and mobilize and the ways in which space, in turn, then also comes to affect their behavior, discourse and exercise of violence. And, strikingly, although mechanism-based explanations have increasingly gained currency in social science in the past decade, few of the spatially aware studies in contentious politics consider the exact processes and mechanisms through which space impacts mobilizations. As a result, despite the initial promise of a broad research agenda which sought to address this main "silence" in contentious politics, there were influential voices in the field who by the 2010s still regretted the lack of progress in grasping the spatialities of contention.[10]

In this book I illuminate the spatially grounded and oriented nature of mobilizations, systematically accounting for the role of Tripoli's physical structure, social fabric and symbolic meaning in Tawhid's genesis and evolution, and by the same token identifying some of the underlying mechanisms through which space affects activism. To begin with I build on the scholarship which views space as a resource for mobilization but, instead of focusing on its physical aspect only, I highlight how movements also utilize the symbolic and social dimensions of space in order to root themselves locally. They may do so by reviving and appropriating local "tales of contention"; or these narratives which associate a certain space like a city to an older, glorified tradition of rebellion. This can help them mobilize by signaling embeddedness and casting activism as a duty in line with local history and identity. They may also enlist the support of "champions of mobilization," or figures bound to their communities by such strong ties of local solidarity that they develop a large personal following and are able to ensure mass recruitment and mobilization in these spaces. By using mechanisms such as the revival of Tripoli's "tales of contention" and the enlistment of "champions of mobilizations" in certain districts, I argue, Tawhid was able to strategically activate the symbolic and social dimensions of space in order to recruit and mobilize locally.

But space, I contend, is not just a resource strategically used by movements to root themselves and operate; instead, it can also significantly affect their behavior and discourse. Developing the insights pioneered by urban sociologists, I claim that as part of their strategy to appeal

[10] Doug McAdam and Hilary Schaffer Boudet, *Putting social movements in their place: explaining opposition to energy projects in the United States, 2000–2005* (Cambridge, Cambridge University Press, 2012), p. 202.

beyond their ideological base and tap into the older and broader pool of discontent locally, some might be willing to act as "spatially oriented movements" which tackle local grievances and identities and seek to achieve a measure of local socio-political change. Yet, although this may bolster their membership, I point to how it then tends to draw them into preexisting antagonisms unrelated to ideology, rendering the nature of their activism more local. I also note another, less conscious aspect to the way space may affect contentious politics: as movements become more embedded in the social fabric and symbolic meaning of a space, they may develop a "habitus of place" or the set of locally rooted historical, cultural and political narratives which impacts the discourse and worldviews of activists, pushing them to interpret the world through partially local lenses while restricting their outside appeal. Tawhid's readiness to act as a "spatially oriented movement" and its "habitus of place," or internalized localism, were two mechanisms which explained how space affected activism, accounting for its strikingly local behavior and discourse and its lack of appeal outside Tripoli.

Naturally not all social, rebel and terrorist movements are as grounded in or oriented toward local space as Tawhid was. But, arguably, all of them are also embedded to at least some extent in specific places; and the physical structure, social fabric and symbolic meaning of these localities significantly impact their worldviews, discourse and behavior at times.

Highlighting the importance of "the local" in studies of contentious politics holds significant implications for the scholarship on Islamism and militant Islamism too. Of course, some scholars of Islamism have taken a city or a neighborhood – in other words, a local space – as a prism through which to analyze how Islamist groups operate more generally.[11] But we still know little about why and how groups which profess an ideology mandating the unity of Muslims globally root themselves very deeply in some spaces especially; with local identities, solidarities and

---

[11] For excellent works that take a local context as a prism through which to view Islamism, but without fully conceptualizing the mechanisms through which "the local" matters or analyzing its effects on the movement under study, see among others: Salwa Ismail, "The popular movement dimensions of contemporary militant Islamism: socio-spatial determinants in the Cairo urban setting" *Comparative Studies in Society and History* (Vol. 42, No. 2, 2000), pp. 363–93; Patrick Haenni, *L'ordre des caïds. Conjurer la dissidence urbaine au Caire* (Paris: Karthala, 2005); Rory McCarthy, *Inside Tunisia's al-Nahda: between politics and preaching* (Cambridge: Cambridge University Press, 2018); Stefan Malthaner, *Mobilizing the faithful: militant Islamist groups and their constituencies* (Chicago: Chicago University Press, 2011); Pascal Menoret, "The suburbanization of Islamic activism in Saudi Arabia" *City and Society* (Vol. 29, No. 1, 2017), pp. 162–86 and Alison Pargeter, "Localism and radicalization in North Africa: local factors and the development of political Islam in Morocco, Tunisia and Libya" *International Affairs* (Vol. 85, No. 8, 2009), pp. 1038–40.

14   Introduction

antagonisms at times shaping their behavior considerably. In a show of the dearth of scholarship on how Islamism relates to local contexts, it is revealing that the literature has produced a trove of excellent research on Islamist groups that operate nationally (e.g. Muslim Brotherhood branches) or transnationally (e.g. pro-Iran Shia Islamist militias, global Salafi-jihadi networks), but has simultaneously overlooked localized Islamist movements – even though this category accounts for a growing part of the Islamist spectrum. In Libya and Syria, in fact, localized Islamist rebel groups have accounted for a large chunk of the Islamist insurgency after 2011.[12] These movements still claim broad goals and remain shaped by larger trends. Yet what characterizes them is that they become bounded to a certain village, quarter, city or region, where they develop relationships that can be so symbiotic that they affect them deeply, rendering their behavior local and restricting their outside appeal. There, these groups can embody the appeal of ideology. But they may also come to epitomize the power of local solidarities or the defense of local communities, which often pushes them to operate through local ties and to claim to embody these spaces and their identities. They are so grounded in space that local contexts can in fact shape them more than ideology.

But factoring in "the local" is not just useful to illuminate the myriad Islamist groups at the subnational level, it can also help us grasp surprising variations in the way national and transnational Islamist movements mobilize and how local dynamics affect their behavior. For example, although nominally the Syrian Muslim Brotherhood is a nationwide movement, it is historically stronger in some parts of the country than in others; and the local solidarities, grievances, traditions and identities of members from the cities of Hama and Aleppo significantly impact how it thinks and operates, at times affecting its internal organization.[13] Even militant global Islamist groups like Al-Qaeda and ISIS can in practice be very local too. These groups are considerably stronger in some localities

---

[12] In the case of Libya, non-exhaustive examples include: the Benghazi Defence Brigades (*Saraya al-Defe'a 'an Benghazi*) in the city of Benghazi, the Consultative Council of the Holy Warriors of Derna (*Majlis Shura Mujahedin Derna*) in the city of Derna or the array of localized rebel groups featuring an Islamist tendency in the city of Misrata which collectively operate as "the Misrata Brigades" (*Kata'eb Misrata*). In the case of Syria, examples include: the Brigades of Darayya (*Saraya Darayya*) formed by Islamist rebels from the town of Darayya who settled in Northern Syria, the Army of Islam (*Jaysh al-Islam*) in the Damascus suburb of Duma, the Falcons of Greater Syria (*Suqur al-Sham*) in the mountainous area of Jabal Zawiya, the Movement of Nur al-Din al-Zenki (*Harakat Nur al-Din al-Zenki*) in the village of Qabtan al-Jabal in the western Aleppo countryside or the Tawhid Brigade (*Liwa al-Tawhid*) in the neighborhoods of East Aleppo.

[13] Raphaël Lefèvre, *Ashes of Hama: the Muslim Brotherhood in Syria* (London: Oxford University Press and Hurst, 2013).

than in others, and spatial variation in their recruitment and mobilization patterns stems partially from their ability to draw on the specific solidarities, narratives and grievances of certain spaces to root themselves locally. Whereas a respective third, two-thirds and up to four-fifths of all Syrians, Moroccans and Libyans who joined Al-Qaeda in Iraq after 2003 hailed specifically from the cities of Deir ez-Zoor and Casablanca as well as the province of Cyrenaica, a fifth of all Tunisians who joined ISIS after 2011 came from Tunis and especially the neighborhood of Ettadhamen.[14] Moreover, in addition to their engagement in violence against targets such as symbols of the state or international organizations, what is often less noted is how these groups also get involved in tribal, ethnic and social conflicts at the subnational level, unrelated to ideology.[15] It is therefore crucial to grasp the rootedness of Islamist movements – the ways in which they not only use space as a resource, but also see their behavior in turn shaped by "the local."

Building on Tawhid's case, I suggest four ideal types to help us think about how Islamist movements use the physical, social and symbolic dimensions of local space to root themselves with sometimes important effects on their behavior; thus introducing a new way of categorizing Islamists not depending on their ideology or their strategy, as existing typologies have it, but depending on the local contexts in which they mobilize too.[16] Thus, I note that movements based in spaces characterized by a strong, longstanding identity like Tripoli may recruit by casting

---

[14] I draw these figures from Brian Fishman and Joseph Felter, *Al-Qa'ida's foreign fighters in Iraq: a first look at the Sinjar records* (Washington, DC: Combatting Terrorism Center at West Point, 2007), pp. 12–15; Nate Rosenblatt, *All jihad is local: what ISIS' files tell us about its fighters* (Washington, DC: New America, 2016), p. 13; and Hatem Achech et al., *Le terrorisme et ses dossiers judiciaires* (Tunis: Forum Tunisien pour les Droits Economiques et Sociaux, 2016), p. 25.

[15] See, for instance, Andrew Lebovich, "The local face of Jihadism in Northern Mali" *CTC Sentinel* (Vol. 6, No. 6, 2013), pp. 4–19; Elizabeth Kendall, "Al-Qaeda and Islamic State in Yemen: a battle for local audiences," chapter 6 in Simon Staffell and Akil Awan (eds.), *Jihadism transformed* (London: Oxford University Press and Hurst, 2016); Mohamed-Ali Adraoui, "The case of Jabhat al-Nusra in the Syrian conflict 2011–2016: towards a strategy of nationalization?" *Mediterranean Politics* (Vol. 24, No. 2, 2019); or Cynthia Ohayon, *The social roots of Jihadist violence in Burkina Faso's North* (Brussels: International Crisis Group, 2017).

[16] Most of the existing typologies in the Islamist politics scholarship categorize Islamist movements either depending on their ideology (e.g. state-oriented and reformist-type Islamism like the Muslim Brotherhood; Umma-oriented and revolutionary-type Islamism like Salafism, sectarian-oriented and anti-Shia-type Islamism like the Islamic State of Iraq) or on the means they employ (e.g. from proselytizing and participation in elections to different forms of violence such as vigilantism and domestic or global terrorism). For a sample of these existing typologies, see, among others, Thomas Hegghammer, *Jihad in Saudi Arabia: violence and pan-Islamism since 1979* (Cambridge: Cambridge University Press, 2010), p. 6, Peter Mandaville, *Global political Islam*

16   Introduction

their Islamism within local cultural and historical narratives, but that this can also push them to espouse a "vernacular Islamism" which taints their discourse and actions with parochialism and restricts their outside appeal. I also point to how, as Tawhid became more embedded in Tripoli and addressed local grievances, it got dragged into older antagonisms which affected the nature of its behavior. For example, it became involved in the feud between the Tripolitan districts of Bab al-Tebbaneh and Jabal Mohsen and justified this ideologically; but what it truly gave rise to was a "neighborhood Islamism" more guided by local concerns and solidarities than ideology. Similarly, as the movement was prepared to embody "subaltern Islamism" in order to court Tripoli's urban poor by providing a conduit for their socio-political revolt, they dragged it into a "social jihad" which was as, if not more, driven by older social tensions than ideology. And finally, Tawhid drew on criminal networks and practices, which allowed it to vastly increase its resources but simultaneously turned it into a vehicle for "Islamo-gangsterism," or a type of behavior systematically prioritizing economic gains over ideological consistency. Far from mutually exclusive, of course, these ideal types can at times overlap and also coexist within one movement, so long as there is evidence that local contexts affect the nature of Islamism. The notions of "vernacular Islamism," "neighborhood Islamism," "subaltern Islamism" and "Islamo-gangsterism" all point to the relevance of viewing Islamism from below; that is, to grasp the local contexts in which these groups operate – and how "the local" shapes them. Table I.1 shows how, as Islamist movements become embedded, local contexts can impact their behavior significantly.

All in all, therefore, exploring how Tawhid strategically used but was then also shaped by Tripoli's physical, social and symbolic structure provides unique insights into the mechanisms through which space affects contentious politics at large and of the ways militant Islamist movements root themselves in certain places, with implications on their behavior.

How Ideology Affects Social, Rebel and Terrorist Movements

Naturally, that Tawhid acted as a spatially grounded and at times even spatially oriented movement should not blind us to the fact that its

(London: Routledge, 2007), Olivier Roy, *The failure of political Islam* (Cambridge, MA: Harvard University Press, 1996), Katarina Dalacoura, *Islamist terrorism and democracy in the Middle East* (Cambridge: Cambridge University Press, 2011), Fawaz Gerges, *Journey of the jihadist: inside Muslim militancy* (London: Wadsworth Publishing, 2007), Laurent Bonnefoy, "Varieties of Islamism in Yemen: the logic of integration under pressure" *Middle East Review of International Affairs* (Vol. 13., No. 1, 2009), pp. 26–36.

How Ideology Affects Movements

Table I.1 *A localism-based typology of Islamist mobilization*

Primary features of the local context	Local manifestation of Islamism	Example of impact on Tawhid's behavior
Need for protection; intense solidarities; history of strongmen	Neighborhood Islamism (channels local concerns, solidarities and practices)	Support for Bab al-Tebbaneh's neighborhood rivalry against Jabal Mohsen
Acute socio-political grievances; revolt against local power structures	Subaltern Islamism (channels local social tensions)	Involvement in a social jihad to undermine Tripoli's elite and usher in a new social order
Identification to and pride in local space; willingness to defend local culture	Vernacular Islamism (channels local collective identity)	Adoption of an Islamist ideology shaped by historical and cultural Tripolitan narratives
Local opportunities to make profits; tradition of engaging in crime	Islamo-gangsterism (channels criminal networks and practices)	Involvement in criminal activities prioritizing economic gains over ideological consistency

behavior was also significantly shaped by its ideology; in other words, by the set of views, values and objectives which taken together forms the militant Islamist beliefs system embraced by the group and provides a program of action. Yet there was also a puzzle about the true extent of ideology's influence in Tawhid: while at first glance its behavior appeared obviously driven by beliefs only, it featured too many variations and inconsistencies to have guided all of the movement's actions, all the time.

Tawhid, of course, took the struggle to the ideological enemies of Sunni Islamism in Tripoli, combating the city's leftist parties and Alawi minority while undermining the secular notables. As it came to control the city through the force of weapons it imposed, sometimes violently, its vision of Islamic law onto local society, prohibiting alcohol, enforcing a ban on eating and drinking during the fast of Ramadan and pressuring women to wear conservative clothes. Even its foreign alliances seemed clearly driven by ideology only as it came to be backed by Fatah's Islamist wing, the Islamic Republic of Iran and Syria's Islamists. But, simultaneously, Tawhid's exercise of violence featured too much spatial and temporal variation to be solely driven by ideology and it also engaged in practices which were in blatant contradictions with its Islamist views. It struck alliances with some of its ideological enemies, engaged in

18   Introduction

criminal activities at odds with its self-professed beliefs, and it soon transpired that many of its members were not truly committed to Islamism. This ebb and flow of ideology's influence on a movement's behavior is not just typical of Tawhid and it raises the broader question of the ways in which ideology affects contentious politics.

What is the role of ideology in social, rebel and terrorist movements? And to what extent as well as through which mechanisms may it come to affect their behavior?

It is only recently that the subfields which make up the scholarship on contentious politics have begun examining these questions. This is something which can appear surprising given the importance of the role of ideology yesterday, in the context of the Cold War, and today, with the proliferation of movements espousing alt-right, anarchist and religious ideologies. And, while the literature has since then flourished, it still remains insufficiently theorized. This stems from many issues, like difficulties to develop sound methods to assess the influence of ideology in movements and a persistent lack of attention to the processes and mechanisms through which ideology matters. But at its core lies the broader challenge of overcoming the binary nature of debates about the role of ideology in contentious politics, for the scholarship has become locked in unsatisfying dichotomies between those who argue that a movement's professed beliefs help predict its behavior and those who disagree, or those who claim members believe in ideologies and those who insist they instrumentalize them.

Social movement theories were the first to discuss the role of ideology in contentious politics. Yet, although the discipline's early pioneers, like Charles Tilly, Doug McAdam and Sidney Tarrow, took the role of beliefs into account, they did not make them their focal point of analysis; something due to the fact that they were in the midst of pushing back against the view that collective action resulted from the manipulation of "mad crowds," which as a result meant that they strove to portray social movement activism as overly instrumental or rational.

It was only with the "cultural turn" of the 1990s that scholars of social movements became more explicitly interested in understanding how ideology could affect activism. Two main perspectives arose which highlighted, but in contradictory ways, the ideational side of collective action and how the broader meaning movements gave to their actions mattered. On the one hand, David Snow and Robert Benford developed the "framing perspective" to argue that movement leaders could strategically articulate the grievances and beliefs of potential activists within a broader set of ideas, or "master frame," in order to recruit them – they emphasized the mobilizing function fulfilled by the process of ideological production.[17] This, however, soon led to a forceful pushback as, on the other hand, other scholars such as Pamela Oliver and Hank Johnston insisted that there was more to ideology than framing. Ideology, they claimed, was not just a set of ideas stitched together to be "resonated with," but was more often than not sincerely embraced and even helped predict behavior.[18] Mayer Zald took this view to its fullest when he famously went as far as calling for the redefinition of social movement behavior as "ideologically structured action,"[19] with the explicit assumption that ideology was often so deeply held that it shaped mobilizations. Debates became heated but the "cultural turn" had brought ideas back into the literature.

Yet by the 2000s and 2010s the scholarship on movements and ideology began to stall. Several reasons accounted for this. First, although the concept of "framing" was a major advance that allowed scholars to think about movement ideologies as the product of a strategic process, rather than assumed as given, it led to a proliferation of work which used this conceptual lens solely. This led to growing confusion between the concepts of "frames" and "ideology," some scholars even complaining that the former was increasingly replacing the latter in the analysis of the role of beliefs in movements. It also delayed work on other important questions, for example what other functions ideologies fulfill during processes of mobilization, or how and to what extent ideology affects movements. A second problem was that, for decades until recently, empirical research on social movements remained confined to the West and in particular to the typically progressive, peaceful and issue-driven movements, in which an ideology was not always clearly articulated. And, while work on mobilizations that seem ideologically driven has recently grown, the scholarship has tended to become compartmentalized between the separate analysis of "extremist," "violent" or "religious" movements instead of clustering around the role of ideology across cases. This has hindered

---

[17] Robert Benford and David Snow, "Framing processes and social movements: an overview and assessment" *Annual Review of Sociology* (Vol. 26, 2000), pp. 611–39. See also: David Snow and Scott Byrd, "Ideology, framing processes and Islamic terrorist movements" *Mobilization* (Vol. 12, No. 1, 2007), pp. 119–36.

[18] Pamela Oliver and Hank Johnston, "What a good idea! Ideologies and frames in social movement research" *Mobilization* (Vol. 5, No. 1, 2000), pp. 37–54.

[19] Mayer Zald, "Ideologically structured action: an enlarged agenda for social movement research" *Mobilization* (Vol. 5, No. 1, 2000), pp. 1–15. Note that Zald's proposal to redefine social movement behaviour as "*ideologically* structured action" stirred up a lively debate, triggering responses by other social movement scholars, like Mario Diani and Bert Klandermans. See: Mario Diani, "The relational deficit of ideologically structured action" *Mobilization* (Vol. 5, No. 1, 2000), pp. 17–24 and Bert Klandermans, "Must we redefine social movements as ideologically structured action?" *Mobilization* (Vol. 5, No. 1, 2000), pp. 25–30.

20   Introduction

the development of a research agenda on ideologies and mobilizations. Third and lastly, the scholarship on social movements has struggled to develop methods other than discourse analysis to assess the role of ideology during episodes of contention. As a result, apart from the cognitive dynamics at play in "framing," little is known about the other processes and mechanisms through which ideology may influence movements. Despite its initial promise, then, this literature has struggled to overcome the binary debate about whether activists believe in or instrumentalize ideologies as well as to develop a conceptual framework broader than "framing," leading some to regret the "paucity"[20] of that scholarship.

Just as the literature on ideology and social movements stalled, the scholarship on terrorism boomed and made the role of ideology in violence one of its key areas of enquiries. Here again pioneers in the field, like Martha Crenshaw or Donatella Della Porta, had long recognized the importance of individual commitment to an ideology in the decision to join a terrorist group and engage in violence, but it was not their central analytical focus.[21] It was the growth of seemingly ideological violence that put the role of ideas in the spotlight. This resulted partially from the shock in the United States of the 1995 Oklahoma City bombing, perpetrated by right-wing terrorists, but more importantly from the fast-increasing number of attacks by Islamist movements, from Hezbollah and Hamas to Al-Qaeda and ISIS.

In theory, this could have provided a golden opportunity to better grasp the ideological underpinnings of terrorist violence, especially as governments invested massively in research. In fact, the field of terrorism can be credited with putting forward a new research agenda which centered on the question of how much ideology affected movement violence. This was especially the case after the growth of a literature on "new terrorism"[22] by scholars such as David Rapoport, Walter Laqueur

---

[20] Aaron McCright and Riley Dunlap, "The nature and social bases of progressive social movement ideology: examining public opinion toward social movements" *The Sociological Quarterly* (Vol. 49, No. 4, 2008), p. 828.

[21] Martha Crenshaw (ed.), *Terrorism in context* (University Park: Pennsylvania State University Press, 1995), Martha Crenshaw, *Explaining terrorism: causes, processes and consequences* (London: Rotutledge, 2010), Donatella Della Porta, "Recruitment processes in clandestine political organizations: Italian left-wing terrorism" *International Social Movement Research* (Vol. 1, 1988), pp. 155–69, Donatella Della Porta, *Clandestine political violence* (Cambridge: Cambridge University Press, 2013).

[22] See: David Rapoport, "Fear and trembling: terrorism in three religious traditions" *American Political Science Review* (Vol. 78, No. 3, 1983), pp. 658–77, David Rapoport, "The fourth wave: September 11 in the history of terrorism" *Current History* (Vol. 100, No. 650, December 2001), Walter Laqueur, *The new terrorism: fanaticism and the arms of mass destruction* (Oxford: Oxford University Press, 1999), Bruce Hoffman, *"Holy terror":*

How Ideology Affects Movements   21

and Bruce Hoffman. They argued that the "new," ideologically driven terrorism including, typically, what their counterpart Mark Juergensmeyer called "religious violence,"[23] had to be distinguished from the more instrumental, independentist or secessionist, type of terrorism – the former being allegedly so irrational that it made the nature of its engagement in violence more indiscriminate and lethal.

Their arguments initially stimulated a lively debate. Some, like Assaf Moghadam and Thomas Hegghammer, agreed that ideology had a causal impact on violence but nuanced their claims, arguing that while it may not always explain all movement behavior ideology still inspired recruits to take action and shaped group perceptions about who the enemy was.[24] Others disagreed entirely. James Piazza and Robert Pape vigorously pushed back against the "religious violence" thesis, the former arguing that goal types are more indicative of lethality than ideology while the latter provided an instrumental account of ideology by suggesting that even when terrorists portray themselves as religiously or ideologically driven allegedly more important goals, like nationalist sentiment, drive their actual engagement in violence.[25]

But although the literature on ideology and terrorism has thus become prolific, even occasionally having an impact on the public debate, it remains mired in debates on whether ideologically driven terrorism is new or old, or stems from irrational or instrumental logics.[26] Moreover,

---

the implications of terrorism motivated by a religious imperative (Santa Monica: Rand Press, 1993) and Bruce Hoffman, *Inside Terrorism* (New York: Columbia University Press, 2006).

[23] Mark Juergensmeyer, *Terror in the mind of God: the global rise of religious violence* (Berkeley: University of California Press, 2001), Mark Juergensmeyer, "Religion as a cause of terrorism," chapter 10 in Louise Richardson (ed.), *The roots of terrorism* (London: Routledge, 2006) and Mark Juergensmeyer, Margo Kitts and Michael Jerryson, *The Oxford handbook of religion and violence* (Oxford: Oxford University Press, 2013).

[24] Assaf Moghadam, "Motives for martyrdom: Al-Qaida, Salafi Jihad and the spread of suicide attacks" *International Security* (Vol. 33, No. 3, 2009), pp. 46–78, Thomas Hegghammer, "The rise of Muslim foreign fighters: Islam and the globalization of jihad" *International Security* (Vol. 35, No. 3, 2010), pp. 53–94 and Thomas Hegghammer, "Should I stay or should I go? Explaining variation in Western jihadists' choice between domestic and foreign fighting" *American Political Science Review* (Vol. 107, No. 1, 2013), pp. 1–15.

[25] James Piazza, "Is Islamist terrorism more dangerous? An empirical study of group ideology, organization and goal structure" *Terrorism and Political Violence* (Vol. 21, No. 1, 2009), pp. 62–88, Robert Pape, "The strategic logic of suicide terrorism" *American Political Science Review* (Vol. 97, No. 3, 2003), pp. 343–61 and Robert Pape, *Dying to win: the strategic logic of suicide terrorism* (London: Random House, 2006).

[26] For good overviews of these debates, see, for instance: Ersun Kurtulus, "The 'new terrorism' and its critics" *Studies in Conflict and Terrorism* (Vol. 34, No. 6, 2011), Jeroen Gunning and Richard Jackson, "What's so 'religious' about 'religious terrorism'?" *Critical Studies on Terrorism* (Vol. 4, No. 3, 2011), pp. 369–88 or, even

22   Introduction

largely relying on large-n datasets, rather than ethnographic research, scholars have failed to identify the mechanisms through which ideology matters. So far, then, they have only had mixed success in grasping ideology's complex role in terrorist movements.

By contrast, the study of civil wars has emerged as the most promising subfield of contentious politics in its treatment of the ways in which ideology affects movements. Despite not featuring prominently when the field emerged in the early 2000s, research on ideology became more common in the 2010s and addressed some of the gaps in the literature. For instance, scholars of rebel groups went further than social movement theories in showing that ideology matters by pointing to the functions it fulfills in rebel movements beyond "framing." Most prominently, Elisabeth Wood and Francisco Gutiérrez Sanín claimed that, in rebel movements composed of combatants who hail from various horizons, ideology can help reinforce group identity and compliance by socializing members into similar discourses and objectives, sometimes even providing the motivations which might lead them to fight; Stefano Costalli and Andrea Ruggeri highlighted how ideology could act as a "pull factor" translating the private grievances of individuals into public grievances, thus attracting them to the movement; and Barbara Walter suggested that ideologies, extremist ones in particular, provide advantages by triggering the external support of radical networks and by allowing for the recruitment of ideologically committed members willing to pay the cost of fighting.[27] Some of these studies were, much like in the field of terrorism, based on rigorous large-n studies. But, interestingly, they also relied more than before on ethnographic and archival research in settings such as El Salvador, Colombia and Italy, thus permitting a more refined

more recently, Simon Cottee, "'What ISIS really wants revisited': religion matters in jihadist violence, but how?" *Studies in Conflict and Terrorism* (Vol. 40, No. 6, 2017), pp. 439–54.

[27] See Elisabeth Wood and Francisco Gutiérrez Sanín, "Ideology in civil war: instrumental adoption and beyond" *Journal of Peace Research* (Vol. 51, No. 2, 2014), pp. 213–26, Juan Ugarriza and Mathew Craig, "The relevance of ideology to contemporary armed conflicts: a quantitative analysis of former combatants in Colombia" *Journal of Conflict Resolution* (Vol. 57, No. 3, 2012), pp. 445–77, Stefano Costalli and Andrea Ruggeri, "Indignation, ideologies and armed mobilization: civil war in Italy, 1943–1945" *International Security* (Vol. 40, No. 2, 2015), pp. 119–57, Barbara Walter, "The extremist's advantage in civil wars" *International Security* (Vol. 42, No. 2, 2017), pp. 7–39, Stathis Kalyvas and Laia Balcells, "Did Marxism make a difference? Marxist rebellions and national liberation movements" *APSA 2010 Annual Meeting Paper* (2010) and Stathis Kalyvas and Laia Balcells, "International system and technologies of rebellion: how the end of the Cold War shaped internal conflict" *American Political Science Review* (Vol. 104, No. 3, 2010), pp. 415–29.

understanding of the multiple functions which ideology comes to fulfill in rebel movements.

Yet, for all the significant contributions the study of civil wars has made to our understanding of the functions fulfilled by ideologies in movements, the literature has also stumbled on the same challenges faced by the other subfields of contentious politics. It has remained locked in a binary debate over whether ideology matters only because it has instrumental value, or instead shapes and therefore helps explain rebel behavior, from the selection of targets and intensity of violence to the movement's institutions and everyday life. This dichotomy is unsatisfying because, while the instrumental perspective leaves little room for ideology to take a life of its own, arguments attributing a causal role to ideology typically assume that beliefs are homogeneous and cause action, whereas in reality even the most outwardly ideological movements feature at least some degree of heterogeneity, and their behavior, far from automatically stemming from their ideas, can at times vary significantly. Moreover, much like in the rest of the literature on ideologies and contentious politics, what is still missing in the scholarship on civil wars is more attention to the mechanisms through which ideology can influence behavior and outcomes. Some scholars, like Jonathan Leader Maynard and Elizabeth Wood, have singled out micro-level cognitive mechanisms, for example the internalization of beliefs, through which ideology may affect the actions of individuals.[28] But the puzzle of the ebb and flow of ideology's influence at the collective level of the movement and its behavior remains unsolved. This, finally, is also reflective of another challenge faced by the other fields of contentious politics – the conceptual and methodological difficulty in assessing the influence of ideology on a movement and to grasp its underlying mechanisms.

In this book I demonstrate ideology's role in contentious politics, systematically exploring to what extent Islamist beliefs impacted Tawhid's discourse, internal dynamics, decision-making process, exercise of violence and foreign alliances, and thereby also identifying some of the mechanisms through which ideology affects movement behavior. My central claim is that, instead of dismissing or assuming the commitment of members, we should disaggregate along a "spectrum of ideological commitment" the degree to which factions and individuals inside movements sincerely believe in and are driven by ideology. Through this notion I mean to conceptualize the heterogeneity of commitments that characterizes even the most outwardly ideological social, rebel and

---

[28] Jonathan Leader Maynard, "Ideology and armed conflict" *Journal of Peace Research* (Vol. 56, No. 5, 2019), pp. 635–49.

24   Introduction

terrorist movements, which are often made up of members who embrace ideology for various reasons. As a result they may be committed to their movement's declaratory beliefs and guided by them to very different degrees. This includes the rank and file but also the leadership for, far from an assumption in the literature according to which commitment to a movement's ideology is pyramidal, leaders being alternatively seen as the most or the least ideological actors, they can also instrumentalize beliefs, be guided by other priorities or see their commitments erode. Depending on their influence and degree of ideological commitment, then, members, cadres and leaders will push the movement to engage in more or less ideologically driven behavior.

This emphasis on internal variation in ideological commitment within movements, and the effect on their behavior, helps overcome two limitations of the instrumental and sincere accounts of ideology, which minimize its influence or assume and risk exaggerating it. First, it allows for the examination of the functions of ideology for the members who instrumentalize it, but also points out that in time they may move along the spectrum and internalize beliefs. This allows for ideology to retain agency even when initially embraced instrumentally. Second, it opens the door to the organizational investigation of how the push and pull toward or away from ideology between members and leaders on the "spectrum of ideological commitment" can explain the ebb and flow of ideology's influence on the movement, when factions seek to steer its behavior in a more or less ideological direction. This breaks with the view of ideology as a disembodied variable, and instead helps locate it within human agency, contingency and a relational context, which all have to be unpacked.

Applying this logic to Tawhid, I disaggregate the ideological commitment of its main factions and groups of individuals and I find that it featured a very diverse pool of members. On the one hand, I argue that entire factions, neighborhoods and constituencies embraced militant Islamism instrumentally as a "protest ideology." That is, many members and even some leaders were not intrinsically attracted by Islamism's deeper set of beliefs but rather by the contentious potential associated with its symbols, vocabulary, practices and infrastructure. As a result they pulled Tawhid toward a behavior unrelated to, and at times at odds with, ideology. On the other hand, I claim that the movement was made up of many committed Islamists too, and I especially illuminate the role of a handful of highly ideologized cadres whom I call the "ideological entrepreneurs." By this notion I mean those actors at the extreme of a movement's "spectrum of ideological commitment" who are not just ideologically driven but also engage in costly efforts to spread their beliefs

How Ideology Affects Movements 25

to other members and to lobby the leaders to take ideologically inspired decisions. By mobilizing their worldviews in order to mold the nature of activism and of the broader environment around them, their "ideological entrepreneurship" acts as a central mechanism through which ideology affects movements. In Tawhid, although these figures only amounted to a few dozen they became influential because they fulfilled crucial functions, which for some time enabled them to push its discourse, exercise of violence and foreign alliances in an ideological direction. And, tellingly, as their influence later waned, Tawhid's behavior became less ideological. I thus trace the ebb and flow of ideology's influence on the movement back to internal interactions and to the push and pull between factions guided by ideology to different extents.

Of course, not all social, rebel and terrorist movements feature the great degree of internal variation which characterized Tawhid. But, arguably, none are ideologically fully homogeneous and all have a more or less wide "spectrum of ideological commitment" – the composition and evolution of which may explain some of the variation in their behavior.

Arguing that even the most outwardly ideological movements feature a surprisingly high degree of heterogeneity also holds major implications for the scholarship on Islamism. This literature, much like the subfields of contentious politics, has become torn between two approaches to the study of ideology in Islamist movements. While one camp largely focuses on Islamist ideologues and concepts and as a result has sometimes tended to overplay the causal role of beliefs in how movements recruit and behave, the rival perspective locates the growth of Islamist militancy not in a "radicalisation of Islam" but rather in an "islamization of radicalism,"[29] which would allegedly stem either from a nihilistic quest for violence or from the grievances of Muslims, an instrumentalist approach explaining ideology away.[30]

---

[29] This is Olivier Roy's term. See Olivier Roy, *Jihad and death: the global appeal of Islamic State* (London: Hurst, 2017) and "Radicalization of Islam or islamization of radicalism?" *Wall Street Journal* (June 16, 2016).

[30] For examples of the first camp, see, among others: Emmanuel Sivan, *Radical Islam: medieval theology and modern politics* (Binghamton: Yale University Press, 1985), Gilles Kepel, *The roots of radical Islam* (London: Saqi Books, 2005), Fawaz Gerges, *The far enemy: why jihad went global* (Cambridge: Cambridge University Press, 2009), William McCants, *The ISIS apocalypse: the history, strategy and doomsday vision of the Islamic State* (New York: St Martin's Press, 2015), Jessica Stern, *Terror in the name of God* (New York: Ecco, 2004), David Cook, *Understanding jihad* (Los Angeles: University of California Press, 2005), and Shiraz Maher, *Salafi-jihadism, the history of an idea* (London: Hurst & Co., 2016). For examples of the second perspective, see, among others: Hrair Dekmejian, *Islam in revolution: fundamentalism in the Arab world* (New York, Syracuse

26   Introduction

Instead, by highlighting the need to investigate the full "spectrum of ideological commitment" of Islamist groups, I point to the range of motivations for which recruits join, and I suggest that this internal variation impacts and therefore helps explain their behavior. Naturally, preexisting commitment to Islamism is an important part of that story, and many initially less committed members may become socialized and educated into these beliefs by "ideological entrepreneurs" in the movement who are striving to spread their worldviews. But acknowledging the heterogeneity of ideological commitments in Islamist movements also means exploring some of the factors beyond ideology which push other people to join. Through the notion of "protest Islamism" I especially point to how militant Islamism replaced revolutionary Marxism in the 1970s and 1980s as the quintessential rebel ideology, one which many people embraced instrumentally in order to express socio-political dissent. Other motivations stemming from the local context may matter too, and ideal types such as "neighborhood Islamism," "vernacular Islamism," "subaltern Islamism" and "Islamo-gangsterism" are again useful. As factions embodying one of these primary motivations gain the upper hand over others, they will steer the movement toward or away from ideology. Figure I.1 shows how, far from being homogeneous, Tawhid was a deeply heterogeneous movement; and Table I.2 illustrates how its main factions had different motivations and were guided by ideology to varying degrees.

Crucially these are not just abstract insights. They can help illuminate the discussion on Islamist "radicalization" or "extremism," which too often posits that indoctrination precedes militancy and tends to overlook the range of motivations for joining violent Islamist groups. Unpacking the heterogeneity of these groups can also help us better grasp their behavior. For instance, although ISIS is often seen as a highly coherent,

University Press, 1995), John Esposito, *The Islamic threat: myth or reality?* (Oxford: Oxford University Press, 1999), Mohammed Hafez, *Why Muslims rebel: repression and resistance in the Islamic world* (Boulder, Lynne Rienner, 2003), François Burgat, *Understanding political Islam* (Manchester: Manchester University Press, 2020) and Olivier Roy, *Jihad and death: the global appeal of Islamic State* (London: Hurst & Co., 2017). Note that the discussion between the two approaches spans beyond the borders of academia and has influenced the terms of the public debate to a great extent. See, for instance: Graeme Wood, "What ISIS really wants," *The Atlantic* (March 2015), Juan Cole, "How 'Islamic' is the Islamic State?," *The Nation* (February 2015); Olivier Roy, "Le djihadisme est une révolte générationnelle nihiliste," *Le Monde* (November 23, 2015), Gilles Kepel and Bernard Rougier, "Radicalisations et islamophobie: le roi est nu," *Libération* (March 10, 2016) or François Burgat, "Les non-dit de l'islamisation de la radicalité," *Le Nouvel Observateur* (November 21, 2016).

Table I.2 *Tawhid's wide spectrum of ideological commitment*

Tawhid faction	Degree of commitment to Islamist ideology
Ideological entrepreneurs	Very strong
Committed Islamists	Strong
Neighborhood Islamists	Medium to weak
Subaltern Islamists	Medium to weak
Islamo-gangsters	Very weak

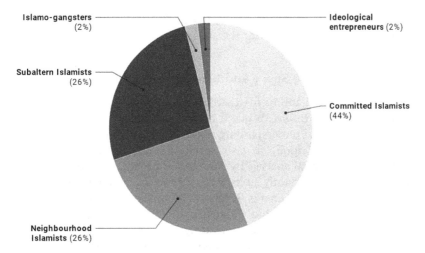

Figure I.1 Tawhid, an ideologically heterogeneous Islamist movement
Note: Ideal types draw on Tawhid factions: (1) Committed Islamists: Soldiers of God and Movement of Arab Lebanon; (2) Neighbourhood Islamists: Popular Resistance; (3) Subaltern Islamists: the bulk of Hashem Minqara's faction in Mina; (4) Ideological entrepreneurs: Tawhid's Education Office; (5) Islamo-gangsters: Anistaz Kouchari's gang.
Source: Estimates of 2,000 Tawhid members gathered from interviews with Tawhid members and from the CIA. See: US Central Intelligence Agency, "Lebanon: Islamic fundamentalism in Tripoli" (Top Secret, NESAR 86-003JX, January 17, 1986)

doctrinaire movement, it actually features a wide "spectrum of ideological commitment." Leaked internal documents suggest that only 5 percent of ISIS's recruits are highly committed Islamists who are advanced students of religion, the rest of them split between 24 percent who say they have an "intermediate" grasp of Islam and a staggering

28 Introduction

70 percent who recognize only having "basic" knowledge of Sharia law.[31] From diehard ideologues and moderately committed Islamists to former Ba'athist officers and even profit-driven smugglers, then, the group features more heterogeneity than is often assumed and it is likely that internal interactions between these factions impact its behavior, pushing it toward ideological but at other points social and criminal violence. Disaggregating ideological commitments is key to grasping the behavior of Islamist groups.

Overall then, investigating the heterogeneity of commitments in Tawhid, and how the push and pull between more or less ideologically driven factions affected movement behavior, provides important perspectives on the mechanisms through which ideology affects contentious politics, with key takeaways for the study of militant Islamist groups.

Researching Space and Ideology in Tawhid

This book is located at the crossroads of three broad epistemological and methodological traditions. While it builds on political sociology by providing a sociological understanding of the phenomenon of Islamist militancy in 1980s Tripoli, it also situates itself in the footsteps of comparative historical analysis by stressing its broader temporal context. But, even more importantly, at its core this book is rooted in the tradition of analytical sociology. That is, it seeks to do more than provide a purely historical account of Tawhid's "Islamic Emirate" in 1982–5 and than contributing to Lebanese/Syrian, Middle Eastern and Islamist politics. Instead it aims to participate to a broader effort at bridging the disciplinary gap between area studies and political science and to use Tawhid to derive lessons applicable to wider debates. Building on analytical sociologists Peter Hedström and Jon Elster, it especially strives to unpack what the latter would have called the "cogs and wheels"[32] of the causal mechanisms through which space and ideology affected the nature of Tawhid's activism. As such, it avoids putting forward general laws and, in the tradition of middle-range theory, instead privileges the partial

---

[31] These figures build on the analysis by Associated Press (AP) of over 3,000 leaked internal ISIS documents. See: "Islam for dummies: IS recruits have poor grasp of faith," *Associated Press* (August 15, 2016). See also: "ISIS: UN study finds foreign fighters in Syria lack basic understanding of Islam," *The Independent* (August 4, 2017).

[32] Jon Elster, *Nuts and bolts for the social sciences* (Cambridge: Cambridge University Press, 1989), Peter Hedström and Petri Ylikoski, "Causal mechanisms in the social sciences" *Annual Review of Sociology* (Vol. 36, 2010), pp. 49–67, Peter Hedström and Peter Bearman (eds.), *The Oxford handbook of analytical sociology* (Oxford, Oxford University Press, 2009) and Charles Tilly, "Mechanisms in political processes" *Annual Review of Political Science* (Vol. 4, 2001), pp. 21–41.

explanation of social phenomena by identifying, through extensive empirical research, the links which allowed space and ideology to shape contention. And, precisely because analytical sociology places such an emphasis on providing ample evidence of the mechanisms at play, or what Derek Beach refers to as their "empirical fingerprints,"[33] three main points on my methodology need to be clarified from the outset.

The first methodological point which must be tackled is the level of the analysis. In order to shed light on Tawhid's behavior, and the role of space and ideology in it, I disaggregate its dynamics of contention and explore the movement's behavior at three levels. The first one, which is most commonly used in studies of contentious politics, involves studying Tawhid's interactions with political actors, both state and nonstate, at the macro level. Tawhid was far from a lone movement in one city completely detached from larger trends. Instead it was impacted by national and regional dynamics and at times shaped them too. It rolled back the influence of the Lebanese government, violently fought the Syrian regime, received backing from and strove to help Fatah and Syria's Islamists and allied with Iran. Analyzing the movement's behavior at the macro level is thus crucial. Yet, to grasp how space enhanced and restricted the prospects of mobilization, a second meso level of analysis is needed. It entails examining Tawhid's relationship to the "local" – how it interacted with the physical structure, social fabric and symbolic meaning of Tripolitan space. Researching this meso level of analysis is key to uncovering the ways Tawhid embedded itself within Tripolitan society and how local identities, solidarities and antagonisms shaped it in turn. To identify the mechanisms through which local space impacted its behavior, I place the emphasis on explaining instances of spatial variation in the patterns of the movement's recruitment, mobilization and engagement in contention and also on accounting for continuities with the behavior of older movements that used to be rooted in the same spaces. Last but not least, a third, micro level of analysis which is required in order to illuminate, this time, the role of ideology in Tawhid involves the investigation of intra and inframovement dynamics. Far from being fully homogeneous, Tawhid was made up of different factions and individuals themselves guided by conflicting motivations and priorities, and which would as a result try to steer the movement in a more or less ideologically driven direction. The disaggregated analysis of where its main factions stood on the "spectrum of ideological commitment" and how this affected its behavior is key to uncovering the role of ideology. And here,

[33] Derek Beach and Rasmus Brun Pedersen, *Process-tracing methods: foundations and guidelines* (Ann Arbor: University of Michigan Press, 2019), pp. 187–90.

30   Introduction

to do so I spend particular effort on process-tracing instances in which Tawhid engaged in typically ideological behavior as well as on unpacking why its behavior at times varied considerably, being often unrelated to and at times even at odds with ideology. All the episodes recounted in this book comprise an integration of the three levels of analysis.

The second point that needs to be clarified is the ontology on which this book draws. To explain the dynamics of contention at the three levels stated above, I interpret social facts and phenomena by relying on the methodological doctrine of "structural individualism." This ontological tradition was spearheaded by two fathers of analytical sociology, Peter Hedström and Peter Bearman, who attributed explanatory importance to the actions of individuals, whether intended or unintended, while stressing their embeddedness in social structures.[34] This simultaneous emphasis on the causal role of both individuals and the broader relational context in which they are situated is crucial. Indeed, it helps to overcome the binary debate in contentious politics between partisans of structures and of agency, and instead places the analytical focus on the mechanisms linking one to the other. This has important implications when researching Tawhid's mobilizations. Whereas most studies of contentious politics tend to either dismiss the role of individuals or to overemphasize the agency of them all in processes of mobilization, this book then highlights the disproportionate causal role of a handful of members and their social embeddedness. Interestingly, these individuals impacted the dynamics of Tawhid's behavior at the three levels of analysis stated above. While, for instance, a select few intermediaries shaped the patterns of Tawhid's relations with its key external allies, Fatah and Iran, a couple of "champions of mobilizations" were able to single-handedly recruit entire neighborhoods and a handful of "ideological entrepreneurs" tried shaping the movement's decisions. Stressing at once the causal importance of some individuals, their social embeddedness and the broader importance of structures and social ties thus lies at the analytical core of this book.

The third point which must be specified is the methods I used to collect the data. Because I placed such a strong emphasis on integrating three levels of analysis, investigating the role of some individuals and unpacking the broader effects of structures, I had to considerably invest in unearthing new primary material. It took four full years and dozens of research trips to Tripoli to gather enough quantitative and qualitative

---

[34] Peter Hedström and Peter Bearman, "What is analytical sociology all about? An introductory essay," chapter 1 in Peter Hedström and Peter Bearman (eds.), *The Oxford handbook of analytical sociology* (Oxford, Oxford University Press, 2009).

evidence about Tawhid before I was then able to inductively make inferences about the role of space and ideology. To collect this data I combined ethnography with archival research, which I detail below.

I began to gather material by adopting three ethnographic techniques. First, I developed insights through participant observation, undertaking dozens of weeks-long research trips to Tripoli between 2012 and 2016, including a five-month immersion in 2014.

Living in the city and its neighborhoods, interacting with residents in routine settings and forging close relationships allowed me to generate bottom-up insights into some of the features which recurrently impact Tripolitan society and politics, like a strong local identity. Then I undertook an oral history of the 1982–5 period, when Tawhid controlled the city. I asked a diverse group of two dozen Tripolitan residents to free-flowingly tell me the story of their lives during this period or first-hand accounts of certain interviews which sometimes lasted for several hours. Naturally I did not take all their accounts at face value, for the narration of some of these stories was evidently biased, either because three decades had passed or because of the suffering and bitterness associated with remembering often violent episodes of contention. But in the context of the lack of written sources, grounding this troubled period of Tripolitan history within human stories, recollections and even simply perceptions was invaluable to help reconstruct the underlying trends in local society and to grasp the mood of the time. The third ethnographic method I used was semi-structured qualitative interviews. Excluding the dozens of informal conversations drawn from participant observation and oral histories, I conducted over 200 interviews with a diverse pool of informants from July 2012 until September 2016, for meetings which sometimes lasted hours and were frequently reiterated. Most of these interviews were arranged by following the technique of snowball sampling – that is, by relying on the social network of interviewees for further contacts, which is particularly useful when trying to reach groups that are not easily accessible. Others also took place after identifying specific figures through the research material, getting in touch through official channels or meeting in unexpected circumstances during my ethnography.

When selecting whom to interview I made every effort to maximize the representativeness of my pool of informants. I interviewed Tawhid leaders but also cadres, rank and file and sympathizers, ideologues and fighters or current and former members. I was especially careful to follow a disaggregated approach, going to all Tripolitan neighborhoods to conduct interviews and interviewing Tawhid members situated on the whole "spectrum of ideological commitment." In addition I also met Tawhid

32   Introduction

allies. They included Sunni and Shia, Lebanese, Syrian and Palestinian Islamist actors in Tripoli and other cities, like Beirut and Sidon, as well as figures linked to Palestinian and Iranian intelligence. Finally, I went to lengths to interview those who were mortal Tawhid enemies and combated it, violently or not; from figures associated with Syrian and Lebanese intelligence to Tripolitan leftist militiamen, notables, independent clerics as well as civil society activists. All these interviews constitute the core of my research material and, even when I do not reference them explicitly in the rest of the book, they were still central in shaping my analysis of Tawhid's involvement in contention, from general dynamics to the tiniest local details.

In order to cross-check facts, ground the perceptions of my interviewees within more objective observations and generate further data at the three disaggregated levels of analysis, I combined ethnography with extensive archival research in Arabic, English and French into Tawhid's private archives, local press sources as well as UK and US institutional records. First, I secured access to Tawhid's archival office, which included its flagship newspaper, *al-Tawhid*, distributed to its members and Tripolitan society at large in 1984–6, as well as troves of other written propaganda material but also many pictures and videos of speeches by some of its clerics and leaders in Tripolitan mosques as well as of mass protests they led. This allowed me to contrast perceptions or recollections of Tawhid – its ideology, views on many issues, inner working etc. – with previously undisclosed and specific details of the movement. Second, I conducted archival research into Tripolitan daily newspaper *al-Incha* for the period 1979–87 and into the local weekly *al-Tamaddon* for parts of the period 1974–2015. This was absolutely crucial in generating fully disaggregated data at the city and subcity level, assessing in detail the extent of Tawhid's rootedness in certain Tripolitan spaces and grounding the movement temporally within older local traditions, identities and narratives. Third, I undertook research into the archives of Lebanese daily newspaper *L'Orient Le Jour* for the period of 1979–87, which allowed me to cross-reference the city-level data gathered through *al-Incha* and *al-Tamaddon* with national data, to generate insights into the way reporters from outside Tripoli viewed the evolution of the situation there in 1982–5 and to grasp how Tawhid's mobilization was grounded in macro, national and geopolitical trends. Lastly, I conducted research into the declassified archives of the UK Foreign Office and the US Central Intelligence Agency (CIA) for the periods respectively of 1920–81 and 1976–87. Obtaining access to foreign institutional records pertaining to Lebanon and Tripoli was important to obtain additional data at the three levels of analysis, contextualize local, national and regional level trends within the insights of particularly well-informed and sometimes on-site observers and, especially with the case of the CIA, to unearth detailed information about Tawhid and to grasp the way Western, security-oriented actors viewed the movement.

Triangulating the material I obtained through this multi-pronged archival research with data from my ethnography allowed me to overcome the challenge of conducting research on events that happened over thirty years ago. I then inductively developed insights into Tawhid and only later "theorized back";[35] that is, reflected on whether and how the results of my research spoke to wider debates, especially on the role of space and ideology in contentious politics.

The Structure of the Book

As this book strives to strike a balance between local empirical details and broader theoretical discussions in political science and sociology, chapters follow and build on each other chronologically while also being structured around key themes and concepts, with the goal of deriving insights from Tawhid but without betraying its multifaceted, at times messy nature. Individual chapters are then organized in the following way. Their introductions present the local puzzles which I seek to answer and lay out the key arguments I make; the body of the text lets the narrative be in the driving seat and occasionally signals through concepts that the empirics may have wider resonance beyond Tripoli; and concluding sections theorize back on how the story which has just been told holds broader insights and implications for the way we should think about the role of space and ideology in social, rebel and terrorist movements.

Chapter 1 provides an introduction to the Tripolitan, Syrian-Lebanese and wider Middle Eastern contexts within which Tawhid would emerge, and it hints at some of the local themes which the movement would address. It explains the rapid growth of Islamist movements in 1970s Tripoli with reference to their readiness to embody the city's older rebel identity and to their ability to tap into its pool of discontent, itself stemming from particularly acute local political and social grievances. These functions used to be fulfilled by leftist movements but I note how their failure to oppose the Syrian regime, which was fast becoming the archenemy of many Tripolitans in the local collective psyche, led to their

---

[35] This is Kevin Ward's term. See: Kevin Ward, "Towards a relational comparative approach to the study of cities" *Progress in Human Geography* (Vol. 34, 2010), pp. 419–35.

34 Introduction

decline and to the rise of Islamist movements instead, a trend also facilitated by the broader sense that Islamism had cultural and political momentum. This sets the scene for understanding the local context within which Tawhid was created and rapidly grew in early 1980s Tripoli.

Chapter 2 zooms in on the Popular Resistance, one of the militant Islamist factions which would merge within Tawhid upon its creation in 1982 and was disproportionately strong in one neighborhood of Tripoli only, Bab al-Tebbaneh. It explains how this originally Marxist group embraced Islamism instrumentally in 1980. This was because its leader, who also acted as the neighborhood strongman or informal local leader, sensed that this ideology would fulfill strategic functions for his district in a new security environment, one especially marked by Syria's 1976 military intervention in Lebanon and occupation of Tripoli. In this increasingly repressive context, Islamist ideology not only allowed the Popular Resistance to continue mobilizing Bab al-Tebbaneh's residents and to keep their local solidarities alive; it also enabled the faction to ally across space and class with resource-rich ideological actors and to enlist the support of militant Islamist militias in the local feud which opposed the inhabitants of the neighborhood to the nearby Alawi and pro-Assad district of Jabal Mohsen. After the Popular Resistance eventually merged with Tawhid in 1982, it would drag the movement into its neighborhood rivalry unrelated to ideology, which affected its behavior.

Chapter 3 provides an account of some of the other factions and individuals which created Tawhid in 1982. One of them, the Movement of Arab Lebanon, was like the Popular Resistance an originally leftist militia which embraced Islamism instrumentally, but its leader and members later became more sincerely committed. Other factions and individuals, like Soldiers of God and scattered groups of Islamist individuals, had for their part always been sincerely committed Islamists. In addition to detailing their respective origins and trajectories, this chapter also traces the root of the merger of all these Tripolitan Islamist factions and individuals back to two regional events which threatened to spill over into Tripoli – Syria's February 1982 Hama massacre and Israel's June 1982 invasion of Lebanon. Tawhid posed as a militant Islamist movement which claimed that it would protect the city from foreign invaders, take the struggle to Syria and Israel and create an Islamic Republic in Lebanon. As a result, it rapidly attracted the constituency of Tripoli's committed Islamists.

Chapter 4 investigates why, despite a grand ideology which in theory had the potential to resonate in Lebanon's entire Sunni Islamist constituency, Tawhid's membership remained overwhelmingly confined to

The Structure of the Book

Tripoli. This, I argue, partially stemmed from the highly fluid and heterogeneous nature of its militant Islamist ideology, which, beyond reflecting the commitment of some members, resulted from the fact that it fulfilled functions. These included outbidding rivals, strengthening internal cohesion and activating bonds of ideological solidarity with like-minded foreign actors to solicit their support. The fluid nature of Tawhid's ideology, which drew on disparate Sunni but also Shia Islamist references, contributed to restricting its appeal among Lebanon's more orthodox Sunni Islamists. Yet, in this chapter I also note another factor which limited the appeal of Tawhid outside of Tripoli: the sense that its Islamist discourse was deeply embedded in local identities and narratives. And, while I partially trace this to a movement strategy to recruit locally, I suggest that it also resulted from its own internalized rootedness, which led non-Tripolitan Lebanese Islamists to conclude that Tawhid was more of a Tripolitan than an Islamist movement.

Chapter 5 explores the dynamics of Tawhid's engagement in low-level violence in Tripoli in 1982–3 and especially of the implementation of an "Islamic Emirate," which amounted to the imposition of its Islamist ideological agenda onto the city. Tawhid's behavior, instead of being homogeneous, came to vary sometimes significantly across space and to feature instances of inconsistencies with its declaratory ideology. This, I claim, originated from its readiness to recruit less or non-ideologically committed members who were often Tripolitan subalterns intent on utilizing the movement as a vehicle for their older social and political revolts. At first these urban poor provided the manpower Tawhid needed to implement its "Islamic Emirate" onto Tripoli. Yet, ultimately, this constituency dragged the movement into the city's preexisting social antagonisms which were unrelated to ideology, pushing it to target the upper class and notables and to overthrow the local order.

Chapter 6 examines what accounts for Tawhid's involvement in high-level, seemingly ideological violence in 1983 against Tripoli's leftist movements and Christians. I acknowledge the causal role of ideology in this exercise of violence, mainly through the activism of a handful of highly ideologized Tawhid cadres who lobbied the leaders to engage in militant Islamist behavior and exacerbated a climate of ideological polarization. But I also note that, in spite of their increasing success in steering the movement's behavior in ideologically driven ways, these figures were a minority. Instead I find that many of the rest of Tawhid's members and leaders were not primarily guided by ideology in their exercise of violence, but rather by considerations of a primarily political, strategic, geopolitical and social nature. The heterogeneity of motivations which

36   Introduction

had led Tawhid to engage in violence became evident as the dynamics of conflict exposed too much variation across space and time to be solely guided by ideology. And, in a show of how the movement's internal diversity could affect its behavior, Tawhid would eventually be penetrated by criminals who steered its behavior and exercise of violence in a direction at odds with its Islamist ideology.

Chapter 7 considers the international relations of Tawhid, accounting for the factors behind its recurring tensions with the Syrian regime as well as its foreign alliances with Syrian Islamists, Fatah and Iran. Here again I point to the role of the handful of Tawhid cadres who, as a result of their strong commitment to Islamist ideology, became the principle handlers of the movement's foreign alliances with like-minded Islamist actors such as Iran. This, I claim, at first reinforced their influence within Tawhid, which they used in order to push its discourse and behavior in an ideological direction and to make shared ideology the cornerstone of the movement's foreign alliances with like-minded actors. But I remark that, as their influence became too strong and their ambition to turn Tawhid into a movement only driven by ideology clashed with the priorities of other factions, a heated debate gripped the movement and violence ensued, leading to the killing of several of them. And, tellingly, the period of late 1984 and early 1985, which corresponds to the decline in the influence of these ideologized cadres, also matches a Tawhid behavior less driven by ideology than before, as it engaged in criminal practices and as its foreign relations turned more pragmatic.

Chapter 8 traces the downfall of Tawhid and analyses in particular what led so many members to mobilize during their doomed struggles against the Syrian army in mid-1985 and in late 1986. These two battles were framed as ideological conflicts pitting fundamentalist militants against partisans of a secular order and I do acknowledge the role of ideology, whether embraced sincerely or instrumentally, as it allowed for the enlistment of new Islamist recruits at the height of the fighting and for support from external Islamist allies. Yet I also note that virtually all Tawhid factions mobilized, including those who were less or not ideologically committed. I argue that this stemmed from the movement's ability to cast the battles as part of a local collective duty in line with Tripoli's history as a rebel city. It also resulted from its readiness to enlist the support of neighborhood strongmen who were linked to their communities by strong ties of solidarity and were thus able to draw in many locals. Despite Tawhid's success at mobilizing so many members, however, the Syrian army and its allies were too strong to be beaten and they ultimately defeated the movement in bloodshed.

Finally, in the conclusion I reflect on the rise and fall of Tawhid in 1980s Tripoli, pulling the story together and summarizing the concepts I developed in my attempt to grasp Islamist movements from below and how space and ideology affect contentious politics. In doing so, I suggest their wider relevance and offer a tentative agenda for future research.

1 Tales of a Rebel City

It is vain to grasp Tawhid without first understanding Tripoli's history and rebel identity. Tawhid was a militant Islamist group which professed to fight for grand goals, at one point even claiming the "Islamization of the entire world." In theory it was thus not concerned with "the local." Yet it is remarkable how, despite an ostensibly transnational Islamist discourse which advocated for the unity of the worldwide Muslim community, Tawhid from its 1982 birth to its 1985 downfall grew considerably versed in local tales of Tripolitan history and identity. The movement came to inscribe itself and its behavior in continuity with the city's prestigious past, rebel instincts and the cross-border solidarities linking Tripoli to nearby Syrian cities. It also extensively addressed Tripolitan grievances, engaging with longstanding narratives of the city's lost glory, immersing itself in local antagonisms and promising to fight Tripoli's historical enemies – the Lebanese government, the Syrian regime and Israel. Tawhid, then, was Islamist but also claimed to embody Tripoli; its people, interests and identity. Naturally this claim would be vehemently challenged by different portions of local society, from leftist movements and notables to religious minorities; and it is worth pointing out from the onset that it never earned the support of more than a minority in the city. But the question of its rootedness in the physical, social and symbolic dimensions of Tripolitan space lingered. This was made even more intriguing by a second puzzle: far from an exception, Tawhid's obsession with all things Tripoli was part of an older local tradition which had seen the birth of many movements embedded in and oriented toward local space. The city had long witnessed a range of social and rebel movements which embraced ideologies that were all different from each other, for example pan-Syrian nationalism, pan-Arabism, radical Marxism and Islamism, but all engaged in a measure of spatially oriented contention; that is, they addressed Tripolitan grievances and identities and spearheaded local collective action. There was something peculiar about Tripoli more generally, then, which had long fueled the growth of spatially oriented movements there, much more than anywhere else in Lebanon.

This chapter explores why Tripoli became a stronghold for a succession of social movements that espoused a variety of rebel ideologies, including but not limited to Islamism. I claim that this resulted from the momentum of their ideologies but, just as significantly, that it also stemmed from the success of these movements to channel the grievances of Tripolitans and cast their activism as part of the "tales of contention" glorifying the city's rebel history. I begin by explaining that one of Tripoli's most remarkable features is the strong collective identity of its residents, their shared sense of belonging to the city as a primary community. This is due to Tripoli's prestigious history as the capital of its own province for centuries and to the role it played for over a millennia as the proud gateway of prosperous Greater Syria. But equally important in Tripolitan identity is a collective bitterness at the city's lost glory. This began to become prevalent from the late nineteenth and early twentieth century onward, when the residents began experiencing an acute sense of decline. Their grievances stemmed in part from the Ottoman Empire's policies, which demoted Tripoli to the status of a secondary city. Even more significant, however, was the French Mandate's landmark decision to cut Tripoli off from the Syrian hinterland, to which residents had a deep social and emotional attachment, and to incorporate it into the newly formed state of Lebanon. This not only enhanced the city's political, economic and administrative marginalization, it also suddenly severed a facet of its collective identity which had long organically associated Tripoli with Syria. Although it had witnessed many previous instances of collective action, it was really then, from the 1920s onward, that Tripoli began earning a reputation as a rebel city, as it started to engage more frequently and more forcefully in contention than any other Lebanese city. Thousands of those I call the "contentious Tripolitans," who were driven by these primarily local grievances and identities and were buoyed by the revival of the city's "tales of contention," poured on to the streets to rebel against the French Mandate and the Lebanese government. With time, the nature of their target broadened. While they continued to display an almost instinctive opposition to successive Lebanese governments, many Tripolitans began engaging in locally oriented collective action against the city's notables who, out of pragmatism, were becoming more favorable to the state. This trend accelerated due to fast-developing social tensions from the 1950s onward, which pitted New Tripoli against the Old City. Finally, in the 1970s, yet another target of the "contentious Tripolitans" would be the Syrian regime which, in addition to occupying the city after the 1976 Syrian

40   Tales of a Rebel City

military intervention in Lebanon, also sought to undermine the armed Palestinian presence, although strong social and emotional ties to Palestine stood at the core of Tripoli's sense of collective identity. Throughout this period, myriad rebel movements espousing a succession of ideologies such as Syrian nationalism, pan-Arabism, radical leftism and Islamism all became popular locally. The strength of these movements partially stemmed from the successive echo of their ideologies in society, or their "cultural momentum." But it was also due to their success at casting their grand beliefs in the context of typically Tripolitan grievances, narratives and identities. As the rest of this book will show, this would be a key to Tawhid's recipe too.

The Strength of Tripolitan Identity

At the core of Tripoli's propensity to nurture social and rebel movements grounded in and oriented toward space is the strong attachment of locals to their city, their collective identity. Indeed, being Tripolitan fits especially well the criteria established by Alberto Melucci, a pioneer of the "cultural turn" in social sciences, who pointed out that at the core of collective identities lay what he called a common "cognitive framework"[1] – the recognition by members of a community that they share a culture and a destiny – that can push people to act together. Tripolitans of all walks of life often intensely identify with their city as a community, proudly speaking about its rich, although at times slightly mythicized, history and culture to the extent that their local collective identity comes close to Benedict Anderson's definition of nationalism as a socially constructed "imagined community,"[2] or group feeling. Many of them even view this community through the lens of perceived kinship, as suggested by the often-used phrase "the sons of Tripoli," which assimilates residents to members of a family. Not all Tripolitans, of course, have exactly the same definition of what it means to belong to the local community and this local identity, far from being fixed, has evolved

---

[1] Alberto Melucci, *Nomads of the present: social movements and individual needs in contemporary culture* (Berkeley: Radius Publishers and University of California Press, 1989), pp. 34–5. On the role of collective identities in activism, see: Francesca Polletta and James Jasper, "Collective identity and social movements" *Annual Review of Sociology* (Vol. 27, 2001), pp. 283–305 and Jeff Goodwin, James Jasper and Francesca Polletta (eds.), *Passionate politics: emotions and social movements* (Chicago, University of Chicago Press, 2001).

[2] Benedict Anderson, *Imagined communities: reflections on the origin and spread of nationalism* (London, Verso, 1983).

through history. But all residents nonetheless share pride in Tripoli and pinpoint common traits to local identity.

This was not only remarked through extensive interviews but by outside observers too. One of them, who authored a landmark study on Tripoli, was bewildered by the "sense of local pride which has travelled through history to the present time," noting how residents frequently boast about their "millennial history" and their "strong collective identity." And, while this sense of belonging to the city as a community is often expressed explicitly, it is sometimes so powerful that this observer also remarked on the presence of a "Tripolitan subconscious," "implanted in the hearts of the people of the city," everyone "inheriting local identity and recalling it like family stories," "remaining alive and close to them and the city." As a result, it was clear to him that Tripolitans, even those from conflicting backgrounds or ideologies, viewed themselves as "one group, one people and one nation" – and that this could lead them into "mobilizing" large groups of residents in locally oriented activism.[3]

Two foundational and interrelated facets of Tripolitan identity channeled by the myriad movements trying to root themselves locally, including Tawhid in the 1980s, are narratives about the city's prestigious past and its social and emotional attachment to Syria.

To begin with, the fact that residents collectively identify with Tripoli as a social and political community stems from its rich history as one of the oldest Middle Eastern cities. Apart from local historians, very few scholars have explored Tripoli's past and evolution, which is a symptom of a broader lack of attention to Arab cities outside the main capitals.[4] Local historical accounts, which widely circulate in Tripoli through

---

[3] Mohammed Abi Samra, *Trablus: Sehat Allah wa mina al-hadatha* [*Tripoli: Allah Square and port of modernity*] (Beirut: Dar al-Saqi, 2011), pp. 50–3.

[4] Note that even studies of Lebanese politics and history tend to overwhelmingly focus on developments in the capital, Beirut, and to relegate Tripoli, the country's second largest city, to the backseat of their narratives. There are only a handful of exceptions. For the few excellent scholarly works that explicitly delve into elements of Tripoli's society, history and politics, see, for instance: John Gulick, *Tripoli: a modern Arab city* (Cambridge, Ma: Harvard University Press, 1967); James Reilly, *The Ottoman cities of Lebanon: historical legacy and identity in the Middle East* (London: I.B.Tauris, 2016); Michel Seurat, "Le quartier de Bab Tebbane à Tripoli (Liban), étude d'une assabiya urbaine," chapter 3 in Mona Zakaria (ed.), *Mouvements communautaires et espaces urbains au Machreq* (Beirut: Presses de l'Ifpo, 1985); Bernard Rougier, *The Sunni tragedy in the Middle East: Northern Lebanon from al-Qaeda to ISIS* (London, Princeton University Press, 2018); and Tine Gade, "Conflit en Syrie et dynamiques de guerre civile à Tripoli, Liban" *Maghreb-Machrek* (Vol. 218, No. 4, 2013), pp. 61–84. Also see Tine Gade, *From genesis to disintegration: the crisis of the political-religious field in Tripoli, Lebanon (1967–2011)* (Paris: Sciences Po, unpublished PhD thesis, 2015).

42   Tales of a Rebel City

popular culture (e.g. books, celebrations, a well-entrenched oral trad-ition passing narratives on to generations), emphasize how the city was created in 700 BC and right away became a strategic hub. Originally it had been created by settlers from the Phoenician towns of Sidon, Tyre and Arwad who, at first, each lived in separate neighborhoods, hence its etymology as *Tri-polis*. What drove them to settle there was the favorable geography of the land. It was surrounded, all at once, by a mountain range that protected it to the east, an agricultural plain to the north, a string of small islands that reduced the strength of the waves reaching the shores; and it was traversed by a generous river stream that passed through its midst. All of this made of Tripoli a safe and valuable location to build a harbor and trade, which soon turned the city into one of Phoenicia's key ports and, later, the seat of its government. Local histor-ical accounts even quote famed ancient Greek historian Diodorus of Sicily describing it as an "important city"[5] in one of the world encyclo-pedias he wrote in 60 BC. The very beginnings of Tripoli's existence over 2,700 years ago, then, are already associated with a sense of self-importance in the widely shared local narratives that still circulate.

Yet Tripoli would have to wait until the seventh century and its capture by the Muslim army of the fast-expanding Ummayad Islamic Caliphate to begin taking a more regional significance. The Ummayad officers, based in their capital Damascus, right away sensed the strategic value of turning the city into their key naval base and gateway to the eastern Mediterranean. The port's location seemed perfectly central on the eastern coast of the Islamic Caliphate, right in between Alexandretta in the north and Gaza in the south (see Map 1.1). It was, moreover, conveniently shielded from the occasional invasions of the time by high-rise mountains to its east which, crucially, still provided through a narrow valley a trade route to the thriving city of Homs, only 90 km east and, from there, safe passage to both Damascus as well as Aleppo. Soon enough, then, the Ummayad rulers transformed Tripoli from the pros-perous city it had become into a hub of regional importance, local narratives even claiming that it came to rival the mythic port of Alexandria for the status of first Arab navy port of the Caliphate.[6] This was probably an exaggeration, but it still reflected local pride in Tripoli's growing status.

---

[5] Diodorus of Sicily quoted in Omar Tadmori, *Tarikh Trablus al-siessi wa al-hadari 'aber al-'asur* [*The political and cultural history of Tripoli through the ages*] (Tripoli: Dar al-Bilad, 1978), Tome 1, p. 31. Note that Omar Tadmori's three-volumes on Tripoli is the best-known and most respected historical account of the city.

[6] Samih al-Zein, *Tarikh Trablus qadiman wa hadathan* [*Recent and ancient history of Tripoli*] (Beirut, Dar al-Andalus, 1969).

The Strength of Tripolitan Identity

It is also to this early era of history that residents refer to when they narrate the roots of what contentious politics scholar James Jasper would have called their lingering "affective commitments"[7] to Syria, even though their city has officially been a part of Lebanon since 1920. For well over a millennia, starting in the seventh century, Tripoli became a central part of the historical sub-region of the Middle East long known as "Greater Syria" (*Bilad al-Sham*). Today sometimes referred to in the West as "the Levant," this large area spanned from Anatolia to the Sinai desert and stretched from the Mediterranean coast to the Euphrates, with its heart in contemporary Syria and the city of Damascus, nicknamed *al-Sham* ("the heaven," in the ancient local language of Akkadian). It was then that, in a show of the organic ties Tripoli developed to Greater Syria, the city became known as *Trablus al-Sham*, which translated into "Tripoli of Syria" or "Tripoli of Damascus." This also conveniently helped distinguish it from its Libyan eponym, *Trablus al-Gharb* ("Tripoli of the West"). Tellingly, reflecting the lingering attachment of their city to the Syrian hinterland, many residents still use the nickname "Tripoli of Syria." In the following centuries, Tripoli continued growing in status and importance. In 999 the city became the theater of a violent power struggle for supremacy in the eastern Mediterranean that pitted the Byzantine Empire against the Islamic Caliphate. Interestingly, the local historical accounts that circulate today often highlight the "heroic resistance"[8] of Tripolitans against the troops of Byzantine Emperor Basil II during the month-long siege of their city. This episode, even if perhaps slightly mythicized, is often remembered in local popular narratives as one of the founding blocs of the "tales of contention" which associate Tripoli with a tradition of rebellion against outsiders. Even Tawhid would come to refer to it.

Shortly thereafter, in 1066, the city's reputation as a hub of strategic, military and economic importance extended to becoming a seat of cultural and intellectual dynamism when the local Banu Ammar dynasty that ruled Tripoli built the "House of Knowledge" (*Dar al-Ilm*). This was a university complex which hosted a library that was said to have boasted up to 100,000 manuscripts, attracting scholars from the entire Middle East.[9]

The period of the Crusades which soon followed is often narrated in ambivalent ways. On the one hand, local accounts emphasize the brutal

---

[7] James Jasper notes how the particular attachment or positive feelings of people for certain causes, ideas or places can develop into "affective commitments," which lie at the heart of the notion of "collective identity." See James Jasper, *The emotions of protest* (Chicago, University of Chicago Press, 2018), pp. 101–27.

[8] Mousbah Rajab, *Le vieux Tripoli (Liban), un espace historique en voie de mutation* (Paris: University of Pantheon Sorbonne, unpublished PhD thesis, 1993), p. 36.

[9] Tadmori, *Tarikh Trablus*, pp. 40–2.

44   Tales of a Rebel City

nature of the conquest of the city by the troops of Raymond de St. Gilles, the Count of Toulouse, even resulting in mass looting. But, on the other hand, they also delve deep into Tripoli's rise to Crusader stardom. The Franks, back then, are said to have entirely rebuilt the city and constructed an imposing medieval castle that overlooked the whole area and its seashore, the Fortress of St. Gilles, which still stands today. The symbolism associated with the castle's longevity, imposing size and role as the quintessential space of resistance would continue to shape the "tales of contention" that glorify a local tradition of collective violence justified as self-defense.

Significantly, the Crusaders also turned the city into the capital of its own province, the County of Tripoli, which alongside Jerusalem arose for the next 200 years as one of the Levant's largest Crusader Kingdoms, reinforcing the local sense of self-importance.[10] Back then, the city of Tripoli became the seat of power of a vast territory extending from the coastal towns of Latakia in the north and Byblos in the south and stretching as far east as Homs, where the Crusaders built the world-famous "Krak des Chevaliers" medieval fortress which was meant to guard entry into the land and protect the valley linking Homs to Tripoli. Local historical accounts of that period remark that it was then that Homs and Tripoli, enclosed for two centuries within one territory and socio-political entity, considerably enhanced their bonds and acquired a reputation as organically linked sister cities. As this book will show, far from disappearing with time, the social and emotional ties binding these cities which nowadays belong to two different states would never be submerged. They would, in fact, resurface frequently and powerfully, including during Tawhid's time in the 1980s.

In 1289, the County of Tripoli was the last Crusader kingdom to fall to the Mamluks. Yet the new Muslim rulers, rather than destroying the city and demoting its status, kept intact the boundaries of the province of which it was the capital and turned it into one of the six provinces (*wilayat*) of the region of Greater Syria. In a reflection of the status, then, of the Province of Tripoli, it was the third most important in rank, behind Damascus and Aleppo. It was then, local accounts narrate, that "Tripoli of Syria" reached its apogee as a major city.

Architecturally the Mamluks invested so much in renovating and constructing buildings that the city became known for some time as

---

[10] For historical accounts of the "County of Tripoli" during Crusader times, see: Tadmori, *Tarikh Trablus*, Tomes 1 and 2; Jean Richard, *Le Comté de Tripoli sous la dynastie toulousaine* (1102–87) (Beirut: Presses de l'Ifpo, 1945) and Kevin James Lewis, *Sons of Saint-Gilles: the Counts of Tripoli and Lebanon in the Twelfth Century* (London: Routledge, 2016).

The Strength of Tripolitan Identity 45

"Tripoli the Renewed One"[11] (*Trablus al-Mustajadda*). The new Muslim rulers built a dozen mosques including some of its largest and most beautiful ones still active today, such as the Great Mosque al-Mansouri, in the vicinity of the Old City, and al-Tawbe, in the heart of the *suq*, the historical covered markets. They also set out an ambitious plan to improve the Old City's overall infrastructure. This included the building of large walls surrounding it as well as a labyrinth of myriad narrow alleyways and military towers to defend it, but also over a dozen schools, four caravanserais, two extensions to the covered markets, three famed *hammams* or public baths, hospitals and an entirely new irrigation system bringing running water to most of the houses. Their imprint was in fact such that Tripoli's Old City came to boast the second largest amount of Mamluk architectural heritage in the Middle East, second only to Cairo, the seat of Mamluk power.[12] And the fact that much of this impressive architectural legacy is still standing today in Tripoli's historical districts perhaps helps reinforce narratives of the city's prestigious past. One observer even argued that this millennial architecture has had a "profound impact" on all those residing in these quarters, acting as a "collective testament to the city's long history."[13]

Economically, this architectural renaissance and general improvement of infrastructure attracted the attention of the merchants in nearby Homs and Hama but also in cities slightly further away, like Aleppo and Damascus, who all bolstered their ties to Tripoli. Growing marriage and business bonds with the merchants and craftsmen of these cities and local sailors and traders allowed them to use Tripoli as a main gateway for their exports, both consolidating its important status and reinforcing its anchoring within the Syrian hinterland. With time, half of Tripoli's population would come to have family ties with people in Syria. The end result was that, by the late fourteenth century, the port had become such a crucial stage for exports coming out of Greater Syria that all European governments interested in trade with this rich region of the Middle East had to send resident consuls to Tripoli, including Venice.[14] Tripoli had now acquired the prestigious reputation of acting as the port of Greater Syria.

---

[11] See, for instance, Omar Tadmori, *Tarikh wa athar masajed wa madares Trablus fi asar al-Mamalek* [*History and legacy of the mosques and the schools of Tripoli during Mamluk times*] (Tripoli: Dar al-Bilad, 1974), pp. 26–7.

[12] Hayaf Salam-Liebich, *The architecture of the Mamluk city of Tripoli* (Cambridge, MA: Harvard University Press, 1975), pp. 11–14.

[13] Abi Samra, *Trablus*, p. 44.

[14] Gulick, *Tripoli*, p. 17. See also Antoine Abdel Nour, *Introduction à l'histoire urbaine de la Syrie Ottomane (16eme-18eme siècle)* (Beirut: Publication de l'Université Libanaise, 1982), p. 44.

46   Tales of a Rebel City

In sum, then, the first 2,000 years of Tripoli's history was an era marked by its rise to strategic importance in Greater Syria and by its growing ties to cities of the Syrian hinterland. This, in turn, powerfully shaped the process of collective identification to Tripoli as a community characterized by shared pride in a grand, if at times slightly mythicized, past, in its undeniable architectural beauty and in its lingering social and emotional ties to Syria. Virtually all the popular political movements in twentieth-century Tripoli, including Tawhid, would later seek to frame their grand ideologies against the backdrop of these elements of local identity.

Narratives of a Lost Glory

Another facet of Tripolitan identity is the sense of bitterness at the city's lost glory, which fueled narratives of local grievances that allowed social and rebel movements to recruit. Interestingly, while most popular accounts and local historical chronicles trace Tripoli's decline to the period of the French Mandate in the 1920s, when the momentous decision of detaching the city from its Syrian hinterland was taken, scholarly analyses and diplomatic dispatches suggest that local grievances were already fast mounting under Ottoman rule.

The Ottoman conquest of Greater Syria in 1516 did not right away weaken the major status that Tripoli had come to take under the Ummayads, Crusaders and Mamluks. Initially the Ottomans kept the administrative and political map that the Mamluks had designed for the subregion of Greater Syria, and as a result Tripoli continued to be the capital of its own province, which rendered it as important a city as Damascus and Aleppo. Gradually, however, its reputation as a well-equipped and safe gateway to the Syrian hinterland crumbled, something that accounts from that period trace to the brutality and lack of care in the city of the Ottoman pashas, or local Turkish rulers, throughout the sixteenth century. Unlike two centuries earlier, when the Mamluks had massively invested in renovating and upgrading the local infrastructure, this period became characterized by the city's degradation. Early Ottoman rule is known to have been marked by corruption in many other cities of the Levant. But in Tripoli levels of carelessness came to reach record highs for, according to a scholar, less than 10 percent of the local taxes levied by the pashas ended up being reinvested in the much-needed renovation of its port and the improvement of infrastructure.[15]

---

[15] Farouk Hoblos, "Public services and tax revenues in Ottoman Tripoli (1516–1918)," chapter 7 in Peter Sluglett and Stefan Weber (eds.), *Syria and Bilad al-Sham under Ottoman rule* (Leiden: Brill, 2010), p. 126.

Moreover, while the Ottomans, whose center of gravity was today's Turkey, had the ambition of turning Aleppo into the cornerstone of their "silk road" between Asia and the West, a plan which in theory could have benefited Tripoli given its status as the port of Greater Syria, they preferred upgrading the harbor of Alexandretta, closer to Istanbul, than investing in Tripoli.

Local accounts highlight how, throughout this time, Tripoli remained linked to Syria. One episode in particular still shapes both narratives of attachment to Syria and the "tales of contention" which associate the city with a tradition of collective rebellion against outsiders. As the power of the Ottoman Empire gradually faded in the 1820s and 1830s, the governor of Egypt, Muhammed Ali, broke away and launched an assault on Ottoman forces to conquer Greater Syria in the First Egyptian-Ottoman War. But when, nearly a decade later, the Egyptian troops began suffering a series of setbacks and came to agree to a settlement wherein they would keep control of the territory south of Tripoli in exchange for a ceasefire, effectively separating the port city from its Syrian hinterland, Tripolitans rebelled en masse. While local historical accounts often narrate this episode in ways emphasizing the collective and heroic nature of the rebellion of "the sons of Tripoli," early diplomatic dispatches match these accounts. They emphasize how, in Tripoli, "the insurgents are in force," having "too many wrongs to redress to remain quiet spectators of what is going on in Greater Syria without making an effort to free themselves from the yoke of the Egyptians."[16] The Tripolitan rebellion of 1840 would significantly weaken Egyptian troops, paving the way for the return of the Ottomans and the reunification of Greater Syria. Although it had suffered from Ottoman rule, Tripoli still preferred attachment to Greater Syria under Ottoman auspices than being swallowed into Egypt and cut from its hinterland.

In the nineteenth century an additional feature of Tripolitan identity emerged: rivalry with Beirut. While Tripoli boasted a prestigious past and had long counted approximately 40,000 inhabitants, Beirut for its part had always been a mere village of 5,000 until this changed in the nineteenth century. By the end of that century, indeed, it had turned into a prosperous city of 50,000. The increase of trade between the Ottoman Empire and Europe had meant a growing Western presence in the

---

[16] Note that Tripoli was among the first Levantine cities to rebel against the Egyptians in 1840, then shortly followed by Latakia, Beirut and more major urban centers such as Aleppo. See, among others, UK Foreign Office, "Colonel Hodges to Viscount Palmerston, Alexandria" (June 16, 1840, No. 49); UK Foreign Office, "Mr Wood to Viscount Ponsonby" (October 10, 1840, No. 11) and UK Foreign Office, "Mr de Lourin to the Baron de Sturmer" (June 18, 1840, No. 39).

48   Tales of a Rebel City

Levant. And Beirut, due to the presence of many Christians, a safe location near Mount Lebanon and its proximity to Damascus, the seat of political and economic power in Greater Syria, soon attracted significant private capital while embassies began opening branches there. This led the Ottomans to invest considerably in upgrading Beirut's infrastructure and to renovate the facilities of its harbor. But this, in the words of a scholar, further accelerated "the decline of the old ports of Sidon, Acre and Tripoli."[17] Tripolitan bitterness at Beirut grew as it became evident that the latter was virtually the only city in Greater Syria to profit from the nineteenth-century liberalization of the Ottoman Empire's economy, which deeply affected Tripoli as it undermined the production of silk and soap by flooding local markets with cheaper European products. Local popular narratives that emphasize the city's traditional rivalry with Beirut also fixate on how, back then, Tripoli was demoted, ceasing to be the capital of its own province and, instead, becoming swallowed into Beirut's. This also reflected the city's decline after a millennia of good fortunes.

The sense that, in local historical accounts, the city's slow demise is not always clearly traced back to Ottoman rule probably stems from the fact that the late Ottoman period was marked by sustained efforts on the part of Istanbul to improve Tripoli's infrastructure. Many of the architectural legacies left behind by the Ottomans are still visible today. In the 1840s and 1850s they introduced a postal delivery system and installed a telegraph, and in the 1870s they set up a horse-drawn tramway that linked Tripoli's Old City to its nearby port of Mina which, at the time, were two distinct geographical areas separated by groves of lemon and orange trees. Two decades later the Ottoman rulers even undertook the construction of key landmarks that are still standing today, including a high-rise clock tower, a mansion of the governor (*serail*) and a city council (*baladiye*). They also built many schools and considerably enlarged the historical covered markets of the Old City. Although, objectively, Ottoman rule therefore marked the beginning of Tripoli's decline, it is not seen in such clear ways locally, principally because the late Ottoman period is recalled as one during which the city witnessed an architectural renaissance with a legacy largely still visible today.

Moreover, even though the late Ottoman period witnessed the demotion of Tripoli and its administrative incorporation into the Province of Beirut, this era of history remains marked by strong persisting social and emotional links between the city and its Syrian hinterland. The discovery

---

[17] Moshe Maoz, *Ottoman reform in Syria and Palestine, 1840–1861: the impact of the Tanzimat on politics and society* (Oxford: Oxford University Press, 1968), p. 181.

of oil in the Persian Gulf and the advent of the railway in the first two decades of the twentieth century even revived local hopes that Tripoli would climb back to glory by once again acting as the port of Greater Syria, from where oil bound to the West would be shipped. Initially Tripoli did attract global interest, as the great powers of the day, including Russia, developed plans early on to make it the pivotal point of their fast-growing trade route linking the oil-rich countries of Kuwait and Iraq to Western and Eastern Europe. As a result, a train station was built in 1909 in Mina, the port neighborhood, whose ruins still stand and for many locals act as a reminder of the city's regional reach at that time. Simultaneously, in a reflection of the degree to which "affective commitments" still bound Tripolitans to the residents of Homs, popular accounts as well as diplomatic dispatches of that time report on how the residents collectively fundraised to build a train line that would link the two sister cities and facilitate safer and quicker travel than the diligence line.[18] Within a few years the Tripoli–Homs railway line took on a more strategic importance. It was used as a terminus for the Orient Express line that linked Tripoli to Aleppo, Istanbul and Paris. Even more importantly, it also connected Tripoli to the thriving trade route spanning Greater Syria and crossing Homs and Palmyra to reach the vibrant city of Baghdad. The sense that Tripoli was experiencing a revival seemed to materialize shortly later when the Iraqi Petroleum Company (IPC) chose the city as its main hub for shipments to Western and Eastern Europe and built a complex to stock, refine and export oil coming from Kirkuk.

Already back then, narratives of Tripolitan hopes of a revival and attachment to its Syrian hinterland were so prevalent that even foreigners began reporting on them. One observer for instance highlighted how the advent of the Tripoli–Homs–Palmyra–Baghdad railway line was experienced in Tripoli as exposing "the entirely fictitious importance" that Beirut had come to take in the preceding decades. The success of the Tripoli–Baghdad line, then, demonstrated that the "historical claims of

---

[18] At the time, the price of setting up the 90 km long railway line between Tripoli and Homs reached £40,000, a considerable amount. It was because Tripolitans organized a local fundraising which gathered half of this amount that the French Damascus Homs Railway Company, which had bought the concession rights, agreed to pay for the rest and build the line in the agreed time. It seems to have become even more popular in the subsequent decades for an observer noted in the 1930s that the line was very busy and that trade through it had developed rapidly. See: UK Foreign Office, "Turkey: annual report" (Confidential 9624, No. 30, 1909); UK Mission in Beirut, "Consul General Sir R Hay-Drummond-Hay to Sir N.O'Connor" (No. 98, November 14, 1907); and UK Mission in Beirut, "Mr Bateman to Mr Eden" (No. 423, E 5488/518/65, August 18, 1936).

50   Tales of a Rebel City

Tripoli as the principal port of Syria" had been unjustly wronged and that the city might now been restored to its "proper importance."[19] Another diplomat, immersed in narratives of a Tripolitan revival, went as far as speculating that the city would now soon reemerge as the main gateway to the eastern Mediterranean and surface as what he called "a dangerous rival to Beirut,"[20] in a telling choice of words. And, in a reflection of Tripoli's lingering connections to its Syrian hinterland and rivalry with Beirut, it would take the Beirut–Tripoli railway line as much as four decades more than for the Tripoli–Homs line to see the light of day, even though the two cities only stood 80 km apart. This showed how, despite the spatial proximity between Beirut and Tripoli, narratives of a rivalry between them and the latter's longstanding attachment to Homs meant that the relations between the two cities were for long kept to a minimum.

Yet the true turning point which, in popular narratives and local historical accounts, is collectively recalled as the one defining event that heralded the city's acute, long-term decline and the rise of local griev-ances was Tripoli's separation from its Syrian hinterland. This momen-tous decision was taken in 1920, in the wake of the Turkish defeat in World War I, as the French and the British dismantled the Ottoman Empire and artificially split the territory of Greater Syria into the newly formed states of Lebanon, Syria, Palestine and Jordan. Interestingly, while the French decision to incorporate Tripoli into Lebanon stemmed from a divide-and-rule strategy to split the Syrian nationalist camp by attaching a Muslim-majority city to Christian-dominated Lebanon, it was met with unease by Lebanese Christian Maronites themselves. One of their key figures, Emile Edde, who would rise to become prime minister and president, even lobbied the French for a decade after the creation of Lebanon to return the city to Syria. His plea, however, was unsuccessful. In 1926 the enactment of the Lebanese constitution enshrined Tripoli's official belonging to Lebanon.

In hindsight, many Tripolitans view their city's detachment from its Syrian hinterland and incorporation into Lebanon as the single most fateful event in Tripoli's entire history. First, it was collectively experi-enced as an attack on the city and its identity, not only for it had long seen itself as "Tripoli of Syria," rather than "Tripoli of Lebanon," but also as the creation of borders within the territory of Greater Syria killed the dreams of many locals that their city would once again act as the main

---

[19] UK Foreign Office, "War Office to Foreign Office" (Secret, 24952, No. 42, July 26, 1907).

[20] UK Mission in Beirut, "Acting Consul General Young to Sir G. Lowther" (No. 46, October 1, 1919).

gateway to the eastern Mediterranean. The Tripoli–Homs–Palmyra–Baghdad railway, for instance, progressively stopped functioning and, for its part, the IPC's Kirkuk–Tripoli oil pipeline became caught in the power rivalries of the newly formed states of Iraq, Syria and Lebanon, which undermined its proper working.

Second, Tripoli's forceful incorporation into Lebanon came to mean that, for centuries the capital of its own province, it was now relegated to the status of secondary city. Indeed, as a centralized state Lebanon concentrated the bulk of resources on its new capital, Beirut, enlarging and improving its harbor at considerable cost while postponing the improvement of infrastructure in other Lebanese cities, including Tripoli, until later. This meant that, by 1936, the port of Beirut had already witnessed the arrival of nearly twice as many shipping boats per year as the port of Tripoli – and, in a sign of where the dynamic was headed, four decades later it had ten times more.[21] For many Tripolitans, then, the city's incorporation into Lebanon had come to mean submission to their bitter rival, Beirut, and it began marking an acute sense of economic, political and administrative marginalization.

Third, from a purely economic perspective, the consequences for Tripoli were dire. The local traders, farmers and small artisans gradually became cut off from their traditional market in the Syrian hinterland, and especially from their sister cities of Homs and Hama. At first the fact that Syria and Lebanon were both under French control in 1920–43 facilitated an economic union between the two countries that helped maintain a level of trade between the port city and its Syrian hinterland. But the break-up of that union in the post-independence era, in 1949, suddenly and painfully severed that historical trade relationship. The introduction of tariff barriers, complex administrative procedures for exports and lengthy verifications at the new Syrian-Lebanese border, only 30 km away from Tripoli, undermined the local production of textiles and citrus crops which traders used to export to Syria. Other parts of Lebanon were also affected by this, such as the Beqaa Valley and South Lebanon, but, according to an observer, the general sense by the early 1950s was that "the repercussions were particularly felt in Tripoli, which acted as the port of the Syrian hinterland."[22]

---

[21] In 1936, while Beirut witnessed the arrival of 256 boats, Tripoli had 145. By comparison, the other Syrian ports of the time, like Alexandretta and Latakia, only had respectively eighty-six and twenty-one boats. Tripoli thus remained a major Syrian port but it had clearly been replaced by Beirut as the most strategic gateway to Greater Syria. See UK Mission in Beirut, "Economic conditions in the Lebanon and Syria during the quarter ended June 30 1936" (Enclosure in No. 73, No. 249, October 22, 1936).

[22] UK Embassy in Beirut, "Lebanon: annual review for 1951" (Confidential, No. 45, EL 1011/1, February 19, 1952).

52   Tales of a Rebel City

It is thus no surprise that, given all these ripple effects, the decision to detach Tripoli from Syria would be collectively experienced as an "attack on the city,"[23] its interests and its identity. This would fuel the local grievances which led to the formation of long-term dissent at the Lebanese government and nurtured the rise of myriad social and rebel movements.

The Contentious Tripolitans

From the 1920s until the 1980s Tripoli witnessed the proliferation of local rebel movements which embraced a variety of ideologies, but were all spatially grounded to a striking extent. Of course, their emergence stemmed from their embrace of ideologies whose momentum grew successively, from pan-Syrian nationalism and pan-Arabism to leftism and Islamism. As a result many members of these movements were sincerely attracted by parts of these ideologies. Yet it is striking how popular narratives and historical accounts highlight not the ideological conviction of these members but, rather, a desire to join "local rebel movements," as if what characterized them primarily was a will to engage in spatially oriented activism. I call the "contentious Tripolitans" those activists who are said to have gotten involved in violent episodes of contention against the authorities not because of ideology per se, but rather because of a deep-seated willingness to defend Tripolitan identity, address local grievances and uphold the "tales of contention" associating the city to a tradition of rebellion. One observer thus noted how many members of these ideologically diverse social and rebel movements seemed primarily driven by a "collective determination to remain faithful to the city's heritage and identity," a "wounded sense of local greatness and aggravated feelings of deprivation" as well as a contentious instinct stemming from "the depths of local history." Guided by "epic narratives about Tripoli," they "mobilized against its external enemies."[24] As a result, Tripoli would for over sixty years witness various waves of activism, which were remarkably larger, more violent and more locally oriented than anywhere else in Lebanon.

As early as in 1920, shortly after the French decision to incorporate Tripoli into the newly formed state of Lebanon, thousands of these "contentious Tripolitans," driven by local identity and grievances, joined the Syrian nationalist movements which back then were fast on the rise, engaging in activism against the French as well as against the new

---

[23] Abi Samra, *Trablus*, p. 41.   [24] Ibid., p. 52.

The Contentious Tripolitans 53

Lebanese authorities. There was, of course, a broader sense of attachment to Greater Syria which animated activists in other parts of Lebanon too. This was especially the case with many Sunni Muslim citizens of the new country, who saw the domination they had long enjoyed under Ottoman rule now being reversed as the Lebanese political system largely advantaged local Christian Maronites. Cities and neighborhoods of the new state of Lebanon that were characterized by Sunni Muslim majorities, like the coastal town of Sidon as well as West Beirut, thus also witnessed early mobilizations which protested against the French decision to dismantle Greater Syria. But, right away, it was Tripoli in particular which became the spearhead of this contention.

Initially the Tripolitan opposition to the French Mandate and to the new Lebanese authorities expressed itself peacefully, through large-scale but largely benign demonstrations as well as through popular petitions handed to officials by local notables, such as Abdel Hamid Karame, the city's religious leader and a prominent Syrian nationalist. Gradually, however, as it transpired that peaceful protests and popular petitions alone would not be sufficient, the local Syrian nationalist movements became more restless and militant. The spatial salience of mobilizations in Tripoli became evident by 1926 when the Lebanese constitution was adopted and enshrined the new country's borders. Observers not only noted that "resentment was strongest in Tripoli," in the form of violent demonstrations, but that while protesters in other Sunni-majority areas such as Sidon and West Beirut were prepared to compromise by proposing a Lebanese confederation in which they would retain autonomy, the Tripolitans who had taken to the streets insisted on full-blown reintegration into Syria.[25] This showed that the mobilizations in Tripoli were largely shaped by local collective identity.

Tension again peaked in 1936 as France and Lebanon were about to sign a Treaty of Friendship and Alliance, which once more confirmed Tripoli's status as an integral part of the new state. As Emile Edde, the Lebanese president, went on a tour of North Lebanon and met with Tripoli's notables, residents welcomed him with a one-week strike as well as slogans of Syrian unity. And, while Sidon and West Beirut remained quiet, Tripoli became restless after the treaty was signed. One external observer then noted that "the reception of the treaty has been stormy, Tripoli has already been more or less closed for the past month as a protest against its retention in Lebanon."[26] Another observer reported

[25] Najla Wadih Atiyah, *The attitude of the Lebanese Sunnis towards the state of Lebanon* (unpublished PhD thesis, London, University of London, 1973), pp. 122–3.
[26] UK Embassy in Beirut, "Acting Consul General Furlonge to Mr Eden" (No. 69, E4804/195/89, July 20, 1936).

54   Tales of a Rebel City

that, days after the treaty was ratified, "a large demonstration hoisted Syrian flags onto Tripoli's mosques" and, as it came into "violent collision" with the police forces, killing three activists, the protest erupted in a "fierce riot lasting three hours and resulting in three or four persons being shot and many injured." His conclusion was that it was "improbable" that those he tellingly called "the hardline" residents of Tripoli would be "as easy to appease as the softer Beirutis."[27] Strong collective identification with the city as a community with a rich history and culture of its own as well as deep-seated local grievances had made Tripoli a stronghold of contention.

In turn, the mechanism which explained the ability of many social and rebel movements to recruit the "contentious Tripolitans" and channel their local identity and solidarities into sustained anti-governmental mobilization was their revival and appropriation of the "tales of contention" associating the city with a rich and glorified tradition of collective rebellions against outsiders, whether the Byzantine Empire, the Crusaders or the Egyptians. One author thus noted how movement leaders succeeded in mobilizing the masses in large-scale protests by putting forward narratives which glorified the "epic millennial history," the "legacies of contention" and the sense of "social cohesion" that bound Tripolitans of all walks of life. Mobilizing against the French Mandate and the Lebanese government was thus cast as acting "in line"[28] with Tripoli's longer history of resistance against external enemies. The revival and appropriation of local "tales of contention" during conflictive times allowed the myriad social and rebel movements on the rise to root themselves locally and recruit many "contentious Tripolitans," making local mobilizations frequent, large in scale and heated.

Later episodes of rebellion in turn continued shaping Tripoli's "tales of contention." One event which took place in November 1943 particularly came to inform the narratives which, until today, exalt the city's strong sense of a community and culture of resistance. Despite the prospect of a Lebanese independence which would keep the country's new borders, the Syrian nationalist movement had not died down – and it was again Tripoli which acted as the spearhead of anti-governmental demonstrations. The French and Lebanese authorities, wary of a reenactment of the scenes of unrest that had gripped Tripoli in 1936, issued a decree forcing the residents of the city to hand in all weapons

---

[27] UK Embassy in Beirut, "Consul General Havard to Mr Eden" (No. 108, E7488/195/89, November 24, 1936).

[28] Abi Samra, *Trablus*, p. 47.

The Contentious Tripolitans

without exceptions. Shortly afterward they imposed a strict curfew and even arrested the local leader of the Syrian nationalist movement, Abdel Hamid Karame, also the Mufti or religious chief of Tripoli. But this, rather than intimidating the "contentious Tripolitans," instead emboldened them. Thousands reportedly poured onto the streets, unarmed, to demand Karame's immediate release and the city's reattachment to Syria. The reaction of the authorities would help forge the narrative that Tripoli is not just a "rebel" but also a "martyr" city in which residents are ready to sacrifice themselves for the defense of their community and its identity. As the authorities failed to disperse protesters, they sent tanks which hurtled their way into the crowd. Local historical accounts talk about a "massacre,"[29] and external observers largely concur, one of them even pointing out that even "some small children" were killed in this incident, which resulted in the death of sixteen "defenceless" protesters as well as the injury of eighty-two.[30] Days later Lebanon proclaimed its independence, and Tripoli remained a part of it. But popular narratives that the city was "coerced" into joining the country still linger, fueling the formation of long-term dissent against the government and providing the backdrop against which myriad revolutionary movements, including Tawhid, would thrive.

As Syria also gained its independence three years later, it became increasingly clear to the "contentious Tripolitans" that their city would remain a part of Lebanon, especially as the Syrian notables, despite regretting the loss of Tripoli, came to accept this new status quo. Yet this never signified a loss of the sense of Tripolitan attachment to the Syrian hinterland. In fact, the observers who toured the city throughout the 1940s and 1950s noticed that residents still displayed "separatist tendencies,"[31] one of them even becoming alarmed that the "secessionist movement" was still so "strong"[32] that it could lead to Lebanon's disintegration.

---

[29] Ibid., p. 46.

[30] UK Foreign Ministry, "General Spears to Minister of State" (E2242/207/89, April 10, 1942); UK Embassy in Beirut, "Weekly political summary Syria and Lebanon" (E2691/207/89, April 30, 1942); and UK Embassy in Beirut, "Weekly political summary, Syria and Lebanon" (No. 85, E711/27/89, November 17, 1943).

[31] UK Embassy in Beirut, "Lebanon: annual review for 1951" (Confidential, No. 45, EL 1011/1, February 19, 1952).

[32] The cable noted a "recrudescence of irredentist movement" among the population of Tripoli and concluded that the secessionist movement was still so strong there that it could burst into a violent struggle for reattachment to Syria. "Such a conflict might release other centrifugal forces and lead to the disintegration of Lebanon as an independent state." See: UK Embassy in Beirut, "Annual review of 1950" (Confidential, No. 3, EL1011/1, January 9, 1951). Interestingly, UK diplomats in Lebanon continued noting this sense of Tripolitan hostility toward the Lebanese state

56   Tales of a Rebel City

But, rather than being expressed through Syrian nationalism, Tripoli's rebel identity and attachment to Syria was now increasingly channeled through pan-Arabism. Many "contentious Tripolitans" were sincerely attracted by parts of this ideology, which included calls for a regional Arab government and radical social and political reforms. Yet what truly attracted them was this ideology's revolutionary undertones, questioning of the state system and advocacy of Arab unity that also implied, to them, Tripoli's reintegration in Syria. The spatial salience of pan-Arabism in Tripoli became evident after the rise of Egypt's Nasser. The new Egyptian president, of course, grew popular throughout the entire Middle East, especially after his bold standoff against the British, French and Israeli armies at Suez. In Lebanon, what became known as "Nasserism" became widely popular with Sunni Muslims, including in Sidon and West Beirut. But it was in Tripoli where it was strongest. There a mass of 30,000 locals enthusiastically took to the streets to celebrate Nasser's successes, which contrasted with the mere 5,000 demonstrators in Sidon, even though the latter was Lebanon's third largest city and considered a main hub of Nasserism in the country.[33] In other words, pan-Arabism as an ideology resonated with tales of Tripolitan culture and identity.

The full extent to which pan-Arabism had grown in Tripoli and came to channel inherently local identities, grievances and "tales of contention" transpired in 1958. Back then a violent conflict gripped Lebanon. It pitted the partisans of the Western-friendly Lebanese government against pan-Arab rebels who advocated for Lebanon's integration and dissolution within the Nasser-sponsored Egyptian–Syrian union, the United Arab Republic. Once again, although the pan-Arab rebels were overwhelmingly popular with the quarter of Sunni Muslims in Lebanon, it was Tripoli which fast became the epicenter of contention. There, pro-Nasser demonstrations which vilified the Lebanese government and glorified the Egyptian–Syrian union quickly grew massive. The army intervened but its violent crackdown only reinforced the resolve of protesters who armed themselves, pushed the security forces out of Tripoli,

---

for much of the 1950s, 1960s and 1970s. While one cable in 1975 noted that "the Sunnis, especially those in Tripoli, could most happily fit into Syria and their stake in Lebanon is not so clear," another diplomat in 1977 went as far as proposing the full-blown "return of the city of Tripoli to Syria" in case a Sunni-dominated government emerged there, remarking that it would remove the Lebanese element "most attached to Syria" and would answer Tripolitan grievances given that the city had "never recovered" from its incorporation into Lebanon. See: UK Embassy in Beirut, "The Lebanon in torment" (No. 244, NFLI/2, October 6, 1975) and UK Foreign Office, "J.L.Y. Sanders to Director of Research" (No. 77, 19/7 CDP, July 1, 1977).

[33] Atiyah, *The attitude of the Lebanese Sunnis*, pp. 257–8.

dug trenches and led a revolt against the government for over four months. Thousands of "contentious Tripolitans" are reported to have taken part in this rebellion and, in a show of how virulent the conflict between the government and the rebels was there, Tripoli would witness twice as many deaths as in Beirut and four times more than in Sidon.[34]

Interestingly, while a key motivation behind the involvement of many "contentious Tripolitans" in the 1958 conflict was to see their city reincorporated into the Syrian hinterland, this attachment between Tripoli and Syria was largely reciprocal for they were backed by sympathizers from Homs, hundreds of whom traveled to bolster the ranks of local rebels. After months of stalemate a series of regional and domestic initiatives succeeded in deescalating the conflict and restoring a form of status quo and a measure of order to the country. Yet in Tripoli this episode bolstered the "tales of contention" which associated the city with a tradition of collective rebellion against those perceived as oppressors and it showed that, despite now being a part of Lebanon, the city still kept strong cross-border ties to Syria.

Political and Social Antagonisms

With time the nature of the target of the "contentious Tripolitans" progressively broadened.

They continued to display an almost instinctive opposition to successive Lebanese governments. But, from the 1950s and 1960s onward, many "contentious Tripolitans" also began engaging in collective action against local notables, increasingly portrayed as outsiders to the community. This led local activists to embrace leftist movements more than before. The rise of radical left-wing movements in the northern city and their frequent engagement in protests of all kinds, in turn, consolidated Tripoli's reputation as a stronghold of contention.

Far from the mythicized local narratives which often highlight the "inner cohesion" of Tripoli, the city was by then witnessing growing cracks in its social fabric. It had long been characterized by sometimes violent internecine conflicts, such as a longstanding feud that opposed the powerful Karame and Muqaddem families. But until then residents of all walks of life were still united as a bloc when they felt their city was

---

[34] See: Nasser Kalawoun, *The struggle for Lebanon, a modern history of Lebanese-Egyptian relations* (New York: I.B.Tauris, 2000), p. 64 and pp. 86–7 and Joumana al-Soufi Richard, *Lutte populaire armée: de la désobéissance civile au combat pour Dieu* (Paris: University of La Sorbonne Nouvelle, unpublished PhD thesis, 1984), p. 38.

58   Tales of a Rebel City

being threatened. Yet, already in the mid-1940s, signs of antagonisms began to emerge between the popular masses and the Tripolitan upper class, made up of notables and businessmen. Politically, first, because the Tripolitan elite, long attached to Syria, pragmatically started entering Lebanese politics. The 1943 National Pact had formalized the power-sharing mechanism wherein the presidency is held by a Christian Maronite, the prime minister is a Sunni Muslim and Parliament is led by a Shia Muslim. This left room for the notables of Tripoli, the second largest city of Lebanon and one overwhelmingly made up of Sunnis, to assuage their political ambitions. In a show of the contradictions this was beginning to lead to, Abdel Hamid Karame, Tripoli's former Mufti and long-time advocate of the city's unity with Syria, became Lebanon's prime minister in 1945, followed by his Tripolitan counterpart S'adi Monla in 1946; Rashid Karame, the son of Abdel Hamid, would later hold the position seven times until 1975. This reconciliation of the Tripolitan upper class with the Lebanese state, which mainly stemmed from self-interest, was perceived as a betrayal by many in the local masses.

This growing political antagonism was worsened by the sense that, despite the fact that the scions of the Tripolitan upper class were frequently in charge of the state apparatus and that the government as a result launched a handful of symbolic projects to improve the city's infrastructure, such as the upgrading of its port and the construction of the Beirut–Tripoli highway, countless residents still continued to "feel neglected"[35] by the state. One slogan coined back then but still largely used today encapsulates especially well the sheer intensity of the grievances and sense of deliberate marginalization felt by many locals: "I am Tripolitan, my right has been eaten"[36] (*ana al-Trabulsi, ma akoul haqi*). Popular bitterness thus began mounting not just at the Lebanese government but also at the Tripolitan notables, seen as complicit in the state's neglect. And, although it did not translate into violence yet, it was still palpable enough for an observer to note that Rashid Karame, who epitomized the notability, was "far from having full popular support in

---

[35] This was the observation of UK diplomats in Beirut who went on a tour of the city in 1953. See UK Embassy in Beirut, "Lebanon: annual review for 1952" (Confidential, No. 27, EL1011/1, February 25, 1953). Note that this sense of persisting local grievances was still largely present in the 1970s. UK embassy staff touring Tripoli in 1978 reported that their interlocutors regretted that the Lebanese government still "overlooked [the city's] needs" and remarked that, as a result, many of them were often inherently "suspicious of the Lebanese government's intentions." See: UK Embassy in Beirut, "Tripoli" (No. 14, NFL014, January 31, 1978).

[36] Abi Samra, *Trablus*, p. 38.

Tripoli," and that "it is quite possible that the events leading to his ultimate downfall may begin there."[37]

Yet the growing antagonism between the elite and masses was not just political, it was fast turning social too. It became particularly evident during and after the 1958 conflict that, although the "contentious Tripolitans" had protested against the government, a prime target of their wrath was the local notability. While, until then, residents of all walks of life had participated in the city's long list of rebellions, the outbreak of contention became from 1958 onward largely confined to the low-income neighborhoods of Tripoli's Old City.

There were several reasons behind the particularly strong spatial salience of mobilizations there. Importantly, these were a string of Mamluk-era quarters. This not only enhanced local identification with a glorious history and a tradition of contention, but its old fortifications and mazes of narrow alleyways also shielded it from mass repression by the security forces. Yet an additional and increasingly important factor was that, although this historical part of Tripoli had long been socially mixed, this began to change in the 1950s. Social tensions emerged and also expressed themselves during outbreaks of anti-governmental violence, when protesters began looting wealthier districts and chanting slogans against local notables.

This transpired in the 1958 conflict as the Tripoli revolt took on a social dimension. It emerged in the Old City and morphed into what a historian called a "questioning"[38] of the traditional leadership embodied by Rashid Karame. This episode, one observer concurred, gave the "contentious Tripolitans" a "taste of rebellion"[39] against the local upper class too, which participated in the rise of radical leftist movements in the city. Later, as this book will show, it would be the turn of Tawhid's militant Islamism to channel local social tensions.

The roots of the social tensions then increasingly plaguing Tripoli are multifaceted, but a key element was the loss of the social diversity that had long characterized the Old City. As in other Levantine cities, Tripoli, geographically long confined to these historical quarters, had always featured a powerful upper class. It was made up of notables and businessmen who derived their wealth and status from longstanding involvement in trade, which meant that many of them inherited large sums of money, fructified it and passed it on to the next generation; and from the fact that seven local aristocratic families called the *ashraf*, or "noble

---

[37] UK Embassy in Beirut, "Lebanon: annual review for 1954" (Confidential, No. 10, VL1011/1, January 7, 1955).

[38] Al-Soufi Richard, *Lutte populaire armée*, pp. 38–45.   [39] Abi Samra, *Trablus*, p. 56.

60   Tales of a Rebel City

ones," had distant ties to the Prophet Muhammed and played key roles in the administration of Tripoli.[40] Significantly, this upper class had been dispersed through the Old City, one historian even reporting that, for centuries, "no quarter was exclusively rich or poor."[41] There was, in fact, a great deal of solidarity between this upper class and the rest of the lower-middle-class population of Tripoli, with interactions between these different social worlds frequently happening not just in the Old City's narrow and intimate alleyways but also taking place within institutional settings such as neighborhood associations and local Sufi lodges. This, however, began to change in the 1950s when Tripoli began expanding westwards from the Old City to what became known as New Tripoli, a series of modern, chic and more spacious boulevards and districts that featured classy shops and better infrastructure.

The migration of Tripoli's upper class from the Old City to New Tripoli drastically accelerated in 1955. Back then a cataclysmic flood of the Abu Ali river, which passes through Tripoli's historical quarters, considerably damaged these neighborhoods. One observer who witnessed the event recounted that "torrential rains in the mountains above Tripoli caused a disastrous flood when waves of trees, rocks and mud swept down a stream on one side of the town."[42] Newspapers reported that the flood had been of such proportions that it killed as many as 200 residents, injured 7,000 and outright destroyed up to 500 shops as well as 90 houses in the Old City. The extent of the destruction meant that 1,000 of the Old City's most deprived residents were displaced.[43] Many of them were later regrouped in supposedly "temporary" housing units built in haste in a nearby neighborhood which would acquire the telling name of al-Mankubin ("The Damaged Ones"). While, in the short term, the flood rendered the Old City a very unhealthy area to live in, with epidemics frequently breaking out, in the medium term it affected the quality of the local infrastructure, which pushed a larger proportion of the upper class to leave the Old City for New Tripoli.

[40] James Reilly, "Past and present in local histories of the Ottoman period from Syria and Lebanon" *Middle Eastern Studies* (Vol. 35, No. 1, 1999), pp. 45–65.
[41] Khaled Ziadeh, *Al-sura al-taqlidiya li al-mujtam'a al-madani: qira' manhajiya fi sijallat mahkamat Trablus al-shara'iya* [*The traditional picture of civil society: methodological reading of the records of the Islamic tribunal of Tripoli*] (Tripoli: Lebanese University Press, 1983) pp. 137–41.
[42] UK Embassy in Beirut, "Lebanon: annual review for 1955" (Confidential, VL1011/1, January 1, 1956). See, also, the excellent four-parts dossier on the role of the Abu Ali river put together by the Tripolitan newspaper, *al-Tamaddon*. "Mujtam'a al-naher fi Trablus" ["The society of water in Tripoli], *al-Tamaddon* (April 6, 2018).
[43] UK Embassy in Beirut, "Lebanon: annual review for 1955" (Confidential, VL1011/1, January 1, 1956).

Political and Social Antagonisms 61

Importantly, these wealthier residents of the historical neighborhoods were not replaced by other upper- or middle-class inhabitants, but by impoverished rural migrants, something which reinforced the sense that the Old City was becoming a markedly poor area.

These rural migrants were attracted by the Old City's cheap rents and had been drawn to Tripoli in the hope of a better life after the agricultural sector fell into profound crisis. Indeed, while the inhabitants of Lebanon's rural areas had long depended on agriculture, their liveli-hoods were severely affected by regional and national-level trends, such as the 1949 break-up of the economic union between Syria and Lebanon or the economic policies of successive governments, which, in attempting to turn the country into the "Switzerland of the Middle East," dismissed agriculture and rather invested in the banking and services industry. This led to speculation on land, a hike in real estate prices, disinvestment in the agricultural sector on the part of private and public bodies and the eventual collapse of the whole sector. As a result rural areas witnessed mass migration to the cities: the Shia Muslim peasants of South Lebanon and the Beqaa Valley moved to Beirut's southern suburbs while the overwhelmingly Sunni Muslim inhabitants of Akkar, a large plain in North Lebanon, and of Dinniye, a mountain range to Tripoli's east, moved nearby to the northern city.[44]

The consequence of all of these trends on Tripoli was twofold. On the one hand, it led to exponential demographic growth, the population of the city suddenly jumping from 110,000 inhabitants in 1952 to 210,000 in 1961 and more than doubling to 400,000 in 1981.[45] On the other hand, because the newcomers were deprived rural migrants who settled in the Old City, it led to further impoverishment and to growing social tensions with New Tripoli.[46]

At first these nascent social tensions were contained, for Tripoli's bustling industries in the 1950s and 1960s were able to absorb the

---

[44] Roger Owen, "The political economy of Grand Liban, 1920–1970," chapter 2 in Roger Owen (ed.), *Essays on the crisis in Lebanon* (London: Ithaca Press, 1976).

[45] Gulick, *Tripoli*, table 1, p. 31 and Seurat, "Le quartier."

[46] The absence of a census since 1932 complicates the task of gathering specific data on Tripoli's population but some scholars, quoted below, have done an excellent job at coming up with estimates that are locally deemed reliable. The figure for 1952 comes from Gulick, *Tripoli*, p. 311, the figure for 961 comes from Rajab, *Le vieux Tripoli*, p. 199 and the figure for 1981 is from Nadine Picaudou, "Mutations socio-économiques du vieux Tripoli" *Annales de Géographie* (Vol. 1, 1981), p. 97, Joumana al-Soufi Richard, "Le vieux Tripoli dans ses structures actuelles" *Annales de Géographie* (Vol. 2, 1981) and Jalal Abs, *Etude et propositions pour une utilisation rationnelle de l'espace à Tripoli-Liban* (Paris: University Paris VII, unpublished PhD thesis, 1981). Michel Seurat, however, mentions 400,000 inhabitants for 1984. See Seurat, "Le quartier."

62   Tales of a Rebel City

unskilled labor that came with rural migration. With fifty-three medium-to-heavy factories providing thousands of jobs to local workers, Tripoli was back then still an important industrial city; coming significantly behind Beirut's 474 plants but ahead of other cities like Byblos, Sidon and Tyre and their respective 10, 9 and 1 plants.[47] Tripoli's light and medium factories were spread between neighborhoods of the Old City while the largest plants were located at the city's extremities. Tripoli's southern district of Bahsas, where the city's power plant was located, became home to massive factories that produced metal blocs, wood, refined sugar and cotton, each employing 500 workers. The northern neighborhood of Beddawi, for its part, was where the IPC had built a major industrial complex to host its oil terminal and refinery, bringing "an influx of capital"[48] there and leading to the hiring of some engineers but of thousands of unskilled workers too. Initially, then, the mass of rural migrants who were settling in Tripoli in the hope of leading a better life and who in majority came to inhabit the Old City saw their expectations fulfilled.

Yet, as the cost of living increased drastically as Lebanon's services-based economy thrived, especially in and around Beirut, work conditions in Tripoli's heavy industries deteriorated. One observer for instance noted that "daily paid unskilled workers nowadays exist dangerously near the starvation limit when they have families to support," making it "impossible for employees, particularly the lower-paid ones, to live."[49] With time, then, these factory workers organized to ask for pay raises and better working conditions, multiplying industrial action, like sit-ins and strikes, and joining trade unions and the Communist Party. But, as their demands were not met by local businessmen, social tensions further increased, a trend which accelerated in the late 1950s and the 1960s due to the closure of many factories.[50]

The subsequent rise of radical leftist parties then became such that, in the Cold War context, Western diplomats found their "success" in Tripoli "disquieting" and that notables reported "considerable concern

---

[47] UK Embassy in Beirut, "Joint report by the commercial and economic representatives of the EC in Lebanon" (No. 79, 4367, December 28, 1978).

[48] UK Embassy in Beirut, "Sources of wealth in the Lebanon" (Restricted, No. 25, E2408/1112/88, February 7, 1949).

[49] UK Embassy in Beirut, "Mr Shone to Mer Bevin" (No. 34, E2088/99, February 21, 1946).

[50] British diplomats reported on the increasingly "dire" employment situation in late 1950s Tripoli, which they attributed to mass layoffs at the IPC oil terminal and at some of the city's largest factories. See UK Embassy in Beirut, "Recent developments in Syrian–Lebanese relations" (No. 1, VL10389/1, January 31, 1957).

over the growing influence of the Communist Party in the area."[51] Communism's popular appeal in Tripoli later vanished with the exception of Mina, the port district, as the heavy industries began closing down and as the party came to revolve around an intelligentsia detached from the actual concerns of the Tripolitan lower class. Yet it was soon replaced by left-wing parties that channeled these social tensions and promoted even more radical agendas, such as the Syrian Social Nationalist Party, the Organization of the Communist Action and, most important of all, the Ba'ath Party.

The meteoric rise of the Ba'ath Party among the Tripolitan masses during the late 1950s and 1960s stemmed primarily from its ability to embody the city's grievances and rebel identity. Here too, some local residents might have been genuinely attracted by Ba'athist ideology, which was a complex mix of secularism, socialism and pan-Arabism. But, by all accounts, many of the "contentious Tripolitans" who joined the movement were attracted by the fact that its leader, Abdel Majid al-Rifa'i, a charismatic Tripolitan doctor, had spearheaded much of the 1958 rebellion and often addressed local identities and grievances.[52] They were also seduced by the concrete way in which he tackled the social tensions plaguing Tripoli and by his explicit attempt to challenge Rashid Karame and the city's notability. By 1955 he had already grown immensely popular with the lower classes because he had spent weeks touring the Old City following the river flood to give free treatment and medicines to the poor, which sharply contrasted with the inaction of the government and the local notables. In later years he also grew popular with the city's educated middle classes as their own ascent was blocked by the feudal practices of the local notability, which routinely conditioned access to health services and to all kinds of municipal jobs to political loyalty.[53] His growing clout translated into myriad popular protests he led throughout the 1960s but truly transpired at the 1972 parliamentary elections when he came well ahead of Rashid Karame.[54] With

---

[51] See: UK Embassy in Beirut, "Communist influence in the Lebanon" (Confidential, No. 173, VL10338/20, October 25, 1956) and UK Embassy in Beirut, "Weekly political summary, Syria and Lebanon" (Secret, E3957/27/89, April 30, 1946).

[52] "Sirat munadel" ["Biography of a combatant"], al-Tamaddon (April 23, 2018) and "Abdel Majid al-Rif'ai, 1927–2017: tarikh madina fi tarikh rajul [Abdel Majid al-Rifa'i, 1927–2017: the history of a city through the history of a man]," al-Tamaddon (April 25, 2018).

[53] Interview with Abdel Majid al-Rifa'i, Tripoli, June 2014 and interview with residents of Tripoli, June 2014.

[54] "Mawaqif wa mahattat hama m'a al-munadil al-kabir al-douktour Abdel Majid al-Rifa'i" [Positions and important stages of the great combatant and the doctor Abdel Majid al- Rifa'i], al-Tamaddon (April 25, 2018) and "Youm' assasna qiyada siyesie li Trablous" [On the day we founded a political leadership for Tripoli], al-Tamaddon (April 25, 2018).

64   Tales of a Rebel City

time, then, Abdel Majid al-Rifa'i's Ba'ath Party became an important movement to be reckoned with in Tripoli. And this, in turn, resulted more from his revolutionary impulse which chimed well with the city's rebel identity as well as from his criticism of the traditional notability, shared by growing sections of local society, than from an intrinsic local appeal for Ba'athism.

By the 1950s and 1960s, in sum, radical left-wing movements in Tripoli had come to embody the city's rebel identity and, increasingly, to channel local grievances such as social tensions – all elements which, decades later, Tawhid would also considerably engage with.

Tripoli's Global Sense of Place

Aside from the Lebanese government and the local notables, the Syrian regime became from the 1970s onward a target for the "contentious Tripolitans," those members of social and rebel movements of all stripes driven primarily by Tripolitan identity and local grievances.

This can seem surprising for, in theory, the notion of local collective identity could be assumed to be inherently parochial and not primarily concerned with the wider world. Yet geographer Doreen Massey has shown that, instead of being only inward-looking, local identities are often traversed by what she calls a "global sense of place,"[55] or narratives and solidarities that organically link these spaces with actors, issues and places elsewhere. In Tripoli this is particularly evident in many residents' attachment to Syria's Sunni hinterland and in particular to Homs and Hama. But the city's "global sense of place" also came to revolve for much of the mid to late twentieth century around local solidarity with the Palestinian cause. This, in turn, would fuel contention against the Lebanese government and the Syrian regime. Local Islamist movements including, in the 1980s, Tawhid, would go to great lengths to embody Tripoli's "global sense of place," its attachment to Palestine and its enmity for the Syrian regime.

Of course, solidarity with the Palestinian people and the rise of pro-Palestinian movements became a general trend in the Middle East and in particular in Lebanese cities like Sidon, Tyre and Beirut in the wake of the Arab defeats against Israel in 1967 and 1973. But this was especially the case in Tripoli, and early on. The city, as the centuries-long capital of its own province in a Greater Syria which included Palestine, had

---

[55] Doreen Massey, "A global sense of place," chapter Six in Doreen Massey (ed.), *Space, place and gender* (Minneapolis: University of Minnesota Press, 2001), especially pp. 154–6.

developed strong social and economic relations with the people of Haifa, Jerusalem and Nablus. Instead of being severed when Palestine fell under British rule in 1920, these social and emotional ties as well as narratives of solidarity binding Tripoli to the Palestinian people became stronger as the city rose as one of the hubs of pro-Palestinian activism in the Middle East.

One episode in particular shaped Tripoli's "global sense of place" and attachment to Palestine – the rise of local pro-Palestinian militant-turned-regional-hero, Fawzi Qawuqji. This Tripolitan military officer who had climbed through the ranks of the Ottoman army rose to fame in the 1920s after he set up a rebel group and recruited hundreds of Tripolitan and other volunteers throughout Greater Syria in order to fight the British army in Palestine.[56] Qawuqji's profile in and outside of Tripoli further grew after his group took on a prominent role in the 1936 Great Arab Revolt, participating in bloody clashes around Nablus and Jenin. By then he had risen to such prominence that, after he temporarily left Palestine, observers remarked that he was welcomed "by thousands" in Damascus and hailed as a true "Arab hero."[57] Unsurprisingly, upon his return to Tripoli he is said to have been "unanimously"[58] celebrated as a figure who epitomized the city's rebel identity and attachment to Palestine. Upon the creation of Israel in 1948, he formed another rebel group, the Arab Liberation Army, which again comprised Tripolitan and Arab volunteers this time to fight local Jewish militias. Qawuqji's proud Tripolitan and Syrian heritage, then, combined with his passion for Palestine, shaped the sense that solidarity with the Palestinians was a part of local identity. Interestingly, when asked why they allied with Palestinian guerrilla organizations in the 1980s, Tawhid members often referred back to the local legacy of Fawzi Qawuqji.

Tripoli's solidarity with Palestine grew even stronger after 1948 when the Arab defeat led to the exodus of hundreds of thousands of Palestinians and to the creation in Lebanon of thirteen refugee camps. Tripoli came to host about 50,000 Palestinian refugees, about a tenth of the displaced who had arrived in Lebanon.[59] They settled in two camps in the northern vicinity of the city, respectively in the areas of Naher al-

---

[56] For more on the life story of Fawzi Qawaqji and his significance in the Palestinian struggle of the 1930s and 1940s, see Laila Parsons' fascinating biography: Laila Parsons, *The Commander: Fawzi al-Qawuqji and the fight for Arab independence, 1914–1948* (New York: Hill and Wang, 2016).

[57] UK Consulate in Beirut, "Consul MacKereth to Mr Eden: Enclosure No. S3, Damascus quarterly report" (Confidential No. 2, E 697/252/89, January 5, 1937).

[58] UK Embassy in Beirut, "Lebanon: summary No. 8" (Restricted, E 3364/909/88, April 23, 1947).

[59] The exact figure of Palestinian refugees in Lebanon is contested for reasons of internal Lebanese politics and also because significant amounts of the refugee population did not

66   Tales of a Rebel City

Bared and Beddawi, with the latter in such proximity with the working-class Tripolitan districts of Mankoubin, Bab al-Tebbaneh and Qobbe that it became an integral part of Tripoli and mixed marriages became common. This further consolidated Tripoli's now quasi-organic attachment to the Palestinian cause.

The full extent to which solidarity with Palestine had become an important facet of local identity transpired in the late 1960s. Back then, in 1968, the Palestinian Liberation Organization (PLO) began using Lebanon to launch commando operations into northern Israel and it soon chose Jeyrun, a mountainous village in the countryside of Tripoli, as its first training camp hosting both Palestinian and Tripolitan volunteers in North Lebanon. Reflecting the popularity of pro-Palestinian mobilization in the city, when the first Tripolitan "martyr" fell in an anti-Israeli attack in late 1968, as many as 30,000 residents poured on the streets to pay tribute to the "heroism" and "sacrifice" of this "son of Tripoli."[60]

Soon enough, Tripoli's "global sense of place" and attachment to Palestine began interacting with other facets of local identity identified earlier, chief among them the city's sense of self-importance, rebel spirit and instinctive hostility to the Lebanese government. One chain of events in particular led to the birth of a spatially oriented rebel movement which channeled these facets of local identity and drew in the "contentious Tripolitans." On October 24, 1969, a young and charismatic Tripolitan known for his vocal support of the Palestinian cause, Faruq al-Muqaddem, gathered hundreds of locals in front of the Old City and defied a curfew to protest the government's attempt to curtail the local presence of the PLO, whose operations against Israel were increasingly attracting reprisals on Lebanon. As the demonstrators were showcasing their solidarity with the PLO and their hostility to the government, a clash ensued with the Lebanese army at the scene, killing four civilians. Muqaddem responded forcefully, leading hundreds of Tripolitans and of Palestinians from the two nearby refugee camps to arm themselves, overrun local police stations and violently push the Lebanese army out of Tripoli. For seventeen days they controlled the city on their own.[61] In

---

register with the UNRWA, the UN agency in charge of Palestinian refugee affairs. Therefore I use the estimates provided by the CIA, which are based on its own observations and off-the-record data from Lebanese political figures and other sources. See: US Central Intelligence Agency, "Palestinians in Lebanon: troubled past and bleak future: a research paper" (Secret, NESA 83-10017, February 1983).

[60] Al-Soufi Richard, *Lutte populaire armée*, p. 102.

[61] By far the best account of the 1969 Tripolitan insurrection and the rise of Muqaddem's 24 October Movement is Joumana al-Soufi Richard's unpublished PhD thesis. See: al-Soufi Richard, *Lutte populaire armée*. See also: US Central Intelligence Agency, "The President's daily brief" (Top Secret, 50 X1, No 19, October 27, 1969).

a highly symbolic move which demonstrated the embeddedness of Muqaddem's men in Tripoli's "tales of contention," the activists took over the medieval fortress, turned it into their headquarters and proclaimed the birth of a "revolutionary government" in the city, thus playing on centuries-old Tripolitan narratives of self-importance, autonomy and rebellion.

Significantly, the strong popularity of Muqaddem with many "contentious Tripolitans" also stemmed from his attempt to address simmering social tensions. Although Faruq al-Muqaddem hailed from an upperclass Tripolitan background, his family had long been hostile to the traditional notability and in particular to the Karame family. He was also able to use his connections with the PLO to train and arm many of the deprived residents of the Old City, where his power base lay, leading a number of them to use the opportunity of his seventeen-day takeover of Tripoli to also engage in acts of urban unrest. In later years Muqaddem would spearhead strikes against the price of basic commodities and riots which, again, would be larger and more violent in Tripoli than elsewhere in Lebanon.[62] This showed how his growing popularity was rooted in his ability to channel Tripoli's "global sense of place" and attachment to Palestine, but also the city's rebel identity and grievances.

Yet, whatever the local nature of the motives held by many demonstrators, the whole episode of the Tripolitan standoff against the Lebanese government on behalf of the PLO received such an echo that Nasser himself convened a meeting in Egypt to solve the crisis. There, Faruq al-Muqaddem, by now the leader of what became known as the Democratic and Socialist 24 October Movement, or simply 24 October Movement (*Harakat Arba wa Ashrin Tishrin*), met with representatives of the Lebanese government and with PLO officials, who all struck a compromise dubbed the Cairo Agreement. This accord sanctioned the armed Palestinian presence in Lebanon by giving the PLO the right to defend itself against Israel.

With time the "global sense of place" which bound many "contentious Tripolitans" to the Palestinian people and had participated in their enmity for a Lebanese government perceived as hostile to the cause eventually also led to animosity toward the Syrian regime. At first glance

---

[62] The April 1974 protest movement featured 15,000 demonstrators in Tripoli, where it was led by Faruq al-Muqaddem, which was considerably more than Beirut's 5,000, Sidon's 800 and Tyre's 300 protestors. A similar protest just months before, in December 1973, had also witnessed "serious riots in Tripoli," in a state of "virtual insurrection," but "less serious demonstrations in Beirut, Sidon and Tyre." See: UK Embassy in Beirut, "Monthly report for December 1973" (NFLI/3DA/46A, December 29, 1973) and UK Embassy in Beirut, "Lebanon" (NFL1/0; 2/4, March 30, 1974).

68   Tales of a Rebel City

this may seem counterintuitive, for Tripolitans had long felt attached to Syria, and the regime there was headed by the Ba'ath Party, which had grown in the 1950s and 1960s in the northern city as a result of Abdel Majid al-Rifa'i's leadership. Yet, by the 1970s the party had begun declining in local popularity as, now a member of parliament, al-Rifa'i lost his revolutionary impulse and no longer chimed with Tripoli's rebel identity. The Lebanese branch of the Ba'ath which he headed also came to suffer under the weight of internal divisions as the Syrian and Iraqi wings of the party split in the 1960s.

Several factors explained why the Syrian Ba'ath Party and, more generally, the Syrian regime became extremely unpopular in Tripoli. First, historically it had been a 1961 coup engineered by Syrian Ba'athist military officers which had led to the dissolution of the short-lived Syrian–Egyptian federation, the United Arab Republic, itself immensely popular in Tripoli as it had revived hopes of a recreation of Greater Syria that would include the city. In local popular narratives Tripolitans continued to blame the Syrian Ba'ath for years for undermining dreams of unity. Second, it had again been the Ba'ath in Damascus that had enacted a sweeping land reform in 1963, which expropriated dozens of landowners from the Syrian hinterland and in particular around the cities of Homs and Hama, pushing them in turn to emigrate to nearby Tripoli and to begin engaging in anti-Ba'ath activism. There the narratives these Syrians hostile to the regime spread cemented local mistrust of the Ba'ath. Third, the split between the Iraqi and Syrian sections of the Ba'ath Party in the mid-1960s gradually came to take on a sectarian coloration as, while the former remained dominated by Sunnis, the latter increasingly came under the wing of Syrian Alawi military officers after 1966. This trend overturned a pattern of centuries of Sunni domination over Greater Syria and heralded a new era in which the Alawi minority, 11 percent of the population, began ruling Syria. This alienated the 80.9 percent of Sunnis in Tripoli who had long felt attached to the Syrian hinterland and to Sunni-majority cities of Homs and Hama, themselves now marginalized. Even before Hafez al-Assad's rise to power, then, Tripolitans mistrusted the Syrian regime.

Yet the most important factor behind the animosity of the Tripolitan masses for the Syrian regime was how Damascus sought to undermine the PLO, which was hugely popular in the city. This Syrian–Palestinian tension crystallized early on as a struggle for influence over Middle Eastern politics, and in particular Lebanese and Palestinian issues, between Hafez al-Assad, who took over Syria in 1970, and Yasser Arafat, the charismatic and independent-minded chairman of the PLO from 1969 and also the leader of its most important subfaction, Fatah.

Tripoli's Global Sense of Place 69

By that time the armed Palestinian presence in Lebanon had drastically increased. This resulted from the 1969 Cairo Agreement, which granted Palestinian militias the right to carry weapons in Lebanon and to rule over the country's twelve refugee camps, and from Jordan's 1970 Black September massacre that pushed PLO leaders to fully relocate to Beirut. From then on the PLO, counting on a generous budget subsidized by the oil money flowing from the Gulf and North Africa, started to sponsor pro-Palestinian Lebanese parties and militias, often on the Muslim and leftist spectrum of politics, to bolster its local influence. This, however, aggravated the simmering crisis between Lebanon's conservative Christians and reformist Muslims, a conflict which eventually erupted into full-blown civil war in 1975. The extent of the PLO's support for the reformist Muslim camp became such that, by March 1976, observers predicted that this Palestinian–leftist alliance would soon gain the "upper hand"[63] in the war. Their victory would have had far-reaching implications for the Syrian regime. It would have brought a revolutionary regime to the doorstep of Damascus, further heightened the PLO's influence in Syria's backyard and, significantly, would have increased the chances of a destructive war between Israel, Lebanon and Syria just as the Syrian army was in the process of recovering from its 1973 loss of the Golan Heights. For all these reasons, therefore, an implicit but highly significant cornerstone of Syrian foreign and security policy under Hafez al-Assad became to tame and undermine the PLO.

The Syrian regime thus began making moves against the PLO's positions in Lebanon. Cautiously at first, in April 1976 it limited itself to undertaking a naval blockade of the Tripoli and Beirut harbors to prevent further shipments of weapons from reaching the PLO and its Lebanese Muslim allies. Then much more openly, in June it sent 30,000 Syrian troops to Lebanon. Officially the Syrian army was intervening militarily in the context of the Lebanese civil war at the behest of President Suleiman Franjiye, a longstanding friend and ally of Hafez al-Assad, in order to help "stop the fighting." Although the Arab League later sanctioned the Syrian military intervention, however, it soon became evident that, far from acting as a neutral arbiter trying to assuage tensions in a bid to end the civil war, the Syrian army's real objective was to "discipline"[64]

[63] US Central Intelligence Agency, "Lebanon: implications of the ascendency of the Lebanese left" (Secret, 25 XI, March 30, 1976).

[64] Fred Lawson, "Syria's intervention in the Lebanese civil war, 1976: a domestic conflict explanation" *International Organization* (Vol. 38, No. 3, 1984), p. 458. See also Adeed Dawisha, "The motives of Syria's involvement in Lebanon" *Middle East Journal* (Vol. 38, No. 2, 1984), pp. 228–36.

70   Tales of a Rebel City

the PLO before it turned too influential in Lebanese politics. In the words of a close observer, Syria had to "rein in"[65] the Palestinians.

The regime's willingness to undermine the Palestinians became evident when, in June–August 1976, Syrian troops began actively helping Lebanese Christian militias besiege and attack Beirut's Palestinian refugee camp of Tal al-Z'atar, a PLO stronghold, in an event known as "Black June" which killed approximately 4,000 Palestinian civilians.[66] Damascus also seemed ready to go to great lengths to tame pro-Palestinian Lebanese militias and figures, as it murdered Kamal Jumblatt, the leader of the pro-PLO front of Lebanese leftists and Muslim parties. Even though by 1978 the Syrian regime had reversed its position and now tacitly supported the Lebanese Muslim camp, mainly out of concern that the Christians were developing too close a political and military relation with Israel, still officially at war with Syria, it continued to weaken the PLO's influence in Lebanon and to keep the status quo. This would lead many "contentious Tripolitans" to engage in activism against the regime.

The Failure of the Left

Naturally, Lebanese Muslim support for the PLO and hostility for the Syrian regime was again a phenomenon visible in other predominantly Sunni areas such as cities like Sidon and neighborhoods like West Beirut. Yet Tripoli's "global sense of place," informed both by solidarity with the Palestinian cause and by strong attachment to Syria's now marginalized Sunni hinterland, meant that anti-regime sentiment became especially prevalent there. Observers touring the northern city after Syria's 1976 military intervention in Lebanon in fact noted how regime troops kept "an iron grip"[67] on Tripoli as they were aware of the "growing

---

[65] US Central Intelligence Agency, "Memorandum: Syrian intentions in Lebanon" (D/NFAC 7E44, September 8, 1981). The CIA analyzed Syria's 1976 intervention in Lebanon in the following way: "Lebanon is militarily important to the Syrians, who believe that control of the Bekaa Valley is necessary to guard against an Israeli flanking attack on Damascus from the west. The Syrian military presence in Lebanon also gives Assad the means to rein in Arafat and to keep him from negotiating without Syrian approval. Assad knows well that he must retain special influence over the Palestinians because they constitute his principal leverage in any future negotiations for a peace settlement and the return of the Golan Heights."

[66] Yezid Sayigh's account, based on reports in the aftermath of the massacre, estimates that 4,280 Palestinian and Lebanese inhabitants of the camp were killed. See Yezid Sayigh, *Armed struggle and the search for a Palestinian state: the Palestinian national movement, 1949–1993* (Oxford: Oxford University Press, 1997), pp. 400–2.

[67] UK Embassy in Baghdad, "Dr Abdul Majid al-Rifa'i" (No. 42, DGOX3W, May 30, 1979).

The Failure of the Left   71

resentment of the Syrian presence there."[68] Crucially, however, in spite of the growing presence of what contentious politics scholars Bert Klandermans and Jacquelien van Stekelenburg would have called a "demand side"[69] for activism against the Syrian regime in Tripoli, neither the leftist parties which had once been popular with the masses in the 1950s and 1960s nor the local notables seemed willing to provide a supply of social and rebel movements to channel local pro-PLO and anti-regime sentiments. The notables, in essence pragmatic local politicians who constantly adapted their rhetoric and stances to the changing environment, were quick to acknowledge the new power dynamic and to vocally back the Syrian regime and its presence as well as policy in Lebanon.[70] This unsurprisingly worsened the political antagonism which was increasingly separating them from many Tripolitans.

What was even more striking was the propensity of leftist movements that had once supported the PLO to gradually back the Syrian regime through the 1970s, which undermined their popularity and pushed the "contentious Tripolitans" to look for alternatives. One well-informed observer recounted that, even though some of these parties had remained "deeply suspicious" of Syria's designs in Lebanon and had "not forgotten"[71] the defeat Syria had inflicted on them and the Palestinians during the Black June of 1976, Israel's 1978 invasion of South Lebanon and its provision of weapons to Lebanese Christian militias made them fear even more a Christian victory in case the Syrian regime now suddenly pulled its troops out of Lebanon. By 1978, therefore, the leaders of many Lebanese leftist movements were now visiting Damascus to urge Hafez al-Assad to keep the Syrian army in Lebanon.

There were also other reasons for the turnaround of these leftist parties and their newfound support for the Syrian regime. Some, like the Syrian Social Nationalist Party and the Lebanese branch of the Syrian Ba'ath

---

[68] UK Embassy in Beirut, "Lebanon: security" (Telegram 60, GR385, February 21, 1979).

[69] By a "demand side" of protest, the two scholars refer to a movement's mobilization potential, which itself consists of the people who sympathize with a certain cause and share grievances and emotions. See: Bert Klandermans and Jacquelien van Stekelenburg, "Fitting demand and supply: how identification brings appeals and motives together" *Social Movement Studies* (Vol. 13, No. 2, 2014), pp. 179–203.

[70] British diplomats reported throughout the 1970s that delegations of Tripolitan notables frequently visited Damascus on what they tellingly called political "pilgrimages" to visit Hafez al-Assad and Syrian regime dignitaries. The "influence of Syria" was visible on Tripolitan politicians but also on businessmen because "the main market for Tripoli's merchants is there." See: UK Embassy in Beirut, "Lebanon" (Restricted, No. 3/23, 3/376, March 26, 1971) and UK Embassy in Beirut, "Tripoli" (No. 14, NFL 014, January 31, 1978).

[71] US Central Intelligence Agency, "Syria's allies and assets in Lebanon" (Secret, 25X1, November 7, 1978).

72   Tales of a Rebel City

Party, began depending on Syrian "arms and money" and as a result turned into what an informed observer called "puppets"[72] of the regime. Others, like the Lebanese Communist Party, at first tried striking a balance between adapting to the new strategic landscape and opposing the Syrian regime's treatment of the PLO. But the 1979 assassination of Abu Hassan Ayyoubi, a vocal supporter of the armed Palestinian presence in Lebanon and one of the party's top officials in Tripoli's Mina district, where it was still strong, pushed the leadership to progressively tone down its anti-regime rhetoric.[73] "We were partisans of a middle ground between the Syrians and the Palestinians," a top Communist official in Tripoli recalled, adding: "However, Syria's influence in Lebanon grew stronger – and we came to recognize this reality."[74] This became all the more the case after Syria and the USSR bolstered their relations in 1980 and signed a Treaty of Friendship.

The two only left-wing parties that refused to unconditionally bow to Syria were the Lebanese branch of the Iraqi Ba'ath Party and the Organization of the Communist Action. The former was by now led by Abdel Majid al-Rifa'i who, as a Tripolitan Sunni, would not conceivably have headed the Lebanese section of the Alawi-dominated Syrian Ba'ath. But, although he spoke out against the Syrian troops' intervention in Lebanon, he had to temporarily seek refuge in Baghdad after dozens of his partisans were imprisoned in Tripoli, which left his movement, already on the decline in the 1970s, severely weakened.[75] The Organization of the Communist Action, for its part, was a revolutionary splinter faction of the Communist Party which continued supporting the Palestinian cause but was too small and dominated by the educated middle classes to hope to be able to attract the Tripolitan masses into its orbit. In theory this state of affairs could have benefited Faruq al-Muqaddem's aforementioned 24 October Movement, which had grown popular a decade earlier thanks to its uncompromising support for the Palestinians and its hostility to the Lebanese government. Yet it had, since then, turned into a mere vehicle for Faruq al-Muqaddem's own political ambitions and no longer chimed with Tripoli's "global sense of

---

[72] US Central Intelligence Agency, "Directory of Lebanese militias: a reference aid" (Secret, NESA 84-10171C, June 1984). See also: US Central Intelligence Agency, "Syria's allies and assets in Lebanon" (Secret, 25X1, November 7, 1978).

[73] It is widely believed that Abu Hassan Ayyoubi was assassinated by a member of the Palestinian Saiqa who was acting on behalf of Syrian intelligence. Interviews with two former leaders of the Lebanese Communist Party and a former head of the Party's militia, June and July 2014, Tripoli.

[74] Interview with Iqbal Saba, Tripoli, June 2014.

[75] Interview with Abdel Majid al-Rifa'i as well as rank-and-file members of the Iraqi Ba'ath, Tripoli, June 2014.

place" after it fell out with the PLO to become, instead, a proxy of Libya.[76] This relationship allowed the movement to continue buying weapons and to operate but it also emptied it of all substance and popularity.

By the late 1970s, then, it had become evident that, despite their previous popular successes in Tripoli, local leftist movements were no longer in a position to channel the primarily local identities and grievances of the "contentious Tripolitans," whose target no longer just included the Lebanese government and local notables but the Syrian regime too. They would be replaced in this endeavor by local Islamist movements – including Tawhid.

Tripoli's Islamists between Ideology and Local Identity

As leftist movements declined in the 1970s, Islamist groups began their rise in Tripoli. Naturally the spread of Islamism as an ideology advocating what scholar Bassam Tibi called a "religionized politics,"[77] or the assertion that religion should inspire, shape and animate social and political activity, was a broad phenomenon which gripped the entire Middle East. Although the mantra that "Islam is the solution" to all the region's ills had been around since the birth of the Muslim Brotherhood in Egypt in 1928, it was really through the 1970s that this Islamist slogan became popular, in the wake of the repeated failures of secular left-wing Arab dictatorships to confront Israel and to provide sustained development for their citizens. This led to the rise of myriad Islamist movements which, either in peaceful or militant ways, began to challenge these governments and to argue for their replacement by a political system adhering to Islamic law, a trend which accelerated after the 1979 Islamic Revolution in Iran.

In Lebanon, Islamism as an ideology grew in many Muslim-inhabited parts of the country, for example in the Beqaa Valley where it would lead

---

[76] Popular accusations that Faruq al-Muqaddem's 24 October Movement turned into a Libyan puppet are widespread in Tripoli. They are also confirmed by research by the CIA on the topic, one cable in 1975 for instance finding "direct evidence" that Muqaddem was the recipient of "more than 1$ million" from Libya. See: US Central Intelligence Agency, "Outlook for Lebanon" (Restricted, OCI No 0857/75, September 23, 1975).

[77] Bassam Tibi's definition of Islamism as a form of "religionized politics," characterized by the promotion of a political order that is believed to emanate from the will of God, is useful insofar as it allows us to grasp the undeniable significance of religion but all while stressing that Islamism is a political ideology which puts forward a certain interpretation of religion, with which many Muslims, including clerics, might disagree. See Bassam Tibi, *Islamism and Islam* (New Haven: Yale University Press, 2012).

74   Tales of a Rebel City

to the rise of Hezbollah among the Shias or in the city and refugee camps of Sidon where Sunni Islamist groups grew strong. But it was Tripoli which undeniably acted as the spearhead of this Lebanese Islamist current. The city arose as the birthplace of the Salafi trend in the 1940s and 1950s and, much more importantly, of Lebanon's Muslim Brothers, the Islamic Group (al-Jama'a al-Islamiya) in the 1950s, 1960s and 1970s, as well as of Tawhid in the 1980s. The especially quick proliferation of these movements there even earned Tripoli the nickname of "Lebanon's Islamist stronghold."[78]

As the next section will show, a fundamental reason for the growth of Islamist movements in Tripoli stemmed from the underlying "cultural momentum" which this ideology was witnessing there. But a condition of their increasing success in the northern city was their ability to simultaneously embody the appeal of ideology and the strength of local collective identity. Indeed, it is remarkable how even the most ideologically committed local Islamists were willing to engage with, at times even seemed inspired by, Tripolitan narratives and grievances. Much like pan-Syrian, pan-Arab and revolutionary leftist movements had done before, they explicitly sought to attract the "contentious Tripolitans" primarily driven by local identities and grievances. On key occasions these Islamist movements were even ready to prioritize loyalty to the city as a community to commitment to their ideology.

It may not be so surprising, after all, that local Islamist movements seemed so keen to engage with Tripolitan identity given that the city itself boasted a rich Islamic legacy. In fact, tales of this Islamic legacy had long been central to the construction of Tripoli's collective identity. They permeated local historical accounts and popular narratives about the city's history, in which they were remarkably often associated with its prestigious past. These local historical accounts claim that Tripoli's rich Islamic legacy dates as far back as the conquest of the city by the Ummayad Islamic Caliphate well over a millennium ago.[79] Yet it is truly with the construction in 1066 of the House of Knowledge (Dar al-'Ilm), a large educational and religious complex said to contain 50,000 copies of the Quran and 20,000 commentaries of the holy texts, that Tripoli arose as a regional hub of Islamic learning in Greater Syria, on a par with Damascus and Aleppo. The Crusaders destroyed the House of

---

[78] This is a phrase especially used in the international and Lebanese media. But it has also come to shape the way some academics of Lebanon discuss the politics and society of Tripoli. See, for instance, Hilal Khashan, "Lebanon's Islamist stronghold" *Middle East Quarterly* (Vol. 18, No. 2, 2011), pp. 85–90.

[79] Abdel Aziz Salem, *Trablus al-Sham fi al-tarikh al-Islami* [*Tripoli of Syria in Islamic history*] (Alexandria: Dar al-Ma'aref, 1967), pp. 65–92.

Knowledge but local historical accounts are quick to highlight that Tripoli later reemerged as a hub of Levantine Islam after the Mamluks conquered it, building many mosques as well as religious schools and Sufi lodges and bolstering the influence of Islam in local society. It is then, local popular narratives insist, that Tripoli became known as "the city of the clerics,"[80] in a show of how Islam became tied to the process of local identity construction.

The importance of religion was then reinforced by the Ottomans, who built additional mosques and eye-catching Sufi lodges. They also gave clerics more clout than ever before by bolstering the judicial and administrative powers of the head of the local courts, the Qadi (or judge) as well as those of the Mufti, the city's most supreme source of religious authority. Tripoli's Islamic legacy reached its apex in the late nineteenth century and early twentieth century when the city became home to two world-famous clerics and public figures; Hussein al-Jisr, who created an Islamic-leaning university, the National Islamic School (*al-Madrassa al-Wataniya al-Islamiya*), and Rashid Rida, a key Muslim scholar and advocate of the Islamic Caliphate.[81]

Tripoli's reputation as a hub of Levantine Islam collapsed during the French Mandate as it was the Sunni-inhabited western quarters of the new capital, Beirut, which began centralizing religious institutions such as Dar al-Fatwa, a governmental body created with the goal of administering Lebanon's mosques and of dealing with the religious affairs of Sunnis. Yet, in spite of this and a general decrease in religious practice in the 1950s and 1960s, the bulk of Tripolitans never ceased to collectively identify with the rich local Islamic legacy. As one observer put it, "until today no one in Tripoli dares to openly disavow the Islamic identity of the city."[82] Of course, residents may not have agreed with each other's definition of what this "Islamic identity" of the city exactly entailed, and in fact local struggles over religious meaning would soon become prevalent. But the very fact that the mindset of many residents still widely associated Tripoli with an Islamic legacy nonetheless gave a local cultural advantage to the Islamist movements on the rise. They strove to frame their calls for more influence of religion in society and politics as chiming with the city's identity and as a way of recalling its prestigious past,

---

[80] Abi Samra, *Trablus*, p. 43.
[81] See, in particular, Abdel Ghani Imad, *Mujtam'a Trablus fi zaman al-tahawulat al-'othmaniya* [*The society of Tripoli at the time of the Ottoman transformations*] (Tripoli: Dar al-Insha', 1999).
[82] Abi Samra, *Trablus*, p. 44.

76   Tales of a Rebel City

addressing its decline and restoring its status.[83] Their engagement with the local cultural backdrop explained part of their growing popularity.

Sometimes the engagement of these Islamist movements with Tripolitan identities, narratives and grievances was such that, when faced with the choice of prioritizing either their city as a community or ideological consistency, even those Islamist activists who appeared to be sincerely committed sacrificed ideology on the altar of solidarity with Tripoli.

A case in point was how Lebanon's branch of the Muslim Brotherhood, the Islamic Group, initially seemed to behave more like a spatially oriented movement in tune with the key themes that shaped Tripolitan identity than as an ideological import coming straight out of Egypt. Although the Islamic Group was formed in 1964, it takes its true roots in the 1958 conflict as Tripolitan pan-Arab rebels sought integration in the Egyptian–Syrian union. Back then, Islamist-inspired Sunni activists from various parts of Lebanon were all part of a religious movement, Worshipers of the Merciful (*'Ibad al-Rahman*), which had been created seven years earlier to spread Islam and achieve Muslim political equality with the Christians.[84] Yet a geographical and ideological rift soon began characterizing it. While its Beiruti members counted on proselytizing and on charitable activities to achieve the movement's aims, its Tripolitan members pushed for engagement in contentious politics. This schism originated from the very different local contexts of the two cities. The Beirutis, for instance, were cautious not to criticize too openly the strong powers given by the 1943 National Pact to the Christian presidency, both because they did not wish to antagonize the authorities in the capital and as Christians were numerous there too. For their part, the fact that Tripolitan members of Worshipers of the Merciful had always been more vocal and virulent in their criticisms of the Lebanese government partially stemmed from their embeddedness in the city's cross-border ties with Syria and with Homs in particular, where contentious activists from the Syrian Muslim Brotherhood were especially strong – Homs had been the birthplace and home of that

---

[83] Interview with members and former members of the Islamic Group, Tripoli, November–December 2014.

[84] For more on the origins, ideology and evolution of Worshippers of the Merciful, see Dalal Bizri's detailed work. Dalal Bizri, *Introduction à l'étude des mouvements islamistes sunnites au Liban* (Paris: Ecole des Hautes Etudes en Sciences Sociales unpublished PhD thesis, 1984) and Dalal Bizri, "Le mouvement Ibad al-Rahman et ses prolongements à Tripoli," chapter 4 in Olivier Carré and Paul Dumont (eds.), *Radicalismes Islamiques Tome 1: Iran Liban Turquie* (Paris: L'Harmattan, 1985).

movement's first leader, Mustafa al-Siba'i.[85] Intense cross-border ties with Syria thus facilitated the spread of dissident ideas to Tripoli.

But the most important factor behind the embrace of contentious politics by Tripolitan members of Worshipers of the Merciful resulted from their rootedness in the "tales of contention" which identified Tripoli as a rebel city, one strongly attached to Syria. The extent to which Tripolitan members of Worshipers of the Merciful appeared perhaps more embedded in inherently local narratives and grievances than in raw Islamist ideology then transpired during the 1958 conflict between the partisans and opponents of the proposal that Lebanon join the United Arab Republic merging the states of Egypt and Syria. In theory, as Islamists committed to ideology, they should have rejected such proposals. This was not only because they originated from Arab nationalist and leftist governments but also out of ideological solidarity with Egypt's Islamists, who were being severely repressed. But instead the Tripolitan members of Worshipers of the Merciful put their Islamist ideology aside for a while and, guided by their city's particularly strong sense of a community, rebel identity and historical attachment to the Syrian hinterland, joined the 1958 rebellion as a bloc, enthusiastically supporting Lebanon's attachment to the Egyptian–Syrian union.

Whereas the Beiruti members of Worshipers of the Merciful maintained a low profile during the conflict, the schism within the movement became too intense to bear as the Tripolitan members, far from just passively supporting the rebels, took an active role in the rebellion. They opened a radio station which broadcast contentious political programs, Free Lebanon Radio (*Sawt Lubnan al-Hurr*), began publishing a local newspaper featuring anti-government pamphlets, *The Revolutionary* (*al-Tha'er*), and even set up a small militia, the Holy Warriors (*al-Mujahidun*), which took part in the violent clashes that rocked Tripoli. More immersed in narratives about Tripoli's attachment to Syria than in Islamist ideology, the Tripolitan members of Worshipers of the Merciful would go as far as flattering Nasser, the initiator of the Egyptian–Syrian

---

[85] Tripolitan members of Worshippers of the Merciful reported having been particularly influenced by the sermons delivered in the northern city by Mustafa al-Siba'i on his frequent trips to Tripoli. In a reflection of the intense social and ideational ties they developed with members of the Syrian Muslim Brotherhood, some of them even travelled to Homs and Hama to witness how the movement prepared and ran for office during Syria's 1956 parliamentary elections. They reported being "impressed" and came back to Tripoli convinced that Worshippers of the Merciful should adopt the Syrian Muslim Brotherhood's views and methods. This draws upon interviews with former Worshippers of the Merciful officials and Islamic Group "founding fathers" Abdallah Babetti, Fayez Iyali and Mohammed Ali Dannaoui, as well as rank-and-file members and former members of both movements, Tripoli, July 2014.

78   Tales of a Rebel City

union who also pushed for Lebanon's integration into it, praising him as a "pious president"[86] even though he was leading a crackdown on Egypt's Islamists. The virulent engagement of the Tripolitan members of Worshipers of the Merciful in contentious politics and their embeddedness in local Tripolitan narratives soon led to an irremediable split within the group, leading them to leave and create the Islamic Group.[87]

From the time of its foundation in 1964 until the mid-1970s, the Islamic Group arose as Lebanon's foremost Islamist movement and then as the official Lebanese branch of the Muslim Brotherhood. But, although it began attracting like-minded Islamist partisans who, from Sidon to West Beirut, also wished to enter contentious politics, its hub remained Tripoli. There the movement recruited some members who were primarily guided by ideology, but for a while it was also able to mobilize some of the "contentious Tripolitans" who, whether committed Islamists or not, at first understood the Islamic Group as a spatially oriented movement which embodied Tripolitan identity, grievances and "tales of contention." Indeed, initially the discourse of the Islamic Group seemed simultaneously versed in ideology and in Tripolitan identity. Catering both to the constituency of committed Islamists and to a growing number of "contentious Tripolitans," the movement called for a "revolutionary Islam," lambasted the "colonial origins" of Lebanon and argued for the country's dissolution within a Greater Syria which, it envisioned, would become ruled by Sunnis and Islamic law.[88] After waves of pan-Syrian nationalism and pan-Arabism had epitomized Tripolitan narratives of hostility to Lebanon and attachment to Syria, it was Islamism's turn to now fulfill that role. Aware of the growing social

---

[86] *Al-Mujtam'a*, Worshippers of the Merciful's newspaper ran by its Tripolitan members only, quoted in Timothy Richard Yousaf, *The Muslim Brotherhood in Lebanon (al-Jama'a al-Islamiya), 1948–2000* (Beirut: American University of Beirut, unpublished MPhil thesis, 2010), p. 27. See also: Amal 'Itani, 'Abdel Qadir 'Ali and Mu'in Manna, *Al-Jama'a al-Islamiya fi Lubnan mundhu al-nash'a hatta 1975* [*The Islamic Group in Lebanon from the inception to 1975*] (Beirut: Markaz al-Zeytuna, 2009), pp. 33–6 and Abdel Ghani Imad, *Islamiyu Lubnan: al-wahda wa al-ekhtilaf 'ala 'arad al-mustahil* [*Islamists of Lebanon: unity and divergence in the impossible land*] (Beirut: Dar al-Saqi, 1998), pp. 10–15.

[87] Interviews with Abdallah Babetti, Fayez Iyali and Mohammed Ali Dannaoui (former officials of Worshippers of the Merciful in Tripoli), Tripoli, July 2014.

[88] See the writings of the Islamic Group's Tripoli-based leader at the time, Fathi Yakan, who emerged as the movement's chief ideologue. Fathi Yakan, *Al-mas'ala al-lubnaniya min manzur islami* [*The Lebanese question through an Islamic perspective*] (Beirut: Mu'assassa al-Islamiya, 1979), pp. 126–40. For more background on Fathi Yakan and an analysis of his evolving positions, see Ali Lagha, *Fathi Yakan: ra'ed al-haraka al-islamiya al mu'asira fi Lubnan* [*Fathi Yakan: pioneer of the Islamic movement in Lebanon*] (Beirut: Mu'assassat al-Risala, 1994) as well as Robert Rabil, "Fathi Yakan, the pioneer of Islamic activism in Lebanon" *Levantine Review* (Vol. 2, No. 1, 2013), pp. 54–65.

tensions plaguing the city, the movement also enhanced its involvement in educational and charitable activities, setting up local schools and dispensaries. By the early 1970s, then, the Islamic Group had already become a political actor to be reckoned with in Tripoli. In 1972 it ran for a seat there at the parliamentary elections, and although it lost it still managed to gather 4,000 local votes, which reflected its growing clout.

Throughout the mid to late 1970s the Islamic Group also strove to portray itself as in tune with Tripoli's "global sense of place," which included sympathy for the Palestinian cause and hostility to the Syrian regime. However, its eventual failure to truly live up to this expectation would eventually pave the way for its decline and for the rise of Tawhid. With the Lebanese civil war looming, the Islamic Group revived the Holy Warrior militia which it had earlier set up and joined the fight on the side of the pro-Palestinian movements. But instead of taking on a significant role the militia confined its involvement to a handful of not-so-strategic battles – in a reflection of this it lost thirteen members, a relatively low number.[89]

As the Islamic Group's presence in Sunni-dominated parts of South Lebanon began to be felt, like in the city of Sidon, it created another militia, the Forces of Dawn (*Quwwat al-Fajr*), which engaged in clashes there with the Israeli army in 1978 and then again in 1982–2000.[90] And, even if in Tripoli, by now occupied by the Syrian army, they had to surrender their weapons and keep quiet on the surface, local Islamic Group members continued speaking out against the Syrian regime and even began helping the regime's number one public enemy, the Syrian Muslim Brotherhood, secretly sheltering some of the sought-after leaders of this main opposition movement and covertly providing it with weapons through the smuggling routes that connected Tripoli's mountain range to Syrian cities where it was strong, like Homs and Hama.[91] This stimulated hopes among the "contentious Tripolitans" that the Islamic Group would eventually channel their growing enmity for the regime.

---

[89] The activities of Holy Warriors remained confined to Tripoli – it only took part in the clashes against Zghorta. See Abdel Ghani Imad, *Al-harakat al-Islamiya fi Lubnan: al-din wa al-siyasa fi mujtam'a mutanawe'a* [*The Islamist movements in Lebanon: religion and politics in a diverse society*] (Beirut: Dar al-Talia, 2006), p. 61.

[90] Fida' 'Itani, *Al-jihadiyun fi Lubnan: min Quwwat al-Fajr ila Fatah al-Islam* [*The Jihadis in Lebanon: from Quwwat al-Fajr to Fatah al-Islam*] (Beirut: Dar al-Saqi, 2008).

[91] One Tripolitan official in particular in the Islamic Group, Abdel Sattar Bakkar, alongside a group of followers engaged in such activities. He suddenly "disappeared" in the late 1970s and many Islamists suspect that Syrian intelligence became aware of his activities and killed him. Interview with former leading Islamic Group officials, Tripoli, September 2016. See also Fida' 'Itani, *Al-jihadiyun fi Lubnan*, pp. 82–4.

80   Tales of a Rebel City

Instead the connections between the Syrian Muslim Brotherhood and the Islamic Group would nearly be fatal for the latter. When in 1979 the Syrian regime discovered a list of Islamic Group members and their close connections to Syrian Muslim Brothers, it arrested its leader, Fathi Yakan, a Tripolitan activist who had long been close to the Syrian Muslim Brotherhood's militant wing in Homs and Hama, and faced him with a dilemma: he would either be released but tell his men to stop helping the regime's enemies, or be jailed and his movement submitted to the ire of Damascus.[92] He chose the former and, from then on, the Islamic Group, which had for a while channeled Tripoli's rebel identity, attachment to the Syrian hinterland and traditions of solidarity with the Palestinians and hostility to the Lebanese and Syrian governments, would now refrain from engaging in contentious politics.

It is against the backdrop of the eventual failure of the Islamic Group to embody Tripoli's "tales of contention" and "global sense of place" in sustained ways that its decline in the 1970s and Tawhid's meteoric rise in 1982 must be viewed. As this book will show, Tawhid would engage with many of the locally specific identities and grievances introduced in this chapter – to the extent that the bulk of its partisans would start seeing it as an ideologically driven, Islamist as much as a spatially oriented, Tripolitan movement.

The Cultural Momentum of Islamism

Another important mechanism which explained why it was Islamism that was now fast on the rise in Tripoli during the 1970s and 1980s, as opposed to leftism or, as even earlier, pan-Arabism and Syrian nationalism, was this ideology's fast-growing "cultural momentum." By this notion I mean to emphasize how political ideologies, far from emerging in a vacuum, tend to achieve a degree of momentum and to be made more widely available to society when their cultural underpinnings become more dominant. In many parts of Muslim-inhabited cities of Lebanon, but in Tripoli especially, three main cultural transformations in the 1970s led to a growth of social conservatism, the spread of a more rigid interpretation of religion and a banalization of sectarian sentiment, which laid the cultural groundwork for Islamism.

The first main transformation which explained Islamism's growing "cultural momentum" was the spread of conservative mores in

---

[92] Interview with the former head of the Islamic Group's political bureau Abdallah Babetti, Tripoli, April 2015; and with the Islamic Group's former leader, Ibrahim al-Masri, Beirut, April 2015.

The Cultural Momentum of Islamism 81

Lebanon's Muslim-majority cities. This was the case in Beirut's southern suburbs, Sidon and Baalbek, but most strikingly so in Tripoli. There the cultural change which took place was particularly stark because, in the 1950s and 1960s, the city and the upper-middle-class neighborhood of New Tripoli in particular had become characterized by a growing liberalization of social mores. This was not only a time when many women began unveiling, attending university and taking part in local politics, it was also a period during which myriad establishments selling alcohol and featuring gambling games opened their doors and thrived in Tripoli. The city became home to the *Cheval Blanc*, Lebanon's only casino before the opening of *Casino du Liban* near Beirut in 1959. It also featured several cabarets, restaurants where wine was served, nightclubs and bars.[93] This change partially stemmed from the dozens of British engineers who worked at the oil terminal from the mid-1940s to the late 1950s and spread a progressive lifestyle. But it was also due to leftism's own "cultural momentum" then and to the fact that upper- and middle-class Tripolitan students attended the Lebanese University which, until 1975, only had a branch in Beirut, thus socializing them into the capital's more progressive lifestyle.

The massive influx of rural migrants to Tripoli in the 1960s gradually reversed that trend for, although they were not necessarily all pious, they still displayed more conservative mores in line with their rural upbringing and few had the opportunity to attend university in Beirut. This resulted in a quick and significant cultural transformation in Tripoli. One scholar noticed that by the 1970s the city was already witnessing the spread of conservative clothing, women for instance increasingly wearing the headscarf, and a growing questioning of the progressive lifestyle which had earlier been prominent.[94] In a cultural context marked by the growth of conservative mores, the Islamist call for a return to religion and tradition was perhaps bound to resonate. Local Islamist movements struck a popular chord as they sought to channel this growth of social conservatism, denouncing the "moral corruption" of parts of society and promising to fight "prostitutes and alcoholics."[95]

The second and related transformation which explained Islamism's growing "cultural momentum" was that rural migration altered the

---

[93] This draws on Khaled Ziadeh's and John Gulick's ethnographic accounts as well as on interviews with residents of Tripoli. See Khaled Ziadeh, *Yum al-Jum'a, yum al-ahad* [*Friday is Sunday*] (Beirut, Dar al-Nahar, 1996) and Gulick, *Tripoli*.

[94] Maha Kayal, *Le systeme socio-vestimentaire à Tripoli (Liban) entre 1885 et 1985* (Neuchâtel: University of Neuchâtel, unpublished PhD thesis, 1989).

[95] Islamic Group Tripoli-based leader Fathi Yakan quoted in Imad, *Al-harakat al-Islamiya fi Lubnan*, pp. 62–78.

82   Tales of a Rebel City

sectarian composition of Lebanon's Muslim-majority cities, undermining diversity and bolstering rigid interpretations of Islam. In Tripoli, aside from significant Alawi migration, the overwhelming majority of the newcomers who settled were Sunni Muslims, something which given the sheer scale of migration meant that entire neighborhoods of the city became homogeneously Sunni Muslim.[96] This stood at odds with Tripolitan history. The city had long been Sunni-dominated, but its Christian minority was historically significant, local Greek Orthodox Christians for instance representing as much as a reported third of the overall local population during Ottoman times. Importantly, this large minority not only practiced its faith freely – it was not touched by the 1840–60 sectarian riots in Beirut – but it was also well integrated in Tripoli's social fabric. Local Christians were long scattered between the Old City's neighborhood of Zehriye, which featured a Street of the Churches, New Tripoli where they built a cathedral and the port district of Mina. They took an active role as leading merchants but also as politicians, some even holding prominent positions in the local Ottoman administration, and as educational entrepreneurs for they participated in the creation of American and French missionary schools in the nineteenth century.[97] Reflecting their integral part in the local social fabric and attachment to the city as a community, a researcher remarked in the early twentieth century that Tripoli was back then known for "the aristocratic pride of its people, Muslims and Christians."[98]

With time, mass migration from Tripoli's Sunni countryside changed this balance, in the space of years bringing down the proportion of Christians to 20 percent of the local population. The decrease in religious diversity that had characterized Tripoli for centuries undermined the appeal of tolerant, coexistence-oriented interpretations of Islam which had long prevailed. In parallel, the sectarian homogenization of some neighborhoods in particular encouraged the spread of more rigid interpretations of religion, with less regard than before for minority rights. There, a researcher thus noted a transformation in the way religion was practiced. She remarked a decline in the Sufi orders that had long been

---

[96] Loïc Ploteau, *Les populations originaires du Haut-Dinniyé à Tripoli (Liban): les dynamiques de ségrégation de citadinisation* (Tours: Tours University, unpublished MPhil thesis, 1997), pp. 15–22.

[97] While John Gulick estimates that during Ottoman and French Mandate times Tripoli was made up of a third of Christians, Mousbah Rajab mentions the figure of a quarter. See Gulick, *Tripoli*, p. 21 and Rajab, *Le vieux Tripoli*, p. 143. For more on the historical background on the Christian presence in Tripoli, see: Khodr Heloui, *La rue des églises* (Paris: L'Harmattan, 2014).

[98] Henry Jessup (1910) quoted in Gulick, *Tripoli*, p. 24.

The Cultural Momentum of Islamism 83

dominant locally and featured liberal and esoteric practices, such as the Mawlawiya and Rifaʿiya, while observing the simultaneous growth of the Naqshbandiya, a Sufi order characterized by its adherence to an orthodox view of Islam.[99] The result was the spread of a more conservative and rigid interpretation of religion. Reflecting this dynamic, it was telling that the movements which, in 1970s and 1980s Tripoli, argued for the full implementation of Islamic law as "sovereignty belongs to Allah alone"[100] first grew popular in Abu Samra, a Sunni district with no Christian presence.

The third main concomitant transformation which explained Islamism's growing "cultural momentum," and would then pave the way for its political and ideological momentum, was the banalization of sectarian sentiment in Lebanon, including in Tripoli. The dynamic of an increasingly violent political and sectarian polarization had been simmering throughout the country since the 1958 conflict and even more since the 1975 civil war. These episodes of contention pitted, broadly speaking, Lebanon's pro-government and Western-friendly Christian Maronite political parties and militias against Muslim-dominated rebel movements which supported the Palestinian resistance. This partially sectarian cleavage trickled down to North Lebanon too, where it crystallized as a struggle between Tripoli's growing number of Sunni Muslims and the nearby villages inhabited by Christian Maronites.

The conflict turned especially bitter with the mountain town of Zgharta. A mere 10 km away from Tripoli, this village was the birthplace and stronghold of Lebanese President Suleiman Franjieh who, importantly, was also known to be loyal to the Syrian regime. Tensions had long been rising between Tripoli's pro-Palestinian Sunni Muslim majority and Zgharta's pro-governmental Christian Maronites and violence eventually broke out in September 1975. Back then, gunmen from the mountain town stopped a bus carrying Tripolitan Muslim passengers on their way to Beirut and killed them all.[101] This triggered armed clashes and mutual shelling between Tripoli and Zgharta, which killed thirty and injured seventy, before the conflict was contained through a buffer zone

---

[99] Daphne Habibis, *A comparative study of the workings of a branch of the Naqshbandi Sufi order in Lebanon and the UK* (London: London School of Economics and Political Science, unpublished PhD thesis, 1985).

[100] Fathi Yakan, the Tripoli- and Abu Samra-based leader of the Islamic Group, quoted in Imad, *Al-harakat al-Islamiya fi Lubnan*, p. 62.

[101] For more background on the history of relations between Tripoli and Zgharta, see: Chawqi Douayhi, "Tripoli et Zgharta, deux villes en quête d'un éspace commun," chapter 3 in Eric Huybrechts and Chawqi Douayhi (eds.), *Reconstruction et réconciliation au Liban* (Beirut: Presses de l'Ifpo, 1999).

84   Tales of a Rebel City

enforced by the Lebanese army. A year later, pro-Palestinian Tripolitan Muslims took revenge for the aforementioned Black June massacre of civilians by Christian militias in the Palestinian refugee camp of Tal al-Z'atar in Beirut by attacking Maronite civilians in the nearby villages of Chekka and Hamat. In Tripoli itself the growing political and sectarian polarization of the Lebanese civil war did not lead to massacres of local Christians, but it nonetheless translated into a wave of sectarian incidents, the shops of known Maronites in the city witnessing "high property damage."[102] This, according to several residents, contributed to the emergence of a "sectarian mindset" at odds with the city's history of Muslim–Christian coexistence, which reinforced the appeal of local Sunni Islamist groups that were critical of religious minorities. Their constant warnings that the "enemies of Islam" were "conspiring against Muslims"[103] grew more popular locally.

These three main transformations which gripped many parts of Lebanon and Tripoli in particular cultivated a new cultural terrain on which Islamist movements, including Tawhid, subsequently gained a measure of political and ideological prominence. Islamism's "cultural momentum" was making it more available to society, paving the way for a marked increase in sincere as well as instrumental embraces of this ideology in the 1970s and 1980s.

Theorizing Back

By exploring the factors behind the engagement of many Tripolitans in locally oriented activism and their corresponding embrace of various ideologies, this chapter draws broader theoretical implications and answers the following questions. What accounts for "rebel cities" that feature recurrent, large-scale collective action throughout their history? And how did some ideologies, like Islamism, become prevalent at a specific point in time?

First, this chapter illuminates how social, rebel and terrorist movements can use the symbolic dimensions of space as a resource in order to root themselves in some localities. The literature on contentious politics is permeated by the assumption that, because of globalization and contemporary technologies, "collective actors are now less likely than in the

---

[102] US Embassy in Beirut, "Tripoli-Zgharta war still rages" (GS-NA, 11301-b, September 9, 1975). See also: US Embassy in Beirut, "The army moves into North Lebanon" (GS-NA, 11423-b, September 11, 1975) and US Embassy in Beirut, "Tripoli-Zghorta area quiet" (GS-NA, 11463-b, September 12, 1975).
[103] Fathi Yakan quoted in Imad, *Al-harakat al-Islamiya fi Lubnan*, p. 74.

past to identify themselves with reference to locality,"[104] as two leading figures of social movements theories claimed. But in other fields it has become evident that what geographer John Agnew called the "sense of place"[105] – or collective identification to a space – remains resilient. This is obvious in the West where, from Catalonia to Flanders, the strength of local narratives and traditions enhances collective identification with space and considerably impacts politics. And, importantly, the significance of local identities is also relevant to the Middle East. There, collective identification with communities at the subnational level such as the neighborhood, the city or the province remains particularly strong given their sometimes-millennial history, an Ottoman legacy of local autonomy, the fragility of state institutions created in the post-independence era and fluid interpretations of the concept of nationhood. In this chapter I unpack the construction of Tripolitan identity. I not only point to its distinctive features and explain its evolution through the ages; I also reveal how, far from only being parochial, it was also traversed by strong solidarity with two larger communities – the Palestinian people and Syrian Sunnis. In the context of locally intense grievances, the identification of residents with their city as a community rendered mobilizations massive and impassioned.

I point to one mechanism in particular through which social, rebel and terrorist movements can take advantage of collective identification with space to recruit and mobilize: the revival and appropriation of "tales of contention" that associate a province, city or neighborhood to an older, sometimes mythicized and often glorified, history of rebellion. Movements can root themselves by building on local narratives that highlight a tradition of contention and by inscribing their mobilization attempt partially within this legacy. Reviving and appropriating these tales will allow them to signal belonging to the local community, activate the solidarities binding residents and cast activism as a duty in line with local history. These "tales of contention" can take a variety of forms, whether written (e.g. pamphlets), oral (e.g. speeches, songs) or visual (e.g. graffiti, memorials); the important point is that they aim at channeling the sense of collective identification to a community and to a particular understanding of its past, one especially putting forward a history of common struggles. In Tripoli's case a succession of movements of all

---

[104] Donatella Della Porta and Mario Diani, *Social movements: an introduction* (London: Blackwell, 2006), p. 94.

[105] By "sense of place," John Agnew meant the personal and emotional attachment of people to a place, which hints at the notion of "collective identity." See: John Agnew, *Place and politics in modern Italy* (Chicago: Chicago University press, 2002).

86   Tales of a Rebel City

ideological stripes successfully revived and appropriated the narratives which associated it with a rebel city in order to root themselves locally – and Tawhid would do so as well, as Chapters 4 and 8 demonstrate. This shows how the symbolic dimension of space can be used as a resource during mobilizations.

Second, I explain why, after pan-Syrian nationalism, pan-Arabism and radical Marxism successively attracted the "contentious Tripolitans," Islamism emerged in the 1970s and 1980s as the ideology which channeled Tripolitan identity and addressed local grievances. One key factor was the declining ability of leftist movements to channel the spatially oriented activism of the "contentious Tripolitans," something due to their growing social elitism but even more so to their unwillingness to oppose the city's new archenemy, the Syrian regime. Local Islamist movements, for their part, had long been more critical of the rulers in Damascus, helped by the fact that Syrian Islamists were at the forefront of the opposition. They also demonstrated a readiness to strike a balance between commitment to ideology and to the city as a community. In one telling instance a group of Tripolitan Islamists vehemently supported the Nasser-sponsored Egyptian–Syrian union because it was widely viewed as in the interest of Tripoli and in continuity with its identity, although it was inconsistent with their ideology at a time marked by Nasser's repression of Egypt's Islamists. As a result of their engagement with local concerns, Islamist movements were able to recruit beyond their ideological base and appeal to a growing number of "contentious Tripolitans."

Another, separate development which bolstered their rise was Islamism's growing "cultural momentum" in 1970s and 1980s Tripoli. By this notion I mean to emphasize how political ideologies, far from emerging in a vacuum, tend to achieve a degree of momentum and to be made more widely available to society when their cultural underpinnings become more dominant (e.g. religious practice, clothing style, social views, artistic genres). In the 1970s and 1980s three main cultural transformations affected the Muslim-inhabited cities of Lebanon and especially Tripoli which gave momentum to Islamism. The first one was the spread of conservative mores, itself due to a massive influx into the city of migrants from the countryside who, although they were not all necessarily pious, still embraced a more traditional lifestyle in line with their rural upbringing. This translated to the spread of conservative clothing and a questioning of the progressive lifestyle that had earlier been prominent. The second cultural change which took place was the gradual transformation of religious practice and the spread of more orthodox interpretations of Islam, itself partially stemming from a broader religious movement affecting the Middle East but also from the sectarian homogenization of entire neighborhoods in Muslim-majority Lebanese cities. And the third cultural transformation which affected Lebanon back then was the growth of sectarian sentiment resulting from the dynamic of political and religious polarization that was gripping the country. These cultural transformations affected many parts of Lebanon but they were particularly acute in Tripoli, where they provided "cultural momentum" to Islamism and bolstered the spread of this ideology. This demonstrates the importance of grasping how the evolution of culture can significantly favor the rise of some ideologies more than others.

2 Neighborhood Islamism

By the late 1970s the growth of Islamism's cultural and ideological momentum in Tripoli tackled in Chapter 1 meant that the city began witnessing the rise of myriad Islamist movements – the most militant of which would create Tawhid in 1982, which Chapter 3 tackles. One of these factions, the Popular Resistance, deserves particular attention for it embraced Islamism only belatedly in 1980, would come to form as much as a quarter of Tawhid's base and became very strong in Tripoli's largest neighborhood, Bab al-Tebbaneh. In fact, all the Popular Resistance's 500 fighters hailed from this district only, and there it could count on an even larger pool of sympathizers – hundreds, sometimes thousands of whom joined in episodes of contention such as Islamist-led demonstrations and risky clashes. They became known for their violent, seemingly ideological enmity for the government, the Syrian regime and Tripoli's Alawi minority in the district of Jabal Mohsen, to the extent that Bab al-Tebbaneh soon acquired a reputation as the hotbed of religious extremism in the city. But the striking degree to which the Popular Resistance had built a spatial base there suggests that something additional, quite apart from the city-wide and broader growth of Islamism's momentum, had to explain the mass embrace of ideology in this neighborhood especially. The phenomenon of the seemingly sudden growth of militant Islamism in Bab al-Tebbaneh was made even more intriguing by a second puzzle. Before suddenly embracing this ideology in 1980, the Islamist-leaning Popular Resistance had been known as a revolutionary Marxist movement – and, back then, it had also drawn the entire neighborhood into radical leftism.

This chapter accounts for the Popular Resistance's remarkable strength in Bab al-Tebbaneh and explores its counterintuitive shift from one ideology to another, arguing that it embraced Islamism instrumentally to prevail in a local conflict and that this led to a "neighborhood Islamism" more guided by local concerns and solidarities than by ideology. I begin by tracing the main social, economic and political characteristics of Bab al-Tebbaneh. Rather than being viewed as a hotbed of religious extremism, I claim that the district should instead be understood as what I call a "stronghold of contention" – a space characterized by its propensity to nurture frequent and sustained episodes of collective action. In the early 1980s this would pave the way for the rise of the militant Islamism of the Popular Resistance and then of Tawhid. But it is noteworthy that, for decades before, Bab al-Tebbaneh had been a hub for revolutionary Marxists and rebels of all stripes. Its status as Tripoli's "stronghold of contention" stemmed from the particular intensity of the grievances suffered by residents there, which shaped their political orientation and rendered them especially hostile to the government, the municipality and the local elite. It also resulted from features unique to the local social fabric, such as the remarkably strong solidarities of neighbors with one another, which facilitated mobilization. While, as a result of this, Bab al-Tebbaneh quickly arose as a propitious place for all kinds of rebel movements to recruit members and to operate, from the 1970s onward it became the birthplace and stronghold of one group in particular, the Organization of Anger. Interestingly, although its ideology was revolutionary Marxism, it behaved more as a neighborhood-oriented than as an ideologically guided movement – it mostly sought to mobilize in and address the grievances of the district. I argue that this was because the Organization of Anger's head, Ali Akkawi, also acted as the informal leader or "champion of mobilization" of Bab al-Tebbaneh, where he thus had an immense aura and following. When Ali passed away in 1974 and his brother Khalil took over as neighborhood leader, he set up the Marxist-leaning Popular Committees and then the pro-Palestinian Popular Resistance. But his two successive movements remained anchored in and oriented toward his district. It was as Bab al-Tebbaneh's grievances came to revolve around a bloody neighborhood rivalry with the Alawi district of Jabal Mohsen and with the Syrian army in Tripoli, in 1980, that Khalil Akkawi ditched his revolutionary Marxism and embraced militant Islamism, attracted by the latter's potential as a "protest ideology" associated with symbols, discourse, practices and infrastructures all useful in this deadly local feud. Many locals who were deeply loyal to him followed through, as a result suddenly becoming Islamists too. At first some highly ideologized Islamist figures bent on spreading their worldviews to the neighborhood tried hard to reinforce the Popular Resistance's commitment to Islamism. But, by and large, the embrace of ideology by Khalil Akkawi's partisans remained instrumental. Their "Islamism," then, was really a "neighborhood Islamism": it was so profoundly shaped by Bab al-Tebbaneh's local context that their behavior and exercise of violence remained more informed by local solidarities, concerns and antagonisms than by ideology. As the Popular Resistance joined Tawhid in 1982, it brought its "neighborhood Islamism" along.

90   Neighborhood Islamism

A Stronghold of Contention

What is most striking about Bab al-Tebbaneh is how, even decades before it became a hub of militant Islamism in the 1980s, it had been known as Tripoli's "stronghold of contention" par excellence: this neighborhood had long been characterized by a particular propensity to nurture regular and often violent episodes of collective action. In the 1950s and 1960s it had acted as a valuable base for some of the social and rebel movements which were proliferating in Tripoli at the time, like the Iraqi Ba'ath and the 24 October Movement, both introduced in Chapter 1. In the 1970s and 1980s the neighborhood ceased to just be a resource for movements to tap into, and instead began to shape the very nature of mobilization. Bab al-Tebbaneh even gave rise to its own, neighborhood-specific movement, one which would successively embrace revolutionary Marxism and then militant Islamism but would remain characterized by its ability to mobilize hundreds of residents in locally oriented activism.

A key reason behind the longstanding prevalence of mobilization in Bab al-Tebbaneh was that many dissident movements saw this space as an invaluable physical, social and symbolic resource. As a result they all made it a priority to recruit and operate in the district.

Most evidently, what attracted these movements to mobilize in Bab al-Tebbaneh were the rich physical resources of the neighborhood, for example its strategic location and useful layout. Situated in the northeastern vicinity of the Old City, the district stretched like a triangle between the Abu Ali river on its left, the hills of Qobbe and Jabal Mohsen to its right flank, all the way north to the coastal road linking Tripoli to its port and the strategically significant oil terminal, the Akkar countryside and eventually to Syria, a mere 30 km away. Bab al-Tebbaneh, then, may not have been the city's geographical center but it still acted as an important node and a key hub for transit connecting Tripoli to the rest of North Lebanon and the Syrian hinterland. Mobilizing in the neighborhood, therefore, not only allowed the social and rebel movements which operated there to paralyze access to the economically vital coastal road and oil terminal by routinely burning tires and leading disruptive strikes, it also brought them closer to the cross-border weapons-smuggling networks that proliferated there.

Bab al-Tebbaneh's urban layout, moreover, usefully provided the adequate "ecological conditions"[1] for the development of contentious

---

[1] Dingxin Zhao, "Ecologies of social movements: student mobilization during the 1989 pro-democracy movement in Beijing" *American Journal of Sociology* (Vol. 103, No. 6, 1998), pp. 1493–529.

A Stronghold of Contention 91

activities, as social movements scholar Dingxin Zhao would have put it; that is, the neighborhood's physical shape was itself conducive to contention. Much like the other historical quarters which together made up Tripoli's Old City, Bab al-Tebbaneh consisted of mazes of narrow streets and alleyways. This allowed the rebels who operated in the neighborhood's vicinity to quickly withdraw when the security forces approached, installing barricades and resisting their entry into the area. And, unlike other parts of the Old City, some of its buildings were partially rebuilt after the 1955 Abu Ali river flood, so sections of the neighborhood also featured many higher-than-normal five-story apartment blocks that provided convenient locations to spot the arrival of security forces and to alternatively hide from or shoot at them. Bab al-Tebbaneh's physical location in proximity to valuable infrastructure and networks as well as an urban layout particularly propitious to the development of contentious activities thus rapidly made it a privileged site for social and rebel movements which, in the 1950s and 1960s, began using the neighborhood as one of their hubs with other districts of the Old City.

Beyond the neighborhood's physical properties, Tripoli's dissident movements were also attracted by the social resources associated with Bab al-Tebbaneh: it had the capacity to act as what Charles Tilly called a "safe space,"[2] or a place where contentious actors could protect themselves from the authorities and where they could carry out their activities freely. This, of course, resulted from the district's physical properties; but even more important was its ability to provide a milieu of support to those involved in social and rebel movements. There locals felt an especially strong sense of belonging to the neighborhood as a community – this implied solidarities which could be activated during episodes of contention.

In the Middle East, strong collective identification to the neighborhood as a community is best signaled by the use of the word *al-hara*. Literally, it means "the quarter." Yet its significance is more profound for it is a concept which not only alludes to a shared physical space but also to a community with a centuries-old history as a thick social fabric; daily life operating through local solidarities and informal institutions. There, residents are particularly close to each other, and local traditions and identities greatly matter to them. Sometimes this identification to the neighborhood as a community can be so strong that it may conflict with other "imagined communities," like the city and the state. In fact, hostility to such higher scales of authority often still lies at the core of the

---

[2] Charles Tilly, "Spaces of contention" *Mobilization* (Vol. 5, No. 2, 2000), pp. 144–6.

92   Neighborhood Islamism

concept of *hara*. Naturally, not all residents everywhere identify with the neighborhood as a strong community. It tends to be especially, although not uniquely, the case for those who live in the historical and popular neighborhoods. There, narrow alleyways, high population density and centuries-old, locally rooted narratives and identities passed on to younger generations foster a particularly acute sense of intimacy, norms of mutual help and a common sense of neighborhood belonging. And this, in turn, often stands at odds with the anonymity, individualism and looser social ties typical of the more modern and wealthier districts.[3]

In Bab al-Tebbaneh, as in other neighborhoods of Tripoli's Old City, the sense of belonging to the local community was strong, with several studies observing the "intense neighborhood relations," "mutual support" and "sense of solidarity and familiarity"[4] which characterized its social fabric. Michel Seurat, a sociologist who authored a landmark study on the district, even argued that local social ties were so tight that they could be compared to a "neighborhood *aasabiya*."[5] This was a reference to a term used by medieval sociologist Ibn Khaldun to describe the sense of "group feeling" which pushed some communities to act as apparent blocs, a concept that has become increasingly common among Middle East scholars to explain sectarian and tribal bonds of loyalty but which Seurat here employed to allude to the intense ties of neighborhood solidarity he saw at play in Bab al-Tebbaneh.

That Bab al-Tebbaneh would be characterized by such a strong sense of local community can seem surprising at first glance, for by the 1970s only a third of its residents originally hailed from the neighborhood and this proportion would continue to go down to a fifth in the later decades.[6] The rest were rural migrants who hailed from Tripoli's northern countryside of

---

[3] For more on identification to the neighborhood as a social and political community in the Middle East, see, among others: Nawal al-Messiri-Nadim, "The concept of the *hara*: a historical and sociological study of al-Sukkariya" *Annales Islamologiques* (Vol. 15, 1979), pp. 313–48; Diane Singerman, *Avenues of participation: family, politics and networks in urban quarters of Cairo* (New Jersey: Princeton University Press, 1995); Salwa Ismail, "The politics of the urban everyday in Cairo: infrastructures of oppositional action," chapter 24 in Susan Parnell and Sophie Oldfield (eds.), *The Routledge handbook on cities of the global South* (London: Routledge, 2014), pp. 269–80; and Salwa Ismail, *Rethinking Islamist politics: culture, the state and Islamism* (London: I.B.Tauris, 2003).

[4] See, for instance: *Tabbaneh: neighbourhood profile* (Beirut: UN-Habitat Lebanon, 2018).

[5] Michel Seurat, "Le quartier de Bab Tebbane à Tripoli (Liban), étude d'une *assabiya* urbaine," chapter 3 in Mona Zakaria (ed.), *Mouvements communautaires et espaces urbains au Machreq* (Beirut: Presses de l'Ifpo, 1985).

[6] While Ali Fa'our found that only 32.7 percent of Bab al-Tebbaneh's residents were originally Tripolitans by the mid-1970s, a recent study by the United Nations suggest that this figure may have now fallen to less than 20 percent. See Ali Fa'our, *Géographie urbaine de la ville de Tripoli (Liban)* (Brussels: Université Libre de Bruxelles, Unpublished PhD thesis, 1975), p. 70 quoted in Seurat, "Le quartier," p. 45 and *Tabbaneh: neighbourhood profile* (Beirut: UN-Habitat Lebanon, 2018), p. 19.

A Stronghold of Contention   93

Akkar and the Syrian hinterland and had settled in the district because of its cheap rents. Yet, far from popular assumptions that sometimes treat deprived rural migrants as uprooted and lost in the masses of large cities, this migration instead reinforced solidarities and a sense of common belonging among local residents. Many such migrants originally hailed from similar villages, which resulted in the presence within the neighborhood of clusters of extended families that trusted and knew each other well. And, although the neighborhood was religiously diverse, with a Sunni majority living side by side with an Alawi minority, strong common identification to the neighborhood as a shared community relegated sectarian loyalties to the backseat, at least until the late 1970s.

Other factors also explained such strong neighborhood solidarities. The district was overcrowded, which fostered intimacy as well as tight networks of mutual support. According to one survey Bab al-Tebbaneh may well have been Tripoli's most densely populated neighborhood by 1970, with a rate of 100,000 inhabitants per square kilometer. This was ten times the city average.[7] Moreover, the historical boundaries of the district and much of its actual shape long remained intact, enhancing the sense of spatial identification to Bab al-Tebbaneh as a geographically delimited *hara*. Like other neighborhoods it was severely affected by the 1955 Abu Ali river flood. But the authorities later rebuilt new housing without modifying the area, unlike several other districts of the Old City, which saw their streets and overall layout significantly altered as part of renovation and modernization projects in the 1960s and 1970s. And finally, the residents of Bab al-Tebbaneh were especially known for their shared pride in inhabiting the neighborhood. This resulted from narratives of a prestigious past that widely circulated through a locally well-entrenched oral tradition. They emphasized how, until the 1950s, the neighborhood had been affectionately known to other Tripolitans as *Bab al-Dhahab* ("Gate of Gold"), a play on words with its actual name as *Bab al-Tebbaneh* ("Gate of Grains"). This hinted at its prominent role for centuries as the especially vibrant and profitable "marketplace"[8] of the city due to its strategic location as a gateway for goods and people transiting to the rest of Northern Lebanon and to Syria. For all these reasons, residents of Bab al-Tebbaneh developed a strong attachment to their neighborhood, something which sharply contrasted with other parts of the city, like modern and wealthy New Tripoli, where an anthropologist noted a striking "loss of community spirit."[9]

---

[7] Fa'our, *Géographie urbaine*, p. 77, quoted in Seurat, "Le quartier."
[8] Interviews with residents of Bab al-Tebbaneh, Tripoli, November 2014.
[9] John Gulick, *Tripoli: a modern Arab city* (Cambridge, MA: Harvard University Press, 1967), pp. 150–1.

94   Neighborhood Islamism

Tripoli's social and rebel movements were thus attracted by the prospect of recruiting in Bab al-Tebbaneh to use it as a milieu of support, which further contributed to turning it into a "stronghold of contention." Operating there allowed the local members of these dissident movements to fall back on neighborhood solidarities when the security forces chased them, enabling them to claim the help of the local population and to hide among it. The degree of willingness of neighbors to risk their lives to protect one of their own was such that it was not uncommon, for some dissidents, to "disappear"[10] inside Bab al-Tebbaneh for several months or years. Ties of resident solidarity were so intense that, activated during episodes of contention, they could result not just in neighbors hiding local outlaws but also in joining a protest or a movement primarily on the mere basis of neighborhood loyalties. As a "safe space," then, the district provided the solidarities which turned it into a milieu of support whenever the locals involved in contentious activities needed help.

The fourth and final factor which turned Bab al-Tebbaneh into a "stronghold of contention" regularly giving birth to violent collective action was a local identity increasingly associating, from the 1960s onward, the neighborhood with the ideal of rebellion against higher forms of institutionalized political authority, both at the city and state level. Of course, as stated earlier, traditions of neighborhood autonomy from and even friction with the municipality and the government often lay at the core of the popular imaginary associated with the notion of *hara* in the Middle East. In Tripoli this was especially true of several districts of the Old City. But in Bab al-Tebbaneh fast-mounting grievances made this rebel identity increasingly prevalent. This helped fashion a local culture of dissent which provided fertile ground for all kinds of militant movements to recruit and operate.

Indeed, while the neighborhood had long been known as Tripoli's "Gate of Gold," in the 1950s and 1960s it became severely affected by some of the wider trends mentioned in Chapter 1, such as the breakdown of the Syrian-Lebanese tariff union, the Abu Ali river flood and the migration of the Old City's wealthiest residents to New Tripoli. The result was a particularly sudden and acute economic downturn and collapse of local infrastructures. Already by the late 1960s, a staggering 90 percent of the neighborhood's inhabitants now belonged to the lower class and "few people older than twenty years have had more than a primary education."[11] One anthropologist who toured Tripoli back then

[10] Nadine Picaudou, "Mutations socio-économiques du vieux Tripoli" *Annales de Géographie* (Vol. 1, 1981), p. 97.
[11] Gulick, *Tripoli*, p. 205.

singled out Bab al-Tebbaneh for its strikingly bad state. He observed that, although it was one of the city's largest neighborhoods with over 40,000 inhabitants, it was "generally dirty and in bad repair, with poorly drained streets, insufficient police protection [and] only two schools."[12]

One consequence of rampant poverty was that, given the ties of local residents to the northern countryside as well as the neighborhood's function as a hub of transit for goods bound for Syria, a growing number of locals got involved in the underground economy to make ends meet – especially smuggling cigarettes, drugs, fuel and weapons. This, however, combined with the fast-growing local consumption of drugs and alcohol due to difficult living conditions, resulted in sporadic and often violent raids by the security forces against local residents, fostering a sense of constant harassment. It also led to the neighborhood's stigmatization by other Tripolitans, especially by the upper-class inhabitants of New Tripoli, as a "tough and dangerous" district with an "ill reputation,"[13] which rendered the proud residents of this neighborhood bitter. By the 1960s, then, there was a growing sense among Bab al-Tebbaneh's residents that they were increasingly "stripped of their rights" and that the municipality, the government as well as the politicians and the upper class at large were all to be blamed for their "neglect." And, importantly, they reported being ready to "use arms if needed"[14] to redress these wrongs, showcasing how the grievances suffered by their neighborhood were laying the groundwork for the proliferation of militant movements. Long known as Tripoli's "Gate of Gold," the district had within the space of years earned the reputation of acting as a "hotbed of dissidence,"[15] one nurturing contention.

In the 1950s and 1960s Bab al-Tebbaneh's physical features, strong local solidarities, rebel identity and fast-mounting grievances all made it especially fertile terrain for movements such as the Iraqi Ba'ath and the 24 October Movement to recruit and operate. Yet, from the 1970s onward this "stronghold of contention" ceased to be merely a set of physical, social and symbolic resources that rebel organizations would tap into. Instead, Bab al-Tebbaneh as a space began to shape the dynamics of contention, producing its own movement made up of locals only who engaged in neighborhood-oriented collective action.

---

[12] Ibid., pp. 204–6.

[13] Ibid. Note that this reputation persists until today. Interview with residents of Bab al-Tebbaneh, Tripoli, November 2014.

[14] *Tabbaneh: neighbourhood profile* (Beirut: UN-Habitat Lebanon, 2018), pp. 24–5.

[15] Mohammed Abi Samra, *Trablus: Sehat Allah wa mina al-hadatha* [*Tripoli: Allah Square and port of modernity*] (Beirut: Dar al-Saqi, 2011), p. 87.

96   Neighborhood Islamism

The *Qabaday*, Champion of Mobilization

The catalyst behind the birth in the 1970s of this new, neighborhood-specific movement in Bab al-Tebbaneh had been the rise of Ali Akkawi as the district's *qabaday*, a popular strongman or informal leader akin to what I call a "champion of mobilization." By this notion I mean a figure with such a high status and large following in his community that he is uniquely placed to activate local solidarities and to channel grievances into collective action. The *qabaday*, because of his role as informal leader bound by intense loyalty to his neighborhood, was able to draw local masses to the protests and movements he was joining.

The role of the *qabaday* as a locally rooted "champion of mobilization" is by no means limited to the 1970s and to Tripoli. It takes its historical roots as far back as the twelfth century in the development of the *futuwwa*; literally groups of chivalrous "young men" who formed militias to defend their quarter, support residents and uphold morals in the popular neighborhoods of Middle Eastern cities at a time when the Islamic Caliphate's authority was fast eroding because of the accumulation of debts, wars and factional splits.[16] In subsequent centuries the broader context changed; yet the concept remained central to the way popular neighborhoods organized themselves and it took on a variety of names such as the *lutis* in Iran or the *qabadayet* (plural of *qabaday*) in Turkey and Greater Syria. Naturally the meaning of the *qabaday* varied depending on the perspective. While some, often in the upper class, viewed this figure as a thug spearheading acts of urban unrest, he was often hailed in his neighborhood as an informal leader who embodied local grievances, identities and strong solidarities; someone prone to act violently and even to die in order to champion the interests and honor of the local community against its enemies.[17] In a reflection of the polarizing nature of these figures, but also of their popularity among corners of society, one scholar remarked that "many Lebanese despised these leaders but it is remarkable how many others admired them."[18] In other

---

[16] Sawsan el-Messiri, "The changing role of the Futuwwa in the social structure of Cairo" in Ernest Gellner and John Waterbury (eds.), *Patrons and clients in Mediterranean societies* (London: Duckworth, 1977), pp. 239–53.

[17] See, among others, Farzin Vejdani, "Urban violence and space: *Lutis*, seminarians and *Sayyids* in Late Qajar Iran" *Journal of Social History* (Vol. 52, No. 4, 2019), pp. 1185–211; Wilson Chacko Jacob, "Eventful transformations: al-Futuwwa between history and the everyday" *Comparative Studies in Society and History* (Vol. 49, No. 3, 2007), pp. 689–712; and Stephanie Cronin (ed.), *Crime, poverty and survival in the Middle East and North Africa: the 'dangerous classes' since 1800* (London: I.B.Tauris, 2020).

[18] Michael Johnson, *All honourable men: the social origins of war in Lebanon* (Oxford: Centre for Lebanese Studies, 2001), pp. 47–8.

The *Qabaday*, Champion of Mobilization 97

words, they came close to what historian Eric Hobsbawm would have described as "social bandits":[19] considered criminals by some, they were seen in their communities as true heroes; fighters for justice and avengers of the poor to be admired and indeed helped because their violence was viewed as legitimate.

In Tripoli these figures especially proliferated in the historical and popular neighborhoods where the authority of the government and the municipality was weakest. This included the quarters of the Old City, including Bab al-Tebbaneh, where they still play a key role. Interviews with dozens of residents of these neighborhoods shed further light on the way locals understand the functions fulfilled by the *qabaday* and the implications of his activism. There, the *qabaday* is still widely hailed as the local community's "protector," a role associated with the ability to spearhead acts of collective violence seen as serving the district. Examples provided to describe the locally oriented nature of this activism included "robbing the rich to give to the poor," "rivaling" with other neighborhoods for control over material resources, perpetuating local traditions of hostility to and even contention "against the municipality and the government," protecting the quarter's "pride, honour and identity" and being ready to "avenge" the local community when it was perceived to be wronged. Therefore, because it was intimately linked to a degree of locally oriented violence, showing "strength," "courage" and "rootedness" was how one of the "sons of the neighborhood" could acquire the coveted status of *qabaday* or chivalrous protector of the community. It was an informal leadership status one had to literally fight for and earn, not a title one inherited.[20]

Depending on the extent of this figure's individual qualities and the degree to which he was prepared to champion the neighborhood, residents were strongly loyal to him. Nearly all stated their willingness to follow the local *qabaday* without much questioning when he spearheaded neighborhood-oriented acts of violence; and a striking number also expressed their readiness to take up weapons and risk their lives if he asked them to, some even pointing out that they stood prepared to

---

[19] Eric Hobsbawm, *Bandits* (London: Weidenfeld and Nicolson, 1969). Note that sociologist Michel Seurat and historian Stephanie Cronin were the first to draw parallels between the figure of the *qabaday* or neighbourhood strongman and the "social bandit" of Hobsbawm. See their excellent works: Seurat, "Le quartier" and Stephanie Cronin, "Noble robbers, avengers and entrepreneurs: Eric Hobsbawm and banditry in Iran, the Middle East and North Africa" *Middle Eastern Studies* (Vol. 52, No. 5, 2016), pp. 845–70.

[20] Interviews with residents of Bab al-Tebbaneh, the Old City, Qobbe and Mina, Tripoli, December 2014.

98   Neighborhood Islamism

avenge him if he was ever to be killed. The *qabaday*, then, did more than embody neighborhood solidarities, identities and grievances; crucially, he also represented his area's potential for dissent. In fact, at times he was so widely followed that he could within moments mobilize hundreds of local residents in collective acts of urban violence allegedly meant to fulfill the "good" of the local community – he epitomized his neighborhood's propensity to engage in spatially oriented contention. This effectively turned a figure which, from the outside, seemed like a mere strongman or a thug, into a culturally, emotionally and spatially rooted "champion of mobilization" whose very activism, for example participation in a movement, protest or clash, could trigger the mass recruitment and mobilization of many of his extremely dedicated followers in the community.

Bab al-Tebbaneh, like the other traditional and popular neighborhoods of Tripoli's Old City, had a long history of *qabadayet* assuming leadership. Yet, far from the glamorous but often mythicized conception of the selfless chivalrous strongmen, some of these figures had developed a tendency to act opportunistically. They still displayed their muscles and talked about the "defense of the district," but in reality a growing number of these local strongmen also started to act more or less openly as informers and occasional enforcers for the security services and notables – a trend which accelerated during the post-independence era in the 1950s and 1960s. This considerably lessened their popular standing and limited their potential to raise the local masses in neighborhood-oriented activism.[21]

It is against this historical and cultural backdrop that Ali Akkawi's rise in the 1970s must be viewed, and his own ability to single-handedly mobilize significant proportions of Bab al-Tebbaneh's residents. His persona awoke the popular imaginary in the neighborhood, where it was experienced as the long-awaited return of the mythicized figure of the chivalrous local strongman. Ali Akkawi looked, at first, like any other typical "son of the neighborhood." He had spent his whole childhood in Bab al-Tebbaneh working at his family's small bakery and, similarly to other local youths, was well versed in narratives of the neighborhood's sense of community and rebel identity. By all accounts, Bab al-Tebbaneh's fast-growing grievances pushed him and four other friends from the area to call themselves "the Five Revolutionaries" (*al-Thuwwar al-Khamsa*) and to engage in intimidation and sporadic acts of violence against some of the city's notables in 1965. Sought by the police, he used

---

[21] Interviews with residents of Bab al-Tebbaneh, Tripoli, November 2014.

Marxism or Spatially Oriented Activism?

knowledge of his neighborhood's physical layout and networks of solidarity to evade scrutiny for a while, before he was eventually arrested and sent to prison for three years. Ali Akkawi's stint in prison, however, combined with the fact that he was only in his early twenties and had dared standing up violently against local politicians who were widely viewed as the "enemies" of the neighborhood, instantly turned him into a local "hero." Upon his release from jail he was welcomed by the masses and celebrated as Bab al-Tebbaneh's true new *qabaday*.[22] Within a short span of time he had shown to the residents of his district that, unlike some of the area's other increasingly opportunistic strongmen, he had been willing to use violence to act in the neighborhood's perceived interest and to uphold its rebel identity – even if this had meant risking his own life. In turn the residents would now be ready to follow him and to engage as a community in locally oriented collective action.

Marxism or Spatially Oriented Activism?

After his release from prison Ali Akkawi set up the Organization of Anger (*Munazzamat al-Ghadab*). Operating between 1968 and 1971, this radical Marxist movement became known in the Lebanese media for the virulence of its anarcho-communist discourse, its ability to raise the masses in protests and riots as well as for its revolutionary violence – to the extent that some outside observers even began calling it a "terrorist organization."[23] At first glance therefore, this movement seemed to perfectly epitomize the growing ideological success of the radical Marxist left which, by the late 1960s, had begun supplanting Nasserism and pan-Arab Nationalism as the intellectual alternative of Arab revolutionaries. Yet, as will be seen, the Organization of Anger was more informed by dynamics specific to Bab al-Tebbaneh than by ideology. Its behavior remained primarily guided by that space's rebel identity, intense grievances, strong solidarities and Ali Akkawi's new status as the local *qabaday*. Behind the group's ostensible embrace of Marxism thus also lay spatially oriented activism.

Officially, the Organization of Anger branded itself as an ideologically pure anarcho-communist movement not bound to any specific city or neighborhood. Initially it was even called Friends of Lenin (*Asdiqa'*

---

[22] Interviews with residents of Bab al-Tebbaneh and partisans of Ali Akkawi, Tripoli, September 2014.

[23] See, for instance: "Le réseau des dynamiteurs de Tripoli démantelé," *L'Orient Le Jour* (September 17, 1971).

100 Neighborhood Islamism

Lenin) to hint at the sense that ideology drove its behavior.[24] But it soon transpired that its embrace of Marxist doctrine had been largely instrumental. Using a markedly leftist rhetoric was first of all a way of signaling ideological proximity with some of the revolutionary Marxist Palestinian guerrilla organizations and Lebanese leftist movements proliferating back then in order to be able to solicit their support. This allowed the Organization of Anger's head, Ali Akkawi, as well as a handful of his loyal followers, to acquire skills and undergo paramilitary training with the Marxist-oriented Popular Front for the Liberation of Palestine active in Tripoli's two Palestinian refugee camps, before benefiting from small funds provided by the Progressive Socialist Party.[25]

But most obviously, embracing a Marxist ideology was a way for the Organization of Anger to express the neighborhood's grievances and channel the local demand for contention against the broader backdrop of leftism's cultural and ideological momentum.

Of course, the movement's propaganda material was filled with references to some of the grand themes developed by the other revolutionary leftist groups back then. Its leaflets fiercely criticized the Lebanese political and economic system, lambasting the government and the security forces for seeking to "impose their sovereignty" at all costs and denouncing a corrupt elite intent on "reinforcing the alliance between the bourgeoisie and political feudalism" through the "masquerade"[26] of elections. It also promised the destruction of Israel, the kidnapping of Lebanese politicians and the advent of a Marxist revolution, and went as far as warning that its members were ready to "die for the people."[27] If one only examined the Organization of Anger's discourse it seemed overwhelmingly driven by ideology, and members did report that their leader Ali Akkawi truly believed in some of these ideas.

Yet it is striking how, despite a broad anarcho-communist discourse which, in theory, had the potential to attract ideologically committed leftist followers throughout Tripoli and even Lebanon, membership in the Organization of Anger remained spatially limited to Bab

---

[24] This information comes from an article on the Organization of Anger published in Lebanese newspaper the *Daily Star* on October 16, 1971, quoted in: Timothy Richard Yousaf, *The Muslim Brotherhood in Lebanon (al-Jama'a al-Islamiya), 1948–2000* (Beirut: American University of Beirut, unpublished MPhil thesis, 2010), p. 61.

[25] Interviews with Fahd Issa, Abu Zghayar and Aziz Allush (former members of the Organization of Anger in Bab al-Tebbaneh and close associates of Ali Akkawi), Tripoli, September 2014.

[26] Organization of Anger leaflet quoted in Dalal Bizri, "Le mouvement des Ibad al-Rahman et ses prolongements à Tripoli," chapter 10 in Olivier Carré and Paul Dumont, *Radicalismes islamiques* (Paris: L'Harmattan, 1992), p. 199.

[27] Seurat, "Le quartier."

al-Tebbaneh. Indeed, it is mostly from this neighborhood only that several dozen inhabitants spontaneously joined it right after its creation. Tellingly, these "Marxist" members were local residents in their teens and early twenties who did not feel any intrinsic sense of appeal for anarcho-communism since most were, in fact, illiterate workers largely unfamiliar with the peculiarities of Marxist doctrine.[28] Instead, what had driven them to join was their loyalty for Ali Akkawi and the sense that the virulence of his movement's discourse chimed particularly well with their neighborhood's grievances and rebel identity, especially as leftism's growing momentum in the late 1960s and early 1970s meant it became the quintessential rebel ideology. Two "participation identities," as sociologist Roger Gould called these identities that are key to mobilization, other than preexisting Marxist convictions, thus informed membership in the Organization of Anger: solidarity for the local *qabaday* and neighborhood identity.[29]

The Organization of Anger's revolutionary undertones helped channel the resentment of Bab al-Tebbaneh's population against the police that cracked down on the local prevalence of the illicit economy as well as the locally widespread anger at the government, the municipality and the city's elite. One of the movement's former rank and file typically explained that radical leftist vocabulary gave him and his comrades a tool to make the neighborhood "heard and visible in local society."[30] As a result, their Marxist discourse was not ideologically sophisticated. Often it boiled down to a succession of "subversive slogans" that advocated for a Leninist revolution and which were written at haste on the walls at Bab al-Tebbaneh's entrance and shouted during demonstrations to justify acts of violence.[31] This nonetheless seemed enough for the movement's members to express dissent and to frame the neighborhood's grievances in a grand way. Within a few years the Organization of Anger's radical Marxism had become Bab al-Tebbaneh's trademark ideology.

Interestingly, despite its Marxist sympathies the Organization of Anger developed a particular sense of hostility against Tripoli's mainstream leftist parties and trade unions. But, once again, rather than resulting

---

[28] "La bande responsable des explosions de Tripoli décapitée, son chef Ali Akkawi a été arrête après un affrontement," *L'Orient Le Jour* (September 16, 1971).

[29] Interviews with Fahd Issa, Abu Zghayar and Aziz Allush (former members of the Organization of Anger and close associates of Ali Akkawi), Tripoli, September 2014. See also Seurat, "Le quartier" and Abi Samra, *Trablus*, pp. 76–84.

[30] Interview with Fahd Issa (former member of the Organization of Anger), Tripoli, September 2014.

[31] "Le réseau des dynamiteurs de Tripoli démantelé," *L'Orient Le Jour* (September 17, 1971).

from the ideological quarrels that often typified elite leftist politics, the Organization of Anger's bitterness against much of the mainstream left had to be understood locally, in the context of Bab al-Tebbaneh's growing mistrust of institutionalized politics. The movement's hostility toward Tripoli's well-established leftist figures largely resulted from the widespread sense, among Bab al-Tebbaneh's residents, that the representatives of left-wing parties and trade unions were often drawn from the upper class in New Tripoli and did not seem to pay much attention to their neighborhood, although it was by far the city's poorest, other than during election time. "Where are the socialist parties [...] that come every four years knock at the doors of the masses to get re-elected?"[32] one of the Organization of Anger's leaflets asked. The way in which the Organization of Anger's criticism of the mainstream left and Bab al-Tebbaneh's rebel identity became two sides of the same coin transpired when a demonstration organized by the movement exited the neighborhood peacefully but then suddenly morphed into a riot when it approached the headquarters of the main trade union, where protesters violently ransacked its offices.[33]

It soon became clear that while Bab al-Tebbaneh's grievances and rebel identity informed the virulence of the Organization of Anger's Marxist discourse, the district also shaped the dynamics of the movement's involvement in violence, to the extent that to well-informed observers the Organization of Anger seemed ever closer to a "neighborhood gang"[34] than to a "terrorist group" guided by anarchocommunism. Indeed, Ali Akkawi's status as the local *qabaday* meant that membership in the movement was overwhelming in his neighborhood, where he personally counted on a following of hundreds, but was inherently limited in Tripoli's other districts. Tellingly, in the rest of the city Akkawi was nicknamed "the Che Guevara of Bab al-Tebbaneh,"[35] which reflected a broader understanding that his activism was at least as spatially as ideologically oriented, aiming to serve goals mostly specific to his neighborhood. In fact, although his movement displayed banners and slogans engaging with wider leftist issues in the dozens of sit-ins and protests it organized, for example the denunciation of the bad conditions suffered by the peasants in Lebanon's northern countryside, the actual claims of its rank and file often revolved around some of their

---

[32] Seurat, "Le quartier."   [33] Abi Samra, *Trablus*, p. 82.

[34] "La bande responsable des explosions de Tripoli décapitée, son chef Ali Akkawi a été arrête après un affrontement," *L'Orient Le Jour* (September 16, 1971).

[35] Interview with Abu Zghayar (associate of Ali Akkawi and former member of the Organization of Anger), Tripoli, May 2014.

neighborhood's own grievances. These involved demands for the construction of more schools and a hospital in Bab al-Tebbaneh as well as the paving of roads and the vaccination of locals against cholera.[36] Behind the engagement for wider and typically leftist causes lay a mobilization which remained considerably neighborhood-oriented.

With time it also transpired that much of the Organization of Anger's self-described "revolutionary violence" merely represented a continuation of the *qabaday*'s tradition of championing locally oriented urban dissent. Indeed, it was sufficient for its leader, Ali Akkawi, to whistle a couple of times in order to gather a crowd of dozens of young men from Bab al-Tebbaneh who on their way would pick up all kinds of weapons, from stones, sticks and kitchen knives to pistols and dynamite sticks, and follow their *qabaday* in acts of violence locally understood as "in defense of the neighborhood."[37] Their targets were revealing for they were overwhelmingly local, resonating in particular with the district's sociopolitical grievances and history as a "stronghold of contention." They comprised police stations in the neighborhood's vicinity, the residence of Tripolitan politicians and local government buildings, but also banks, pharmacies and grocery shops – the content of which was widely said to have been handed out in its entirety to Bab al-Tebbaneh's inhabitants.[38]

The best example of the full extent to which neighborhood dynamics shaped the Organization of Anger's behavior and violence occurred on October 15, 1971. On that day the movement had called on Tripoli's masses to go on strike for a "Day of Popular Anger" (*"yawm ghadab al-sha'ab"*) allegedly meant to mark the beginning of a wide-ranging "popular revolution" to "improve general livelihoods."[39] But, although the vocabulary of anarcho-communism helped frame the event in grand revolutionary leftist ways, it quickly became evident that it was the neighborhood, rather than ideology, which was in the driving seat. The protest began in Bab al-Tebbaneh and was mostly made up of the district's residents who had followed Ali Akkawi spontaneously, showing once again the great deal of agency of the *qabaday* and his crucial role in activating local ties of solidarity and championing neighborhood mobilization. His leadership made the demonstration massive. Yet it also quickly rendered it chaotic and increasingly violent – at odds, in other words, with the more peaceful and better organized kinds of protests

---

[36] Interviews with former sympathizers of the Organization of Anger in Bab al-Tebbaneh, Tripoli, October 2014.
[37] Interview with residents of Bab al-Tebbaneh, Tripoli, October 2014.
[38] Abi Samra, *Trablus*, pp. 79–84. [39] Seurat, "Le quartier."

104   Neighborhood Islamism

typical of the mainstream leftist parties and the trade unions.[40] Moreover, some of the demonstration's main slogans, like "fighting until the death," were locally understood as hinting at Bab al-Tebbaneh's rebel identity. The demonstration soon broke out into a full-blown riot as soon as it exited the neighborhood, providing yet another opportunity for Akkawi's followers to engage in the type of local collective violence which they saw as serving their district.[41]

As violence quickly escalated and protesters began to throw dynamite sticks at the police units which were approaching the scene, the security forces engaged in a fierce gunfight and eventually managed to injure and capture Akkawi as well as a dozen of his followers. Even then, however, the bonds of neighborhood solidarity and sense of loyalty that tied the *qabaday* of Bab al-Tebbaneh to local residents were so intense that the police feared that his partisans would enter the hospital and try to free him. In a bid to "avoid any attempt at intimidation,"[42] the Lebanese judiciary later decided to send the judge in charge of the affair to sentence Akkawi while in prison rather than taking the risk of bringing him to the court. They may have been right to be worried for, a while later, some of Akkawi's partisans would go as far as going to Beirut and taking forty customers hostages at a local branch of the Bank of America in order to negotiate, albeit unsuccessfully, the freedom of their *qabaday*.[43] All in all, although the Day of Popular Anger may have sounded, from the outside, like a gathering of Tripoli's diehard and ideologically committed anarcho-communists, it came to act as a platform to express dissent in the context of Bab al-Tebbaneh's grievances, as a vehicle to continue an older tradition of urban violence and as an embodiment of the intense bonds of loyalty tying the *qabaday* to his neighborhood.

Ali Akkawi died three years later in prison as a locally acclaimed "martyr." It is likely that the actual reason for his death in jail had more to do with an appendicitis than with murder. But in Bab al-Tebbaneh it was nonetheless widely interpreted by residents as a "political assassination" and part of a "broader conspiracy"[44] allegedly meant to silence a district known for its rebellious inclinations. This was also an implicit recognition, once more, of the role Ali Akkawi had come to play as a

---

[40] "Sept explosions à Tripoli," *L'Orient Le Jour* (October 15, 1971).

[41] Interview with former sympathizers of the Organization of Anger, Tripoli, October 2014.

[42] "Les dynamiteurs de Tripoli seront interrogés en prison," *L'Orient Le Jour* (October 20, 1971).

[43] Interviews with sympathizers of the Organization of Anger in Bab al-Tebbaneh, Tripoli, August 2014.

[44] Interview with residents of Bab al-Tebbaneh and former sympathizers of the Organization of Anger, Tripoli, October 2014.

community champion single-handedly able to draw the local masses into locally rooted and neighborhood-oriented mobilization.

The extent to which Ali Akkawi had, within such a short span of time, become a "champion of mobilization," the key figure behind the efforts of Bab al-Tebbaneh's residents to produce a spatially oriented, if ostensibly leftist, social movement, is also reflected in the popular memories he left behind after his death in 1974. Observers noted that up to a decade after his passing away, portraits of him were still widespread on the walls of Bab al-Tebbaneh, and that he was still widely hailed as a "saint" there,[45] the long-awaited and widely regretted chivalrous strongman who had championed and defended the area until his death. In interviews with dozens of elderly residents all of them could recount, forty years later, some of the exploits the local *qabaday* was still remembered for, for example when he allegedly robbed banks to give money to the poor, ransacked pharmacies to hand out vaccines to the sick, blew up police stations to distribute arms to residents or led riots with his local followers.[46] Accompanying this was a constant thread: the idea that his behavior and his movement's engagement in violence had been virtuous; not because it had been "Marxist" but because it had been spatially rooted and neighborhood-oriented – seen as serving Bab al-Tebbaneh's best interests and upholding its tradition as a "stronghold of contention."

Upon Ali Akkawi's death in September 1974, it was his younger brother, Khalil, who soon emerged as the new *qabaday* of Bab al-Tebbaneh. In fact, Khalil Akkawi or, as he became known locally, "Abu Arabi," would come to play an even more important role than his elder brother in acting as Bab al-Tebbaneh's "champion of mobilization" until his assassination in February 1986 – a watershed moment in the history of the neighborhood, as tackled in Chapter 8. Like the rest of this chapter shows, the solidarities and emotional bonds tying him to the district would in fact become such that hundreds of local residents followed his decisions largely spontaneously and picked up weapons whenever he asked, to the point that even though they had proudly described themselves as "revolutionary Marxists," many locals would, under his leadership, soon be ready to switch to "Islamism" – albeit a type which, unsurprisingly, would be grounded in and oriented toward the district.

Ideology to Ally across Space and Class

Khalil Akkawi's embrace of Islamism only matured in the late 1970s and early 1980s, but it stems from a key feature which, early on, distinguished

[45] Seurat, "Le quartier."
[46] Interview with residents of Bab al-Tebbaneh, Tripoli, October 2014.

106   Neighborhood Islamism

him from his older brother. Khalil would go further than Ali in instrumentalizing ideology to ally across space and class with actors external to Bab al-Tebbaneh. At first this pushed him to use Marxism to ally with ideologically driven, resource-rich leftists. Later he would reframe his discourse to ally with Palestinian and Islamist actors, again with the logic that it would benefit Bab al-Tebbaneh.

The two brothers, of course, shared a lot of traits in common. Khalil had long acted as his older sibling's right-hand man at the helm of the Organization of Anger and he had been patiently learning in his shadow. It is not surprising, then, that he rapidly acquired a similar reputation for acting as Bab al-Tebbaneh's chivalrous strongman. Indeed, much like Ali, Khalil became seen as ready to use violence and to put his life on the line in order to "defend" the neighborhood and uphold its rebel identity. It is telling, for instance, that upon rising as Bab al-Tebbaneh's new *qabaday*, his first act was to place 2 kg of dynamite under the car of a prominent Tripolitan businessman who was despised for having made large profits out of selling flour at an abnormally high price to the deprived residents of the district during a period of bread shortage.[47] The attempted assassination failed but it showed to Bab al-Tebbaneh's inhabitants that, much like his brother before, Khalil Akkawi would not compromise on his neighborhood's perceived interests – even if this meant attracting the wrath of Tripoli's powerful and well-connected business leaders. Shortly afterward, he and his partisans plotted the bombing of a Tripolitan police station in an act which was widely understood as revenge for Bab al-Tebbaneh's perceived harassment by the security forces and payback for their alleged role in Ali Akkawi's death.[48] By showing the same willingness to spearhead acts of violence in the "defense of the neighborhood" as his regretted brother, as well as displaying a similar sense of "courage" and "rootedness," the new *qabaday* of the district soon acquired the status of uncontested local "leader" and "protector"[49] of the area.

Yet, despite common traits, Khalil Akkawi differed from his older sibling in three significant respects, which eventually resulted in them pursuing different political strategies.

A first key difference was personality. The elderly residents of Bab al-Tebbaneh who got to know the two brothers equally well typically recall that, while Ali had an "impulsive," "sanguine" and "uncompromising"

---

[47] Interview with Aziz Allush (close aide to Ali and Khalil Akkawi), Tripoli, October 2014.
[48] Interview with Abu Zghayar (close aide to Ali and Khalil Akkawi), Tripoli, October 2014.
[49] Interviews with residents of Bab al-Tebbaneh, Tripoli, October 2014.

character which sometimes led him to "act before thinking," Khalil was more "patient" and "resourceful," and had better "manners." He is said to have been someone who, by all accounts, did not shy away from using violence, but who also much enjoyed exchanging views with others, was open minded and showed a striking ability to learn from his mistakes and evolve. He was said to be guided by Bab al-Tebbaneh's long-term, strategic interests more than just short-term gains.[50]

A second crucial difference between them was leadership style. For Khalil, acting as Bab al-Tebbaneh's *qabaday* did not just mean spearheading acts of collective violence to physically champion the neighborhood, its values and interests. To him, being the area's leader also had a much broader significance. It meant that he had to actively avoid internecine conflicts and keep alive the neighborhood's particularly strong sense of community. Even more than his older brother, Khalil came to embody Bab al-Tebbaneh's inner solidarities and most intimate concerns. Residents remember how he came to act as a "role model" even in the "details"[51] of the district's everyday life. He routinely toured the neighborhood, mediating when petty disputes erupted among neighbors, participating in the cleaning of the streets, trying to limit the growing local use of drugs and even handing out small amounts of financial assistance to help young men in getting married. In a bid to further strengthen social ties and networks of mutual support he personally organized weekly football tournaments in the wastelands of the district's vicinity. Participants in these games revealingly tell of how Khalil would often simultaneously perform the functions of coach, captain and referee all at once. This showed how his status as *qabaday* meant that he was not only acting as the neighborhood's leader during episodes of contention but in daily life too. A former local football player elaborated that Khalil's behavior on and off the sports field was "exemplary," being "tough" but "fair."[52] Whether fully accurate or not, this was nevertheless reiterated in dozens of interviews, reflecting popular acceptance of his role and the degree of emotional attachment many residents felt for him, which rendered them extremely loyal. A local inhabitant summed up the feeling that still prevails today when he stated that "the neighborhood lived in safety, justice and dignity under the authority of Khalil Akkawi."[53] When he was assassinated in 1986, tens of thousands of emotional locals carried

---

[50] Interviews with former associates of Ali and Khalil Akkawi, Tripoli, October 2014.

[51] Interview with Mazen Mohammed (figure close to Khalil Akkawi), Tripoli, October 2014.

[52] Interview with a former football coach of al-Shahid team, Tripoli (Beddawi camp), August 2014.

[53] Interview with residents of Bab al-Tebbaneh, Tripoli, October 2014.

108   Neighborhood Islamism

his body to the grave. Within the space of years the new *qabaday* had come to personify, more than his brother, Bab al-Tebbaneh's strong sense of community.

The third contrast between the two neighborhood strongmen sprang naturally from their different characters and visions of leadership: they ended up developing dissimilar political strategies to ensure their district's perceived best interests. While the two brothers both used revolutionary Marxism as an ideology to cast Bab al-Tebbaneh's grievances against the broader backdrop of radical leftism's cultural and ideological momentum and to justify acts of neighborhood-oriented urban violence, Khalil went further in instrumentalizing ideology, using it to build a more sustainable movement providing concrete services to the residents of his deprived district. One activist from Bab al-Tebbaneh who "served" under the two successive strongmen put it the following way. "Whereas Ali used to rob pharmacies to steal medicines and give them away [to the residents of the district], Khalil would fundraise to build a local clinic."[54] For the latter this meant using radical leftist ideology not just to frame local grievances and justify urban violence in a grander way but also as a tool to forge alliances with resource-rich, ideologically driven Marxist actors from outside of Bab al-Tebbaneh with the ultimate goal of benefiting his neighborhood. Khalil, in other words, would go to great lengths to use ideology to operate wider alliances across space and class for the sake of the "defense" of Bab al-Tebbaneh.

Khalil Akkawi's willingness to use anarcho-communist ideology in order to engage in alliance-making crystallized in 1974 with the formation of the Popular Committees (*al-Lijan al-Sha'abiya*). Much like the Organization of Anger before, this new, ostensibly Marxist, social movement was still undoubtedly spatially grounded and oriented. This stemmed from Khalil Akkawi's status both as founder and leader of the Popular Committees and as the *qabaday* of Bab al-Tebbaneh, which meant that any demonstration he spearheaded there was bound to enjoy an especially high turnout. It also continued acting as a neighborhood-oriented movement, a close observer noting that, in spite of its grand anarcho-communist ideology, "Bab al-Tebbaneh remained the main focus of the Popular Committees."[55]

This time, however, a key difference with the Organization of Anger was that Khalil Akkawi sought to actively broaden the appeal of his movement. First, he wished to widen its spatial base. He did so by enticing the inhabitants of Tripoli's other impoverished neighborhoods,

---

[54] Interview with Aziz Allush (close aide to Ali and Khalil Akkawi), Tripoli, October 2014.
[55] Abi Samra, *Trablus*, p. 91.

for example in the Old City, Qobbe and Jabal Mohsen, to join the Popular Committees in demonstrations which, despite their revolutionary leftist slogans and regular focus on Bab al-Tebbaneh, often tackled the concrete urban issues touching all of Tripoli's deprived districts, such as the lack of road paving and water shortages. This rendered the protests organized by the Popular Committees larger than ever before, something which proved to an extent successful in attracting the attention of the Tripolitan municipality and the Lebanese government to some of the concerns raised. But, even most importantly, Khalil Akkawi also wanted to widen the social base of his movement and to appeal to the ideologically driven and typically resource-rich Tripolitan Marxists, with the hope that such an alliance would bring tangible benefits to his neighborhood. This led him to forge close connections with a group of middle-class Tripolitan Marxists who were high school teachers, doctors and university students hailing from various neighborhoods and who had in the early 1970s all split from leftist movements, such as the Lebanese Communist Party and the Iraqi Ba'ath, as they no longer considered them revolutionary and ideologically pure enough.

In turn, what pushed these two dozen highly committed revolutionary Marxists to join the Popular Committees was the opportunity they saw in gaining a foothold in Bab al-Tebbaneh and, through Khalil Akkawi's dual status as head of the movement and *qabaday* of the neighborhood, to influence the local masses and spread radical leftist ideology. By the mid-1970s Bab al-Tebbaneh had clearly emerged as Tripoli's "stronghold of contention" par excellence due to the combination of the Organization of Anger's legacy, the district's older rebel identity and its reputation as the city's most marginalized area by far. Spreading true revolutionary Marxism in the neighborhood thus became viewed as an opportunity, almost a duty, for these highly committed leftist figures, who sometimes regretted that the Organization of Anger had used the language of anarcho-communism without its members being sincerely convinced and driven by ideology.[56] One observer noted that joining the Popular Committees allowed these figures to use Bab al-Tebbaneh as a "laboratory" in which they would try to "inject"[57] ideology, turning the contentious potential inherent to the neighborhood into a reservoir of truly committed revolutionary leftists and transforming the instrumental embrace of ideology into more sincere commitments. In other words, these were what I call "ideological entrepreneurs," or highly ideologized

---

[56] Interview with revolutionary leftist figures who joined the Popular Committees, Tripoli, November 2014.
[57] Abi Samra, *Trablus*, pp. 87–8.

110 Neighborhood Islamism

individuals who mobilize ideas and seek to shape the nature of activism, trying to render it ideological.

This first experience in engineering coalitions across space and class proved successful for Khalil Akkawi and his partisans. While it made the demonstrations of the Popular Committees larger than ever before, which put the spotlight on some of the grievances long suffered by Bab al-Tebbaneh's inhabitants, it also attracted the goodwill of the Marxist "ideological entrepreneurs," who in return allocated some of their resources to the neighborhood. Naturally, given that these new members came from more privileged socio-economic backgrounds and neighborhoods the resources they brought to the Popular Committees and, therefore, to Bab al-Tebbaneh, were sometimes financial. They contributed to the movement's "fundraising," which allowed Khalil Akkawi to open a handful of small charity shops distributing free food and clothes to the inhabitants of his neighborhood.[58] No less important, the services which these well-educated and ideologically committed Marxists rendered were also nonmaterial. For instance, while several of the doctors who had joined the Popular Committees began regularly visiting Bab al-Tebbaneh to provide free treatment and medicines to the area's sick and elderly people, members who were teachers for their part offered to help the local youths who struggled at school.[59] Crucially, this new alliance across space and class also gave renewed pride and dignity to residents who had long felt stigmatized due to their neighborhood's ill reputation. The attention these deprived residents now drew from outside of Bab al-Tebbaneh by Marxist "ideological entrepreneurs" who sometimes treated them like "superstars" made many feel once again "connected to a larger world."[60] Overall, then, Khalil Akkawi's first attempt at using ideology to forge alliances across space and class proved a fruitful experience that largely benefited his neighborhood.

A Fateful Rapprochement

Yet, for all the success of the Popular Committees, this movement soon fell into disarray when the *qabaday* of Bab al-Tebbaneh engineered a rapprochement with Fatah a year later, in 1975, a dynamic which culminated with the creation of the Popular Resistance (*al-Muqawama al-Sha'abiya*). The logic was similar to that which had led to the formation of the Popular Committees. Khalil Akkawi was still intent on forging

[58] Interview with residents of Bab al-Tebbaneh, Tripoli, November 2014.
[59] Interview with former members of the Popular Committees, Tripoli, November 2014.
[60] Abi Samra, *Trablus*, p. 89.

A Fateful Rapprochement 111

close connections with resource-rich actors outside of Bab al-Tebbaneh, but this time it involved allying with the Palestinian guerrilla organization – a scheme which promised to be even more lucrative than the alliance he had earlier forged with the group of Tripolitan Marxists. Yet, although it was meant to benefit his district, the alliance between the Popular Resistance and Fatah instead progressively drew Bab al-Tebbaneh in a violent neighborhood rivalry. This considerably affected Khalil Akkawi, contributing to his embrace of militant Islamism and ultimately to his decision to join Tawhid's alliance of Islamist movements in 1982.

Three reasons pushed Khalil Akkawi to ditch the Marxist-inspired Popular Committees and create, instead, the pro-Palestinian Popular Resistance: grand politics, preexisting ties and neighborhood interests. The most obvious factor of all, of course, was the political climate of the day. By the mid-1970s, popular enthusiasm was fast growing among Lebanese Muslim leftists for the Palestinian guerrilla organizations that were part of the PLO. This was chiefly due to the humiliation of the successive Arab military defeats against Israel in 1967 and 1973, which undermined the credibility of national armies and put the spotlight onto Fatah – the PLO's most powerful guerrilla organization that quickly became very successful at waging bloody commando operations into Israel from South Lebanon and the West Bank. For reasons explained in Chapter 1, this momentum surrounding Fatah was particularly strong in Tripoli, where various militias began forming to support the armed Palestinian presence in Lebanon at a moment when the issue was increasingly stirring up heated domestic controversies. In late 1974 a conversation took place within the Popular Committees on the opportunity of also creating a pro-Palestinian militia that would be ready to engage on the side of Fatah in the looming Lebanese civil war, which by early 1975 all "could feel coming."[61] This debate pitted the group of middle-class Marxist "ideological entrepreneurs," who supported the Palestinian cause but did not want to become personally dragged in a full-blown military struggle, against Khalil Akkawi's partisans in Bab al-Tebbaneh, who had experience in urban violence and were attracted both by the revolutionary zeal of the guerrilla group and by the aura of its leader, Yasser Arafat.

The second set of reasons that pushed Khalil Akkawi to create the Fatah-backed Popular Resistance had to do with social ties. The family of the *qabaday* had Palestinian roots, something which, at a period of history

---

[61] Interview with former members of the Popular Resistance, Tripoli, November 2014.

112 Neighborhood Islamism

now considered a turning point in the Arab–Israeli conflict, triggered further bonds of solidarity with Palestinian guerrilla organizations active in Tripoli. The Akkawis, as their name indeed suggests, originally hailed from the Palestinian port of Acre (*Akka*) and had only emigrated to Tripoli and Bab al-Tebbaneh after the Arab defeat of 1948. So, while Ali, as mentioned earlier, had received military training by the the Popular Front for the Liberation of Palestine, Khalil for his part attended Fatah military training camps in the Beqaa Valley and in Syria. Preexisting social ties thus bound the *qabaday* of the neighborhood to the Palestinian guerrilla organization. Yet it was not just the Akkawis, in Bab al-Tebbaneh, who shared kinship and social bonds with the Palestinians. The neighborhood itself was, in fact, located in the immediate vicinity of the Beddawi Palestinian refugee camp and boasted cheap rents, which meant that a higher-than-normal proportion of Palestinian refugees also lived and worked there as well as intermarrying with locals, enhancing bonds of solidarity. As a result of these political factors and kinship ties, Khalil Akkawi's followers in Bab al-Tebbaneh soon split from the Popular Committees in order to create, instead, the Popular Resistance as a local militia ready to mobilize on behalf of Fatah in their neighborhood.[62]

But there were also other, even more locally specific, reasons behind Khalil Akkawi's rapprochement with Fatah and formation of the Popular Resistance. One significant local factor was the growing need for physical "protection"[63] felt by the inhabitants of Bab al-Tebbaneh. By 1975, indeed, Khalil Akkawi and a dozen of his followers in the district were now actively wanted by the Lebanese judiciary for their involvement in the aforementioned bombing of a police station in Tripoli and their role in organizing and leading mass anti-governmental protests that had often ended in scenes of urban violence. To escape the security forces they went underground in Bab al-Tebbaneh, using the neighborhood's tight networks of mutual support and sense of community in order to hide from house to house for a few months. Allying with Fatah, which militarily controlled the nearby Palestinian refugee camp of Beddawi where, by virtue of the 1969 Cairo Agreement, the Lebanese police could not enter, this time provided them with full protection and the opportunity of leading relatively normal lives without having to constantly hide. "At first, Fatah protected Khalil Akkawi against the Lebanese state,"[64] stated a figure close to the *qabaday* of Bab al-Tebbaneh.

---

[62] Interviews with former members of the Popular Resistance and residents of Bab al-Tebbaneh, Tripoli, November 2014.

[63] Interview with residents of Bab al-Tebbaneh, Tripoli, September 2014.

[64] Interview with Bilal Matar (former political adviser to Khalil Akkawi and member of the Popular Resistance), Tripoli, November 2014.

A Fateful Rapprochement   113

The second local factor that pushed Khalil Akkawi to engineer a rapprochement with Fatah was that by 1975 it had clearly emerged as the most powerful Palestinian guerrilla organization, one generously funded by petrodollars from the Gulf. This meant that it was ready to pay hefty amounts to Lebanese movements willing to support its cause. At a time when Bab al-Tebbaneh was greatly suffering from the deterioration of the socio-economic situation, Fatah's financial backing allowed Akkawi and his men to support the residents of their neighborhood in more concrete ways than ever before. Of course, they continued operating the small charity shops which they had opened as part of the Popular Committees. But with all the additional money they now received they also began to pay actual salaries to dozens of young men in the neighborhood, who would then become full-time militiamen for the Popular Resistance, as well as to give small handouts to other residents. From a financial perspective their alliance with Fatah was looking more profitable to their district than their earlier coalition with the middle-class Marxist "ideological entrepreneurs" had been.[65]

The third and last local factor that led Khalil Akkawi to enter into an alliance with Fatah was that the Palestinian guerrilla organization was also ready to provide his followers with "truckloads of weapons" and "training sessions"[66] in guerrilla and combat skills. Until then, during some of the contentious episodes which had marked the existence of the Organization of Anger and the Popular Committees, the sympathizers of Ali and Khalil Akkawi had engaged in acts of urban violence mostly using rudimentary weapons such as sticks, stones, kitchen knives and a handful of old-fashioned pistols and dynamite sticks. But now Fatah actually proposed to provide them with dozens of Kalashnikovs, bazookas, machine guns and TNT explosives with, in addition, the option of undergoing a quasi-professional military course at the nearby Palestinian refugee camp of Beddawi. This was an attractive alternative for many residents in a neighborhood where countless locals were involved in the trafficking of cigarettes, drugs and fuel and, therefore, increasingly needed armaments of quality and in quantity in order to deter the security forces from cracking down too harshly on the local prevalence of the illicit economy as well as to face off against gangs from rival districts.[67]

[65] Interview with former members of the Popular Resistance, Tripoli, October 2014.
[66] Interview with Samir Hassan, Abu Zghayar and Aziz Allush (military commanders in the Popular Resistance), Tripoli, November 2014.
[67] Interview with former members of the Popular Resistance, Tripoli, October 2014.

114   Neighborhood Islamism

By all accounts these three neighborhood-specific, local reasons were key in pushing Khalil Akkawi to create the Fatah-backed Popular Resistance when the opportunity arose on the eve of the Lebanese civil war. Yet, rather than contributing to the "defense" of the district, as the *qabaday* had originally envisioned, this alliance with the Palestinian guerrilla organization would instead draw all of Bab al-Tebbaneh into an unexpectedly bitter and bloody struggle with the adjacent neighborhood of Jabal Mohsen, just meters away.

In return for providing protection as well as generous amounts of funding and weaponry to the neighborhood-based Popular Resistance Fatah expected nothing less than the movement's full support and loyalty. As the Lebanese civil war was fast looming, in early 1975, this meant activating the ties of neighborhood solidarity binding the leader and members of the Popular Resistance to the residents of Bab al-Tebbaneh, Tripoli's most populated area back then, in order to organize mass protests. These demonstrations no longer just tackled the "poverty" or the "injustice" suffered by the neighborhood, but this time also vocally supported the armed Palestinian presence in Lebanon and hailed its "resistance"[68] against Israel. This served Fatah well at a time when its public relations strategy was to demonstrate to its foes that significant portions of the Lebanese population actively supported its cause and its presence in Lebanon.[69] As the first military battles flared up in mid to late 1975 between the Lebanese opponents and supporters of the PLO, Fatah also began expecting the Popular Resistance to join the struggle and fight on its behalf. This is what Khalil Akkawi's men did by joining the coalition of pro-Palestinian Tripolitan Muslim movements which fought the pro-governmental Christian Maronite militias in the North Lebanon towns of Zgharta and Chekka. Yet, as Chapter 1 showed, soon enough a new line of fracture in the Lebanese civil war no longer just pitted Muslims against Christians, but increasingly the supporters and opponents of Syria's June 1976 military intervention in Lebanon, which was designed to rein in the Palestinians. Fatah pressured Khalil Akkawi's

---

[68] After the beginning of the Lebanese civil war, Bab al-Tebbaneh emerged as the "stronghold of contention" from where pro-Palestinian demonstrators in Tripoli would gather and make claims, drawing in neighborhood inhabitants but also other Tripolitans and Palestinian refugees from the nearby camps of Beddawi and Naher al-Bared. See, for instance, "Tazahurat tad'am al-intifada fi Filastin" ["Protests in support of the struggle in Palestine"], *al-Incha'* (November 21, 1979) or "Ahl Trablus yusirun min Bab al-Tebbaneh ila Sehat al-Koura ahtijajan 'ala al-'alaqat bein Misr wa Isra'il" ["The people of Tripoli march from Bab al-Tebbaneh to Koura Square in protest of the relation between Egypt and Israel"], *al-Incha'* (January 26, 1980).

[69] Interview with current and former Fatah militants and commanders, Beddawi refugee camp, November 2014.

men into entering a fateful struggle against the followers of Ali Eid, the pro-Syrian *qabaday* of the Alawi-dominated Tripolitan district of Jabal Mohsen, situated just meters from Bab al-Tebbaneh. This chain of events would, in the mid-1970s, draw the two areas into a spatially rooted antagonism which, in the late 1970s and the 1980s, would violently spiral out of control and lead to an all-out slum war that still simmers today. It would be in the context of this violent local rivalry that Khalil Akkawi would draw his neighborhood into embracing militant Islamism, both as a "protest ideology" and as a way of operating alliances across class and space with resource-rich and battle-hardened Islamist actors.

Neighborhood Rivalries

In the early and mid-1970s, few expected the neighborhoods of Bab al-Tebbaneh and Jabal Mohsen to enter into the feud which developed shortly afterward. Residents from these two Tripolitan districts were not traditionally rivals; in fact they had a lot in common. To begin with, their proximity resulted in the sense among many locals that they belonged to a shared space. The area of Jabal Mohsen comprises a relatively high hill which, from the top, overlooks Bab al-Tebbaneh, but then goes steeply down until the bottom of the hill, where the two neighborhoods merge to an extent, becoming only visibly separated by Syria Street – an artery that links them both to the coastal road linking Tripoli to the North Lebanese countryside of Akkar and eventually to Syria. In a reflection of the degree to which they were largely considered part of the same geographical space, the two neighborhoods were long officially one, belonging to the same administrative subsection of the city of Tripoli.

In demographic and sectarian terms, of course, Jabal Mohsen came to acquire a reputation as the hub of Tripoli's and Lebanon's Alawi community, in contrast to the Sunni-dominated Bab al-Tebbaneh. But even this dynamic of sectarian homogenization was a decade-long process. Jabal Mohsen had long been a scarcely inhabited hill made up of olive trees, some apartment buildings and shacks, an area inhabited in equal proportion by Sunnis and Alawis. The neighborhood's demographic balance began changing in the late 1960s and early 1970s after it witnessed the mass arrival of impoverished Alawi migrants who hailed from the North Lebanese and Syrian countryside. In search of a job, they had settled there due to cheap rents and to the indigenous presence of deprived Tripolitan Alawis, which implied a degree of sectarian mutual help. Progressively, then, Jabal Mohsen became more homogeneously

116 Neighborhood Islamism

inhabited by Alawis, to the extent that it would come to host over half of Lebanon's total Alawi population of 80,000 people, the rest remaining scattered between myriad remote villages in the North Lebanese countryside near the border with Syria.[70]

Interestingly, however, rather than stirring up sectarian tensions with the Sunni-dominated neighborhood of Bab al-Tebbaneh, this Alawi migration to Jabal Mohsen initially strengthened the bonds between the adjacent districts. This stemmed from the fact that Bab al-Tebbaneh had itself long featured an indigenous Alawi minority too which was so well integrated in the fabric of the neighborhood that, there, mixed Sunni–Alawi marriages were until the 1970s relatively common. Unlike in other parts of North Lebanon and in Syria, therefore, Sunni–Alawi tensions were not a part of Bab al-Tebbaneh's history and identity.

The ties between the mostly Sunni residents of Bab al-Tebbaneh and the Alawi inhabitants of Jabal Mohsen also resulted from shared grievances. Like Bab al-Tebbaneh, Jabal Mohsen rapidly became overcrowded. Within years, between 30,000 and 40,000 Alawi newcomers had migrated there and, according to an anthropologist who toured Jabal Mohsen, they rapidly settled in "shantytowns." The Alawi residents of Jabal Mohsen also acquired the reputation of being so desperate for jobs that they seemed ready to undertake "the kinds of work that no one else is willing to do."[71] Poverty thus prevailed, with 85 percent of Jabal Mohsen's population reportedly belonging to the lower class – a rate coming very close to the 90 percent who were lower class in Bab al-Tebbaneh. In addition to being economically deprived, these Alawi rural migrants also felt an acute sense of political marginalization. This was due to the fact that the constitutional existence of Lebanon's small Alawi community was not recognized by the 1943 National Pact, which effectively prevented them from entering a civil service characterized by sectarian quotas, except at its lowest echelons.[72] Out of convenience, some nominally converted to Sunni or Shia Islam; yet this nonetheless stirred up their resentment for the Lebanese political system.[73] Their political marginalization also resulted from growing tensions within Tripoli's

---

[70] Interviews with residents of Jabal Mohsen, Tripoli, December 2014.

[71] Gulick, *Tripoli*, p. 206.

[72] In the 1970s Lebanon's Alawis were not represented in the first and second echelons of the state bureaucracy. Only one member of the community worked at the third echelon as the head of the topography department in Tripoli. Most were employed at the fourth, fifth, and sixth echelons of the bureaucracy (e.g. as assistants). Interview with an Alawi rights activist in Jabal Mohsen, Tripoli, August 2014.

[73] Sheikh Ahmad Assi, the Mufti or religious leader of Lebanon's Alawis, asserted that since the early 1970s over half of the community switched religion to Sunni and Shi'ite Islam to avoid discrimination and to qualify for government jobs. The figure is probably

Alawi community itself. These tensions pitted the small but powerful group of well-educated, wealthy Tripolitan Alawi notables, who professed to speak on behalf of the community but without experiencing its grievances, against the masses of impoverished and illiterate Alawi workers originally from the countryside who had settled in Jabal Mohsen and did not feel represented by upper-class Alawis living in New Tripoli. All in all, therefore, Jabal Mohsen's Alawis shared the animosity of the largely Sunni residents of Bab al-Tebbaneh for the Lebanese politico-economic system and the local Tripolitan elite.

Unsurprisingly, then, many inhabitants of Jabal Mohsen came to support Ali Akkawi's Organization of Anger and Khalil Akkawi's Popular Committees in the 1970s. They were not full-blown members for they were both to a large extent spatially oriented movements rooted in Bab al-Tebbaneh. But they still sporadically joined the protests organized by the two movements when they exited the neighborhood and supported their virulent criticism of the Tripolitan municipality, the upper class and the Lebanese government. It may have helped, too, that the two movements espoused explicitly secular, leftist ideologies and were widely known to attract Bab al-Tebbaneh's Sunni majority as much as its Alawi minority in their pleas for the "defense" of the neighborhood. Up until the early 1970s, therefore, Bab al-Tebbaneh and Jabal Mohsen may have been respectively inhabited by a majority of Sunnis and Alawis, but this by no means prevented the inhabitants of the two neighborhoods from sharing a degree of common political agenda and sporadically socializing and mobilizing across space and sect in order to protest against their conditions.[74]

Yet this drastically changed within the space of years after Jabal Mohsen came under the wing of its own *qabaday*, Ali Eid, an Alawi "champion of mobilization." Like Khalil Akkawi in Bab al-Tebbaneh, he was keen on entering wider alliances to benefit his neighborhood. But, for his part, he would ally with Fatah's nemesis – the Syrian regime.

The son of a small Alawi farmer from the North Lebanese countryside who had emigrated to Tripoli in the 1950s, Ali Eid had moved to Beirut in 1970 where, in a bar late at night, he was involved in a brawl with the nephew of Saudi Arabia's King Faisal, Abdel Mohsen bin Saud. The fight had turned so heated that the Saudi man had taken a dagger out and

---

exaggerated but the pattern of conversions is nevertheless significant. See: "Lebanon's Alawis: a minority struggles in a 'Nation' of sects," *Al-Akhbar* (November 8, 2011).

[74] Interviews with residents of Jabal Mohsen and Bab al-Tebbaneh as well as with former partisans of the Organization of Anger and of the Popular Committees, Tripoli, December 2014.

118   Neighborhood Islamism

stabbed his rival several times in the back, causing Ali Eid severe injuries. Because of the perpetrator's status as a member of the Saudi royal family, the brawl made the headlines in the Lebanese media and the judiciary sentenced him to paying Ali Eid, who had barely survived, a substantial financial compensation. While the incident had revolved around a competition between the two men over a woman, given the aforementioned socio-economic and political discriminations suffered by Lebanon's Alawis the incident nonetheless soon turned Ali Eid into a hero and living martyr for many local Alawis – he had shown, his partisans say, an ability to stand up to bullying and to defend the honor of his community.[75]

Ali Eid later fully recovered, moved back to Tripoli and soon settled in Jabal Mohsen. There, with the compensation money, he built a large villa and began wanting to capitalize on his incident's momentum in order to rise as the uncontested champion of Lebanon's Alawi community. To do so he encouraged the Alawi rural migrants who were newcomers to Tripoli to permanently move to and settle in Jabal Mohsen, and with the rest of the money paid by his Saudi rival formed the Movement of the Alawi Youth (*Harakat al-Shabab al-Alawi*) in 1972. Nominally this was a civil society organization supposed to raise awareness about the discrimination suffered by Lebanon's Alawis and to lobby the government regarding more rights to this community. But, although it routinely used the discourse of sectarian victimization, it gradually came to act in clearer and more systematic ways as a vehicle to enhance Ali Eid's own mobilization potential in Jabal Mohsen, by now the stronghold of the Alawis. Through this movement, Ali Eid started providing services to the mass of impoverished Alawi residents of the neighborhood, such as free medical treatment and food for the poor. By putting local Alawi thugs on the movement's payroll, he also offered protection to those who were increasingly trying to make ends meet by engaging in petty crime and the smuggling business.[76] Within the space of years, then, the Movement of the Alawi Youth had turned Ali Eid into the locally powerful *qabaday*, or "champion of mobilization," of Jabal Mohsen and of its increasingly homogeneous Alawi population.

However, as the *qabaday* of Jabal Mohsen began to search for resource-rich allies to further solidify his own status and to benefit his

---

[75] "Trois pourvois dans l'affaire de l'Emir Abdel-Mohsen," *L'Orient le Jour* (October 20, 1971). Note that Tine Gade has written about this in detail in an excellent article on the relation between Tripoli and Syria: Tine Gade, "Sunni Islamists in Tripoli and the Asad regime; 1966–2014" *Syria Studies* (Vol. 7, No. 2, 2015), esp. pp. 31–3.

[76] Interviews with former members of the Movement of the Alawi Youth, Tripoli, December 2014.

neighborhood, he entered into a fateful alliance with the Assad regime. Indeed, in Damascus too, Ali Eid's stabbing incident and his subsequent rise as the informal leader of Tripoli's Alawis in Jabal Mohsen had not gone unnoticed. The early to mid-1970s were sensitive times for the new Syrian president, Hafez al-Assad, an Alawi officer who had come to power in November 1970 through a coup against another Alawi, Salah Jedid, and was thus in dire need of new, fully loyal allies in the wider Lebanese and Syrian Alawi community to help him consolidate his power base. Moreover, the president, according to a member of his inner circle, also felt "threatened"[77] by Tripoli's proximity to Syria, in no small part due to the fact that many Alawis in Jabal Mohsen originally hailed from the Syrian countryside and still entertained strong social ties with relatives back home. This, combined with the fact that Tripoli remained effectively outside of the Syrian regime's reach until 1976, raised the distinct possibility that Jabal Mohsen would sooner or later turn into a hub of anti-Assad Alawi dissidence, a "safe space" capable of nurturing the kind of indigenous opposition potentially leading to another Alawi coup in Syria, this time against Hafez al-Assad. Since 1967 Tripoli had been home to Mohammed Omran, a former Syrian defense minister turned leading Alawi opponent of the new Syrian president. According to a member of the Syrian Ba'ath Party close to the intelligence services, Omran was about to use Tripoli as a base to "destabilize Hafez al-Assad." "He was planning a comeback to Syria and he represented a real threat to the president,"[78] this well-informed source recalled. Omran was assassinated at his Tripoli home in March 1972, most likely on orders from the Syrian regime. Yet Hafez al-Assad's perceived need to keep Tripoli's Alawis in check and to gain allies in Jabal Mohsen persisted.

It is in this context that the Syrian regime's willingness to develop an alliance with the *qabaday* of Jabal Mohsen must be viewed. Damascus would provide Ali Eid with significant financial, political and military backing to help him further expand his local influence. In return, the *qabaday* would act as the Syrian intelligence's eyes, ears and mouth in Tripoli, a figure entirely loyal to the Assads and popular enough, locally, to prevent the emergence of new Alawi critics of the Syrian regime. Hafez al-Assad displayed his interest for Ali Eid early on, in 1972. Back then, in a show of the importance the *qabaday* of Jabal Mohsen had quickly come to take, the Syrian president dispatched his younger brother and right-

---

[77] Interview with a high-ranking Syrian politician who used to be close to Hafez al-Assad, Paris, April 2015.

[78] Interview with a high-ranking official in the Syrian Ba'ath Party, Tripoli, September 2014.

120   Neighborhood Islamism

hand man, Rif'at al-Assad, to provide financial support to Ali Eid upon the formation of the Movement of the Alawi Youth. The relationship between Ali Eid and Rif'at al-Assad soon became so personal that the former even called his second son Rif'at as a mark of allegiance to the latter. On the eve of the Lebanese civil war, then, Ali Eid had established a strong alliance with the Syrian regime, which furthered his ability to provide services and protection in Jabal Mohsen and to act as the uncontested leader of the district.[79] Yet it also meant that, given Khalil Akkawi's simultaneous rapprochement with Fatah in a broader geopolitical context marked by the fast-escalating tensions pitting the Palestinian guerrilla organization against Damascus, Ali Eid's alliance with the Syrian regime was going to set the Tripolitan neighborhoods of Bab al-Tebbaneh and Jabal Mohsen on a collision course.

Although the conflict which developed between Khalil Akkawi's Sunni-dominated Popular Resistance and Ali Eid's Movement for the Alawi Youth is often described as "religious,"[80] it had more to do with grand politics and neighborhood rivalries than with any notion of Sunni–Alawi sectarianism. The conflict only burst out in late 1975 when, answering a call from Fatah to attack pro-Syrian Tripolitan movements, fighters from the Bab al-Tebbaneh-based Popular Resistance exchanged gunfire a couple of hundred meters away at the Jabal Mohsen offices of the Movement of the Alawi Youth, whose members they rapidly outgunned and overran. In retrospect the fighters of the Popular Resistance thus portray their attack as part of the broader "political" battle pitting local supporters of Fatah against the backers of the Syrian regime and insist that they had only acted "on behalf of the Palestinians."[81] But it also drew on much more local and nascent neighborhood rivalries.

By 1975 the growing socio-economic grievances suffered by residents of Bab al-Tebbaneh and Jabal Mohsen, which had earlier been channeled in a degree of cross-spatial and cross-sectarian socialization and mobilization, was now beginning to give rise to increasingly recurrent conflicts over the only resource, external patronage aside, that residents of the two deprived districts still had access to – Tripoli's illicit economy. Under the respective protection of Ali Eid and Khalil Akkawi, groups of youths in

---

[79] Interview with Mahmud Shehade (Ali Eid's adviser and right-hand man), Tripoli, September 2016.

[80] In his otherwise good account of Islamist movements in Tripoli, Robert Rabil for instance mentions the "religious line" pitting partisans of Khalil Akkawi and of Ali Eid against each other. See Robert Rabil, *Salafism in Lebanon, from apoliticism to transnational jihadism* (Washington, DC: Georgetown University Press, 2014), p. 77.

[81] Interviews with former members of the Popular Resistance in Bab al-Tebbaneh, Tripoli, October 2014.

Neighborhood Rivalries 121

Jabal Mohsen and Bab al-Tebbaneh had developed networks of petty crime and smuggling. The revenues generated from this involvement in the illicit economy helped many residents to make ends meet. Yet they also began to trigger sometimes very heated rivalries. A violent feud especially developed between Jabal Mohsen's main gang headed by Mohsen Eid, Ali Eid's older brother and a man with a reputation as a violent criminal who had gone to prison for killing his ex-wife's new husband, and another gang in Bab al-Tebbaneh led by Mahmud al-Aswad, a Sunni smuggler who was a close associate of Khalil Akkawi. Due to the tight bonds of resident solidarity in Jabal Mohsen and Bab al-Tebbaneh, this feud soon broadened into a wider sense of competition between the residents of the two districts, and unsurprisingly also crystallized as a power struggle between the two areas' respective *qabadayet*, Ali Eid and Khalil Akkawi.[82] Simmering rivalries between bands of local youths over control of Tripoli's illicit economy and, behind it, a broader competition over local resources, status and neighborhood pride thus provides the background for understanding the Popular Resistance's promptness in answering Fatah's call to attack the Movement of the Alawi Youth.

The battle that took place in late 1975 was thus more fueled by a combination of neighborhood rivalries and grand politics than driven by Sunni–Alawi sectarian tensions. It was physically and symbolically violent, to be sure. The attack only lasted two days, yet it was bloody, resulted in the Popular Resistance's near-complete destruction of the offices of the Movement of the Alawi Youth and even led to the ransacking of Ali Eid's own villa. This represented a true humiliation for the pro-Syrian *qabaday* of Jabal Mohsen. Alongside his followers he even had to escape Tripoli for a few months and to find refuge in Tartus, a nearby Syrian coastal town within the heart of the Assad regime's Alawi power base.[83]

Yet the dynamics of the Popular Resistance's struggle against the Movement of the Alawi Youth were not, in and of themselves, driven by sectarianism. In fact, although the Popular Resistance was unmistakably Sunni-dominated, this spatially oriented movement epitomized Bab al-Tebbaneh's sense of community. This meant that it also included a dozen Alawi fighters from the district for whom neighborhood identity prevailed over sectarian loyalty.[84] Moreover, rather than forcibly taking over Jabal Mohsen, killing local Alawis and trying to repopulate the

---

[82] Interviews with former partisans of Khalil Akkawi and of Ali Eid, Tripoli, October–November 2014.

[83] Interviews with partisans of Ali Eid in Jabal Mohsen, Tripoli, October 2014.

[84] Concurring sources in the Popular Resistance suggested that among the dozen military commanders the movement had, up to six were Alawi residents of Bab al-Tebbaneh, including Mohammed Sleiman, Ibrahim Habib, Mohammed Ghanet, Issam Chadid, Mohammed Hassan Hamama and Samir Hassan – the last of whom would even assume

122   Neighborhood Islamism

neighborhood with Sunnis, as would perhaps have been the case had the conflict dynamics actually been sectarian, the Popular Resistance showed sensitivity toward Jabal Mohsen's Alawi population. Khalil Akkawi, indeed, sent one of his closest Alawi followers from Bab al-Tebbaneh, Ibrahim Habib, who in the absence of Ali Eid and his Movement of the Alawi Youth began ruling Jabal Mohsen on behalf of the Popular Resistance. And, by all accounts, the mostly Sunni fighters of the Popular Resistance did not engage in sectarian killings of local Alawis. Behind the 1975 struggle between the two movements therefore lay grand politics and a spatially rooted antagonism in the form of a neighborhood feud – Sunni–Alawi sectarianism did not play a significant role back then.

A Slum War

Yet these local rivalries soon spiraled out of control and morphed into an all-out "slum war,"[85] as scholar of urban conflicts Dennis Rodgers would have qualified the spatially confined but viciously violent struggle over resources, status and neighborhood pride which came to pit the deprived residents of Jabal Mohsen and Bab al-Tebbaneh against one another. It is precisely as Bab al-Tebbaneh was about to lose this slum war in 1979 and 1980 that Khalil Akkawi and his Popular Resistance came to embrace militant Islamism instrumentally.

Throughout the late 1970s the neighborhood rivalries which had burst into the open during the Popular Resistance's attack on the Movement of the Alawi Youth in 1975 progressively assumed much greater proportions. Months after the 1975 attack on Jabal Mohsen, Syria had launched a full-blown military intervention in Lebanon in June 1976, which offset the progress of pro-Palestinian Lebanese Muslim militias throughout the country and reempowered pro-Syrian regime movements, chief among them the Movement of the Alawi Youth in Tripoli. Given the imbalance of forces, the Popular Resistance quietly withdrew back to Bab al-Tebbaneh without putting up a fight and bitterly witnessed Ali Eid coming back to Tripoli as a victor. The *qabaday* of Jabal Mohsen had

important political and military functions in the Popular Resistance and then in Tawhid. This was confirmed by one of the Popular Resistance's main rivals, Mahmud Shehade, who was a close aide to Ali Eid. Interviews with former Popular Resistance members, Tripoli, September 2014 and interview with Mahmud Shehade, Tripoli, September 2016.

[85] Dennis Rodgers, "Slum wars of the 21st century: gangs, mano dura and the new urban geography of conflict in Central America" *Development and Change* (Vol. 40, No. 5, 2009), pp. 949–76.

A Slum War 123

returned to his neighborhood stronger than ever after a months-long exile in Tartus. His right-hand man recalls that, while in Syria, Ali Eid's tight relationship with Rif'at al-Assad had allowed him and his men to acquire high-quality weapons and undergo an intense paramilitary course. They even came to embed themselves in the Defense Brigades (*al-Saraya al-Difa'a*), a powerful, Alawi-dominated Syrian military strike force which Hafez al-Assad's younger brother supervised. The Movement of the Alawi Youth's alliance with the Syrian regime had therefore turned considerably "stronger"[86] during its months-long exile in Tartus. Its members came back to Jabal Mohsen in mid-1976 battle hardened, armed to the teeth and well-connected.

Ali Eid's men came back to Tripoli fully determined to undermine the longstanding dominance of Bab al-Tebbaneh's gangs over Tripoli's illicit economy. They began by arresting Mahmud al-Aswad, Khalil Akkawi's associate in the Popular Resistance who headed a smuggling ring and had been a rival of Mohsen Eid's gang, using their Syrian connections to arrange for al-Aswad to be sent to prison in Damascus for two years.[87] Then, having intimidated their rivals in Bab al-Tebbaneh with the full extent of their newfound power, they strengthened their grip over the Tripolitan underworld. The Alawi gangs supervised by Mohsen Eid expanded their reach outside of Jabal Mohsen. They took over large parts of the smuggling business on which residents of Bab al-Tebbaneh had long had the upper hand, which further exacerbated their neighborhood rivalry. They came to exercise sway in the northern neighborhood of Beddawi, where they taxed with full impunity the companies that stocked petroleum at the oil terminal. They even expanded their influence to the port area of Mina. From there they got involved in piracy off the coast of Tripoli. In 1979 alone they were allegedly responsible for the theft of the content of as many as thirty-one commercial boats, leading Western observers to raise alarm bells about the "nefarious" increase in "gangster activities in the Tripoli area particularly affecting shipping."[88] With the blessing of their Syrian patron, Rif'at al-Assad, the gangs of Jabal Mohsen even began running a large-scale, cross-border drug trafficking and smuggling ring.[89] A figure close to Syrian intelligence

---

[86] Interview with Mahmud Shehade, Tripoli, September 2016.

[87] Interviews with Aziz Allush and Abu Zghayar (former commanders in the Popular Resistace), Tripoli, October 2014.

[88] See: UK Embassy in Beirut, "Piracy" (Confidential 469 34, No. 489, July 11, 1979); and "Piracy" (Confidential ZCZCm No. 7, August 1, 1979).

[89] This was reported repeatedly in interviews with sources in Lebanese intelligence and sources close to Syrian intelligence in Tripoli. The CIA also reported in several of its cables dedicated to Syria and Lebanon on Rif'at al-Assad's involvement in drug

124   Neighborhood Islamism

acknowledged their staggering post-1976 rise in the illicit economy by quipping, with a smile, that the Movement of the Alawi Youth had by then turned into the "Movement of the Tripolitan Mafia."[90] Within the space of years after his return to Tripoli in 1976, Ali Eid had clearly emerged as the most prominent figure of Tripoli's underworld and was reportedly making tens of millions of dollars, parts of which he spent by providing services and further protection in Jabal Mohsen to reinforce his aura as the area's *qabaday*.

But soon enough Ali Eid began to want more than just undermining the position of Bab al-Tebbaneh's gangs and rising as the boss of Tripoli's illicit economy. He now also wished to exact revenge for the true humiliation he and his men had suffered at the hands of the Popular Resistance when they had been forced to escape Jabal Mohsen in 1975. In the words of one observer, Ali Eid's men had returned to Tripoli in 1976 animated with deep "enmities" and a thirst for "vengeance" against those who lived "just meters away"[91] in Bab al-Tebbaneh. The late 1970s were thus marked by the Movement of the Alawi Youth's involvement in a growing number of violent incidents targeting members of the Popular Resistance in Bab al-Tebbaneh. Tripolitan Alawi militiamen began to raid the homes of known Popular Resistance figures whom they intimidated and sometimes allegedly tortured and killed. They seemed so confident in their newfound power that they routinely engaged, in broad daylight, in sporadic gunfire against gatherings of their rivals in Bab al-Tebbaneh's vicinity. They even went as far as orchestrating the attempted assassination of Khalil Akkawi, by now Ali Eid's arch-rival, even though their operation failed and only ended up adding fuel to the fire by exacerbating the neighborhood rivalry. Yet their thirst for revenge and sense of invulnerability also became such that, in early and mid-1980, it started to translate into increasingly murderous acts of urban violence – shoot-outs but also actual bombings. Their attacks no longer just targeted individual Popular Resistance members. This time they were also aimed at residents of Bab al-Tebbaneh at large, whom they suspected of harboring disproportionate sympathy for this locally rooted and neighborhood-oriented movement.[92]

---

trafficking and its alliance with Ali Eid's gangs in Jabal Mohsen. See, for instance, US Central Intelligence Agency, "Heroin trafficking: the Syrian connection, an intelligence assessment" (Top Secret, GI 85-10046C, February 1985).

[90] Interview with a high-ranking official in the Syrian Ba'ath Party, Tripoli, September 2016.

[91] Abi Samra, *Trablus*, p. 103.

[92] See, among others, "'Arbat enfijarat fi leila wahida fi Trablus" ["Four explosions in one night in Tripoli"], *Al-Incha* (December 6, 1979); "Mu'tamar fi Bab al-Tebbaneh hawl artife'a as'ar al-m'aishat wa al-wad'a al-amni" ["Conference in Bab al-Tebbaneh on the increase of the price of living and on the security situation"], *Al-Incha* (December 11,

The tipping point which turned these increasingly violent neighborhood rivalries into an all-out "slum war" was reached in April 1980. Back then a brawl erupted in a Tripolitan nightclub between groups of youths from the two rival districts. Yet, as it once more quickly morphed into a shootout in which a resident of Bab al-Tebbaneh was killed and another two injured, the Popular Resistance this time decided to fight back, whatever the consequences. Khalil Akkawi ordered his fighters to erect barricades to protect Bab al-Tebbaneh from further raids by Ali Eid's men. They began exchanging heavy gunfire at the nearby positions of the Movement of the Alawi Youth in Jabal Mohsen, whose militiamen then answered by throwing rocket-propelled grenades back down the hill toward Bab al-Tebbaneh, thus starting a spatially confined but rapidly escalating and especially violent cycle of tit-for-tat attacks.[93]

The April 1980 clash may have "only" killed three but, according to observers present at the scene, it had also been "particularly violent"[94] in several other ways. It had involved the mutually indiscriminate shooting and shelling of both neighborhoods, which caused severe injuries to a dozen civilians and further plunged the two areas in a circle of revenge. This was not missed by a local reporter who rightly predicted after the clash had ended that it would probably be followed by "persisting tension"[95] between the two districts. In fact, such rounds of violence would continue to be a familiar feature of Tripoli in the early and mid-1980s as well as, again, in the 2000s and 2010s. Moreover, because it lasted for four days the April 1980 clash was unexpectedly long and frightening. Although the struggle remained confined to the two districts, the sporadic gunfire and explosions could be heard and seen throughout Tripoli, including in the city's wealthier area of New Tripoli. There, as a result of the eruption of violence, the traffic came to a standstill, businesses closed down for days, schools sent children home and no one dared to stay outside. Even though most were Sunnis, the upper-class residents of New Tripoli became so bitter to see their own relaxed lifestyle being disrupted that they began increasingly resenting the Sunni residents of Bab al-Tebbaneh as much as the Alawi residents of Jabal Mohsen, without distinction between sects.[96] This reinforced the stigma suffered

---

1979) or "Atlaq nar fi Bab al-Tebbaneh" ["Shooting in Bab al-Tebbaneh"], *Al-Incha* (January 22, 1980).

[93] "Qatil wa jarihen fi qital fi malha bi Trablus" ["One dead and two injured in a fight in a cabaret in Tripoli], *Al-Incha*, (April 22, 1980).

[94] "Ebullition et accrochages à Tripoli: 3 morts et 9 blessés en deux jours," *l'Orient Le Jour* (April 23, 1980).

[95] "Tension persistante à Tripoli," *L'Orient Le Jour* (April 23, 1980).

[96] Interviews with upper-class residents of New Tripoli, Tripoli, December 2014.

126   Neighborhood Islamism

by the two districts and furthered their socio-economic isolation. The April 1980 clash, then, marks the turning point which transformed the neighborhood rivalry between Jabal Mohsen and Bab al-Tebbaneh into a slum war waged mercilessly by residents of the two districts, a conflict that became so violent that it began triggering the impatience and resentment of the upper middle class in New Tripoli.

The April 1980 clash had another especially important effect in Bab al-Tebbaneh. It crystallized the growing bitterness of virtually all the inhabitants of that neighborhood no longer just toward the Lebanese government, Tripoli's political and economic elite and, now, Jabal Mohsen, but also toward the Syrian regime. As Chapter 1 tackled, with the exception of the Movement of the Alawi Youth and a handful of small leftist parties, dislike for the Syrian regime was widespread in Tripoli. Yet this became particularly the case in Bab al-Tebbaneh. There, residents began to intensely resent both the open support of Damascus for the Movement of the Alawi Youth and the increasingly obvious meddling of the Syrian army in Tripoli in the neighborhood rivalry opposing Jabal Mohsen and Bab al-Tebbaneh.

Between 1976 and 1980 the Movement of the Alawi Youth's relationship with the Syrian regime had further deepened – particularly the bonds that tied it to Syria's powerful Defense Brigades. It is revealing, in fact, that this elite Syrian military unit had chosen Jabal Mohsen to set up its Tripoli headquarters during the time of the Syrian military occupation of Lebanon. Of course, the Defense Brigades had reasons of their own to settle on this neighborhood, such as because their preexisting alliance with Ali Eid's men guaranteed that this was a safe place for Syrian Alawi officers and soldiers and because Jabal Mohsen's location on a hill overlooking all Tripoli rendered it a strategically and symbolically important space to set up a military base.[97] But this also had the effect of further empowering the Movement of the Alawi Youth and attracting the widespread sense that it was fast becoming difficult to distinguish Syrian and Tripolitan Alawis in Jabal Mohsen. Ali Eid's men deliberately entertained this ambiguity and it seemed to serve them well. They became known for attacking homes and shops in Bab al-Tebbaneh while wearing Defense Brigades uniforms and carrying badges from the Syrian military unit, which allowed them to act with full impunity. According to a Lebanese intelligence officer in Tripoli at the time, the relationship between the Movement of the Alawi Youth and the Defense Brigades had by 1980 become so tight that the former could be

---

[97] Interviews with a former Syrian officer in post in Tripoli, London, September 2015.

A Slum War   127

considered an "integral part of the Syrian security apparatus."[98] Even Western intelligence reported on this increasingly symbiotic relationship by pointing to the significant support "Rif'at al-Assad's Defense Brigades" provided to Ali Eid's men, whom the regime used to "strengthen Syria's hand"[99] in Tripoli.

Unsurprisingly, Syria immediately took the side of the Movement of the Alawi Youth when the April 1980 clash broke out, which gave the sense to Bab al-Tebbaneh's residents that the regime had crossed a line by openly meddling in the rivalry opposing them to Jabal Mohsen's inhabitants. The Defense Brigades units stationed on Jabal Mohsen did not ostensibly participate in the fight. But, according to a figure close to Ali Eid, they helped the Tripolitan Alawi fighters to man some of the high-quality weapons they had earlier provided them with.[100] Moreover, other Syrian army units rapidly came to encircle Bab al-Tebbaneh. Officially this was meant to prevent Fatah forces in the nearby Palestinian camp of Beddawi from resupplying Popular Resistance fighters with weapons and ammunition. But in reality it may have also been aimed at creating dissensions in Bab al-Tebbaneh by making it harder for local residents, who were exhausted and weakened after days of violence, to access food and water supplies. Yet, far from creating divisions in this tight community of local residents, the erection of Syrian military checkpoints at the neighborhood's entrance was collectively interpreted as an open act of hostility that deserved a violent response. On the third day of the clash a group of local residents and fighters from the Popular Resistance approached the largest nearby Syrian checkpoint and attacked a patrol, injuring two soldiers in the process.[101] This episode would trigger a wave of Syrian arrests of residents and would mark the beginning of the feud that has opposed the inhabitants of Bab al-Tebbaneh to the Syrian regime ever since, and which would culminate with the December 1986 massacre, a topic tackled in Chapter 8. From 1980, therefore, Bab al-Tebbaneh's rebel identity and tradition of locally oriented violence became increasingly associated with the need to "resist" the Syrian army and Ali Eid's men in Jabal Mohsen to "defend" the district.

---

[98] Interview with a Lebanese intelligence officer formerly in post in Tripoli, Beirut, January 2015.

[99] US Central Intelligence Agency, "Directory of Lebanese militias: a reference aid" (Secret, NESA 84-10171C, June 1984).

[100] Interview with Mahmud Shehade (Ali Eid's adviser and right-hand man), Tripoli, September 2016.

[101] "L'effervescence persiste à Tripoli: 2 soldats de la FFA blessés," L'Orient Le Jour (April 25, 1980).

128   Neighborhood Islamism

By the spring of 1980 it was now fast becoming clear to the residents of Bab al-Tebbaneh that they were about to lose the slum war against Jabal Mohsen. This was already starting to have dire economic and security consequences for the neighborhood, with significantly less revenues than before being generated from involvement in the illicit economy and a tide of shootings and bombings aiming at local shops and groups of residents.[102] One resident recalled that the late 1970s and early 1980s were a period during which "our neighborhood became the victim of injustice and oppression on a daily basis."[103]

Of course, Syria's open support for Ali Eid's men in the neighborhood rivalry only intensified this resentment and, although the alliance between the two actors had been the product of shared interests, it nonetheless began being viewed as an "Alawi plot" to undermine Sunni-dominated Bab al-Tebbaneh and control Tripoli at large. This sense was reinforced by the Defense Brigades' reputation as a nest of chauvinistic Alawi officers whom Syria's own former defense minister, Mustafa Tlass, once described as "sectarian fundamentalists"[104] due to their alleged dislike of Sunnis, and by Mohsen Eid's reputation as a brutal man who routinely engaged in what some, in Bab al-Tebbaneh, called "sectarian killings" against Sunni residents. Local narratives that emphasized more than before the sectarian element of the neighborhood rivalry between Jabal Mohsen and Bab al-Tebbaneh thus started spreading. "Just like in Syria, Jabal Mohsen's Alawis started ruling the area,"[105] was a typical complaint from a resident of Bab al-Tebbaneh. It is in this local context that Khalil Akkawi suddenly embraced Islamism, drawing with him many inhabitants of Bab al-Tebbaneh who, not long before, would have still called themselves "revolutionary Marxists."

Militant Islamism as a Protest Ideology

Strikingly, almost forty years later the elderly residents of Bab al-Tebbaneh can still remember the approximate date on which a significant portion of the neighborhood's young men suddenly became "Islamists" – it was during the summer of 1980. Back then dozens of

---

[102] See, for instance: "Enfijar qunbla laylan fi Bab al-Tebbaneh" ["Explosion of a bomb at night in Bab al-Tebbaneh"], *Al-Incha* (May 20, 1980); "Enfijaren fi Trablus" ["Two explosions in Tripoli"], *Al-Incha* (May 27, 1980) or "Enfijaren fi Trablus" ["Two explosions in Tripoli"], *Al-Incha* (June 13, 1980).

[103] Interview with residents of Bab al-Tebbaneh, Tripoli, October 2014.

[104] Mustafa Tlass, *The mirror of my life* [*Mirat Hayati*] (Vol. 4) chapter 87 (Damascus: Dar Tlass, 2004), p. 22.

[105] Interview with residents of Bab al-Tebbaneh, Tripoli, October 2014.

Militant Islamism as a Protest Ideology

them had reportedly emulated Khalil Akkawi who, during the holy month of Ramadan, had set foot in a mosque for the first time to pray. From then on he and his followers soon began to regularly perform their five prayers a day, grow beards, organize religious demonstrations, ostensibly hold the black banners of jihad, initiate the building of new mosques and multiply sermons that featured more or less explicit Islamist references.

Naturally, from the outside, it seemed like a contradiction in terms that a neighborhood strongman who had once proudly described himself as a "revolutionary Marxist" and had never set foot in a mosque was, just months after the violent April 1980 clash with Jabal Mohsen, now suddenly becoming pious and turning to militant Islamism. Yet the timing mattered. Far from a standalone incident, the April 1980 clash which had erupted into an all-out slum war was symptomatic of a period during which Ali Eid's men, with Syrian complicity, began carrying out attacks on Popular Resistance members and residents of Bab al-Tebbaneh at large that were more frequent and murderous than before. In mid-August 1980, for instance, they carried out what the Lebanese media called a violent "vendetta"[106] by firing mortar rounds and rockets into the neighborhood, killing dozens of local civilians and leading residents of the district to demand "security from persecution."[107]

Slowly but surely crumbling, Khalil Akkawi's Popular Resistance had to devise a strategy quickly to get back at Ali Eid's men and the Syrian regime and to impose a power balance. While revolutionary Marxism had once allowed it to channel the grievances of Bab al-Tebbaneh's residents, militant Islamism would now act as what I call the movement's new "protest ideology"; a corpus of symbols, discourse and practices embraced instrumentally because of the contentious potential they are associated with more than because of their intrinsic appeal per se. Through this concept I mean to place the analytical emphasis on the Popular Resistance's rebel orientation and on the protest strategies of its leader and members, more than on the alleged causal role of ideology. The instrumental shift from one "protest ideology" to another was thus the mechanism which explained the Popular Resistance's switch from revolutionary Marxism to militant Islamism. As Bab al-Tebbaneh's context became marked by new threats and opportunities, the embrace of militant Islamism as a "protest ideology" served a range of strategic functions for the movement. They included expressing dissent in a religious language which was blurry enough to avoid repression, allowing

---

[106] "Un tué à Tripoli," *L'Orient Le Jour* (August 17, 1980).
[107] "Tensions persistante hier à Tripoli," *L'Orient le Jour* (August 25, 1980).

130   Neighborhood Islamism

for the continued socialization and mobilization of members through a local network of mosques and the post-Friday prayer march and allying across class and space with ideologically driven Islamist actors prepared to help it address Bab al-Tebbaneh's grievances.

The fact that the Popular Resistance embraced Islamism is not only remarkable due to its Marxist origins but also because Bab al-Tebbaneh, which acted as its spatial base, had until 1979–80 not been as affected by this ideology's otherwise growing cultural and political momentum, described in Chapter 1. The neighborhood may have been overwhelmingly inhabited by Sunni rural migrants who espoused a traditional lifestyle, but it was most importantly characterized by its sheer degree of poverty. There, Islam had long been dismissed as a "conservative" beliefs system, many residents reporting that they used to view piety as an issue of importance mostly to those in the middle and upper classes who could afford to be concerned, indeed at times to be guided, by religious and moral principles. In contrast with this "elitist" preoccupation for Islam, then, the deprived and mostly illiterate inhabitants of Bab al-Tebbaneh had developed survival and coping strategies which at times stood in flagrant contradiction with religion, such as the involvement of locals in petty crime and urban violence or the locally widespread consumption of drugs and alcohol. Tellingly, for several decades before 1980 this large neighborhood of 40,000 inhabitants only featured one mosque – and, by all accounts, it had long been mostly "empty."[108]

Given Bab al-Tebbaneh's rebel history and identity, it was only after the 1979 Iranian Revolution that Islamism began witnessing some cultural and ideological momentum there, when it gradually became seen as the new quintessential rebel ideology. Circles of followers of Khalil Akkawi and residents of Bab al-Tebbaneh formed to discuss and collectively follow, through radio or television, the series of events that were witnessing the overthrow of the secular Shah of Iran and the coming to power of an Islamic Republic headed, initially, by a coalition of revolutionary leftists and Islamists. They were intrigued and quickly attracted by the rhetoric of Ali Shariati. The Iranian Revolution's leading ideologue argued for a "Red Islam" which would combat the socio-economic and political injustices found in society. This even provided the inspiration behind the rise of the People's Mujahedin (*Mojahedin-e Khalq*), an Iranian rebel movement that sought to reconcile revolutionary Marxism and Islamism. Akkawi's followers then became in awe of the Ayatollahs, or senior clerics, who soon took charge of Iran's new Islamic Republic

[108] Interview with residents of Bab al-Tebbaneh, Tripoli, October 2014.

more exclusively and, through their involvement in the hostage crisis at the US embassy in Tehran, militant support for the Palestinian cause and call for a worldwide jihad against oppressive regimes, popularized the notion that Islamism could act as a revolutionary ideology.[109] The Islamic Republic was led by Shias, of course, but the simultaneous proliferation of Sunni Islamist movements that soon also began to call for revolutions, from Saudi Arabia to Egypt, where militant Islamists even killed the president, Anwar al-Sadat, further demonstrated Islamism's contentious potential and its ability to act as a "protest ideology." The circles of Popular Resistance members and residents of Bab al-Tebbaneh which had formed to follow these regional events in late 1979 and through 1980 came to the opinion that, despite different outlooks, revolutionary Marxism and militant Islamism had "a lot in common."[110]

While such a statement may have seemed incongruous for ideologically committed Marxists, who often believe that "religion is the opiate of the people," the use of leftist ideology by residents of Bab al-Tebbaneh had never been synonymous with a full-blown, doctrinally rigorous embrace of all Marxist tenets. As the cases of the Organization of Anger and the Popular Committees showed, revolutionary Marxism had been instrumentally and selectively embraced. At best it had acted as a tool to channel Bab al-Tebbaneh's socio-political grievances, express dissent and operate coalitions across space and class to benefit the neighborhood. At worst it had merely been a pseudo-intellectual justification for the continued involvement of some residents in the tradition of locally oriented contention. Moreover, although drugs and alcohol were rife, Bab al-Tebbaneh had otherwise always remained a traditional neighborhood characterized, for instance, by conservative relations between men and women. Perhaps unsurprisingly, then, members of the Popular Resistance and many residents of the district at large reported finding it "natural," indeed even "comfortable,"[111] to shift the way they expressed dissent from Marxism to Islamism. Even Bab al-Tebbaneh's religious minorities, who had long lived in the neighborhood and therefore also made up a portion of the Popular Resistance, seemed to understand militant Islamism's ability to serve as a "protest ideology." One of them, long close to Khalil Akkawi, explained that, although he was not a

---

[109] Interviews with rank-and-file members of the Popular Resistance in Bab al-Tebbaneh, Tripoli, October 2014.

[110] Interview with Aziz Allush (former military commander in the Popular Resistance), Tripoli, October 2014.

[111] Interviews with rank-and-file members of the Popular Resistance in Bab al-Tebbaneh, Tripoli, October 2014.

132   Neighborhood Islamism

Muslim, he grew "fascinated" by Islamism's contentious potential. "Many of us used to view Islam as an inherently conservative religion," he recounted. "But 1979 showed that it could be both popular and revolutionary."[112]

Militant Islamism's potential to act as the quintessential "protest ideology" further transpired months later when militant Syrian Islamist movements violently took on the Syrian regime which had, by now, risen as Bab al-Tebbaneh's archenemy. Throughout 1980, groups such as the Fighting Vanguard (*al-Tale'a al-Muqatila*) and the Syrian Muslim Brotherhood (*al-Ikhwan al-Muslimin al-Suryin*) spearheaded a series of strikes, demonstrations and insurgent attacks, which then multiplied to such an extent that Hafez al-Assad's power seemed about to crumble.[113] This earned them the "admiration" of many residents of Bab al-Tebbaneh who were now, by their own account, "obsessed"[114] with their dislike of the Syrian regime. It also helped that these two Islamist movements were particularly strong in the Syrian cities of Homs, Hama and Aleppo. All three were intimately tied to Tripoli's symbolic and social fabric, as was seen in Chapter 1, and this was especially felt in Bab al-Tebbaneh, where some local inhabitants originally hailed from the Syrian hinterland. The residents of the district therefore followed with considerable enthusiasm the daily developments of the Syrian insurgency, openly cheering for the Islamist opposition. Tellingly, the inhabitants of Bab al-Tebbaneh recall that 1980 became the year during which the figure of Che Guevara was replaced in the local imaginary by the likes of Marwan Hadid and Adnan Uqla, the "heroes" of the Syrian jihad who led bloody operations against regime forces, as true revolutionaries to be "admired" and "emulated."[115] In other words, within the space of months Bab al-Tebbaneh had witnessed Islamism's growing cultural and ideological momentum, and it arose as a new and appealing ideological option. Although this area was not known for the piety of its residents, militant Islamism nonetheless became seen as an effective "protest ideology," one containing the potential to express dissent and to undermine the regime's local grip as well as that of Ali Eid's men. Figure 2.1 illustrates how the Popular Resistance embraced Islamism just as Bab al-Tebbaneh began facing increasingly frequent and murderous attacks in mid-1980.

---

[112] Interview with Haj Nikoula (former adviser to Khalil Akkawi), Tripoli, November 2014.

[113] For more on this period, see Raphaël Lefèvre, *Ashes of Hama: the Muslim Brotherhood in Syria* (London: Oxford University Press and Hurst, 2013).

[114] Interviews with Mazen Mohammed, Abu Zghayar, Aziz Allush, Samir Hassan, Abu Jandah and Bilal Matar (former members and commanders of the Popular Resistance in Bab al-Tebbaneh), Tripoli, October 2014.

[115] Interview with residents of Bab al-Tebbaneh, Tripoli, October 2014.

Militant Islamism as a Protest Ideology

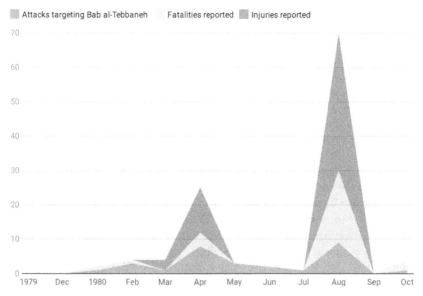

Figure 2.1 The timing of the Popular Resistance's ideological shift
Source: Tripolitan daily *Al-Incha* and Lebanese daily *L'Orient Le Jour*

The result was the rise throughout the summer of 1980 of what I call "protest Islamism": an instrumental embrace of religion and ideology aimed at expressing dissent with an existing socio-political situation and at using the contentious potential inherent in Islamist symbols, vocabularies, practices and infrastructure. Of course, from the outside performing simple acts such as going to the mosque five times a day, taking part in demonstrations to celebrate the birthday of the Prophet, clandestinely distributing pictures of the heroes of the Syrian jihad or writing Islamist slogans on the walls of Bab al-Tebbaneh might seem tantamount to very small-scale forms of mobilization. But in the repressive context that characterized Tripoli in 1980, with the head of Syrian intelligence in Lebanon, Mohammed Ghanem, even threatening to take "special measures"[116] to enforce order, embracing these routine religious practices, symbols and vocabularies became for many of Bab al-Tebbaneh's residents a way to engage in what anthropologist James Scott called "everyday resistance."[117]

---

[116] "Reprise des affrontements à Tripoli: 2 morts, 21 blessés," *L'Orient Le Jour* (August 23, 1980).
[117] James C. Scott, *Weapons of the weak: everyday forms of peasant resistance* (New Heaven: Yale University Press, 1987).

134   Neighborhood Islamism

When it came to expressing dissent against the Syrian regime and Ali Eid's men in Jabal Mohsen, the embrace of Islamism as a "protest ideology" had particularly appealing comparative advantages over revolutionary Marxism, both rhetorically and organizationally.

Rhetorically, Islamism boasted an especially rich panoply of concepts and symbols to be used for the sake of dissent – especially against the Syrian regime and Ali Eid's men. Whereas the Popular Resistance struggled to find in Marxist ideology the concepts which would allow it to express its enmity for the Syrian regime and Ali Eid's men, other than by rather weakly suggesting that the rulers in Damascus were "bourgeois," Islamism offered a new array of possibilities.[118] To begin with, the very embrace of Sunni Islamist ideology had the advantage of implicitly singling out the "Alawism" of both the Syrian regime and Jabal Mohsen's Movement of the Alawi Youth precisely when the sectarian question was fast becoming delicate for Damascus. This was a time marked by fatwas, or religious rulings, by Syrian Islamist opposition movements that deemed the Alawi community "not Muslim," which stirred up Sunni–Alawi tensions throughout Syria in 1980. In this context the Popular Resistance began using a religious and ideological vocabulary which suggested that the aggressions suffered by Bab al-Tebbaneh's Sunni majority at the hands of Jabal Mohsen and the Syrian regime were driven by "pro-Alawi," "anti-Muslim" sentiment. Its propaganda material implied in deliberately blurry but locally clear terms that there were certain "forces" which were bent on "clearing out Muslims from their land" and on "eliminating the Islamic presence."[119] At a time of growing Sunni–Alawi tensions, casting the attacks and arrests suffered by Bab al-Tebbaneh's residents as though they were driven by Alawi chauvinism and anti-Sunni sentiment had the effect of putting the Syrian regime and its allies in Jabal Mohsen much more on the defensive than accusing them of being "bourgeois."

A second rhetorical advantage of Islamism was that the very fact of using a religious discourse, even if not outwardly political or militant in nature, in itself displayed low-key opposition to the Syrian regime and its allies in Jabal Mohsen. Indeed, while Hafez al-Assad routinely used secular and socialist rhetoric as an ideological blanket to justify his domestic and foreign policy decisions, Ali Eid began emulating the Syrian president and soon transformed his Movement of the Alawi

---

[118] Interview with Abu Zghayar (Popular Resistance commander close to Khalil Akkawi), Tripoli, October 2014.

[119] Undated sermon by a Popular Resistance member in Bab al-Tebbaneh, Tripoli, video given to the author.

Youth into an Arab Democratic Party (*al-Hizb al-Arabi al-Dimuqrati*) which also ostensibly mobilized the discourse of secularism and socialism. Adopting religious speech that lambasted leftism therefore became a way for the Popular Resistance to highlight its dual opposition to the Syrian regime and to Ali Eid's men – even if it meant embracing a critique of an ideology that the movement and local residents had previously embraced. Popular Resistance members, who had once been "comrades," then began calling each other "brothers in faith." They now expressed their pride in making up "the nation of the Quran" and even started explicitly lambasting those whose leftist ideologies "disfigure the character of the Muslim nation."[120] Embracing religious vocabulary, even if in initially superficial ways, became a tool to single out and denounce the purported "socialism" and "secularism" of the Syrian regime and Ali Eid's Arab Democratic Party.

Organizationally the embrace of Islamism had another crucial advantage over revolutionary Marxism. In an increasingly repressive context it provided the Popular Resistance with access to Bab al-Tebbaneh's arguably last "safe space" – the local mosque. After the April 1980 clash, the neighborhood's only mosque progressively came to play the role of what contentious politics scholar Doug McAdam called an "indigenous infrastructure":[121] it provided dissenters with access to an already existing structure of support and a resource the Popular Resistance could tap into in order to continue mobilizing local residents. To the movement's members it seemed very likely that the Syrian regime and Ali Eid's men, on the defensive after they became accused of behaving brutally with locals out of anti-Sunni sentiment, would not wish to be further associated with controversial "anti-Muslim" practices like violating the sanctity of a worshiping place. As a result, Bab al-Tebbaneh's mosque rapidly became the cornerstone of the Popular Resistance's strategy to mobilize members and residents at large under duress.[122] While, for instance, the five prayers a day allowed locals to gather inside the mosque in large groups and discuss things in safety, which enabled the neighborhood's sense of a community and strong solidarities to persist, the Friday sermon provided an opportunity for the continued spread of contentious speech and the subsequent march enabled the low-key socialization and mobilization of members. In spite of their officially nonpolitical

---

[120] Undated sermon by a Popular Resistance member in Bab al-Tebbaneh, Tripoli, video given to the author.

[121] Doug McAdam, *Political process and the development of black insurgency, 1930–1970* (Chicago: University of Chicago Press, 1982), pp. 43–4.

[122] Interviews with rank-and-file members of the Popular Resistance in Bab al-Tebbaneh, Tripoli, October 2014.

136   Neighborhood Islamism

character, then, these three religious practices nonetheless contained a high potential to be used for the sake of contention.

Of course, while raiding Bab al-Tebbaneh's mosque was a red line for the Syrian regime and Ali Eid's men, they could still send spies or crack down on any religious street demonstration that featured even the slightest explicit call for the neighborhood's residents to rebel. Yet, here again, another advantage of embracing religious discourses, symbols and practices was how fluid and ambiguous they had the potential to be all while mobilizing the local residents. They offered plausible deniability, but also expressed dissent effectively. In one sermon, for instance, Khalil Akkawi lengthily referred to the *Hijra* – the forced exile of Muhammad from Mecca to Medina – and vaguely compared the "disbelief, injustice, corruption and tyranny" which the Prophet was facing then to the "oppression"[123] Muslims faced today. The sermon once again implicitly targeted the Syrian regime and its allies in Jabal Mohsen but, couched in the language of religious historical reference and avoiding explicit mentions to the situation in Tripoli, it went unnoticed by Syrian intelligence.

At times the very use of religious rhetoric even allowed for a degree of militant zeal to be expressed within the boundaries of socio-political acceptability. This enabled the Popular Resistance to keep Bab al-Tebbaneh's rebel identity and sense of community alive and to continue spreading a measure of contentious speech among residents. For instance, the reference to "jihad" became common in Popular Resistance propaganda and, while it was not immediately clear whether it referred to the internal "greater struggle" against one's own temptations or to the "lesser struggle" advocating for resistance against perceived enemies, it was locally understood as a reframing of the neighborhood's identity as a "stronghold of contention." Another example is a sermon Khalil Akkawi gave which exalted the audience present in the local mosque:

Today, we are rising up from within the ruins to make it clear to all the tyrants, with the loudest of our voices, that this nation, the nation of Muhammed – peace be upon him – will continue to exist regardless of how much it suffers and regardless of the presence of rocket launchers, tanks and missiles. Were the flames of the world pour onto its head, it would still stay on its feet, with God's help![124]

---

[123] Undated sermon by Khalil Akkawi in Bab al-Tebbaneh's Harba mosque, Tripoli, video given to the author.

[124] Undated sermon by Khalil Akkawi in Bab al-Tebbaneh's Harba mosque, Tripoli, video given to the author.

Speeches of that type, by implicitly framing the grievances suffered by Bab al-Tebbaneh at the hands of Jabal Mohsen and the Syrian regime in such passionate, almost messianic, religious terms, lifted the morale of the residents and kept the neighborhood's rebel spirit alive during challenging times.

As a result, from the summer 1980 onward the Friday prayers and the march that often followed became the one weekly occasion around which the socialization and mobilization of the Popular Resistance's members and Bab al-Tebbaneh's residents at large occurred. Tellingly, as the examples above suggest, it was often the former Marxist, Khalil Akkawi, rather than an experienced Muslim preacher who delivered the Friday sermons, thereby guaranteeing by virtue of his status as the local *qabaday* or "champion of mobilization" that the prayers would be well attended. And they were. Videos of some of his sermons that still circulate today consistently show a jam-packed mosque whose worshipers enthusiastically cheered at every second sentence uttered by the beloved strongman of the neighborhood.

Therefore, if the Popular Resistance embraced Islamism suddenly in mid-1980, it was to serve as a "protest ideology" whose symbols, discourse and practice aimed at expressing dissent and at continuing resident mobilization. Khalil Akkawi himself acknowledged as much when, in one of his Friday sermons, he explicitly asked his local followers to adopt Islam as a "revolution" and an "instrument of change."[125] In a show of how popular his call for a "protest Islamism" had been, back then the neighborhood's only mosque soon became overcrowded and the Popular Resistance had to initiate the construction of as many as four additional mosques in Bab al-Tebbaneh.[126] And the names they acquired, from Holy War (*al-Jihad*) and Martyr (*al-Shahid*) to the Spear (*al-Harba*) and Solidarity (*al-Tadamun*) – most of them highly unusual names for mosques but ones that resonated with Bab al-Tebbaneh's rebel spirits, solidarities and grievances – encapsulated the full extent to which Islamism had been embraced for its potential to act as the neighborhood's "protest ideology."

From the *Hara* to the *Umma*?

Yet, if the Popular Resistance had initially embraced religion for its instrumental value, the discourse of Khalil Akkawi and the behavior of

---

[125] Undated sermon by Khalil Akkawi in Bab al-Tebbaneh's Harba mosque, Tripoli, video given to the author.

[126] Interview with Mazen Mohammed (member of the Popular Resistance and cleric), Tripoli, October 2014.

138   Neighborhood Islamism

some, albeit a small minority, of his followers appeared for a while to have become genuinely driven by Islamist ideology.

The discourse of the *qabaday* of Bab al-Tebbaneh progressively became steeped in a militant and transnational Islamist rhetoric. He began stepping up interventions in the neighborhood's mosques to urge the residents to embrace Islam no longer just as an "instrument of change," but as a deeper conviction leading to "martyrdom under the banner of God Is Great (*Allahu Akbar*)" and to "jihad" against the "oppressors who threaten the Muslims." In addition to being increasingly militant, his speeches also became more global and ideological in the themes they tackled. Khalil Akkawi thus started to call for the transformation of the "Islamic awakening" which Tripoli and Bab al-Tebbaneh were witnessing into a much wider and more ambitious "total Islamic project" that would "unify the Muslim nation and order its ranks to face the enemies." Of course, he continued referring in mostly implicit ways to the situation faced by his neighborhood, but he now also began to engage more openly than before with wider Lebanese and Palestinian issues as well as to talk with passion about the challenges affecting the worldwide "Muslim nation" – the *umma* – at large. Two ostensible targets of his wrath in his Friday sermons became the United States and Israel. He stated that "the Western superpowers, tyrants of this age, have understood that the Islamic awakening constitutes the gravest of threats to their interests." He continued in a passionate tone. "It is Islam that for the first time in the history of the struggle defeated the Israeli army, it is Islam that defeated the American navy, it is Islam that has become a power whose spark reaches inside Israel!" Tellingly, he often came to conclude his sermons with the need for his partisans to "break the barrier standing between the neighborhood (*al-hara*) and the worldwide Muslim nation (*al-umma*)."[127] Within the space of a few months, then, the *qabaday* of Bab al-Tebbaneh, a former leftist who had always been neighborhood-oriented, had turned into a militant Islamist now ostensibly driven by ideological aims. Once guided by concern for the *hara*, he now seemed driven by the *umma*.

The root of the transformation of Khalil Akkawi's discourse lay in his gradual socialization and education into a more ideologically driven form of Islamist speech in 1981 and 1982 as a result of his growing ties to a movement known as the Line of Islamic Justice (*Khat al-'Adel al-Islami*). This was an intellectual club, a salon, more than a formally structured organization, which regularly brought together a dozen middle-class

---

[127] Undated sermon by Khalil Akkawi in Bab al-Tebbaneh's Harba mosque, Tripoli, video given to the author.

From the *Hara* to the *Umma?*

former Tripolitan Marxist intellectuals who had turned into committed Islamists in the mid to late 1970s. One observer noted that their primary goal became to carry out "proselytization"[128] activities – they tried to spread their worldviews and make Tripolitan society more receptive to Islamism. They had become Islamist "ideological entrepreneurs," or highly ideologized individuals who mobilize a beliefs system and strive to mold the nature of activism around these worldviews.

Interviews with a handful of current and former members of the Line of Islamic Justice shed light on the degree to which their ideology – and even their vocabulary – seemed to have shaped Khalil Akkawi's. Their main argument, indeed, was that the "Islamic awakening" gripping Tripoli should be used not to advance local interests but, instead, to contribute to the advent of a true religious political system, an "Islamic third way," the only one in their minds able to "destroy the West." The enemy of these "ideological entrepreneurs," then, was not the Syrian regime or its allies in Jabal Mohsen but, rather, "the West." They singled out the United States, the United Kingdom and France for their "democratic hypocrisy" which, in their view, had resulted in the massacre of thousands of Muslims in Palestine and Algeria, the rise of Israel and Western domination over the Middle East. The solution they proposed was straightforward. A member of the group explained it in the following way: "We had to go back to our Islamic roots and study the factors behind the failure of the Islamic Caliphate in order to unify, once again, the ranks of the Muslim nation in preparation for the final struggle against the West." To do so they would have to turn the growing embrace of Islam in Tripolitan society into a more genuine "cultural and ideological movement" that would "infuse" the revolutionary aspects of Islamic doctrine. This would eventually lead to a worldwide Islamic "revolution" that would pave the way for the advent of an Islamic political system "by and for the masses,"[129] one devoid of Western influence. Far from being guided by neighborhood or city-wide aims, then, the outlook of the Line of Islamic Justice was driven by an unmistakably transnational and militant Islamist ideology.

By all accounts, Khalil Akkawi was to some extent genuinely attracted by the Islamist ideas developed by the Line of Islamic Justice. He had become familiar with them through the preexisting social ties that bound him to the movement's head, Bassem Miqati, a former high school teacher and revolutionary Marxist whom he had earlier met, albeit

---

[128] Abi Samra, *Trablus*, p. 124.
[129] Interviews with current and former members of the Line of Islamic Justice, Tripoli, August 2014.

140   Neighborhood Islamism

briefly, in the Popular Committees. Accompanied by a handful of his lesser strongmen, the *qabaday* of Bab al-Tebbaneh began to attend the weekly meetings of the Line of Islamic Justice in 1981. They soon fell under the spell of Bassem Miqati who, in a display of the ideological influence he came to have over this small group, became known as "the professor" and even as "the godfather."[130] One of Akkawi's followers who attended these meetings remembered being "subjugated" by Miqati's views and "breadth of Islamic knowledge." "He taught us that Islam is more than a religion or a dogma; it is an ideology, a culture."[131] Another Popular Resistance member recalled that, whereas he had until then fought for his neighborhood "without thinking about the meaning of ideology," whether Marxist or Islamist, after attending the meetings organized by Miqati he continued to fight, but this time "for ideas."[132] The activism of the Line of Islamic Justice's "ideological entrepreneurs," then, was the mechanism through which a handful of Popular Resistance cadres who had initially embraced Islamism for its instrumental value became more ideologically committed and driven.

Khalil Akkawi himself seemed to some degree influenced by the ideological aims of the Line of Islamic Justice. Since the April 1980 clash with Jabal Mohsen and the Syrian army, along with the series of violent attacks that followed it, he had begun wondering about the "broader significance" of Bab al-Tebbaneh's plight and had been "searching for meaning."[133] In a display of Bassem Miqati's influence during this period, Khalil Akkawi sometimes spent one to two entire days per week "locked up" in the apartment of the head of the Line of Islamic Justice, with whom he would exchange views all night until dawn.[134] Members of the salon boasted that Miqati had allegedly convinced Akkawi to turn the Popular Resistance into a movement that would not just be neighborhood-oriented but also committed to "changing society" at large and would turn its members into "militants who think."[135] Some thus argue that the period of Khalil Akkawi's attendance of the meetings of the Line of Islamic Justice, in 1981 and 1982, was marked by the *qabaday*'s more sincere conversion to Islamism.

---

[130] Interview with Popular Resistance members and partisans of Khalil Akkawi, Tripoli, September 2014.

[131] Interview with Ali Agha (Popular Resistance fighter and cleric), Tripoli, October 2014.

[132] Interviews with Jamil Raad (Popular Resistance fighter), Tripoli, September 2014.

[133] Interview with a member of the Line of Islamic Justice, Tripoli, August 2014.

[134] Interview with Mazen Mohammed (figure close to Khalil Akkawi who attended the Line of Islamic Justice's meetings), Tripoli, November 2014.

[135] Interview with a member of the Line of Islamic Justice, Tripoli, August 2014.

Yet for all of Khalil Akkawi's outward display of harmony with Bassem Miqati and the appearance of ideological proximity with the Line of Islamic Justice, his rapprochement with these "ideological entrepreneurs" was, once more, at least partially guided by concern for Bab al-Tebbaneh. Just as in 1974, when he had used Marxist ideology to trigger an alliance with middle-class leftists as part of the Popular Committees, he was again in the midst of engineering a coalition across space and class with resource-rich, this time Islamist, "ideological entrepreneurs." It helped that some of the members of the Line of Islamic Justice had earlier been committed revolutionary Marxists who had joined the Popular Committees. Therefore they not only knew Khalil Akkawi well from this experience but also appreciated his ability to learn fast and to engage in deep conversations about grand ideas. They had regretted, but also respected, his choice to ditch the Popular Committees and create, instead, the Fatah-backed Popular Resistance as a movement ostensibly dedicated to supporting the armed Palestinian presence in Lebanon, and therefore saw with great satisfaction his willingness to reactivate his ties with them. Perhaps more importantly, just like when they had been Marxists, as Islamist "ideological entrepreneurs" they were keenly aware of the potential effect a newfound alliance with Akkawi, the popular *qabaday* of Bab al-Tebbaneh, could have in terms of spreading Islamist ideology to this large, aggrieved and rebel neighborhood and turning many of its residents into committed militant Islamists.[136]

This alliance soon materialized in myriad ways. It did not involve an organizational merger, mostly because the Islamist "ideological entrepreneurs" were wary of becoming dragged into the Popular Resistance's frequent skirmishes with the Syrian army and Ali Eid's men in Jabal Mohsen. Yet this coalition across space and class did crystallize through a series of clandestine meetings between Khalil Akkawi's followers, who hailed from Bab al-Tebbaneh, and members of the Line of Islamic Justice, many of whom lived in the middle-class neighborhood of Abu Samra. Going by car up to the hill of Abu Samra, where the meetings were held, only took between fifteen and twenty minutes for Akkawi's followers, but it represented a real journey which gave them a sense of social equality. "All the participants in these meetings were slaves of God,"[137] one of them pointed out tellingly, who as a petty trader from Bab al-Tebbaneh began feeling the equal of members of the Line of

---

[136] Interviews with current and former members of the Line of Islamic Justice, Tripoli, August 2014.
[137] Interview with a former Popular Resistance member who became a cleric, Tripoli, August 2014.

142   Neighborhood Islamism

Islamic Justice, themselves middle-class high school teachers, doctors or university students. Participating in these sessions allowed Popular Resistance members to overcome their social marginalization.

Another way in which this alliance across space and class materialized was through the establishment of a full-blown school that the Islamist "ideological entrepreneurs" set up and funded in Bab al-Tebbaneh's Harba mosque, which had just been built. The school was mid-way between an indoctrination camp and a small popular university. It provided well-qualified teachers from outside of Bab al-Tebbaneh, often themselves members of the Line of Islamic Justice, who lectured and tutored local youths on Islamist ideology, of course, but also science, languages, economics and even health. This seemed like a mutually profitable scheme. The "ideological entrepreneurs" saw a golden opportunity to mobilize their worldviews and spread a genuinely Islamist "intellectual atmosphere" in Tripoli's largest and most aggrieved neighborhood in order to turn local youths into the new generation of ideologically committed Islamist militants.[138] Khalil Akkawi, for his part, was by all accounts enthusiastic about the unique opportunity the school's presence represented. He knew some of the Islamist "ideological entrepreneurs" since their time as Marxists in the Popular Committees. He appreciated how much they had done for the neighborhood back then and he was convinced that they would be committed to teaching and providing services to the mostly illiterate local residents. Moreover, the creation of a full-blown school in Bab al-Tebbaneh's Harba mosque also provided another chance to further the low-key socialization and mobilization of the Popular Resistance's members and inhabitants of Bab al-Tebbaneh at large while burnishing his movement's newfound Islamist credentials.[139]

Interestingly, however, the reaction of the neighborhood's own inhabitants was more mixed. Some, of course, attended the school and appeared to have enjoyed it. One felt proud of the very presence in Bab al-Tebbaneh of university-educated middle-class residents from other Tripolitan districts whom he called, full of admiration, "big brains." For deprived inhabitants used to having their neighborhood stigmatized, this coalition across space and class breathed fresh air and gave a renewed sense of pride in their tight community. Others appreciated

---

[138] Interviews with current and former members of the Line of Islamic Justice, Tripoli, August 2014.

[139] Interviews with Popular Resistance members Mazen Mohammed and Abed Merkabawi who attended the Line of Islamic Justice's indoctrination camps, Tripoli, November 2014.

From the *Hara* to the *Umma*?   143

attending the school. Since many youths were unemployed or worked part-time, going to one of the Line of Islamic Justice's six-days-a-week lectures at Bab al-Tebbaneh's Harba mosque, where they might meet their neighborhood champion, Khalil Akkawi, made them enthusiastic and helped fill in their day.[140] One committed resident who attended all the classes remembered that the year would typically begin with a dozen students enrolled and would often end up with double and sometimes triple that amount.[141]

Yet many other Popular Resistance members and residents of the neighborhood at large did not seem to look as favorably upon the Line of Islamic Justice's school in Bab al-Tebbaneh. One of them called it "intellectual masturbation"[142] to highlight the extent to which some of the Islamist themes and concepts tackled by the "ideological entrepreneurs" were detached from the local reality of persecution, poverty and stigmatization. This was particularly the case as the period of the Line of Islamic Justice's efforts at proselytizing in Bab al-Tebbaneh was also one during which residents felt they were "fighting for survival" and were as a result more preoccupied with their own day-to-day security and socioeconomic concerns than with deeper debates about ideology. One resident and member of the Popular Resistance quipped that "the frog sees the world from the bottom of the well."[143] This drove home the sense that, while many locals embraced Islamism to make sense of their localized grievances and express dissent at the Syrian regime and Ali Eid's men, very few became truly indoctrinated into ideology and driven by it. Another one acknowledged that dozens of Bab al-Tebbaneh's young men had attended the school, but also pointed out that most had used it as a vehicle to socialize and mobilize rather than out of an inherent sense of ideological appeal for the Line of Islamic Justice's grander goals.[144] Several more concurred and remarked that the enterprise of Islamist ideological indoctrination had largely failed, with the exception of a handful of men around Khalil Akkawi. Members of the Popular Resistance and countless inhabitants of Bab al-Tebbaneh may well have embraced "protest Islamism" but, just as with Marxism before, most would not be ready to sacrifice spatially oriented activism on the altar of

---

[140] Interviews with residents of Bab al-Tebbaneh, Tripoli, October 2014.

[141] Interview with Jamil Raad (Popular Resistance member who attended the Line of Islamic Justice's indoctrination camp at Bab al-Tebbaneh's Harba mosque, Tripoli, September 2014.

[142] Interview with Abu Zghayar (Popular Resistance commander), Tripoli, September 2014.

[143] Interview with Haj Nikoula (former adviser to Khalil Akkawi), Tripoli, November 2014.

[144] Interview with a resident of Bab al-Tebbaneh, Tripoli, October 2014.

144   Neighborhood Islamism

what they saw as largely abstract, grand ideological aims. Despite all the efforts of the Line of Islamic Justice, therefore, the *hara* still prevailed over the *umma*.

Neighborhood Islamism

While from mid-1980 onward the Popular Resistance and then Tawhid's local faction in the district may well have adopted Islamism, their embrace and practice of ideology remained so grounded in and oriented toward Bab al-Tebbaneh that I call it "neighborhood Islamism" – it was more guided by inherently local solidarities, concerns and traditions than by ideology. From the outside, the Marxist-turned-Islamist Popular Resistance increasingly looked and sounded like some of the other ideologically committed militant Islamist groups proliferating in Tripoli. But the nature of this movement – its composition, underlying goals and exercise of violence – remained largely informed by Bab al-Tebbaneh's local context, itself traversed by strong local solidarities, intense grievances and Khalil Akkawi's status as the *qabaday* of the neighborhood. At times the type of Islamist practice which spread in Bab al-Tebbaneh seemed even more embedded in social features inherent to the neighborhood than in any genuine embrace of Islamist ideology. And, revealingly, any tension which would arise between loyalty to the neighborhood as a community and commitment to ideology would be systematically settled in favor of the former. The Popular Resistance's Islamism thus remained disproportionately anchored in, driven by and oriented toward Bab al-Tebbaneh. Once again, therefore, behind the embrace of ideology also lay spatially oriented activism.

Like a decade earlier when revolutionary Marxism had seemed fast on the rise, the two participation identities which explained engagement first in the Islamist-leaning Popular Resistance and then in Tawhid after the 1982 merger were neighborhood identity and loyalty for the local *qabaday* or "champion of mobilization." When asked why they committed acts which appeared, from the outside, like Islamist militancy, such as going as self-styled "Islamist commandos" near Syrian military checkpoints guarding Jabal Mohsen's entrance and unloading their guns at the soldiers posted there while shouting "God is Great," members and local residents who fought during that period of time replied that they had only sought to "defend" and "avenge"[145] Bab al-Tebbaneh. Their involvement in violence took the shape of militant Islamism because, for reasons

---

[145] Interviews with former rank-and-file Popular Resistance members, Tripoli, October 2014.

seen previously, this "protest ideology" provided them with more effective conceptual and organizational tools than radical leftism to express dissent at the Syrian regime and Ali Eid's men in Jabal Mohsen. Yet it still remained intrinsically driven by Bab al-Tebbaneh's concerns, rebel spirits and strong local solidarities. Despite the ostensible process of ideological change from Marxism to Islamism there was therefore a great deal of continuity in the Popular Resistance's targets and the nature of its violence. Becoming an Islamist in the early 1980s became a way for many local young men of "enacting neighborhood,"[146] as geographer Deborah Martin put it; that is, it turned into a practice and a signal that demonstrated attachment to Bab al-Tebbaneh as a tight community through engagement in spatially oriented, if ostensibly Islamist, collective action.

Back then the extent to which becoming a self-styled Islamist signaled commitment to the local community was such that several Alawi residents of Bab al-Tebbaneh for whom neighborhood identity prevailed over sectarian loyalty either converted to Sunni Islam or grew a beard and appeared as "Islamists" too. Samir Hassan was one of these Alawis from Bab al-Tebbaneh. He would speak and look like an Islamist, regardless of his deeper convictions, because this beliefs system had shown "more efficiency"[147] in acting as the "protest ideology" of his beloved neighborhood. By all accounts, his effort to "blend in" was locally much appreciated and, as a result, he rapidly rose as one of the Popular Resistance's most trusted and powerful "Islamist" commanders. Of course, far from all of Bab al-Tebbaneh's Alawis became Islamists back then. In fact, many felt uncomfortable with the Popular Resistance's embrace of Islamism and these either refused to take part in its involvement in Islamist contention or left the neighborhood entirely. But it is telling that, even then, some are still reported to have "stayed in touch"[148] with their former friends and neighbors, at times clandestinely giving them a hand during episodes of contention.

In addition to neighborhood identity, the other crucial and partially overlapping factor which explained the prevalence of Islamism in Bab al-Tebbaneh was the deep sense of loyalty which bound many residents to Khalil Akkawi, who had announced his Islamist coming-out in the summer of 1980. It is remarkable how, by simple virtue of his status as the *qabaday* or informal leader of the neighborhood, his sudden embrace

---

[146] Deborah Martin, "Enacting neighbourhood" *Urban Geography* (Vol. 4, No. 5, 2003), pp. 361–85.

[147] Interview with Samir Hassan (military commander in the Popular Resistance), Tripoli, November 2014.

[148] Interviews with Abu Zghayar (military commander in the Popular Resistance), Tripoli, November 2014.

146 Neighborhood Islamism

of militant Islamism had triggered the almost automatic conversion of dozens of young men – some of whom, just months earlier, had still been calling themselves "revolutionary Marxists." Of the two dozen interviewed former leftist fighters of the Popular Resistance who became militant Islamists back then, all of them mentioned "emulating" Khalil Akkawi as a key factor behind their ideological conversion. This does not mean that they were devoid of agency. In a show of how some internalized beliefs, a handful of them later attended the indoctrination camp run by the "ideological entrepreneurs" at the local Harba mosque and some even became clerics. Yet the degree of influence which Khalil Akkawi exercised on many of the district's young men nonetheless points to the particular importance of the *qabaday* as a "champion of mobilization," an informal leader with such a large following in his community that, by activating local solidarities, he could spur locally oriented, if ostensibly Islamist contention.

A resident who back then was a self-described Islamist fighter in the Popular Resistance thus explained that he had embraced a more religious way of life and Islamist discourse after he had seen Khalil Akkawi doing the same. Like many other local youths, he "trusted" and "admired" the *qabaday*, whom he claims was "present in the hearts of all the residents"[149] of Bab al-Tebbaneh. It seemed obvious to follow in his footsteps. Akkawi's "courage," "charisma," "sincerity" and history of championing the neighborhood were consistently given as factors that had pushed many of Bab al-Tebbaneh's young men, in the early 1980s, to join the Popular Resistance and embrace Islamism in open ways.[150] One former fighter, now incidentally a local cleric, seemed to speak for many others when he passionately remembered, while bursting into tears, that "Khalil Akkawi took all of Bab al-Tebbaneh with him into Islam – he was our cleric, our guide, our ideal."[151] To the point that many outside the neighborhood decried what they felt was nothing short of idolatry or, as a resident of another district put it mockingly, "the religion of Abu Arabi,"[152] Akkawi's nickname. The ability of the "champion of mobilization" to activate local solidarities and channel them into activism therefore acted as the underlying mechanism through which many of Bab al-Tebbaneh's residents were recruited and mobilized into Islamist collective action.

[149] Interview with Ali Agha (Popular Resistance member turned cleric), Tripoli, October 2014.
[150] Interviews with residents of Bab al-Tebbaneh, Tripoli, October–November 2014.
[151] Interview with Mazen Mohammed (Popular Resistance member), Tripoli, October 2014.
[152] Interview with a resident of New Tripoli, Tripoli, November 2014.

Neighborhood concerns and loyalty for the *qabaday*, then, more than any sincere appeal for Islamism's deeper set of beliefs, informed many local young men's embrace of Islamism. And this, in turn, meant that the local context of the neighborhood also shaped in at least three ways the type of Islamism which began characterizing the Popular Resistance.

First, this "neighborhood Islamism" revolved around the persona of Khalil Akkawi. The strongman of Bab al-Tebbaneh surrounded himself with a leadership of a dozen street commanders or lesser strongmen who met him daily either at his home in the district, the local Harba mosque or, at times, in the Beddawi refugee camp where he took refuge when the Syrian army and Ali Eid's men searched for him during episodes of contention. But ultimately Akkawi alone made all the decisions. Tellingly, one of these street commanders who was part of the Popular Resistance's leadership summed up that he "just followed orders."[153] The intense ties of loyalty tying the *qabaday* of Bab al-Tebbaneh to his followers thus meant that the Popular Resistance was overly dependent on Akkawi's leadership and charisma and lacked well-trained cadres and broader ambitions. But it also signified that its fighters were fully committed to Akkawi, and thus to the movement. They would stand ready to engage in neighborhood-oriented acts of collective action like mass protests or risky battles whenever he would order them to. The intensity of the bonds tying Akkawi to local fighters was on full display upon his assassination at the hands of the Syrian regime on February 9, 1986. Then, members and local residents at large launched an anti-Syrian regime uprising in Bab al-Tebbaneh which, although it was cast as Islamist, was first and foremost guided by a thirst for revenging his murder – a topic tackled at length in Chapter 8. The intense loyalty binding Popular Resistance members to their leader meant that the movement soon earned a reputation for being highly cohesive and tightly centered around the persona of Khalil Akkawi, his partisans ready to do whatever he would ask of them.[154]

Second, the rise of "neighborhood Islamism" meant that the spatial base of the Popular Resistance would be overwhelming in Bab al-Tebbaneh. The movement was weak, arguably nonexistent, in other Tripolitan districts. But in his neighborhood Khalil Akkawi's dual status as the head of the Popular Resistance and local *qabaday* was enough to secure a virtually never-ending pool of local recruits who were young men in their late teens, twenties and sometimes thirties. Unlike

---

[153] Interview with Abu Zghayar (Popular Resistance commander and figure close to Khalil Akkawi), Tripoli, October 2014.

[154] Interview with Islamist militants from Soldiers of God, Tripoli, December 2014.

148   Neighborhood Islamism

organizationally more rigid Islamist movements, such as the Muslim Brotherhood, there were no constraints on membership – in fact, there seemed to be no such policy at all – nor complex procedures or lengthy indoctrination.[155] Hailing from the neighborhood appeared to be enough. "Anyone could pick up a gun and join," recalled a former member of the Popular Resistance. "We quickly grew – even fifteen-year-old kids from the neighborhood wanted to join us!"[156] With the money it received from Fatah for good and loyal services, the movement could pay modest salaries to between 150 and 200 local fighters. But its actual base in the neighborhood was much more significant than that. While Western intelligence agencies, like the CIA, were at first wary of the local strength of this militant Islamist movement and estimated that it had over 300 fighters, sources in Palestinian intelligence suggested that the figure was double that amount, and Khalil Akkawi himself estimated that it was closer to 500 members – the large majority of them unpaid.[157] What is even more striking was the movement's ability to mobilize well over a thousand additional local residents who sporadically joined during episodes of contention, for example during violent clashes or mass protests.[158] The spatial base of the Popular Resistance may have been limited to Bab al-Tebbaneh, but its sheer numerical strength there rapidly turned the "neighborhood Islamists" into an impressive movement to be reckoned with in Tripoli.

Last but not least, the spread of "neighborhood Islamism" as a locally rooted and oriented form of Islamist contention meant that the embrace of ideology was bound to remain instrumental and doctrinally superficial. The rank and file of the Popular Resistance now looked and

---

[155] Interviews with Abu Jandah and Ahmed Harrouq (Popular Resistance members), Tripoli, October 2014.

[156] Interview with Aziz Allush (former Popular Resistance commander), Tripoli, October 2014.

[157] Interview with Abu Marwan (Fatah intelligence officer in North Lebanon), Tripoli, February 2015. See also: US Central Intelligence Agency, "Lebanon: Islamic fundamentalism in Tripoli" (Top Secret, NESAR 86-003JX, January 17, 1986). Khalil Akkawi's own estimate is quoted in Abi Samra, *Trablus*, p. 106.

[158] Interviews with Popular Resistance members, residents of Bab al-Tebbaneh and observers of Tripolitan politics and society, Tripoli, October–November 2014. Akkawi's ability to raise thousands of local residents would be on full display after his assassination at the hands of the Syrian regime in February 1986 when a staggering 50,000 people, most of them inhabitants of Bab al-Tebbaneh, carried his body from the neighborhood's main mosque to the cemetery of Tripoli. I draw this figure from interviews with residents of Bab al-Tebbaneh and it is confirmed in news reports. *Associated Press* reported that "50,000 Sunni Moslems attended a funeral for Khalil Akkawi, the Sunni fundamentalist leader who was assassinated in an ambush the day before." See: "Four killed, including one Syrian, in Tripoli gunfights," *Associated Press* (February 1986).

sounded Islamist, to be sure. But their new, ostensible religious practice remained more anchored in the social features specific to the neighborhood than in ideology per se. Because, before 1980, the neighborhood had never featured a particularly active religious life, it was not home to enough qualified local preachers and, in fact, critical masses of its Sunni Muslim residents were themselves unfamiliar with even some of the most basic requirements of Islamic faith. This was particularly striking to pious observers from outside of Bab al-Tebbaneh who, intrigued by the Popular Resistance's rising profile back then and attracted by its outwardly Islamist credentials, initially went to the local Harba mosque a handful of times for Friday prayers. They remarked that Khalil Akkawi's speeches represented an idiosyncratic mixture of militant Islamist slogans and neighborhood references which contrasted with the more mainstream and less localized religious discourse of typical Muslim clerics. This led them to doubt whether he was sufficiently knowledgeable in Islamic doctrine to "properly"[159] lead prayers and deliver Friday sermons.

Even more shockingly, these observers also noted that the behavior of the crowd present in the Harba mosque did not resemble the attitude of other Tripolitan worshipers. They were appalled, in fact, to see locals initially entering the mosque for Friday prayers without having washed their hands, although it is considered a basic pillar of Islamic practice, and to then shamelessly cheer and shout during Khalil Akkawi's sermons. They even reported seeing some of the local worshipers later exiting the Harba mosque and spending the afternoon engaging in practices widely regarded as against Islamic faith, like drinking alcohol. An outsider who regularly used to visit the neighborhood quipped that "old habits die hard" and explained that "at the time one of the only places in Tripoli where one could still find whiskey was ... Bab al-Tebbaneh!"[160] Even a former "Islamist" street commander in the Popular Resistance acknowledged the unorthodox type of ideology which spread in the neighborhood when he recalled, with a smile, how his fighters started praying and fasting after they witnessed Khalil Akkawi do the same while, simultaneously, continuing to drink beer at night.[161] Other fighters denied this was a widespread trend yet its occurrence, even if sporadically, and the fact that the Popular Resistance never seriously tried to rein it in, still showed how its Islamism was spatially rooted in, even shaped

---

[159] Interviews with residents, Tripoli, October 2014.
[160] Interview with Elias Khlat, Tripoli, October 2015.
[161] Interview with Abu Zghayar (former commander in the Popular Resistance), Tripoli, October 2014.

150   Neighborhood Islamism

by, older local practices. This differed from the doctrinal vision of the more orthodox Islamist movements which, tellingly, would never gain any significant spatial base in Bab al-Tebbaneh. "Our Islamism was deeply anchored in the neighborhood,"[162] acknowledged a figure long close to Akkawi. The ostensible embrace of Islamism by the Popular Resistance and its leadership therefore never fully translated into a full adoption of its basic ideological tenets by members at large.

"Neighborhood Islamism," then, was more about the neighborhood than about Islamism. And, in case it is still not clear enough, any tension between loyalty to Bab al-Tebbaneh as a community and commitment to ideology would systematically be resolved in favor of the former. A revealing incident was the case of Fu'ad al-Kurdi's eviction from the neighborhood. This resident of Bab al-Tebbaneh was a military commander in the Popular Resistance and a figure close to Khalil Akkawi. By all accounts, the *qabaday* took him to the meetings of the Line of Islamic Justice, which he then continued attending assiduously. Rapidly, however, al-Kurdi grew so subjugated by Bassem Miqati's views that he himself also turned into an Islamist "ideological entrepreneur." That is, he became highly committed to ideology and began to mobilize his Islamist worldviews so as to turn the instrumental embrace of Islamism by the Popular Resistance into more sincere beliefs. He then transformed into such an ardent defender of the Islamic Republic of Iran that he even opened a small bookshop selling copies of Khomeini's books.[163] As Chapter 7 shows, through 1983 and 1984 al-Kurdi would become one of the Islamic Republic's most vocal advocates in Tawhid and a key relay with Iranian intelligence. This showed that the efforts of the Line of Islamic Justice had not been in vain. But, interestingly, this outward display of sincere ideological commitment to Islamism was not appreciated by members of the Popular Resistance and the neighborhood's residents at large. They began accusing al-Kurdi of "caring more about Iran than about Bab al-Tebbaneh"[164] and lambasted him for seeking to turn the Popular Resistance's locally oriented activism into a more ideologically driven form of mobilization. He was subsequently asked to leave the district, underlining the paramount importance of loyalty first and foremost to the neighborhood as a community.

The full extent to which it was the neighborhood, more than Islamist ideology, which shaped the Popular Resistance's behavior and exercise of

---

[162] Interview with Bilal Matar (political adviser to Khalil Akkawi), Tripoli, October 2014.
[163] Interview with Ali Agha (Popular Resistance member), Tripoli, November 2014.
[164] Interview with Abu Zghayar (Popular Resistance commander), Tripoli, October 2014.

violence transpired when a new series of bloody clashes erupted between Bab al-Tebbaneh and Jabal Mohsen in August 1980, September 1981, February 1982 and May 1982. By then the Popular Resistance was portraying itself as a group "close to militant Syrian Islamist movements" bent on eliminating the pro-Assad, "Alawi" Arab Democratic Party. Its members became known in the media for their propensity to shout slogans to the glory of "jihad" and to conduct violent attacks on Jabal Mohsen in conjunction with Tripoli's other militant Islamist factions, thus making the clashes "exceptionally violent"[165] and weakening Ali Eid's men and Syrian troops.

Yet what had triggered these clashes was not the Popular Resistance's embrace of militant Islamist ideology but the preexisting neighborhood rivalry between Bab al-Tebbaneh and Jabal Mohsen and the sense that local residents continued to be "persecuted" by Syrian troops and Ali Eid's men. The only actual demand of the Popular Resistance, then, was not the instauration of some kind of Islamist order but simply the "neutralisation"[166] of the Arab Democratic Party in Jabal Mohsen as well as the withdrawal of Syrian troops from Bab al-Tebbaneh's vicinity. To achieve that aim, Khalil Akkawi had used Islamist ideology to operate an alliance across space and class with Soldiers of God (*Jund Allah*). This was an ideologically driven, militant Tripolitan Islamist faction which had long been deeply opposed to the Syrian regime and was driven by a sectarian dislike for Tripoli's Alawis. Crucially, this well-trained Islamist militia had a strong spatial base in the middle-class district of Abu Samra as well as in Qobbe, two areas conveniently situated in proximity to Jabal Mohsen. Allying with Soldiers of God therefore allowed Khalil Akkawi to considerably raise the stakes when a battle erupted. Indeed, the clashes would immediately spread to Abu Samra and Qobbe, which considerably relieved the Bab al-Tebbaneh front. This also suddenly added pressure on Ali Eid's men and on Syrian troops, retrenched in Jabal Mohsen and now attacked not just from one but from several sides. With a total of 193 people killed between August 1980 and May 1982, these clashes were particularly deadly.[167] The Syrian army soon recognized that, alongside Ali Eid's men, it had been especially affected by them,

---

[165] "Calme précaire à Tripoli et sa banlieue nord," *L'Orient Le Jour* (August 22, 1980) and "Cessez le feu effectif à Tripoli où les combats ont fait 15 morts et 40 blessés," *L'Orient Le Jour* (August 24, 1980).

[166] "Tension persistante hier à Tripoli," *L'Orient Le Jour* (April 25, 1980).

[167] I draw these figures from my analysis of Tripolitan daily *Al-Incha*, Lebanese daily *L'Orient Le Jour* and an article by Tripolitan researcher Adib N'ame: Adib N'ame, "Al-amen fi Trablus, 1980–1985" ["The security in Tripoli, 1980–1985"], *Nada' al-Shamal* (undated, copy given to the author).

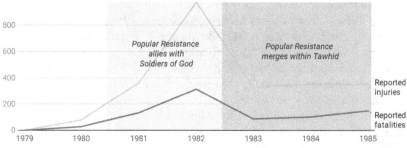

Figure 2.2 Neighborhood Islamism: ideology and localized concerns
Note: This graph reflects the localized violence which resulted from the feud between Bab al-Tebbaneh and Jabal Mohsen (e.g. armed clashes, bomb attacks, gunfire) – it does not take into account broader patterns of violence in Tripoli.
Source: Tripolitan daily *Al-Incha*; Lebanese daily *L'Orient Le Jour* and Adib N'ame, "Al-amen fi Trablus, 1980–1985" ["The security in Tripoli, 1980–1985"], *Nada' al-Shamal* (November 1985)

acknowledging that it had caused a "particularly high"[168] loss of lives among its ranks. Progressively this had the effect of installing a precarious local balance of terror between the pro and anti-Syrian camps (see Figure 2.2). Whereas the Syrian regime had for a time attempted to strike the Popular Resistance with an "iron fist,"[169] and still acknowledged the "gravity"[170] of the situation in Tripoli, Damascus now seemed too concerned that all-out repression might trigger a violent Islamist backlash which would undermine its position and its allies.

It was in the context of this apparent success of the Popular Resistance's alliance across class and space with Soldiers of God and out of the acute sense that Bab al-Tebbaneh would in the future again be "persecuted" by the Syrian regime and Ali Eid's men that Khalil Akkawi began to socialize and mobilize with Tripoli's other militant Islamists in 1982. Unlike the leftist parties whose revolutionary zeal had died down or the Tripolitan notables who vehemently professed their "disapproval"[171] every time clashes erupted between the two neighborhoods, most of Tripoli's militant Islamist factions supported the Popular

---

[168] "Reprise des affrontements à Tripoli: 2 morts, 21 blessés," *L'Orient Le Jour* (August 23, 1980).
[169] "Calme précaire à Tripoli et sa banlieue nord," *L'Orient Le Jour* (August 22, 1980).
[170] "Cessez le feu des plus précaires à Tripoli: 3 tués, plusieurs blessés," *L'Orient Le Jour* (May 13, 1982).
[171] "Cessez le feu des plus précaires à Tripoli: 3 tués, plusieurs blessés," *L'Orient Le Jour* (May 13, 1982).

Theorizing Back 153

Resistance in this local feud and shared its animosity toward the Syrian regime and Ali Eid's men. Khalil Akkawi's right-hand man tellingly recalled that the main factor behind his participation in Tawhid's creation in mid-1982 was because he felt he needed "all the help he could get" in a bid to "defend"[172] the neighborhood more effectively. In the Popular Resistance, not everyone agreed with Akkawi's judgment that Bab al-Tebbaneh's best interest lay in joining a coalition of militant Islamists from all over Tripoli.[173] But, in a display of loyalty to the *qabaday*, few questioned his decision and most joined Tawhid too.

The Popular Resistance's "neighborhood Islamism," or engagement in a type of behavior and violence more rooted in and driven by local concerns and solidarities than ideology, would then become a key feature of Tawhid during the early to mid-1980s.

Theorizing Back

By tackling the Popular Resistance's strong spatial base in the Tripoli neighborhood of Bab al-Tebbaneh as well as the dynamics of its embrace of Islamism, this chapter also answers the following questions, with theoretical implications related to the role of space and ideology in contentious politics. How are social, rebel and terrorist movements able to engage in the mass recruitment and mobilization of the residents of specific spaces? And what accounts for patterns of collective ideological change when some movements switch their ideologies?

First, I continue to show the ways in which social, rebel and terrorist movements can use the physical, symbolic and social dimensions of space to root themselves in some localities, and I demonstrate how space can then considerably inform the nature of activism. In the case of Bab al-Tebbaneh, what attracted many of Tripoli's social and rebel movements to seek to establish a foothold in the neighborhood was its spatial layout, tactical location, longstanding rebel identity and intense grievances, all of which they strategically utilized for the sake of mobilization during episodes of contention. But I point to one mechanism in particular through which movements can activate the social dimension of space as a resource: the enlistment of figures I call "champions of mobilization." These figures are tied to their community, here the neighborhood, by such strong solidarities that they develop a large following and are able to ensure mass recruitment and mobilization there. This is precisely what explained the ability of the Popular Resistance, and later of Tawhid, to

---

[172] Interview with Bilal Matar (political advisor to Khalil Akkawi), Tripoli, October 2015.
[173] Interview with Abu Zghayar (Popular Resistance commander), Tripoli, October 2014.

154   Neighborhood Islamism

root themselves so deeply in Bab al-Tebbaneh; both movements indeed relied on Khalil Akkawi's extremely large personal following in the neighborhood to recruit and mobilize. I trace Akkawi's role as Bab al-Tebbaneh's "champions of mobilization" back to his status as the neighborhood's *qabaday* or strongman; a culturally, emotionally and spatially rooted figure in the traditional districts of Middle Eastern cities who takes up his area's leadership informally by virtue of his ability to defend, often violently, the local community and of the bravery he shows when seeking to address local grievances and antagonisms. Earning the status of *qabaday* turned this figure into the holder of neighborhood solidarities and networks, which he would then channel during episodes of locally oriented contention. Simultaneously, however, while movements which overly rely on a "champion of mobilization" might succeed in recruiting massively in his community, it also tends to make them dependent on his choices and persona and may render the nature of activism very local. Through Akkawi's agency, then, the Popular Resistance and Tawhid's local branch were able to recruit hundreds, sometimes thousands of residents of Bab al-Tebbaneh, yet these locals always remained more loyal to their strongman than to the ideologies of these movements. Enlisting "champions of mobilization" who can activate local solidarities to recruit in their communities thus allows movements to use the social dimension of space to root themselves.

Second, by addressing what accounts for the Popular Resistance's seemingly counterintuitive shift from revolutionary Marxism to militant Islamism, I demonstrate the need to overcome the dichotomy between instrumental and sincere accounts of the role of ideology in social, rebel and terrorist movements. On the one hand, I illuminate how a central mechanism through which individuals, factions and movements may adopt a certain beliefs system is through their instrumental embrace of a "protest ideology." That is, they adopt this ideology because of the contentious potential associated with its symbols, discourse, practices and infrastructure, more than because of its content per se. Through this concept I thus mean to emphasize the rebel political orientation as well as the agency and protest strategies of those who tend to embrace ideologies instrumentally. It is through the lens of this instrumental embrace of a "protest ideology" that the Popular Resistance's sudden shift from revolutionary Marxism to militant Islamism must be viewed. As Bab al-Tebbaneh's context became marked by new threats and opportunities, the movement's embrace of militant Islamism as a "protest ideology" served a range of strategic functions. These included expressing sociopolitical dissent in a religious language blurry enough to avoid repression, allowing for the continued socialization and mobilization of members through a local network of mosques and the post-Friday prayer march, and allying across class and space with ideologically driven Islamist actors ready to help the movement out of ideological solidarity. The very fact that this process of collective ideological change from leftism to Islamism took place within the space of mere months, and without translating into a truly significant change in the worldviews, targets and everyday practices of Popular Resistance and then Tawhid members in Bab al-Tebbaneh, confirmed the sense that it resulted, at least for most, from a superficial shift from one "protest ideology" to another, undertaken for instrumental reasons. Through the notion of a "protest ideology," then, I highlight the need to go beyond the assumption that ideology automatically causes behavior, and instead to empirically investigate the nature of the embrace of ideology by movements as well as the extent to which it trickles down in an equivalent adoption in the grassroots' worldviews and practices.

On the other hand, far from presenting a purely instrumentalist account dismissing beliefs as mere tools, I also claim that, even when they are initially embraced as a "protest ideology," they can take on a life of their own, be internalized and create path dependencies. I introduce one mechanism and type of actor in particular through which ideology can influence movement beliefs and behavior – the "ideological entrepreneurs." Chapter 6 explores in detail the background, worldviews and influence on Tawhid of these figures. But at this point suffice is to say that the category of "ideological entrepreneurs" refers to actors at the extreme of a "spectrum of ideological commitment" who are not just ideologically driven but also mobilize their worldviews to shape the nature of activism, seeking to turn the instrumental embrace of ideology by some into sincere commitments. Here I highlight the impact of the "ideological entrepreneurship" of a handful of committed Tripolitan Islamists on some of the Popular Resistance's members and cadres, suggesting that, through their mobilization of Islamist ideology, they succeeded in affecting parts of the movement's discourse, cementing the beliefs of some cadres and precipitating their decision to join Tawhid in 1982. This indicates how, even when initially embraced instrumentally, beliefs can still take on a life of their own and create path dependencies.

3   The Emergence of Tawhid

Tawhid was created in mid-1982 out of the merger of Tripolitan factions and figures which came from different backgrounds, but all embraced a militant Islamist ideology. This right away included the Popular Resistance's "neighborhood Islamists," who adopted militant Islamism instrumentally. Tawhid's "spectrum of ideological commitment" would later continue to grow even wider as, to root itself locally and bolster its numerical strength, it would recruit other constituencies instrumentalizing ideology too, most obviously the "subaltern Islamists" and the "Islamo-gangsters." Still, though, in the months surrounding Tawhid's foundation, the movement's center of gravity undeniably lay with its most ideologically committed Islamist factions and individuals. Two factions whose members were committed Islamists participated in its creation and became influential. While the first, Soldiers of God, had for years been Tripoli's foremost militant Islamist militia frequently engaging in ideologically driven violence, the second, the Movement of Arab Lebanon, had been a Maoist group which, much like the Popular Resistance, had embraced militant Islamism instrumentally as a "protest ideology," but had then internalized beliefs. In addition to these two factions sincerely committed to Islamism, Tawhid also attracted Tripoli's most vocal, ideologically driven Islamist figures or "ideological entrepreneurs," two of them even joining the movement's leadership otherwise made up of the founding factions' leaders. And, finally, the fact that the movement was led by Sa'id Sha'aban, a cleric known for his militant Islamist sermons in Tripoli's mosques, attracted even more committed Islamists to its orbit. However wide Tawhid's "spectrum of ideological commitment" may later have grown, therefore, the momentum which initially accompanied the movement's rise was primarily due to its ability to appeal to many of Tripoli's sincerely committed Islamists, to the extent that shortly after its creation it had already turned into the city's largest Islamist group by far.

This chapter traces the process behind Tawhid's emergence and accounts for the immediate success it met among Tripoli's ideologically committed Islamists, who would form half of the movement's total number of members of between 2,000 and 3,000. It builds on Chapter 2 and continues to introduce Tawhid's founding factions and figures, their levels of ideological commitment and the degree to which ideology shaped their behavior. I begin by showing the sheer diversity of a Sunni Islamist field too often reduced, in the Islamist politics literature, to either the Muslim Brothers or the Salafis, pointing out that Tawhid became composed of members hailing from various subcurrents of Islamism. Some of them did hail from the Islamic Group – Lebanon's Muslim Brotherhood – from which they split in the mid-1970s after it sought to become politically more institutionalized. But many others came from other ideological traditions found in Lebanese Sunni Islamism. For instance, while some were "Sufi jihadis" animated by the politically revolutionary and socially conservative breed of Naqshbandi Sufism increasingly spreading in Tripoli, others were "Sunni Khomeinists" whose goal was to spread the Iranian model of leading an Islamic Revolution and implementing an Islamic Republic in Lebanon, by force if necessary, and who explicitly backed Iran's post-1979 bid for Islamic leadership in the Middle East. I then introduce the movement's leader, Sa'id Sha'aban, a cleric whose fiery sermons buoyed many. All these Islamist factions, currents and figures soon merged within Tawhid and I highlight the importance of the timing of its birth, in a climate marked by the new threats and opportunities triggered by the Syrian regime's February 1982 Hama massacre and Israel's June 1982 invasion of Lebanon. The sense that Tripoli was stuck between the Syrian anvil and the Israeli hammer would allow the new movement to outbid its rivals by framing its rise as a response to popular demands to "defend the city" and "wage jihad" against its enemies. Tawhid subsequently did its best to appear as a socially inclusive, organizationally flexible and ideologically driven Islamist movement, which attracted even more Islamists to its orbit.

The Islamic Group Gets Outclassed

It is remarkable how, despite its rising profile in Tripoli in the 1960s and early 1970s, the Islamic Group would come to face severe difficulties just a few years later. It was in Tripoli that the Lebanese branch of the Muslim Brotherhood was originally created. The root of its initial popular success there stemmed, as was seen in Chapter 1, both from the growth of Islamism's "cultural momentum" and the movement's ability, at first, to epitomize Tripolitan aspirations of reattachment to Syria, narratives of a local Islamic legacy, rejection of the Lebanese state and

158   The Emergence of Tawhid

solidarity with both the Palestinian cause and the Syrian opposition. In other words, the Islamic Group came, for a while, to embody simultaneously the appeal of Islamism as an ideology as well as local, Tripolitan narratives and identities. This, in turn, explained the particular strength it acquired early on in the northern city. Yet signs were already emerging in the mid-1970s to suggest that the ideological commitments of the Islamic Group's own leaders were fast eroding under the dual effect of the movement's increasing institutionalization and oligarchization. From then on, the sense that the Islamic Group was betraying its ideals was a key factor which pushed some of its most militant figures to split, join the more radical Soldiers of God militia and ultimately Tawhid in 1982. By the 1980s, then, the Islamic Group had been outclassed as Tripoli's foremost Islamist movement.

It may seem surprising, at first glance, that the Islamic Group's revolutionary zeal began dying down as early as the mid-1970s. This, after all, was a period during which its leader, Fathi Yakan, was still publishing books which celebrated the legacy of Sayyid Qutb, the ideologue of the militant wing of the Egyptian Muslim Brotherhood and someone best known for instilling a revolutionary twist into Islamist ideology.[1] In a similar vein, the leader of the Islamic Group began advocating for the rise of what he called a "revolutionary Islam." Fathi Yakan's vision involved rejecting participation in institutionalized politics – an approach he called "gradualism." Instead, what Yakan envisaged was overthrowing the "illegitimate" Lebanese polity and replacing it with an "Islamic system" dominated by Muslims in which there would be "no compromise," with sovereignty belonging "to Allah alone."[2] If one only examined the declaratory ideology of the Islamic Group's leaders it was evident that they were still sincerely committed to a militant Islamist worldview.

But although this revolutionary Islamist discourse was striking a chord with many of its youths, the Islamic Group's leaders started entering the game of Lebanese politics. The movement ran for a parliamentary seat in Tripoli in 1972 and, after interpreting its defeat as a symptom of its isolation on the local and national political scene, it doubled down on the path of institutionalization. In 1973 it took a leading role in the

---

[1] For more background on Fathi Yakan and an analysis of his evolving positions, see: Ali Lagha, *Fathi Yakan: ra'ed al-haraka al-islamiya al mu'asira fi Lubnan* [*Fathi Yakan: pioneer of the Islamic movement in Lebanon*] (Beirut: Mu'assassat al-Risala, 1994) and Robert Rabil, "Fathi Yakan, the pioneer of Islamic activism in Lebanon" *Levantine Review* (Vol. 2, No. 1, 2013), pp. 54–65.

[2] Fathi Yakan quoted in Abdel Ghani Imad, *Al-harakat al-Islamiya fi Lubnan: al-din wa al-siyasa fi mujtam'a mutanawe'a* [*The Islamist movements in Lebanon: religion and politics in a diverse society*] (Beirut, Dar al-Talia, 2006), p. 62.

The Islamic Group Gets Outclassed 159

creation of the Islamic Gathering in the North (al-Tajamm'u al-Islami fi al-Shamel). This platform gathered North Lebanon's Sunni politicians of all stripes, whether Islamists or not, who engaged in wider consultations and alliances to lobby parliamentarians on "Muslim issues" such as granting citizenship to the stateless Sunni tribes of Wadi Khaled, in the northern countryside, or keeping Friday as a day off. But even though the platform became increasingly active in the mid to late 1970s it yielded little practical results. This pushed the Islamic Group's leadership to persist on the path of institutionalization. It continued its efforts to forge alliances and make compromises in order to have a greater impact in politics, at times even allying with Rashid Karame who, as we saw in Chapter 1, epitomized the embrace by Tripolitan notables of the Lebanese political system.[3] This attempt at becoming a more mainstream part of politics would actually prove fruitful, at least eventually, for it would earn the Islamic Group three seats in parliament in the first postwar legislative elections of 1992. But, in the mid-1970s, the movement's by-now apparent institutionalization began to give rise to severe internal tensions. A conflict started pitting the leaders who, for all their revolutionary discourse, showed growing pragmatism and a patent desire to become an active part of Lebanese politics, against a younger generation that had initially been enthusiastic about Fathi Yakan's call for a "revolutionary Islam" but was now increasingly disappointed by the direction the movement was taking. Tellingly, a joke which circulated back then among its militant youths was that their leaders no longer represented the "Islamic Group" (al-Jama'a al-Islamiya) but, instead, the "Lebanese Group" (al-Jama'a al-Lubnaniya).[4] This play on words conveyed grassroots disapproval with the movement's institutionalization.

Another criticism formulated by the Islamic Group's rank and file was the sense that, as they pursued institutionalization, their leaders were fast becoming motivated by self-serving goals rather than by commitment to the movement's ideology; that is, they were increasingly turning "oligarchized"[5] as sociologist Robert Michels would have said. Several of the

---

[3] Interview with Mohammed Ali Dannaoui (Islamic Group candidate at the 1972 election), Tripoli, July 2014. See also Timothy Richard Yousaf, *The Muslim Brotherhood in Lebanon (al-Jama'a al-Islamiya), 1948–2000* (Beirut: American University of Beirut, unpublished MPhil thesis, 2010), p. 43.

[4] Interviews with leading Islamic Group officials, Islamists who split and rank-and-file, Tripoli, July 2014.

[5] See: Robert Michels, *Political parties: a sociological study of the oligarchical tendencies of modern democracy* (New York City, Free Press, [1911], 1962) and Elizabeth S. Clemens and Debra C. Minkoff, "Beyond the Iron law: rethinking the place of organizations in social movement research," chapter 7 in David Snow, Sarah Soule and Hanspeter Kriesi

160   The Emergence of Tawhid

members who split back then thus reported feeling disenfranchised by the way a small clique of "founding fathers" began concentrating power and dismissing the concerns of the often younger rank-and-file activists, thus fueling the sense that these figures were more interested in keeping a hold of the movement's leadership than in fulfilling its ideology.[6] Reflective of this, it is telling that only one figure, Fathi Yakan, acted as the head of the Islamic Group for nearly thirty years, from 1964 until 1992, and that the other "founding fathers" around him confiscated the reins of the movement's other internal institutions. With time, the Islamic Group's institutionalization and oligarchization would fuel a sense among the base that the leaders, who once appeared sincerely dedicated to mobilizing "revolutionary Islam," were instrumentalizing ideology and no longer seemed truly committed to it.

Of course, as mentioned in Chapter 1, when the Lebanese civil war erupted in 1975 the Islamic Group engaged once again in contentious activities. Like most other Lebanese parties at the time it formed a full-blown militia, named the Holy Warriors (al-Mujahidun). Yet the very process of putting the movement's institutionalization on hold for a few years, and instead to suddenly militarize, proved controversial internally. The leaders, by their own account, were "cautious"[7] not to become trapped in feuds with other Lebanese Muslim and Christian forces that could negatively impact their future political prospects, especially as success in the Lebanese political system often depends on the ability to strike wider alliances. Under the pressure of an increasingly restless base the leaders still agreed, albeit reluctantly, that the Islamic Group form a militia, but they insisted that this militarization should be "well pre-pared" and "thought through." The relatively slow emergence of the Holy Warriors and the militia's subsequently modest role in the early stage of the Lebanese civil war, with involvement in clashes limited to the Tripoli-Zghorta front in 1975, would be a key factor in the split of dozens of militant youths who left the Islamic Group in the mid-1970s.

One of them, Fawwaz Hussein Agha, was a militant Tripolitan cleric who had long been at odds with the Islamic Group's growing embrace of institutionalization within the Lebanese political system. He was dismayed that the same leaders who, just years earlier, had been calling for a "revolutionary Islam" now seemed slow to grasp that the advent of

---

(eds.), *The Blackwell companion to social movements* (Oxford, Blackwell Publishing, 2007), pp. 155–71.

[6] Interviews with former Islamic Group members, Tripoli, August–July 2014.

[7] Interview with Abdallah Babetti (former head of Islamic Group political bureau), Tripoli, August 2014.

The Islamic Group Gets Outclassed 161

the civil war provided a golden opportunity to deliver on their professed objectives, such as support for the Palestinian cause, a profound change of the Lebanese political system and the nationwide implementation of Islamic law. After he split from the Islamic Group on the eve of the Lebanese civil war, Fawwaz Hussein Agha formed a new Islamist movement which immediately answered the call for a "revolutionary Islam" and would ultimately join Tawhid upon its formation in 1982. The very name of Agha's new faction, Soldiers of God (*Jund Allah*), hinted at the full extent to which it would not go down the path of institutionalization and oligarchization. Instead it sought to convey the sense that, contrary to the Islamic Group, this militia would be made up of sincerely committed militant Islamists guided by ideology.[8] One of its co-founders proudly remembered that it was the first "real" Tripolitan Islamist movement in the mid-1970s which "raised the black flag of jihad," its members dismissing Lebanon as a "Christian creation" and calling on local Sunnis to take up arms to "defend their religion."[9] Soldiers of God would never develop any intention of entering parliamentary politics, and instead advocated engaging in Islamist violence. Through the late 1970s, Soldiers of God gradually outclassed the Islamic Group as Tripoli's foremost Islamist movement, one popular with many local youths, until it merged into Tawhid in 1982.

At first, Soldiers of God's engagement in Islamist mobilization was peaceful. It began organizing religious demonstrations in the streets of Tripoli during which weapons would be brandished and militant Islamist slogans critical of the Lebanese government and of the country's Christians would be shouted, but without erupting into all-out violence. The goal of these demonstrations was unmistakably to recruit new members and earn a reputation as an ideologically committed and driven Islamist movement. "Soldiers of God soon became Lebanon's only true Islamist movement back then,"[10] recalled a former member proudly. And its strategy seemed to be successful. According to observers its religious demonstrations quickly grew "bigger and bigger," particularly as the "cultural momentum" of Islamism was growing in Tripoli, as described in Chapter 1. One such event, held on the occasion of the Prophet's birthday in 1975, was reportedly attended by several thousand Tripolitans.[11]

---

[8] Mohammed Abi Samra, *Trablus: Sehat Allah wa mina al-hadatha* [*Tripoli: Allah Square and port of modernity*] (Beirut: Dar al-Saqi, 2011), p. 138.
[9] Interview with Kan'an Naji (co-founder and later leader of Soldiers of God), Tripoli, August 2014.
[10] Interview with Hashem Minqara (former member of Soldiers of God), Tripoli, August 2014.
[11] Abi Samra, *Trablus*, p. 137.

162   The Emergence of Tawhid

Yet, as the Lebanese civil war erupted the same year, Soldiers of God also engaged in violence. In contrast with the Islamic Group's militia, the Holy Warriors, which was not only slow to emerge but then only took on a modest share in the fighting, Soldiers of God's members soon acquired a reputation for being committed and ruthless Islamist militants. They were fully loyal to Fatah and in particular to its underground Islamist wing, whose role is studied in greater depth in Chapter 7, undergoing intense paramilitary training in Palestinian refugee camps and then playing leading roles in several key battles which opposed the Muslim and Christian militias of North Lebanon, for example at Zghorta and Chekka in 1975 and 1976. There the involvement of Soldiers of God was such that the movement was even accused of engaging in what critics called sectarian massacres, although Islamist fighters deny these allegations, arguing that they merely "waged jihad."[12] They did not elaborate, but this was a hint that their behavior may have been ideologically driven.

The Syrian army's 1976 military intervention in Lebanon temporarily forced the militants to flee to South Lebanon, where there were no Syrian troops. There they not only fought the Israeli army, gaining further combat skills, but also forged connections with leading militant Syrian Islamists who were also in South Lebanon hiding from Syrian intelligence. The connection between Tripoli's and Syria's Islamists is also explored in Chapter 7, but at this point suffice it to say that the bond between them became sufficiently strong that Soldiers of God later came back to the northern city convinced to "wage jihad" against the "secular" Syrian army and its "infidel" Alawi allies in Jabal Mohsen, now both seen as the mortal ideological enemies of militant Sunni Islamism.[13] It was then, in 1980–2, that Soldiers of God began allying with the Popular Resistance whenever violent clashes erupted with Ali Eid's pro-Assad Arab Democratic Party, as Chapter 2 remarked. Yet, by then Soldiers of God's anti-regime views had already turned so ideological that its members also took the considerable risk of logistically helping Syrian Islamist groups like the Fighting Vanguard and the Syrian Muslim Brotherhood, providing them with weapons and ammunition and even sheltering and hiding them when members clandestinely visited Tripoli.[14] "We had no choice, we had to combat

[12] Interview with Abu Othman (military commander of Soldiers of God), Tripoli, September 2016 and interviews with rank-and-file Soldiers of God militants, Tripoli, August–September 2014.
[13] Joumana al-Soufi Richard, *Lutte populaire armée: de la désobéissance civile au combat pour Dieu* (Paris, Sorbonne University, unpublished PhD thesis, 1984), pp. 282–6.
[14] Interviews with current and former Soldiers of God members and Tripolitan Islamists, Tripoli, August 2014.

tyranny,"[15] argued a member of Soldiers of God. This forced the militia's leaders and members to operate clandestinely to a large extent and to take considerable risks. In fact, some of its officials were arrested and never seen again. Yet Soldiers of God's very willingness to stand by its militant Islamist ideology, in spite of the sometimes significant costs this entailed, and to take key roles in the successive struggles against Christian militias, the Israeli army, the Syrian regime and Tripoli's Alawis, rapidly turned it from a mere split of the Islamic Group into a movement attracting to its midst hundreds of committed Tripolitan Islamists. Showing sincere commitment to militant Islamism thus allowed Soldiers of God to ideologically "outbid"[16] the Islamic Group, as Donatella Della Porta might have said, and gain credibility.

By contrast the Islamic Group may have officially professed its solidarity for Syria's Islamists, in particular for the Syrian Muslim Brotherhood with which it had historically entertained strong relations and helped at the beginning of its struggle against the regime, but it soon stopped supporting them. This was partly a consequence of the movement's growing institutionalization in Lebanon's political system, which would have rendered continued interference in the domestic affairs of Syria, the powerful neighbor, very controversial. But it was also the product of the Syrian regime's own intimidation campaign. In 1979 and 1980 the Syrian authorities raided the Islamic Group's office in Tripoli and arrested its head, Fathi Yakan, and another of its top figures, the Tripolitan cleric Faysal Mawlawi.[17] They were both soon released but the arrest, even if temporary, of two of its most important figures nonetheless pushed the Islamic Group's leaders to be more cautious and to completely distance themselves from the Syrian Muslim Brotherhood. "The Syrian regime was too strong,"[18] argued an official. Yet this had a devastating effect on the Islamic Group's ideological credentials, especially with the militant youth that had already expressed frustration with the movement's institutionalization. "We really wanted the movement to do something about the situation in Syria," explained a former member

---

[15] Quoted in al-Soufi Richard, *Lutte populaire armée*, p. 285.

[16] Donatella della Porta, "Radicalization: a relational perspective" *Annual Review of Political Science* (Vol. 21, 2018), pp. 461–74.

[17] "Al-Jama'a al-Islamiya fi Trablus tanshur bayan 'an ekhtifaf Fathi Yakan" [The Islamic Group in Tripoli releases a statement on the kidnapping of Fathi Yakan], *Al-Incha* (November 17, 1979) and "Al-Jama'a al-Islamiya tushaker al-Ra'is Franjie 'ala muse'adtu fi qadiat ekhtifaf Fathi Yakan" ["The Islamic Group thanks President Franjieh for his help in the case of the kindapping of Fathi Yakan"], *Al-Incha* (November 18, 1979).

[18] Interview with Ibrahim al-Masri (leading official and then leader of the Islamic Group), Beirut, August 2014.

164   The Emergence of Tawhid

who left the Islamic Group because of its "passive"[19] attitude toward the Syrian opposition in the late 1970s. A former leader confirmed that the reluctance to get drawn in the Islamist struggle against the Syrian regime had allowed the Islamic Group to come out of this troubled period unscathed and even to secure a good working relationship with Damascus, something important to becoming more institutionalized, but that it cost the movement dearly in terms of its popularity.[20] Many of those who left the Islamic Group back then joined Soldiers of God, which stepped up its cooperation with the Popular Resistance after it embraced Islamism in 1980 and took a key role in the struggle against the Alawis and Syrian troops in Tripoli.

A last difference between Soldiers of God and the Islamic Group was the different social and spatial base the two Islamist movements came to cultivate. From the time of its creation in 1964, the Islamic Group had been composed of middle- and upper-middle-class doctors, lawyers, teachers and engineers who were sometimes even the scions of well-established Tripolitan families. In fact, the very process of becoming a member of the Islamic Group in itself seemed tailored to those generally well-educated Tripolitans. It involved graduating from eight courses on the Islamic Group's history and rules as well as on Islamist ideology (a stage called "the rings" or *al-halaqat*), before gradually moving into a series of "families" (*al-'usar*) meant to test the degree of loyalty of prospective members. Only after spending years going through this vetting process could candidates officially become members and later be considered for junior leadership positions.[21] This earned the Islamic Group a reputation for being socially elitist for, by definition, it excluded the growing number of illiterate Tripolitans, particularly the recently arrived mass of rural migrants and those whose work was so low paid, demanding and unstable that they could not afford to commit to such side activities.[22] Tellingly, the Islamic Group's offices in Tripoli were in Mina and Abu Samra, two middle-class neighborhoods. And its candidate for the 1972 parliamentary elections had been Mohammed Ali Dannawi, a lawyer from a longstanding Tripolitan family traditionally allied with the Karames, who epitomized the notability. The Islamic Group's embeddedness within Tripoli's economic and political power structures helps explain why the movement's leaders rapidly toned down

[19] Interview with former members of the Islamic Group who split in the 1970s, Tripoli, August 2014.
[20] Interview with Abdallah Babetti (former head of Islamic Group political bureau), Tripoli, August 2014.
[21] Imad, *Al-harakat al-Islamiya fi Lubnan*, pp. 79–83.
[22] Interviews with Islamist activists, Tripoli, August–September 2014.

The Islamic Group Gets Outclassed   165

their calls for a "revolutionary Islam" and instead attempted to become an institutionalized part of Tripolitan and Lebanese politics.

Of course, because Soldiers of God originally emerged as a split from the Islamic Group, a sizable proportion of its own members were at first solidly middle class too. The faction's stronghold was in parts of the Tripolitan middle-class district of Abu Samra, and it also came to exercise influence in Mina. Yet its social and spatial base rapidly expanded. In contrast with the Islamic Group, Soldiers of God did not require its potential recruits to go through any lengthy or sophisticated indoctrination process. Instead it was enough to attend the Friday sermons of its clerics and get a grasp of militant Islamist ideology. This opened the movement up to members of local society who had not always benefited from a full education, for example the Tripolitan lower middle class and rural migrants.[23] Its leader, Fawwaz Hussein Agha, and his powerful deputy, Kan'an Naji, themselves originally hailed from Tripoli's countryside of respectively Dinniye and Koura. In addition, the willingness of Soldiers of God to engage in contentious politics was proving increasingly attractive to a constituency that was fast becoming more impoverished through the mid to late 1970s. Sometimes Soldiers of God's obvious thirst for contention seemed enough to attract potential recruits who may have been more or less ideologically committed Islamists but also saw in militant Islamism a "protest ideology" channeling their socioeconomic and political grievances and reformulating in an Islamist frame local narratives of Tripoli as a "rebel city." It was no surprise, therefore, that the spatial base of Soldiers of God soon expanded from Abu Samra and Mina to parts of lower-middle-class neighborhoods such as the Old City and Qobbe, both characterized by much older histories of involvement in urban dissent.

For all these reasons, therefore, Soldiers of God gradually outclassed the Islamic Group as Tripoli's foremost Islamist movement through the mid to late 1970s; one with a reputation for being both more ideologically committed and socially open than its rival. According to Western intelligence assessments, it soon became composed of 250 members ready to engage in contention, the vast majority of them committed Islamists who had split from the Islamic Group.[24] They would soon merge within Tawhid upon its creation in 1982.

---

[23] Interviews with current and former members of Soldiers of God, Tripoli, August 2014.
[24] I draw the estimated number of Soldiers of God militants from interviews with members and leaders of the organization as well as from the CIA's own figures. See; US Central Intelligence Agency, "Lebanon: Islamic fundamentalism in Tripoli" (Top Secret, NESAR 86–003JX, January 17, 1986).

166   The Emergence of Tawhid

The Growth of Sufi Jihadism

In addition to the myriad splits which began plaguing the Islamic Group and to the simultaneous rise of Soldiers of God, another development that would comfort militant Islamism's growing momentum in Tripoli was the emergence of "Sufi jihadism." The politically revolutionary and socially conservative breed of Sufism which started spreading back then would contribute to Tawhid's rise, eventually also providing it with some of its most ideologically committed militants who pushed for involvement in Islamist violence.

At first glance the concept of "Sufi jihadism" to describe the politically revolutionary and socially conservative breed of Sufism which became prevalent in late 1970s Tripoli can seem counterintuitive. It may even appear a contradiction in terms given the extent to which Sufism has gained a reputation as a mystical and apolitical religious practice, one often described as carrying the potential to act as a counterweight to militant Islamist movements. Yet, while this may be true in a number of cases, scholars have also shown that, during times of instability, Sufi orders (*tariqat*) can also be politically active and even contentious.[25] The Sanusiya, after all, inspired wars of national liberation in Sudan and Libya. And, in the case of Syria and Lebanon, it would be the Naqshbandiya which would fulfill this mobilizing role.

The Naqshbandiya Sufi order was created in the twelfth century with a focus on strictly adhering to Islamic law. It spread from the Arabic peninsula to India, the Caucasus and Turkey, in all of which it played a role in stirring up contention against the authorities. In Syria the order became divided in the 1950s between an apolitical branch headed in Damascus by Ahmed Kuftaro, who passively supported the Syrian regime and became the Grand Mufti, and a politically active, contentious one centered on the city of Hama.[26] The "master," or head, of the Naqshbandiya there, Muhammad al-Hamid, was even the co-founder of the Syrian Muslim Brotherhood, and some of his pupils would join the group's militant offshoot, the Fighting Vanguard, in the 1970s.[27] In

---

[25] See, for instance, Itzchak Weismann's excellent volume: *The Naqshbandiyya: orthodoxy and activism in a worldwide Sufi tradition* (London: Routledge, 2007).

[26] Paulo Pinto, "Dangerous liaisons: Sufism and the state in Syria" *Crossing Boundaries* (Vol. 14, 2003), pp. 4–9.

[27] For more on the dynamics informing the local relation between Sufi orders and the Muslim Brotherhood in Hama see Itzchak Weismann's well-researched articles. Itzchak Weismann, "The politics of popular religion: Sufis, Salafis and Muslim Brothers in Twentieth Century Hamah" *International Journal of Middle East Studies* (Vol. 37, 2005), pp. 39–58 and Itzchak Weismann, "Sa'id Hawwa and Islamic revivalism in Ba'thist Syria" *Studia Islamica* (Vol. 85, 1997), pp. 131–54.

The Growth of Sufi Jihadism 167

Hama Sufi circles associated with the Naqshbandiya thus acquired the reputation of engaging in contention against the regime.

The developments taking place within Hama's Sufi religious scene were perhaps bound to affect Tripoli. As we saw in Chapter 1, Tripoli entertained particularly close geographical, historical, economic and social bonds with the Syrian hinterland, especially with the cities of Homs and Hama, and Sufism had long been an essential component of Islamic life in North Lebanon. It was therefore no surprise that the Naqshbandiya's rise in Hama would encourage its growth in Tripoli too. In turn, the mechanism behind this cross-border diffusion of ideas were world-renowned Sufi masters who toured the centuries-old Sufi lodges of Homs, Hama, Aleppo and Tripoli and spent much of their time teaching and trying to persuade locals to embrace Naqshbandi Sufism. Their activism already stood, in the 1920s and 30s, behind the embrace of the Naqshbandiya by a handful of deeply conservative Tripolitan figures, such as Rashid Rida. They also pushed members, in Tripoli as in Hama, to become more virulent in their criticism of the unorthodox practices characterizing more liberal Sufi orders such as the Mawlawiya and the Rifa'iya – famous for featuring rotating dances, fire eating and snake charming. The influence of the Naqshbandiya further grew in the 1970s as social mores became more distinctively conservative in Tripoli. The order reached its apogee in the city during the late 1970s when the port district of Mina came to host Muhammad Nazim al-Haqqani. This world-renowned Turkish Sufi master of the Naqshbandiya order strove to spread a contentious breed of Sufism to the Syrian cities of Hama and Aleppo, where he was teaching at the time, as well as to Tripoli, where he used to stop on his journeys between Syria and his home in Cyprus.[28] He acted as an "ideological entrepreneur," a highly committed figure mobilizing "Sufi jihadi" worldviews and seeking to mold the nature of activism and of the broader ideological environment around them.

Because this "ideological entrepreneur" did not wish to be arrested by the authorities for subversive activities, the type of religious discourse he preached was not openly political. He did not, for instance, call as such for the overthrow of secular Arab regimes or for the advent of Islamic revolutions like in Iran. Yet the millenarian and often violent rhetoric he espoused nonetheless paved the way for the spread of what one scholar of Tripoli's Sufis called an "apocalyptic ideology."[29] Muhammad Nazim al-

---

[28] Daphne Habibis, *A comparative study of the workings of a branch of the Naqshbandi Sufi order in Lebanon and the UK* (London: London School of Economics and Political Science, unpublished PhD thesis, 1985) pp. 59–119.

[29] Daphne Habibis, "Millenarianism and Mahdism in Lebanon" *European Journal of Sociology* (Vol. 30, No. 2, 1989), p. 235.

168   The Emergence of Tawhid

Haqqani was particularly known for the prophecies he formulated regarding the imminent return of the Mahdi – the Islamic equivalent of the Messiah. In a 1979 sermon in Tripoli he typically expressed his belief that "the divine sword of the Mahdi" will soon "come to cut off all the evils and devils now governing the world." He continued: "For every period there is a limit [...] Now we are in the period of tyrants. They have their limit and then, finished! [...] Every day the world is approaching this limit. It is the Third World War."[30] The contentious way in which the Sufi cleric framed his prophecies rapidly found a local echo in a context marked by Syria's military occupation of Tripoli, the plight suffered by Palestinian refugees, a seemingly never-ending Lebanese civil war and the growing deterioration of socio-economic conditions. The Mahdi's return, indeed, would come to signal the end of all these ills and herald Islam's victory against the *dajjal* – a satanic figure embodying the "unbelievers," however one chose to define them. And what made the appeal of these prophecies even more powerful in the northern city was the Sufi cleric's insistence that, while the Mahdi was momentarily hiding in Saudi Arabia, he would publicly appear in 1979 and make his way to Tripoli before the world would end. If one wanted to be a true Sufi, then, one would have to be prepared to fight for the Mahdi. The apocalyptic and contentious breed of Sufism mobilized by this "ideological entrepreneur" rapidly met a degree of success in Tripoli, where his lectures and prayer circles became overcrowded as he rapidly formed a pool of over 400 dedicated local followers. Longstanding cross-border ties thus facilitated the diffusion of militant Islamist ideas in Tripoli which Sufi Naqshbandi "ideological entrepreneurs" were spreading in Hama.

Their millenarian prophecies set the stage for the radicalization of many Tripolitan Islamists. This became especially the case after rumors spread that Juhayman al-Utaybi, a prominent Saudi Islamist figure critical of the Saudi regime, had also dreamed that the Mahdi would return in November 1979. In a show of how such prophecies played a considerable role in stirring up contention, the Saudi Islamist gathered dozens of followers and seized Mecca's Great Mosque, taking thousands of worshipers hostage for two weeks and waiting for the Mahdi to appear before launching a full-blown revolution.[31] The event prompted a group of half a dozen Tripolitan Islamists who had been inspired by Muhammad

---

[30] Ibid.

[31] On this important yet often overlooked event of Middle Eastern history and politics, see the excellent work of Thomas Hegghammer and Stéphane Lacroix: "Rejectionist Islamism in Saudi Arabia: the story of Juhayman al-'Utaybi revisited" *International Journal of Middle East Studies* (Vol. 39, 2007), pp. 103–22.

The Growth of Sufi Jihadism 169

Nazim al-Haqqani's "apocalyptic ideology" to buy tickets for Saudi Arabia. They hoped to fight with Juhayman al-Utaybi and to give allegiance (*al-bay'a*) to the Mahdi when he would appear, which would then lead to wider Islamist revolutions throughout the Middle East.[32]

One of the Tripolitan Islamists who was inspired by such prophecies was Ali Mer'aib, who was best known in the city as "Abu Imara." In his early thirties, he had been one of the many youths who had split from the Islamic Group out of the combined dislike of its oligarchization, institutionalization, growing withdrawal from any form of contentious politics and sense of social elitism. Although he was not a committed Sufi himself, he had been inspired by the millenarian and contentious ideology of Muhammad Nazim al-Haqqani. Upon his arrival at Riyadh's airport, however, the Saudi authorities arrested him right away. According to a figure close to him, Abu Imara then spent the next year and a half in a single cell, a period during which he read dozens of books by militant Islamist thinkers and further radicalized his views on Arab regimes and in particular on the Syrian regime.[33] He was released in September 1981 and returned to Tripoli, where he became celebrated as a true "jihadi hero" in militant Islamist circles. Abu Imara, by the simple virtue of having tried to join "the Mahdi," al-Utaybi, of having been sent to jail in Saudi Arabia and of having read dozens of Islamist books, then self-styled himself as a militant "cleric," forcibly taking over a large mosque in the lower-middle-class neighborhood of Qobbe and rapidly building a large following of local youths who admired his "courage."[34] Abu Imara would a year later join Tawhid upon its creation and rise as one of its most vocal "ideological entrepreneurs" until his death in 1984, constantly lobbying for the movement to engage in ideological behavior.

The rest of those Tripolitan Islamists who had traveled to "rescue" Juhayman al-Utaybi made it safely to Saudi Arabia. And, in a show of how important the prophecies of Muhammad Nazim al-Haqqani seem to have been, rumors still circulate today that at least one member of this group, Hashem Minqara, "met with the Mahdi"[35] while in Saudi Arabia. The millenarian and contentious prophecies had had a particularly powerful effect on Hashem Minqara for he was a deeply committed Sufi. In fact, his father was a prominent Sufi master himself and even acted as the Tripolitan representative of Uthman Sirajeddine

---

[32] Abi Samra, *Trablus*, p. 140.

[33] Interview with Ibrahim Antar (Islamist militant close to Abu Imara), Tripoli, August 2014.

[34] Interviews with former partisans of Abu Imara, Tripoli, August 2014.

[35] Interview with Ibrahim Saleh (Islamist official formerly close to Hashem Minqara), Tripoli, August 2014.

170   The Emergence of Tawhid

al-Naqshbandi, an Iraqi Sufi cleric and the famed head of the Naqshbandi-Qadiri order. "My first step when I was born was to walk in the direction of the prayer circles (*al-dhikr*) led by my father,"[36] remembered Hashem Minqara in all seriousness. He started learning passages of the Quran by heart and, according to Tripolitans who heard him speak back then, he was particularly skilled at reciting them with passion to the public. Yet, unlike his father, who was purely interested in religion and not in politics, he became driven by the contentious breed of Naqshbandi Sufism which Muhammad Nazim al-Haqqani was spreading in the port neighborhood of Mina, where the Minqara family had just settled. This pushed him, as early as his twenties, to join Soldiers of God, for there seemed to be no other Islamist movement willing to take up the mantle of "jihad" at the time. It also helped that the deputy head and soon-to-be-leader of Soldiers of God, Kan'an Naji, had himself religious roots in the Tabligh, a grassroots Islamic movement with origins in Sufism. Hashem Minqara and Kan'an Naji both felt committed to Islam in mystic ways, "more through emotion than through reason," as the former explained. The 1979 seizure of Mecca's Great Mosque by Juhayman al-Utaybi deeply inspired them both and they began dreaming that the "Islamic waves"[37] unleashed from Saudi Arabia, Iran and Syria would soon reach the shores of Tripoli. The emotional and millenarian breed of militant Islamism which they began spreading, one full of grand ideological certainties, would be a feature of Tawhid's discourse and become key to motivating, indeed to galvanizing, some members to engage in ideologically driven violence.

From One Protest Ideology to Another

Another development which bolstered the local ideological momentum of militant Islamism in the late 1970s was the embrace by a group of Tripolitan Maoists of a type of Islamism which I describe, in the next section, as "Sunni Khomeinism," for their striking commitment to the ideological aims espoused by the Islamic Republic of Iran. Chapter 2 already tackled how the embrace of militant Islamism as a "protest ideology" was the mechanism which explained the Popular Resistance's instrumental shift from revolutionary Marxism to Islamism, because the latter became seen after the 1979 Iranian Revolution as the quintessential rebel ideology that would channel neighborhood grievances into activism. Yet, for its part, the case of the ideological conversion of the

---

[36] Interview with Hashem Minqara, Tripoli, August 2014.
[37] Interviews with Hashem Minqara and Kan'an Naji, Tripoli, August 2014.

From One Protest Ideology to Another 171

Tripolitan Maoists to Islamism differed from that of the Popular Resistance in two significant respects. First, their shift was not guided by local concerns but, rather, by the willingness to cast in locally popular frames their preexisting and broader commitments, for example attachment to the Palestinian cause and to a wider anti-imperialist agenda. And, second, while their embrace of Islamism was also initially instrumental, it progressively transformed into more sincere commitments.

Unlike the case of the Popular Resistance, then, the ideological conversion of these Tripolitan Maoists from one "protest ideology" to another was not a neighborhood- or city-specific phenomenon. It was, instead, reflective of a much wider trend which affected an entire pool of anti-imperialist and pro-Palestinian leftist activists of Fatah scattered all throughout Lebanon and who went on to join Islamist groups such as Tawhid, Hezbollah and Islamic Jihad.[38] Originally these activists belonged to the Student Brigade (*al-Katiba al-Tulabiya*). This faction within Fatah comprised Lebanese and Palestinian student activists and young intellectuals. They came from diverse religious backgrounds, whether Sunni, Shia or Christian; yet all saw in the "Palestinian revolution," as the PLO called the struggle for self-determination, not only a noble political cause worthy of support but also a starting point for broader revolutionary change in the Arab world. Most of these young activists had initially been attracted by pan-Arab ideologies. But the humiliation of the 1967 and 1973 Arab defeats against Israel and the beginning of the Egyptian–Israeli peace process had pushed them to embrace more revolutionary breeds of leftism such as Marxism and, shortly later, Maoism. Behind their embrace of successive "protest ideologies," then, stood preexisting commitments to the Palestinian cause as well as to an anti-imperialist political orientation.

In a show of the large degree of continuity hiding behind an ideological conversion which, from the outside, seemed sudden and contradictory, three elements had drawn these student activists toward Maoism which would later also find expression in Islamism.

First, they were inspired by the Maoist concept of the *khatt al-jamahir* ("line of the masses") which poses as a condition for a successful revolution that its leaders must immerse themselves in the masses and their

---

[38] Historian Nicolas Dot Pouillard has written extensively on the trajectory and profile of these Maoists-turned-Islamists. See his well-researched work: Nicolas Dot Pouillard, "De Pekin à Teheran en regardant vers Jerusalem: La singulière conversion à l'islamisme des 'Maos du Fatah'" *Cahiers de l'Institut Religioscope* (No. 2, December 2008) and Wissam Alhaj and Nicolas Dot Pouillard, *De la théologie à la libération? Histoire du Jihad Islamique palestinien* (Paris: La Decouverte, 2014).

172   The Emergence of Tawhid

mindset in order to relate to people's conditions.[39] A former Student Brigade militant recalled that this philosophy pushed him, an upper-middle-class student at a prestigious Lebanese university, to seek to "build bridges"[40] with populations on the ground. The activists typically did so by going to live in South Lebanon where they fought the Israeli army and lost over forty men in battles between 1976 and 1978. A second element which brought these pro-Palestinian militants closer to Maoism was their deep-seated anti-imperialism. They may have been opposed to the United States, which they saw as unconditionally backing Israel's existence and expansion in the region, yet they were also mistrustful of the Soviet Union – this became especially prevalent after the 1979 Soviet invasion of Afghanistan. And third, in their quest to create the conditions for the rise of a "people's war" targeting Israel, the United States and the Soviet Union, they sought to devise a "theory of liberation" with indigenous undertones. Another Student Brigade militant thus stressed the emphasis the group placed on respecting local traditions while in South Lebanon. This was seen as a key factor behind the success of a revolutionary movement like the Vietcong. The group's leaders dismissed Marxist rhetoric, which was seen as polarizing, and instead revived concepts coined centuries ago by Arab intellectual Ibn Khaldoun such as *hadara* ("civilization"), *moumana'a* ("resistance") and *ghalaba* ("domination"). These concepts that had a long history, and thus a resonance, in the Arab world allowed Student Brigade activists to frame their commitment to anti-imperialism in terms that would be understood locally.[41] What had initially pushed the Student Brigade to embrace Maoism, then, was its ability to act as a "protest ideology" casting the Palestinian and anti-imperialist causes in locally understandable frames. This, in the context of Islamism's broader cultural and political momentum in the late 1970s and 1980s, would now push them to embrace this ideology.

The 1979 Iranian Revolution and the ways in which Iran, once led by the pro-Western, secular and autocratic Shah, was now guided by revolutionary clerics who not only seemed to have the support of large chunks of the population but also rapidly took the helm of the global anti-imperialist movement, left a deep mark on the Student Brigade militants.

---

[39] This paragraph draws on a lengthy interview given by Fatah official Munir Chafiq to Nicolas Dot Pouillard and on observations made by Manfred Sing in an excellent article retracing the transformation of some Student Brigade fighters from Maoism to Jihadism. See Manfred Sing, "Brothers in arms: how Palestinian Maoists turned Jihadists" *Die Welt des Islams* (Vol. 51, 2011), pp. 10–16.

[40] Interview with a former Fatah Student Brigade militant, Beirut, June 2014.

[41] Interviews with former Fatah Student Brigade militants, Beirut, June 2014.

From One Protest Ideology to Another

While not all of the group's Maoist activists then became Islamists, patterns of ideological conversion were still sufficiently stark that it even affected some of its Christian members. The best known of them was Munir Shafiq. A high-ranking Palestinian Christian official in Fatah, he was the Maoist intellectual who had been the brains behind the Student Brigade. One scholar who studied this figure's ideological and religious transformation in depth dates his "Islamic coming-out"[42] back to 1981 when he published an important book. In it he celebrated the 1979 Iranian Revolution, and in particular its popular, pro-Palestinian and anti-imperialist dimensions. These elements pushed him to embrace Islamism. "We rediscovered a culture and a civilization, Islam," he said. "The conditions for a revolution can only come from within the history of a society and its deep interior. And, in this deep interior, there is Islam, whether you like it or not, whether you want it or not."[43] For Munir Shafiq Islamism was thus a "protest ideology" to be embraced instrumentally. Because it was based on a religious discourse and practice that was, given the "cultural momentum" of Islamism in the late 1970s, becoming widespread in the Middle East, articulating a pro-Palestinian and anti-imperialist agenda around it had the potential to attract the masses to his revolutionary cause. Using religious concepts that had a long history and were sometimes associated with a high contentious potential, like jihad and the need to defend the *umma*, or community of believers, was likely to resonate locally and form the basis of the anti-imperialist revolution. In a show of the lengths to which he was ready to go in his embrace of Islamism as a "protest ideology" meant to channel his pro-Palestinian and anti-imperialist orientation into activism, Munir Shafiq converted to Islam and sponsored the rise of Islamic Jihad (*al-Jihad al-Islami*).

Because Munir Shafiq had initially played a leading role in the Student Brigade, his embrace of Islamism as the new "protest ideology" to articulate commitments to the Palestinian cause and to anti-imperialism influenced many of the group's Maoist members who were scattered throughout Lebanon – including in Tripoli, where they were led by Esmat Murad. This Tripolitan medical doctor had grown close to Fatah's Student Brigade after becoming committed to the "Palestinian revolution" and to a broader anti-imperialist agenda as a student in Toulouse, France, where he had joined Maoist networks in the fever of May 1968. A figure who knew him well and studied with him in Toulouse recounted that while there he became key to three overlapping

---

[42] Manfred Sing, *Op. cit.*, p. 5.
[43] Quoted in Pouillard, "De Pekin à Teheran en regardant vers Jerusalem," p. 25.

174   The Emergence of Tawhid

social movements that shaped his political orientation.[44] While, in the *Comité Palestine*, he organized pro-Palestinian marches in several French cities, he coordinated with Lebanese students in the *Union Générale des Etudiants Libanais de France*, and was in addition very active in the Maoist-inspired *Comité de Liaison Anti-Impérialiste*. The 1973 Arab defeat was a "trauma,"[45] according to his brother, one which prompted him to return to Lebanon and join the "Palestinian revolution" as a fighter. He developed a strong relationship with Abu Jihad (Khalil al-Wazir), the Palestinian official responsible for overseeing Fatah's paramilitary activities and who, conscious of Esmat Murad's preexisting commitments, capacity to build networks and ability to mobilize, tasked him with returning to Tripoli and recruiting a group of committed pro-Palestinian militants. There Esmat Murad attracted to his cause dozens of educated middle-class youths, and his Maoist-inspired faction expanded to Beirut and the Beqaa Valley. This culminated in the 1975 creation of the Union of the Nationalist Youth (*Ittihad al-Sha'abib al-Watani*) which became, upon Israel's 1978 invasion of South Lebanon, the Movement of the Earth (*Harakat al-Ard*), and shortly thereafter the Movement of Arab Lebanon (*Harakat Lubnan al-'Arabi*).[46]

According to a high-ranking Palestinian official, although the Movement of Arab Lebanon ostensibly acted as an ideologically Maoist and politically independent Lebanese militia, it always remained a "trump card"[47] in Fatah's hands, or a faction fully dedicated to the Palestinian cause and to fighting its enemies, both Israel and right-wing Lebanese militias. Tellingly, its reputation as a Lebanese mouthpiece and forward arm for the Palestinian guerrilla organization was such that in Tripoli it was jokingly known as the "Movement of the Lebanese Fatah"[48] (*Harakat Fatah al-Lubnaniya*). Fighters from Esmat Murad's Maoist movement shared the same training camps as those from the Student Brigade. Moreover, they often carried out joint operations in South Lebanon. Together, for instance, they fortified Beaufort Castle (*Qala'at al-Shafiq*), a Crusader fortress lying on a hill above the Litani River, from where they launched rockets against the Israeli army and its local allies. A Fatah commander who was a key to the pro-Palestinian Maoist network formed by the Movement of Arab Lebanon and the

---

[44] Interview with Ghassan Ghose, Tripoli, June 2014.
[45] Interview with Nasser Murad, Tripoli, June 2014.
[46] Interviews with former members of the Movement of the Arab Lebanon, Tripoli and Beirut, June–July 2014.
[47] Interview with a high-ranking Palestinian security official in Fatah, Beirut, May 2014.
[48] Interview with Abu Zghayar (military commander in the Popular Resistance), July 2014.

Student Brigade explained that the only real difference between them both was that the former had "more space to express its political identity"[49] because it was made up of exclusively Lebanese activists and was therefore not officially integrated into Fatah's organization chart. This may explain why Esmat Murad's Maoist movement ended up embracing Islamism so openly and early on – an ideological conversion which, significantly, took place before Munir Shafiq's own conversion in 1981.

Instrumental or Sincere Embrace of Khomeinism?

The Movement of Arab Lebanon's shift from Maoism to Islamism did not primarily reside in the influence of Munir Shafiq's writings, which would merely accompany and bolster the dynamic of ideological conversion already at play within Esmat Murad's group. Instead, the origin of the Movement of Arab Lebanon's embrace of Islamism stemmed from its growing ties to a group of highly committed Iranian Islamists who were partisans of Ayatollah Ruhollah Khomeini and were fighting Israel in South Lebanon in 1977–8. Socialization and education into ideology through close interactions with these "ideological entrepreneurs" largely explained Esmat Murad's own conversion to Islamism and clarified why he came to embrace a breed of Islamism which I qualify as "Sunni Khomeinism" for its striking commitment to the aims espoused by the Islamic Republic of Iran. Importantly, although at first he embraced Islamism instrumentally as a "protest ideology," it would gradually turn into sincere commitments. In fact, when a few years later the Movement of Arab Lebanon joined Tawhid, it would provide it with some of its most committed Islamists and a strong link to Iran, tackled in Chapter 7. This shows the fluidity of ideological commitments and the possibility that instrumental embraces of ideology turn more sincere.

The seeds of the Movement of Arab Lebanon's ideological shift were planted before Munir Shafiq's conversion in 1981. They originate in the exile of a dozen upper-middle-class Iranians who were highly committed Islamists and, persecuted by the Shah, escaped in the mid and late 1970s to Lebanon, where they participated in the struggle against Israel waged by Palestinian guerrillas and by their Lebanese allies.[50] A figure close to Iranian intelligence explained that, from his Iraqi exile of Najaf, Ayatollah Khomeini coordinated their arrival in Beirut so that they could

---

[49] Interview with Anis Naqqash, Beirut, June 2014.
[50] Interview with Selim Lababidi (former commander in the Movement of Arab Lebanon), Beirut, May 2014.

176   The Emergence of Tawhid

gain fighting experience there.[51] Once they landed, Abu Jihad, the senior official in Fatah in charge of coordinating paramilitary activities, dispatched these Iranian volunteers to Palestinian training camps in South Lebanon. He chose to send them to the camps controlled by the Maoist network made up of the Movement of Arab Lebanon and the Student Brigade, for members of the two groups may have been leftists but, as was seen, they were also respectful of traditions, well educated and shared the anti-imperialist and pro-Palestinian political orientation of the newcomers. The Iranians thus quickly felt "at ease,"[52] said a militant who took a leading role in these camps where transnational Khomeinist networks interacted with Lebanese and Palestinian Maoists.

One such Iranian Islamist volunteer fighter, Jalaleddine al-Farsi, grew particularly close to Esmat Murad during his time in Fatah's South Lebanese camps.[53] The two men had much in common. The Iranian figure, like him, was well educated and had always been an ardent anti-imperialist. He had, in fact, earned fame in Iran in the 1950s as a prominent advocate of nationalist Prime Minister Muhammad Mossadegh, who was critical of the West and had eventually been overthrown by a US-backed coup d'état in 1953. Unlike the Maoist Esmat Murad, however, Jalaleddine al-Farsi had become more religious in the 1960s and 1970s and was even said to have translated a version of the Quran into Persian. One man who knew him well described him as a "Shia jihadist"[54] to highlight the extent to which, although he had once been a nationalist, he had turned by the 1970s into a highly committed Islamist "ideological entrepreneur" seeking to spread a militant breed of Shia Islam. Sought by the powerful intelligences services of the Shah of Iran, he left Tehran precipitately and came to Lebanon where he fought for several years alongside the Movement of Arab Lebanon. There, by all accounts, he spent a lot of time conveying his support for Ruhollah Khomeini, who was back then still a leading opposition cleric.[55] His backing for the Ayatollahs would be rewarded after the revolution when the clerics nominated him as a candidate in Iran's 1980 presidential

---

[51] Interview with Anis Naqqash (former Fatah commander close to Iranian intelligence), Beirut, June 2014.

[52] Interview with Selim Lababidi (former commander in the Movement of Arab Lebanon), Beirut, May 2014.

[53] Interview with Ibrahim Saleh (former Tawhid official close to Esmat Murad), Tripoli, April 2014.

[54] Interview with Anis Naqqash (former Fatah commander close to Iranian intelligence), Beirut, June 2014.

[55] Interviews with former militants from the Movement of Arab Lebanon, Tripoli and Beirut, June 2014.

elections.[56] In the meantime he had also socialized and educated Esmat Murad into "Khomeinism," underlining how interactions with "ideological entrepreneurs" can be an underlying mechanism behind shifts from one ideology to another.

By a "Khomeinist" ideology, I allude to the breed of Islamism spearheaded by Iran after 1979, which consisted not only in supporting the overthrow of secular regimes and the establishment of Islamic Republics characterized by clerical guidance over politics, but also in backing Iran's post-1979 anti-imperialist foreign policy and bid for regional leadership.

At first glance the notion of "Sunni Khomeinism" can appear exaggerated. Although much has been written about the 1979 Iranian Revolution's influence on Shia Islamist movements in the Middle East such as Hezbollah, the extent of the influence of this watershed moment of regional history on Sunni Arabs remains largely overlooked.[57] Moreover, the sense that the Sunni–Shia sectarian gap was always too large to bridge comforts analyses that dismiss the Iranian Revolution's impact on Sunni Islamist movements. Yet it is striking how myriad such movements, as was seen in the case of the Popular Resistance in Chapter 2, applauded the Iranian Revolution whether they were Islamists or not. The Movement of Arab Lebanon, with its anti-imperialist instincts, was particularly vocal in its support for the anti-Israeli and anti-American dimensions of the Shah's downfall. To its members, the revolution represented first and foremost a "strike against imperialism."[58] In Tripoli, for instance, they started celebrating Quds Day, the "International Day for Jerusalem" initiated by the new Iranian leaders to show support for the Palestinian cause.[59]

Soon enough, however, the Movement of Arab Lebanon went further than most of the other Sunni movements which, whether Islamist or not, had at first applauded the Iranian Revolution but quickly became more

---

[56] This builds on interviews with figures close to Esmat Murad, Tripoli, October–November 2014. Note that although al-Farsi was nominated as candidate, he was later disqualified as his father was from Afghanistan.

[57] The only works to explicitly tackle the Revolution's impact on Sunni Islamists are: Mohammad Ataie, "Revolutionary Iran's 1979 endeavour in Lebanon" *Middle East Policy* (Vol. 10, No. 2, 2013); Toby Matthiesen, "The Iranian Revolution and Sunni Political Islam" *POMEPS Studies* (Vol. 28, 2017), pp. 36–9 and Shadi Hamid and Sharan Grewal, "Emboldened and then constrained: repercussions of Iran's Revolution for Sunni Islamists," chapter 22 in Suzanne Maloney (ed.), *The Iranian Revolution at Forty* (Washington DC: Brookings Institution Press, 2020).

[58] "Iran wal thawra: tasfa'a al-imbiryaliya" ["The Iranian Revolution: a strike against imperialism], *Sawt al-Shabiba al-Wataniya* (July 15, 1979).

[59] "Nashatat Harakat Lubnan al-'Arabi: ittihad al-shabiba al-wataniya fil shamal ["The activities of the Movement of Arab Lebanon: the national youth union in the North"], *Sawt al-Shabiba al-Wataniya* (September 1, 1979).

178   The Emergence of Tawhid

skeptical of its increasingly Shia and Khomeinist aspects. Esmat Murad's Maoist movement, indeed, acquired a reputation as a staunch backer of the Ayatollahs. At a time marked by murky and violent power struggles within Iran's new political and security galaxy, the Movement of Arab Lebanon went as far as taking a stand, vehemently defending the deeds of the hardline faction sponsored by the Ayatollahs. In its publications the movement started openly praising Mohammed Montazeri, a clerical and military figure who had been key to the network of Iranian volunteers in South Lebanon, became a founding member of the Islamic Revolutionary Guards and acted as an Islamist "ideological entrepreneur."[60] The movement also lambasted the 1979 Kurdish rebellion in Iran for being backed by "foreign conspirers" trying to stir up a Sunni–Shia conflict to undermine the new regime. It supported the Islamic Republic's bloody crackdown on Kurdish rebels, which caused 12,000 deaths, by stating that "we must protect [the revolution] in any way we can." It openly called on "all faithful Muslims and true revolutionists" to "stand by Islam and the revolution" and to "support Khomeini's leadership" as he "always presented a good example of how to destroy enemies and lead the revolution to a safe conclusion in spite of all the obstacles."[61] The movement's loyalty to the hardliners in Iran was rewarded as early as 1980. Back then, Esmat Murad was invited for a high-profile visit to Tehran, where he reportedly met with prominent political and security officials and developed close relationships with them. In the next two years he would go back to Iran eight more times, underlining the extent to which these relationships quickly deepened.[62]

By then, inspired by Jalaleddine al-Farsi, Esmat Murad had become a practicing Muslim, yet Maoism continued to structure his thinking for a few additional years, showing once again the overlaps and great deal of continuity between the two "protest ideologies." First he wanted to immerse himself in the masses in order to learn from them and design a locally appealing ideology that would mobilize around the struggle against imperialism. Whereas he had previously spent some time fighting Israel with his faction in South Lebanon, he decided to go back to his hometown of Tripoli where he began residing and even opened a small clinic. It soon became clear to him that in Tripoli, in which Sunni

---

[60] "Iran wal thawra: tasfa'a al-imbiryaliya" ["The Iranian Revolution: a strike against imperialism], *Sawt al-Shabiba al-Wataniya* (July 15, 1979).

[61] "Ishtidad al-ta'amur 'ala al-Thawra al-Iraniya yazid min ilifafina hawlaha wa sanabqa: m'a al-Islam, m'a intisar al-Thawra 'ala al-ad'a'a" ["The more they conspire against Iran, the more firmly we will support it: for Islam and for the Revolution's victory over all enemies"], *Sawt al-Shabiba al-Wataniya* (September 1, 1979).

[62] Abi Samra, *Trablus*, p. 136.

Muslims made up over 80 percent of the population, Islam was the "obvious ideology"[63] around which his agenda had to be formulated. As a result he started giving speeches in mosques and holding charity events there. One such event, in September 1979, led to the collection of clothes which were then distributed to 300 poor children in Tripoli.[64] The success of this charity event showed that Islam had the local capacity to bring people together and provide a platform upon which to mobilize.

The second way in which Maoism continued to structure Esmat Murad's thinking, despite the fact that he had by now become a practicing Sunni Muslim, was his attempt to "speak to the masses" in understandable terms. That is, he was guided by the goal of framing his grand anti-imperialist instincts in a manner that would sound appealing locally. Interestingly, he did so by openly embracing some of the local "tales of contention" which historically associated Tripoli with a "rebel city," as Chapter 1 showed. Drawing parallels between Tripoli's legacy of resistance against external enemies and Israel's aggression against Lebanon, Syria's occupation of Tripoli and US expansionism in the Middle East allowed Esmat Murad to make his sympathizers better grasp the importance of fighting imperialism.

In one of his articles, for instance, he hinted at the need to struggle against the growth of Western cultural, political and military influence by recounting Tripoli's collective resistance and heroic victory against the powerful Christian emperor of Byzantium, Basil II, in 995. He concluded his article by stating that "Byzantium's raid on Tripoli" had ended because Basil II's troops "could not defeat the determination of the city's people despite their small number." "The Tripolitans did not surrender in the face of the [emperor's] huge army, numerous ships, and long siege,"[65] he insisted. This underlines how, by reviving local "tales of contention," movements seek to signal belonging to the community, activate the solidarities that bind its members and frame activism as a duty in line with local history.

In a show of how successful the Movement of the Arab Lebanon's growing mix of an embrace of Islamist rhetoric and of the Tripolitan "tales of contention" were becoming, Murad's movement, once

---

[63] Interview with Abu Shawqi (former official in the Movement of Arab Lebanon), Tripoli, August 2014.

[64] "Nashatat Harakat Lubnan al-'Arabi: ittihad al-shabiba al-wataniya fil shamal ["The activities of the Movement of Arab Lebanon: the national youth union in the North"], *Sawt al-Shabiba al-Wataniya* (September 1, 1979).

[65] "Intisarat al-'arab: Trablus tatahadda hisar al-binzantiyin" ["Victories of the Arab: Tripoli overcomes the Byzantine siege," *Sawt al-Shabiba al-Wataniya* (January 1, 1980).

180   The Emergence of Tawhid

composed of a few dozen members, soon enlarged to include 300 activists, mostly educated Tripolitan youths and traders from middle-class backgrounds.[66] Tellingly, they mostly hailed from the neighborhood of Zehriye, where tales of Tripolitan history were particularly widespread because of its own architectural beauty dating to Ottoman times, and its proximity to the Old City, built by the Mameluks 800 years ago.[67]

Third, and lastly, Esmat Murad inherited from Maoism key anti-imperialist concepts which he reframed in the Islamist vocabulary back then used by the Islamic Republic of Iran, demonstrating again the great degree of continuity between the two "protest ideologies" of revolutionary leftism and Islamism. Thus the Maoist category of "the oppressed" became "the Islamic world" since the Third World was anyway composed of Muslims by "more than half." The Third World's semantic opposition to "the oppressor" transformed into "a battle between good and evil." The latter category, according to Murad's Maoist thinking, was made up of a "first enemy," the United States, "trying to provoke the West into a war against Islam," and a "second enemy," the Soviet Union, whose "cruel intention" was to "suppress the Afghan Islamic Revolution." All-out war against both was inevitable but victory would now only come through the "sword of religion." "We realize that one of the most supreme objectives of Islam is to defeat the tyrants and the oppressors," wrote Esmat Murad. "Islam can be a great weapon in the hands of the Muslims and all the oppressed people around the world."[68] Comparing religion to a "weapon" in the struggle against imperialism showed how initially instrumental Esmat Murad's embrace of Islamism as a "protest ideology" had been. Figure 3.1 illustrates how, in 1979–80, the magazine of Esmat Murad's Maoist-leaning Movement of Arab Lebanon featured themes and a discourse increasingly characterized by the ideological imprint of Khomeinist Islamism.

Yet, with time the rhetoric employed by the Movement of Arab Lebanon took on a life of its own, becoming more distinctively and homogeneously Islamist. There seemed to be a self-fulfilling prophecy at play. Initially used as a "protest ideology" because of its high contentious potential and its ability to reframe Murad's preexisting commitments to anti-imperialism and the Palestinian cause, the "Khomeinist"

---

[66] This draws on the CIA's own estimate. See: US Central Intelligence Agency, "Lebanon: Islamic fundamentalism in Tripoli" (Top Secret, NESAR 86–003JX, January 17, 1986).

[67] Interviews with former members and officials of the Movement of Arab Lebanon, Tripoli, June 2014.

[68] "Al-islam: hadha al-silah al-'adhim dodd al-jabbarin wal-mustakbirin" [Islam: the great weapon in the battle of the oppressed against the tyrants and the oppressors], *Sawt al-Shabiba al-Wataniya* (January 16, 1980).

Instrumental or Sincere Embrace of Khomeinism? 181

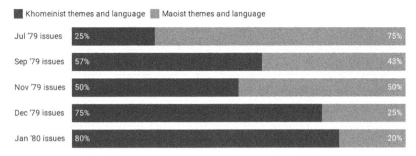

Figure 3.1 Esmat Murad's shift from Maoism to Khomeinist Islamism
Note: This chart is based on my analysis of the content and language of articles published in the Movement of Arab Lebanon's magazine in July 1979–January 1980; though the August and October 1979 issues are missing.
Source: *Sawt al-Shabiba al-Wataniya* magazine (1979–80)

breed of Islamism gradually appeared to have been embraced more sincerely by the Movement of Arab Lebanon, at times even driving its entire thinking. Progressively, Esmat Murad stopped referring to Islam as a mere "weapon" in the struggle against imperialism. Instead he began calling on Muslims to "adhere to Sharia, the Quran and the Sunna" and to all of "Allah's commands."[69]

In one of his most locally celebrated articles, Esmat Murad analyzed what Islamic law had to say about leadership and politics. His prose, punctuated by verses from the Quran, shows that he had acquired within the space of a few years a deep knowledge not just of the sacred texts but also of "Khomeinist" doctrine. In the article, Esmat Murad argued that Muslim leaders should only make decisions based on the Quran and the Sunna, for they would otherwise "give preference to personal views over Sharia," something which would lead to "hypocrisy and polytheism," thus weakening the Islamic world from within. Therefore, in his eyes, the best system of government which could emerge was one entirely based on divine law. "Some people may think that strict abidance to Sharia and Allah's orders will lead us to doom," he wrote, "yet the contrary is the truth."[70] Esmat Murad recognized that these ideas would be difficult to implement in a country like Lebanon, characterized by religious and political diversity, and might stir up controversies and even lead to a

---

[69] "Al-mawqif al-siessi lil-shari'a (1)" ["The political stance of Shari'a (1)], *al-Tawhid* (July 27, 1984).
[70] Ibid.

182   The Emergence of Tawhid

backlash against his movement. Yet he remained fiercely optimistic. "Muslims have always suffered from hardships while holding tightly to their faith despite temptations and even physical torture," he went on. "True faith is the main source of Muslim power – it is the reason why [Allah] will grant them victory."[71] The "Khomeinist" imprint was evident throughout the text. In the space of a few years he had turned from a Maoist instrumentally using the ideological discourse of the Ayatollahs into someone more sincerely committed to a "Khomeinist" breed of Islamism, fully embracing all of its tenets and ready to spread them. As a result, many of the 300 members of his movement also became sincere "Khomeinists."[72]

While Esmat Murad did not explicitly call for *velayat al-faqih* ("the rule of the jurisprudent," which gives a right of political supervision to Shia clerics in Iran but is controversial with Sunnis), he nonetheless clearly hinted at the importance which clerical guidance should hold in politics. To him an Islamist movement would not be entirely "Islamic" until it was spearheaded by a cleric acting as "leader and guardian," someone whose religious authority would be sufficiently great to settle internal disputes and "lead it to victory."[73] Esmat Murad and his Movement of Arab Lebanon would find that cleric in the person of Sa'id Sha'aban who would rise, in 1982, to become head of the Tawhid movement.

The Emir of Tripoli

What is most striking about Sa'id Sha'aban was the sudden transformation of his social and spatial base from a traditional cleric preaching in a middle-class neighborhood into a militant preacher idolized by many Tripolitans, especially in the city's poorest districts. This stemmed from his ability to simultaneously engage with militant Islamist themes and champion much more local, Tripolitan concerns and identities, which soon earned him the affective nickname of "Emir of Tripoli" or informal political and religious leader of the city. The full extent to which he had grown into a popular figure with many Tripolitans, one able to draw the local masses, transpired after his death from a heart attack in June 1998, when a procession made up of 30,000 residents carried his body through

---

[71] "Al-mawqif al-siessi lil-shari'a (2)" ["The political stance of Shari'a (2)], *al-Tawhid* (August 2, 1984).
[72] Interviews with former members and officials of the Movement of Arab Lebanon, Tripoli, June 2014.
[73] "Al-mawqif al-siessi lil-shari'a (2)" ["The political stance of Shari'a (2)], *al-Tawhid* (August 2, 1984).

the streets of Tripoli.[74] Much of this transformation occurred after he split from the Islamic Group in the late 1970s.

It is not an easy task to unpack the reasons which may have pushed Sa'id Sha'aban to leave the Lebanese Muslim Brotherhood. He had been, after all, a committed activist of the movement for over a decade. Like many others, he had first been a member of Worshipers of the Merciful in Tripoli, which he left after the movement's 1958 split, a topic tackled in Chapter 1, in order to continue his studies in Cairo. There he developed strong personal and ideological relations with leading Egyptian members of the "mother" organization, in particular Sayyid Qutb and Yusuf al-Qaradawi.[75] His connections with the Muslim Brotherhood extended to other branches of the movement in Morocco and Iraq, where Sha'aban taught religion in the early 1960s. In 1965 he returned to Tripoli where he naturally joined the Islamic Group. Given his experience with Islamist groups abroad and his preexisting social ties with Tripolitan Islamists who had left Worshipers of the Merciful in 1958, he rapidly rose through the ranks of the movement, even becoming head of its Tripolitan branch. "Sa'id Sha'aban was a pure product of the school of thought espoused by the Muslim Brotherhood,"[76] summed up an Islamist figure who knew him well.

Today, Islamic Group officials typically dismiss Sa'id Sha'aban's split as a by-product of his "pro-Iranian" ideological inclination. His "fervent" support for the 1979 revolution is thus said to have stood in stark contrast with the rest of the leadership's "independence."[77] In reality, however, Sa'id Sha'aban's ostensibly enthusiastic embrace of the Islamic Republic was partially guided by personal interests, as we see in Chapter 7 – he may have vocally supported the Ayatollahs but he was not committed to the point of turning into an "ideological entrepreneur" constantly mobilizing "Khomeinist" Islamism. Moreover, while it is true that he was supportive of the Iranian Revolution right away, this was also the case for the Islamic Group which, like other Muslim Brotherhood branches throughout the Middle East, applauded the overthrow of the secular Shah and his replacement by a political system in which religion and clerical guidance came to play significant roles. The Islamic Group, in fact, had even sent one of its own members to Tehran in January 1980 to attend an Islamic conference which had been organized by the new

---

[74] Abi Samra, *Trablus*, p. 151.

[75] Interview with Fayez Iyali (Islamic Group co-founder and figure close to Said Sha'aban), Tripoli, June 2014.

[76] Interview with Maher Hammoud (former Islamic Group cleric), Sidon, June 2014.

[77] Interview with Ibrahim al-Masri (former leader of the Islamic Group), Beirut, July 2014.

184 The Emergence of Tawhid

Islamic Republic.[78] Sa'id Sha'aban would also travel to Iran but his first trip there would only occur a year later.[79] Thus, despite official claims to the contrary, ideology did not lie at the heart of Sa'id Sha'aban's split from the Islamic Group. Instead it was motivated by disagreement over the Islamic Group's growing institutionalization and social elitism, fueled, in the background, by tension with its head, Fathi Yakan – and a bitter rivalry for power between their wives.

Sa'id Sha'aban had always had his own vision of what the Islamic Group, and Muslim Brotherhood branches more generally, should look like. To begin with, he was a proponent of turning the group from a tight-knit "organization" (*tanzim*) into a more open "movement" (*haraka*). This view only sharpened with time as he witnessed frustrated youths starting to leave the organization from the mid-1970s onward. He was also concerned that the combination of the Islamic Group's growing institutionalization, oligarchization, sense of social elitism and organizational rigidity meant it was fast becoming an "end in itself" to be a member while "work for God"[80] seemed to be relegated to the back seat. This state of affairs, in his eyes, felt like a betrayal of the Muslim Brotherhood's originally ambitious ideological aims and also stood in flagrant contradiction of Fathi Yakan's own call for a "revolutionary Islam." He was critical of the erosion of the Islamic Group's ideological commitments.

Sa'id Sha'aban seemed particularly bitter about the increasingly bureaucratic and oligarchic way the Islamic Group was operating, something perhaps informed by personal experience too. His son and political heir recalled one instance in which his father was "prevented" by the leadership from traveling to Pakistan to learn from the experience of the Tabligh, a grassroots Islamic movement. On another occasion, three "founding fathers" or senior members came late one evening to their house to complain about Sa'id Sha'aban's latest sermon given in a Tripolitan mosque controlled by the Party of Liberation (*Hizb al-Tahrir*), a more radical Islamist organization and a competitor of the Islamic Group.[81] His supporters thus argued that he left the movement when he realized that, firmly on the path of institutionalization,

---

[78] Interview with Anis Naqqash (Lebanese Islamist militant close to Iranian intelligence), Beirut, June 2014.

[79] Interview with Bilal Sha'aban (son of Said Sha'aban and leader of Tawhid), Tripoli, August 2014.

[80] Interview with Ibrahim Saleh (former Tawhid official and adviser of Said Sha'aban), Tripoli, July 2014.

[81] Interview with Bilal Sha'aban (son of Said Sha'aban and leader of Tawhid), Tripoli, August 2014.

oligarchization and growing social elitism, he was never going to be able to change it from within. His former colleagues in the Islamic Group, however, pointed more to incompatibilities of behavior between him and the rest of the leadership. "He was impulsive and took too many initiatives on his own," explained a former leader. "As a *tanzim* we have clear rules and we all need to respect the final decisions. Sa'id Sha'aban wasn't disciplined enough – he had to say and do anything that came to his mind!"[82] Tension simmered between Sa'id Sha'aban and Fathi Yakan, the group's leader from 1964 until 1992.

The tipping point was reached in 1978. Tension between Sa'id Sha'aban and Fathi Yakan crystallized as a struggle for power between their respective wives, Najah al-Nazir and Mona Haddad. They were both members of the Islamic Group's women branch in Tripoli, which in the late 1960s had founded the movement's first Islamic nursery and primary school, called Paradise of the Children (*Janet al-Atfal*). Najah al-Nazir and Mona Haddad both took a leading role in administering the school but it is said that the latter had a particularly "strong personality" and that she "took the institution for herself,"[83] becoming director and sidelining Sa'id Sha'aban's wife. A source who was in the leadership of the Islamic Group back then and acted as a confidant of Sha'aban explained that the cleric's wife, herself a teacher and a founding member of the school, was also ambitious and that a "conflict"[84] developed between the two women. Sa'id Sha'aban left the movement shortly afterward. Revealingly, one of Sa'id Sha'aban's later moves as head of Tawhid would be to set up a network of Islamic schools too, the Islamic Message *(al-Risala al-Islamiya)*, to compete with the Islamic Group's – and to nominate his wife as the director.

Sa'id Sha'aban's split from the Islamic Group also allowed him to act free from organizational, social and ideological constraints and, ultimately, to exponentially increase his own social and spatial base. For years he had remained a relatively traditional cleric. He had studied at Tripoli's private Islamic College *(al-Kuliya al-Islamiya)*, attended Egypt's prestigious Al-Azhar University and, once back in Lebanon, had become a preacher at Tripoli's Mohammed al-Amin mosque, situated close to his home in Abu Samra, a middle-class residential area which also happened to act as a hub for the Islamic Group. Sha'aban marked a clear break with much of that privileged background by deciding to move to the Tawbe

---

[82] Interview with Abdallah Babetti (former Islamic Group head of political affairs), Tripoli, August 2014.
[83] Interviews with former officials in the Islamic Group, Tripoli and Beirut, June 2014.
[84] Interview with Maher Hammoud (former Islamic Group cleric), Sidon, June 2014.

186   The Emergence of Tawhid

mosque, one of Tripoli's largest and most ancient mosques built during Mameluk times and located in the heart of the Old City, a heavily populated and low-income neighborhood. There his sermons became more popular and attracted much larger crowds than before, and by all accounts he soon built for himself a considerable following.

The root of Sa'id Sha'aban's popular success as the orator of the Tawbe mosque in the late 1970s resided in his dual ability to address older local narratives of Tripolitan identities and grievances and to embody the growing appeal of militant Islamist ideology. Unlike some of Tripoli's other well-known preachers back then, like the Islamic Group's Fathi Yakan, who reportedly spoke in ways people outside his movement "could not fathom,"[85] Sa'id Sha'aban became known as a charismatic figure who was especially skilled at framing local concerns in grand ways, drawing on Islamic history and classical Arabic vocabulary. One scholar who researched the cleric's background and attended his sermons in the late 1970s and early 1980s was particularly struck by the way he would hint at local grievances and identities by frequently employing the Arabic word for "the city," *al-madina*, to the extent it was at times deliberately unclear whether he was referring to Tripoli or to Medina, the Saudi city which acted as the capital of Muhammad's early Muslim empire. This was an elegant way of framing Tripolitan concerns against the grand backdrop of Islamic history and references. The researcher described the "puffs of enthusiasm" that his sermons would thus unleash, producing "an aesthetically pleasing effect, undeniably linked to the emotional; an effect arousing a state of harmony and inner clarity in the listener."[86] Sha'aban's implicit, but locally clear, engagement with Tripolitan concerns and identities, especially in the ancient setting of the Tawbe mosque, drew hundreds to his speeches.

Beyond his ability to address local issues, Sa'id Sha'aban also became known in the late 1970s and early 1980s as a revolutionary cleric espousing a particularly militant breed of Islamism, someone whose views had become at odds with the Islamic Group's and its growing institutionalization. In his speeches he often tackled deeply ideological issues. For instance, he advocated for worldwide Islamic revolutions and the establishment of Islamic Republics in the Middle East, or lambasted the "enemies" of Islam, from Israel and secularism to the West. A journalist who reported on his sermons thus remarked that they became "very heated" and even "provocative." Sha'aban, he said,

---

[85] Interview with residents, Tripoli, July 2014.
[86] Dalal Bizri, *Introduction à l'étude des mouvements islamistes sunnites au Liban* (Paris: Ecole des Hautes Etudes en Sciences Sociales, unpublished PhD thesis, 1984), p. 265.

vehemently criticized "the state, the government, the presidency, the Christian parties and militias, and everything non-Islamic in Lebanon, as well as the autocratic Arab countries, regimes and leaders – he even urged the people of Tripoli to rise against them all through jihad and weapons."[87] This contrasted with the cautious wording of Tripoli's other, more traditional clerics whose speeches catered to a more socially elitist and politically conservative audience. His readiness to engage both with local Tripolitan concerns and identities and with militant Islamist themes turned him into Tripoli's most popular cleric by far in the early 1980s.

Sa'id Sha'aban started being invited to deliver sermons in mosques throughout the city, including in the embattled neighborhood of Bab al-Tebbaneh, Tripoli's "stronghold of contention" par excellence and a hub of anti-Assad activism, where his call to arms of course resonated with many. From early 1982 onward he also began preaching regularly at Tripoli's historical Great Mosque of al-Mansuri, located right at the entrance of the Old City, thus reinforcing his religious credentials and ability to draw even larger crowds. It did not take long for militant Islamist factions such as Soldiers of God, the Popular Resistance and the Movement of Arab Lebanon to take notice of the cleric's rising profile and militant rhetoric. Despite their different backgrounds and varying levels of commitment to religion and ideology, they shared a similar militant Islamist discourse and agreed on many aspects of local politics. These three factions began socializing and mobilizing, and in August 1982 finally merged to create Tawhid. Sa'id Sha'aban rose as their leader. He would become the "Emir" of Tripoli and exercise a great deal of power over the city for the next three years.

The Syrian Hammer and the Israeli Anvil

The timing of Tawhid's birth in mid-1982 is worth considering for it would emerge in a particularly tense broader context, one marked by new threats and opportunities. Within a few months, two key regional events featuring exceptionally high levels of governmental violence had just taken place and threatened to spill over into Tripoli: Syria's February 1982 Hama massacre and Israel's June 1982 invasion of Lebanon. Many Tripolitans, and especially the city's militant Islamists, began fearing for their fate, feeling squeezed between the Syrian hammer and the Israeli anvil. It was in response to this need for protection that Tawhid framed

---

[87] Abi Samra, *Trablus*, p. 123.

188   The Emergence of Tawhid

its birth as a bid to "defend the city" and "wage jihad" against the enemies.

It is remarkable that, despite being one of the bloodiest episodes of repression in the Middle East, the February 1982 Hama massacre has long remained outside careful scrutiny.[88] The Syrian regime's crackdown on the Islamist-led Sunni opposition was neither limited to February 1982 nor to Hama. It was part of an older struggle dating back to 1976, which intensified in 1979, spread too all major Syrian cities and indeed culminated in Hama in 1982 as rebels from the Syrian Muslim Brotherhood and the Fighting Vanguard took over the city. The collective punishment inflicted by the regime on Hama's entire population would defy comparison. Relentless shelling and raids by the security forces resulted in the deaths of some 25,000 people and the exile of 100,000 residents within the space of a month, nearly suppressing all forms of contentious politics inside the country until the 2011 uprising. The regime, through this brute show of force, regained control of Hama. But what is less known is that, although it crushed the anti-Assad movement inside Syria, the February 1982 Hama massacre intensified the challenges faced by the Syrian army in North Lebanon. This raised the possibility that it would lead to another brutal repression, this time in Tripoli.

Paradoxically, the Hama massacre initially considerably bolstered the anti-Syrian regime camp in Tripoli. Most obviously, it disrupted Tripoli's demographic and sectarian make-up in ways unfavorable to the rulers in Damascus. A researcher estimated that, given Tripoli's proximity to Hama and the cross-border social and historical ties between the two cities, the port welcomed as many as 20,000 Sunni refugees.[89] By all accounts most were civilians, but the tales of sheer horror and the anti-regime narratives they spread contributed to exacerbating the abhorrence many Tripolitans historically held for the Syrian regime. Moreover, of all these Syrian refugees now staying in Tripoli, a

---

[88] For some of the more recent works that tackle the 1982 Hama massacre, see: Salwa Ismail, *The rule of violence: subjectivity, memory and government in Syria* (Cambridge: Cambridge University Press); Thomas Pierret, *Religion and state in Syria: the Sunni Ulama from coup to revolution* (Cambridge: Cambridge University Press, 2013); Michel Seurat, *L'état de barbarie* (Paris: Presses Universitaires de France, 2012 edition); Raphaël Lefèvre, *Ashes of Hama: the Muslim Brotherhood in Syria* (London, Oxford University Press and Hurst, 2013); Nora Benkorich, "La tentation de la lutte armée contre le pouvoir baasiste en Syrie Passé (1976–1982) et présent (2011)" *Le Débat* (Vol. 168, No. 1, 2012), pp. 155–67 and Dara Conduit, "The Syrian Muslim Brotherhood and the spectacle of Hama" *The Middle East Journal* (Vol. 70., No. 2, 2016), pp. 211–26.

[89] Interview with Amer Arnaout (Tripolitan researcher and former activist in the 1980s), Tripoli, May 2014.

not insignificant proportion had also acted as rebel fighters for the Muslim Brotherhood and the Fighting Vanguard. Western intelligence cables from that time confirmed that "many Sunni dissidents fled to the Tripoli area in North Lebanon after the Hama uprising in 1982."[90] The vast majority of these militants merely used Tripoli as a gateway to safer destinations like Saudi Arabia and Iraq. But a handful nonetheless settled in Tripoli, where they intended to continue their struggle against the Syrian regime. The nature and extent of their impact is assessed more thoroughly in Chapter 7, but at this point suffice it to say that their deep-seated anti-regime views, local status as heroes and military expertise reinforced Tripoli's Islamists.

Another way in which the Hama massacre bolstered the anti-Syrian regime camp in Tripoli was by spurring a vast spate of violence targeting the Syrian army's presence in the northern city as well as its local allies. This bolstered the momentum of Tripoli's Islamists. With an estimated half of the Tripolitan population having relatives in Homs and Hama and over a millennia of shared historical narratives between these cities, the ties that bonded the inhabitants of Tripoli to those of Hama were not merely social – they were also emotional. Several locals who back then began joining militant Islamist factions known for their extreme anti-regime views and involvement in contention, like the Popular Resistance or Soldiers of God, explained they did so in the wake of the February 1982 massacre to "avenge Hama."[91] But the thirst for revenge against the regime ran even deeper, with officials in several Tripolitan political parties and militias explaining that their youths became "uncontrollable" and that, at the time, some took matters into their hands by engaging in anti-regime violence.[92]

February 1982 and the following weeks, then, would be the bloodiest months by far for the Syrian army and its allies in Tripoli since the 1976 military intervention in Lebanon.

While the Syrian Ba'ath Party's Tripoli office was blown up and unidentified youths machine-gunned a police station hosting Syrian officers, a Syrian army outpost in the Old City came under such fire that soldiers had to use rockets to repel the attack and a kidnapping and assassination campaign began targeting Syrian intelligence officials in

---

[90] US Central Intelligence Agency, "Syria: Sunni opposition to the minority Alawite regime" (Secret, NESA 85-10102, June 1985).

[91] Interviews with former members of Soldiers of God and the Popular Resistance, Tripoli, September 2014.

[92] Interviews with officials of the local branches of the Iraqi Ba'ath Party and the Organization of the Communist Action in Lebanon, Tripoli, August–September 2014.

190   The Emergence of Tawhid

the northern city.[93] Militant demands crystallized on the immediate withdrawal of Syrian troops from Tripoli.

But it was not just the Syrian army's local presence which was the target of that wrath, for Tripoli's pro-Syrian regime parties and militias also came under severe fire. This was the case with the Syrian Social Nationalist Party, a party-cum-militia notoriously close to Damascus, which only had a small presence in Tripoli but whose office nonetheless became a target of bombings.[94] Yet it was most obvious with pro-Assad militias in Jabal Mohsen.

As we saw in Chapter 2, Tripoli's district of Jabal Mohsen was entirely inhabited by Alawis, came under the wing of a pro-Assad strongman, Ali Eid, and developed a bitter neighborhood rivalry with the adjacent, Sunni-dominated neighborhood of Bab al-Tebbaneh. Violent clashes began opposing Ali Eid's militia, the pro-Assad Arab Democratic Party against the Popular Resistance's faction of "neighborhood Islamists" in Bab al-Tebbaneh. By September 1981, clashes had been contained through a precarious local balance of terror. But the emotional shock from news about the February 1982 Hama massacre, alongside the spate of violence targeting the Syrian army's presence in Tripoli, rekindled these clashes, Clashes that took place during that month alone killed as many as forty-two and injured sixty. Subsequent, nearly weekly, local rounds of fighting cost the lives of an additional thirteen locals in April, fifty-eight in May, fourteen in June and twenty-two in July, with hundreds injured.[95] Entire blocks of the two districts were devastated by the indiscriminate shelling and shooting. This included Syria Street, the main artery separating the two districts but also a highly strategic place for anti-regime fighters to target because Syrian soldiers had to pass through it on their way between Tripoli and Syria, and its name also symbolized the Syrian regime's local prominence. According to journalists who had reported on previous episodes of violence, these clashes between the anti-regime neighborhood of Bab al-Tebbaneh and the pro-Syrian area of Jabal Mohsen were of a "rare violence,"[96] causing "considerable" material damage and loss of life. They observed that "all kinds

---

[93] See: "Enfijar amam maktab Hizb al-Ba'ath al-Arabi al-Eshtiraki fi Trablus" ["Explosion in front of the Syrian Baath in Tripoli"], *Al-Incha* (February 5, 1982); "Atlaq nar istahdef hajiz al-jaysh al-Suri fi Trablus" ["Gunfire targets a checkpoint of the Syrian army in Tripoli"], *Al-Incha* (February 18, 1982).

[94] "Atlaq nar istahdef maktab Hizb al-Qawmi al-Suri" ["Gunfire aims at the bureau of the Syrian Social Nationalist Party"], *Al-Incha* (January 12, 1982).

[95] I draw these figures from my analysis of the fatalities and injuries reported in Tripolitan daily *Al-Incha* and Lebanese daily *L'Orient Le Jour* for the time of February–July 1982.

[96] "13 tués, 12 blessés dans les affrontements de Tripoli," *L'Orient Le Jour* (April 24, 1982).

The Syrian Hammer and the Israeli Anvil

of weapons" were used by fighters in the two districts, from "light automatic weapons" all the way to "semi-heavy weapons like rockets and mortars."[97] The Popular Resistance in Bab al-Tebbaneh was backed up by Soldiers of God and myriad militant Islamist figures and their followers in the neighborhoods of Qobbe and Abu Samra, themselves in the vicinity of Jabal Mohsen, which had the effect of opening the fight on new fronts and exerting additional pressure on Ali Eid's men, retrenched and attacked by all sides. Because many blamed the February 1982 Hama massacre on Alawis at large, perhaps due to the role of Rifa'at al-Assad's Alawi-dominated Defense Brigades in these killings, they engaged in sectarian revenge attacks by targeting local Alawi civilians and shops in Tripoli.[98] By the spring and summer of 1982, then, the Islamist-led anti-Syrian regime camp in the northern city seemed about to gain the upper hand on the Syrian army and its local allies.

Yet, instead of pressuring Damascus into withdrawing its troops from Tripoli, the series of defeats and humiliations the Syrian army and its local allies suffered began raising the possibility that the regime would undertake a Hama-style brutal crackdown on the city. This was an option which Syria's local allies, under great pressure, were actively pushing for. They asked the head of Syrian intelligence in Lebanon, Mohammed Ghanem, "for help" to put an end to an "unbearable situation," calling for the implementation of a "total and radical solution" which would eliminate "those who do not understand the language of softness."[99] The Syrian regime seemed ready to follow through. Its foreign minister, Abdel Halim Khaddam, explained that Damascus was "conscious" of the situation in Tripoli, shortly followed by a statement from Hafez al-Assad in which he solemnly announced his readiness to do the "utmost in order to re-establish security in Tripoli once and for all."[100]

These threats raised the specter of a Hama-style crackdown on Islamist factions in the city, which prompted them to socialize together, to mobilize more and to begin unifying. The myriad militant Islamist militias and figures which had all been on the rise since the late 1970s and early 1980s began to organize joint events more regularly in the spring of 1982. Of

---

[97] "Nouvelle flambée de violence à Tripoli," *L'Orient Le Jour* (May 8, 1982).

[98] "Munawashat fi Bab al-Ramel" ["Skirmish in Bab al-Ramel"], *Al-Incha* (March 19, 1982); "Enfijar amam matjar fi manteqat al-Qobbe" ["Explosion in front of a store in the area of Qobbe"], *Al-Incha* (April 9, 1982); and interviews with residents of Bab al-Tebbaneh and Jabal Mohsen, September–October 2014; "Découverte macabre à Bohsas," *L'Orient Le Jour* (April 11, 1982).

[99] "Les combats redoublent d'intensité à Tripoli," *L'Orient Le Jour* (May 9, 1982).

[100] "Cessez le feu des plus précaires à Tripoli: 3 tués, plusieurs blessés," *L'Orient Le Jour* (May 13, 1982) and "Normalisation à Tripoli," *L'Orient Le Jour* (May 15, 1982).

192   The Emergence of Tawhid

course, they sometimes had different backgrounds and trajectories, but all were staunchly against the Syrian regime and shared militant Islamist views – whether held instrumentally or sincerely. While the Popular Resistance deeply resented the Syrian army's presence in Bab al-Tebbaneh's vicinity and its backing for Ali Eid's men in Jabal Mohsen, Soldiers of God was driven by more ideologically Islamist views of the "infidel" Syrian regime and local Alawis, and for its part the Movement of Arab Lebanon argued that the Syrian pressures on Tripoli had to be offset as Damascus was "standing in the way of struggling against Israel."[101]

The bold anti-Assad stances of these Islamist movements contrasted sharply with the cautious positions of Tripoli's other political parties and figures. Some, like the Islamic Group, tried to remain neutral. The movement, as we saw, had gradually withdrawn from contentious politics as it sought institutionalization and as some of its leaders had been intimidated and detained by the Syrian regime a couple of years earlier. Yet at such a critical time of Tripoli's history it further alienated its militant youths, more of whom split from it.

Others, especially in the Tripolitan upper class, were openly critical of the spate of violence that had targeted the Syrian army's presence and its local allies from February 1982. The city's wealthy business elite, wary about the rapid spread of the clashes well beyond the usual front line of Bab al-Tebbaneh and Jabal Mohsen to wealthier residential and commercial districts, advocated for a "firm attitude" to "stem the insecurity reigning in Tripoli."[102] Similarly, the city's traditional Sunni clerics, for their part feeling increasingly threatened by the more radical and, often, more popular competitors in the myriad Islamist factions on the rise, also asked for an "end to be put" to what they went as far as calling the "criminal folly"[103] by then gripping the city. And, of course, the notables whose standing was fast declining were quick to take the regime's side and call for a crackdown. Rashid Karame, who as we saw in Chapter 1 epitomized the Tripolitan notability, called on "President Hafez al-Assad to help us save our city" for "we can no longer bear this state of affairs."[104] His vocally supportive stance for the presence of more Syrian troops in Tripoli was such that it earned him a reputation among observers of Lebanese politics for acting as one of the regime's main

---

[101] Interviews with members and officials of the Popular Resistance, the Movement of Arab Lebanon and Soldiers of God, Tripoli, October 2014.

[102] "Calme total mais barricades pas encore démantelées dans la capitale du Nord," *L'Orient Le Jour* (May 16, 1982).

[103] "L'hémorragie a fait 19 tués et 40 blessés de plus," *L'Orient Le Jour* (May 11, 1982) .

[104] "Les combats redoublent d'intensité à Tripoli," *L'Orient Le Jour* (May 9, 1982).

Sunni "puppets," the type who "faithfully adheres to the Syrian line on all issues."[105] This attracted Hafez al-Assad's goodwill, which was key in enabling him to become prime minister. But in his home city his leadership became contested as a result. He began receiving death threats and, months later, survived a car bomb loaded with 70 kg of TNT.[106] By contrast, Sa'id Sha'aban's popularity received a boost as he came to embody Tripolitan opposition to the Syrian regime. Some of his statements which were critical of Damascus were amplified, for example when he provocatively called on Syrian soldiers "not to follow the orders they receive as they are in contradiction with God's orders"[107] or as he warned that Tripoli might use its right of "jihad" as "self-defence"[108] against the regime.

The months that followed the February 1982 Hama massacre and the sudden rise of violence in Tripoli triggered a dynamic of socialization and mobilization between Tripoli's militant Islamist factions and figures. On April 2, 1982 they led a joint protest which started in Bab al-Tebbaneh, again showing the neighborhood's status as Tripoli's "stronghold of contention," and then crossed all of the districts where the Islamists had influence, like Qobbe and Abu Samra, to finish in the Old City where Sa'id Sha'aban preached.[109] A day later Fatah's Student Brigade and the Movement of Arab Lebanon jointly invited Sa'id Sha'aban to deliver a sermon at the Great Mosque of Tripoli, where partisans of the Popular Resistance and Soldiers of God also came to see with their own eyes the phenomenon he now represented.[110] This triggered a further increase in joint events held in the following months. In early May, for instance, another pro-Palestinian rally was held at the Great Mosque, and this time not only Sa'id Sha'aban but militant clerics from Soldiers of God and others who had split from the Islamic Group all delivered speeches.[111] The process seemed to be finally coming to a head on June 2, 1982, after the leaders of the Popular Resistance, Soldiers of

---

[105] US Central Intelligence Agency, "Syria's allies and assets in Lebanon" (RPM 78-10411, November 7, 1978).

[106] "Sayara mufakhakha amam munzal Rashid Karami fi Trablus" ["Car bomb in front of the house of Rashid Karame in Tripoli"], *Al-Incha* (August 23, 1982).

[107] "Situation à Tripoli," *L'Orient Le Jour* (November 10, 1983).

[108] "Le Tawhid tend la main à la Syrie," *L'Orient Le Jour*, (December 17, 1983).

[109] "Mahrajen Trablus d'ama lil-muqawama al-filastinia" ["Festival in Tripoli in support of the Palestinian resistance"], *Al-Incha* (April 2, 1982).

[110] "Mahrajen wa khitab al-Sheikh Sa'id Sha'aban fi Jam'a al-Mansuri" ["Festival and the speech of the cleric Sa'id Sha'aban at the Great Mosque al-Mansuri"], *Al-Incha* (April 3, 1982).

[111] "Mahrajen fi Jam'a Mansuri" ["Festival at the Great Mosque al-Mansuri"], *Al-Incha* (May 2, 1982).

194   The Emergence of Tawhid

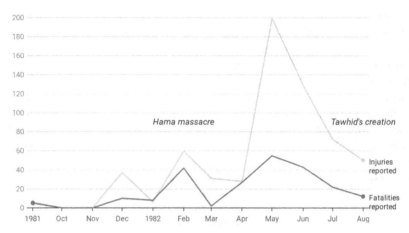

Figure 3.2 Violence between pro- and anti-Assad forces in Tripoli in 1982
Note: This graph reflects the number of injured and killed in Tripoli in attacks and clashes between pro- and anti-Assad forces.
Source: Tripolitan daily *Al-Incha*; Lebanese daily *L'Orient Le Jour* and Adib N'ame, "Al-amen fi Trablus, 1980–1985" ["The security in Tripoli, 1980–1985"], *Nada' al-Shamal* (November 1985)

God and the Movement of Arab Lebanon, alongside local Islamist figures, issued a joint statement declaring that "Islamic unity is an obligation."[112] They intended to merge within one movement headed by Sa'id Sha'aban which could claim leadership of Tripoli and the Sunni community, face off the Syrian threat and finally implement an Islamic Republic. Figure 3.2 indicates how Tawhid's creation and promise to defend Tripoli from the Syrian army came within a context marked by an escalation of violence in the city between pro- and anti-Syrian regime forces following the February 1982 Hama massacre.

Yet it was the Israeli intervention in Lebanon, on June 6, 1982, which would provide the impetus for Tawhid's official launch. The Israeli troops' quick advance on Beirut caught many militants by surprise. "It came as a shock to us all – it was the first time Israel was reaching and occupying an Arab capital!"[113] remembered one of these Islamists. In a show of how unexpected it had been, Sa'id Sha'aban and some of his followers had just landed in Tehran, where they were attending a meeting

[112] "Mu'tamar Trablus: al-wahda al-islamiya wajib" ["Conference of Tripoli: Islamic unity is an obligation"], *Al-Incha* (June 2, 1982).
[113] Interview with Samir Hassan (Popular Resistance commander), Beirut, July 2014.

The Syrian Hammer and the Israeli Anvil 195

with Lebanese and Iranian clerics. They rushed to return to Tripoli where they declared "jihad"[114] against the Jewish state. Rumor was fast spreading that the Israeli army would soon march toward the northern city. By early August it had reached the ancient harbor of Byblos, a mere twenty-four miles away from Tripoli. "The Tripoli area appears a likely Israeli target,"[115] reported the *New York Times* back then.

Officially it was therefore to counter this threat that the Movement of the Islamic Unification (*Harakat al-Tawhid al-Islami*, known locally just as Tawhid) was formed. "We had to prepare our city for war against Israel,"[116] recalled one of the founding figures in the movement. In Beirut the Israeli army defeated the Palestinian militants and their Lebanese Muslim allies in the space of two months and it later oversaw the killing of thousands of Palestinian refugees in the Sabra and Shatila camps. Quick military gains paved the way for the election of Israeli-backed Bashir Gemayel, head of the right-wing Christian Maronite Phalange Party, as Lebanon's new president. At the time many Muslim politicians pragmatically accepted, to varying degrees, the new status quo. Some, like Beirut's Saeb Salam, the head of the National Islamic Congress, an alliance of Sunni notables, quickly recognized the "legitimacy" of Bashir Gemayel's election and started criticizing the "backward mentality"[117] of pro-Palestinian forces. Others, like Tripoli's Abdel Majid al-Rifa'i and Rashid Karame, were at first more cautious but progressively endorsed the new Israeli-backed Lebanese government. Their compromising stance left a wide space open for the emergence of more militant voices. Islamist movements like Hezbollah and Tawhid would use this political opportunity to show off their militant credentials and quickly fill that gap. Tawhid's very founding charter thus framed the movement's creation as answering the "need for an Islamic force to counterbalance Israeli power and protect Lebanese Muslims."[118]

There is evidence to suggest that Tawhid's promptness to sanction "jihad" against Israel, indeed its injunction that it was a "religious duty" to seek martyrdom against what it called "the Zionist enemy," proved an instant popular success in Tripoli, even though the Israeli army later

---

[114] "Masheyekhs Trablus id'aun al-muslimin lil-jihad dodd Israyil" ["The clerics of Tripoli invite the Muslims to jihad against Israel"], *Al-Incha* (June 12, 1982).

[115] "North Lebanon fears Israeli drive," *New York Times*, August 20, 1982.

[116] Interview with Ibrahim Saleh, Tripoli, August 2014 and interview with Abu Shawqi, Tripoli, August 2014.

[117] "Pierre Gemayel approuve les conditions du congrès islamique," *L'Orient Le Jour*, September 9, 1982.

[118] *Al-khutut al-asasia li-muntalaqat wa mabade wa ahdaf Harakat al-Tawhid al-Islami* [The fundamental premises, principles and objectives of the Islamic Unification Movement] (copy given to the author, undated).

196   The Emergence of Tawhid

withdrew from Byblos and never made it to North Lebanon. Tawhid's steep anti-Israeli rhetoric and the timing of its creation immediately attracted young Tripolitans of all backgrounds, but especially the militant Islamists, who recalled having been seduced by its willingness to stand by the Palestinians and defend Tripoli.[119] Tawhid would, in the next few years, considerably help Fatah, as we see in Chapter 7. But it would only do so by protecting the Palestinian guerrilla organization's presence in Tripoli against attacks by the Syrian regime – not by militarily confronting Israel. Still, the sense that the city was increasingly stuck between the Syrian hammer and the Israeli anvil had triggered the process of unification which finally gave birth to Tawhid in August 1982 and immediately provided it with strong momentum among Tripoli's Islamist constituency.

Tawhid's Rise to Islamist Stardom

What is remarkable about Tawhid's beginnings is how, mere months after its creation, it had already risen as Tripoli's strongest political movement by far. Naturally it is always difficult to precisely evaluate the sense of momentum of a movement. And this is all the more the case when assessing events that date back nearly forty years. Yet local reports concur that Tawhid's rise in Tripoli was "sudden and overwhelming."[120] One scholar who was living in the city and researching the Islamist movement shortly after its emergence in mid-1982 similarly noted that it soon acquired the capacity to mobilize a "considerable" number of members and sympathizers and that the crowds it gathered in protests and other episodes of contention were often "enormous and enthusiastic."[121]

Outside observers formulated similar assessments. The CIA, for instance, at first alarmed by Tawhid's fast-rising profile, estimated that although membership of the movement fluctuated to an extent, it should be considered "the largest Sunni fundamentalist group in Lebanon," one which had close to 2,000 members.[122] This, of course, may seem relatively modest when compared to some of the other Lebanese militias operating back then, for example the 5,000 Christian fighters of the

---

[119] Interviews with residents of Tripoli and with Islamist activists, Tripoli, July–August 2014.
[120] "A Tripoli le Sheikh Shaaban dispense la justice par téléphone," *L'Orient le Jour* (October 20, 1983).
[121] Al-Soufi Richard, *Lutte populaire armée*, pp. 251–62.
[122] US Central Intelligence Agency, "Lebanon: Islamic fundamentalism in Tripoli" (Top Secret, NESAR 86-003JX, January 17, 1986).

Lebanese Forces, the 5,000 Shia members of Amal or the 6,000 Druze fighters of the Progressive Socialist Party. However, these movements operated over large swathes of Lebanese territory while Tawhid remained confined to Tripoli. In fact, the CIA's estimate that Tawhid had 2,000 fighters is far from insignificant if compared to other city-based militias, for example the Beirut-based Murabitun which was the other Sunni rebel group of the Lebanese civil war and had 500 Sunni activists, or Islamic Amal, made up of 800 Shia militants from Baalbek who later joined Hezbollah.[123] Other sources mention that Tawhid had closer to 3,000 members.[124] And, of course, the 30,000 locals who attended the funeral of its leader, Sa'id Sha'aban, suggests that it had a much larger pool of sympathizers who mobilized more sporadically.[125]

As this book shows, many of Tawhid's 2,000–3,000 members and its thousands of sympathizers were less ideologically committed activists who were motivated by factors other than ideology. But it is nonetheless undeniable that the momentum which surrounded its emergence was due to its success in attracting the constituency of Tripoli's Islamists.

This partially stemmed from the fact that it had been created as the merger of Tripoli's three largest militant Islamist factions, which provided it with a backbone of 1,000 fighters. As was remarked, the Popular Resistance, Soldiers of God and the Movement of Arab Lebanon had merged in a security and political context marked by volatility and in particular by the threats and opportunities unleashed by Syrian and Israeli actions in 1982. They hoped that by pooling their resources they would withstand a potential Syrian or Israeli attack and recruit new members attracted by the ideal of jihad to defend the city. Moreover, although the three groups each had their leaders, trajectories and varying levels of commitment to religion and ideology, all nonetheless featured a broadly similar Islamist discourse around which they agreed and could gather. They also trusted Sa'id Sha'aban. As a revolutionary cleric popular with many Tripolitans, his leadership of the movement would provide further religious and militant credentials and a strong base. It also helped

---

[123] I draw the figures on membership to Lebanese militias from: US Central Intelligence Agency, "Directory of Lebanese militias: a reference aid" (Secret, NESA 84-10171C, June 1984).

[124] See, for instance, security sources quoted in "Tripoli, la consolidation du cessez le feu se fait attendre," *L'Orient Le Jour* (November 13, 1983) and Voice of Lebanon radio report quoted in "Military strength of the warring sides in Tripoli," *BBC World* (October 1, 1985). In addition, it is also widely reported that, upon Tawhid's creation in Tripoli's Tawbe mosque in August 1982, an estimated 3,000 people had pledged allegiance to its leader Sa'id Sha'aban – this is the estimate of a researcher who was inside Tripoli. Al-Soufi Richard, *Lutte populaire armée*, p. 261.

[125] Abi Samra, *Trablus*, p. 151.

198   The Emergence of Tawhid

that he was widely seen as an independent-minded figure, someone with no partisan affiliation since his split from the Islamic Group and whom the leaders and members of the three Islamist factions felt could mediate between them if disputes were to arise.[126] One of them, Soldiers of God, initially preferred enhanced cooperation to the prospect of an actual merger between the three of them. But, reflective of the enthusiastic atmosphere which surrounded Tawhid's creation, it then rapidly confirmed its participation and dilution in the new movement as its leader began being afraid of losing out on the sense of momentum.[127]

However, beyond attracting the members of these three militant Islamist factions, what also explained Tawhid's momentum was its ability to recruit hundreds of independent Islamists. A first factor which appealed to these independent Islamists was Tawhid's willingness to break with the sense of organizational rigidity and social elitism which had come to characterize the Islamic Group and had led to splits from it. Instead of spending months or even years going through an indoctrination and vetting process, it was easy to become a Tawhid member. All the new recruits had to do was to promise to abolish their previous loyalties and to work together to defeat Israel, struggle against the Syrian regime, bring down the Lebanese government and participate in the establishment of an Islamic Republic.[128] The low cost of joining Tawhid played a key role in attracting many independent Islamists who had been disenfranchised by the Islamic Group's social elitism and organizational rigidity.

A second factor which attracted the Islamist constituency was Tawhid's promise to unify the subcurrents which had long fragmented the local Islamist scene. The very fact that the factions which merged within Tawhid themselves hailed from diverse traditions, like "Sufi jihadism," "Sunni Khomeinism" or "neighborhood Islamism," proved key to attracting dozens, perhaps hundreds more Islamists attracted by the idea of unity. In fact, Tawhid made "Islamic unification" its trademark organizational identity. That concept even stood at the origins of the name that the founders chose for the movement. *Tawhid* had the dual advantage of literally meaning "unification" but of also referring to the "oneness of God," a key tenet of Islamic faith. It also drew on verse three

---

[126] Interviews with Tawhid founders Ibrahim Saleh, Hashem Minqara, Kan'an Naji, Tripoli, July–August 2014 as well as former commanders and members of the Popular Resistance, Soldiers of God and the Movement of Arab Lebanon, Tripoli, July–August 2014.

[127] Interview with Kan'an Naji (leader of Soldiers of God), Tripoli, August 2014.

[128] Interview with current and former Tawhid members, Tripoli, July–August 2014.

of the Quran's Surat al-Imran, repeatedly quoted in many Tawhid publications, which states the following:

And hold firmly to the rope of Allah all together and do not become divided. And remember the favour of Allah upon you – when you were enemies and He brought your hearts together and you became, by His favour, brothers. And you were on the edge of a pit of the Fire, and He saved you from it. This is how Allah explains to you His revelations so that you may have the right guidance.[129]

In Tawhid's founding charter, much was also made of the need for pious Sunni Muslims to "unite until they become one body" in order to "share a common sentiment as well as work toward a collective objective on behalf of God."[130] The movement's openness to a wide array of ideological subcurrents within Islamism and its ostensible commitment to the divine injunction of "Islamic unity"[131] sharply contrasted with the Islamic Group, which had developed a reputation for using religion out of self-interest. "Working for God," then, rather than for the sake of a partisan entity, initially attracted many committed activists who joined Tawhid because of its promise to unify Tripoli's faithful.

The third and final factor which appealed to the constituency of Tripolitan Islamists was the sense that Tawhid had strong ideological credentials. This resulted from various reasons. One was that, unlike the Islamic Group which was fast institutionalizing, Tawhid's founding charter stressed it was "not a political party" about to run for elections and looking for its self-interest, but instead a self-described "popular" and "jihadi" group calling for the formation of an "Islamic state" and "preparing members of the nation for a moral, spiritual and physical struggle against the enemies."[132] It also helped, of course, that Tawhid's three founding factions had never considered running for office and had always been known for their embrace of a militant breed of Islamism. The other reason behind the sense that Tawhid had strong ideological credentials was its ability early on to attract to its cause Tripoli's most famous Islamist "ideological entrepreneurs," figures known locally for their high commitment to Islamist ideology who mobilized their worldviews with

---

[129] See, for instance, "Al-qiyada al-islamiya fi Trablus" ["The Islamic leadership in Tripoli"], *Al-Taqwa* (Vol. 20, April 1985).

[130] *Al-khutut al-asasia li-muntalaqat wa mabade wa ahdaf Harakat al-Tawhid al-Islami* [The fundamental premises, principles and objectives of the Islamic Unification Movement] (copy given to the author, undated).

[131] "Al-aftitahiya: al-Tawhid" ["Editorial: the Tawhid"], *al-Tawhid* (June 20, 1984).

[132] *Al-khutut al-asasia li-muntalaqat wa mabade wa ahdaf Harakat al-Tawhid al-Islami* [The fundamental premises, principles and objectives of the Islamic Unification Movement] (copy given to the author, undated).

200   The Emergence of Tawhid

the goal of spreading them to society and of shaping the nature of activism. Two of these figures, Fu'ad al-Kurdi and Abu Imara, even integrated Tawhid's "Consultative Council" (*Majlis al-Shura*), which acted as the movement's decision-making body, an institution presided over by Sa'id Sha'aban that gathered six other influential founding figures. That these "ideological entrepreneurs" known for their sincere commitment to Islamism and their willingness to spread ideology had integrated Tawhid reinforced its Islamist credentials.

Tellingly, the grand ceremony which officially marked the birth of Tawhid in August 1982 featured one of these "ideological entrepreneurs," Abu Imara, who had introduced Sa'id Sha'aban during Friday prayers at Tripoli's Tawbe mosque by publicly pledging allegiance to him as "Emir of all the believers," or leader of the faithful, in front of a crowd of thousands. The very fact that Abu Imara had taken such a prominent role in the ceremony was designed to suggest to Tripoli's Islamists that Tawhid's ideological credentials would be impeccable.

Many pious Tripolitans who attended the ceremony were also inspired by the parallels this drew with Islamic history and in particular the way in which tribes had sworn allegiance (*al-baya'a*) to the Prophet – a tradition then perpetuated under successive Islamic Caliphates. The way in which Abu Imara had addressed the audience had itself seemed straight out of Islamic history and, by all accounts, inspired many of those attending to also join Tawhid.[133] "Oh Muslims!" Abu Imara started in a loud, dramatic voice. "Hear what I say and do what I do! We proclaim that we choose Sa'id Sha'aban, may God protect him, as cleric of all the mosques and as Emir of Tawhid, so repeat after me!" he continued, while turning toward the cleric by his side. "Oh, leader of all fighters, we pledge allegiance to you and promise to stand by you through thick and thin and to obey to God, His prophet and His holy book!"[134] Many of those who attended reported feeling "subjugated"[135] by the event, some recalling that Tawhid's leaders, with Sa'id Sha'aban at their helm, had even concluded the ceremony by officially declaring Tripoli an "Islamic Emirate" – that is, a land only ruled by Islamic law. Sources diverge on this issue but all concur that the ceremony had been very successful in attracting committed Islamist recruits, one observer noting that "thousands of Tripolitans" had reportedly "swarmed inside and in front of the

---

[133] Interview with current and former Tawhid members, Tripoli, July–August 2014.
[134] Text of Abu Imara's speech provided by Ibrahim Antar (figure close to Abu Imara), Tripoli, August 2014.
[135] Interview with Salem al-Rafe'i (former Tawhid cleric nowadays a Salafi cleric), Tripoli, July 2014.

Tawbe mosque in the Old City in order to pledge allegiance to its orator and imam, sheikh Sa'id Sha'aban, as their Emir."[136] Tawhid's instant religious and ideological credentials bolstered the momentum around its formation.

The actions undertaken by Tawhid just a short while after its creation also rapidly reinforced its growing status as the incontestable movement of Tripoli's Islamist constituency. Tawhid began organizing a series of religious public events like open-air lectures and Quran recitation competitions, as well as large-scale religious demonstrations throughout the city in commemoration of episodes of Islamic history or holy days like Eid or the Prophet's birthday. The movement, as its clout grew in Tripoli, also went to lengths to ornate the city with Islamic decoration and symbols, even at one point erecting a massive sign of God on the central square and another, smaller one at the entrance of the port neighborhood of Mina. Moreover, Tawhid formulated an ideology which, if it was idiosyncratic because it drew on Sunni as well as Shia references, was unambiguously Islamist and militant in character, calling for an Islamic revolution in Lebanon, the implementation of Islamic law and even for bombing attacks to be undertaken against the United States and the West to avenge Palestine. It also attempted to spread its revolutionary Islamist concepts to all Tripolitans through its growing control over mosques and indoctrination camps, as well as by taking over the teaching of religion in the city's schools and forcibly imposing its vision of Islamic norms onto society. Even Tawhid's foreign relations seemed largely driven by Islamist ideology as the movement allied with Syrian Islamist groups, Fatah's underground Islamist wing and the Islamic Republic of Iran. All of this satisfied the constituency of Tripolitan Islamists who, even when they did not join Tawhid, still sympathized with it and viewed its growing clout as epitomizing a "golden age of Islam."[137]

Tawhid's fast-increasing popularity with Tripoli's militant Islamists also resided in its readiness to engage in what appeared to be ideologically driven violence. In the weeks that followed its creation in mid-1982, the new movement undermined what was left of the Lebanese government's authority in Tripoli by forcibly taking over police stations and by intimidating the local detachment of the Lebanese army into remaining confined to its military barracks.[138] It also continued engaging in

---

[136] Abi Samra, *Trablus*, p. 113.
[137] Interview with Bilal Hidara (Salafi cleric), Tripoli, July 2014.
[138] "Tension dans le Nord," *L'Orient Le Jour* (August 25, 1982) and "Aggression contre les Forces de Sécurité Intérieures à Tripoli," *L'Orient Le Jour* (September 8, 1982).

202   The Emergence of Tawhid

contention with the Syrian army and its local allies. The combined weight of the Islamist factions who had allied within Tawhid meant that it rapidly outgunned Tripoli's pro-Syrian forces, chief among them the Arab Democratic Party made up of Alawis in Jabal Mohsen. Clashes between Tawhid and the Arab Democratic Party killed twelve in August 1982, fifteen in September, twenty-seven in October, sixty in December and finally as many as seventy-six in January 1983.[139] The death toll in the Arab Democratic Party's ranks was such that it pushed Ali Eid's men to hole themselves up in their gated neighborhood of Jabal Mohsen and to refrain from engaging in hostilities. Concomitantly, Tawhid's military strength had grown to the extent that, after months of skirmishes with the Syrian army units still posted in Tripoli, the regime had to finally announce the full withdrawal of its troops from the northern city.[140] This represented a major victory for the new militant Islamist movement, which took over the checkpoints and military posts occupied by the Syrian army, upon which it erected its own flags made up of black and green, respectively the colors of jihad and Islam. Days later the constituency of Tripoli's militant Islamists, already very pleased by all of Tawhid's actions, was even more satisfied to see the movement bloodily cracking down on a criminal group involved in drug dealing, the "Hashasheen," killing nine and injuring eighteen, and solemnly announcing it would continue to "clean Tripoli of its gangsters and drug addicts."[141] Weeks later Tawhid would eliminate with bloodshed what was left of Tripolitan leftist parties, paving the way for the movement's complete military control of the northern city. By mid-1983, then, on the first anniversary of Tawhid's creation, rumors even began spreading that the movement would proclaim the birth of an Islamic Republic in Tripoli.[142] This ultimately did not occur but it still epitomized how powerful the Islamist movement had grown by then.

Yet the puzzle of Tawhid's sudden and overwhelming rise in Tripoli is that the movement's ideological credentials alone do not account for its high mobilizing capacity. Many of the actions mentioned above did

---

[139] I draw these figures from my analysis of the fatalities and injuries reported in Tripolitan daily *Al-Incha*, Lebanese daily *L'Orient Le Jour* and Adib N'ame: Adib N'ame, "Al-amen fi Trablus, 1980–1985" ["The security in Tripoli, 1980–1985"], *Nada' al-Shamal* (undated, copy given to the author).

[140] "Nouvelle nuit d'enfer àTripoli," *L'Orient Le Jour* (June 22, 1983).

[141] "Attaque du Tawhid contre le domicile d'Abu Bilal à Tripoli," *L'Orient Le Jour* (June 23, 1983).

[142] Lebanese daily *L'Orient Le Jour* reported that "rumours circulate in Tripoli according to which the president of Tawhid, Sheikh Sa'id Sha'aban, has the intention to proclaim on 15th August the birth of an Islamic Republic." See "Violents accrochages à Tripoli," *L'Orient Le Jour* (August 2, 1983).

attract the constituency of ideologically committed Tripolitan Islamists to its cause. But, although a handful of them became "ideological entrepreneurs" with influence in the movement, these committed Islamists did not represent more than 1,000–1,250 members – that is, about half of Tawhid's overall membership.[143] The numerical weight of the committed Islamists in the movement can be further contrasted to the 30,000 people who carried Sa'id Sha'aban's body for his funeral, who can be viewed as Tawhid sympathizers but who were less or not committed to Islamist ideology. In one of the cables it dedicated to the movement, the CIA itself recognized Tawhid's high heterogeneity, noting that it was made up of factions "each committed in varying degrees"[144] to militant Islamist ideology. In other words, it featured what I call a wide "spectrum of ideological commitment." This significant internal variation in ideological commitment transpired when Tawhid appeared to engage in what at first glance looked like ideologically driven Islamist violence. Its exercise of violence featured such spatial, temporal and organizational variation and witnessed such stark inconsistencies with its self-professed beliefs system that it could not possibly have been guided by ideology only. Finally, even if ideology alone could explain Tawhid's behavior and sudden rise in Tripoli, it would still not account for why the broader constituency of Lebanese, as opposed to just Tripolitan, Sunni Islamists – active in Sidon and Beirut – never joined the movement.

Tawhid came to attract only Tripolitans and only certain types of Tripolitans. As this chapter has shown, they included many sincerely committed Islamists. But Tawhid was also made up of factions which had instrumentalized militant Islamism and, on its "spectrum of ideological commitment," stood on the less or not ideologically committed side. This included Bab al-Tebbaneh's "neighborhood Islamists," who were guided by local concerns, practices and solidarities as well as by loyalty to Khalil Akkawi, now in Tawhid. There were also the "subaltern Islamists," or urban poor, who joined the movement because of its readiness to address their grievances and to channel older social tensions through involvement in a type of violence closer to "social jihad" than to ideology. Moreover, many local rebels motivated by Tripolitan identity and concerns also sporadically joined during key episodes of contention,

---

[143] This is an estimate of the numerical weight of the members from Soldiers of God, the Movement of Arab Lebanon and independent Islamists who were all known committed Islamists and joined Tawhid, based on interviews with current and former members as well as on a CIA cable. US Central Intelligence Agency, "Lebanon: Islamic fundamentalism in Tripoli" (Top Secret, NESAR 86-003JX, January 17, 1986).

[144] US Central Intelligence Agency, "Shaykh Shaban: Lebanon's radical Sunni cleric" (Top Secret, NESAR 85-003CX, January 18, 1985).

204   The Emergence of Tawhid

for example during the September 1985 battle between Tawhid and the Syrian regime, attracted by the movement's "Tripolitan habitus" and by its engagement with local issues. Finally, in a show of how wide Tawhid's "spectrum of ideological commitment" truly was, it also drew in "Islamo-gangsters" or recruits who were attracted by the prospect of controlling Tripoli's underground economy even when it meant violating Islamist ideology. The following chapters continue to analyze these phenomena in more detail and assess the extent to which internal variation in ideological commitment affected Tawhid's discourse and behavior, from its engagement in violence to its foreign alliances.

Theorizing Back

By tracing the process of Tawhid's emergence in mid-1982 and exploring the trajectory of the militant Islamist factions which joined it, this chapter also draws three broader theoretical implications to better understand the role of ideology in social, rebel and terrorist movements.

First, building on Chapter 2, I point to the need to investigate collective shifts from one ideology to another and to scrutinize their potential continuities. While, in Chapter 2, what was striking about the Popular Resistance's shift from Marxism to Islamism was that neighborhood concerns and loyalty to the local "champion of mobilization" guided patterns of collective ideological conversion, the Movement of Arab Lebanon's successive embrace of Maoism and Khomeinism was driven by broader preexisting political commitments to the Palestinian cause and anti-imperialism. The reasons which pushed the two movements to embrace Islamism may have differed, then, but in both cases what remained at stake was an instrumental shift from one "protest ideology" to another.

Second, I delve into another mechanism, already signaled in Chapter 2, through which ideology mattered – the "ideological entrepreneurship" of deeply committed Islamist figures who mobilize an Islamist beliefs system and strive to mold the nature of activism and of the broader environment in which they operate around these worldviews. In this chapter I point to the "ideological entrepreneurship" of two figures in particular, the Sufi master al-Haqqani, who spread "Sufi jihadist" views in Hama and Tripoli, and the Iranian volunteer fighter in South Lebanon, al-Farsi, who was key in convincing the Movement of Arab Lebanon's own leader to embrace Khomeinism at first instrumentally and then sincerely. This highlights the role of "ideological entrepreneurs" in shaping the broader ideological environment and in the decision of individuals and movements to embrace an ideology. I also

Theorizing Back

suggest toward the end of the chapter that the fact that local figures of this status joined Tawhid instantly gave it ideological credentials and thus committed recruits.

Third and lastly, I demonstrate that ideological commitment can be highly fluid. Far from an assumption in the literature which treats ideological commitment as given and fixed, the degree to which individuals sincerely believe in and are guided by an ideology can sometimes evolve considerably over time – in a more or in a less committed direction. For instance, one of the reasons for which the Islamic Group witnessed splits in the mid to late 1970s was the growing sense among its members that, for all their Islamist discourse, its leaders no longer appeared sincerely committed to ideology and instead were increasingly concerned with keeping a hold over the movement's leadership and running for office. In other words, once sincere believers, their ideological commitment had gradually eroded. By contrast, while the Movement of Arab Lebanon had initially embraced "Khomeinist" Islamism instrumentally, its leader and members became sincerely committed to ideology. Such fluidity shows the utility of the concept of a "spectrum of ideological commitment," which allows for the analysis of how ideological commitments may evolve over time.

Through the story of Tawhid's emergence in 1982, then, this chapter underlines broader points related to the role of ideology in contentious politics, such as the ways in which some movements shift their beliefs system from one "protest ideology" to another, the role "ideological entrepreneurs" play in socializing and educating members into new ideologies and in cementing their beliefs, and the fluidity of ideological commitment.

4 A Vernacular Islamist Ideology

Given the speed at which Tawhid gained momentum in the constituency of Tripoli's committed Islamists in 1982, external observers began predicting its concomitant spread to Lebanon's other Sunni strongholds where Islamism held some sway, like Beirut and Sidon. The CIA, which dedicated two full cables to the rise of Tawhid, seemed particularly nervous about this prospect. What worried it was the allegedly "clearcut fundamentalist ideology" which it said animated the movement as it drew on "orthodox and inflexible Islam." Tawhid, the cables noted, had shortly after its creation transformed Tripoli into an "Islamic city" where "Sharia law is applied," with strict rules governing "every aspect of human behavior from dress codes to the prohibition of liquor consumption."[1] Intelligence officers were therefore anxious that, if the movement ever spread outside of Tripoli, it might seek to implement its model of Islamic governance on the whole country. They also seemed especially concerned about Tawhid's declared readiness to engage in "revolutionary violence." It would violently overthrow the Lebanese government and create an Islamic Republic; but what was equally frightening was that it might also target the West, given that the movement's ideology was "vehemently anti-Western" and had on several occasions "threatened the United States and the West with operations on their territory."[2] Yet in spite of the efforts of some members, as tackled in Chapter 7, Tawhid never acted on the grand goals of its ideology and, instead of spreading to all of Lebanon, it remained confined to Tripoli. This was made even more intriguing by a second puzzle. Behind the outward appearance of a group driven by uniform, deterritorialized Islamist beliefs, its ideology was highly eclectic and shaped by local narratives and identities. What, then, accounted for these idiosyncrasies?

---

[1] US Central Intelligence Agency, "Shaykh Shaban: Lebanon's radical Sunni cleric" (Top Secret, NESAR 85-003CX, January 18, 1985).

[2] US Central Intelligence Agency, "Lebanon: Islamic fundamentalism in Tripoli" (Top Secret, NESAR 86-003JX, January 17, 1986).

A Vernacular Islamist Ideology

This chapter explores the many facets of Tawhid's ideology, striving to account for the remarkably heterogeneous and local character of its ideological production and arguing that these two features restricted the movement's appeal in Lebanon's wider Islamist community. It builds on the analysis of Tawhid's corpus, which comprises its founding charter but also articles published in its flagship newspaper and oral statements made in sermons and the media. I begin by describing the movement's unambiguously Islamist and rigidly conservative views of society. These especially stemmed from the influence exerted on Tawhid by two Egyptian and Syrian ideologues of the radical wing of the Muslim Brotherhood in the 1960s and 1970s, Sayyid Qutb and Sa'id Hawwa. A second broad theme which emerges from Tawhid's ideological corpus is a virulent revolutionary political orientation advocating for the overthrow of the Lebanese government by force, and more broadly for the advent of Islamic revolutions throughout the Middle East. I notice that, in this respect, Tawhid drew on some of the radical Sunni Islamist movements and figures back then on the rise, such as Egyptian Islamic Jihad or Abdallah Azzam, a Jordanian ideologue who called for a worldwide "jihad" against the Soviet Union. The third theme which is strikingly present in Tawhid's intellectual production is the movement's admiration for the ideological model offered by the Islamic Republic of Iran. This model, transposed by Tawhid to Lebanon, included calls for the establishment of an Islamic Republic, an injunction that the country's Sunni and Shia Muslims unite to undermine the political dominance of the Christians and threats of a bombing campaign against the West. Tawhid's deployment of these three grand ideological themes is what made it look so threatening from the outside. But, in the community of more orthodox Islamists, its willingness to draw on such eclectic strands of Sunni and Shia Islamism was perceived as too idiosyncratic or, some said, incoherent, with many raising doubts as to what the ultimate purpose of Tawhid's ideological production was. Moreover, I also point out that, when looking closer at the movement's full ideological corpus, a fourth theme emerges and equals or outweighs the others– engagement with all things Tripoli. Tawhid went to great lengths to cast its grand Islamist ideology within Tripoli's symbolic meaning and within the local narratives, grievances and identities linked to it. At first glance this seemed to primarily result from a pragmatic strategy to recruit heavily in Tripoli by making its Islamism more vernacular, or chiming with the local cultural backdrop. Yet it soon transpired that the movement itself was also imbued in a "Tripolitan habitus"; that is, it had become so embedded in a Tripolitan context traversed by a particularly strong collective identity and longstanding local historical narratives that it

208   A Vernacular Islamist Ideology

had internalized these local features which came to significantly inform the nature of its Islamist ideology. This "habitus of place" made many members interpret the world through Tripolitan lenses, at times rendering the themes they tackled and the vocabulary they employed very local. Far from being guided by deterritorialized goals only, therefore, Tawhid's ideology could best be described as a "vernacular Islamism" cast in and shaped by local narratives and concerns. Deploying such a "vernacular Islamism" allowed the movement to root itself deeply in Tripoli's symbolic meaning and mobilize locally, but it restricted its appeal outside the city.

On the Radical Fringes of the Muslim Brotherhood

This and the next two sections examine the socially conservative and politically revolutionary facets of Tawhid's Islamist ideology, which drew on strikingly eclectic references. I argue that a key reason for the heterogeneity of its ideological corpus, which breaks with dominant views of ideologies as rigid and uniform, was that the enterprise of ideological production fulfilled strategic functions in the movement. These included outbidding rivals, strengthening internal cohesion and activating the bonds of ideological solidarity tying Tawhid to external actors. These three strategic functions of ideological production in Tawhid were not mutually exclusive, often overlapped with other functions of ideology already identified in the literature – like "framing" to enlist new recruits, galvanize members and justify movement behavior – and, crucially, always coexisted with the presence of sincere believers. This heterogeneity was further reinforced by internal variation in commitments within the movement, because the process of ideological production was being carried out jointly by cadres and leaders who used ideology for the functions laid out above but also by "ideological entrepreneurs" driven by a genuine will to spread their Islamist worldviews (and whose background and degree of influence will be studied in greater detail in Chapter 6). As a result, Tawhid's discourse drew on highly eclectic strands of militant Islamism, something which made it sound threatening to the West but, in the community of Lebanese Islamists, gave way to the sense that its ideology was incoherent and restricted its appeal.

A first important aspect of the trove of ideological statements produced by Tawhid, whether through its founding charter, flagship newspaper or the lectures delivered by its officials, was a socially very conservative framework for understanding society. In this respect its views drew unambiguously on the radical fringes of Muslim Brotherhood thinking.

On the Radical Fringes of the Muslim Brotherhood 209

A case in point was the frequent use by Tawhid of the term "ignorance" (*jahiliya*). This Quranic term was developed by conservative Islamic thinker Ibn Taymiyya in the early fourteenth century and popularized in the 1950s by Pakistani Islamist Abul Ala Maududi to refer to the "barbaric" nature of the polytheist beliefs and practices which used to prevail in the Arabian Peninsula before the spread of Islam. The term was then more fully conceptualized by the ideologue of the radical wing of the Egyptian Muslim Brotherhood, Sayyid Qutb, who most importantly developed a parallel between the "ignorance" of pre-Islamic times and the "new ignorance" allegedly characterizing the contemporary Middle East. Qutb was writing in the early 1960s, a period marked by the predominance of the left in Egyptian society and by Jamal Abdel Nasser's harsh repression of Islamist movements.[3] Large popular support for the Egyptian president's policies led Sayyid Qutb to argue that society, despite "claiming to be Muslim," had in fact returned to a state of pre-Islamic "ignorance." "Everything around is ignorance,"[4] he wrote, "People's ideas and beliefs, manners and morals, culture, art and literature, laws and principles." Sayyid Qutb's writings, and especially his conceptualization of the term of "ignorance" and application to contemporary politics, became extremely controversial back then – even the Muslim Brotherhood officially distanced itself from him. This was because, by branding Muslims who were not Islamists as "ignorant" and therefore as impious Muslims, Sayyid Qutb religiously and ideologically legitimized the use of violence against them. His concept of "ignorance" later gained traction with the growing cultural and political momentum of Islamism in the 1970s and 1980s and it fueled the rise of militant Islamist movements in Egypt and throughout the Middle East.[5] Yet, for the more mainstream Islamist movements, Sayyid Qutb's concept of "ignorance" remained taboo.

While Lebanon's Muslim Brotherhood, the Islamic Group, also officially rejected the use of the concept of "ignorance" as it was fast becoming more institutionalized, as Chapter 3 showed, Tawhid for its part right away made the term a cornerstone of its ideology. In a mark of its significance it mentioned the concept in one of its newspaper's editorials and it even dedicated a lengthy additional article to it, entitled

---

[3] Fawaz Gerges, *Making the Arab world: Nasser, Qutb and the clash that shaped the Middle East* (Princeton: Princeton University Press, 2018).

[4] Sayyid Qutb quoted in Jeffrey Kenney, *Muslim rebels: Kharijites and the politics of extremism in Egypt* (London: Oxford University Press, 2006), p. 93.

[5] Gilles Kepel, *Jihad: the trail of political Islam* (Cambridge, MA: Harvard University Press, 2003).

210   A Vernacular Islamist Ideology

"Ignorance returns in the twentieth century."[6] In the vein of Sayyid Qutb, the authors lambasted the "moral crisis" which, in their view, was in the process of engulfing local society. "We have associations for homosexuals, clubs for people who commit adultery, governments for gamblers, and societies for criminals, alcoholics and drug junkies," the article stated. "How hideous is this picture! Isn't the world today much gloomier than the 'ignorance' of the sixth century?" it wondered. The article concluded with a call to action. "This volatile world is about to collapse. It desperately needs to be saved." The main culprits, in Tawhid's eyes, were the West because of the Anglo-American and French influence in Lebanon and the local Maronites whom it suspected of being pro-Western. In another article, Tawhid also blamed local leftists whose defense of "personal freedoms" and "secularization" had spread "ignorance." Only a "return to religion" could prevent the "ignorance" from turning Lebanon into a "jungle society."[7] Unlike the Islamic Group, then, Tawhid fully embraced Qutb and proudly brandished his concept of "ignorance."

Tawhid also drew on another Islamist thinker who followed in Qutb's footsteps, Sa'id Hawwa, who was the ideologue of the radical wing of Syria's Muslim Brotherhood. Hawwa is less known than Qutb but he is widely seen as having developed even more radical ideas, leading mainstream Islamist groups in the Middle East to officially distance themselves from him – including the Syrian Muslim Brotherhood and the Islamic Group in Lebanon. Writing in the late 1970s as the struggle between Syria's Islamists and the Ba'ath regime was heating up, Hawwa espoused Qutb's diagnosis on the "ignorance" of society. Yet, while a degree of ambiguity continued to surround the exact meaning of Qutb's writings because he had died shortly after publishing them, Hawwa was crystal clear about the need to carry out armed struggle against those he called the "disbelievers." Indeed, he went as far as specifying a timing for the "jihad" against them and even established categories of "disbelievers," arguing that the struggle had to be waged instantly against the "hypocrites" and "apostates,"[8] a category to which the less religious Muslims who were members of secular leftist parties

---

[6] "Al-jahiliya min jadid fi al-qarn al-'ashrin" ["The ignorance returns in the twentieth century"], al-Tawhid (June 20, 1984).

[7] "Hiwar m'a al-Duktur al-Shaykh Muhammad 'Ali al-Juzu: hel yusbih Lubnan Jumhuriya Islamiya?" ["An interview with sheikh Dr. Mohammed Ali Jouzou: will Lebanon become an Islamic Republic?"], al-Tawhid (July 27, 1984).

[8] For more on Sa'id Hawwa's thought, see the excellent article: Itchak Weismann, "Sa'id Hawwa and Islamic revivalism in Ba'thist Syria" Studia Islamica (No. 85, 1997), pp. 136–7.

On the Radical Fringes of the Muslim Brotherhood   211

belonged. This laid the groundwork for the use of violence by Syrian Islamist movements in the 1970s and early 1980s, justifying religiously and ideologically the killing of members of the Ba'ath Party and more broadly of regime sympathizers – especially those who were Alawis. For these reasons, Sa'id Hawwa became controversial and Lebanon's Islamic Group, which tried to maintain a working relationship with the Syrian regime, did not spread his writings.[9]

Once more, for its part Tawhid engaged significantly with Sa'id Hawwa, its ideological production featuring many of the Syrian ideologue's key concepts and arguments. One such example was an article which was fully dedicated to trying to reformulate in relatively simple terms Hawwa's conceptualization of "hypocrisy" and "apostasy." "[Pious Muslim believers] must be aware [of the difference] between those who believe and those who do not," the article started. "But between the categories [of] the believers and disbelievers there is a third category," it read. "This grey category, the category of hypocrites, is a real danger and threatens the Islamic position" because "it functions like a shiny gate of polytheism which appeals to Muslims who are not wise or bright enough." The article ended with a warning to these "hypocrites" that they were running a "great danger" and would soon have to face "Allah's anger."[10] Beyond singling out the Alawis, Tawhid once again drew on Hawwa to also lambaste secular parties. Another article explicitly assimilated the category of "hypocrites" with "leftist parties." "They want to mislead the believers!"[11] it claimed. Openly embracing Hawwa's concepts again distinguished Tawhid from the Islamic Group.

Inspired by the writings of Sayyid Qutb and Sa'id Hawwa, Tawhid's ideological production featured remedies to the presence of "ignorance" and of all kinds of "disbelievers" in society. One of its proposals was to put Muslims back on to "the correct path that the Prophet had taken,"[12] which would involve redefining the social norms considered lawful or unlawful according to Islamic teachings. This included entering into the details of private life. One of Tawhid's "ideological entrepreneurs" thus

---

[9] For more on the Islamic Group's policy of self-distancing from Sayyid Qutb's and Sa'id Hawwa's writings, see: Abdel Ghani Imad, *Al-harakat al-Islamiya fi Lubnan: al-din wa al-siyasa fi mujtam'a mutanawe'a* [*The Islamist movements in Lebanon: religion and politics in a diverse society*] (Beirut: Dar al-Talia, 2006).

[10] "Al-mawqif al-siessi al-shar'ai (2)" ["The political stance of Sharia law (2)], *al-Tawhid* (August 2, 1984).

[11] "Al-mawqif al-siessi al-shar'ai (1)" ["The political stance of Sharia law (1)], *al-Tawhid* (July 27, 1984).

[12] *Al-khutut al-asasia li-muntalaqat wa mabade wa ahdaf Harakat al-Tawhid al-Islami* [The fundamental premises, principles and objectives of the Islamic Unification Movement] (copy given to the author, undated).

212 A Vernacular Islamist Ideology

explained to his audience that while it was, for instance, "permissible to wear the clothes of modern civilization," Islam's "mission" consisted of "preventing moral decay in nightclubs, beaches and in bars." In the movement's view, then, religion acted as "a comprehensive system regulating all aspects of life – from the top to the bottom." It had to "allow what is good for society and prohibit what is wrong." It bluntly asserted that "real freedom is not the freedom of [having] sex, absolute freedom of expression or the freedom of an individual to run a state."[13] Another proposal of Tawhid to fight the "ignorance" plaguing society and to eliminate the "disbelievers" was to embark on a peaceful campaign of "proselytizing" (da'wa) to convince sectors of society to change their beliefs and ways of life. And, in case peaceful social and religious activism was not enough, Tawhid's "ideological entrepreneurs" hinted that the use of violence would be justified. While one article stated that "if our youth tried to fight moral corruption they would be doing the right thing,"[14] the movement's founding charter unequivocally pushed Muslims to "take responsibility for upholding Islamic principles" and to "overcome their fear of action."[15] Tawhid also suggested that "cultural momentum" for its religious ideology was on its side. The mosques of Lebanon and of Tripoli in particular, they claimed, had become "jam-packed with young men," women had "returned to wearing the headscarf" and Muslims at large were ready to fight "to defend their mission."[16] Throughout the trove of statements published by Tawhid, the social conservatism and ideological authoritarianism of thinkers often positioned on the radical fringes of the Muslim Brotherhood fully transpired.

Yet, in addition to reflecting the sincere commitments of some, the fact that Tawhid took so much inspiration from Sayyid Qutb and Sa'id Hawwa also resulted from the sense that drawing on these thinkers and their concepts would fulfill three strategic functions.

First, and perhaps most obviously, referencing two famous Islamist ideologues whose concepts were considered controversial but which, given the growth of Islamism's momentum, were still getting increasing

---

[13] "Hiwar m'a al-Duktur al-Shaykh Muhammad 'Ali al-Juzu: hel yusbih Lubnan Jumhuriya Islamiya?" ["An interview with sheikh Dr. Mohammed Ali Jouzou: will Lebanon become an Islamic Republic?"], al-Tawhid (July 27, 1984).

[14] Ibid.

[15] Al-khutut al-asasia li-muntalaqat wa mabade wa ahdaf Harakat al-Tawhid al-Islami [The fundamental premises, principles and objectives of the Islamic Unification Movement] (copy given to the author, undated).

[16] "Al-'alam fi al-gharb y'akis khawfahum min al-Islam wal-Muslimin" ["The media in the West reflects their fear of Islam and of Muslims"], al-Tawhid (June 20, 1984).

On the Radical Fringes of the Muslim Brotherhood   213

attention allowed Tawhid to outbid its rival, the mainstream Islamic Group, by signaling more ideological purity. In contrast with a rival portrayed as looking out for its own interests and as increasingly out of touch with its Islamist constituency, Tawhid cast itself as ideologically pure and true to its Islamist ideals.

Second, drawing on Qutb and Hawwa was essential internally because, as an official in Tawhid explained, the movement was made up of a "cocktail"[17] of subcurrents of Sunni Islamism. Many members and some leaders originally hailed from the Islamic Group, which they had left precisely because of the perceived erosion of the organization's commitment to a "revolutionary Islam." Tawhid's head himself, Sa'id Sha'aban, originally came from the Islamic Group. According to his son he had long been "fond"[18] of Qutb and Hawwa, and he had been particularly disenfranchised with the way the organization had made them taboo thinkers in the 1970s. Two other factions in Tawhid which were especially inspired by the two ideologues were the "ideological entrepreneurs" who, as Chapter 6 details, often mobilized their world-views, and the committed Islamists who before the 1982 merger had been members of Soldiers of God – a group which directly drew its name from one of Sa'id Hawwa's most celebrated books.[19] Not everyone in Tawhid was equally attracted by Qutb and Hawwa. Yet to preserve internal cohesion in the context of a movement which had merged subcurrents of Islamism, of which members inspired by the radical wing of the Muslim Brotherhood were a key part, Tawhid's corpus made space for the two thinkers.

Third, the prominence of Hawwa's concepts and arguments in Tawhid's ideological production within a broader context marked by the constant threat of a Syrian military crackdown on Tripoli between 1982 and 1985 suggests that some Islamist officials may have strategically drawn on the Syrian ideologue to construct the appearance of ideological proximity with Syrian Islamists inspired by his writings. They may have hoped to activate bonds of ideological solidarity and to entice the dozens of Syrian militants who had escaped Syria and taken refuge in Tripoli after the 1982 Hama massacre into supporting Tawhid. These militants knew how to fight and they vehemently opposed the Syrian regime, but

---

[17] Interview with Ghassan Ghoshe (Tawhid official close to Esmat Murad and Iran), Tripoli, August 2014.

[18] Interview with Bilal Sha'aban (Sa'id Sha'aban's son and political heir, leader of Tawhid), Tripoli, July 2014.

[19] Interview with Abu Meriam Khassouq (former head of the Education Office), Tripoli, September 2014 and interviews with Soldiers of God leader Kan'an Naji, as well as commanders and members, Tripoli, July 2014.

214   A Vernacular Islamist Ideology

many of them did not share aspects of Tawhid's ideology. Specifically drawing on Hawwa, then, might have helped in convincing some to nonetheless join the movement more actively.

Peppering Tawhid's ideological production with concepts drawn from Qutb and Hawwa therefore fulfilled some of the functions already laid out in the literature, for example "framing" to enlist recruits, galvanize members and justify violence. But, importantly, it also allowed it to outbid rivals, bolster internal cohesion and signal interest for external backing.

A Revolutionary Political Orientation

The second core theme which clearly emerges from Tawhid's ideological corpus is a revolutionary political orientation advocating the overthrow of the Lebanese government. This section first details the contours of the movement's revolutionary discourse and then argues that a function of ideology was again to outbid the mainstream Islamic Group. Throughout the section it also transpires that Tawhid's revolutionary political orientation played other roles, for example "framing" the political and social grievances which affected the wider community of Lebanon's Sunnis in a militant Islamist discourse to enlist new recruits.

Tawhid developed a particularly virulent critique of Lebanon's political system, or "regime" (*nizam*), as it called it pejoratively. To begin with the Islamist movement vehemently opposed the democratic nature of Lebanese politics. It was clear right away that, besides reflecting the belief of many of its members, this criticism was aimed at channeling a broader sense of disenchantment with politics in society. Developing a revolutionary and populist Islamist discourse, Tawhid insisted that "we reject democracy in favour of Islam" and argued against participation in elections, claiming that "the majority is not always right – one man alone may often hold the truth while all others are mistaken."[20] Unlike the Islamic Group which had taken part in Lebanon's 1972 parliamentary elections and would later continue running for office in the 1990s and 2000s, Tawhid thus unambiguously rejected institutionalization. Its founding charter stated that "Islam does not permit any human jurisdiction as this is regarded as a form of slavery."[21] The movement also played on a much

---

[20] "Le leader du MUI: l'Islam au lieu de la démocratie," *L'Orient Le Jour* (October 19, 1983).
[21] *Al-khutut al-asasia li-muntalaqat wa mabade wa ahdaf Harakat al-Tawhid al-Islami* [The fundamental premises, principles and objectives of the Islamic Unification Movement] (copy given to the author, undated).

A Revolutionary Political Orientation

wider disenfranchisement with political parties in Lebanon which, whatever their ideology, were seen as corrupt, self-interested vehicles ready to act on behalf of the highest bidder. As a result it harshly lambasted them as "creations of colonial powers" which had been designed to "divide Muslims" and asked the latter, instead, to "unite under the banner of God."[22] This was a hint to its name, for *Tawhid* literally meant "Islamic unification." The movement therefore went to great lengths to pose as an alternative to Lebanon's traditional parties by framing itself as "neither a political organization nor a constricted party succumbing to partisan leadership" but rather, as a "popular" movement seeking to "mobilize the masses" and to "unite Muslims under submission to God's will."[23] In other words, Tawhid was framing its ideology as answering a growing demand for noninstitutionalized politics.

Tawhid's critique of the "Lebanese regime" also targeted the Christian Maronite monopoly over the Lebanese presidency and control of key institutions, a central political issue at the time and a main source of grievance for Lebanon's Muslims. One of Tawhid's "ideological entrepreneurs" thus typically argued that "democracy has no meaning in Lebanon" since one community had "seized power for itself" and "robbed the country's treasures."[24] A central objective of the movement thus became to undermine what it called "political Maronism" – those ideologies and parties based on Christian collective identity concerned with representing and furthering the interests of the Maronite community. Undermining "political Maronism" involved launching vehement attacks on one of its symbols, the Phalanges, a right-wing Christian party. Tawhid's ideological corpus featured violent verbal attacks against Amine Gemayel, the party's leader and the new Lebanese president following the assassination of his brother Bashir in September 1982. He was accused of being a "tyrant" and of treating Muslims like "servants."[25] In addition, he was also suspected of plotting to forge "close relations" with Israel. This led the movement to equate the "Israeli regime" with what it now began calling the "Phalangist Lebanese regime." One piece of evidence Tawhid's ideological corpus pointed to was the Phalanges Party's involvement in the 1982 Sabra and Shatila massacre of Palestinians.[26] This was an act

---

[22] "Le drapeau de l'état hébreu piétiné à la mosquée de Bir Abed," *L'Orient Le Jour* (November 9, 1984).

[23] *Al-khutut al-asasia li-muntalaqat wa mabade wa ahdaf Harakat al-Tawhid al-Islami* [The fundamental premises, principles and objectives of the Islamic Unification Movement] (copy given to the author, undated).

[24] "Hiwar m'a al-Duktur al-Shaykh Muhammad 'Ali al-Juzu: hel yusbih Lubnan Jumhuriya Islamiya?" ["An interview with sheikh Dr. Mohammed Ali Jouzou: will Lebanon become an Islamic Republic?"], *al-Tawhid* (July 27, 1984).

[25] "Shaaban renvoie à dos Kataeb et Geagea," *L'Orient Le Jour* (March 15, 1985) and "Shaaban: saper les bases de l'Etat maronite phalangiste même si tout s'effondre avec lui," *L'Orient Le Jour* (March 9, 1985).

216   A Vernacular Islamist Ideology

which it deemed worthy of judgment by a "military tribunal," and as a result it swore to "disobey" the president until justice was done. It also used news of the massacre and other instances of sectarian strife to mobilize followers using the theme of self-defense. While one statement predicted that Lebanese Muslims will be eliminated, "like Palestinians were expelled from Palestine," the leader Sa'id Sha'aban expressed his belief that "the Crusaders and Jews," a reference to the Phalanges and to Israel, "are planning to throw Muslims out of their homelands."[27]

The reference to the "Crusaders" also showed that Tawhid's Islamist critique of Christian Maronite domination of Lebanon was on the verge of becoming sectarian. It espoused a provocative language which contributed to blurring the lines between, on the one hand, legitimately targeting "political Maronism," and on the other lumping all of Lebanon's Christians together in scathing sectarian attacks. This was perhaps done deliberately in a bid to channel the "cultural momentum" of Islamism which, as was tackled in Chapter 1, included a growth of sectarian animosity. Sa'id Sha'aban himself gained particular notoriety throughout the country after calling Lebanese President Amine Gemayel a "pig," a reference to his Christian background, and ordering him to "convert to Islam" and "start applying Islamic law."[28] The head of Tawhid routinely dismissed the plurality of views expressed in the Christian community and instead argued that "there is no way to get along with the Maronites." He argued that their presence in Lebanon was part of a "Maronite–Zionist conspiracy." He explained to his audience that members of the community were "brought up in Israel where they were taught how to lie and hate."[29] In his view, the alliance between the Phalange Party and Israel stemmed not from a temporary and pragmatic bargain but rather from a longstanding "Christian preference for Jews and Israel." This was one of the reasons which, accordingly, pushed Lebanese Christians to carry out a "cultural invasion" and to do their utmost to "distance Muslims from their religion." This

[26] It is worth noting that while Tawhid publications consistently blame the Phalange Party for the Sabra and Shatila massacre, the killings were actually carried out by Elie Hobeiqa, a Lebanese Forces military commander.

[27] "Al-sheikh Sa'id Sha'aban: silah al-Muslimin wajib shara'i wa ilwa' al-silah ma'siya li-lla" ["Sheikh Sa'id Sha'aban: the armament of Muslims is a Shari'a duty and surrendering is a grave sin"], *al-Tawhid* (April 26, 1984).

[28] "Shaaban: saper les bases de l'Etat maronite phalangiste même si tout s'effondre avec lui," *L'Orient Le Jour* (March 9, 1985) and "Shaaban répond à Gemayel: 'je ne suis pas fanatique mais ... '," *L'Orient Le Jour* (March 22, 1985).

[29] "Al-sheikh Sa'id Sha'aban: silah al-Muslimin wajib shara'i wa ilwa' al-silah ma'siya li-lla" ["Sheikh Sa'id Sha'aban: the armament of Muslims is a Shari'a duty and surrendering is a grave sin"], *al-Tawhid* (April 26, 1984).

A Revolutionary Political Orientation 217

"conspiracy" disqualified them from holding important positions in Lebanese politics. Sha'aban bluntly told them that "you Christians have proved that you are unable to run the country."[30] By using the language of Sunni Islamism to legitimize sectarian statements, Tawhid hoped to appeal to Lebanese Muslims whose view of religious coexistence in society had been affected by the civil war.

Besides "framing" the issues faced by many Lebanese Sunnis in an Islamist discourse in the hope of enlisting their support, a key function of much of this politically revolutionary aspect of Tawhid's ideological production was again to outbid its rival, the Islamic Group, which had toned town its criticism of Lebanon's political system to become institutionalized. In contrast with an Islamic Group ready to strike compromises to enter the game of Lebanese politics, then, Tawhid for its part unambiguously called for the downfall of the "Phalangist regime" through what it called a "victorious Islamic revolution." This Islamic revolution would have to be total, leaving no possible room for compromise with "regime" elements. Reflecting Tawhid's objective to outbid the Islamic Group, some of the movement's officials welcomed a delegation of Sudanese Islamists but then spent all their time publicly lambasting the institutionalized approach of Muslim Brotherhood branches throughout the Middle East, including the Islamic Group, criticizing these movements for being naïve and instead arguing that they "need to understand that a revolution cannot take place from within a regime."[31] To overthrow the Lebanese government, Tawhid explicitly justified the use of revolutionary violence, using religious arguments to claim that "the armament of Muslims is a duty in Islamic law" and that "surrendering is a grave sin."[32] Its very political charter, in fact, framed the movement in reference to violence, priding itself as being "revolutionary and jihadi."[33] This was again a way of outbidding the Islamic Group by appearing more ideologically daring.

---

[30] "Shaaban: non à un Liban athée," *L'Orient Le Jour* (April 13, 1985) and "Shaaban: le musulman ne peut être gouverné par un non-croyant," *L'Orient Le Jour* (December 1, 1984). See also: "Fi hadith li fadilat al-Sheikh Sa'id Sha'aban: eshtidad al-azma sayu'addi ila al-enhiyar" ["In a conversation with Sheikh Sa'id Sha'aban: the intensification of the crisis will lead to collapse"], *al-Tawhid* (April 18, 1986).

[31] "Shaaban invite les chrétiens à 'embrasser l'Islam'," *L'Orient Le Jour* (March 7, 1985) and "Shaaban: honte à Noumeyri," *L'Orient Le Jour* (March 26, 1985).

[32] "Al-sheikh Sa'id Sha'aban: silah al-Muslimin wajib shara'i wa ilwa' al-silah ma'siya li-lla" ["Sheikh Sa'id Sha'aban: the armament of Muslims is a Shari'a duty and surrendering is a grave sin"], *al-Tawhid* (April 26, 1984).

[33] *Al-khutut al-asasia li-muntalaqat wa mabade wa ahdaf Harakat al-Tawhid al-Islami* [The fundamental premises, principles and objectives of the Islamic Unification Movement] (copy given to the author, undated).

218   A Vernacular Islamist Ideology

Intellectually, Tawhid drew much of the revolutionary aspects of its ideological corpus from some of the most militant Sunni Islamist thinkers of the 1980s. One of them was Abdallah Azzam, a Jordanian Islamist ideologue who became controversial among more mainstream Islamist ranks because he religiously justified jihad as armed struggle, calling it "Islam's forgotten obligation," and made it a central tenet of his writings.[34] He is also infamous for having advocated a worldwide armed struggle against the Soviet Union after its invasion of Afghanistan in 1979. Showcasing Tawhid's stated affinity with the thought of Abdallah Azzam, its newspaper was filled with regular references to the "exploits" of the "Islamic resistance in Afghanistan"[35] which the Jordanian ideologue spearheaded. Another reference on which the movement drew was Egyptian Islamic Jihad (*al-Jihad al-Islami al-Misri*), the militant Islamist group which carried out the assassination of Egyptian President Anwar Sadat in 1981 and would later go on to merge with Al-Qaeda. In one of the articles of Tawhid's newspaper, tellingly entitled "Holy warriors against tyrants," the movement reproduced a series of Egyptian Islamic Jihad statements about the need for revolutionary violence and it concluded by praising Khalid Istambuli, the mastermind of Sadat's assassination who was later executed, going as far as calling him "a martyr."[36] Throughout its ideological corpus, Tawhid promised it would use violence to bring down the Lebanese government and even hinted that it might kill President Gemayel, calling him, in reference to Sadat's nickname, "Lebanon's Pharaoh," although it never executed its threats.

Making the Islamic Republic of Lebanon

The third theme which emerges from Tawhid's ideological production was as grandiose and ambitious – the movement allegedly wanted to import the "Iranian model" to Lebanon.

Ideology fulfilled several functions here. One of them was evidently to outbid the Islamic Group. Explicitly arguing for Lebanon to become an "Islamic Republic,"[37] a controversial concept, allowed Tawhid to pose as

---

[34] For more on Abdallah Azzam, see Thomas Hegghammer's excellent book: Thomas Hegghammer, *The caravan: Abdallah Azzam and the rise of global jihad* (Cambridge: Cambridge University Press, 2020).

[35] "Al-muqawama al-islamiya fi Afghanistan" ["The Islamic resistance in Afghanistan"], *Tawhid* (July 27, 1984).

[36] "Al-mujahidun fi wajh al-tugha" ["The mujahedeen against the tyrants"], *al-Tawhid* (August 2, 1984).

[37] "Hiwar m'a al-Duktur al-Shaykh Muhammad 'Ali al-Juzu: hel yusbih Lubnan Jumhuriya Islamiya?" ["An interview with sheikh Dr. Mohammed Ali Jouzou: will Lebanon become an Islamic Republic?"], *al-Tawhid* (July 27, 1984).

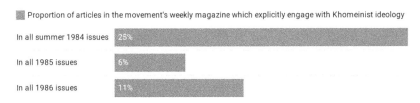

Figure 4.1 Temporal variation in Tawhid's Khomeinist ideology
Note: Pre-1984 issues of Tawhid's magazine are unavailable but a survey of the movement's statements to the Tripolitan and Lebanese media suggests that its engagement with Khomeinist Islamism was relatively weak.
Source: *Al-Tawhid* magazine

ideologically pure and to make the contrast starker with a rival which had abandoned its call to implement Islamic law across the country. Another function was to bolster internal coherence by drawing on "Khomeinism" – this breed of Islamism calling for clerical guidance over politics and for an anti-imperialist foreign policy. This was important because, as was seen in Chapter 3, "Sunni Khomeinism" was a major subcurrent of Lebanese Islamism which had merged within the movement. Several "ideological entrepreneurs" were genuinely attracted by the "Iranian model" as well as by the prospect of implementing an Islamic Republic, as Chapter 7 details. Yet, most strikingly, ideology also played the role of signaling ideational proximity with the Islamic Republic of Iran to activate ties of ideological solidarity and obtain Tehran's support. In fact, while Tawhid's ideological corpus had from the start featured implicit references to the "Iranian model," they did not become frequent until the summer of 1984, when it witnessed a peak of ideological production drawing on explicitly "Khomeinist" thinkers and concepts. In other words, when it came to taking inspiration from the pro-Iran, "Khomeinist" strands of Islamist thinking, Tawhid's ideological corpus presented clear temporal variation (see Figure 4.1).

In turn, what accounts for the timing of this variation was Tawhid's urgent need for Iranian diplomatic support in the summer of 1984. This was a time marked by a sudden increase in violence between the Islamist movement and a local pro-Assad militia, which raised the specter of a Syrian crackdown on Tripoli (see Figure 4.2).[38] The exponential growth

---

[38] In late July 1984, Hafez al-Assad ordered the Syrian army contingent in Lebanon to move to the vicinity of Tripoli, which raised the likelihood of a Syrian military intervention to dislodge Tawhid. See: "Accord Président Assad – Premier Ministre Karamé sur l'extension du plan de sécurité: l'armée très bientôt dans la montagne et à

220   A Vernacular Islamist Ideology

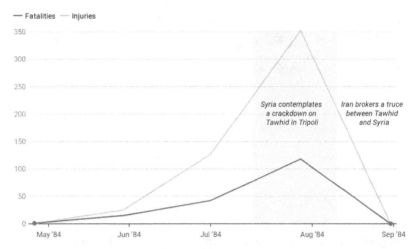

Figure 4.2 The sudden increase of violence in Tripoli in mid-1984
Note: This chart reflects the sudden increase in violence in Tripoli between Tawhid and the pro-Assad Arab Democratic Party (ADP) over the summer 1984.
Source: Tripolitan daily *Al-Incha*; Lebanese daily *L'Orient Le Jour* and *Adib N'ame* (1985)

in the number of Tawhid statements drawing on "Khomeinism" may have been duly noted by the Islamic Republic of Iran. The dynamics of the relationship between Tawhid and its external backers, including Iran, are fully explored in Chapter 7. At this point suffice it to say that when the Iranian president, Ali Khamene'i, went to Damascus on a "surprise visit"[39] after tensions peaked in Tripoli, he asked a Tawhid delegation to join him and he attempted a "reconciliation" between the movement and Hafez al-Assad. This lull would be brief, but it still allowed Tawhid to continue controlling Tripoli for a year longer. The shift in Tawhid's ideological production in a markedly pro-Iranian Islamist direction by

Tripoli," *L'Orient le Jour* (July 27, 1984). I draw the figures of the number of casualties in Tripoli through the summer 1984 from a survey of Tripolitan daily *Al-Incha*, Lebanese daily *L'Orient Le Jour* and Adib N'ame's study: Adib N'ame, "Al-amen fi Trablus, 1980–1985" ["The security in Tripoli, 1980–1985"], *Nada' al-Shamal* (undated, copy given to the author).

[39] Note that, although the Iranian mediation formally took place during the visit of Khamene'i to Damascus on October 7, 1984, it was already well under way in late August and through September. See: "Le président iranien à Damas," *L'Orient Le Jour* (October 7, 1984), "Shaaban à Damas pour des entretiens avec les autorités syriennes," *L'Orient Le Jour* (October 8, 1984) and "Téhéran engage une médiation," *L'Orient Le Jour* (October 9, 1984).

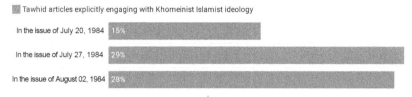

Figure 4.3 Soliciting external support, a strategic function of ideology.
Source: *Al-Tawhid* magazine

no means suggests that it was insincere, for some cadres and leaders were genuinely attracted by "Khomeinism." Yet its timing and effect suggest that it helped signal ideational proximity with Iran, activate bonds of ideological solidarity and enlist its diplomatic support.

In late July and early August Tawhid began producing more ideological statements explicitly drawing on the "Khomeinist" strands of Islamism; calling for the establishment of Islamic Republics with clerical guidance over politics, expressing support for Iran's post-1979 anti-imperialist foreign policy and bid for regional primacy and even advocating for Lebanon's Sunnis and Shias to unite within a pro-Iranian movement. In a mark of the temporal variation in Tawhid's ideological production and of its stark shift in a pro-Iranian direction, statements featuring typically "Khomeinist" Islamist content in its weekly magazine nearly doubled from mid-July 1984 to late July and early August 1984 (see Figure 4.3), and while this proportion stood at a staggering 25 percent for the overall period of the summer 1984, it fell back to an average 9 percent of all magazine articles published in 1985–6 (see Figure 4.1). No other theme in Tawhid's corpus featured as much temporal variation as "Khomeinism" (see Figure 4.3).

Although it was a Sunni Islamist movement, Tawhid thus began praising the Shia-led Islamic Republic of Iran in the most explicit of ways, thereby also suggesting that Sunni–Shia relations were not at the time marked by the animosity which later developed. In fact, Tawhid branded the 1979 Iranian Revolution and the 1982 birth of pro-Iran Hezbollah in Lebanon as Islamic, rather than narrowly Shia, achievements, even going as far as stating that "no Islamic movement since the first Islamic Caliphate has been able to recreate the [Islamic] state, except for the Khomeini movement in Iran."[40] Tawhid thus started openly calling for the "Iranian model" to be imported to Lebanon. Until then the movement had sometimes referred to the need for an Iranian-style Islamic Republic, but this had always remained vague and not a central

---

[40] Abi Samra, *Trablus*, p. 154.

222 A Vernacular Islamist Ideology

part of its ideological production. By contrast, in late July and early August 1984 it published a trove of much more explicit statements detailing what the Islamic Republic of Lebanon would look like if Tawhid succeeded in overthrowing the government.

Unsurprisingly, this Lebanese Islamic Republic would take a "Khomeinist" flavor. Drawing on a Shia tradition in which clerics are an important source of social and political authority, Tawhid envisioned Lebanon's preachers also beginning to rule the country. "The way toward establishing the Islamic state is for Muslim clerics to have more power,"[41] thus argued an article in its newspaper. Another one justified this by reference to Muhammad's life. "[The Prophet] used to sign treaties, form political and military alliances, formulate the policy of the Muslim community and draw boundaries – therefore it is the duty of religious scholars to do the same."[42] It is important to note that this did not mean that Tawhid would as such call for the application in Lebanon of the specifically Iranian concept of *velayat-e-faqih*, or "rule of the jurisprudent," which would have meant officially submitting Lebanon to Ayatollah Khomeini's authority. Yet the movement nonetheless implicitly referred to it when it titled one of its newspaper's articles in the summer 1984 "Religious clerics are the heirs of the Prophet"[43] which, in addition to being a well-known hadith, famously formed the basis of Ayatollah Khomeini's argument in favor of *velayat-e-faqih*. Moreover, although Tawhid did not explicitly endorse the concept, it was telling that at this point it opened the columns of its newspaper to the most prominent Lebanese proponent of the "role of the jurisprudent" back then, the pro-Iran Shia cleric Mohammed Hussein Fadlallah, who also acted as the spiritual guide of Hezbollah. Fadlallah, in his article for *al-Tawhid*, recognized the difficulty of importing the "rule of the jurisprudent" to Lebanon, because the Sunnis notoriously disliked it. But he also expressed his hope that "the problem can be solved," reducing this "Khomeinist" concept to a mere "theory of leadership" and arguing that "the characteristics of the *faqih* which is being proposed are those that the Sunnis demand and endorse."[44] This was a controversial statement to

[41] "Hiwar m'a al-Duktur al-Shaykh Muhammad 'Ali al-Juzu: hel yusbih Lubnan Jumhuriya Islamiya?" ["An interview with sheikh Dr. Mohammed Ali Jouzou: will Lebanon become an Islamic Republic?"], *al-Tawhid* (July 27, 1984).

[42] "Al-'ulama' warathat al-'anbiyat" ["[Religious] scholars are the heirs of the prophet"], *al-Tawhid* (August 2, 1984).

[43] Ibid.

[44] "Hiwar m'a al-'Alim Sayid Muhammed Hussayn Fadl Allah: la khilaf bein al-Sunna wal-Shi'a" ["Interview with Sayed Mohammed Hussein: there is no conflict between the Sunnis and the Shias"], *al-Tawhid* (July 27, 1984).

Making the Islamic Republic of Lebanon 223

make in a newspaper destined for a Sunni Islamist audience – publishing it showed how far Tawhid was ready to go to signal ideational proximity with Iran. Soon thereafter a Tawhid delegation visited Mohammed Hussein Fadlallah and, although the officials did not say whether they agreed with the content of his article, they nonetheless expressed their "admiration and support" for the "wise"[45] nature of his positions.

In addition to suggesting its appeal for the Iranian model of an Islamic Republic featuring clerical guidance over politics, in the summer of 1984 Tawhid's ideological corpus became marked by statements steeped in an anti-Western rhetoric closely resembling Iran's and by clear attempts at engineering a rapprochement with Hezbollah, Iran's key ally in Lebanon.

Naturally, as a militant Islamist movement, Tawhid and its founding factions had always used an anti-Western rhetoric. While it had stated early on, in its founding political charter, that one of its goals was to "mobilize the masses against the international Zionist movement" and against "imperialism,"[46] the movement would continue to espouse such rhetoric after the summer 1984 too. In November 1984, for instance, Tawhid would proclaim a "jihad to liberate not only Palestine but also the entire Islamic world of imperialist hegemony."[47] In January 1985 it even would go as far as threatening the United States with a wave of bombings on its soil, promising that "America will be subject to operations on its own country to avenge the people of South Lebanon and Palestine" and explicitly warning that "the Islamic tide [...] has begun to knock at the door of the White House."[48] But, although Tawhid's anti-Western positions were thus a constant, the summer of 1984 was marked by a peak in rhetoric implying harmony with Iran's anti-imperialist foreign policy.

Within the space of two months Tawhid visibly radicalized its ideological positions on foreign policy issues, systematically bringing them closer to "Khomeinism." Over the summer 1984 Tawhid published statements espousing a specifically anti-imperialist language. It lambasted those "giant devils who are ruling the world," which comprised "a crusader West led by America" as well as "an atheist East led by

[45] "Wafd Harakat al-Tawhid yaltaqi ba'd al-shakhsiyat wa al-f'aliyat" ["A delegation from the Tawhid movement meets figures and attends events"], *al-Tawhid* (August 2, 1984).

[46] *Al-khutut al-asasia li-muntalaqat wa mabade wa ahdaf Harakat al-Tawhid al-Islami* [The fundamental premises, principles and objectives of the Islamic Unification Movement] (copy given to the author, undated).

[47] "Shaaban: Israel n'évacuera pas le sud par les négociations et ne sera pas vaincu par les pourparlers mais par les fusils et les bras des combattants mujahedeen musulmans," *L'Orient Le Jour* (November 17, 1984).

[48] "Shaaban menace les Etats-Unis d'opérations sur leur propre territoire," *L'Orient Le Jour* (January 14, 1985).

224 A Vernacular Islamist Ideology

Russia."[49] And, even if its ideological corpus had always featured a harsh anti-Israeli rhetoric, it reached new heights then too. The movement not only called for an "Islamic jihad" against Israel and stated that "Islam is the most effective weapon against the Jews and Crusaders,"[50] it also promised that it would "soon mobilize all our men to do their duty in South Lebanon,"[51] occupied by the Israeli army since 1982, although this would only remain empty words.

During the summer of 1984 Tawhid's ideological corpus also became marked by attempts at engineering a rapprochement with Hezbollah, Iran's key Shia ally in Lebanon. Tawhid, despite being made up of Sunnis, thus praised the Shia Islamist militia in the most laudatory of ways, hailing the "devotion to Allah" of its members and the "heroic attacks" which they had begun launching against the Israeli forces stationed in South Lebanon. "They are not seeking anyone's rewards or thanks," one of its articles then stated, conveying admiration for their struggle against Israel. "They want nothing but victory or martyrdom."[52] However, back then Tawhid did more than just congratulating Hezbollah for its "jihad against Zionism." It also suggested that it was ready to enter into an alliance with the Party of God in order to unite what it portrayed as Lebanon's two strongest proponents of "Khomeinism," something which would shortly lead to a formal proposal on the part of the movement to merge the country's Sunni and Shia Islamists in one group "under the banner of God."[53] Uniting Tawhid and Hezbollah was a groundbreaking proposal which, if it had succeeded, would have bolstered the appeal of "Khomeinism" and strengthened Iran's hand in Lebanon. Once again, some "ideological entrepreneurs" in the movement were genuinely attracted by this idea, and they engaged in costly efforts to make it happen, as Chapter 7 details. Yet the very fact that this proposal surfaced in the summer of 1984 and came within Tawhid's much broader effort to steer its ideological production in a "Khomeinist" direction showed that even if it was sincerely

---

[49] "Al-jahiliya min jadid fi al-qarn al-'ashrin" ["The ignorance returns in the twentieth century], al-Tawhid (June 20, 1984).

[50] "Al-muqawama al-filastinia tatajeh nahu tariq masdud" ["The Palestinian resistance is headed towards a dead end"], al-Tawhid (August 2, 1984).

[51] Tawhid statement quoted in: "Téhéran engage une médiation," L'Orient Le Jour (October 9, 1984).

[52] "Al-'ulama' yaqudun al-mujahidin fi al-m'araka dod Isra'il," al-Tawhid (June 20, 1984).

[53] "Hiwar m'a al-shaikh Maher Hammud: la yakhtalif al- 'ulama' hawl al-ahdaf al-niha'iya" ["Interview with Sheikh Maher Hammud: the religious scholars do not disagree on the ultimate goals], al-Tawhid (August 2, 1984). See also: "Le drapeau de l'état hébreu piétiné à la mosquée de Bir Abed," L'Orient Le Jour (November 9, 1984) and "Jérusalem nous voici," L'Orient Le Jour (November 9, 1984).

Vernacular Islamism

embraced by some, it was also meant to solicit Iranian support. It soon transpired that the movement's strategy was successful for, while the summer of 1984 witnessed the first joint communiqué between Tawhid and Hezbollah, the Party of God's spiritual leader, Mohammed Hussein Fadlallah, expressed his enthusiasm in his interview to Tawhid's newspaper, hoping that "a common [Sunni–Shia] framework"[54] can be created.

All in all then, temporal variation in Tawhid's ideological production demonstrated that a key function of ideology was to solicit external support. The marked shift in the movement's discourse in a "Khomeinist" direction in the summer of 1984 especially allowed it to activate latent bonds of ideological solidarity with Iran, which triggered the Islamic Republic's diplomatic support and enabled Tawhid to dodge the Syrian threat. Yet at the same time Tawhid's functionalist use of ideological production meant it drew on highly eclectic references, which made its Islamism look "fuzzy"[55] from the outside. This contributed to restricting its influence among Lebanon's more orthodox Sunni Islamists.

Vernacular Islamism

Beyond Tawhid's strategic use of ideology, which rendered its corpus heterogeneous or, some might have said, incoherent, another factor which limited its appeal in Lebanon's broader Islamist community was the remarkably local character of much of its ideological production – that is, the movement's considerable engagement with all things Tripoli. Tawhid would go to great lengths to cast its grand Islamist ideology in Tripolitan narratives and identities. This and the next section explore the two mechanisms through which the symbolic dimensions of space – local narratives and identity – interacted with Tawhid's Islamism. At first glance the embeddedness of its discourse within Tripoli's symbolic meaning seemed to result merely from a pragmatic strategy to recruit heavily in the city by constructing a "vernacular ideology," a beliefs

---

[54] "Hiwar m'a al-'Alim Sayid Muhammed Hussayn Fadl Allah: la khilaf bein al-Sunna wal-Shi'a" ["Interview with Sayed Mohammed Hussein: there is no conflict between the Sunnis and the Shias"], *al-Tawhid* (July 27, 1984). Tawhid's first joint communiqué with Hezbollah was issued on August 5, 1984, in which the two movements promised that they would "take revenge against the murderers of Tripoli" at a time when Tawhid's struggle against the local pro-Assad militia, the Arab Democratic Party, was fast intensifying. See: "Tripoli: le cycle de la violence se poursuit inlassablement," *L'Orient Le Jour* (August 5, 1984).

[55] US Central Intelligence Agency, "Shaykh Shaban: Lebanon's radical Sunni cleric" (Top Secret, NESAR 85-003CX, January 18, 1985).

A Vernacular Islamist Ideology

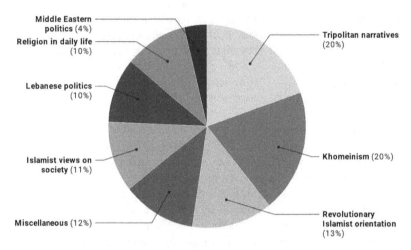

Figure 4.4 Tawhid's ideological production: eclectic and vernacular
Note: This graph represents the primary theme of the articles published in the movement's weekly magazine in 1984–6. Note that the "miscellaneous" category gathers non-ideological themes such as internal Tawhid matters.
Source: *Al-Tawhid* magazine (1984–6)

system chiming with the local cultural backdrop. But it soon transpired that Tawhid also became imbued in a "Tripolitan habitus": as it rooted itself in Tripoli's symbolic meaning, local narratives and identities started to affect its ideology too. This and the next section therefore show that, although Islamist ideology is often seen as universalistic and deterritorialized, it can also be rooted in the symbolic meaning of local spaces to a remarkable degree. Sometimes, in fact, Islamist engagement with local concerns and identities can be such that it amounts to what I call a "vernacular Islamism." Through this term I mean to emphasize the rootedness of some Islamist movements in "the local" to the extent that their ideology becomes visibly shaped by local culture, concerns and identity.

Tripoli thus emerges as the fourth main theme of Tawhid's ideological corpus and, strikingly, it proportionately equals or outweighs the three other themes this chapter explores. As Figure 4.4 indicates a remarkable fifth of all articles published in its newspaper concerned the city, recurrently addressing Tripoli's history, distinctive grievances and strong sense of collective identity. First, the most obvious mechanism through which space affected Tawhid's Islamism was the making of a "vernacular ideology," or the ways in which movements try to recruit locally by

Vernacular Islamism

transmitting their grand or complex ideology in the language of local grievances, identities and cultural and historical narratives. Partially viewing space as a symbolic resource to be exploited, Tawhid went to great lengths to recruit in Tripoli by inscribing its Islamism in the context of the city's longstanding antagonisms and of its strong breed of local identity.

One example of Tawhid's "vernacular Islamism" was the movement's considerable ideological engagement with Tripoli's foremost locally rooted antagonism back then, the neighborhood rivalry which pitted Bab al-Tebbaneh against Jabal Mohsen. The main features of this rivalry have already been tackled in Chapter 2, but at this stage it should be repeated that Bab al-Tebbaneh was a Sunni-majority district with strong anti-Syrian regime inclinations and that Jabal Mohsen was an Alawi-only neighborhood supporting the Assads. Initially this neighborhood feud had very little to do with Sunni–Alawi tensions. Yet from the early 1980s onward it became characterized by a degree of sectarian animosity as it gradually intensified and engulfed nearby Sunni-majority districts. From its creation in 1982 onward Tawhid was very strong in Bab al-Tebbaneh. Its spatial salience there was not the product of the sincere commitment of its residents to Islamism, but rather stemmed from their instrumental embrace of Islamism as a "protest ideology" and from their loyalty to the neighborhood's strongman or "champion of mobilization," who had joined the movement and thus drew them in with him. In that neighborhood very few were leading a properly religious way of life. Tawhid therefore engaged ideologically with Bab al-Tebbaneh's rivalry against Jabal Mohsen with the hope of making the residents of the former more receptive and committed to the movement's Islamist ideology. This would also allow it to recruit in the Sunni-dominated adjacent districts of Qobbe, Beddawi and parts of the Old City, whose residents had overwhelmingly taken Bab al-Tebbaneh's side.

Tawhid went to considerable lengths to "place-frame"[56] its grand ideology in the context of this neighborhood rivalry, as geographer Deborah Martin would have said. At times the movement used a non-ideological language to address this antagonism, for instance explicitly mentioning "the fight between Jabal Mohsen and Bab al-Tebbaneh" or the legitimacy of "defending one's area."[57] But most frequently it

---

[56] Deborah Martin, "Place-framing as place-making: constituting a neighbourhood for organizing and activism" *Annals of the Association of American Geographers* (Vol. 93, No. 3, 2003), pp. 730–50.

[57] "Khitab Amir Harakat al-Tawhid al-Islami al-Shaykh Sa'id Sha'aban" ["Speech by the Emir of Tawhid the cleric Sa'id Sha'aban], *al-Tawhid* (August 2, 1984).

228   A Vernacular Islamist Ideology

ideologized the rivalry. This was no longer a mere local feud between rival "champions of mobilization" and bands of youths over the control of the underground economy, neighborhood pride and the degree of influence of the Syrian army in Tripoli. Instead it had now allegedly become an ideological struggle: one pitting those in Bab al-Tebbaneh and the adjacent Sunni districts whom Tawhid tried to recruit and glorified as "Muslims who desire to live the life of Islam" and "refuse any other authority than God" against the Alawi "non-Muslims" who were not only denied Islamic legitimacy but were also called outright "disbelievers" and "intruders in the Muslim society."[58] They were even framed as "local Jews" involved in an "international conspiracy" to "burn the houses" of Muslims and "evict them"[59] so that they could take over their land. This allowed Tawhid to cast the use of violence against Jabal Mohsen's Alawis in a grand ideological frame in order to legitimize it, for it was permissible to "chastise" those who held "infidel and disgusting beliefs and principles" to "keep the Muslim society clean and pure."[60] In a language reminiscent of Qutb's and Hawwa's, Tawhid portrayed the slightest attack by Jabal Mohsen's militias against the adjacent Sunni districts as a proof of pre-Islamic "ignorance" which had to be mercilessly combated. By contrast, it eulogized the Sunni fighters who fell in this local feud between 1982 and 1985 as true "martyrs under God."[61] Tawhid promised to the local fighters that, if they joined the dynamic of "Islamic unity," in a hint at its name, they would prevail for the movement would play an "effective role" on the ground by providing "security through Islam" and upholding "Islamic honour and dignity."[62] Tawhid, then, instead of distancing itself from a neighborhood rivalry which, as Chapter 2 demonstrated, had little to do with Islamist ideology, dedicated a large amount of its intellectual production seeking to cast its grand Islamist beliefs within this very local context.

Another example of Tawhid's attempt to recruit locally by transmitting its Islamist ideology in a local, vernacular language was its engagement with Tripolitan identity, whose facets were introduced in great detail in

---

[58] "Kalimat lil-'akh Kan'an Naji" ["A speech by the brother Kan'an Naji"], al-Tawhid (September 19, 1985).

[59] "Al-Shaykh Sa'id Sha'aban: kel min yuhawel tamziq al-Muslimin huwa khadim lil-yahud" ["The cleric Sa'id Sha'aban: anyone who attempts to tear the Muslims apart is a servant of the Jews"], al-Tawhid (September 18, 1985).

[60] "Kalimat lil-'akh Kan'an Naji" ["A speech by the brother Kan'an Naji], al-Tawhid (September 19, 1985).

[61] Speech by a Tawhid official at Bab al-Tebbaneh's Harba mosque, Tripoli (undated, video given to the author).

[62] "Al-qiyada al-islamiya fi Trablus" ["The Islamic leadership in Tripoli"], Al-Taqwa (Vol. 20, April 1985).

Chapter 1. In much of its ideological production the movement went to great lengths to "place-frame" its grand ideology against the backdrop of the city's sense of community and rich Islamic legacy. In one article, for instance, it hailed "the people of Muslim Tripoli" and went as far as portraying its Islamist ideology as the quasi-messianic embodiment of the city, claiming that "Muslims are not just a party or a movement; they are Tripoli, for everyone knows that Tripoli is an Islamic city."[63] Another article in its newspaper epitomized how far Tawhid was ready to go to construct a "vernacular Islamism" which would channel local identity and allow it to recruit locally. The article began by calling on the "dear brothers and sisters who are still far from Allah" to stop following their "lusts and whims," and instead "hurry and join the growing masses who support Allah's cause in Tripoli." "Allah's name is now all over Tripoli because the people love Him and want to see His Name everywhere." Importantly, it concluded by asking residents to continue "fearing" God because "this is the city of Allah and His messenger."[64]

This exclusionary breed of Tripolitan identity was only shared by a minority, because the city had long featured Christians, Alawis and leftists of all stripes. Yet Tawhid's very attempt to transmit its grand ideology in the language of local concerns and identities and construct a "vernacular Islamism" chiming with the local cultural backdrop still showed how far the movement was ready to go to root itself within Tripoli's symbolic meaning.

Tawhid's Tripolitan Habitus

Nominally, then, Tawhid merely considered space as a resource to articulate a "vernacular ideology" – casting its beliefs in a local cultural context would allow it to enlist new recruits. This is even what its founding charter suggested, as it acknowledged that "the movement geographically centres on Tripoli" but insisted that "this does not imply that its ideology is local," because Tawhid instead covered "all of Lebanon" and was driven by "global goals."[65] All identities other than being a Muslim and belonging to the *umma* – the worldwide community of Muslim believers – were said to be "secondary,"[66] including being Tripolitan. However, had space only been a resource useful to build a

---

[63] Ibid.

[64] "Ma nad'eu al-nas?" ["What are we calling people to?"], *al-Tawhid* (June 20, 1984).

[65] *Al-khutut al-asasia li-muntalaqat wa mabade wa ahdaf Harakat al-Tawhid al-Islami* [The fundamental premises, principles and objectives of the Islamic Unification Movement] (copy given to the author, undated).

[66] Quoted in Seurat, *L'état de barbarie.*

230   A Vernacular Islamist Ideology

"vernacular ideology" with the sole goal of recruiting, one would have expected Tawhid to draw on the antagonisms and identities of Sidon and Beirut, the two other cities where Lebanese Sunnis were numerous. Yet the movement engaged comparatively little with the issues specific to those two cities. If it did, it was always for purposes other than to cast its ideology in local identities to recruit Sunnis, for example when it praised Hezbollah's role in the south to portray itself as "Khomeinist." Moreover, when its officials met the representatives of other non-Tripoli-based Islamist movements, these would often be shocked by the sense that Tawhid, more than strategically using space as a resource to recruit locally, was at times so embedded in Tripolitan narratives and identities that it seemed to have internalized them and that they shaped its ideology.[67] Something else about space, then, seemed at play which affected the movement's Islamism.

This section explores the second mechanism through which space came to affect Tawhid's ideology. Drawing on Pierre Bourdieu's concept of "habitus"[68] as internalized dispositions shared by people of similar background and which shape their views, I point to how the embeddedness of actors in a space characterized by strong historical, cultural and political narratives can turn into a "habitus of place" – an internalized localism which pushes actors to view the world through at least partially local lenses and which affects their ideologies. The symbolic dimension of space was no longer just a resource but affected the nature of activism. Tawhid's "Tripolitan habitus," or internalized localism, would come to significantly influence the movement's ideology – its choice of themes and even its vocabulary.

One reflection of the effect of this "habitus of place" on Tawhid's Islamist ideology was the way inherently Tripolitan narratives had visibly penetrated, indeed at times seemed to shape, much of its ideological corpus. This turned it from an Islamist movement with "global" aims into a locally oriented one, something placing it in striking continuity with Tripoli's older tradition of giving birth to spatially oriented movements which, whatever their ideological inclinations, consistently sought to channel local grievances and identities.

For instance, much like the city's revolutionary leftist and pan-Arab movements before it, Tawhid dedicated much of its ideological corpus to the critique of Lebanon's very existence as a country and a nation. Of course, at times it framed this anti-Lebanese inclination in an ideological

---

[67] Interview with Hezbollah official Hani Fahs, Beirut, August 2014 and interview with Sunni Islamists active in the 1980s, Sidon and Beirut, August 2014.
[68] Pierre Bourdieu, *The logic of practice* (Cambridge: Polity Press, 1992).

Tawhid's Tripolitan Habitus 231

and religious way, for example by asserting that "Islam does not permit Muslims" to be part of a country dominated by Christians because, while "Islam provides a comprehensive system of rules to follow in life" which Muslims are "obliged to follow," "Christianity gives no specific regulations."[69] But remarkably often its critique of Lebanon as a country and a nation whose existence, sixty years after its creation, was no longer challenged anywhere except in Tripoli, drew on explicitly local narratives and grievances. Perhaps bearing in mind the violent protests which gripped Tripoli in the 1920s, 1930s and 1940s when it was forcibly brought into Lebanon, Tawhid viewed the country as an artificial entity that had been "imposed" upon Tripolitans. "We cannot recognize the entities established by the colonizers and we must resist them as much as we can until they are abolished,"[70] an article in its newspaper stated. Showing the extent to which the movement's discourse was embedded in historical narratives of collective bitterness at Tripoli's sense of decline, its ideological corpus was peppered with reminders that the city had been repeatedly "discriminated against"[71] in its history and had become marginalized in post-independence Lebanon. In turn, this reading of Tripolitan history, which as we saw in Chapter 1 was especially widespread locally, may explain the particular virulence with which Tawhid rejected the legitimacy of Lebanon's existence. In a typical statement a Tawhid official thus lambasted Lebanon for having been built on the basis of "injustice and corruption," perhaps a hint at Tripoli's demotion to the benefit of its arch-rival Beirut, and then had harsh words for state institutions which resonated locally. "They ask us to support the state's legitimacy under the pretext that the country is close to the abyss. I tell them: may the Lebanese state disappear!" He went as far as to call for its complete destruction: "We will be doing our utmost to undermine the basis of the state [...] even if it means that the Lebanese Pound, houses, cities and villages will have to collapse to be rebuilt on the basis of faith."[72]

---

[69] "Al-d'awa lil-Islam laysat bida'a ta'efiya" ["Calling for Islam is not a sectarian heresy"] al-Tawhid (June 20, 1984).

[70] "Hiwar m'a al-Duktur al-Shaykh Muhammad 'Ali al-Juzu: hel yusbih Lubnan Jumhuriya Islamiya?" ["An interview with sheikh Dr. Mohammed Ali Jouzou: will Lebanon become an Islamic Republic?"], al-Tawhid (July 27, 1984). See also: Al-khutut al-asasia li-muntalaqat wa mabade wa ahdaf Harakat al-Tawhid al-Islami [The fundamental premises, principles and objectives of the Islamic Unification Movement] (copy given to the author, undated).

[71] "Khitab Amir Harakat al-Tawhid al-Islami al-Shaykh Sa'id Sha'aban" ["Speech by the Emir of Tawhid the cleric Sa'id Sha'aban], al-Tawhid (August 2, 1984).

[72] "Shaaban: saper les bases de l'Etat maronite phalangiste même si tout s'effondre avec lui," L'Orient Le Jour (March 9, 1985).

232 A Vernacular Islamist Ideology

Another example of the way the "habitus of place" affected Tawhid's choice of themes in its ideological corpus – to the extent that, at times, it seemed to have more in common with Tripoli's older spatially oriented movements than with other Islamist groups – was its obsession with the recreation of a Greater Syria to which the city would be attached. Here again, Tawhid sometimes cast its pan-Syrian rhetoric within Islamist ideology. It argued that Greater Syria with its capital Damascus had been the seat of the Umayyad Islamic Caliphate and that Islamic law should be implemented all over it. But most often Tawhid used nonreligious and nonideological arguments to advocate for Lebanon's dilution within Greater Syria, for example by borrowing from the language of Tripoli's longstanding social and emotional attachment to the Syrian hinterland. The movement, continuing in the vein of its critique of the country, thus boldly stated that "the Lebanese question is irrelevant – can anyone spot Lebanon on a map?" It kept insisting that Lebanon had always been an "integral part of Syria," had been "detached by colonization" and should therefore be "totally reunited"[73] within a Greater Syria to which Tripoli would naturally belong. The movement, having visibly internalized its "Tripolitan habitus" as its discourse was in this respect more spatially oriented than ideologically driven, even went as far as explicitly noting that the recreation of Greater Syria would benefit Tripoli immensely. The city, it noted, had suffered from the "substantial" decrease in trade with its Syrian hinterland due to colonialism and due to the breakdown of the Lebanese–Syrian tariff union, although trade had previously "reached 25 million pounds [...] – this point must not be overlooked."[74] Given Tawhid's enmity for the Syrian regime, it never actively pursued the project of Tripoli's reintegration into Syria or the recreation of Greater Syria. But the very presence of a vigorously pan-Syrian rhetoric in its ideological corpus suggests the extent to which historical narratives about Tripoli's cross-border ties to Syria had penetrated its ideology, shaping its choice of themes.

Yet what most antagonized Lebanese Islamists outside of Tripoli, for example in Beirut or Sidon, was that Tawhid's vocabulary turned so parochial that they felt that the movement was more informed by – and perhaps loyal to – local identity than Islamist ideology. It was as if Tawhid, more than strategically articulating a "vernacular ideology" making its Islamist beliefs chime with the local cultural backdrop, had become guided by a "Tripolitan habitus." Far from its official view that local identity was a secondary

---

[73] "Le leader du MUI: l'Islam au lieu de la démocratie," *L'Orient Le Jour* (October 19, 1983) and "Téhéran engage une médiation," *L'Orient Le Jour* (October 9, 1984).

[74] "Iqtisad Trablus ila ayn?" ["The Tripolitan economy, where to?"], *al-Tawhid* (June 20, 1984).

Tawhid's Tripolitan Habitus 233

substance, then, the movement regularly used a vocabulary which suggested that the sense of belonging to Tripoli as a community played more than a strategic role and was in fact driving parts of its behavior.

Examples abound about how Tawhid's Islamist ideology was deeply affected by this "Tripolitan habitus." For instance, although the movement was in theory addressing non-Tripolitan Islamists too, it began to routinely use phrases such as "our loved city"[75] or "for the sake of the people of Tripoli."[76] But one of the statements it issued back then epitomized particularly well how it had internalized local historical and cultural narratives to the extent that they came to shape the nature of its ideology, rendering it distinctly local. This statement aimed at recruiting Sunni Islamists outside of Tripoli as well, and in fact it began by addressing the dangers facing "the entire Muslim population in Lebanon." But it soon verged toward a type of parochialism which was puzzling for a group driven by "global goals." It proudly asserted that "the main leaders of the Muslim world" were mere "representatives" of the Islamist groups present in Tripoli, with Tawhid at their helm. Perhaps aware of the incongruous nature of such a statement, the author of the article continued his reasoning. "This is not an exaggeration, for Tripoli has been, and still is, the centre for Muslims throughout the world ever since it was conquered by the companions [of the Prophet]." Taking for granted that all of his readers must have been fully conscious of the city's sense of self-importance, deep-seated grievances and strong identity, he wondered: "who amongst us does not know the history of Tripoli from the Crusades all the way to French colonialism, when the ancient city of Tripoli was targeted, its role distorted and its people silenced?" Local narratives, an air of Tripolitan pride and the "tales of contention" seen in Chapter 1 permeate the entire article – even though it sought to recruit non-Tripolitan Muslims too. The author repeatedly hailed "this city" for having "maintained its Islamic characteristics despite difficult situations." He concluded on a telling note, framing Tawhid's rise in Tripoli as part of an "Islamic awakening" but also playing into older local narratives by casting it as a development which had the potential of restoring long-overdue prestige to the northern city. "This gives hope to the Muslims of Tripoli that the city's role will be revived on the eastern coast of the Mediterranean Sea, from Alexandria to Alexandretta, for Tripoli is the city where the light of Islam shines bright and directs its

---

[75] "Al-qiyada al-islamiya fi Trablus" ["The Islamic leadership in Tripoli"], *Al-Taqwa* (Vol. 20, April 1985).

[76] "Khitab Amir Harakat al-Tawhid al-Islami al-Shaykh Sa'id Sha'aban" ["Speech by the Emir of Tawhid the cleric Sa'id Sha'aban"], *al-Tawhid* (August 2, 1984).

234   A Vernacular Islamist Ideology

warmth upon everyone, is it not indubitable?"[77] That a publication aimed at all Lebanese Muslims was so imbued in local identities and narratives showed how Tawhid's "Tripolitan habitus" was affecting parts of its ideology.

Interestingly, over thirty years later several current and former Tawhid officials recognize that, far from having been guided by deterritorialized global ideological aims, the movement had always been "local"[78] in its thinking. Several of its leaders and many of its members were reportedly driven by the goal of "making Tripoli the greatest Islamic city."[79] This "habitus of place," or set of internalized local narratives and identities which pushes activists to see the world through partially local lenses and affects their ideology, was in fact very obvious to other Islamist activists from outside of Tripoli who interacted with Tawhid regularly, and all observed the Tripolitan bias of the movement and of its ideology. One of them, a Beiruti leader in Hezbollah, remembered being shocked by Tawhid's obsession with Tripoli. He had met its officials in 1984 as part of their growing cooperation. He then engaged in a conversation with them and recalled realizing, after a while, that their ultimate goal, beyond references to launching "Islamic revolutions" and building an "Islamic Republic," was to restore prestige to Tripoli by making it the capital of any future Islamic political system. "They were extremely enthusiastic about that,"[80] he recalled with a smile.

Space, then, was much more than the mere resource which Tawhid claimed it was. Instead it gave rise to a sense of place which was so pervasive that it affected parts of the movement's Islamist ideology – even shaping its choice of themes and its vocabulary. Tawhid's "Tripolitan habitus," alongside the highly heterogeneous Islamist references on which it drew, largely contributed to restricting its appeal outside of the northern city.

Theorizing Back

By uncovering what stood behind the highly heterogeneous and local aspects of Tawhid's Islamist ideology, this chapter also draws broader theoretical insights and answers the following questions related to the role of ideology and space in contentious politics. What are the strategic functions fulfilled by

[77] Ibid.
[78] Interview with Abu Othman (Tawhid commander, former Soldiers of God official), Tripoli, October 2017.
[79] Interviews with current and former Tawhid officials and members, Tripoli, July–September 2014.
[80] Interview with Hani Fahs (former senior official in Hezbollah), Beirut, August 2014.

the process of ideological production? And why is the ideology of some social, rebel and terrorist movements sometimes so local deep down?

First, this chapter lays out some of the functions of ideologies beyond "framing" for social, rebel and terrorist movements. Tawhid engaged in a rich ideological production. Its officials ran a newspaper, made speeches and delivered statements; in all of these they laid out the basic tenets of their ideology and strove to convey it. Strikingly, this corpus was eclectic, drawing on highly heterogeneous Islamist references. Of course, one reason behind the movement's keen interest in ideology stemmed from the sincere commitments of the cadres who engaged in the task of ideological production and were often "ideological entrepreneurs" bent on mobilizing worldviews and trying to spread them to society. But, although most of Tawhid's "ideological entrepreneurs" did actively take part in this enterprise, not all of those who produced ideological statements were guided only by beliefs, and other, less ideologically driven, members cadres and leaders also participated in this. Tawhid's interest in ideology, then, was also driven by the sense that it fulfilled functions.

In this chapter I continue to identify some of the functions fulfilled by ideology. I thus build on Chapter 2, in which I pointed out how ideology could be utilized in order to operate alliances across class and space or to gain access to a set of symbols, discourses, practices and infrastructures, all of which are useful when devising effective protest strategies. Beyond "framing" to enlist new recruits and galvanize existing members, the functions of ideology which I identify in this chapter and that are overlooked in the rest of the literature therefore include: (1) outbidding rivals, in the context of an ideology's growing "cultural momentum," by frequently referring to concepts and thinkers that may be considered controversial or radical but which, because of this, also signal ideological purity; (2) strengthening internal cohesion in a movement that merges subcurrents of a broader ideology by drawing on each of their intellectual references and influences to suggest inclusivity – even at the cost of being seen from the outside as eclectic or, worse, incoherent; and (3) soliciting the external support of like-minded foreign actors by pushing ideological production in a direction closer to their views to activate the bonds of ideological solidarity.

Identifying the strategic functions which ideology played in Tawhid does not suggest that the movement only viewed Islamism instrumentally, for it featured a wide "spectrum of ideological commitment," with some members being extremely committed to its ideology. Instead it shows once more the need to overcome the dichotomy between instrumental and sincere accounts of the role of beliefs in movements, because while the "ideological entrepreneurs" engaged in intellectual production to spread their worldviews, others used ideology to outbid the

236   A Vernacular Islamist Ideology

movement's rivals, bolster internal cohesion and get external backing. It is precisely this internal variation in motivations to engage in ideological production which explains why Tawhid's ideology was so eclectic, drawing on various strands of Islamism.

Second, by accounting for the strikingly Tripolitan character of Tawhid's Islamist ideology, this chapter shows how movements use the symbolic dimension of space to root themselves locally, but may then see their discourse and worldviews shaped by space too. On the one hand, then, I point to how social, rebel and terrorist movements try to appeal to populations in certain spaces by constructing what I call a "vernacular ideology" – they cast their grand belief systems against the backdrop of local identities, concerns and narratives. Partially viewing space as a resource to be exploited, Tawhid went to lengths to recruit in Tripoli by inscribing its ideology in the context of the city's longstanding identity and by Islamizing older local antagonisms, like neighborhood rivalry. This emphasis on the vernacular dimension of ideologies, or the local language in which they are sometimes transmitted, shows that despite often being treated in the literature as rigid and uniform, they are in fact malleable and adaptable to local contexts. In turn, this explains why movements that construct vernacular versions of ideologies can root themselves deeply in some spaces.

On the other hand, however, I also indicate that, as social, rebel and terrorist movements become more rooted in a local space, and therefore in its symbolic meaning too, they may develop a "habitus of place." This set of locally rooted historical, cultural and political narratives then begins to impact the discourse and worldviews of the activists, pushing them to interpret the world through partially local lenses while restricting their outside appeal too. The case of Tawhid's embeddedness in a "Tripolitan habitus" was particularly striking. The movement, far from sporadically and strategically using space as a resource, developed a discourse considerably imbued in the narratives which had long lambasted the creation of Lebanon, advocated the recreation of Greater Syria and glorified Tripoli's prestigious past, rebel tradition and sense of a community. Tawhid's discourse turned so parochial that observers from outside the city felt that its ideology was at times more informed by local identity than by Islamism. The development of such a "habitus of place" shows how space, far from just being a resource, can profoundly affect movement behavior and discourse, both enhancing but at times also restricting the potential for mobilization.

5   Social Jihad

As its clout grew over Tripoli in 1982 and 1983, Tawhid became known as the only movement of the Lebanese civil war which went as far as imposing its ideology. While ambiguity lingers as to whether it officially declared Tripoli an "Islamic Emirate," it certainly ruled as if it were one; observers noting that "Sharia is applied in the city's judicial system, drugs and alcohol have been eliminated, Western dress for women is criticized and Tawhid members enforce the fast during Ramadan."[1] Yet there was a puzzle to Tawhid's engagement in this ideological behavior and to its exercise of low-level physical and symbolic violence. Although the movement had attracted the constituency of Tripoli's committed Islamists, as we saw in Chapter 3, many of its members were less or not ideologically committed, and paradoxically some of them imposed ideology onto the city especially zealously. They might have internalized ideology after being socialized and educated into militant Islamism by the "ideological entrepreneurs," whose role is studied in detail in Chapter 6. But many others were urban poor who had long engaged in locally oriented social and political violence against the city's upper middle class, intelligentsia and notables in New Tripoli through involvement in revolutionary leftist and criminal movements. Tawhid recruited them as it needed manpower to rule the city and to implement its agenda; yet they instrumentalized its ideology, joining the movement to become empowered and using the Islamist injunction to govern morals to continue waging their struggle for the city. This explained why they imposed Tawhid's ideology with such vehemence over New Tripoli. What was less visible was that their mobilization affected the nature of the movement's Islamism, drawing Tawhid in their older social antagonism and widening its "spectrum of ideological commitment" to the extent that variation in its behavior and inconsistencies with its ideology began to emerge. Behind Tripoli's "Islamic Emirate" lay many sheds of gray.

---

[1] US Central Intelligence Agency, "Shaykh Shaban: Lebanon's radical Sunni cleric" (Top Secret, NESAR 85-003CX, January 18, 1985).

238   Social Jihad

This chapter explores Tawhid's remarkably strong social and spatial base with Tripoli's urban poor – a constituency which was less or not ideologically committed. I examine how the mass recruitment of the urban poor at first bolstered the movement's numerical strength, but also ended up affecting the nature of its behavior, arguing that its exercise of low-level, seemingly ideological violence in 1982–3 amounted to a "social jihad" which was as, if not more, driven by preexisting local tensions than by ideology. I begin by analyzing these older social tensions. I note that they stemmed from the growing intensity of the grievances suffered by Tripoli's subalterns who lived in the Old City and its extensions and suffered from economic, social, political and cultural domination at the hands of the locally rooted power structures, themselves controlled by the city's upper middle class, intelligentsia and notables in New Tripoli, who were all intent on keeping the status quo. These social tensions gradually took the shape of a local antagonism pitting the Old City and its extensions against New Tripoli, with young residents of the former so revolted by their condition that they began targeting key sites of the latter district. In the 1960s this locally oriented social and political violence of the urban poor was channeled by revolutionary leftist groups. Yet I especially note the less intuitive but remarkable case of how a criminal organization, the State of the Outlaws, was able to tap into this socio-spatial antagonism and to become the movement of the subalterns in the Old City in the 1970s. It is against the backdrop of this increasingly violent struggle for the city that Tawhid's instant success in Tripoli's impoverished neighborhoods and slums must be viewed. This, I claim, reflected the movement's ability to embody "subaltern Islamism." Through this term I counter the prevailing assumption of some scholars of terrorism and of Islamism, according to whom there is little relationship between marginalization and engagement in militancy, and instead I highlight how certain Islamist groups are able to court a subaltern base by offering the urban poor a conduit for their social and political revolt and by ushering in a new local order. In fact, Tawhid went to particular lengths to recruit Tripoli's subalterns. Even more than revolutionary leftist and criminal organizations, the militant Islamist movement not only addressed the grievances of the urban poor and provided them with a platform to continue their locally oriented social and political violence; it also went as far as overturning the local power structures and placing them at the center of the new order it was creating. The extent to which Tawhid was ready to go to court the subalterns, even if it meant immersing itself in older social conflicts, transpired when the movement appeared to have torn down from the city's central square the statue of Abdel Hamid Karame, a notable from a locally powerful family, erecting in its place a giant, three-dimensional sign of the name "God." This epitomized the success of Tawhid's "subaltern Islamism": it was an Islamist group concerned with wider issues, of course, but it simultaneously acted as a "spatially oriented movement" too – one engaging with local grievances, identities and antagonisms. The "Islamic Emirate" it implemented materialized its ideology but it also reflected an older struggle for the city.

Tripoli's Subalterns

Tawhid's rise epitomized the agency of those who, in the tradition of history from below and counter-hegemony, are known as the "subalterns." This term was originally developed by Antonio Gramsci to designate the dominated groups in society who lack representation and are denied citizenship.[2] It was picked up in the 1980s by historians of South Asia, chief among them Ranajit Guha, who were critical of local narratives traditionally glorifying the political consciousness of Indian elites and sought, instead, to highlight the lesser known but equally important mass resistance of the "labouring population" against the colonial state.[3] Through their work, the concept of "subalterns" no longer just referred to the subordination of parts of society to the dominant order, but also began to allude to their potential to act as key agents of contentious politics taking part in social movements and rebellions. The term soon spread beyond the confines of scholarship on Indian history as it resonated with growing efforts in the 1990s and 2000s in the fields of Latin American and Middle Eastern studies to resist the culturalist and economistic assumptions that often treat marginalized social actors as lacking political agency. This resulted in the emergence of a large, cross-regional body of work investigating the various ways in which nonelite groups of people who are subordinate whether because of race, gender, class or religion, actively resist against power structures, thus allowing for a new reading of contention from below.[4]

---

[2] Antonio Gramsci, *Selections from Antonio Gramsci's prison notebooks* (London: Elecbook, 1999), pp. 202–308.

[3] See, among others: Ranajit Guha, "On some aspects of the historiography of India," chapter 2 in Ranajit Guha and Gayatri Chakravorty Spivak (eds.), *Selected subaltern studies* (Oxford: Oxford University Press, 1988), pp. 37–45; Gayatri Chakravorty Spivak, "Scattered speculations on the subaltern and the popular" *Postcolonial Studies* (Vol. 8, No. 4, 2005), pp. 479–86; or Ananya Roy, "Slum dog cities: rethinking subaltern urbanism" *Journal of Urban and Regional Research* (Vol. 35, No. 2, 2011), pp. 223–38.

[4] For some excellent works applying a subaltern lens to the Middle East specifically, see: Salwa Ismail, "Urban subalterns in the Arab revolutions: Cairo and Damascus in comparative perspective" *Comparative Studies in Society and History* (Vol. 55, No. 4,

240   Social Jihad

The use of the term the "subalterns" is particularly relevant in the Tripolitan context. As this and the following two sections show, the mass of impoverished rural migrants who had come in the 1950s and 1960s to the city in search of jobs had, by the 1970s and 1980s, become subordinate and marginalized in every way. Although most were Sunni Muslims like the vast majority of Tripolitans, these urban poor were not only economically exploited but were also socially stigmatized, politically sidelined and even culturally excluded. Describing them as the city's "subalterns" thus points to the fact that their marginalization was not just about poverty – it had to do with much wider, locally rooted power structures. It also echoes the way they often described themselves and their peers, in interviews, as "the oppressed ones" (al-mazloumin). This alluded to their conscious subalternity and, in addition, hinted at their sense of belonging to a wider community of people sharing similar grievances.[5] Yet just as the term of the "subalterns" highlights the shared, severe grievances of the subordinate sectors of society, it also suggests their potential to engage in contention. In Tripoli many subalterns would revolt by getting involved in urban violence through revolutionary movements and criminal organizations, before they joined Tawhid en masse. This would result in what I call, in the rest of this chapter, "subaltern Islamism": Tripoli's subalterns joined Tawhid not as they were intrinsically attracted by Islamism but because they viewed it as a platform to overturn power structures, wage a "social jihad" more driven by their grievances than by ideology and erect a new order in which they became the masters.

Most strikingly, what characterized Tripoli's subalterns was their economic condition. They all belonged to the lower and lower middle classes, from families originally hailing from the impoverished Sunni countryside of Dinniye, a mountain range to Tripoli's east, and from Akkar, a plain to its north, and which had migrated to the city in hope of a better life. Chapter 1 described how, at first, their expectations were fulfilled. Until the 1960s and early 1970s Tripoli had dozens of bustling medium- to large-sized industries that never seemed to run out of work to provide to unskilled laborers in sectors as diverse as sugar, cotton, metal and perfume or the mass manufacture of furniture and textiles.

2013), pp. 865–94; Stephanie Cronin, *Subalterns and social protest: history from below in the Middle East and North Africa* (London: Routledge, 2011); Joel Beinin, *Workers and peasants in the modern Middle East* (Cambridge: Cambridge University Press, 2001); and John Chalcraft, *Popular politics in the making of the modern Middle East* (Cambridge: Cambridge University Press, 2016).

[5] Interview with subaltern residents of the Old City, Mina and Mankubin, Tripoli, May–October 2014.

Tripoli's Subalterns

The city also featured some heavy industries that hired thousands of workers, for example a power plant and a large oil refinery that belonged to the IPC.

However, the IPC installations gradually stopped functioning, with dire consequences for employment. While its oil refinery and terminal had long provided up to 60 percent of Lebanon's domestic fuel needs, the company stopped investing in its Tripoli infrastructures after it became nationalized in 1973.[6] Three years later the rise of geopolitical tensions between Iraq and Syria pushed Baghdad to halt its export of crude to Damascus, which undermined the pipeline's working.[7] But it was the recurrent outbreaks of fighting in the refinery's vicinity, both at the nearby Beddawi Palestinian refugee camp and between the close by neighborhoods of Bab al-Tebbaneh and Jabal Mohsen, which dealt the petroleum installations a nearly fatal blow. The refinery and terminal had to stop functioning during these episodes of contention and they were sometimes even hit by shells. This severely degraded the installations. In one case stray rockets that landed on the oil installations caused a series of blasts that were so massive it took days for firefighters to extinguish the blaze. In the meantime up to twenty-eight reservoirs of fuel and gas had been destroyed, for a staggering loss of $150 million.[8] By the 1980s, then, the IPC no longer functioned properly and it had to lay off most of the thousands of workers on its payroll.

Similar incidents caused significant damage to Tripoli's other plants and factories, to the extent that, while two years into the civil war a fourth of them had to already close down, a few years later it was most of them which would go bankrupt and start laying off workers.[9] Apparently aware of the social danger which this might constitute, the Lebanese government granted a $50 million loan to the Association of Industrialists of North Lebanon to invest in repairs and resume the activities of Tripoli's industries. Yet a well-placed economic source remembered that the money was pocketed by the association's executive board, made up of members of Tripoli's elite, without ever being reinjected into the local economy.[10] Whether true or not, these anecdotes began to quickly

[6] US Embassy in Beirut, "Lebanese takeover of IPC" (Confidential, 03139b, March 19, 1973) and US Embassy in Beirut, "Crude supplies to Tripoli refinery" (Limited official use, 03692b, April 26, 1976).
[7] "Interruption du transit du brut irakien vers Tripoli," *L'Orient Le Jour* (April 11, 1982).
[8] "Tripoli au-delà du désespoir: les combats tournent à la guerre totale," *L'Orient Le Jour* (January 5, 1983) and "Tripoli: pressions accrues sur Arafat," *L'Orient Le Jour* (November 12, 1983).
[9] Interview with Hassan Monla (head of Tripoli's Chamber of Commerce in the 1980s), Tripoli, July 2014.
[10] Interview with a prominent Tripolitan businessman, Tripoli, August 2014.

242 Social Jihad

circulate among Tripoli's subalterns, fostering a sense of economic exploitation and social exclusion at the hands of the local elite.

Partially as a result of the collapse of Tripoli's industrial sector, another crucial part of the local economy which witnessed a severe downturn in the 1970s and 1980s was the port. The neighborhood of Mina, Tripoli's westernmost enclave where the port installations are located, had until then long boasted vibrant activity, despite competition with Beirut's port. Yet the decline of local industrial production combined with the crisis of the agricultural sector meant that within the space of a mere four years Tripolitan exports dropped from 65,242 tons per year to 12,529 tons per year, considerably affecting the activity of the port.[11] The socio-economic situation in the neighborhood of Mina worsened because of the virtual disappearance of another sector of the economy closely associated with that of the port – the fishing industry. By the 1960s and 1970s Tripoli's many fishermen, by then estimated at between 650 and 1,000, had to start competing with the larger Greek and Italian boats as well as with the growth of cheaper imports from the West. They soon became unemployed.[12]

No longer able to pay their rent, Mina's subalterns settled in the fast-expanding shantytowns of the port area. Some of these slums, such as al-Hara al-Jadide and al-Masaken al-Sha'abiye, were overcrowded collective residences built in haste by the government in the 1970s.[13] Others, like Hosh Abid, were longstanding informal housing units situated at the neighborhood's extremity, being geographically isolated and lacking the most basic infrastructure, as they were neither paved nor even connected to the city's electricity grid. The economic situation of Mina's subalterns had become dramatic so quickly that many of them began squatting a large abandoned *khan*, or medieval caravanserai. It had the advantage of being located just across the port installations, for when job opportunities sporadically came up, but the *khan* was so old that it threatened to collapse and was so overcrowded that diseases regularly broke out, threatening to contaminate its hundreds of residents all at once.[14] Mina, long known as an economically vibrant middle-class neighborhood, thus began to struggle with pockets of severe poverty concentrated in slums at the district's extremities. One survey estimated that as many as 66 percent of its residents were either poor or very poor, the remaining

---

[11] I draw this figure from Gulick, *Tripoli*, p. 92.

[12] Interview with a former member of the Mina municipality, Tripoli, August 2014.

[13] "Un programme général pour l'habitat," *L'Orient Le Jour* (September 7, 1971).

[14] Interview with subaltern residents of the neighborhood of Mina, Tripoli, July–August 2014.

Tripoli's Subalterns

44 percent belonging to the upper middle class being either well off or wealthy.[15] Tripoli's subalterns, who had benefited from the city's industrial boost in the 1950s and 1960s, now had to struggle with high poverty rates and with fast-worsening living conditions.

Of course, not all of the subalterns became unemployed. Many, in fact, found new jobs, but the problem was that these were often low paid, temporary and subcontracted. This was a symptom of the wider rise of the "informal proletariat," as urban social historian Mike Davis called this new phenomenon which began affecting countless cities of the global south. The term designated the shift of masses of jobs "from the factory line to the slum street or marketplace."[16] Workers were no longer hired to collectively manufacture items in large factories, they were now individually subcontracted to sell already produced goods and services. And, while they used to benefit from job stability and social security, their new activities pushed them toward the informal economy, with no regulations protecting them.

As an example, one area of Tripoli which became particularly affected by the rise of the "informal proletariat" with significant social and political consequences was the Old City. For centuries before the 1970s this string of Mameluk-era historical neighborhoods had been known throughout Lebanon and Syria for the high quality of its handicrafts. It was so renowned for the skills of its artisans who produced items as diverse as soap, jewelry, leatherwork and glasswork that, until the 1970s, it was not uncommon for wealthy Lebanese from all over the country and of all religions to do their luxury shopping in Tripoli's Old City. Yet the outbreak of the civil war and the deterioration of the security situation in the city as well as on the Tripoli–Beirut road negatively affected the economy of the old quarters. Moreover, the artisans had to begin competing with much cheaper Western imports, which put them under additional economic stress. While, for instance, a local shoemaker could craft a maximum of three shoes per week, a workshop using Western-imported leatherwork and machines was able to produce as many as 220 pairs in the same time, albeit of lower quality.[17] The result was a dramatic decrease in the number of handicraft shops in Tripoli's Old City. Within the space of a few years these jobs had disappeared to the extent that the total number of shops which crafted and sold Tripolitan soap and glasswork, for long two of their most popular

[15] I draw this figure from Gulick, *Tripoli*, p. 184.
[16] Mike Davis, *Planet of slums* (London: Verso, 2006).
[17] Nadine Picaudou, "Mutations socio-économiques du vieux Tripoli" *Annales de Géographie* (Vol. 1, 1981), pp. 37–41.

244   Social Jihad

items, barely came to represent 3 percent of the Old City's total number of shops.[18]

Instead these handicraft shops were replaced by larger workshops exclusively employing unskilled workers who operated automated machines. Yet, because competition for jobs was so fierce as unemployment was on the rise, this workforce became "unstable." In other words, these workers benefited from no job security whatsoever, being frequently laid off and perpetually in search for their next, low-paid and short-term, position. This situation was not just typical of the larger workshops, it came to characterize the new local economy. Workers were either subcontracted or became self-employed, acting one day as a petty coffee seller or shoe shiner while the next being a construction worker or vegetable seller. One researcher suggested that by the early 1980s a staggering 75 percent of the workforce in the Old City had become "unstable,"[19] characterized by a permanent struggle for survival.

The way in which the Old City's artisans were rapidly replaced by this "informal proletariat" had several important social and political implications. To begin with, having to alternate between menial jobs and unemployment worsened the already difficult economic condition of the subalterns. The Old City, once known for being a socially mixed area, became more distinctively marked by poverty. Surveys indicate that approximately 75 percent of its residents became "poor" or "very poor,"[20] which corresponds to the locals who were part of the "informal proletariat." Sometimes they got involved in petty crime and avoided paying taxes to the authorities, but this was rarely enough to make ends meet. Many of the wealthier shopkeepers who had stayed in the area started to desert it and to relocate to safer and richer New Tripoli, in the western vicinity of the old quarter. Moreover, the fact that these workers were individually subcontracted or became self-employed signified that they did not develop a culture of organized collective labor. This meant that there was close to no trade union presence in the Old City. In fact, a gap began separating the concerns of the trade unions and of the mainstream left from those of the "informal proletariat," many of whose members no longer felt socially and politically represented. And finally, the individualized nature of their work also meant that they had virtually no bargaining power with the machine owners or the wealthier clientele

---

[18] Joumana al-Soufi Richard, "Le vieux Tripoli dans ses structures actuelles" *Annales de Géographie* (Vol. 2, 1981), pp. 50–1.

[19] Ibid.

[20] I draw the figure from Gulick, *Tripoli*, p. 184 and from Adib N'ame, *Al-Faqr fi madinat Trablus* [*Poverty in the city of Tripoli*] (Beirut: United Nations, 2014), p. 55.

they sold their goods and services to, enhancing the workers' sense that they were being economically exploited. This began translating into resentment for the middle and upper middle classes in New Tripoli.

These mounting social tensions were also fueled by a loss of social mixity in the Old City. While many of the well-off inhabitants of New Tripoli originally hailed from the Old City and had long kept social and economic ties there, visiting regularly and buying much of their furniture, clothes and jewelry locally, this began to change in the 1970s. The Old City had not only lost its reputation for producing quality handicrafts, it had also become known as an area rife with crime, with social tensions constantly on the verge of breaking out. One researcher who studied the Old City's society and economics back then thus noted the "contempt" with which Tripoli's middle and upper middle class, especially in New Tripoli, started to view the residents of the old quarters. As a result, the shops of the Old City gradually shifted toward relying on the lower and lower middle classes, who came to constitute over two-thirds of all their customers.[21] All of these developments dramatically accentuated the sense of social exclusion, economic exploitation and political alienation suffered by the residents of the Old City. Although this sense was particularly acute there, the deterioration of the conditions of Tripoli's subalterns was a general trend.

A Tale of Two Cities

Crucially these tensions between Tripoli's subalterns and the upper class built on a dynamic of urban segregation, and as a result gradually turned into a spatially rooted antagonism. Tripoli had for centuries been a socially mixed city, with richer and poorer inhabitants routinely socializing in neighborhood alleyways, Sufi *zawiyas* (lodges) or in the Old City's many *hammams* (public baths). But, by the 1970s and 1980s it became increasingly torn by a cleavage pitting the subalterns in the Old City and its extensions against the upper middle class in New Tripoli. To the outside this growing socio-spatial antagonism may not have been as visible as Tripoli's other, much more publicized struggle – the neighborhood rivalry between the Alawi hilltop of Jabal Mohsen and the Sunnidominated district of Bab al-Tebbaneh tackled in Chapter 2 – but it would play as important a role in Tawhid's rise.

Spatially, New Tripoli comprised the gentrified set of boulevards and districts built in the 1940s, 1950s and 1960s. This area stretched

---

[21] Mousbah Rajab, *Le vieux Tripoli (Liban), un espace historique en voie de mutation* (Paris: University of Pantheon Sorbonne, unpublished PhD thesis, 1993), p. 339.

246   Social Jihad

horizontally from the vicinity of the Old City westwards in the direction of Mina and southward in the direction of the Tripoli–Beirut highway, with a string of private beaches, hotel complexes and real estate developments, as well as Balamand University and the newly built Tripoli campus of the Lebanese University. This was where the city's political and financial heart was also located for it concentrated the municipality building, the seat of the governor of North Lebanon and up to a dozen banks. Shops on these boulevards featured the latest Western trends. They included women's hairdressers and shops selling pricy Italian shoes and clothes as well as French cosmetics. The clientele not only had to be wealthy but also educated to enter these salons and shops for everything in there was either written in French or, to a lesser extent back then, in English, from brochures and price tags to discount vouchers and even the shop signs at the entrance.[22] Socially, then, it was no surprise that the neighborhood was very privileged, one study reporting that 90 percent of its population was either upper middle class, well off or very rich.[23]

New Tripoli also concentrated the city's entertainment and cultural infrastructure. Some of its cafes, like the *Café Americain*, the *Café Bresilien* and *Le Negresco*, served as socializing places for the neighborhood's residents and as working spaces for the notables who debated or read a newspaper while drinking their espresso and savoring fine pastries. They sometimes also met at the Cultural League (*al-Rabita al-Thaqafiye*), an impressive and elegant building which acted as a sort of gentlemen's club and also had a lecture hall open to members of the wider public, although most were locals, for theater plays and choir concerts. New Tripoli also featured up to ten cinemas that all belonged to the city's wealthiest families. Unsurprisingly this was where virtually all of the restaurants were located too, and it also concentrated some of Tripoli's more controversial entertainment places such as a casino, *Le Cheval Blanc*, a French restaurant where alcohol was served, *La Barique*, three cabarets that featured Turkish belly dancers and even a few fancy bars and nightclubs. New Tripoli thus quickly emerged as the new seat of the city's political, economic and cultural power.

Importantly, New Tripoli became spatially segregated from the city's poorer areas through two key landmarks which came to bear socially loaded connotations for the subalterns. To its east the chic neighborhood

---

[22] I draw some of the ethnographic observations in this section on interviews with residents of Tripoli in June–August 2014 as well as on two books on the evolution of Tripolitan society; Khodr Heloui, *La rue des églises: il était une ville paisible, Tripoli au Liban nord* (Paris: L'Harmattan, 2014) and Khaled Ziadeh, *Neighbourhood and boulevard: reading through the modern Arab city* (New York: Palgrave Macmillan, 2011).

[23] I draw this figure from Gulick, *Tripoli*, p. 184.

A Tale of Two Cities   247

was separated from the Old City by a large roundabout, where its wide boulevards also ended. At the center of this roundabout, which symbolically acted as Tripoli's main square, lay a giant bronze statue of Abdel Hamid Karame, the father of Rashid Karame, who embodied the local notability. The statue was so large and central that it even earned the site the name of "Abdel Hamid Karame Square" or "Square of the Statue." As the later part of this chapter will show, it became a key target of the subalterns who saw as provocative the location of a statue of the father of the city's most powerful scion at the very junction that separated New Tripoli from the poorer districts.

To its southwest, the chic neighborhood became isolated from the slums of Mina, the port area, through the construction of the city's International Fair. One scholar of urbanism in Tripoli argued that this project, which absorbed a massive amount of virgin land, was designed to act as a "protection"[24] shielding New Tripoli from the spread of slums nearby. The International Fair, in fact, epitomized the way in which space was "socially produced,"[25] as urban thinker Henri Lefebvre put it; that is, how it reflected and perpetuated power relations. Although officially the project meant to restore the status of the city and kick-start its economy, it was actually intended to benefit first and foremost the residents of New Tripoli. Tellingly, the funds for the fair were allocated during Rashid Karame's tenure as prime minister in 1975, and even foreign observers seemed to agree that its "main object"[26] was to satisfy the Tripolitan upper middle class that voted for him and largely inhabited New Tripoli. In addition to protecting the chic neighborhood from the spread of slums to its southwest, the presence of the fair also provided a "justification"[27] for the exponential increase in real estate prices in the area and it allowed the upper class access to a unique infrastructure. The "Rashid Karame International Fair," as the site was called in a reflection of its wider social and political importance, did not just comprise a large

[24] Charbel Nahas, "La foire internationale et Tripoli, quel avenir?" (paper delivered at the Safadi Foundation, Tripoli, December 15, 2007), also available at: http://charbelnahas .org/textes/Amenagement_et_urbanisme/Maarad_Tripoli.pdf. For more on the history of Tripoli's Rashid Karame International Fair, see also: Mousbah Rajab, "Les grands projets de Tripoli: systèmes de décisions et besoins de réappropriation" in *Conquérir la ville* (Beirut: Presses de l'Ifpo, 2006); Bruno Dewailly, "L'espace public à travers le prisme du pouvoir: quelques réflexions à partir du cas tripolitain (Liban)" *Geocarrefour* (Vol. 77, No. 33, 2002), pp. 297–307; and Bruno Dewailly, *Pouvoir et production urbaine à Tripoli al-Fayha (Liban)* (Tours: Université Francois Rabelais de Tours, unpublished PhD thesis, 2015).

[25] Henri Lefebvre, *The production of space* (Cambridge: Blackwell, 1991).

[26] "25 millions de Livres pour la Foire de Tripoli," *L'Orient Le Jour* (September 13, 1974) and UK Embassy in Beirut, "Lebanon" (Confidential NPLN1/2, August 2, 1975).

[27] Nahas, "La foire internationale et Tripoli."

248   Social Jihad

building where world-class exhibitions could be held. It also included a series of very useful amenities such a parking lot with a capacity of 2,000, a luxury hotel, fountains, gardens and even a helicopter landing strip. Visually the fair gave grandeur to New Tripoli for it was designed by world-renowned Brazilian architect Oscar Niemeyer who realized eye-catching, futuristic buildings such as a giant arch visible from afar, an auditorium and a large dome. However, the site was so badly damaged by revolutionary leftist movements and criminal organizations that it only opened its doors in 1995. This showed how, for the many subalterns who made up these movements, the fair came to epitomize Tripoli's socio-spatial antagonism.

Across from that social and spatial frontier lay a completely different face of Tripoli. Of course, the rest of the city was not entirely and homogeneously inhabited by subalterns. Some neighborhoods were still solidly middle class. Chief among them was the hill of Abu Samra, in the southeastern vicinity of Tripoli. This was a modern residential district entirely inhabited by Sunni Muslims, a large portion of them socially conservative. Before the rise of Tawhid, Abu Samra had been the strong-hold of the Lebanese Muslim Brotherhood, known as the Islamic Group, and of Soldiers of God, as Chapter 3 showed. Yet, apart from Abu Samra, and to a lesser extent the boulevards of Mina where as we saw a portion of the district was middle class too, much of the rest of this other Tripoli was poor. In New Tripoli's northeastern vicinity, right across "Abdel Hamid Karame Square," lay the ancient but run-down and overcrowded neighborhoods that together made up the Old City. This large area no longer represented a geographically coherent unit since the 1955 Abu Ali river flood had destroyed the local infrastructure and the authorities had created new roads. It stretched vertically from a southern edge in the old quarter of Bab al-Ramel, famous for its car repair shops and its ancient mosques, through the maze of *souqs* or covered markets all the way to a northern edge constituted by the restive neighborhood of Bab al-Tebbaneh.

Aside from these historical and deprived districts, Qobbe was another area of Tripoli which came to be overwhelmingly constituted of subal-terns. This neighborhood, situated on a hill overlooking the Old City and located very close to the Alawi district of Jabal Mohsen, was a formerly middle-class area that was increasingly made up of deprived rural migrants. Qobbe was most strikingly characterized by its blocs of unfin-ished concrete, newly built but already overcrowded housing units, wastelands and a generally dysfunctional infrastructure. There were three more areas where Tripoli's subalterns lived. One was Mankubin, whose translation means "the damaged ones" and, although it was meant

A Tale of Two Cities 249

to allude to the status of the area's inhabitants after they became homeless during the 1955 flood, could well describe the terrible social conditions in which they still continued to live decades after the disaster. Behind Mankubin was the deprived district of Beddawi, with its large Palestinian refugee camp. And westwards in the direction of Mina lay the infamous slums of the port district.

This "other Tripoli" made up of the subalterns, then, did not represent a geographically coherent unit, and each neighborhood featured its own peculiarities. However, all shared similar social characteristics. Most struggled with extreme poverty. Unemployment was rife too. While, for instance, there were over twice as many unemployed in the Old City than in New Tripoli, there were four times as many in Bab al-Tebbaneh.[28] And, as suggested in the previous section, when the inhabitants of these deprived districts were not unemployed they were often part of the "informal proletariat," perpetually being in search of new daily, hard and low-paid work. These neighborhoods were also overcrowded, benefiting from no public space, and suffered from antiquated infrastructure.

This resulted in sometimes disastrous health conditions locally. For instance, the bad state of the pipes polluted the water which, in turn, resulted in the spread of skin disease and cancer. One researcher who authored a remarkable study on the quality of running water in Tripoli thus reported a major divide between New Tripoli and the city's subaltern-inhabited districts. While water was polluted in only 21 percent of the households of the chic neighborhood, it was contaminated in a staggering 83 percent of Qobbe's households, going up to 89 percent in the Old City. There the health situation was close to a complete disaster, with up to 35 percent of the locals in Qobbe reporting that they either suffered from cancer, typhoid or skin disease. And, as worryingly, when residents from these deprived areas called the engineering department of Tripoli's municipality to carry out repairs, they were likely to receive no response at all. This contrasted with the well over half of residents of New Tripoli who acknowledged that the authorities had "responded fast" to their demands for reparation.[29] In other words, these areas constituted black holes on the municipality's socio-urban map. And, tellingly, while the Old City for instance hosted over a tenth of Tripoli's population, it was equipped with neither a single school nor a

---

[28] I draw this figure from Rajab, *Le vieux Tripoli*, p. 386.

[29] I draw these figures from the excellent study of Maha Kayal on the quality of water in Tripoli per neighbourhood: Maha Kayal, *Al-mai fi al-mujtam'a* [*Water in Society*] (Beirut: Mukhtarat, 2007), pp. 116–20.

clinic. It could only count on one doctor and had no pharmacy.[30] This reflected the extent of the marginalization of Tripoli's most impoverished districts and the dynamic of segregation separating them from New Tripoli.

In addition to being socially and economically marginalized, Tripoli's poor districts also became the target of what sociologist Loïc Wacquant called "territorial stigmatization."[31] That is, when an inhabitant of, say, Qobbe, the Old City, Bab al-Tebbaneh or Mina's slums had to interact with a resident of New Tripoli, in routine settings like a job interview, for a business transaction or in a shared taxi, the very fact of mentioning his or her area of residence would trigger deeply entrenched reactions, most often a mix of contempt and fear. Sometimes there was not even a need to mention it, for the very accent, clothing style and look of the uneducated subaltern was enough to formulate assumptions about his or her rural background and likely residence in one of Tripoli's deprived and infamous districts. There was a pronounced cultural component too to this territorial stigmatization, one resulting from rampant tension between the inhabitants of New Tripoli, who could trace their family's local presence to generations – sometimes to hundreds of years – and thus felt they owned the city, and rural migrants who were newcomers in search of a sense of citizenship. This tension became acute in the 1970s when migration to Tripoli reached its peak, with a staggering 38 percent of its population now made up of rural migrants living in poor districts.[32]

In interviews, in fact, it was common to hear residents of New Tripoli recalling this period as one during which "the countryside invaded the city."[33] A wealthy inhabitant from a historical Tripolitan family explained she began feeling like a "foreigner" in her "own city."[34] "I would go out and look at people's faces but there was no longer anyone I could recognize." These indigenous Tripolitans often felt "contempt" for the rural-inherited lifestyle of the migrants; for instance mocking the "farm feel" of Qobbe, where cows and chickens began to wander in the streets, or disparaging the traditional dress worn by women in areas like the Old City. This stigmatization, even rejection, of the rural- and subaltern-inhabited poorer districts did not go unnoticed.

---

[30] Al-Soufi Richard, *Lutte populaire armée*, p. 45.

[31] Loïc Wacquant, *Urban outcasts: a comparative sociology of advanced marginality* (Cambridge: Polity Press, 2008).

[32] I draw the figure from Mousbah Rajab's doctoral research on Tripolitan society: Rajab, *Le vieux Tripoli*, p. 199.

[33] Interview with residents of New Tripoli, Tripoli, August 2014.

[34] Interview with an upper-class resident hailing from a historical local family, Tripoli, July 2014.

Criminal Violence as Contentious Politics

One researcher who studied in depth the attitudes of Tripolitan subalterns originally from the mountainous rural area of Dinniye who had settled en masse in the Tripoli districts of Qobbe and Abu Samra reported that up to 56 percent of them felt a sense of "unease" and a denial of their citizenship as Tripolitans on the part of indigenous locals.[35]

By the 1970s and 1980s, then, an important local cleavage was the growing social and spatial segregation between wealthy New Tripoli and the much poorer Old City as well as its extensions. This was about much more than wealth against poverty. It was about two very different kinds of social worlds on a collision path; one whose residents felt they owned the city and where the seats of political, economic and cultural power were located, and another one scarred by an acute sense of subordination and territorial stigmatization. Segregation between these spaces, of course, was never total. In fact, the spatial proximity of New Tripoli to Mina's slums and the Old City, or the fact that many subalterns routinely commuted to the chic neighborhood for petty jobs in areas such as construction, meant that they were not fully isolated from the relaxed lifestyle of the upper middle class. This is precisely what bred the paradoxical mix of resentment and envy felt by the subalterns which they began channeling through participation in revolutionary and criminal groups. Tawhid, by engaging considerably in Tripoli's social tensions and in this spatially rooted antagonism, would later provide the conduit through which they would wage "social jihad."

Criminal Violence as Contentious Politics

A remarkable feature of subaltern politics in Tripoli is how the urban poor expressed these social and political grievances in sometimes very different and rapidly changing ways. While, as one might expect, they began to protest against their condition by adhering to revolutionary leftist groups that got involved in locally oriented social and political violence, like the 24 October Movement and the Organization of Anger, tackled in Chapters 1 and 2, in this section I discuss the less intuitive case of how, by 1974, many of them had joined a criminal group. There were of course a range of nonpolitical reasons behind the social and spatial salience with the subalterns of the gang known as the "State of the Outlaws" (*Dawlat al-Matloubin*). Yet the main source of this

---

[35] Loïc Ploteau, *Les populations originaires du Haut Daniyye à Tripoli Liban: dynamiques de ségrégation et de citadinisation* (Tours: University of Tours, unpublished Master's dissertation, 1997), p. 71.

252 Social Jihad

criminal movement's popularity lay in its ability and willingness to address the grievances of the subalterns and to channel them into a type of collective action which seemed like "criminal violence" at first glance but was, at heart, inherently political. Through a succession of revolutionary and criminal groups in the years before Tawhid's advent, the subalterns were increasingly engaging in locally oriented contentious politics.

A key factor which accentuated the desire of the subalterns to join movements engaging in locally oriented social and political violence, linked to but distinct from social tensions with New Tripoli, was the acute sense of political exclusion which many of them felt. This stemmed from the gap that separated them from the mainstream left and the trade unions, whom they lambasted for being socially elitist and detached from subaltern concerns. But, even more obviously, the subaltern disenfranchisement with institutionalized politics was due to the fact that they were effectively denied participation in local decision-making. Indeed, in Lebanon the absence of a census since 1932 means that people vote not in their current place of residence but instead in their city or town of origin. This signified that most of the subalterns in Tripoli's impoverished districts, who were largely rural migrants or their descendants, were not eligible to vote in the city. For instance, while two-thirds of Qobbe's inhabitants were politically excluded from the decision-making process in this way, a shocking four-fifths of Bab al-Tebbaneh's residents were not able to vote in Tripoli.[36]

This had two implications. The first was that many subalterns fell outside of the scope of the patronage networks sponsored by the local political parties and notables competing for seats in the Tripoli constituency during parliamentary elections or for the municipal elections. This meant that many were unlikely to benefit from the petty jobs and the small but crucial services, like free healthcare, often provided by local political bosses seeking to get reelected. In addition to fueling resentment it enhanced the sense that they were rejected as citizens.[37] A second implication of their exclusion from the decision-making process was the reinforcement of the domination of historical, upper-class Tripolitan families over the city. One example was the way in which the Tripolitan municipality continued to act as a vehicle enabling the reproduction of old elites, even though local society had become more diverse. Tellingly

---

[36] See *Qobbe: neighbourhood profile* (Beirut: UN-Habitat Lebanon, 2018) and *Tabbaneh: neighbourhood profile* (Beirut: UN-Habitat Lebanon, 2018).

[37] Interview with residents of the deprived districts of the Old City, Qobbe and Mankubin, Tripoli, June 2014.

the heads of the Tripolitan municipality from 1944 to 1998 comprised Mohammed Karame, Moustafa Karame (for three mandates), Rashed Sultan, Akram Uwayda, Mohammed Misqawi (for two mandates), Abdel Karim Uwayda and Ashir al-Daye.[38] They were all either representatives of the Karames or members of the upper class in New Tripoli.

Excluded from participating in political life in institutionalized ways, many subalterns began turning to contentious politics to make themselves heard in local society. While in the late 1960s and early 1970s they were known to be particularly numerous in revolutionary leftist movements that engaged in urban violence, officially on behalf of the "Palestinian cause" or "Marxism," like the 24 October Movement or the Organization of Anger, the subalterns soon embraced the State of the Outlaws when it emerged in 1974.[39]

At first glance this gang of Tripolitan criminals could hardly be considered a vehicle for "collective political struggles,"[40] as the definition of contentious politics puts it. The foundations for the State of the Outlaws were laid out in 1970 when two dozen criminals wanted by the judiciary for murders and robberies teamed up, entered Tripoli's Old City and used its labyrinth of alleyways to prevent the police forces from pursuing them. Their motivations, therefore, were clearly self-serving. They soon began to call themselves the "Movement of the Outlaws" and to expand their criminal enterprise to the entire Old City, to the extent that by April 1974 they even declared it to be their own "state" – the "State of the Outlaws."[41]

It is then that the Old City's subalterns joined the criminal movement en masse. Figures vary but it is estimated that from two dozen in 1970, the State of the Outlaws had now grown to hundreds of gang members who erected checkpoints and barricades at the Old City's entrance and together conducted sporadic raids on Tripoli's banks and luxury shops. The movement's leader, Ahmed Qaddur, boasted that he could raise 1,500 fighters during episodes of violence[42] – this was probably an

---

[38] Interview with Rashid Jemali (former Mayor of Tripoli) and with members of the Tripoli municipality, Tripoli, July 2014.

[39] See Maha Kayal and Atef Atiya, *Trablus min al-dahkal* [*Tripoli from the inside*] (Beirut: Dar al-Mokhtarat, 2004), pp. 156–73.

[40] Charles Tilly and Sidney Tarrow, *Contentious politics* (London: Paradigm Publishers, 2007), p. 7.

[41] "Al-qissa al-kamila la Dawlat al-Matlubin fi Trablus sanat 1974, (1)" ["The full story of the State of the Outlaws in Tripoli in the year 1974 (1)"], *al-Tamaddon* (February 26, 2018). I draw most of this section on archival research into Lebanese daily *L'Orient Le Jour* and on a trove of archives published in Tripolitan weekly *al-Tamaddon*.

[42] "Ra'is 'Dawlat al-Matlubin' yurwi qussatu rifaqu," *al-Nahar* (November 10, 1974), republished in "Al-qissa al-kamila la Dawlat al-Matlubin fi Trablus sanat 1974, (6)" ["The full story of the State of the Outlaws in Tripoli in the year 1974 (6)"], *al-Tamaddon* (March 4, 2018).

254   Social Jihad

exaggeration but it is undeniable that the State of the Outlaws counted on a much larger pool of sympathizers than its membership base. The media, in fact, was soon bewildered by the sheer "popularity" of this group of criminals. One journalist called it "a small army."[43] Another one, reporting on a vast offensive by the police on the State of the Outlaws in September 1974, noted how the "popular pressure" in the Old City, through the help of "local inhabitants who took up weapons"[44] and joined the criminals, had caused five deaths and forced the security forces into a humiliating retreat. This pushed the notables to solemnly ask the subaltern residents of the Old City to "turn their back"[45] on the Outlaws and instead support the governmental authorities – but to no avail. The State of the Outlaws had effectively become the movement of the Old City's subalterns.

There were several reasons for the criminal group's striking social and spatial salience with the subaltern residents of the Old City. Predictably, one factor was profit. Leaders of the State of the Outlaws had originally come to the Old City with suitcases of cash and they were prepared to pay salaries to those who would join them. For the subalterns who were part of the "informal proletariat" and struggled with menial jobs, this provided a measure of stability. The strength of the Outlaws in the Old City also allowed the subalterns to continue engaging in petty crime, which had long enabled them to make ends meet, this time on a larger scale. The period ranging from April 1974 until January 1975, when the State of the Outlaws collapsed, thus marked a drastic increase in the involvement of locals in robberies, extortion and the black market, from the trafficking of hashish all the way to weapons smuggling. Crucially, this was also a period characterized by the complete control of the Outlaws over the Old City, which prevented the entry of the authorities in the area for a full nine months – this fitted the local residents well for it allowed them to avoid paying taxes during this time. But the smell of profit, however important, was only one factor among others explaining the social and spatial salience of the State of the Outlaws with many subalterns in the Old City.

Another important factor was the way in which the Outlaws successfully embedded themselves in the neighborhood's social fabric. Although the initial backbone of the State of the Outlaws was made up of criminals who originally hailed either from the northern countryside or from

[43] "50,000 Livres Libanaises pour qui aiderait à retrouver Ahmed Qaddour," *L'Orient Le Jour* (January 7, 1974).
[44] "Troubles à Tripoli," *L'Orient Le Jour* (September 27, 1974).
[45] "Journée calme à Tripoli hier," *L'Orient Le Jour* (December 4, 1974).

Criminal Violence as Contentious Politics 255

deprived districts of Tripoli other than the Old City, many married locals and one of them, its leader Ahmed Qaddur, had even grown up there as a child. This meant that, in the minds of many locals, they belonged to the Old City as a community.[46] As we saw in Chapter 2, these bonds of neighborhood belonging and the resulting sense of solidarity which tied residents with one another could be so powerful that, when activated, they led locals to help each other, even if that required taking considerable risks with their lives. Another way in which the State of the Outlaws embedded itself in the neighborhood was by portraying its "criminal violence" as fitting with local narratives that had long associated the Old City with a tradition of contention against the authorities, like the police. "In this district, there is an automatic willingness of a large group of residents to support the movements of resistance,"[47] explained a journalist in reference to the area's centuries-old reputation as a heart of "disobedience" against perceived "enemies" of the neighborhood. For local residents, then, helping the Outlaws resist the security forces may have been a way of defending their community and of upholding its identity as a stronghold of contention. This especially became the case after the State of the Outlaws was joined by most of the Old City's *qabadayet* in mid-1974. These strong-arm neighborhood heroes epitomized the ideal of the defense of the local community and, as Chapter 2 showed, their very adherence to a movement could trigger the subsequent joining of dozens of their extremely loyal followers. The participation of these spatially grounded "champions of mobilization" to the State of the Outlaws was key in explaining the spatial salience of this criminal group in the Old City.[48]

Yet, even though the smell of profits and the activation of neighborhood solidarities therefore mattered, the most central factor behind the popularity of the State of the Outlaws with the Old City's residents was its ability to channel the subaltern demand for contention. The criminal group, of course, was not a social movement in the traditional sense that it organized political gatherings, led street demonstrations or explicitly challenged the state. But it did embody the extent to which criminal

---

[46] "Al-qissa al-kamila la Dawlat al-Matlubin fi Trablus sanat 1974, (2)" ["The full story of the State of the Outlaws in Tripoli in the year 1974 (2)"], *al-Tamaddon* (February 26, 2018) and "Qaddour réussit à se réfugier dans le jurd," *L'Orient Le Jour* (January 12, 1975).

[47] "Al-qissa al-kamila la Dawlat al-Matlubin fi Trablus sanat 1974, (1)" ["The full story of the State of the Outlaws in Tripoli in the year 1974 (1)"], *al-Tamaddon* (February 26, 2018).

[48] For evidence of their role, see: "La flambée de violence de mardi à Tripoli," *L'Orient Le Jour* (November 7, 1974) and "Un jeune qabaday déchiqueté par l'explosion d'une grenade à Tripoli," *L'Orient Le Jour* (December 19, 1974).

256   Social Jihad

groups can, at times, be considered key actors of contentious politics. Indeed, although the State of the Outlaws' first public demand, written on a large banner put up at the Old City's entrance in April 1974, simply asked the police for "equality"[49] and demanded that it does not go at the area's outlaws more fiercely than it would elsewhere in Lebanon, the criminal group's rhetoric soon turned more political. It began printing tracts in which it prided itself as a "resistance movement" opposing "the power," explaining that "our cause has always been the cause of every citizen who rejects injustice, deprivation, arbitrariness and of all those who lead protests and carry out revolts."[50] Some of its leaders gave interviews in which they portrayed themselves as the spokespersons for the Old City's subalterns. One of them for instance engaged with the territorial stigmatization which locals often felt the victims of, regretting that the area's residents were routinely seen in other parts of the city "as criminals, even when they are actually innocent." They also defended "the poor people" living there and even hailed their "restlessness in demanding their rights"[51] as a good way of lobbying the authorities to improve their livelihoods. From mid-1974, the State of the Outlaws had begun developing a political rhetoric which, if it was not sophisticated, still explicitly engaged with the area's grievances.

But the true root of the criminal movement's ability to channel the subaltern demand for contention stemmed from the way in which it framed its rule over the Old City as an alternative political order, one empowering the locals and giving them a platform to revolt. Indeed, the timing of its spectacular rise in popularity in the area from April 1974 onward is perhaps not a surprise for it precisely matched its rebranding from the "Movement of the Outlaws" into the "State of the Outlaws." This rebranding of the criminal movement as a "state" was far from neutral. It reflected its efforts to implement tentative governance structures in the Old City, through the provision of small jobs, financial help and basic healthcare to the needy families of the neighborhood.[52] In

---

[49] "Al-qissa al-kamila la Dawlat al-Matlubin fi Trablus sanat 1974, (1)" ["The full story of the State of the Outlaws in Tripoli in the year 1974 (1)"], al-Tamaddon (February 26, 2018).

[50] "Al-qissa al-kamila la Dawlat al-Matlubin fi Trablus sanat 1974, (2)" ["The full story of the State of the Outlaws in Tripoli in the year 1974 (2)"], al-Tamaddon (February 26, 2018).

[51] "Ra'is 'Dawlat al-Matlubin' yurwi qussatu rifaqu," al-Nahar (November 10, 1974), republished in "Al-qissa al-kamila la Dawlat al-Matlubin fi Trablus sanat 1974, (6)" ["The full story of the State of the Outlaws in Tripoli in the year 1974 (6)"], al-Tamaddon (March 4, 2018).

[52] "L'accès de la Vieille Ville est interdit aux investigateurs," L'Orient Le Jour (December 20, 1974).

Criminal Violence as Contentious Politics 257

this respect it rapidly outperformed the nearly nonexistent services of the government and the local municipality. Even more importantly, the State of the Outlaws also came to signify the enactment of an alternative sociopolitical order in which it was the subalterns who now took center stage. Many locals tellingly called it the "Republic of the Outlaws," and not the "State," because the former term referred not just to institutions providing services but also to a wider social and political system, underpinned by shared values, which gave people the last word.[53] This "Republic" had "ministers," a "spokesman" and even a "president," Ahmed Qaddur, who was so "ardently admired"[54] by local residents that many had his picture in their homes. They hailed him as a modern "Robin Hood,"[55] someone whose criminal group had empowered the subalterns more than any previous social movement or rebel group.

The State of the Outlaws implemented this alternative political order by encouraging the Old City's subalterns to assert themselves and challenge power structures. The criminal group had stockpiles of light but also heavy weapons, from pistols and grenades all the way to Kalashnikovs, machine guns and bazookas, which it put at the disposal of any of its members willing not just to raid banks but also "to impose their own law"[56] on Tripoli. The Old City's subalterns, then, may have been economically exploited, socially stigmatized, culturally excluded and marginalized from the local decision-making process but, through the State of the Outlaws, they could now express their grievances and exert political agency. Indeed, while the nature of the violence they came to exercise often appeared "criminal" at first glance, it was social and political at its core, observers even calling it outright "terrorism."[57] The list of their targets speaks for itself. From April 1974 until January 1975, a police station in the vicinity of the Old City was blown up, the seat of the governor was targeted, a series of bombs exploded during Independence Day, explosives were thrown into the factories that had laid off many workers and belonged to the prestigious Ghandour family, the mansions of local notables were shot at and even some of Tripoli's private schools

---

[53] "Dans la République des Hors La Loi avant le grand nettoyage," *L'Orient le Jour* (January 13, 1975).

[54] "Tripoli: Qaddour avoue une dizaine de crimes crapuleux," *L'Orient Le Jour* (January 18, 1975).

[55] "Tripoli: l'armée donne l'assaut à la République des Hors La Loi," *L'Orient Le Jour* (January 5, 1975).

[56] "Tripoli: l'insécurité provoque un début d'exode," *L'Orient Le Jour* (January 3, 1975).

[57] "Dans la République des Hors La Loi avant le grand nettoyage," *L'Orient le Jour* (January 13, 1975).

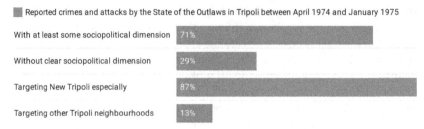

Figure 5.1 Tripoli's Outlaws between criminal and political violence
Note: By "no social or political dimension" I refer to crimes or attacks primarily driven by profit (e.g. running a brothel, attacking shopkeepers) and by "some social or political dimension" I refer to crimes or attacks underpinned by social and political tensions (e.g. murdering a trade unionist, attacking the seat of the governor).
Source: Data gathered from Tripolitan weekly *al-Tamaddon* and Lebanese daily *L'Orient Le Jour*

were vandalized.[58] Figure 5.1 indicates how most of the criminal group's violence had social and political meaning and targeted New Tripoli more than any other neighborhoods.

Even when the choice of the target seemed more driven by criminal intent than by political contention, it transpired that the violence built on preexisting social tensions. This was a period during which the State of the Outlaws imposed "protection taxes" on dozens of luxury shops, but virtually all were in New Tripoli. And some of them, despite paying their due, were still ransacked and bombed. In a show of the degree of sociopolitical anger which animated the perpetrators, one luxury shop that belonged to a scion of one of the area's historical and prestigious families was bombed as many as three times in a matter of weeks.[59] Also, acts of urban unrest often assumed an implicit social and political coloration. In one telling instance which occurred on New Year's Eve, the State of the Outlaws raided New Tripoli's restaurants to force owners to pay a tax on the benefits they were realizing. And, instead of immediately withdrawing back to the Old City, members celebrated in their own way by "having fun"[60] bothering local residents and throwing dynamite sticks

---

[58] "Al-qissa al-kamila la Dawlat al-Matlubin fi Trablus sanat 1974, (1)–(11)" ["The full story of the State of the Outlaws in Tripoli in the year 1974 (1)–(11)"], *al-Tamaddon* (February 26, 2018) and (March 4, 2018).
[59] "Plastiquage d'un magasin à Tripoli," *L'Orient Le Jour* (December 19, 1974).
[60] "Tripoli: les Hors La Loi se déchainent pour les fêtes," *L'Orient Le Jour* (December 28, 1974).

Criminal Violence as Contentious Politics 259

throughout New Tripoli all night long. Even the rapes committed by the gang seemed to build on that social cleavage. In a shocking case, the State of the Outlaws kidnapped two women in their twenties "from a family of the Tripolitan bourgeoisie" and took them to the Old City where they were reportedly imprisoned for weeks and abused by local young men "for their own pleasure."[61] Murders became rife too but, here again, the criminal group's kill list, which included historical Tripolitan families in New Tripoli, police officers and even the leader of a trade union, seemed more to speak to the grievances of the subalterns than to be profit-driven.[62] Observers noted that forty-five people were murdered in this way by the group, which tripled Tripoli's murder rate from 1973 and made of 1974 the city's most violent year in sixteen years.[63]

The result of all of this seemingly "criminal" violence was thus inherently social and political for it gave way to the effective overturn of local power structures for a full nine months. Thanks to their participation in the State of the Outlaws, the Old City's subalterns, once marginalized in every way, now dominated the upper middle class and the notables in New Tripoli – not formally or institutionally, of course, but through the sheer force of weapons. Two Tripolitan sociologists argued that the criminal group had empowered the subalterns, allowing them to carry out attacks that may have appeared criminal but were driven by a sense of political and social "revenge"[64] against an elite guilty of both "neglecting" their condition and, even more importantly, of "denying their very existence as citizens of Tripoli." Tellingly, one of the State of the Outlaws' slogans back then was "destroying the city for one Lebanese Pound" – the price of a dynamite stick. This epitomized the extent to which "sowing fear, terror and chaos"[65] in New Tripoli, where power was located, was a key goal.

Through the dread of raids, bombings and murders the Old City's subalterns who made up the State of the Outlaws became Tripoli's new masters. One Tripolitan man, anonymous but well educated and pre-

---

[61] "Le nettoyage du Vieux Tripoli," *L'Orient Le Jour* (January 9, 1975).
[62] "Al-qissa al-kamila la Dawlat al-Matlubin fi Trablus sanat 1974, (1)–(11)" ["The full story of the State of the Outlaws in Tripoli in the year 1974 (1)–(11)"], *al-Tamaddon* (February 26, 2018) and (March 4, 2018).
[63] "Al-qissa al-kamila la Dawlat al-Matlubin fi Trablus sanat 1974, (9)" ["The full story of the State of the Outlaws in Tripoli in the year 1974 (9)"], *al-Tamaddon* (March 4, 2018).
[64] Maha Kayal and 'Atef 'Atiya, *Tahawulat al-zaman al-akhir* [*Transformations of the recent past*] (Beirut: Dar al-Mokhtarat, 2001), pp. 186–7.
[65] "Tripoli: l'insécurité provoque un début d'exode," *L'Orient Le Jour* (January 3, 1975).

260   Social Jihad

sumed to be an upper-class resident of New Tripoli, talked about this period as one during which he and his neighbors were "hurt" in their "pride and ego."[66] They felt like "strangers" in their "own city," limiting their moves during the day and locking themselves up in the evenings, "only to hear blasts and gunshots all night long." The police presence gradually dwindled in the northern city, many officers fearing assassination. New Tripoli's families stopped sending their children to schools, luxury shops closed down for months and the media even reported an "exodus"[67] of the upper class from Tripoli. By early January 1975 the extent to which the State of the Outlaws had overturned local power structures was such that one newspaper called the whole of Tripoli, and no longer just the Old City, the "kingdom"[68] of the criminals and subalterns, who are "reigning over the city and impose their law, the law of the strongest," in which people are killed "for a yes or a no." It had by now become obvious to all that the State of the Outlaws, far from simply a group of criminals, had in fact enabled a wider "social revolt"[69] in the city. One journalist called this period a "quasi-civil war"[70] because, instead of just pitting criminals against the security forces, it opposed Tripolitans from competing social worlds who scrambled for domination.

Eventually the State of the Outlaws collapsed. There were several reasons for this. One was that, behind the grand façade of the alternative "state" it proposed to create, the criminal movement became plagued with bitter internecine divisions and rivalries for power. As the clout of the Outlaws grew over Tripoli, a struggle for the leadership of the movement began opposing Ahmed Qaddur to one of his ambitious young deputies, Faysal al-Atrash. Violent skirmishes erupted between rival factions, killing three in two separate incidents.[71] Moreover, with time the most profit-driven members within the State of the Outlaws began engaging in practices which shocked some of the Old City's

---

[66] "Dans la République des Hors La Loi avant le grand nettoyage," *L'Orient Le Jour* (January 13, 1975).
[67] "Tripoli: l'insécurité provoque un début d'exode," *L'Orient Le Jour* (January 3, 1975).
[68] "Nouvelles révélations du Hors La Loi tripolitain," *L'Orient Le Jour* (January 27, 1975).
[69] "Al-qissa al-kamila la Dawlat al-Matlubin fi Trablus sanat 1974, (8)" ["The full story of the State of the Outlaws in Tripoli in the year 1974 (8)"], *al-Tamaddon* (March 4, 2018).
[70] "9 heures d'enfer hier à Tripoli: assiégés dans Vieille Ville, les Hors La Loi tiennent tête aux FSI," *L'Orient Le Jour* (November 8, 1974).
[71] "Tripoli: l'enquête sur le meurtre des deux qabaday impossible," *L'Orient Le Jour* (December 20, 1974) and "Al-qissa al-kamila la Dawlat al-Matlubin fi Trablus sanat 1974, (7)" ["The full story of the State of the Outlaws in Tripoli in the year 1974 (7)"], *al-Tamaddon* (March 4, 2018).

socially conservative residents. In one instance allegations even surfaced that elements within the movement were using the area's ancient mosques as brothels.[72] This might have led some, although not all, local residents to reconsider whether they truly shared values with the State of the Outlaws. Eventually the Lebanese government, which had for months been calling the criminal group the country's "No.1 Public Enemy," decided to launch an unprecedented offensive. In a reflection of the movement's sheer military might, the government dispatched as many as forty army tanks and 1,000 soldiers and policemen to Tripoli in a bid to encircle the Old City.[73] Even then, however, the ties between the State of the Outlaws and local residents were still so strong that, for all of the shelling that took place, the movement resisted two full days.

Even after the security forces penetrated the area, killing and arresting many, the leadership of the State of the Outlaws could still count on such powerful bonds with the local residents that six criminals, including the "president," Ahmed Qaddur, disappeared for days. The locals, who knew the Old City like their pocket, had taken the movement's leadership through the maze of narrow alleyways and smuggled them in the underground tunnels which, since medieval times, had connected Tripoli's historical neighborhoods with one another.[74] These tight bonds with locals is what allowed Ahmed Qaddur to escape the Old City, before he was eventually arrested two weeks later as he was about to board a boat to flee Tripoli. In the meantime the State of the Outlaws had collapsed and 300 locals were arrested. Nearly all of them young residents of the Old City who originally hailed from the countryside, were part of the informal proletariat as day traders, coffee sellers or construction workers, and sometimes had a background with revolutionary leftist movements such as the 24 October Movement. This confirmed the State of the Outlaws' subaltern base in the Old City.[75] It had been a murderous gang, undoubtedly; yet it had also addressed the grievances of the subalterns, allowing them to engage in contention and to overturn local power structures. Criminals, then, despite seeming profit-driven, can also be key actors of contentious politics.

---

[72] "Tripoli: Qaddour avoue une dizaine de crimes crapuleux," *L'Orient Le Jour* (January 18, 1975).

[73] "Tripoli: l'armée donne l'assaut à la République des Hors La Loi," *L'Orient Le Jour* (January 5, 1975).

[74] "La fuite de Qaddour," *L'Orient Le Jour* (January 14, 1975).

[75] "Al-qissa al-kamila la Dawlat al-Matlubin fi Trablus sanat 1974, (1)–(11)" ["The full story of the State of the Outlaws in Tripoli in the year 1974 (1)–(11)"], *al-Tamaddon* (February 26, 2018) and (March 4, 2018).

262   Social Jihad

Subaltern Islamism

The rest of this chapter explains how it was precisely these subaltern sectors of society who joined Tawhid en masse after it was created in 1982, providing the movement the manpower it needed to impose itself on Tripoli but also dragging it into the city's older social conflict.

Tawhid's sudden and overwhelming popularity with the subordinate parts of society epitomized what I call "subaltern Islamism." This term hints at the argument made in the rest of the chapter according to which the urban poor, who overall had fluid ideological allegiances as the shift of some of them from revolutionary leftist to criminal groups showed, did not join Tawhid because they were sincerely attracted by its ideology but, rather, because they saw in militant Islamism a "protest ideology" to carry on their locally oriented social and political revolt and to justify their continued involvement in subaltern practices such as petty crime, urban unrest and protest masculinity. Tawhid's behavior may have been in some cases driven by Islamist ideology, then, but the subalterns viewed it even more than the State of the Outlaws before as a "spatially oriented movement" articulating their local grievances and striving to overturn Tripoli's social order. In turn, their adherence to Tawhid initially boosted the movement's numerical strength, which proved key to its attempt to impose its ideology onto the city and to wage the battles tackled in Chapters 6, 7 and 8. But with time this widened its "spectrum of ideological commitment" to the extent that stark instances of variation in its behavior began occurring and severe inconsistencies with its ideology would emerge. Behind the sense that Tawhid ruled Tripoli as an "Islamic Emirate" therefore also lay a "social jihad" which was more driven by preexisting local social antagonisms than by ideology.

By pointing to the remarkably strong social and spatial base of Tawhid with Tripoli's urban poor, the notion of "subaltern Islamism" sheds new light on the long-debated relationship between poverty, social conflict and engagement in militant Islamist movements. Over the past two decades scholars of political violence such as Alan Krueger or Marc Sageman have repeatedly asserted that militant Islamism is not the movement of the "underprivileged and impoverished," but rather of the "middle" and "upper middle class."[76] Their quantitative analyses

---

[76] See Alan B. Krueger, *What makes a terrorist: economics and the roots of terrorism* (Princeton: Princeton University Press, 2007) pp. 33–5 and 44–6; Alan B. Kruger and Jitka Malečková, "Education, poverty and terrorism: is there a causal connection?" *Journal of Economic Perspectives* (Vol. 17, No. 4, 2003), pp. 119–44 and Marc Sageman, *Leaderless Jihad: terror networks in the 21st century* (Philadelphia: University of Pennsylvania Press,

Subaltern Islamism 263

constituted good first steps in the direction of stimulating a debate on the crucial questions of whether there is a nexus between "Islamist violence" and poverty and of what motivates people to join militant Islamist movements. But their data were biased. To begin with, they created databases of the social backgrounds of transnational terrorists by relying on media reporting, even though this disproportionately focused on the leadership rather than the rank and file and additionally failed to account for more localized Islamist militancy. Even more problematic was their use of country-level correlates of poverty because, since it was not disaggregated, the data often hid stark variations between areas within countries.

Nonetheless, their argument was echoed by some scholars of Islamism, chief among them Asef Bayat, who concurred that militant Islamism is a "movement of the educated middle class." If, accordingly, Islamist groups do not attract the poorer sectors of society, it is primarily because they are allegedly obsessed with questions of religion and ideology and therefore they have "never articulated an alternative urban order around which to mobilize community members." This famously led him to conclude that "the identity of Islamism does not derive from its particular concern for the urban disenfranchised."[77] However, although Bayat may be right when it comes to institutionalized Islamist groups such as the Muslim Brotherhood, which are typically made up of the middle and upper middle classes, evidence advanced by scholars who have undertaken in-depth research in severely impoverished contexts such as the suburbs of Cairo, Algiers or Tunis suggests that militant Islamists in some cases do attract the poor.[78]

2008), pp. 48–50. They are seconded by several scholars of terrorism. See, among others, James A. Piazza, "Rooted in poverty? Terrorism, poor economic development and social cleavages" *Terrorism and Political Violence* (Vol. 18, No. 1, 2006), pp. 159–77 and Graeme Blair et al., "Poverty and support for militant politics: evidence from Pakistan" *American Journal of Political Science* (Vol. 57, No. 1, 2013), pp. 30–48.

[77] See Asef Bayat, *Life as politics: how ordinary people change the Middle East* (Stanford: Stanford University Press, 2013), p. 44, p. 71; Asef Bayat, "From 'dangerous classes' to 'quiet rebels': politics of the urban subaltern in the Global South" *International Sociology* (Vol. 15, No. 3, 2000), pp. 533–57 and Asef Bayat, "Radical religion and the habitus of the dispossessed: does Islamic militancy have an urban ecology?" *International Journal of Urban and Regional Research* (Vol. 31, No. 3, 2007), pp. 579–90.

[78] See, among others: Salwa Ismail, "The popular movement dimensions of contemporary militant Islamism: socio-spatial determinants in the Cairo urban setting" *Comparative Studies in Society and History* (Vol. 42, No. 2, 2000), pp. 363–93; Patrick Haenni, *L'ordre des caïds: conjurer la dissidence urbaine au Caire* (Paris: Karthala, 2005); Luis Martinez, *La guerre civile en Algérie* (Paris: Karthala, 1999); Meriem Verges, "Genesis of a mobilization: the young activists of Algeria's Islamic Salvation Front," chapter 25 in Joel Beinin and Joe Stork, *Political Islam* (London: I.B.Tauris, 1997) pp. 292–309; Fabio Merone and Francesco Cavatorta, "Salafist movement and sheikh-ism in the Tunisian democratic transition" *Middle East Law and Governance* (Vol. 5, No. 3, 2013),

264   Social Jihad

The qualitative and quantitative evidence I derive from Tawhid's case suggests that militant Islamism may attract the subaltern sectors of society; not because of the intrinsic appeal of its deeper values and beliefs but because of its ability to act a "protest ideology" against the existing local order and the opportunity the subalterns may see to instrumentalize the Islamist injunction to govern morals as a conduit for their own social and political revolt.

I draw the qualitative evidence from interviews, access to archives and secondary material. The overwhelming majority of the dozens of current and former Tawhid rank and file whom I interviewed, even including some leaders, were themselves often subalterns. They or their family originally hailed from the Tripolitan countryside, most lived in the city's impoverished neighborhoods like Bab al-Tebbaneh, the Old City, Qobbe or Mina's slums and before joining Tawhid they were either unemployed or part of the informal proletariat. This was not the case with all, since a minority was also of middle-class background and lived in the residential district of Abu Samra, but it was still a clear trend. Naturally, it is difficult to know whether the sample of interviewed current and former members was exactly representative of the movement's social and spatial base in the 1980s. Yet additional qualitative and quantitative evidence suggest that this was probably the case. Archives of Lebanese newspapers noted Tawhid's social and spatial salience among Tripoli's subalterns living in impoverished districts.[79] For its part, the CIA, which authored two detailed reports on the movement, noted in the first one that its social base lay with the "rural Muslims" and "unemployed workers"[80] who had moved to Tripoli to find jobs and observed in the second one that a key factor behind Tawhid's growth had been "increased unemployment and underemployment" which had fueled conflicts over resources and status. The latter cable was considerably detailed in its description of how the movement was made up to a significant extent of members of the "lower-class Muslim community" in Tripoli. It even highlighted the instrumental nature of their adhesion to militant Islamism, asserting that "the success of Islamic fundamentalism in Tripoli is rooted in the Tawhid leadership's ability to translate economic and social grievances into political causes," and going as far as concluding that the movement had

pp. 308–30; and Olfa Lamloum and Mohammed Ali Ben Zina (eds.), *Les jeunes de Douar Hicher et d'Ettadhamen: une enquête sociologique* (Paris: Arabesque, 2015).

[79] For instance, Lebanese daily *L'Orient Le Jour* notes that Tawhid members and leaders hail from Tripoli's "slums." See: "A Tripoli, le sheikh Shaaban dispense la justice par téléphone," *L'Orient Le Jour* (October 20, 1983).

[80] US Central Intelligence Agency, "Shaykh Shaban: Lebanon's radical Sunni cleric" (Top Secret, NESAR 85-003CX, January 18, 1985).

been used as a "vehicle for military and social mobilization."[81] Secondary material concurred, for example doctoral dissertations and books by observers of Tripoli.[82]

I also bring quantitative evidence confirming Tawhid's strength with the subalterns. Because the archives of the movement which I accessed did not contain a specific list of all its members in 1982–5, it was difficult to gather precise data about its social base as such. Yet through interviews with dozens of Tawhid members, former members and residents of Tripoli, I reconstructed where in the city the movement primarily recruited and mobilized. For instance, data collected on the location of its mosques in 1982–5 suggest that Tawhid was particularly strong, in order of importance, in Bab al-Tebbaneh (for specific reasons seen in Chapter 2), where it controlled all local mosques; in Qobbe, the Old City and Mina, where it controlled nearly two-thirds of the mosques; and in Abu Samra, where it controlled half; the rest of the mosques were affiliated with independent clerics, notables or rival Islamist groups. By comparison, the movement had control over none of New Tripoli's nine mosques. Thus, when matching the spatial salience of Tawhid in Tripoli with indicators of poverty disaggregated at the neighborhood level, it transpires that the movement was twice as strong in subaltern districts than in middle-class districts and was virtually absent in wealthy areas (Table 5.1). This indicates the importance of obtaining data fully disaggregated at the neighborhood level. The location of Tawhid's indoctrination camps per district also confirmed this analysis (see Figure 5.2).

Tawhid's "Social Jihad"

The key to explaining Tawhid's success in recruiting so many subalterns, in addition to its already existing backbone of Islamist militants, lies in its ability to act as a "spatially oriented movement." By this I mean those movements which are not just based in but also directed toward space, engaging explicitly with local grievances and/or identities and striving to achieve a measure of local social and political change – "the local" is what

---

[81] US Central Intelligence Agency, "Lebanon: Islamic fundamentalism in Tripoli" (Top Secret, NESAR 86-003JX, January 17, 1986).

[82] Mohammed Abi Samra notes the overwhelmingly subaltern background of one Tawhid faction in particular, Hashem Minqara's group in the port neighborhood of Mina, who were "early school dropouts, either illiterate or semi-illiterate" and before the economic crisis of the 1970s had been employed in unskilled, physical work. They lived a "rugged and mischievous lifestyle" and "spent most of their time in the streets" of Mina's slums. See Abi Samra, *Trablus*, pp. 170–1. See also: Joumana al-Soufi Richard, *Lutte populaire armée: de la désobéissance civile au combat pour Dieu* (Paris: Sorbonne University, unpublished PhD thesis, 1984).

266   Social Jihad

Table 5.1 *Social and spatial variation of Islamist mobilization in Tripoli*

Neighborhoods of Tripoli	Local poverty rate (%)	Number of local mosques	Tawhid-controlled mosques	Tawhid indoctrination camps
Bab al-Tebbaneh	90	4	4	1
Old City	75	14	8	0
Qobbe	69	5	3	1
Mina	66	5	3	2
Abu Samra	40	6	3	1
New Tripoli	10	9	0	0

Source: I draw local poverty rates disaggregated at the neighborhood level from figures gathered by John Gulick (1967) and Adib N'ame (2014). Information related to the location of Tawhid mosques and indoctrination camps comes from my interviews with officials.

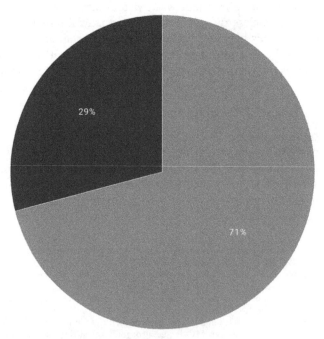

Figure 5.2 Subaltern Islamism, or how Tawhid courted Tripoli's poor

Tawhid's "Social Jihad" 267

they are primarily about. The concept of a "spatially oriented movement" builds on Manuel Castells' older notion of "urban social movements,"[83] which designated movements engaged in mobilizations tackling local issues of collective consumption, struggles for urban meaning and a desire for local autonomy, but without falling into his fairly restrictive definition and while steering clear of the debates about the specificity of the "urban" which it gave rise to. Tawhid, then, was an Islamist group, yet it simultaneously acted as a "spatially oriented movement." It not only provided the poor with a conduit for their socio-political revolt but also addressed their concerns, engaging with their local grievances, channeling their criticism of Tripoli's power structures and erecting them as masters of the new social order. But, while this provided it with a massive pool of subaltern members and sympathizers, it also drew Tawhid into Tripoli's older social antagonism to the extent that its behavior at times turned into a "social jihad" driven by preexisting local tensions more than by ideology.

In order to show the impact of the older social and political revolt of Tripoli's subalterns on Tawhid's behavior, the social context preceding its rise must be introduced. Tripoli, in the years immediately preceding Tawhid's advent, witnessed the exacerbation of the socio-spatial antagonism pitting the subalterns in the Old City and its extensions against the upper middle class in New Tripoli. The period of 1980–2, in fact, was reminiscent of 1974–5 when the subalterns had rebelled, except that their actions were now disjointed. No social movement seemed able to reiterate the experience of the State of the Outlaws, which had channeled subaltern grievances in a partially criminal, partially political project. In addition, while in the mid-1970s the Lebanese police and army had contained the Outlaws and eventually dealt them a fatal blow, by the early 1980s the security services effectively no longer functioned – they still existed but, in the context of the worsening of the civil war, they were plagued by splits and had little authority, remaining confined to their barracks. As a result of these factors, the socio-spatial antagonism between the Old City and its extensions and New Tripoli took the form of what observers called "anarchy":[84] unorganized groups of subalterns spontaneously engaged in acts of locally oriented social and political violence.

Much like in 1974–5, 1980–2 was thus marked by a wave of violent incidents which targeted the spaces associated with the relaxed lifestyle of

[83] Manuel Castells, *The city and the grassroots: a cross-cultural theory of urban social movements* (Berkeley: University of California Press, 1983).
[84] "Un hold-up audacieux à Tripoli," *L'Orient Le Jour* (February 26, 1981).

268   Social Jihad

New Tripoli's upper class. These two years witnessed the looting of luxury shops, dynamite sticks thrown onto brand-new cars, the explosion of a restaurant, raids on a nightclub and bomb attacks on cinemas.[85] New Tripoli's cafes which attracted a notoriously affluent clientele, like *Le Negresco*, frequented by the city's businessmen and notables, were bombed with much bloodshed.[86] The racketeering of wealthy shopkeepers and historical Tripolitan families reached new heights.[87]

By comparison the social tensions palpable in 1980–2 were in some ways more severe than in 1974–5 because, by then, the sense by the subalterns that they were being economically and socially exploited at the hands of the city's elite was even more acute. This was because scandals surfaced which shocked local society and the subalterns in particular. The city's businessmen were accused of speculating on the price of basic commodities such as wheat and flour, sometimes artificially bolstering their price. The local elite that made up the executive board of the Qadisha, Tripoli's private electricity company, was suspected of engaging in "corrupt" practices.[88] And, even more outrageously, allegations spread that some of the city's doctors and pharmacists were involved in a large scheme to sell expired medication to the poor.[89] These were not just accusations thrown in the air. Even the former head of Tripoli's Chamber of Commerce acknowledged, in retrospect, the existence of cases in which the elite "took advantage"[90] of the deterioration of the situation to maximize its profits. Doctors and pharmacists thus became targets. A large explosion destroyed the Halabi pharmacy in the vicinity of New Tripoli and, shortly afterward, two doctors were murdered.[91] The notables and local governmental representatives were

---

[85] See, among others: "Tripoli: un pourrisement continu," *L'Orient Le Jour* (January 1, 1981); "Enfijar fi cinema al-Hamra" ["Explosion in al-Hamra cinema"], *Al-Incha* (November 6, 1981); and "Enfijar amam matjar fi sher'a Azmi" ["Explosion in front of a shop on Azmi Street," *Al-Incha* (March 21, 1982).

[86] "Enfijar amam maqha neghresku" ["Explosion in front of the Negresco cafe"], *Al-Incha* (April 8, 1980).

[87] "Attentat à l'explosif dans une rue commerçante de Tripoli," *L'Orient le Jour* (April 16, 1980).

[88] "Fadihat fased tat'alaq bi-bi'a al-dawa'" ["Corruption scandal regarding the sale of medication"], *Al-Incha* (March 21, 1980) and "La farine était avariée," *L'Orient Le Jour* (March 13, 1980).

[89] "Ejtime'a qadat Trablus hawl ertife'a as'ar al-tahin" ["Meeting of the leaders of Tripoli concerning the increase in the prices of flour"], *Al-Incha* (November 21, 1979).

[90] Interview with Hassan Monla (former head of Tripoli's Chamber of Commerce), Tripoli, August 2014.

[91] See, among others: "Enfijar amam saydaliyat Al-Halabi fi manteqat al-Zehriye" ["Explosion in front of the Halaby pharmacy in the area of Zehriye"], *Al-Incha* (December 7, 1979); "Atba' Trablus yahtajun 'ala maqtal zamilthum Sam'an Qatrib" ["The doctors of Tripoli protest against the killing of their colleague Sam'an Qatrib"],

Tawhid's "Social Jihad" 269

also not spared. One demonstration whose original goal had been to "protest against high prices" turned out to be massive. It morphed into a riot as soon as it approached Abdel Hamid Karame Square, which separated New Tripoli from the poorer ancient neighborhoods of the Old City. There, protesters threw projectiles at the nearby mansions of politicians and went as far as entering the seat of the governor of North Lebanon before ransacking his office and even taking him hostage.[92] They released him a few hours later but he continued receiving death threats for months.[93] By 1982, then, the antagonism between New Tripoli and the Old City and its extensions had exacerbated and, although the reaction of the subalterns was largely disjointed, their locally oriented social and political violence had reached an all-time high. In this context all they needed was an organized city-wide social movement which would engage in locally oriented contentious politics, empowering them and helping them to overthrow Tripoli's social order.

It can seem puzzling, in this context, that it was a militant Islamist group, more so than a trade union, a left-wing party or even the Lebanese Muslim Brotherhood, which capitalized on this antagonism and posed as the movement of the subalterns par excellence. But, irrespective of their declaratory ideology, as this and previous chapters showed these actors were all institutionalized and controlled by the Tripolitan upper middle class. Therefore, they appeared detached from the broader grievances of the subalterns, which included the traditional issues of poverty and unemployment but also concerns regarding cultural and territorial stigmatization, political marginalization and a sense of exclusion from the city. Even when they sporadically engaged with some of the grievances of the subalterns, then, they lacked the credibility to gain their full support – and in any case they rarely tried hard to do this.

By contrast, Tawhid was neither institutionalized, as was seen in Chapters 3 and 4, nor led by the city's upper middle class. Most of its leaders hailed from Tripoli's countryside, which spoke to subalterns feeling discriminated against because of their rural origins. Indeed, apart from Hashem Minqara, who was born in the impoverished Tripoli district of Bab al-Tebbaneh, no other leader in Tawhid's Consultative

---

Al-Incha (March 25, 1980); "Enfijar fi Sehat Abdel Hamid Karame" ["Explosion in Abdel Hamid Karame Square"], *Al-Incha* (March 27, 1980); "Enfijar amam markez tibi fi Trablus" ["Explosion in front of a medical centre in Tripoli"], *Al-Incha* (April 22, 1980); "Enfijar amam mustachfa al-Bissar" ["Explosion in front of the Bissar Hospital"], *Al-Incha* (May 27, 1980).

[92] "Calme précaire à Tripoli," *L'Orient Le Jour* (January 1, 1980).

[93] "Nouvelles menaces de mort contre le Mohafez du Liban Nord," *L'Orient Le Jour* (March 5, 1980).

270   Social Jihad

Council or leadership were indigenous locals – although it certainly did not imply that they did not "feel" Tripolitan. From its head, Sa'id Sha'aban, to the small group of leaders who met every few days to discuss the movement's matters and politics, like Esmat Murad, Fu'ad al-Kurdi, Kan'an Naji, Khalil Akkawi and Abu Imara, all originally hailed from the nearby countryside; with the exception of Khalil Akkawi, who was the son of a Palestinian refugee. And, interestingly, only Abu Imara came from a traditionally privileged family in the plain of Akkar with a history as feudal lords. But, even then, very few were aware of this fact as he had deliberately assumed a pseudonym in lieu of his real name, Ali Mer'abi. Moreover, apart from Esmat Murad and Sa'id Sha'aban, who studied medicine and religion at university, none of the half a dozen first-rank leaders had more than a high school education. And, while there was a small group of educated second-rank activists around them who acted as Tawhid's "ideological entrepreneurs" and hailed from the middle class, the majority of the movement's cadres were subalterns living in Tripoli's marginalized districts.[94] By contrast with other political actors in Tripoli, then, Tawhid resembled the profile of the subalterns.

As Tawhid's clout grew in 1982–3 it began needing manpower to impose itself onto Tripoli more forcefully, by implementing an "Islamic Emirate" and battling its enemies. To attract the numerically large constituency of subalterns it was ready to act as a "spatially oriented movement" which would articulate their local concerns, engage with the antagonism that pitted them against New Tripoli and provide a platform for their older social struggle. Although Tawhid comprised committed Islamists and its discourse was steeped in ideological rhetoric, the movement began referring to the local issues of the subalterns unrelated to Islamism. It started addressing "the weak and the oppressed," a reference to the subalterns, criticizing "those who have lust for power, wealth and prestige" and sternly warning that the "shame and humiliation" of "those who have been wronged" will not go on indefinitely. Serving "God's cause," it added, was not just about adhering to religious precepts in one's own life, it was also about leading a much wider "struggle against injustice and corruption."[95]

Yet, by acting as a "spatially oriented movement" Tawhid did more than blurrily articulate social tensions in an ideological rhetoric; instead it addressed explicitly the concrete and local concerns of Tripoli's subalterns and suggested an alternative social order. For instance, it tackled at length the issue of unemployment and the rise of the informal proletariat, and took

[94] I draw all of this information from interviews with Tawhid leaders, cadres and members, Tripoli, June 2014.
[95] Speech by a Tawhid cleric in a mosque in Tripoli (undated, video given to the author).

Tawhid's "Social Jihad"

clear sides in the city's simmering social conflict. It regretted the earlier shutdown of the industries, specifically naming the Ghandour wood factory, the Arida-Jisr textile factory and the Beddawi glass factory, and squarely blaming their closure and the rise of poverty on the "greediness" and relentless "pursuit of wealth"[96] of Tripoli's upper classes. Similarly, the movement addressed growing concerns among the subalterns about the deterioration of their health situation. For example, it engaged with the "state of the hospitals in Tripoli." It fiercely criticized its "managers" for "not trying to renovate the equipment and the laboratories" and it lambasted "wealthy Tripolitans" for seeking medical treatment in Beirut's hospitals and abroad while "the poor" had to use "the city's neglected hospitals." Crucially, Tawhid also formulated concrete solutions to resolve these issues – and the nature of these solutions confirmed its attempt to court the constituency of Tripoli's subalterns. Indeed, it suggested to invest in "productive projects," like handicraft workshops and manufacturing plants, in a bid to "absorb labour and help reduce unemployment in the city." And, in case money would be lacking, the movement explained that it would be prepared to "withdraw funds from the banks" and "collect taxes"[97] to invest in development. Tawhid, then, was Islamist, but also sporadically acted as a "spatially oriented movement" articulating the specific grievances of the subalterns and drawing the contours of a new Tripolitan order.

In addition to explicitly articulating their grievances, Tawhid provided Tripoli's subalterns with a conduit to carry on their locally oriented social and political violence and to continue their involvement in practices such as petty criminality and urban violence, which they had earlier channeled through engagement with revolutionary and criminal groups. For instance, by stating that it was prepared to redistribute the money sleeping in the city's banks, the movement was in the midst of theorizing the acceptability for its subaltern members of continuing to target symbols of an upper middle class perceived as exploitative, even giving it a veneer of religious legitimacy by reminding its audience that "Islam prohibits interest."[98] Similarly, it blessed the imposition of "protection taxes" – or, said plainly, racketeering – on luxury shops by arguing that it was part of the "*zakat*," the alms giving that is mandatory in Islam.[99] And any act of urban violence against New Tripoli, where many upper-class residents led a socially progressive lifestyle, would for its part be justified as part of the broader attempt on the part of the movement to punish, sometimes

---

[96] "Iqtisad Trablus ila ayn?" ["The Tripolitan economy, where to?"], *al-Tawhid* (June 20, 1984).
[97] Ibid.   [98] Interview with Amir Rʿad (former Tawhid cleric), Tripoli, September 2016.
[99] Interviews with residents of Tripoli, May–July 2014.

272   Social Jihad

harshly, any transgressions of Islamic law. The result was the emergence of a type of behavior that appeared Islamist at first glance, because it was legitimized in religious and ideological ways, but which at its core reflected the longstanding practices and struggles of the subalterns more than ideology. This "social jihad," as I call the effect of Tawhid's "subaltern Islamism" on the movement's involvement in violence, began by translating early on into a rise in acts of unrest targeting New Tripoli.

Much like the State of the Outlaws before, Tawhid provided a platform for the subalterns to carry on their revolt against the symbols of power in New Tripoli. To the outside, of course, the new subaltern members of Tawhid looked like any other "fundamentalists," instantly recognizable by their "bushy black beards and close-cropped hair," a Kalashnikov in hand and "passages of the Quran printed on their uniforms."[100] But, behind the appearance of ideological change, they continued engaging in their older social struggles. The targets of the Islamist movement's low-level violence in 1982–3, which corresponds to the solidification of its control over Tripoli, were indeed reminiscent of those in 1974–5 and 1980–2. The city's banks in New Tripoli, symbols of the social and spatial segregation between the chic neighborhood and the impoverished districts, were frequently attacked. The incidents reported in the media back then only constituted the tip of the iceberg, and within the space of months they already included the looting of the Arab-Lebanese Bank's branch as well as the raiding of the French-Lebanese Bank whose director was humiliated, kidnapped and later released in exchange for a ransom.[101] The manager of an important bank in Tripoli, who hailed from a historical and wealthy local family, remembered with still palpable anguish that the period 1982–3 was "negative" for his business and his employees. "Tawhid militants were engaged in pressure, intimidation and persuasion in different ways," he recalled. He evoked a previously undisclosed case in which Mohammed Sufi, a prominent Tripolitan businessman and the local head of the Arab Bank, Tripoli's wealthiest, was "smuggled away in a car boot." He added: "militants had asked him to pay one million Lebanese Pounds in exchange for his safety but he had refused so they kidnapped him." The board of the bank eventually paid the large ransom. He explained that, years later, Sa'id Sha'aban personally acknowledged Tawhid's responsibility for his kidnapping.[102]

---

[100] This draws on the observation of a foreign journalist in Tripoli. See: "Battered Tripoli girds itself for new wave of bloodletting," *Washington Post* (December 10, 1983).

[101] "Accrochage d'ampleur limitée à Tripoli," *L'Orient Le Jour* (April 9, 1983); "Pillage de la Banque Libano-Arabe à Tripoli," *L'Orient Le Jour* (November 24, 1983); "Attentat contre la banque Libano-Française à Tripoli," *L'Orient Le Jour* (January 7, 1985).

[102] Interview with the former director of the Tripolitan branch of a major bank, Tripoli, October 2014.

Concurrently, robberies against luxury shops in New Tripoli as well as sporadic raids on cafes, cinemas or passers-by in the chic neighborhood multiplied, both as a continuation of petty crime and as an expression of social anger.[103] A journalist reported that late 1982 and 1983 witnessed a sudden increase in attacks and shootings by masked Tawhid gunmen firing from speeding cars into restaurants, chic shops and crowded beaches in New Tripoli.[104] In parallel, the racketeering of richer residents became frequent. This trend was so marked, in fact, that even foreign observers reported on Tawhid's involvement in "eliciting financial and material backing from wealthy citizens of Tripoli in the form of protection money."[105] The head of the Chamber of Commerce recalled that a growing sense of fear among local businessmen prompted some to close down their shops and leave Tripoli indefinitely.[106]

Tawhid's "social jihad," in addition to providing a conduit for the subaltern practices of petty crime and urban violence, also targeted the symbols of local and national power structures. Again, in a way reminiscent of 1974–5 but also, more recently, of 1980–2, the seat of the governor of North Lebanon, located near Abdel Hamid Karame Square, was attacked. Interestingly, this incident soon became "one of the most famous acts committed by members of Tawhid"[107] as it had involved a group of Islamist youths who "entered the office of the Governor and made him fall on the ground by pulling the carpet from under his feet," thus reinforcing the sense that the movement was turning power structures on their head. Tawhid members also machine-gunned his office and repeatedly shot at a nearby national flag.[108] Symbols of local power structures were not spared either. In one telling case militants led a riot on the municipality, which was then headed by Ashir al-Daye, a figure close to Rashid Karame and the upper middle class in New Tripoli. They accused him of "indifference" toward the subalterns and Tripoli's impoverished districts at large and, in particular, of denying

---

[103] See, among others, "Enfijar fi Sher'a al-Monla" ["Explosion in Monla Street"], *Al-Incha* (March 18, 1983); "Incident isolé à Tripoli," *L'Orient Le Jour* (January 23, 1983); "Insécurité et anarchie persistante à Tripoli," *L'Orient Le Jour* (March 2, 1983); "Accrochages d'ampleur limitée à Tripoli," *L'Orient Le Jour* (April 9, 1983); "Deux vols à main armée à Tripoli," *L'Orient Le Jour* (June 1, 1985).

[104] "Battered Tripoli girds itself for new wave of bloodletting," *Washington Post* (December 10, 1983).

[105] US Central Intelligence Agency, "Lebanon: Islamic fundamentalism in Tripoli" (Top Secret, NESAR 86-003JX, January 17, 1986).

[106] Interview with Hassan Monla (former head of Tripoli's Chamber of Commerce), Tripoli, August 2014.

[107] Abi Samra, *Trablus*, p. 44.

[108] "Tirs sur le sérial de Tripoli," *L'Orient Le Jour* (May 21, 1983).

274 Social Jihad

them access to paved roads and quality water infrastructure. Dozens of Tawhid fighters thus went down to the municipality building, located in the vicinity of New Tripoli, encircled it, brandished their weapons and threatened the employees with harm if roads were not paved and water distributed throughout the deprived districts.[109] As municipal workers had still not responded to their demands days later, they entered the building and, according to a journalist present at the scene, "scared"[110] the staff. They were behind the theft, months later, of much of the municipality's equipment and cars.[111] Attracted by its readiness to act as a "spatially oriented movement" which would engage with their grievances and provide them with a platform to continue their social revolt, the subalterns joined Tawhid but simultaneously dragged it into struggles and practices unrelated to its ideology.

Tawhid's "subaltern Islamism," or the movement's involvement in a type of behavior which was closer to a "social jihad" than to "religious violence," was thus much more in continuity, rather than a break, with earlier forms of subaltern politics that had seen revolutionary and criminal groups become popular with subordinate sectors of society. Like these movements, Tawhid articulated, albeit in its own vocabulary, the grievances of Tripoli's urban marginalized and it gave them a platform to continue their social revolt.

Overcoming Spatial Barriers

Beyond enabling the continuation of their revolt and their involvement in practices such as urban violence and petty crime, what also attracted the subalterns to Tawhid more than to other contentious movements was the opportunity they saw in using the discourse and practice of Islamism as a tool to overcome the "spatial barriers" standing among them. By "spatial barriers" I mean the ways in which space can hinder broad-based collective action, either because of distance and the built environment or, as importantly, because of the socially and symbolically consequential local rivalries and the sometimes conflicting priorities, traditions and identities of spatially proximate spaces. These local rivalries and differences may be such that even those sharing similar grievances across space may see their

---

[109] "Des éléments armés encerclent le siège de la municipalité de Tripoli," *L'Orient Le Jour* (November 30, 1984).
[110] "Mejmu'a musalaha tahajam mabna baladiyet Trablus" ["An armed group attacks a building of the Municipality of Tripoli"], *Al-Incha* (December 3, 1984).
[111] "Bayan min baladiyet Trablus hawl sareqat mu'addat al-tanzif" ["Statement of the municipality of Tripoli on the theft of cleaning equipment"], *Al-Incha* (May 29, 1985).

Overcoming Spatial Barriers

attempt at building a broad-based collective action undermined by such "spatial barriers."

In Tripoli's case, the "spatial barriers" standing among the subaltern-inhabited districts had long limited the willingness and capacity of the urban poor to mobilize together. These neighborhoods may have shared social characteristics, as was stated earlier, but they did not form a geographically coherent unit. In fact, although objectively, on a map, they did not seem that far from each other, with a maximum of six kilometers standing between them, it could take an hour and a few successive shared taxi rides to commute from Mina's slums, situated at the western extremity of the port district, all the way to the eastern hill of Qobbe. In other words, it took time and resources to mobilize across Tripoli's pockets of poverty.

Moreover, social and political life in these neighborhoods was largely self-enclosed and collective action was organized locally, each district counting on its own *qabaday* or spatially grounded, but also bounded, "champions of mobilization" to spearhead activism. Chapter 2 for instance tackled how, through the Akkawi brothers, who were the "champions" of Bab al-Tebbaneh, movements such as the Organization of Anger and the Popular Resistance mobilized en masse there, but then also remained confined to this district. Similarly, while the 24 October Movement was popular with many subalterns throughout Tripoli, the support it drew from *qabadayet* in the vicinity of the Old City, in particular in the historical neighborhood of Zehriye, meant that the bulk of its members hailed from there.[112] This was also the case with the State of the Outlaws, which chiefly acted as the movement of the Old City's subalterns as it mobilized *qabadayet* but also local grievances and narratives. The local prevalence of these movements in certain neighborhoods in particular resulted in the fragmentation of subaltern politics for, despite sharing similar concerns, Tripoli's subalterns continued mobilizing in relative social and political isolation from each other, indeed at times in competition against each other as local rivalries and turf wars resurfaced. None of these movements, then, had been able to mobilize Tripoli's subalterns across space.

In this respect, the discourse and practice of militant Islamism offered new promises. Tawhid's "vernacular" ideology, a mix of militant Islamist doctrine and Tripolitan habitus, actively advocated socialization across neighborhood lines. For instance, one leader, in a speech delivered in one of the deprived districts, lambasted the "narrow factionalism" typical

---

[112] Kayal and 'Atiya, *Tahawulat al-zaman al-akhir*, pp. 185–6.

276   Social Jihad

of local subaltern politics which had long pitted "this neighborhood against that quarter." Instead, he advocated "renouncing local interests" and "ordering the ranks" around the "banner of Islamic unity," a reference to Tawhid's name, "to be victorious."[113] Tawhid's emphasis on the idea of a double belonging to the Islamic community and to Tripoli provided a shared ideological language through which the subalterns could mobilize across space.

But, beyond discourse, it was especially the practice of Islamist mobilization which encouraged Tripoli's subalterns who hailed from different neighborhoods to join hands. Tawhid's Friday prayers, led by Sa'id Sha'aban at the Tawbe mosque, would provide the occasion for the socialization and mobilization of Tripoli's subalterns across space. This was a historical and prestigious mosque built 800 years ago. But what truly mattered for the subalterns was its location right at the center of Tripoli, between Mina and Qobbe, on the Old City's edge and by a main artery. In other words, it acted as a convenient gathering point. Going there once a week, especially on a Friday, the day off, and in the morning, when work was quiet, provided a low-cost way to connect across their disparate neighborhoods. This was not just about getting to know each other and socializing, it was also about creating bonds of solidarity outside of the traditional limits of the neighborhood through sharing the emotionally powerful experience typical of Sa'id Sha'aban's sermons, seen in Chapter 3. Crucially, Friday prayers were often concluded with a massive march that followed the network of mosques controlled by Tawhid in the deprived districts and ended as a protest in the city's central square. This enabled the mobilization of the subalterns across space.

Therefore the "spatial routines"[114] associated with Tawhid's Friday prayers, as contentious politics scholar William Sewell described the social actions that regularly bring many activists together in special places and at particular times, encouraged the socialization, identification and mobilization of those whose actions had until then been largely disjointed. Of course, this did not mean that the socially and symbolically consequential "spatial barriers" were fully overcome, as the resilience of "neighborhood Islamism" in Tawhid will show. But the "spatial routines" of Tawhid's Friday sermons and post-prayer march brought the

---

[113] Sermon by a Tawhid cleric delivered in a mosque of Tripoli (undated, video given to the author).

[114] William H. Sewell Jr., "Space in contentious politics," chapter 3 in Ronald Aminzade et al. (eds.) *Silence and voice in the study of contentious politics* (Cambridge: Cambridge University Press, 2001), pp. 62–4.

Becoming Emirs

city's subalterns together in a way that no other social movement had previously done. Islamism thus provided the urban poor with their first opportunity to mobilize across space.

Becoming Emirs

Another factor which explained Tawhid's prevalence in Tripoli's impoverished neighborhoods was its promise to empower its subaltern members to an unprecedented extent. They would climb its ladders and hoped, one day, to become "Emirs."

Tawhid's membership policy, in fact, seemed tailored to Tripoli's subalterns. Unlike mainstream leftist parties or even the Lebanese Muslim Brotherhood which, as we saw in Chapter 3, required would-be members to go through a lengthy indoctrination and loyalty-testing process, something that by and large did not fit with the lack of education and the short-termism of the subalterns, Tawhid had relatively flexible membership procedures. Naturally, candidates to join the movement had to show a degree of interest in its ideology by regularly attending a Tawhid mosque and going to a Friday sermon. Those who wanted to make a good impression and were not previously familiar with Islamism could also attend one of the indoctrination camps ran by Tawhid's "ideological entrepreneurs," tackled in Chapter 6. These camps were located in Tripoli's impoverished districts of Qobbe, Bab al-Tebbaneh, Beddawi and the slums of Mina, with three additional ones situated in the nearby rural provinces of Akkar, Miniye and Dinniye.[115] This suggested that Tawhid's "ideological entrepreneurs" would try reinforcing the Islamist convictions of the new subaltern adherents.

But, on the whole, Tawhid was not characterized by any lengthy and demanding vetting process. One could join without having read the key texts of militant Islamism by Sayyid Qutb and Sa'id Hawwa, indeed one could join without knowing how to read at all. All one had to do, then, was to promise to abolish previous loyalties and swear to work together to defeat Israel and the Syrian regime and bring about an Islamic revolution. Even Sa'id Sha'aban personally reminded his crowds that the Prophet thought that reciting the *shahada*, or the Muslim declaration of faith, was a "sufficient way to show conviction."[116] Many subalterns thus viewed joining Tawhid as a low-cost move that seemed worth a try.

---

[115] Interview with Ibrahim Saleh (Tawhid official and right-hand man of Sa 'id Sha'aban), Tripoli, July 2014.

[116] Al-Soufi Richard, *Lutte populaire armée*, p. 254.

278 Social Jihad

This was especially the case as the movement promised high returns to those who showed commitment to its cause, implemented its ideology and fought on its behalf. These loyal members would be rewarded by getting promoted and may one day become an "Emir." "Becoming Emir" was thus heard repeatedly in conversations with subaltern militants and former members as an answer to why they or their comrades had become loyal to Tawhid. Literally, "Emir" means "Prince" and is a religiously and historically loaded word, for it refers to one of the titles of the Prophet and to generations of rulers in the Islamic world. But to many subalterns it essentially boiled down to notions of authority and respect; earning the title of Emir thus became associated with a transformation of their social status. This was especially the case as, within Tawhid, being an Emir was linked to the right to exercise authority on the movement's behalf in the "Islamic Emirate" of Tripoli, which often boiled down to wielding military control over some streets or a neighborhood.

Tawhid, indeed, was led by its general Emir or head, Sa'id Sha'aban, who decided on the issues of utmost importance, but he was seconded by a Consultative Council which also took part in the decisions, had a right of veto and helped to manage the movement. This Council was made up of the six other founding figures who were called Emirs and had split Tripoli among themselves in zones of influence where they ruled as they pleased. Officially these Emirs were supposed to "implement Islamic law"[117] in the neighborhoods where they exercised power. But in reality they often wielded much wider prerogatives for their installation of checkpoints, control over hundreds of fighters and the provision of security as well as limited social services gave them local status as well as authority. And, while in official Tawhid rhetoric only the movement's seven key leaders, with Sa'id Sha'aban at their helm, were referred to as Emirs, on the ground lesser commanders and street leaders also began referring to themselves that way – and requesting their subordinates to do so too.[118] Tripoli during that time therefore witnessed the rise of dozens of "big" and "small" Emirs. This phenomenon rapidly empowered members in all echelons of the movement and it additionally proved appealing to the subalterns as it seemed to resonate with a tradition of local strongmen in subaltern politics who traditionally provided security and low-level services.

---

[117] Interview with former Tawhid Emirs Kan'an Naji and Hashem Minqara, Tripoli, July–August 2014.
[118] Interview with former and current Tawhid members, Tripoli, May–June 2014.

Becoming Emirs

The full extent to which Tawhid's flexible membership policy and the promise of empowerment through the spread of Emirs appealed to the subalterns was reflected by the movement's integration of militants who had been members of criminal and leftist groups. This may not have been a widespread phenomenon. The leader of a revolutionary Marxist movement remembered that "only a dozen"[119] of his members defected to join Tawhid back then. Still, the very occurrence of rapid switches from criminal and leftist groups to the emerging Islamist movement showed how the ideological commitment of the subalterns was fluid. "You could pledge allegiance to Sa'id Sha'aban, get a gun, join as a fighter and even one day hope to become an Emir,"[120] explained a Tawhid militant, who acknowledged that this unavoidably meant that many of those who joined were less or not ideologically committed. The leader of another leftist militia thus also recounted having witnessed some of his "comrades" becoming attracted by the growing presence of the Islamist movement. They grew a beard and joined Tawhid, he recalled, only to shave and escape after battles flared up with the Syrian army in 1985. "They were attracted by power and money – not by ideology,"[121] he said. Becoming an "Islamist," then, was sometimes about plain opportunism.

Hashem Minqara's meteoric rise from anonymity to Emir of Mina embodied the promises of "subaltern Islamism" and acted as a magnet for the poor seeking empowerment. This typical subaltern was born in the impoverished district of Bab al-Tebbaneh to a lower-class family which in 1971 moved to the port area of Mina, where he grew up. As a teenager he attended a technical high school in the deprived neighborhood of Qobbe. One of his former teachers described him as an "introverted" student who got "poor grades."[122] He then obtained a job as a low-paid worker in a maintenance company that fixed elevators for the high-rise apartment buildings in New Tripoli and on Mina's upper-class boulevards.[123] Hashem Minqara, in other words, was long a typical subaltern who worked for the elite. Through the religious education he received from his father as a passionate Sufi, however, he joined the militant Islamist faction, Soldiers of God, and became close to its military leader, Kana'an Naji. Upon Soldiers of God's merger in Tawhid in

---

[119] Interview with Jamil Safiye (official in Tripoli's branch of the Communist Party), Tripoli, June 2014.

[120] Interview with Ibrahim Antar (former Tawhid member close to Abu Imara), Tripoli, August 2014.

[121] Interview with a former leftist militia commander, Tripoli, July 2014.

[122] Interview with Rashid Jemali (former engineer and teacher at Qobbe's high school), Tripoli, July 2014.

[123] Abi Samra, *Trablus*, p. 145.

280   Social Jihad

1982, Hashem Minqara showed such commitment to the new movement's cause that he rapidly climbed through its ranks, and later Sha'aban asked him to join the leadership and to become the Emir of Mina.[124]

Hashem Minqara's rise acted as a magnet for Mina's subalterns who lived in the slums of the port district. He embodied perfectly the degree to which joining the Islamist movement could empower them and participate to the advent of an alternative urban order. As Emir of Mina, his status, authority and even personal wealth greatly expanded. Chapter 6 tackles in detail the dynamics of how behind his engagement in seemingly "religious violence" in Mina lay, among other factors, a "social jihad," and the ways in which he made a fortune by controlling the port and allying with gangsters. But at this point, suffice it to say that his authority soon came to supersede that of the mayor of the area. Mina, indeed, had its own municipality distinct from Tripoli's because, in the past, it had long been a village on a western peninsula detached from the rest of the city by groves of orange trees. The head of the municipality, who was a figure close to Rashid Karame and embodied the political class that had long ruled the village-turned-neighborhood, recalled feeling bitter about the rise of Hashem Minqara, an "elevator fixer," "from anonymity to Emir of Mina." "Minqara was previously unknown to us," he remembered, referring to the local political elite to which he and municipality members belonged. "But he came to behave as if he was the Governor of Mina – and, on the ground, he certainly wielded more power than I did."[125] The Emir, for his part, in a rare interview recounted with thinly veiled pride having "imposed order." "Locals began visiting me more regularly to solve their problems,"[126] he remembered. Hashem Minqara's dazzling rise to prominence from anonymity to Emir of Mina epitomized Tawhid's promise of a new local order in which the subalterns would now take center stage.

In a reflection of how Tawhid's Emir in Mina became a magnet for the subalterns who lived in the slums of the port, he rapidly surrounded himself with many local followers. Figures are disputed. While Hashem Minqara boasted having "one thousand" militants, the mayor of Mina spoke about "hundreds," informed observers putting the number at

---

[124] Interview with Kana'an Naji (leader of Soldiers of God and former Tawhid Emir), Tripoli, July 2014.
[125] Interview with Abdel Qader Alameddin (Mayor of Mina), Tripoli, July 2014.
[126] Interviews with Hashem Minqara (Tawhid Emir in the neighborhood of Mina), Tripoli, July–August 2014.

300–500.[127] Yet what is certain is that he particularly attracted the area's subalterns and that his ability to mobilize this constituency during key episodes of contention was by all accounts significant. Tellingly, he did not focus on recruiting experienced Islamists, but rather many of the fishermen who had been forced to quit their occupation years earlier as well as dozens of locals who had until then been members of revolutionary leftist movements and criminal organizations. This became even more the case after he set up his headquarters in a mosque which he built in one of the slums situated at the western extremity of the port. There and in the surrounding lower-class areas he began being perceived more as a spatially grounded strongman providing security and social services – a *qabaday* – than as an Islamist per se.[128] By uniting Mina's subalterns, themselves scattered between different slums and collective housing units, Minqara would, through the sheer force of weapons, take control of the entire neighborhood and considerably empower the locals who had long remained marginalized. The Emir of Mina embodied the promise of empowerment inherent in "subaltern Islamism."

A New Cultural and Social Order

Crucially, the promise of a new social order implicit in "subaltern Islamism" did not just concern the concrete, physical, empowerment of the subalterns who, by joining Tawhid, began ruling Tripoli through the sheer force of weapons; it also had to do with the movement's zealous imposition of Islamic norms, which turned the cultural order on its head. Once again, this challenges the prevailing assumptions of some scholars of Islamism, such as Asef Bayat, who view the interest of Islamist movements with questions of morality and religion as antonymic to the more urgent concerns of the subalterns with bread-and-butter issues. Tawhid's case instead shows how the subalterns can use the Islamist aspiration to govern morals and impose religious precepts as a "protest ideology" to overturn the structures of symbolic domination and enact a new cultural order in which they take center stage.

As was hinted at earlier, the dynamic of social and spatial segregation which was gripping Tripoli was also beginning to result in cultural

---

[127] While the CIA estimated that Minqara's Tawhid faction comprised 300 members, informed observers put the figure at 500. See: US Central Intelligence Agency, "Lebanon: Islamic fundamentalism in Tripoli" (Top Secret, NESAR 86-003JX, January 17, 1986) and interviews with observers of Tawhid, Tripoli and Beirut, June 2014.

[128] Interviews with former Tawhid members in Mina and with local residents, Tripoli, July 2014.

282   Social Jihad

inequalities and differentiation. What came to distinguish New Tripoli or the boulevards of Mina from, say, Qobbe, the Old City or the slums of the port area, was no longer just very different social, economic and political conditions, but also cultural norms and practices that seemed at odds with each other. On the one hand, then, the inhabitants of the city's chic neighborhoods, and in particular the youth, increasingly adopted a Western lifestyle that entailed following the latest trends such as speaking French or English, dressing in Beatles fashion, socializing with women in public, going to the beach or hanging out in cafes or restaurants and having an active nightlife. On the other hand, the impoverished districts featured more traditional mores in line with the rural upbringing of many of their residents, for example an insistence that women wear the headscarf and remain confined to the private sphere, and they benefited from no leisure infrastructure. Of course, as we saw earlier, segregation between these spaces was never fully total. In fact many subalterns were in regular contact with the relaxed lifestyle led by richer boys. However, although this lifestyle reflected a wider trend and fashion in Lebanese society, the subalterns could not access it. It was not just that they did not belong to these spaces of affluence, but also that they often lacked the cultural and social codes needed to blend in. A local observer recalled that, as a result, the subalterns in Tripoli's deprived neighborhoods began developing a counterintuitive mix of "envy and resentment" for the lifestyle found in wealthier districts. Many, he reported, became animated by a thirst for "cultural revenge."[129]

Tawhid's militant Islamism equipped the subalterns with a "protest ideology" whose discourse and practices enabled them to turn structures of symbolic domination on their head by justifying the imposition of norms heralding a new cultural and social order. And, while the imposition of these Islamist norms disproportionately targeted New Tripoli's entertainment infrastructure, it also came to center on domination over wealthier young men and women through challenging understandings of masculinity and policing dress codes.

Tawhid's militant Islamism provided the subalterns with the rationale and the vocabulary to disrupt the relaxed lifestyle of the upper class in New Tripoli. As was tackled in Chapter 4, the movement explicitly called on its members to intervene in society and in private lives to enforce "morality." Tawhid clerics often reminded their audience that "Islam's mission" consisted in large part of fighting what they called "social decadence," which would involve forcefully preventing the occurrence

---

[129] Abi Samra, *Trablus*, p. 171.

A New Cultural and Social Order   283

of "morally corrupt practices" by closing down spaces of entertainment such as "nightclubs, bars and beaches." This was justified because Allah, according to Tawhid's ideological reading of the sacred texts, "allows what is right but prohibits what is wrong," and therefore religion was seen as "regulating all aspects of life from top to bottom, including political and social affairs."[130] "Allowing what is right" and "prohibiting what is wrong" thus became the motto of the subaltern members of Tawhid. Yet, behind the veneer of their grand calls to return to a "pure Muslim society" and to "morality," many began using religion and ideology selectively with the goal of continuing their social revolt by disrupting the relaxed lifestyle of the upper class.

This pushed the subalterns to go further than physically targeting New Tripoli's entertainment infrastructure, like they had done in 1974–5 and 1980–2, for Islamist ideology now allowed them to impose not just taxes but also a new cultural and social order. They prohibited alcohol in chic restaurants, prevented men from working as hairdressers in New Tripoli's women salons, bothered the customers sitting at the terrace of affluent cafes during prayer times or pressured those listening to Western music to switch to Quranic songs. They also closed down the remaining cabarets and even checked whether the breath of the privileged youths who used to party in Beirut smelled of spirits when they returned to Tripoli.[131]

Importantly, much of the symbolic violence which these subaltern Islamists exerted seemed more driven by preexisting social tensions than by true ideological commitment. In a show of how instrumentalist the embrace of ideology by its subaltern members had often been, Tawhid began featuring instances of spatial variation in its behavior, its harsh implementation of Islamic norms disproportionately focusing on New Tripoli. And it even witnessed stark inconsistencies between its ideology and the behavior of some members.

Anecdotes abound about the way the movement's subaltern members implemented Islamism especially zealously on New Tripoli all while engaging in practices at odds with ideology. One resident of the chic neighborhood recalled a Tawhid member from a deprived neighborhood entering one of the city's most reputed cafes in order to prohibit betting on horse racing, an activity popular among the upper class but one largely seen as un-Islamic, only to discreetly force the owner to gamble on his

---

[130] "Hiwar m'a al-Duktur al-Shaykh Muhammad 'Ali al-Juzu: hel yusbih Lubnan Jumhuriya Islamiya?" ["An interview with sheikh Dr. Mohammed Ali Jouzou: will Lebanon become an Islamic Republic?"], al-Tawhid (July 27, 1984).

[131] Interviews with residents of Tripoli, July–September 2014.

284 Social Jihad

behalf.[132] Similarly, while Tawhid members enforced a strict ban on selling and consuming alcohol in New Tripoli's chic cafes and restaurants, it was not uncommon for small circles of militants not primarily guided by ideology to discreetly gather and drink whiskey or beer. In one striking instance, in Mina subaltern militants who had ransacked a shop selling wine and local spirits were spotted hours later visibly drunk in a back alley.[133] As Chapter 6 shows in more detail, several Tawhid members would even be involved in the trafficking of alcohol and hashish. Significantly, the movement's leadership knew about these inconsistencies between its ideology and the behavior of some of its subaltern members but it never tried reining it in. Countless such anecdotes suggest how Tawhid's Islamism channeled the counterintuitive mix of resentment and envy of the subalterns for the relaxed lifestyle found in New Tripoli by providing a rationale to impose "Islamist" norms and overturn the cultural and social order.

Protest Masculinity

Another factor pushing many subalterns to support Tawhid was that the Islamist movement was in the midst of redefining prevailing understandings of manhood by developing a "protest masculinity" which undermined the status of richer boys and empowered the poor. Back then Tripoli's subaltern men were facing an unprecedented crisis of masculinity. Manhood had long been locally defined as the combined ability to get married to a woman, have children and provide for one's family – and, crucially, to do all of this early on in life. Yet in the 1970s and 1980s the subalterns began finding it increasingly difficult to get married. High unemployment rates, the rise of the informal proletariat, which was not just low-paid but also insecure, and the spread of extreme poverty all made it challenging for poorer young men to pay the dues (al-alameh) they traditionally owed to the family of their future bride. This prevented many from getting married and having children, and as a result their manhood and social status, already severely degraded, were being questioned even further. Moreover, even when some managed to get married and form a family, they were often unable to provide their wife and children with secure prospects, which felt humiliating. Marriage's central

---

[132] Interview with a resident of New Tripoli, Tripoli, August 2014.

[133] Note that this was far from an isolated event. Other residents reported witnessing similar incidents and former Tawhid members recognize that this period was marked by the spread of "morally corrupt practices." Interviews with residents of Tripoli and with current as well as former Tawhid members, July–September 2014.

Protest Masculinity

importance to the notion of masculinity was best exemplified by the haste at which Hashem Minqara got married upon becoming the wealthy Emir of Mina – and his telling choice of the sister of glamorous Lebanese actress Shams al-Barudi for a wife. Minqara's case, however, was the exception to the rule for, although Tawhid began giving funds to assist its members in getting married, it was not enough to make a difference for all.[134]

What made matters worse was that, while understandings of masculinity were shared across the social and spatial boundary between the city's impoverished neighborhoods and New Tripoli, the plight of young subaltern men did not seem shared by the richer boys. On the contrary in fact, for the latter seemed to have it all. One journalist recalled how, in the years preceding the advent of Tawhid, New Tripoli witnessed its richer boys socializing with the district's "fashionable and trendy women" in local cafes, restaurants and cinemas. "Those who would later become militants could not dream of getting near one of these girls."[135] As a result they soon began developing what sociologist Raewyn Connell called a "protest masculinity"[136] – a set of norms and practices through which they contested their subordinate position by challenging prevailing understandings of masculinity and formulating new ones. In Tripoli's impoverished neighborhoods the meaning of manhood stopped simply revolving around getting married and forming a family, and instead began centering on other notions, such as the ability to use violence to defend one's own "honor" and that of women.

Tawhid seemed well suited to channel the "protest masculinity" of subaltern men. Drawing on militant Islamist ideology, the movement had developed a discourse which emphasized how "real" men were accordingly characterized by their chivalrous readiness to exercise violence to right the wrongs, for "Muslim men will remain men."[137] Moreover, in terms of practice, Tawhid placed much emphasis on the physical fitness of its members and their ability to fight – not just with guns but also their bare hands. Tellingly, the new fashion for subaltern men under Tawhid's rule over Tripoli was no longer to try to imitate the Beatles fashion spreading in New Tripoli, but instead to signal one's readiness to be violent by dressing as an Afghan mujahedeen and

---

[134] Interviews with subaltern residents of Tripoli and with former Tawhid members, Tripoli, June–July 2014.

[135] Abi Samra, *Trablus*, p. 170.

[136] R.W. Connell, *Masculinities* (Cambridge: Polity Press, 1995), pp. 109–19.

[137] "Al-sheikh Sa'id Sha'aban: silah al-Muslimin wajib shara'i wa ilwa' al-silah ma'siya li-lla" ["Sheikh Sa'id Sha'aban: the armament of Muslims is a Shari'a duty and surrendering is a grave sin"], *al-Tawhid* (April 26, 1984).

286   Social Jihad

carrying a rifle on the back.[138] This militarized masculinity idealized values at odds with the quieter lifestyle of richer boys. In addition, Tawhid's insistence on the need for gender segregation allowed the subalterns to express their protest masculinity by targeting richer males who were known as womanizers. A resident of New Tripoli, at the time a handsome man in his twenties, recounted how he was often harassed. He recalled that, to escape Tawhid's scrutiny, his female friends and he used to leave the city to go to a beach which was outside the movement's reach to undress, swim and socialize. "But, when going back home in late afternoons, the militants, aware of the trick, would copiously spit and insult me while assaulting my girlfriends,"[139] he recounted. And, finally, the insistence in Tawhid's Islamist discourse on "morality" and in particular on the need for men to "defend" women from "corrupt practices"[140] provided the rationale for its subalterns to reassert their domination over women by regulating their public behavior. Sometimes accusing women of "decadence" allowed Tawhid's subaltern men to express their "protest masculinity" violently at these women. This was a period during which shocking incidents were reported, such as the brutal collective rape of the female director of a private school and the public flagellation of another woman – both accused of "depravity."[141] "Subaltern Islamism" seemed to effectively channel the protest masculinity of the urban poor.

Tellingly, one factor which intensified the violence of Tawhid's subaltern men against women was that the vast majority of the city's socially progressive women came from the upper class in New Tripoli. The symbolically and physically violent "protest masculinity" which they exercised against them thus partially stemmed from preexisting social tensions. One anthropologist indeed noted how, in the 1960s and 1970s, upper-class Tripolitan women had started unveiling, buying lingerie, wearing skirts and carrying purses. These styles sharply contrasted with the more conservative mores typical of the city's more deprived districts, where rural migration had encouraged the spread of headscarves and long dresses.[142] Tawhid's rise and call for the application of its version of

---

[138] Interviews with residents of Tripoli and with former Tawhid members, Tripoli, July–August 2014.

[139] Interview with a resident of New Tripoli, Tripoli, June 2014.

[140] "Hiwar m'a al-Duktur al-Shaykh Muhammad 'Ali al-Juzu: hel yusbih Lubnan Jumhuriya Islamiya?" ["An interview with sheikh Dr. Mohammed Ali Jouzou: will Lebanon become an Islamic Republic?"], al-Tawhid (July 27, 1984).

[141] "Flagellation publique d'une femme à Tripoli," L'Orient Le Jour (November 3, 1984) and "Reprise des combats à Tripoli," L'Orient Le Jour (October 16, 1984).

[142] See: Maha Kayal, Le système socio-vestimentaire à Tripoli (Liban) entre 1885 et 1985 (Neuchâtel: University of Neuchâtel, unpublished PhD thesis, 1989), pp. 214–19.

Islamic law may have provided a chance for its subaltern members to gain a sense of empowerment by imposing their own cultural norms onto Tripoli's upper class and overturning patterns of symbolic domination.

By all accounts, Tawhid did not uniformly coerce women into wearing a headscarf. But its officials acknowledged that they did engage in "pressures" and that the "conservative atmosphere" gripping Tripoli prevented women from dressing "immodestly."[143] One example of the type of "pressures" the movement applied on the city's socially progressive women who dressed liberally was by spreading certain horrific rumors, according to which Tawhid's members would throw acid on those who did not cover their hair and legs. Even though officials recognized that such rumors circulated but vehemently denied that it ever occurred, a doctor affirmed having treated female patients injured in this way.[144] Whether true or not, the rumors were widespread and may have intimidated many women.

Another way through which "pressures" were exercised on wealthier, socially progressive women was through the checkpoints Tawhid installed in the city. Manning one of these numerous checkpoints fulfilled an important social function of control. Even Tawhid's lowest-ranking members could arbitrarily decide whether a woman was worthy of being allowed to pass. Invoking clothing codes and religion thus became a way for many to wield authority and get a sense of empowerment. The type of violence taking place at checkpoints was not always physical, it could also be symbolic. A militant from one of the deprived neighborhoods who was manning a checkpoint in the vicinity of New Tripoli in the 1980s thus insisted that he always showed "restraint." "Whenever I would see a woman who was not dressed decently, I would stop her and tell her to go home and change. But I never beat any of them!"[145] he reported. This showed the extent to which Tawhid's rise allowed subalterns who had long felt stigmatized to overturn patterns of cultural domination. The result, then, was a drastic change in the way women dressed in the early to mid-1980s. One sociologist who studied the evolution of women's dress throughout the twentieth century noted that, during Tawhid's rule, "Tripolitan women avoided wearing sleeveless shirts" as well as skirts and other clothes deemed too Western, and instead many started wearing the headscarf. She argued that Tawhid

---

[143] Interview with Amir R'ad (former Tawhid cleric), Tripoli, September 2016.

[144] Interview with a former official in the Lebanese Red Cross, Tripoli, April 2014. While most Tawhid officials deny this practice ever took place, one former senior member acknowledged that it occurred "occasionally."

[145] Interview with a former Tawhid militant from Qobbe, Tripoli, August 2014.

288   Social Jihad

"was the only militia to have tried to extend the limits of its power by imposing clothing rules,"[146] in reference to the context of the Lebanese civil war. The movement's rise had effectively heralded a new cultural and social order in which the subalterns became dominant. They would now redefine the essence of Tripolitan identity.

A Struggle for Tripolitan Identity

Enforcing Islamic precepts constituted a first step in Tawhid's broader attempt to redefine Tripolitan identity so as to mold it to reflect its ideology – and the interests of the subalterns. This, in turn, showed again Tawhid's propensity to act as a "spatially oriented movement" mobilizing over local issues. It engaged in contention not just against actors at the macro level like the state, as the traditional definition of social movements has it, but just as prominently with some of the local actors which embodied Tripoli's power structures. The movement became especially involved in a local struggle for what Henri Lefebvre and David Harvey called "the right to the city," or the "claim to some kind of shaping power"[147] over Tripoli and its symbolic meaning as a way of asserting citizenship. Tawhid grew interested not just in obtaining resources, imposing its power and heralding a new cultural and social order, but also in engaging with questions about local identity such as what Tripoli was about, who had the right to speak on its behalf and ultimately who "owned" it. And, while Tawhid framed its activism ideologically, the stakes were unmistakably social and political too for, as sociologist Manuel Castells pointed out, conflicts over "urban meaning"[148] often reflect underlying struggles for the city between socially antagonistic actors. Revealingly, Tawhid's struggle for Tripolitan identity and, in turn, for the right to the city, was spearheaded by Hashem Minqara, whose faction in Mina embodied "subaltern Islamism." Behind Tawhid's battle for the soul of Tripoli lay the longstanding struggle of the subalterns to become a more integrated part of the city and acquire a sense of Tripolitan citizenship.

Tawhid's struggle for Tripolitan identity crystalized as a confrontation with the Cultural League (*al-Rabita al-Thaqafiya*), another movement made up of Sunni Muslims but who, as the historical elite in New

---

[146] Kayal, *Le système*, pp. 185–6.

[147] See Henri Lefebvre, *Le droit à la ville: espace et politique* (Paris: Economica Anthropos, 2001 [1968]); Henri Lefebvre, *La Révolution Urbaine* (Paris, Gallimard, 1970); and David Harvey, *Rebel cities: from the right to the city to the urban revolution* (London: Verso, 2012).

[148] Castells, *The city and the grassroots*.

Tripoli, hailed from a different social world. At first this tension expressed itself through heated encounters and disagreements. But by 1983 it had become so acute that Tawhid began to intimidate the Cultural League's members, even going as far as trying to assassinate some of them and to bomb their headquarters. "Tawhid militants harassed us permanently," explained Rashid Jemali, the long-time head of the Cultural League and a key Tripolitan notable, who later even became mayor of the city. "They intimidated us and threatened us – I survived three assassination attempts," he added. For Rashid Jemali, the reason behind this violence was crystal clear. "The Islamist militants were trying to change the city's identity, but we were standing against them," he said. "They told us to leave Tripoli as our activities supposedly did not represent the soul of the city."[149]

It was not surprising that Tawhid's struggle for local identity targeted the Cultural League. It had long acted as Tripoli's most influential "civil society" organization and frequently claimed to represent the city as well as embodying its identity. This was because it was one of the city's oldest associations and had considerable legitimacy with historical Tripolitan families. It was created in 1943, originally as an alumni association gathering the graduates of the city's first private Muslim high school, the House of Islamic Education and Teaching (*Dar al-Tarbiya wal T'alim al-Islamiya*), itself set up in 1921 and gifted with a reputation for excellence. Given that the vast majority of Tripoli's notables and members of the historical Sunni Tripolitan elite attended the school, the Cultural League rapidly reached a thousand members, many of whom became some of the most important actors in the city's political, economic and cultural life.[150] The Cultural League thus epitomized the Tripolitan upper class' tendency for self-reproduction and longstanding domination over the city.

This would transpire in 1975 when the advent of the civil war, the collapse of state institutions and the breakdown of order pushed the Cultural League's members to style themselves as the city's "enlightened vanguard" and to take a more visibly prominent role. They were key in setting up the National Gathering for Social Work (*al-Tajamm'u al-Watani lil Amal al-Ejtime'i*), a local alliance which gathered Tripoli's political parties, civil society associations, professional unions and trade unions to "prevent local conflicts and restore order." However,

[149] Interview with Rashid Jemali (Cultural League's former head and Mayor of Tripoli), Tripoli, August 2014.
[150] Interview with current and former members of the Cultural League, Tripoli, June–July 2014.

290 Social Jihad

throughout it was evident that it was the Cultural League, more than its partner associations, which was truly in the driving seat, to the extent that it came to host the activities and reunions of the National Gathering for Social Work at its own headquarters. Thus, its former head concluded that the Cultural League had become "the voice of Tripoli." "Somebody had to express the needs and requirements of this city – that was our goal as we debated and lobbied to propose solutions to local authorities and the government."[151] The Cultural League, and through it the local elite, thus claimed to speak on behalf of all Tripoli.

But if all residents identified some common traits to Tripolitan identity, as was seen in Chapter 1, aspects of the Cultural League's vision for it were at political, religious, cultural and social odds with that of Tawhid and its constituents, which triggered a conflict. Politically most of the Cultural League's members were secular Arab nationalists, as exemplified by the bronze statue of Egyptian President Jamal Abdel Nasser in the garden behind the League. Moreover, while they were all Sunni Muslims and, as Tripolitans, had to publicly express a degree of dislike for the Syrian regime, they did not actively oppose its military presence in Lebanon, and some had longstanding and important friendships in Damascus. Sometimes this pushed them to engage in the indirect promotion of the regime in Tripoli, for instance by regularly inviting Ahmad Kuftaro, the Mufti of Syria but a Sunni Muslim cleric first and foremost known for his loyalty to Hafez al-Assad, to deliver talks at the League. This evidently put them at odds with Tawhid, whose growing clout they intensely opposed. This enmity did not translate into military clashes because the members of the Cultural League were notables who had neither military training nor the appetite to fight violently. However, the League provided an informal opposition platform at a time when a growing number of political parties and civil society organizations were about to leave Tripoli. One opponent of the Islamists recalled that the Cultural League became "the only breathing space we had left"[152] after Tawhid turned the city's library into one of its offices.

Culturally and religiously, the Cultural League was also completely at odds with Tawhid. Members mounted theater plays every week, led the most famous choir of North Lebanon, al-Fayha, and organized art exhibitions – one of them, in a show of the Cultural League's secularism, featuring statues of naked women by celebrated Syrian artist Mohammed Haffar. Religiously, members of the Cultural League may have regularly

---

[151] Interview with Rashid Jemali (Cultural League's former head and Mayor of Tripoli), Tripoli, August 2014.
[152] Interview with a Tawhid opponent, Tripoli, September 2016.

A Struggle for Tripolitan Identity   291

hailed Tripoli's "Islamic heritage" but their vision of how this translated concretely had nothing to do with Islamism. On the contrary, they prided themselves for being at the forefront of Islamic "modernism."[153] Rashid Jemali asserted that the school affiliated with the League was "Islamic in name only,"[154] religious lessons being given an hour a week by "enlightened" Sorbonne graduate cleric Sobhi Saleh and a partnership linking it to Christian schools in Tripoli and Beirut. Despite being both made up of Sunni Muslims residing in Tripoli, Tawhid and the Cultural League developed fundamentally different visions of what their city stood for. One defended a narrow understanding of the city's religious heritage and traditions while the other strove to make it open to diversity and pluralism. Hashem Minqara, whose subaltern-dominated faction was behind Tawhid's campaign against the Cultural League, vehemently argued that its members were "not Islamic enough" and that, although "we were both Muslims," points of view on the meaning of Tripoli "diverged too much"[155] to be reconciled. Rashid Jemali, for his part, was adamant that the Cultural League strove to "show the real face of this city."[156] What was at stake was a struggle for local identity – and for who had the right to embody it.

Yet what triggered Tawhid's violence was that, behind this contest over the political, cultural and religious aspects of Tripolitan identity, the Cultural League had long ascribed to the city an elitist social meaning which effectively excluded the subalterns from belonging. The Cultural League had long acted as a forum allowing for the reproduction of the elite and the promotion of its interests, a situation that stemmed from the high fees the private school associated with it imposed, which prevented social diversity. Members, of course, preferred to pride themselves as embodying "civil society,"[157] especially as they were key in steering the National Gathering for Social Work as mentioned above. But for all their claims, as the city's notables, businessmen, professionals and high-ranking civil servants they were hardly representative of the Tripolitan society they claimed to embody. One critical former member even recalled that "there was not a single worker in the Workers

---

[153] Interview with current and former members of the Cultural League, Tripoli, June–July 2014.
[154] Interview with Rashid Jemali (Cultural League's former head and Mayor of Tripoli), Tripoli, August 2014.
[155] Interviews with Hashem Minqara (Tawhid Emir in the neighborhood of Mina), Tripoli, July–August 2014.
[156] Interview with Rashid Jemali (Cultural League's former head and Mayor of Tripoli), Tripoli, August 2014.
[157] Interview with current and former members of the Cultural League, Tripoli, June–July 2014.

292   Social Jihad

Subcommittee."[158] And, tellingly, its headquarters were situated on Culture Street (*Sher'a al-Thaqafa*), in the heart of New Tripoli, which indicated again how the chic district concentrated local power structures.

Members of the Cultural League saw Tawhid as a mortal threat to "their" Tripoli; not just because it was an Islamist movement with opposing political, cultural and religious values, but because it had empowered the subalterns and heralded a new social order. They grasped the "subaltern Islamism" of Tawhid for what it truly was: a conduit for the subalterns to wage a "social jihad" by allowing them to undermine local power structures, struggle for the city and its identity and erect themselves as masters of the new local order. Behind the battle for Tripoli's soul thus lay a conflict between socially antagonistic actors. One member of the Cultural League revealingly recalled this period as "dark times" during which "everyday people" – the subalterns – "controlled all aspects of our city by the force of weapons,"[159] referring to Tawhid's imposition of Islamist norms and military supremacy. Interestingly, Tawhid members understood their struggle with the Cultural League in similar terms. "Our conflict with the Cultural League was deeply social," reflected Hashem Minqara. "Their members were the elite while we represented the people,"[160] he proudly claimed.

A key aspect of this underlying social struggle between Tawhid and the Cultural League was the latter's refusal to acknowledge that Tripoli's demographics had changed and that, therefore, the city's meaning and power structures might have to be more inclusive too. Members of the Cultural League largely held negative views of the mass of rural migrants who made up the subalterns, stigmatizing them and not seeing them as real Tripolitans. Many for instance despised the easily recognizable accent of the Akkar and Dinniye countryside, which reminded them of the rural background of the subalterns; and others viewed their sheer number, lack of education and conservative mores as outright threats to their own lifestyles. The political, cultural and social ascent of these subalterns, through Tawhid, repulsed them. "We felt as if our city was occupied by foreign fighters," explained Rashid Jemali, in a telling choice of words. "We did not know any of the militants manning Tawhid's checkpoints. They had strange faces and were aggressive, impolite and uneducated – they did not belong to our society."[161] This socially loaded view of Tawhid

[158] Interview with a former member of the Cultural League, Tripoli, September 2016.
[159] Interview with current and former members of the Cultural League, Tripoli, June–July 2014.
[160] Interviews with Hashem Minqara (Tawhid Emir in the neighbourhood of Mina), Tripoli, July–August 2014.
[161] Interview with Rashid Jemali (Cultural League's former head and Mayor of Tripoli), Tripoli, August 2014.

A Struggle for Tripolitan Identity 293

members, many of whom were local subalterns, reflected the full extent of the stigmatization and exclusion they had long suffered.

In a gross attempt to suggest that Tawhid, the movement which had empowered the subalterns and heralded the advent of a new social order, would never truly be Tripolitan, no matter how hard it tried, the upper class began spreading the word that Sa'id Sha'aban was a Shia. Of course, this was an overtly sectarian attempt at reclaiming Tripoli's Sunni Islamic heritage by hinting at the supposedly "un-Tripolitan" nature of Tawhid's alliance with Shia Iran. Yet, even more shockingly, it was also meant to emphasize the rural background of its leader in a way that was implicit but largely understood by the elite in Tripoli. Indeed, suggesting Sa'id Sha'aban was a Shia helped remind indigenous, upper-class Tripolitans that the cleric, for all the "Tripolitan habitus" displayed by his movement, did not hail from the city. He was born twenty miles south from Tripoli in the coastal town of Batroun and his father, a peasant, used to go up to farm and raise sheep in a nearby, mountainous Shia hamlet. Investigation of the cleric's family records and Batroun's administrative archives confirmed that Sa'id Sha'aban had always been a Sunni, but rumors he was a Shia lingered for a long time. This gross attempt at denying Sa'id Sha'aban a sense of Tripolitan citizenship reflected the wider efforts of the notables to preserve their hold on local identity and power structures and to keep Tawhid's rural and deprived subaltern members at bay – even if only symbolically. What was at stake, then, was the question of who truly belonged to Tripoli as a community.

The Cultural League's adamant refusal to acknowledge the Tripolitan belonging and sense of citizenship of residents who had emigrated decades ago, or were in many cases born in the city of parents who had originally come from the countryside, infuriated the subalterns. They may not have shared the political, cultural and religious orientation of the upper class yet they felt deeply attached to Tripoli. In fact, as this and Chapter 4 demonstrate, Tawhid embodied at once the empowerment of the subalterns and, through their "Tripolitan habitus" and constant references to local narratives and history, their deep identification to Tripoli too. In interviews members often proudly stated how, by fighting against the Syrian regime, a topic tackled in Chapters 7 and 8, they upheld Tripoli's "honor," "safety" and "dignity," as well as its longstanding identity as a rebel city. And, in its statements, the movement typically accused the regime of "forcing Tripoli onto its knees to disgrace it."[162]

---

[162] See, for instance, a Tawhid statement in: "Violents accrochages à Tripoli," *L'Orient Le Jour* (June 15, 1983).

294   Social Jihad

The identification of Tawhid's subaltern members to Tripoli and their sense of belonging to the city as a community made their exclusion from it by the elite painful. One Tawhid fighter felt "humiliated" by the way his values and persona were routinely rejected. "I sacrificed a lot for the sake of Tripoli," he bitterly recounted. "We fought to make the whole city, not just our areas, safe and proud," he said, referring to Tawhid's violent struggle against the Syrian regime's presence in North Lebanon, "yet wealthier people kept dismissing us as thugs (*za'aran*)."[163] Their socio-political anger at local power structures was widespread among subalterns and led Tawhid to bomb the headquarters of the Cultural League in 1983. Newspapers reported that two people were hurt and that the material damage was "very considerable."[164] It resulted in members of the Cultural League withdrawing from local politics and society during the remainder of Tawhid's rule over the city. Tellingly, they would be among the first to lobby the Syrian regime to crack down on Tawhid in Tripoli in mid-1985. Sources within Tawhid for their part confirmed the movement's involvement in the bombing of the Cultural League and suggested that it was ordered by "people at a high level."[165] This showed the degree to which "subaltern Islamism" became explicitly rooted in Tawhid's behavior – and how far it was prepared to go in order to wage its "social jihad."

Taking on the Notability

After it consecutively empowered the subalterns, heralded the advent of a new cultural and social order and engaged in a struggle with the Cultural League over the meaning of Tripolitan identity, Tawhid's next step would be to take on the traditional notability which had long ruled over the city's politics – most prominently the Karame family. This struggle would first translate into a rhetorical confrontation between Sa'id Sha'aban and Rashid Karame. But the most powerful way through which Tawhid undermined the notability was by tearing down the statue of Abdel Hamid Karame from Tripoli's central square, erecting in its place a sign of the word "God" and renaming it "Allah Square." This seemed to reflect the importance of religion and ideology in Tawhid. In fact, the

---

[163] Interview with Aziz Allush (Tawhid fighter in Bab al-Tebbaneh), Tripoli, August 2014.
[164] According to Tripolitan daily *Al-Incha*, the damage was worth 150,000 LL – a considerable amount at the time. See: "Enfijar amam al-Rabita al-Thaqafiye," *Al-Incha* (December 13, 1983) and "Double attentat à la bombe à Tripoli," *L'Orient Le Jour* (December 14, 1983).
[165] This is alleged to be Hashem Minqara. Interview with Ibrahim Saleh, Tripoli, August 2014.

new shape and name of Tripoli's central roundabout resulted from the lobbying of the two dozen "ideological entrepreneurs" who pushed the movement to take decisions guided by Islamism. But appearances can be deceptive too. The root of the transformation of "Abdel Hamid Karame Square" into "Allah Square" lay not only in religion and ideology but, as importantly, in a much wider rejection of the traditional notability in Tripolitan society. This enabled a counterintuitive coalition across space, class and ideology among actors who hailed from different social worlds but all agreed on the goal of undermining the Karame family, and it energized the subalterns who had long used the square as a space of protest and unrest. This would show how some spaces can be "sites of transcendence" enhancing mobilization. The overthrow of the Karame statue and the erection of an immovable sign of God in its place would herald the symbolic and actual downfall of the family's domination over Tripoli.

The main reason behind the fast-growing dislike of parts of Tripolitan society for Rashid Karame was that he embodied a supreme kind of notability, whose family had politically ruled the city for over a century and was intent on continuing to behave as feudal lords. The Karames were a historical Tripolitan family that had long exercised important positions of power in Tripoli from the Ottoman period onward. In a reflection of their strong ties to Istanbul and local prominence, the Ottomans had even granted them the status of "Effendis," a rare aristocratic title placing them at the very top of Tripoli's social hierarchy.

At times they benefited from relative popularity, especially as social tensions had not yet fully developed. Rashid Karame's father and grandfather, for instance, had acted as popular Muftis of Tripoli, or the highest-ranking religious figure with a degree of social and political influence too. Crucially, moreover, both of them had also been fervent supporters of the popular pan-Syrian movement advocating Tripoli's reattachment to Syria. This had even caused Rashid's father troubles with the French authorities during the Mandate period, which had heightened the local popular support he came to enjoy in the 1930s and 1940s. Rashid Karame used their legacy to become, in 1955, Lebanon's youngest prime minister at thirty-four years old. He would then hold this position seven more times until Tawhid's emergence in the 1980s, making him both Tripoli's most prominent representative in government and also the most powerful local notable by far, known as the city's *za'im*, or political boss.

Yet Rashid Karame's rise to local and national power, far from turning him into the consensual figure his father and grandfather were, instead began to polarize Tripolitans. In fact, even foreign observers noted how,

296   Social Jihad

although he may have "inherited the political influence and prestige of his ancestors," he never achieved genuine local popular support.[166] Three sectors of an evolving Tripolitan society particularly came to oppose Rashid Karame and would, under Tawhid's rule, discreetly ally and plot to tear down the statue of Abdel Hamid Karame from the city's central square and replace it with an immovable sign of God. This would herald the end of the Karames' century-old political domination over Tripoli.

Historically the first part of society to oppose the Karames' quasi-monopoly over Tripolitan politics was the Muqaddem family and their allies, another upper-class and historical family which had long been prominent before the ascent of the Karames but were not "Effendis." The Muqaddems viewed the decline in their power and the rise of the Karames with intense resentment, which led them to engage in violent competition against their rivals. A history of bad blood developed between the two families that both belonged to the elite. The period of the French Mandate, which redistributed the cards among the Tripolitan elite, accentuated their power rivalry and translated into bloody incidents and a cycle of revenge. While, in 1936, one of the Karames had used his family's influence in local institutions to kill a Muqaddem and evade justice, in 1944 it was the turn of Rashid Muqaddem, by then leader of the family, to extract revenge by leading a "murderous attack"[167] on the Karames. Tensions ran so high between the two families that it shortly engulfed the city in a cycle of clashes pitting their supporters against each other, thus threatening stability and causing the "considerable concern"[168] of the government – it had become a matter of national importance. The feud turned so bitter and violent that it even took on geopolitical proportions, as each family sought the support of the UK and France, which were competing for influence in the Levant. While diplomats in Beirut observed that Abdel Hamid Karame began portraying himself as "pro-British," they noted that Rashid Muqaddem had turned into an "associate of the French."[169] The drama culminated when the power of the Karames again grew as the Mandate period came to a close. They arranged for Rashid Muqaddem to be exiled to an island off Syria where he died, members of his family asserting that the Karames

---

[166] UK Embassy in Beirut, "Lebanon: annual review for 1955" (Confidential, VL1011, January 1, 1956).
[167] UK Embassy in Beirut, "Weekly summary, Syria and Lebanon" (Secret, No. 141, December 13, 1944).
[168] UK Embassy in Beirut, "Lebanon: weekly summary no. 3" (E1154/909/89, February 6, 1947).
[169] UK Embassy in Beirut, "Weekly political summary: Syria and the Lebanon" (E248484/27/89, April 28, 1943).

poisoned him.[170] Ever since, the feud between the Muqaddems, the Karames and their respective allies never subsided. With their prestige diminished in the post-independence era, the Muqaddems began allying across class and space with subalterns in the Old City to target the Karames. This culminated in the 1960s with the rise of the 24 October Movement, which as was seen in Chapter 1 embodied Tripoli's "global sense of place" and attachment to the Palestinian cause, but also social tensions as the subalterns used it to engage in sporadic urban violence. This revolutionary leftist movement, led by Faruq al-Muqaddem, then soon fell into disarray and the status of his family further receded. Yet tensions between the two families lingered. "We are the nemesis of the Karames,"[171] a representative of the Muqaddems thus still asserts.

The second part of Tripolitan society which intensely opposed Rashid Karame was the newly educated middle class whose economic and social ascent was blocked by the virtual monopoly of the Karames and their local allies over the city's economy and politics. Rashid Karame, indeed, behaved like his ancestors as a true feudal lord, conditioning access to jobs and business opportunities to the sole political loyalty of residents voting in Tripoli. Both as scion of a family with longstanding influence in local institutions and as *za'im* of the city who was every few years either minister or prime minister, Rashid Karame exercised a great deal of influence over the local economy. Through his connections he could help make a business thrive or collapse and he also controlled access to patronage networks, routinely staffing Tripoli's municipality, port, post office, hospitals and even mosques with loyalists. But, although this enabled him to secure enough local votes to be constantly reelected to parliament through the 1950s, 1960s and 1970s, it blocked the ascent of the educated middle class. This translated both into resentment for Rashid Karame and support for his chief rival during this period, Abdel Majid al-Rifa'i, head of the Tripoli branch of the Iraqi Ba'ath Party. Although al-Rifa'i was at first popular with many subalterns, his party's base came to revolve more distinctively around the anti-Karame Tripolitan middle class in neighborhoods like Abu Samra, where his offices were located. The support of the middle class for al-Rifa'i was key in helping him come out on top in the 1972 parliamentary election, ahead of Rashid Karame. Another party which channeled the resentment of the middle class for the Karames was the Organization of the Communist Action, a small revolutionary leftist movement.

---

[170] Interviews with members and allies of the Muqaddem family, Beirut and Tripoli, July 2014.

[171] Interview with a representative of the Muqaddem family, Tripoli, July 2014.

298   Social Jihad

The third and last part of Tripolitan society which opposed Rashid Karame were the subalterns in the lower classes who, since the 1960s and 1970s, had become marginalized in every possible way. They blamed him for the deterioration of their conditions, pointing to his connections to the upper-class Tripolitan families involved in corruption scandals and mass layoffs at factories in the 1970s and to his control of the levers of local and national power. Moreover, they also disliked Rashid Karame because he personified the structures of power which had left the subalterns feeling stigmatized and undermined by elites in New Tripoli. Tawhid, despite being an Islamist group, explicitly engaged as a "spatially oriented movement" with their local grievances. This crystallized in a rhetorical confrontation between Sa'id Sha'aban and Rashid Karame which drew on their sense of social exclusion. The cleric, for instance, in his public appearances began mockingly calling the *za'im* "His Excellency the Son of Tripoli" to ridicule Rashid Karame's pride in his aristocratic background, or lambasting "Rashid Effendi who does not represent Tripoli" to underline the gap between his pretense to embody the city and his lack of support from "the people."[172] And, in a show of how Tawhid's "social jihad" was anchored at the heart of its "subaltern Islamism," even the interviewed rank-and-file Islamists did not shy away from using the socially loaded anti-Karame rhetoric of revolutionary leftist movements when they criticized his "arrogance" and "political feudalism."[173] One of them even stated that "Rashid Karame thought of himself as the leader of Tripoli while he was merely the leader of the bourgeoisie."[174] Tawhid channeled the subaltern dislike of the notability in explicit ways.

Tawhid's attacks on Rashid Karame were, of course, also framed in a less socially loaded and much grander, political and ideological, discourse. The movement began attacking Karame on his record as prime minister, especially after he agreed to become premier again in 1984 under Amine Gemayel's presidency, although he had earlier criticized him as "an agent of Israel." Tawhid did not miss this chance. It multiplied statements accusing Karame of being "complicit in the crimes committed by the fascist party," a dig at Amine Gemayel's Phalange Party, or of "having gone down to the level of these killers [...], monkeys

---

[172] "Shaaban se déchaine contre Karamé," *L'Orient Le Jour* (March 23, 1985) and "Shaaban longuement reçu à Moukhtara par Joumblatt," *L'Orient Le Jour* (April 11, 1985).

[173] Interviews with current and former Tawhid members, Tripoli, June–August 2014.

[174] Interview with Aziz Allush (former Tawhid commander, close to Khalil Akkawi), Tripoli, August 2014.

and pigs."[175] Tawhid's rhetorical attacks turned even fiercer after Rashid Karame endorsed the idea of starting UN-sponsored negotiations between Lebanon and Israel in the border town of Nakura. It undermined Karame's pretense to speak on behalf of Sunni Muslims when it stated that "Muslims reject the Nakura talks" and that "nobody should negotiate on our behalf." "We deny your right to talk in the name of Muslims as you serve the Jews and the Crusaders," it concluded, calling Karame's attempt at making peace with Israel a "betrayal."[176] This episode was the prelude to an even more violent Tawhid campaign against the *za'im* of Tripoli. The movement lambasted the Muslim ministers in the Karame government for "not being Muslims." It accused the prime minister of "going to the infidels" and of "underestimating the power of Muslims and of the Tawhid movement."[177] Allegations even surfaced that Rashid Karame could well become the target of a Tawhid assassination. Ultimately this did not happen, but the movement's violent verbal escalation probably inspired some of its subaltern members to take matters into their own hands, because it was followed by gunshots targeting his Tripolitan residence and by a car bomb on his nephew.[178] Tawhid, then, soon succeeded in significantly undermining the authority of Rashid Karame.

From Karame Square to Allah Square

More than Tawhid's verbal attacks and intimidation, what truly heralded the end of the Karame family's century-long reign over Tripoli was the destruction of the giant statue of Abdel Hamid Karame on the city's central square, its replacement with an even more massive metal structure of the name "God" and the renaming of the area as "Allah Square." This reflected Tawhid's "spatial agency,"[179] as contentious politics scholar William Sewell called the ability of social movements to change the meanings and uses of spaces. While at first sight it seemed evident that it was religion and ideology which had pushed Tawhid to exert its

---

[175] "On ne peut pas soutenir un régime dont le chef devrait être condamné," *L'Orient Le Jour* (March 9, 1985).

[176] "Shaaban à Beyrouth: les Chrétiens ont divisés le Liban," *L'Orient Le Jour* (November 10, 1984).

[177] "Khitab al-Sheikh Sa'id Sha'aban" ["Discourse of Sa'id Sha'aban"], *Al-Incha* (December 28, 1984) and "Shaaban: un 'complot,'," *L'Orient Le Jour* (March 12, 1985).

[178] "Tripoli: l'attentat contre la mosquée a fait 8 morts et 66 blessés," *L'Orient Le Jour* (February 2, 1985) and "Echange de tirs entre l'Armée du Liban Arabe et l'Armée Libanaise," *L'Orient Le Jour* (May 17, 1985).

[179] Sewell, "Space in contentious politics," pp. 55–6.

300   Social Jihad

spatial agency in such ways, another crucial factor behind the square's transformation was how it symbolized the wide rejection of the Karames in Tripolitan society, leading to the formation of a game-changing coalition and to heated mass mobilizations there.

It had been the dozen "ideological entrepreneurs" in the entourage of Sa'id Sha'aban who had pushed the leader of Tawhid to order the construction of the metal sign of God.[180] It would act as what we might call an "ideological artifact" meant to indoctrinate local society into Islamist ideology by projecting its ideas visually and spatially. The "ideological entrepreneurs," as highly committed Islamist figures constantly mobilizing their worldviews and striving to mold the nature of activism and of the broader environment around their beliefs, had always been critical of the presence of the Karame statue, for "Islam prohibits idols." In its place, they argued, Tawhid should take God out of the mosque and enforce His presence on Tripoli's most symbolic and central public square. This would anchor in the heart of urban space, and therefore in the local collective psyche, the Islamist injunction to implement "God's rule on Earth," making it appear almost natural. "What is nicer than seeing the name of the Almighty when entering and leaving Tripoli?" asked one of them, before adding: "remember that you are the slave of Allah and that you live on His land and below His mercy."[181] The "ideological entrepreneurs" also lobbied so that the sign of the word Allah would be surrounded by large black flags of jihad. The flags bore the profession of faith of the Prophet and advocated the "oneness of God" (al-tawhid), which hinted at Tawhid's hegemony and at the ascent of its Islamist ideology.[182] And, finally, they encouraged the movement's leadership to install a massive marble stele, visible from afar, which read:

[180] Interview with Abu Othman (Tawhid military commander close to Sa'id Sha'aban), Tripoli, October 2015.

[181] "Sehat al-Nur wa kafa" ["Square of the Light and that's enough"], al-Tamaddon (September 20, 2002). See also the broader debate which took place in 2002 in the columns of Tripolitan weekly al-Tamaddon on the shape and name of Allah Square: "Al-Sheikh Fathi Yakan: al-Islam leis al-sha'arat" ["The cleric Fathi Yakan: Islam is not about banners"], al-Tamaddon (September 20, 2002); "Tawdih min al-Jama'a al-Islamiya hawl Sehat al-Nour" ["Clarification from the Islamic Group on the Square of the Light"], al-Tamaddon (August 30, 2002); "Bahes fiqhi fi bayan hakm idafa lafaz al-jalale ila Sehat al-Nour" ["Jurisprudential research on the permissibility of using the name of Allah on the Square of the Light"], al-Tamaddon (September 6, 2002); and "Qissat Sehat Abdel Hamid Karame min al-khamsiniyat hata al-youm ... wa eqtirah hloul" ["The story of Abdel Hamid Karame Square from the 1950s until today ... and recommendations for solutions"], al-Tamaddon (September 13, 2002).

[182] This draws on interviews with Ibrahim Saleh (Tawhid official close to the "ideological entrepreneurs"), Tripoli, August 2014, with Bilal Sha'aban (Tawhid's leader), Tripoli, June 2014 and with Abu Meriam Khassouq (Tawhid's head of Education Bureau and a leading ideological entrepreneur), Tripoli, July 2014.

"Tripoli is the fortress of the Muslims" (*Trablus qal'at al-muslimin*). This embodied Tawhid's "vernacular ideology," a mix of militant Islamism and "Tripolitan habitus," which established its fighters as the first defenders of their own vision of a militarized and Islamized Tripoli. Of course, by essentializing the city in this way the inscription on the marble stele targeted the presence of Christian and especially Alawi minorities. But it also echoed Tripoli's longstanding identity as a stronghold of contention and in particular the local tradition of opposition to the Syrian regime. "Allah Square" (*Sahat Allah*) or "Square of the Light" (*Sahat al-Nour*), as the area became known, thus epitomized Tawhid's explicit interest for Tripolitan identity as well as its willingness to spatially mark the city with the ideological imprint of Islamism. In a reflection of how successful the efforts of "ideological entrepreneurs" were in erecting this "ideological artifact" in the heart of Tripoli, Allah Square has outlived Tawhid and is still dominating the city today, also demonstrating the long-term effects that "ideological artifacts" can at times have on society.

But, beyond the roles played by religion and ideology, what enabled the destruction of the Karame statue, the rise of the sign of God and the renaming of the area as "Allah Square" was that space's unique ability to embody the wider rejection of the Karames in society. Despite their different social, spatial and political worlds, then, and each for their own reasons, the subalterns, parts of the middle class and some historical, anti-Karame upper-class families coordinated and mobilized to replace the Karame statue with an immovable sign of divinity. This shows how some spaces can act as "sites of transcendence": their location, shape and history may have such salient meanings that they have the potential to enhance mobilization. Indeed, they may both politically transcend older cleavages to enable coalitions across class, space and ideology as well as emotionally transcend activists who will rally there en masse.

Before the destruction of the statue and the renaming of the area, Abdel Hamid Karame Square had come to symbolize the extent of that family's supremacy over Tripoli. The roundabout's central location, shape, name and history reminded Tripolitans on a daily basis of the family's feudal practices, sense of self-importance and degree of political influence. The area, in a show of its strategic location, was Tripoli's largest square by far and acted as a key node connecting four main arteries and two lesser roads. At its heart lay a giant bronze statue which featured Abdel Hamid Karame, "slim bareheaded, dressed in a western suit and striding forward with one arm raised as if greeting."[183] The statue was so massive, in fact, that it had given

---

[183] Gulick, *Tripoli*, p. 215.

302   Social Jihad

its name to the area, which from its erection to its destruction became known as "Abdel Hamid Karame Square" or "Square of the Statue."[184] All of this was deemed provocative by critics of the Karames. While the Muqaddems and their allies were bitter to see their rivals so centrally linked to the production of space and the construction of Tripolitan identity, the middle class lambasted how the square and the statue embodied the feudal practices of the Karames. The subalterns, for their part, shared the two criticisms, but in addition were infuriated that such an expensive bronze statue of a notable was erected at the precise location that separated New Tripoli from the much poorer Old City. The history of the statue itself further enraged them all. The expensive costs were paid for not by the Karames themselves but, in a show of their power, by the Lebanese government. The order for its manufacture, in fact, had been personally placed by Rashid Karame after he became prime minister for the second time in 1958 with the justification that his father had been a leader of the independence movement. This demonstrated to all how Rashid Karame at times used his influence at the heart of the government to engage in self-serving practices. Abdel Hamid Karame Square thus symbolized everything critics disliked about the Karames.

Signs that the square was starting to violently polarize Tripolitans surfaced in the early days of the civil war, in 1975, when it was the target of two bombings by middle-class activists from the Organization for the Communist Action and the Iraqi Ba'ath Party who "wanted political feudalism dead,"[185] as a figure close to them remembered. As a result the bronze statue was severely damaged. The Karame family later organized its temporary removal from the square so that repairs could swiftly be made. But it was then that Tawhid used the vacant space to manufacture and install the massive metal sign of God.

The story that follows shows how some spaces can act as "sites of transcendence" which may politically transcend traditional cleavages and emotionally transcend activists. Tawhid, indeed, engaged in the words of one of its top officials in a "complex coalition"[186] across class, space and ideology which helped the movement construct the metal sign of God. The significant costs of the manufacture of the large, three-dimensional monument were paid not by Tawhid but by money provided by anti-Karame, historical families in New Tripoli. Chief among them were the

---

[184] Khaled Ziadeh, "Place Abdel Hamid Karamé ou Place de la Lumière à Tripoli: conflits de dénominations," chapter 5 in Franck Mermier (ed.), *Liban, espaces partagés et pratiques de rencontre* (Beirut: Presses de l'Ifpo, 2013), p. 112.

[185] Interview with Ahmed al-Amin (Organization for the Communist Action official), Ehden, June 2014.

[186] Interviews with Ibrahim Saleh (Tawhid official close to Sa'id Sha'aban), Tripoli, July–August 2014.

Bissars, a prestigious and upper-class Tripolitan family but one that historically despised the Karames as they intermarried and allied with the Muqaddems. The alliance between the Bissars and the Muqaddems ran deep in local history and was in fact such that, when Rashid Muqaddem was forced into exile in the 1940s, the Karames also banished Abdelatif Bissar, the leader of his family clan, from Tripoli for several years. From then on his descendants continued backing the Muqaddems and frequently tried running for local and national office against the Karames.[187] It was the Bissars, then, who paid for most of the expenses associated with the construction of the sign of God and publicly supported Tawhid's rebranding of "Abdel Hamid Karame Square" into "Allah Square," and rumor has it that one of their scions, Kheireddine Bissar, even shortly joined the movement. Today the representatives of the Bissar family recognize the existence of a short-term, game-changing "understanding" between them and Tawhid, although they are adamant that "this did not constitute an alliance per se" and that they rejected the Islamist movement's broader values. Still, they like to recall that "everybody used to hate the Karame statue" and how, by supporting Tawhid's rebranding of the city's central square, they helped put an end to the "cycle of oppression and humiliation" which had touched the Muqaddems and their allies. "The Karame statue belonged to the family's backyard, not to the center of Tripoli – a sign of the word God was more welcoming!"[188] concluded the head of the Bissar family with pride. This shows how some spaces can act as "sites of transcendence" which, because of the salient meaning associated with their location, shape and history, have the potential to enable short-term and single-issue, but game-changing, coalitions across class, space and ideology.

As the Bissar family strategized with Tawhid's leadership to install the metal structure of Allah in the vacant space on the square, allies of the Karames began publicly arguing that "God belongs to the sky"[189] in a bid to advocate for the Karame statue's return. This, however, was rapidly followed by a mass mobilization of Tawhid's subaltern members. They had long used the city's central square to protest. The meaning associated with the area and its proximity to mansions of Tripolitan notables, the seat of the governor and several banks allowed them to make claims aimed at both the local and national power structures. The downfall of the Karame statue and the erection of the sign of God emotionally transcended them further, turning the area into Tripoli's space of

---

[187] Interview with Leila Bissar, Tripoli, July 2014.
[188] Interview with Abdallah Bissar, Tripoli, August 2014.
[189] Interview with a figure close to Rashid Karame, Tripoli, July 2014.

304   Social Jihad

mobilization par excellence. The square's new configuration gave implicit divine backing to the demands of the subalterns for the "right to the city," adding grandeur to their claims and making them sound inevitable. It was now the turn of the subalterns to occupy the square that happened to separate chic New Tripoli from the impoverished and overcrowded neighborhoods of the Old City. The presence of the sign of God and the black flags of jihad gave them additional rationales to march there after Friday prayers and engage in locally oriented violence, casting their occupation of the area and their involvement in unrest as religiously driven and legitimate. It was also now their turn to shape the identity of Tripoli. Long stigmatized as thugs who were not real Tripolitans, they were now "soldiers of God" claiming to defend their city. And, finally, the square's new shape and name epitomized the advent of the new social order of Tawhid in which it was the subalterns, rather than the notables, who literally took center stage. Once relegated to the margins of society and stigmatized in every possible way, then, the subalterns imposed their political, cultural and social domination onto the city. They had such power, it seemed, that they had been able to reshape Tripoli's highly symbolic central square to their liking. All these meanings associated with the site's new setup transcended the subalterns, leading them to mobilize there en masse and to prevent the return of the statue.

Eventually, the transformation of Abdel Hamid Karame Square into Allah Square performed a variety of functions, for instance allowing Tawhid to impose its ideology on Tripoli in spatial and visual ways and to reshape urban identity to its liking. But its main, immediate effect was to undermine the notability and especially the Karames. Much like Abdel Hamid Karame Square had symbolized the family's long domination over the city, the destruction of the statue and its replacement with a sign of God epitomized its downfall. It was one thing to be an occasional target of the rhetorical attacks of Tawhid. Yet it was quite another for Rashid Karame, by then prime minister, to see his leadership and the longstanding legacy of his family challenged in his home city in such ostensible ways. This episode did not just represent a symbolic defeat for him, which national opponents of all stripes quickly took advantage of; it also called into question the inevitability of the city's power structures, and in particular the centrality of the Karames' historical role. Especially because, now that God's name was erected at the center of Tripoli, a city with such a rich and proud Islamic legacy, it would surely prove controversial to change the new status quo. "Who wants to take the responsibility for bringing God down from Tripoli?"[190] asked a local notable to highlight the difficulty of bringing the

---

[190] Interview with a figure close to Rashid Karame, Tripoli, July 2014.

Karame statue back to the square. In fact, one upper-class ally of the Karames explained that the family at first tried to bring the statue back to the square and to rename the area but that "by fear of tension" it stood back. Interestingly, Allah Square has remained the key site of mobilization for all sectors of society including but not limited to the subalterns, where until today they engage in protest against local and national power structures, earning it the nickname "Square of the Revolution."[191]

This episode, then, is a striking demonstration of the degree to which space can be the stake of contention. In some cases the meanings associated with local space can be so salient that they turn it into a "site of transcendence" characterized by heated mobilizations as well as coalitions across class, space and ideology. It also showed, once more, Tawhid's propensity, despite its grand Islamist agenda, to engage as a "spatially oriented movement" in local struggles for the city, and it epitomized the promises of "subaltern Islamism" for a new social order, one based on alternative power structures.

Theorizing Back

By revealing what explained Tawhid's involvement in a type of behavior resembling a "social jihad" more shaped by local antagonisms than by Islamist ideology, this chapter also draws broader theoretical implications related to space and ideology in contentious politics and it answers the following questions. Why are some movements not just grounded in but also considerably oriented toward local space, targeting primarily local power structures? Why are constituencies which are less or not ideologically committed sometimes attracted by ideological movements, and what is the effect of their joining on movement behavior?

First, by exploring Tawhid's base with Tripoli's subalterns this chapter illuminates the locally oriented nature of much of contentious politics. It demonstrates how space or "the local" can be a target for social, rebel and terrorist movements and shapes their activism. In Tripoli's case the subalterns had long engaged in locally oriented contention. This partially stemmed from the fact that, although some of the grievances from which they suffered reflected wider national and regional trends, they tended to

---

[191] For a more comprehensive history of Tripoli's central square from the 1980s until today, see among others: Khaled Ziadeh, "Place Abdel Hamid Karamé"; the excellent thesis by Sylvain Mercadier, *Logiques de la contestation et symbolique spatiale: l'exemple de la place Abdel el Hamid Karameh à Tripoli (Liban)* (Beirut: Université Saint Joseph, unpublished Master's thesis, 2015); and "Hyde Park al-Nour fi Trablus: sehat al-tahawwulat al-ejtimeʻaiya" ["Hyde Park of the Light in Tripoli: Square of the social transformations"], *al-Akhbar* (October 25, 2019).

306   Social Jihad

materialize themselves in spatially uneven ways, concentrating in their neighborhoods especially. But, significantly, it also resulted from their economic, social, political and cultural subjugation at the hands of typically local power structures, which therefore became one of their primary targets. This explains why their resulting mobilization was locally oriented to an extent and that the revolutionary and criminal movements that sought to channel the grievances of the city's subalterns targeted so vehemently symbols of local power structures located in New Tripoli.

In this vein, what explained Tawhid's social and spatial salience with the subalterns was its striking willingness and ability to act as a "spatially oriented movement." Through this concept, I mean those movements which are not just based in but also directed toward space, explicitly engaging with local grievances and/or identities and striving to achieve a measure of local social and political change – space or "the local" is what they are primarily about. The concept of a "spatially oriented movement" builds on Manuel Castells' older notion of "urban social movements,"[192] which designated movements engaged in mobilizations tackling local issues of collective consumption, struggles for urban meaning and a desire for local autonomy, but without falling into his fairly restrictive definition and while steering clear of the debates about the specificity of the "urban" which it gave rise to. The central mechanism which accounted for Tawhid's subaltern base was therefore its willingness to act as a "spatially oriented movement" which was Islamist but also explicitly engaged with the local concerns of the poor and tried to overturn Tripoli's social order. This shows the relevance of researching locally oriented contentious politics at the subnational level – space is not just a resource but also a target of movements that shapes their behavior.

I also identify two additional ways in which space matters in contentious politics which have not yet been conceptualized in the literature. Taking the example of Tawhid's short-term but game-changing coalition with other actors to turn Tripoli's "Abdel Hamid Karame Square" into "Allah Square," I point to the use by movements of "sites of transcendence" as a mechanism through which space enhances the prospects for mobilization. These spaces, by virtue of their location, shape and/or history, may have such salient meanings that they have the potential to enhance mobilizations, both by politically transcending older cleavages

---

[192] Manuel Castells, *The city and the grassroots: a cross-cultural theory of urban social movements* (Berkeley: University of California Press, 1983).

Theorizing Back

to enable coalitions across class, space and ideology and by emotionally transcending activists who rally there. Space, however, does not automatically act as a resource which benefits movements, it can also restrict the prospect for mobilization. While in Chapter 9 I identify the mechanism of "spatial repression" through which governments seek to transform a "safe space" into a "repressed space," this chapter points to the recurrent presence of "spatial barriers" or the ways in which space hinders broad-based collective action, either because of distance or the built environment or, as importantly, because of the socially and symbolically consequential local rivalries, different traditions and identities as well as the conflicting priorities of different spaces. To mobilize constituencies that share similar grievances across space, then, social movements like Tawhid have to develop discourses and practices which help overcome these "spatial barriers." This shows the important role of space in enhancing and restricting the prospect of activism.

Moreover, this chapter also makes three broad points related to the role of ideology in contentious politics, which form the analytical base on which I then build in Chapter 6. First, by showing that many subalterns joined Tawhid not because of the appeal of its ideology per se but more because it acted as a "spatially oriented movement" providing a conduit for their social revolt, I point to the significant numerical presence of less or not ideologically committed members in movements that are ostensibly guided by ideology. This demonstrates the utility of going beyond the assumption of ideological homogeneity in movements and instead considering their full "spectrum of ideological commitment," disaggregating the motivations of lesser committed constituencies and analyzing their effect on movement behavior. Second, and relatedly, this and Chapter 6 call for the more careful deconstruction of movement behavior which may appear as ideologically motivated. I acknowledge the importance of ideologically committed activists in Tawhid, especially the role of "ideological entrepreneurs," but I suggest that behind the sense that the movement behaved ideologically also lay other factors and older struggles, which have to be unpacked. Contextualizing Tawhid's seemingly ideological behavior in time and space to understand its underlying logics is crucial because it then illuminates the sometimes stark instances of variation in the movement's exercise of violence and it helps to grasp some of the inconsistencies which arose between its ideology and the behavior of some of its members. Finally, I continue to lay out the functions fulfilled by ideology for those instrumentalizing it. For many subalterns, then, Islamism acted as a "protest ideology" to oppose the upper class in New Tripoli. Islamism's discourse, practice and infrastructure also allowed the urban poor to overcome the "spatial

308   Social Jihad

constraints" which had long prevented effective mobilization across space. Last but not least, I also use the case of Tawhid's erection of a massive metal sign of God on Tripoli's central roundabout in order to point to how the construction of "ideological artifacts" helps indoctrinate society by projecting the power of ideas visually and spatially.

6   The Illusion of Religious Violence

As Chapters 2 and 5 showed, Tawhid came to be composed of some factions which were less or not ideologically committed and used Islamism as a "protest ideology" to express dissent in different local contexts, like the "neighborhood Islamists" and the "subaltern Islamists." Yet it is important to note that, however wide Tawhid's "spectrum of ideological commitment" grew as a result, ideology also mattered beyond its instrumental value. The movement, after all, also included members who were sincerely committed Islamists. In fact, in mid-1983 Tawhid's behavior gradually shifted from the low-level type of physical and symbolic violence described in Chapter 5 to more large-scale, organized and brutal battles which seemed to be unmistakably characterized by "religious violence." The term of "religious violence" has become ubiquitous in much of the public and academic debate since the wave of Islamist terrorism which targeted the Middle East and the West in the 2000s and 2010s; proponents of the concept such as Mark Juergensmeyer[1] explain it as a distinct, especially lethal subcategory of political violence carried out by religious activists who allegedly hold a "total ideological vision"[2] and whose behavior thus becomes irrational. At first glance, then, Tawhid's exercise of violence in 1983 seemed to match this category. After solidifying its rule over Tripoli and starting to implement its "Islamic Emirate," the movement led a bloody crackdown on its ideological enemies, the city's secular leftist parties, some of its officials describing the battles as religiously and ideologically inspired. Tawhid later intimidated the Christians and religiously sanctioned the

---

[1] Mark Juergensmeyer, *Terror in the mind of God: the global rise of religious violence* (Berkeley: University of California Press, 2001).

[2] Magnus Ranstorp, "Terrorism in the name of religion" *Journal of International Affairs* (Vol. 50, No. 1, 1996), p. 49. In the same vein, see: Walter Laqueur, *The new terrorism: fanaticism and the arms of mass destruction* (Oxford: Oxford University Press, 1999), Bruce Hoffman, *"Holy terror": the implications of terrorism motivated by a religious imperative* (Danta Monica: Rand Press, 1993) and Bruce Hoffman, *Inside Terrorism* (New York: Columbia University Press, 2006).

310   The Illusion of Religious Violence

killing of its enemies. But behind the initial sense that this demonstrated the utility of the category of "religious violence" lay a puzzle. If ideology was supposed to largely shape the dynamics of Tawhid's involvement in violence in Tripoli in 1983, why did it actually behave differently across time, space and leftist organizations, and engage in practices which violated its declaratory beliefs?

This chapter explores the relative causal weight of ideology in Tawhid's exercise of violence in 1983, assessing its role compared to other factors and concluding that, even in this seemingly obvious example of "religious violence," the causal linkage between ideology and behavior lying at the heart of the concept was ultimately weaker than anticipated – it entertained an illusion which overshadowed an array of factors that were as, if not more, important. This should not be taken to mean that religion and ideology, as genuinely held beliefs, did not matter in Tawhid's exercise of violence. In fact, I begin this chapter by emphasizing their role through the "ideological entrepreneurship" of highly committed Islamists who strove to mold the nature of activism around their worldviews – they translated ideology into action. These figures, who were Tawhid cadres, impacted the movement's exercise of violence in mid-1983 in two ways: they lobbied the leaders to undertake a crackdown on Tripoli's leftists and they mobilized a vehement ideological discourse which galvanized members and upset rivals. Through their "ideological entrepreneurship," ideology affected Tawhid's violence. Yet I also note that, in spite of their occasional success in steering Tawhid's behavior in an ideological direction, these figures were only in the dozens and constituted a minority, even if a vocal one. Many of the movement's 2,000–3,000 members as well as some leaders were not chiefly guided by ideology in their exercise of violence, but rather by considerations of a primarily political, strategic, geopolitical and social nature. This transpired when Tawhid led a crackdown on Tripoli's leftist parties, but with such temporal, spatial and organizational variation that its ideology alone could not explain it. Indeed, the movement chose mid-1983 in particular to engage in this high-level violence and, while it spared the lives of leftists from the Organization of the Communist Action, it attacked Tripoli's branch of the Iraqi Ba'ath Party and the 24 October Movement but did so with relative restraint and waged total war on the city's Communists, carrying out horrific exactions in the neighborhood of Mina especially. There it also brutalized the Christian minority. But, rather than stemming from any locally high levels of religious or ideological commitment, the reason for Tawhid's brute violence in Mina had more to do with the strength of "subaltern Islamism" in the port district and with how the ideological cleavage between Islamism and leftism there overlapped with particularly salient, preexisting local antagonisms. The way many members in Mina had instrumentalized religion and ideology as a conduit for their social revolt and personal gain was further exposed when some of them later dragged Tawhid into a behavior completely at odds with religious teachings, as shown by the development of "Islamo-gangsterism" – those criminal activities prioritizing economic gain over ideological consistency. Ideology played distinct roles in Tawhid's engagement in violence in 1983, then, but the sense that all its members were driven by high levels of ideological commitment was an illusion. For many of them this was a "social jihad" more than a "holy war."

Tawhid's Ideological Entrepreneurs

The perception that Tawhid began to engage more clearly in "religious violence" in mid-1983 stems from the fact that, by then, its "ideological entrepreneurs" had grown especially influential, raising the possibility that, through them, ideology had driven the violence. Because these figures constantly engaged in efforts to maximize Tawhid's ideological commitment, therefore, one way of evaluating the impact of ideology on the dynamics of contention is to analyze the nature of their role and extent of their influence in the movement.

In Tawhid, various actors matched the broad category of "ideological entrepreneurs" as figures at the extreme of a movement's "spectrum of ideological commitment," who are not just ideologically driven but also mobilize their beliefs to shape the nature of activism. For instance, they included some independent Islamists close to but nominally outside the movement, such as the members of the Line of Islamic Justice, mentioned in Chapter 2. But the most influential ones belonged to a gathering of two dozen highly committed Islamist Tawhid figures who set up the Education Office (*al-Maktab al-Tarbawi*) through which they mobilized as a faction in order to shape the movement's behavior, trying to render it ideological. Most of them had been drawn to Tawhid either after splitting from the more institutionalized Islamic Group or, in other cases, as they had been a part of the three currents that merged within Tawhid in 1982, especially the "Sunni Khomeinists" and the "Sufi jihadis" introduced in Chapter 3. They hailed from a range of backgrounds, and had each for their own reasons come to espouse deeply militant Islamist views and to turn from rank-and-file social movement activism to the more costly enterprise of ideological lobbying. While some were influenced by other "ideological entrepreneurs," others radicalized their views in prison, as several examples drawn from Chapters 2,

312   The Illusion of Religious Violence

3 and 7 suggest. Despite diverse trajectories, however, the overwhelming majority hailed from middle-class backgrounds, had often at least graduated from high school and sometimes attended university. They teamed up as they all wished to make Tawhid's behavior more ideological and to see its leaders and members embrace militant Islamism wholeheartedly. These "ideological entrepreneurs" rarely belonged to the leadership for most Tawhid leaders, including its head Sa'id Sha'aban, had to balance ideological considerations with other imperatives and were even themselves sometimes not primarily driven by ideology. Out of the seven figures who formed the movement's Consultative Council and were leaders, in fact only two, Fu'ad al-Kurdi and Abu Imara, can be viewed as "ideological entrepreneurs." The few dozen other such figures were instead movement cadres who acted as intermediaries between the leaders and the members at large and were recruiters, preachers and thinkers.

Although most of Tawhid's "ideological entrepreneurs" were thus cadres and not leaders, their influence in the movement rapidly became significant in 1982–3 and became significant. This, in turn, stemmed from their unique ability to activate and mobilize militant Islamist ideology, which allowed them to perform functions that became essential for Tawhid.

From the start, leaders realized that the very presence of "ideological entrepreneurs" in the movement would give it strong Islamist credentials. Some of them, like Abu Imara, had long been known as passionate advocates of militant Islamist ideology, and their high-profile endorsement of the movement in mid-1982 had thus provided it with ideological momentum. Others, who were less prominent but no less ideologically driven, had begun to fulfill the equally important task of articulating and disseminating Islamist ideology. It helped that they were, by their own account, a relatively "well-educated"[3] group of activists who enjoyed to read and write and knew how to mobilize complex ideas in simple ways. This pushed them to initiate the publication of Tawhid's flagship propaganda newspaper and to become highly prominent voices on its radio and TV channels – they spearheaded the process of ideological production. As Chapter 4 showed, their considerable engagement with the militant strands of Sunni and Shia Islamist thinking was key in enabling Tawhid to ideologically outbid the Islamic Group and to rapidly attract the

---

[3] This section draws heavily on my interviews with several Tawhid "ideological entrepreneurs," including Abu Meriam Khassouq, Husam Sbat, Salem al-Rafe'i, Amir Raad, Mohammed Imam and Abu Shawqi ("ideological entrepreneurs" and cadres in Tawhid's Education Office), Tripoli, June–August 2014.

constituency of Tripoli's committed Islamists to its cause. As importantly, their vocal advocacy of militant Islamist ideology triggered early on the interest of the Islamic Republic of Iran, which was in search of a strong ally in Lebanon's Sunni community. As Chapter 7 demonstrates, they would thus become Tawhid's intermediaries with Iran, which brought the movement funds and diplomatic backing. From the beginnings of Tawhid in mid-1982, their ability to activate and mobilize militant Islamist ideology fulfilled key functions, which gave them occasional influence over the leadership.

Moreover, by going to lengths to mobilize militant Islamist worldviews, the "ideological entrepreneurs" also socialized and educated Tawhid's members into ideology. The movement was made up of members and factions who had joined it for sometimes very different reasons and were as a result guided by ideology to wildly varying extents – Tawhid featured a wide "spectrum of ideological commitment." Naturally, many members were ideologically committed Islamists. But, as we saw in Chapters 2, 3 and 5, many others had also adhered to Tawhid for instrumental reasons; for instance, out of inherently local concerns and solidarities, like the "neighborhood Islamists," or as a conduit to continue waging their social revolt, like the "subaltern Islamists." Tawhid's "ideological entrepreneurs" were thus keenly aware that large proportions of the movement's base viewed militant Islamism as a mere "protest ideology" – in fact, these figures had often been key in channeling the socio-political grievances of members into Islamism – and they were now bent on turning this instrumental embrace of ideology into more sincere beliefs. This became the central function of the Education Office, an institution within the movement which they set up in early 1983 as part of their attempt to mobilize as a faction in order to formalize and enhance their efforts at molding the nature of Tawhid's activism around their worldviews. The former head of the Education Office thus explained that the main motivation of the faction was to "consolidate the Islamist beliefs of Tawhid members and Tripolitans."[4]

The Education Office socialized and educated members into ideology in several ways. The "ideological entrepreneurs" obtained funds to set up a network of a dozen what they called religious "summer schools" – this was merely a euphemism, for in reality they were more akin to Islamist indoctrination camps. In them they taught members the basics of Islam, for example instructions on how to pray, but also the fundamental tenets of militant Islamist ideology. The former head of the Education Office

---

[4] Interview with Abu Meriam Khassouq (first head of Tawhid's Education Office), Tripoli, June 2014.

314   The Illusion of Religious Violence

himself acknowledged that they exerted particular efforts to mobilize and disseminate the ideas of radical Islamist thinkers Sa'id Hawwa and Sayid Qutb, tackled in Chapter 4, to build a pool of firmly committed Islamist militants. Tellingly, these Islamist "summer schools" were all free to attend –food was even provided for the day – and took place in those Tripolitan neighborhoods where Tawhid members were most notoriously known to be primarily driven by motivations other than ideology, such as in Bab al-Tebbaneh, Mina's slums, Qobbe or Beddawi.[5] To socialize local youths into ideology and encourage them to attend these summer schools, the "ideological entrepreneurs" sometimes organized games, such as Quran recitation competitions but also football tournaments. While these weekly and sometimes even daily events provided a chance for the mostly unemployed and bored youth to interact with the "ideological entrepreneurs" and with each other, it contributed to cementing the Islamist beliefs of others. Concurring sources suggest that each of the dozen Islamist summer schools was attended by 300 participants every summer until 1985, even though it remains difficult to ascertain their success at turning the instrumental embrace of ideology by many into sincere commitments.[6]

Crucially, as part of their efforts to socialize Tawhid members into Islamist ideology, the "ideological entrepreneurs" also organized frequent activities which fulfilled the additional function of bringing the movement's various constituencies closer together. Former members of the Education Office recalled giving weekly open-air lectures, delivering Friday sermons and organizing demonstrations for religious holidays, which provided occasions for the socialization and mobilization of members from different backgrounds. As the frequent activities they held increasingly played the role of relational incubator, or social and ideational glue stitching together factions and members who had joined Tawhid for different motivations, the activism of the "ideological entrepreneurs" helped consolidate organizational solidarities and initially prevented the development of factional disputes. In other words, their activities were key to cementing internal coherence in the movement.

Another crucial task performed by the "ideological entrepreneurs" in 1983 was the marginalization of Tripoli's traditional Muslim clerics, which enabled them to take over two dozen local mosques and to teach religion in their place in the city's public schools. This not only gave the

[5] Interview with Ibrahim Saleh (Tawhid official close to the "ideological entrepreneurs"), Tripoli, August 2014.
[6] Interviews with several current and former Tawhid officials and rank-and-file members, Tripoli, July 2014.

movement control over valuable infrastructure, it also allowed these figures to mold the broader ideological environment in which Tawhid was operating and to make local society more receptive to its militant Islamist message, thus securing an ever larger pool of sympathizers. The ability of the "ideological entrepreneurs" to indoctrinate local society into militant Islamism from early 1983 further reinforced their influence in the movement. They then successfully lobbied Tawhid's leaders to crack down on Tripoli's leftists in mid-1983.

In turn, the root of their success in marginalizing Tripoli's traditional clerics and in claiming that their ideologized and militant version of Islam represented "true religion" stemmed from a crisis of trust which was affecting the representatives of establishment Islam. Tripoli's traditional clerics were back then criticized for acting more as high-ranking civil servants detached from local reality than as true preachers, and their authority was challenged. "Many people mistrusted the clerics at the time,"[7] the former head of the Education Office claimed. "They looked Muslim but, deep down, there was little Islamic substance: some had a bad reputation, others were poorly educated and most were out of touch with the people, considering their job like any other in the bureaucracy!" Crucially, this sense seemed largely shared by many Tripolitans unaffiliated with Tawhid. One resident, pious but not an Islamist, typically recalled being "profoundly bored" when attending Friday prayers in the 1970s. The advent of Tawhid, with the energetic and militant discourse mobilized by the "ideological entrepreneurs," changed things. "Their preachers directly addressed us, the youths; they showed passion and talked about politics and making revolutions, we liked that!"[8] he said. By activating and mobilizing militant Islamist ideology at a time marked by the crisis of trust plaguing Tripoli's establishment Islam, Tawhid's "ideological entrepreneurs" were able to pose as an alternative source of authority and to shape the broader religious environment.

Tension simmered between Tripoli's clerical elite and Tawhid's "ideological entrepreneurs," who claimed to be preachers yet had rarely graduated with a degree in religion. It soon crystallized as a struggle for religious legitimacy with Dar al-Fatwa, the governmental institution nominating Sunni clerics and delivering Islamic education in high schools. Unsurprisingly, much of the animosity which developed between the representatives of establishment Islam and Tawhid's "ideological entrepreneurs" revolved around ideology. While the traditional

---

[7] Interview with Abu Meriam Khassouq (first head of Tawhid's Education Office), Tripoli, June 2014.
[8] Interview with a local resident, Tripoli, June 2014.

316   The Illusion of Religious Violence

clerics were on Dar al-Fatwa's payroll, constituted an integral part of the bureaucracy and thus toed the government's line on even the most controversial issues, Tawhid's "ideological entrepreneurs" held deeply ideological and militant views of Islam.[9] The two camps thus began to engage in sometimes heated arguments. Whereas, for instance, the former committed to defend the "legal authorities" and supported Lebanese President Amine Gemayel, although he was intensely disliked by Tripolitans because of his Phalange Party's involvement in a 1982 massacre of Palestinians, the latter instead called for an Islamist "revolution" and a "confrontation" with the "clerics who are defending Gemayel."[10] Tensions were heating up and the "ideological entrepreneurs" were gaining the upper hand.

However, if the struggle between Tawhid and Dar al-Fatwa was fast turning acrimonious, it was also perhaps linked to the sense that, for the "ideological entrepreneurs," their confrontation with the clerical elite was also partially social. This shows how ideological commitment can be genuine while at the same time being driven by underlying interests.

Dar al-Fatwa's establishment Islam, indeed, had long been seen as socially elitist – and this was not entirely unwarranted. Its Beiruti branch was dominated by clerics co-opted by Saeb Salam, the capital's most prominent Sunni notable, whereas in Tripoli it was Rashid Karame and his allies who exercised considerable sway over the religious institution. As a prominent Tripolitan notable, Karame was given a formal say in the local nominations of top clerics, and his family's legacy in Tripoli's Dar al-Fatwa branch reinforced his clout. One researcher noted that he regularly got involved in the institution's tiniest matters, even shaping Friday sermons to fit his own interests.[11] This not only meant that he directly influenced the religious discourse of establishment Islam, therefore striking a fatal blow to the institution's public claims to independence, but that he also controlled the very patronage networks to which access was necessary in order to become a fully salaried cleric in Tripoli. Dar al-Fatwa, it seemed, was fast becoming an additional tool of social reproduction in the hands of the Tripolitan upper class. Tellingly, in the decades preceding Tawhid's advent, all of Tripoli's successive Muftis, or

---

[9] Interview with Taha Sabunji (Mufti of Tripoli in the 1980s and head of Dar al-Fatwa), Tripoli, August 2014.

[10] See: "Allégeance totale au Liban," *L'Orient Le Jour* (October 28, 1983); "Khaled: appui sans équivoque a la légalité et au plan sécurité," *L'Orient Le Jour* (November 22, 1984); and "Shaaban invite les chrétiens a 'embrasser l'Islam'," *L'Orient Le Jour* (March 7, 1985).

[11] Joumana al-Soufi Richard, *Lutte populaire armée: de la désobéissance civile au combat pour Dieu* (Paris: Sorbonne University, unpublished PhD thesis, 1984), pp. 205–7.

leaders of the local Dar al-Fatwa branch and figures considered to be the highest-ranking religious authorities, hailed from the city's wealthiest families in New Tripoli which acted as Karame allies. They included Abdel Hamid Karame, Rashid Miqati, Abdel Karim Uweida, Kazam Miqati, Nadim al-Jisr and Taha Sabunji.[12]

For their part, Tawhid's own would-be preachers and "ideological entrepreneurs" hailed from a different social world. They may not have been subalterns per se, since they often hailed from middle-class backgrounds and had at least attended high school and even sometimes university. But as Tripolitan residents who, like much of Tawhid's membership, mostly hailed from the countryside originally and thus could not vote in the city, they were frequently excluded from Rashid Karame's patronage networks. It also did not help that Taha Sabunji, the Mufti of Tripoli, notoriously despised them for "not being educated enough."[13] Joining Tawhid, therefore, granted them the religious authority that Dar al-Fatwa denied them. This was especially the case as the movement began bypassing Dar al-Fatwa by issuing its own "certificates in Islamic law" which turned its "ideological entrepreneurs" into "clerics."[14] Tawhid made it particularly easy for them as it even issued an official statement clarifying that graduating from a famed Islamic university was not a requirement to become a cleric. "A scholar may not necessarily wear a turban," it quipped, hinting at the red and white hat worn by the traditional clerics who often graduated from prestigious universities like Al-Azhar. Instead it set as conditions to be considered a "religious scholar" to be merely "knowledgeable" in Islamic jurisprudence and the *hadith* and to have been brought up in an "Islamic environment."[15] These requirements were easy to meet for the "ideological entrepreneurs," many of whom as a result "graduated" from Tawhid with the veneer of legitimacy they needed to call themselves "clerics" and spread their own version of Islam. Behind the contest for religious authority thus lay the social struggle seen in Chapter 5.

This underlying social struggle between the "ideological entrepreneurs" and Dar al-Fatwa's clerical elite added fuel to the fire of an already deteriorating relationship and perhaps explains the vehemence with which Tawhid sidelined Tripoli's traditional clerics. Such tension

---

[12] Interviews with officials in the local branch of Dar al-Fatwa, Tripoli, June–July 2014.
[13] Interview with Taha Sabunji (Mufti of Tripoli in the 1980s and head of Dar al-Fatwa), Tripoli, August 2014.
[14] Interview with Abu Shawqi (former head of Tawhid's Education Office), Tripoli, August 2014.
[15] "Al-'ulama' warathat al-'anbiyat" ["[Religious] scholars are the heirs of the prophet"], *al-Tawhid* (August 2, 1984).

318   The Illusion of Religious Violence

did not manifest itself physically. Taha Sabunji, the Mufti of Tripoli and local head of Dar al-Fatwa, reported receiving death threats only once and remained unharmed.[16] But Tawhid's "ideological entrepreneurs" did their utmost to undermine the religious and moral authority of the traditional clerics. They did so by forcibly taking over two dozen Tripolitan mosques in early and mid-1983 as well as the one-hour weekly religious class in high schools that the representatives of establishment Islam had until then performed. This was a watershed moment that consecrated the influence of Tawhid's "ideological entrepreneurs" for it gave them control over infrastructure that was invaluable for the movement and provided further opportunities to socialize and educate society into ideology. They would now be able to mold the broader ideological environment in which Tawhid operated, making local society more receptive to the movement's militant Islamist views. These figures still remember with pride how, instead of teaching mainstream religion the way the traditional clerics had long done, they "talked a lot about jihad."[17] To mark the contrast with the traditional robes of elite clerics they even started to wear the dress worn by the Afghan mujahedeen, which drove the point home about the need for jihad. The result was that, by mid-1983, Tawhid's "ideological entrepreneurs" had largely succeeded in marginalizing Dar al-Fatwa's clerics, came to monopolize local religious discourse and infrastructure and were in the midst of attracting growing numbers of recruits to their cause. Although they were mostly movement cadres, the key functions they came to perform turned the "ideological entrepreneurs" of the Education Office into important figures to be reckoned with in 1982–3, allowing them to lobby the leaders into a crackdown on Tripoli's leftists.

There is little doubt that the growing influence of Tawhid's "ideological entrepreneurs" in 1982–3 acted as a key mechanism through which ideology shaped parts of the movement's behavior – including but not limited to its exercise of violence in 1983. The creation of the Education Office in early 1983 as an internal institution directly reporting to the leaders provided them with a vehicle to lobby as a faction and translate ideology into action. Moreover, they were acutely aware that their ideological activities served other essential functions for the movement. These included bolstering Tawhid's religious credentials to outcompete rivals, recruit committed activists, leverage external support

---

[16] Interview with Taha Sabunji (Mufti of Tripoli in the 1980s and head of Dar al-Fatwa), Tripoli, August 2014.
[17] Interview with Abu Meriam Khassouq (first head of Tawhid's Education Office), Tripoli, June 2014.

or socialize and educate members into Islamist ideology, which not only helped turn the instrumental embrace of ideology by many into firmer commitments but also cemented internal coherence. They also shaped the broader ideological environment in which Tawhid mobilized, which made significant parts of Tripolitan society more sympathetic to their militant Islamist views. In a telling recognition of the strategic roles they played, Tawhid's Consultative Council or leadership decided to grant them, through the Education Office, a budget of $10,000 a month to continue carrying out their activities – a significant amount for the movement back then.[18] Another, less obvious factor which helped the "ideological entrepreneurs" secure influence over the leadership was the fact that many hailed from the middle-class district of Abu Samra, where Sa'id Sha'aban also resided. Local social ties and opportunities to socialize with Tawhid's leader allowed them to lobby him into making some ideologically driven decisions. Among their key victories was a decision by Tawhid's leadership to impose Islamist precepts on Tripoli in 1982–5, such as by prohibiting the sale and consumption of liquor or by issuing a ban on eating during the day through the fast of Ramadan – even though not all of the movement's members and leaders were favorable to such enforcement. They also steered Tawhid in an ideological direction by lobbying the leadership to transform Abdel Hamid Karame Square into Allah Square and to issue threats and engage in skirmishes with the Syrian army and the Lebanese security forces. They were even able to push it to forge an initially strong alliance with the Islamic Republic of Iran, even though this backfired after their internal rivals resisted, as Chapter 7 shows.[19]

Of course, the growing influence of Tawhid's "ideological entrepreneurs" over the movement in 1982 and 1983, despite being real and tangible, should not be exaggerated. While the leaders and other factions sometimes pushed back against their lobbying efforts, the extent of their sway over the grassroots can also be questioned. For instance, they wanted Tawhid to officially declare Tripoli to be an "Islamic Emirate," or a small Islamic Republic in which religious law would be applied. But although the term became widely used in conversations between Tawhid members, the movement's Consultative Council refused to make it public as the leaders feared it might trigger a Syrian military intervention. Similarly, the "ideological entrepreneurs" had lobbied Sa'id Sha'aban

---

[18] Ibid.
[19] Interviews with Abu Meriam Khassouq, Husam Sbat, Salem al-Rafe'i, Amir Raad, Mohammed Imam and Abu Shawqi ("ideological entrepreneurs" in Tawhid's Education Office), Tripoli, June–August 2014.

320   The Illusion of Religious Violence

hard to set up "Islamic tribunals" which would have been responsible for issuing sentences for reported violations of the religious norms imposed on Tripoli; yet Tawhid's leader had rejected the idea as, according to his right-hand man, he feared that it would start a spiral of tit-for-tat retribution and chaos. "Sha'aban was reasonable,"[20] this figure added, while noting that the leader, known for his heated diatribes in his Friday sermons, actually behaved as a pragmatist inside the movement – he only seemed to follow the advice of the "ideological entrepreneurs" when it suited him. Their broader influence over Tawhid's behavior can also be nuanced for the movement became dragged deeply into preexisting local antagonisms sometimes unrelated to ideology, like older neighborhood rivalries and social tensions. In fact, from mid to late 1984 onward their sway over the movement would significantly decline, something resulting from pushback by other factions which were increasingly fearful about their degree of influence and led one of these rivals to order the murder of several leading "ideological entrepreneurs." The concomitant spread of "Islamo-gangsterism" finally showed that their efforts at turning the instrumental embrace of Islamism by some into firmer commitments had often failed. In sum, by mid-1983 the "ideological entrepreneurs" had become important voices who were able to steer parts, but not all, of the movement's behavior in ideologically driven ways (see Figure 6.1).

It is in this context that the influence of the "ideological entrepreneurs" acted as a mechanism through which ideology shaped parts of Tawhid's exercise of high-level violence. The "ideological entrepreneurs" had always been fiercely critical of Tripoli's leftist parties, calling for violence by equating them with the category of "hypocrites," which was even worse than the category of "disbelievers" as "hypocrites want to mislead the believers." This category thus represented "a great danger" for Islam and all "hypocrites" would sooner or later be "deserving of Allah's anger and resentment."[21] In order to avoid the wrath of God, the "ideological entrepreneurs" encouraged the "guardians" of Islam to "confront the followers of falsehood and those who support them amongst the hypocrites."[22] Their "ideological entrepreneurship" enabled them to affect Tawhid's violence in two ways. To start with, through their lobbying efforts, they pushed the leaders to order a

[20] Interview with Ibrahim Saleh (right-hand man of Sa'id Sha'aban), Tripoli, August 2014.
[21] "Al-mawqif al-siessi al-shar'ai (2)" ["The political stance of Sharia law (2)"], al-Tawhid (August 2, 1984). Note that this article is not authored but figures in Tawhid recall that it was written by Esmat Murad, a prominent "Sunni Khomeinist" introduced in Chapter 3 who was close to the movement's "ideological entrepreneurs."
[22] Ibid and "Al-qiyada al-islamiya fi Trablus" ["The Islamic leadership in Tripoli"], Al-Taqwa (Vol. 20, April 1985).

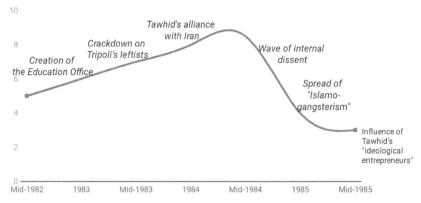

Figure 6.1 The ebb and flow of the influence of the "ideological entrepreneurs" in Tawhid

Note: The vertical axis is meant to represent an estimation of the degree of influence of the "ideological entrepreneurs" over Tawhid's leadership and membership from 0 (no influence at all) to 10 (absolute influence). "Influence" refers to the extent to which these actors are able to affect the movement's behavior.

crackdown on Tripoli's leftist parties, even though not all factions believed in the need to use violence. And, on top of that, their mobilization of radical ideological content galvanized some members into taking risks to fight as well as antagonized rivals, worsening a climate of polarization. This exacerbated ideological cleavages and had path dependencies which triggered conflict.

Controlled Violence in Abu Samra

While the "ideological entrepreneurship" of a handful of highly committed Islamist cadres acted as a central mechanism through which ideology affected Tawhid's behavior, the role of beliefs in its exercise of violence in mid-1983 should not be overestimated. Had high levels of commitment to militant Islamism guided all movement members and leaders, as the "religious violence" thesis suggests, their crackdown would not have varied as wildly across time, space and leftist organizations and it would not have featured internal dissent. As I indicate in this and the next sections, the fundamental features of Tawhid's violence such as its extent, motivations and timing had therefore less to do with ideology than anticipated. The "ideological entrepreneurs" fueled the conflict, but they did not drive violence per se. Instead, factors other than ideology

322   The Illusion of Religious Violence

had more causal weight, such as political orientation, strategic imperatives, geopolitics, dynamics of "social jihad" and older local antagonisms. In addition to casting doubts on the analytical utility of the concept of "religious violence," this and Chapters 7 and 8 also unearth material shedding light on these overlooked events. Remarkably, nearly forty years on, still very little is known about the violent conflicts that gripped Tripoli back then. This is a symptom of the gap in the literature on the Lebanese civil war, which has tended to focus disproportionately on developments in the capital, Beirut, although Northern Lebanon comprises 20 percent of the population and also witnessed brutal battles.[23]

Tawhid's first real battle, rather than the low-level violence it had mostly engaged in until then, occurred in August 1983 against the Tripolitan branch of the Iraqi Ba'ath Party in the district of Abu Samra, followed by another brief battle against the 24 October Movement.

Of course, the rhetoric of an "Islamist struggle against leftism" soon became the "master narrative"[24] of that battle, as political violence scholar Stathis Kalyvas calls the official macro cleavage which comes to characterize a conflict but often hides its underlying roots. The rise of this "master narrative" of Islamism versus leftism was primarily the doing of "ideological entrepreneurs" from both sides, who each mobilized polarizing ideological content and lobbied their respective leaders into using violence, thus fueling the conflict. Buoyed by the diatribes of Tawhid's "ideological entrepreneurs" against the secular leftists whom

---

[23] There has been a flurry of publications on the Lebanese civil war, but they refer only in passing – or not at all – to some of the violent episodes which especially gripped Tripoli and northern Lebanon. These events include Tawhid's crackdown on Tripoli's leftists in mid-1983, the bloody struggle between Fatah and Fatah al-Intifada in Tripoli's Palestinian refugee camps in late 1983, the locally confined but extremely violent feud between the Tripolitan neighborhoods of Bab al-Tebbaneh and Jabal Mohsen or Syria's mid-1985 conflict with Tawhid and the killing of hundreds of civilians in the district of Bab al-Tebbaneh in December 1986. Despite their lack of scrutiny of these episodes, some of the standard accounts of the Lebanese civil war are nonetheless excellent for understanding the general dynamics. See, among others: Jonah Shulhofer-Wohl, *Quagmire in civil war* (Cambridge: Cambridge University Press, 2020); Elizabeth Picard, *Liban, état de discorde: des fondations aux guerres fratricides* (Paris: Flamarrion, 1988); Sara Fregonese, *War and the city: urban geopolitics in Lebanon* (London: Bloomsbury, 2019); Robert Fisk, *Pity the nation: Lebanon at war* (Oxford: Oxford University Press, 2001); Fawwaz Traboulsi, *A history of modern Lebanon* (London: Pluto Press, 2007); Theodor Hanf, *Coexistence in wartime Lebanon: decline of a state and rise of a nation* (London: I.B.Tauris, 2015); and Sune Haugbolle, *War and memory in Lebanon* (Cambridge: Cambridge University Press, 2010).

[24] Stathis Kalyvas, "The ontology of political violence: action and identity in civil wars" *Perspective on Politics* (Vol. 1, No. 3, 2003), pp. 475–94. See also Stathis Kalyvas, *The logic of violence in civil war* (Cambridge: Cambridge University Press, 2006), pp. 384–90.

they branded as "hypocrites" worth killing, Tawhid members fiercely denounced the "progressive" nature of the claims made by the Iraqi Ba'ath Party and the 24 October Movement on issues such as women's rights or the role of religion and minorities in society. And, similarly, the members of these two leftist movements, who believed in respectively Ba'athist and Nasserist leftist ideology and disliked Islamism, were galvanized by their own "ideological entrepreneurs" who framed growing tensions with Tawhid as an inevitable "ideological struggle between Islamism and progressivism."[25] This added fuel to the fire of an already deteriorating relationship. They went as far as casting Tawhid as a "terrorist group" and pushing for violence themselves, arguing that "we must confront the struggle which is led on behalf of jihad."[26] "Ideological entrepreneurs" on both sides thus activated latent ideological cleavages and brought tensions to new heights.

Yet, although the "ideological entrepreneurs" thus stoked leftist–Islamist tensions, what also lay behind this ideological cleavage was a clash between political orientations. While the two leftist movements had once been characterized by their revolutionary instincts and involvement in contentious activities against the government, which had earned them a great deal of popular support in Tripoli (as Chapter 1 explained), by the 1980s they had kept their leftist ideology but gradually shifted their political orientation in support of the state.

This growing institutionalization of the Iraqi Ba'ath Party and the 24 October Movement was primarily due to the fact that their leaders, Abdel Majid al-Rifa'i and Faruq al-Muqaddem, had turned into ambitious politicians who coveted the Sunni-reserved post of prime minister. To achieve that aim in a parliamentary system characterized by the need for cross-sectarian alliances, they had to appear as consensual beyond their immediate power base. This meant that they had to engage with and support the Israeli-sponsored Lebanese presidential candidate, Bashir Gemayel, and, following his assassination, his brother Amine Gemayel, at first cautiously and then more openly, despite their unpopularity in Tripoli. Whereas Abdel Majid al-Rifa'i began calling for the government to "shoulder its responsibilities"[27] and deploy the Lebanese army to all areas of the country, including Tripoli, Faruq al-Muqaddem argued for a

---

[25] Interview with several current and former members of the local branch of the Iraqi Ba'ath Party as well as with Abdel Majid al-Rifa'i (longtime leader of the local branch of the Iraqi Ba'ath), Tripoli, June 2014.

[26] "Tripoli: l'embarras de Damas," *L'Orient Le Jour* (November 20, 1983).

[27] "Tripoli: capitale de la violence," *L'Orient Le Jour* (June 17, 1983).

324   The Illusion of Religious Violence

reconciliation with the state under the slogan "Lebanon above all,"[28] which seemed ironic as, by then, he had turned into a proxy for Egypt and Libya. Their increasingly compromising stances and support for the Phalange-dominated government in 1982 and 1983, perhaps more than their embrace of progressive ideologies per se, is what fueled tension with Tawhid, whose orientation was vehemently anti-government. Tellingly, skirmishes only occurred after Tawhid accused them of "playing the enemy's game" by "placing hope in the criminal and crusader legality"[29] – a hint at the government.

Ideological animosities between committed leftists and Islamists may have fueled tensions, then, but they were underpinned by a deeper struggle between increasingly clashing political orientations, the leftists supporting the government while Tawhid opposed it. "Abdel Majid al-Rifa'i and Faruq al-Muqaddem became supporters of Gemayel – the clash was inevitable,"[30] argued one of the Tawhid leaders who, alongside the movement's "ideological entrepreneurs," was also pushing for the crackdown. And, revealingly, Tawhid would not take the struggle to Tripoli's branch of the Organization of Communist Action. The members of this movement were also leftists committed to progressive values who opposed Islamism as an ideology, yet they had remained true revolutionaries and opponents of the Lebanese government – therefore, they shared Tawhid's political orientation and had its trust. Behind the "master cleavage" of an ideological rivalry between leftism and Islamism which was supposed to explain the August 1983 battle therefore lay a deeper clash over political orientations.

One implication of this struggle over political orientation between the anti-government Tawhid and the institutionalized Iraqi Ba'ath Party and 24 October Movement was that the Islamists began suspecting that these two movements had become stooges for the Lebanese intelligence services, who might in turn soon instruct them to undermine the group. "These movements were infested with spies who made threats against our lives,"[31] recalled a Tawhid fighter who took part in the battle in mid-1983. "We had to finish them," he argued. Clashing political orientations heightened Tawhid's mistrust about the two movements and led to the growing sense that there was a strategic imperative in ridding Tripoli of them.

---

[28] "Voiture piégée près du siège du Mouvement 24 Octobre," *L'Orient Le Jour* (20 August 1983). See also the comprehensive account of the 24 October Movement by al-Soufi Richard, *Lutte populaire armée*, pp. 180–200.
[29] "La terreur frappe de nouveau au Nord," *L'Orient Le Jour* (6 August 1983).
[30] Interview with Kan'an Naji (Tawhid Emir in Abu Samra), Tripoli, August 2014.
[31] Interview with a former fighter in Tawhid, Tripoli, September 2014.

Claims that the Iraqi Ba'ath Party and the 24 October Movement were tools in the hands of the security services are exaggerated. But there is evidence to suggest that they were close to a criminal gang in Tripoli, the Hashashin, which, for its part, was known to have a tight relationship with the Second Bureau (*al-Maktab al-Theni*), Lebanon's military intelligence, before Tawhid cracked down on members of the gang as part of its "Islamic Emirate." The rationale behind this complex alliance was explained by a former intelligence officer in post in Tripoli. The root of that relationship, he said, dated back to the beginning of Sleiman Franjieh's term as Lebanese president in 1970. "President Franjieh secured power in a context of rising chaos by recruiting new agents for the Second Bureau – this sometimes included penetrating the lowest sectors of society such as gangs in order to get information." "The Hashashin gathered intelligence for us in Tripoli,"[32] he confirmed. The fact that the two leftist movements were in close contact with the remnants of that gang frightened Tawhid members and heightened their suspicion that all these actors were plotting to undermine Tawhid. This mistrust became even more palpable after a Tawhid mosque in the district of Qobbe was the target of a massive car bomb that killed nineteen and injured seventy in mid-1983.[33]

In this context, the sense among Tawhid leaders and members that there was a growing strategic imperative to launch a battle against the Iraqi Ba'ath Party and the 24 October Movement was further amplified by the fact that, despite their dwindling popularity, these two movements were still well armed and counted on a hundred armed partisans each. This raised the real possibility that, if and when pushed by the Lebanese security services to lead clashes against Tawhid, the leftists would inflict great damage, especially as they retained influence in some of the Tripoli districts considered most strategic by the movement. The Iraqi Ba'ath Party, for instance, was still strong in the residential area of Abu Samra, a hill overlooking the city where its leader Abdel Majed al-Rifa'i had long lived but where Sa'id Sha'aban now also resided, thus making local security a paramount need for Tawhid. The 24 October Movement, for its part, still had partisans in similarly strategic areas, for example in the vicinity of the Old City, where it had its headquarters, and around Tripoli's medieval fortress, at the crossroads of Tawhid strongholds like the Old City, Qobbe and Abu Samra. The strength retained by these two movements meant that they could gather information about Tawhid to

---

[32] Interview with a former Lebanese military intelligence officer in post in Tripoli, June 2014.

[33] "La terreur frappe de nouveau au Nord," *L'Orient Le Jour* (August 6, 1983).

326   The Illusion of Religious Violence

pass on to the intelligence services and even carry out bomb attacks. "They were still influential," summed up a Tawhid fighter who pointed at their nuisance capacity. "We had to do something about that,"[34] he stated to justify the 1983 crackdown. Launching a battle to rid Tripoli of their presence increasingly seemed a strategic imperative.

Yet, even if ideological polarization, a clash over political orientation and strategic imperatives explain why tension was, by the own account of Islamist and leftist commanders, fast rising in early and mid-1983, they do not explain the timing of the battle on 30 August. After all, skirmishes between Iraqi Ba'ath Party partisans and Tawhid militants had already killed two on July 3, but without erupting in all-out conflict in the way it did in August.[35] While Abdel Majed al-Rifa'i suggests that what triggered it was Sa'id Sha'aban's "hurt ego"[36] after he was insulted by leftists as he passed by the Ba'athist compound in Abu Samra, Tawhid militants who took part in the battle for their part claim that the "nervous behavior"[37] of leftist fighters who began shooting in the air prompted them to act first. These situational accounts certainly capture the tense atmosphere in Abu Samra and there is no doubt that, with everyone on edge, large-scale fighting was bound to erupt soon enough.

But it is perhaps the geopolitical climate of the day which best explains the battle's timing in late August 1983. At the time Tawhid had developed particularly privileged relations with Fatah but, sensing the Palestinian organization's slow demise, it was starting to hedge its bets by engineering a rapprochement with the Islamic Republic of Iran. The geopolitics of Islamism is tackled in greater depth throughout Chapter 7, but it is worth noting at this point that the timing of Tawhid's crackdown on local Ba'athists was far from coincidental: it took place shortly after the Ba'athist regime of Saddam Hussein in Iraq began using chemical weapons against Iranian civilians in Piranshahr in August 1983. Sa'id Sha'aban was acutely aware that a Tawhid crackdown on the Iraqi Ba'ath Party's Tripoli branch at this turning point of the Iran–Iraq war would draw Tehran's attention and perhaps even earn its gratitude as it would be perceived as payback for the chemical attack.[38] This was all the more the case as the Iraqi Ba'ath Party's Tripoli branch was known to be particularly important for the Iraqi

[34] Interview with a former Tawhid fighter, Tripoli, August 2014.
[35] "Affrontements Baas Irak vs Tawhid: 2 blessés," *L'Orient Le Jour* (July 3, 1983).
[36] Interview with Abdel Majid al-Rifa'i, Tripoli, June 2014.
[37] Interviews with Ibrahim Antar and Hashim Yaghmour (Tawhid fighters in Abu Samra), Tripoli, June 2014.
[38] Interview with Ibrahim Saleh (Tawhid official and right-hand man of Sa'id Sha'aban), Tripoli, August 2014.

regime, for it was not just Lebanon's largest but also acted as the power base of its national head, Abdel Majed al-Rifa'i who was personally very close to Saddam Hussein. Tellingly, an Islamist official recounted that Tawhid's battle with the Iraqi Ba'ath Party at a critical time in Iranian–Iraqi relations caught the attention of Tehran which, from then on, developed a closer interest in the movement and later backed it.[39] The timing of the August 1983 battle had therefore more to do with geopolitics than ideology.

Surprisingly, given the high stakes, much of the violence which Tawhid exercised against the Iraqi Ba'ath Party was restrained and remained under control. Naturally this does not mean that the movement entirely refrained from employing symbolic and physical violence against its opponent. In a show of the role of ideology, in fact, it was evident that the diatribes of Tawhid's "ideological entrepreneurs" against the progressivism of the Iraqi Ba'ath Party, especially regarding societal issues, had galvanized some Islamist fighters and shaped the rituals of symbolic violence. Their first act as they forcibly entered the Ba'athist compound was to head to the private quarters of its head, Abdel Majed al-Rifa'i, and seize bottles of whiskey and his wife's underwear before displaying the items in public for days. This epitomized their resentment of the secular lifestyle led by the head of the Iraqi Ba'ath Party and of the role played by his wife, Leila, who not only used to wear skirts and sleeveless shirts but also saw herself as the vanguard of secularism and women's rights in an increasingly conservative society and had, furthermore, begun playing a more prominent role in her husband's party. "Symbolically, Tawhid's violence was huge,"[40] a figure close to the Ba'athist leader recalled. "It was clear that they were intent on humiliating Abdel Majed al-Rifa'i and his ideals – they wanted to destroy his image, his political potential and legacy."

Yet, for all the ideological hostility which animated Tawhid, the physical violence it exercised remained controlled. Some even suggest that the Islamist movement was ready to spare Ba'athist lives. "Sa'id Sha'aban had taken the decision to eliminate the Iraqi Ba'ath but he wished to avoid a bloodbath," recalled Tawhid's military commander in charge of the fighting in Abu Samra. "For my part I wanted to launch the hostilities by attacking the residence of Abdel Majed al-Rifa'i but Sha'aban refused and asked me to convince the Ba'athists to leave

---

[39] Interview with Abu Shawqi (Tawhid cadre close to Iran), Tripoli, August 2014.
[40] Interview with Bashir Mawas (member of the Iraqi Ba'ath Party in Tripoli), Tripoli, May 2014.

328   The Illusion of Religious Violence

peacefully."[41] Negotiations failed and, given the tense atmosphere, the battle erupted violently, leaving in a space of hours twelve dead and sixty injured, mostly within the ranks of the Ba'athists.[42] However, even then, and despite all the ideological polarization, clashing political orientations and the high strategic and geopolitical stakes at play, Tawhid showed restraint and did not engage in executions or post-battle exactions. And, while dozens of Ba'athists were taken prisoner, they were subsequently released.

The root of that paradox lies in the fact that, in the neighborhood of Abu Samra, the Islamist–leftist divide was only ideological and political – unlike other parts of Tripoli it did not reflect preexisting sectarian and social antagonisms. The hill of Abu Samra was almost entirely inhabited by Sunnis, many of whom originally hailed from the countryside and, although a sizable proportion were middle to lower middle class, there were no slums. There was, in fact, a great degree of social mixing and a sense of a "tight community,"[43] many expanded families living side by side and entertaining close relations with their neighbors. Social ties were thus strong and, although ideological polarization may have affected them to an extent, it did not fully supersede them. In fact, in that neighborhood the social and spatial base of the Ba'athists and the Islamists largely overlapped. Residents reported that it was common to find partisans of both movements "in the same streets and groups of friends."[44] It was even considered "normal" for Abu Samra's families to have within their midst some relatives who were Ba'athists while others were Islamists, without this significantly affecting relations. One Islamist militant in the district who fought against the Iraqi Ba'ath thus recalled how he told his Ba'athist brother of the battle in advance so that he would not show up to the compound that day and explained having fought carefully to avoid bloodshed during the battle.[45] The resilience of social ties across ideological boundaries contributed to limiting the violence which Tawhid wielded against the Iraqi Ba'ath Party during and after the battle.

Ideology, then, played a role in the case of Tawhid's crackdown on the Iraqi Ba'ath Party in Abu Samra, mainly through "ideological entrepreneurs" who activated the latent Islamist–leftist cleavage, stoked tensions, galvanized members into fighting and shaped the rituals of violence. Yet

[41] Interview with Hashim Yaghmour (Tawhid military commander), Tripoli, July 2014.
[42] "Echtibaket bein hizb al-Ba'ath al-Iraqi wa al-Tawhid fi Trablus" ["Clashes between the Iraqi Ba'ath Party and Tawhid in Tripoli"], Al-Safir (September 1, 1983).
[43] Interviews with residents of Abu Sarmra, Tripoli, June–September 2014.
[44] Interview with a resident of Abu Sarmra, Tripoli, June–September 2014.
[45] Interview with a Tawhid fighter, Tripoli, July 2014.

ideology's explanatory power should not be overestimated for, despite the "master narrative" of an ideological clash, what drove the timing and motivations of the battle had more to do with clashing political orientations, strategic interests and geopolitics.

Bloody Wednesday in Mina

The defeat of the Ba'athists and the humiliation suffered by Abdel Majed al-Rifa'i were enough to push Faruq al-Muqaddem to order the members of his 24 October Movement to surrender and hand over the strategically significant fortress of Tripoli to Tawhid.[46] There was little bloodshed in the process, again due to the fact that, despite its leftist and Nasserist ideology, the 24 October Movement had long acted as a vehicle for Tripoli's subalterns, a constituency that now supported Tawhid but kept some social ties to Muqaddem's fighters. This restraint, however, would not be on display in October 1983 during Tawhid's crackdown on its other ideological rival – Tripoli's branch of the Lebanese Communist Party.

In fact, there was not only a great deal of difference in the restrained way Tawhid dealt with members of the Iraqi Ba'ath Party and of the 24 October Movement, on the one hand, and the bloody and nightmarish fate awaiting local Communists, on the other; there would also be a striking spatial variation in levels of violence across Tripoli neighborhoods. As I argue in the next section, the key to understanding this differential lies in how, in the area of Mina where most of the violence took place, the Islamist–leftist divide reflected preexisting local cleavages, pitting impoverished Sunnis against their wealthier coreligionists and Christians. There, in other words, Tawhid members used the battle to carry out their "social jihad."

This is not to say that ideology played no significant role in fueling this conflict. After Tawhid's victories against the Iraqi Ba'ath Party and the 24 October Movement, its "ideological entrepreneurs" successfully lobbied the leaders into casting the rise of tensions with the Communists as an "ideological struggle,"[47] as Sa'id Sha'aban himself put it then. Through their efforts, ideology thus became once more the conflict's "master narrative." Their arguments also justified, and maybe partially inspired, the brutality which shook Mina. Tawhid's local Emir or leader

---

[46] "Harakat 24 Tishrin tansaheb min Qal'at Trablus" ["The 24 October Movement withdraws from the Fortress of Tripoli"], *Al-Safir* (2 September 1983).

[47] "Al-Sheikh Sa'id Sha'aban hawl al-wad'a fi Trablus: m'arakatna m'a al-shuyu'ain aydulujiya" ["The cleric Sa'id Sha'aban on the situation in Tripoli: our battle with the Communists was ideological"], *Al-Safir* (October 19, 1983).

330   The Illusion of Religious Violence

in that neighborhood, after all, was Hashem Minqara. As was seen in Chapters 3 and 5, Minqara led the "subaltern Islamists" but was also known to be inspired by the "ideological entrepreneurs" and held views drawn from "Sufi jihadism." Tellingly, in retrospect, Minqara justified Tawhid's violence against the Communists by mobilizing a rhetoric close to that of the "ideological entrepreneurs" when he claimed that "the believers" had killed "the atheists." "This tension between good and evil was rising," he recalled. "I am very much against any ideology pretending that God is absent from Earth."[48] This framing of the battle's "master narrative" as a cosmic struggle may have partially been window dressing, as will be seen in the next section, but ideology mattered to an extent too.

Another role played by ideology in fueling the conflict was that, in Mina, there were particularly strong preexisting Islamist–leftist cleavages, which Tawhid's "ideological entrepreneurs," through their diatribes against Communism, then reactivated with force. Clashes had sporadically opposed Islamist and Communist fighters in Tripoli, for example on Square of the Star (*Sehat al-Nejme*) near New Tripoli, where the Communist city headquarters was located.[49] But it was in Mina where tensions were already most acute, even before the October 1983 battle. This district had long been known to many leftists as "Lebanon's Stalingrad,"[50] epitomizing the extent to which it displayed the typical features of a Communist bastion. Historically, Mina acted as the hub of Tripoli's trade union activism given its proximity to the port, itself a short distance from the oil terminal and some factories. It was also a religiously mixed area with a Sunni majority living side by side with a Greek Orthodox Christian minority, which further turned it into a propitious place for the development of Communism. And, although the closure of heavy industries, the decline of the port and the rise of the "informal proletariat" had meant that the Communist Party's branch in the district had seen its numbers dwindle it could still count on hundreds of sympathizers.[51] Mina's branch of the Communist Party was thus still Tripoli's largest by far.

Ideological tensions began surfacing as Islamist movements emerged through the 1970s. Initially these local frictions were benign. Accounts of

---

[48] Interview with Hashem Minqara (Tawhid Emir in Mina), September 2014.
[49] There, clashes had opposed a Tawhid faction to local Communists in March 1983. See "Nouveaux combats à Tripoli," *L'Orient le Jour* (March 15, 1983).
[50] Interviews with current and former members of the Lebanese Communist Party, Tripoli, June–July 2014.
[51] Interview with Iqbal Sabal (head of the Tripoli branch of the Lebanese Communist Party) and with Jamil Safiye (head of the Mina section of the Tripoli branch of the Lebanese Communist Party), Tripoli, June 2014.

Mina in the mid to late 1970s report a growing number of ideological provocations pitting Islamists from the Islamic Group and Soldiers of God against local Communists, but these were mostly petty. For instance, they involved the former reciting Quranic verses in front of the Communist office in the district, before the latter answered back with songs considered to be "blasphemous."[52] But with time it seemed as though there was an increasing likelihood that any such petty provocations would suddenly get blown out of proportion and turn into more violent incidents. This was the case once in 1980 when a local street fight ended up inbloodshed, killing three and injuring five, and it then appeared to escalate further as 1982 was marked by the assassination of a local leader of Soldiers of God in Mina and then by a massive car bomb.[53] Importantly, this ideological tension was underpinned by pre-existing, local sectarian and social antagonisms, as I argue in the next section. But the spiral of tit-for-tat retribution that was pitting Mina's Communists against the Islamists had set up a dynamic of its own which, by 1983, put Mina on edge. The polarizing rhetoric of Tawhid's "ideological entrepreneurs" provided the spark needed to reactivate cleavages and turn looming tension into violence.

The mobilization of a radical Islamist ideological content by these figures also had indirect path dependencies which fueled the October 1983 conflict. It made Mina's Communists especially anxious that, now that Tawhid had eliminated the Iraqi Ba'ath Party and the 24 October Movement, they would be the next victims of what they saw as Islamism's inexorable struggle against the forces of progress. This might seem surprising as the previous section showed how Tawhid's August 1983 battle had more to do with clashing political orientations, strategic imperatives and geopolitics than with an ideological struggle. In fact, it had spared the lives of leftists from the Organization of the Communist Action, a secular Marxist movement but one which shared Tawhid's anti-governmental views. But the "master narrative" of Islamism versus leftism, even if not fully accurate, was mobilized with such vehemence by Tawhid's "ideological entrepreneurs" that it was subsequently absorbed by the Communists who started fearing for their fate. This set a dynamic

---

[52] Mohammed Abi Samra, *Trablus: Sehat Allah wa mina al-hadatha* [*Tripoli: Allah Square and port of modernity*] (Beirut: Dar al-Saqi, 2011), p. 179.

[53] See, among others: "Week-end sanglant à al-Mina: 3 tués, 5 blessés," *L'Orient le Jour* (April 5, 1980) "Fusillade à Tripoli-Mina: 2 tués, une vingtaine de blessés," *L'Orient Le Jour* (May 24, 1982) "Aghtiyal qa'ed fi Jund Allah" ["Assassination of a leader in Soldiers of God"], *Al-Incha* (March 23, 1982) and "Voiture piégée à Tripoli: 2 tués, une cinquantaine de blessés dans le quartier d'al-Mina," *L'Orient Le Jour* (September 12, 1982).

332   The Illusion of Religious Violence

of its own by heightening the already tense local atmosphere and by pushing the Communists to arm themselves and launch a doomed preemptive clash. In the context of polarization and mistrust characterizing Mina, this would lead to a brutal conflict.

A Communist military officer in Mina recalled these events in detail. "Our relations with the Islamists had always been uneasy but, after they declared that Tripoli was an Islamic Emirate and eliminated the other parties, we knew we would soon be their next target." Rather than surrendering before the battle erupted, the officials of the local Communist Party branch, who "did not trust" local Tawhid members, instead decided to prepare for the clash. They gathered a few hundred of their most capable fighters in and around the party's Mina headquarters while setting up barricades as well as distributing weapons to their sympathizers. This may have attracted the attention of the Islamists who sent one of their own on a reconnaissance tour. "But their man came too close and began shooting so we killed him."[54]

Tawhid's own situational narrative differed slightly. Hashem Minqara evoked the "aggressiveness" of fighters in the neighborhood branch of the Lebanese Communist Party. "The man they killed was Naji Faoual, one of my street commanders, who was only guilty of passing by their headquarters on a motorcycle," the Emir recounted with still visible anger. "We became anxious that they might be the ones launching the battle against us," he went on, "so when Naji Faoual was killed and the Communists refused to hand over his murderer to me, I ordered a full-scale attack." Hashem Minqara obtained the backing of Sa'id Sha'aban who gave him the green light to begin the hostilities. He cut off all telephone lines between Mina and the rest of the outside world and asked his troops to "finish off the atheists."[55] Preexisting ideological tensions were thus violently reactivated through the fiery rhetoric of Tawhid's "ideological entrepreneurs" and the nervousness of mistrustful local Communists.

The battle which then burst out gripped the city for two days, on October 12 and 13, 1983. It especially focused on both Tripoli's downtown area of Square of the Star, where the Communist city headquarters was located, and on the party's local office in Mina. Yet it was actually in the latter district that the violence started and where a staggering 92 percent of the killings took place (Figure 6.2). There, Tawhid's exercise of violence stood at odds with the behavior it had displayed in Abu Samra, where it had cracked down on the Ba'athists but with restraint. In other

[54] Interview with a former commander in the Mina section of the Lebanese Communist Party, Tripoli, July 2014.
[55] Interview with Hashem Minqara (Tawhid's Emir in Mina), September 2014.

Bloody Wednesday in Mina 333

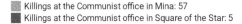
Killings at the Communist office in Mina: 57
Killings at the Communist office in Square of the Star: 5

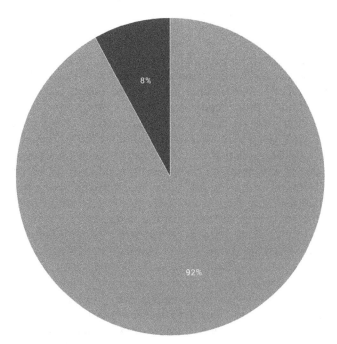

Figure 6.2 Spatial variation in Tawhid's violence against the Communists.
Source: *L'Orient Le Jour*, *Al-Safir*

words, Tawhid's anti-leftist violence varied across space and leftist organizations.

In Mina, indeed, it was clear that the movement had gone in with the goal of slaughtering local Communists, as Hashem Minqara's order to his men to "finish off" the leftists suggests. The media reported that Tawhid rapidly mobilized its hundreds of militants in the port district and that they started moving toward the Communist compound, where dozens of local leftists armed to the teeth had gathered.[56] Shells and gunfire began to be exchanged from 10.30 am, killing one leftist and two Islamist fighters. The Communist military commander explained that, now aware of the blatant asymmetry of forces, "we tried to initiate

[56] "Asbah al-wad'a fi Trablus" ["The situation in Tripoli has become dangerous"], *Al-Safir* (October 13, 1983), "Mercredi rouge à Tripoli," *L'Orient Le Jour* (October 13, 1983).

334   The Illusion of Religious Violence

negotiations so as to evacuate peacefully."[57] Some Communist fighters took advantage of the lull to escape and leave the district. Minqara's deputy and military commander during the battle confirmed that, for a few hours, matters calmed down as talks were under way but that, when Sa'id Sha'aban was asked his opinion, he ordered them to "finish the battle until victory" – but, also, he insisted, "without excesses."[58] Gunfire then intensified throughout the night and Tawhid began using its heavy weaponry. "It became much more violent than earlier," the Communist commander reported. "Tawhid bombed our office for several hours with rocket-propelled grenades, mortars and gunfire – I was myself blinded by an explosion then." Another leftist fighter who took part in the battle explained that, by dawn, he and his comrades were running out of ammunition. "We were trapped and the Islamists were about to come in to butcher us[59]," he remembered. The restraint that Tawhid had shown in Abu Samra was not the order of the day in Mina.

Yet the most striking difference in the dynamics of Tawhid's violence against the leftists in these two districts was that in Mina the fight was marked by post-battle exactions. Despite Sa'id Sha'aban's order to Tawhid fighters that they should not commit "excesses," the morning and afternoon of 13 October witnessed Minqara's men engaging in atrocities. Ideology, here, may have played the role of justifying and perhaps even partially inspiring violence by shaping some of its most extreme rituals. One leftist survivor who was taken for dead, for instance, recalled having heard a group of Islamist militants entering the building, seizing the remaining Communist fighters and shooting some of them dead. "One Tawhid commander kept telling his militants that whoever would find and kill leftist activists would go to heaven while another one was busy searching for gas to burn his prisoners alive."[60]

However, the particularly intimate nature of the violence in Mina suggests that something else beyond ideology was at play. For instance, Minqara's men issued a list of wanted local Communists who had escaped during the lull and they began spreading the rumor that they would be chased, tortured and then either burned on the beach, buried alive or placed in cement and thrown into the sea. One Communist official explained that five members died that way.[61] In another example

---

[57] Interview with a former commander in the Mina section of the Lebanese Communist Party, Tripoli, July 2014.
[58] Interview with Abu Meriam Khassouq (military commander of Minqara's faction in Mina), Tripoli, June 2014.
[59] Interview with a member of the Lebanese Communist Party, Tripoli, July 2014.
[60] Interview with a member of the Lebanese Communist Party, Tripoli, July 2014.
[61] Interview with Jamil Safiye (head of the Mina section of the Tripoli branch of the Lebanese Communist Party), Tripoli, June 2014.

of the strikingly intimate nature of the post-battle exactions that took place, an observer recounted that Tawhid fighters selected the youngest of their leftist prisoners alive, killed them in front of their families and forced relatives to spit on their dead bodies.[62] The media reported that fourteen Communists were shot in such killings.[63] Several others were "arrested at their homes, dragged through the streets and gunned down." Sources still diverge on the number of casualties in Mina, with figures oscillating between fifty-two and seventy-five killings and dozens of bodies having additionally "disappeared."[64] But what is clear is that there was another factor, beyond ideology, which had pushed Tawhid's fighters in Mina to behave in such brutally intimate ways. The movement's head, Sa'id Sha'aban, recognized that "abuses" took place but dismissed them by saying they had been perpetrated by "uncontrollable elements."[65] Even Minqara's deputy in charge of the battle in the port acknowledged that events "got out of hand," although he denied all the exactions. "My fighters had a lot of frustration and too much energy," he said, before arguing that this led them to commit "excesses,"[66] even though he refused to elaborate on what he meant by this. Under the cloak of anonymity, a Tawhid leader acknowledged that "this wasn't a battle like the others – it was a true massacre."[67] "We became trapped in a chain of events and a web of factors," he said. Ideology may have been an element, then, but only one among others. This casts doubt over the validity of the strong causal linkage between ideology and violence which lies at the heart of "religious violence" as a distinct subcategory of political violence.

Holy War or Social Jihad?

The main factor which accounts for variation in Tawhid's anti-leftist violence is that, while in Abu Samra the base of the Islamists and the Ba'athists overlapped, in Mina the Islamist–Communist divide reflected

---

[62] Abi Samra, *Trablus*, p. 176.

[63] "A Tripoli, le Sheikh Shaaban dispense la justice par téléphone," *L'Orient Le Jour* (October 20, 1983).

[64] While *Al-Safir* reported that seventy-five had been killed in the battle and in post-battle exactions, *L'Orient Le Jour* put the figure at fifty-seven deaths. See: "Trablus: fashilat muhawalat jama'iye li-waqf al-muqatilin" ["Tripoli: a collective attempt at stopping the fighters has failed"], *Al-Safir* (October 14, 1983) and "Mercredi rouge à Tripoli," *L'Orient Le Jour* (October 13, 1983).

[65] "A Tripoli, le Sheikh Shaaban dispense la justice par téléphone," *L'Orient Le Jour* (October 20, 1983).

[66] Interview with Abu Meriam Khassouq (military commander of Minqara's faction in Mina), Tripoli, June 2014.

[67] Interview with a former leader of Tawhid, Tripoli, August 2014.

336   The Illusion of Religious Violence

the port area's preexisting sectarian and social antagonisms. Behind the "master narrative" of an ideological and religious struggle lay primarily local conflicts such as a contest for neighborhood primacy and dynamics of "social jihad." For their part, factors such as the geopolitics of Fatah and Syria explained the battle's timing.

It is noteworthy that, in the months and years immediately preceding Tawhid's massacre of local Communists, Mina witnessed an especially acute rise in social tensions. By the 1970s the port district had already become an area where minor, everyday issues like traffic incidents had a propensity for turning violent. It had also turned into such an unsafe neighborhood rife with crime that residents petitioned to have night guards patrolling it.[68] Because of its proximity to the port installations, Mina had long been an economically vibrant district with a relatively large local upper middle class, one made up of many Orthodox Christians and some Sunnis. But, as we saw in Chapter 5, the 1970s brought a drastic rise in poverty which affected the new Sunni residents originally from rural areas, who settled in slums. This new sectarian and social cleavage manifested itself as ideological tension between Communism and Islamism and burst out violently during the 1983 battle.

In sectarian terms, Mina's branch of the Communist Party was mostly, albeit not entirely, made up of the neighborhood's Christian Orthodox minority. This was not just the product of ideological sympathy on the part of some for Communism but, as importantly, an extension of their deep sense of loyalty felt for Russia and its Orthodox religious leadership. Collective identity, then, as much as sincere beliefs, drove their membership of the party. A local Communist explained:

We were Communists because we had Russian sympathies, not because we all loved Marxism. In fact, in Mina, most of us were pious Orthodox Christians – we went to mass every Sunday and religious celebrations such as Easter and Christmas were very important to us.[69]

The particularly strong Christian composition of the Communist Party branch in Mina, and that party's prominent local role, explains why Tawhid's Sunni fighters began perceiving their looming battle with the

---

[68] See, among others: "Tragique incident sur la route Tripoli-Mina," *L'Orient Le Jour* (March 19, 1974); "Week-end sanglant à al-Mina: 3 tués, 5 blessés," *L'Orient le Jour* (April 5, 1980); or "Fusillade à Tripoli-Mina: 2 tués, une vingtaine de blessés," *L'Orient Le Jour* (May 24, 1982) .

[69] Interview with a member of the Mina section of the Tripoli branch of the Lebanese Communist Party, July 2014 and interviews with Christian residents of Mina, Tripoli, July–August 2014.

Holy War or Social Jihad? 337

Communists in Mina as a struggle for neighborhood primacy with Christian residents allegedly bent on "eliminating Muslims."[70] These Sunni–Christian tensions were not purely sectarian, they were underpinned by local power structures, as we see in the next section, but they surely contributed to Tawhid's violence in Mina. A Tawhid official in Mina confirmed in retrospect that the sectarian aspect of the battle against the Communists partially "helped explain"[71] some of its brutality.

Yet interviews with survivors of the massacre and their opponents alike suggest that Tawhid members were as determined to slaughter Sunni as well as Christian members of the Communist Party in Mina. This implied that something else, beyond the local sectarian struggle for neighborhood primacy, must have motivated their vehemence and brutality. The district's own preexisting, simmering social antagonisms played that important role.

In social terms it was striking how Tawhid's faction in Mina under the aegis of the local Emir, Hashem Minqara, was mostly composed of poor Sunnis who had originally come from the countryside to work before they became unemployed and settled in slums.[72] They epitomized, as Chapter 5 showed, the "subaltern Islamism" of Tawhid. If their battle with Mina's Communists had turned so intimate and brutal, as shown by their unrestrainable willingness to frighten and kill their opponents while shaming their families, it was because, beyond ideology and religion, they were driven by a will for social revenge.

While it may seem counterintuitive from the outside, the Lebanese Communist Party had by the 1970s largely turned into a refuge for those members of the politically ambitious Sunni Tripolitan upper class whose role had become somewhat marginalized by the monopoly of Rashid Karame and his allies over local politics and who, in addition, had been socialized into progressive ideologies after studying in the West in the wake of May 1968.[73] Far from empowering the subalterns, then, Tripoli's branch of the Communist Party had become with time socially elitist to a large extent. And, revealingly, the reins of its leadership rotated exclusively between the hands of Tripoli's most historical upper-class families such as the Shahal, Mazloum, Ma'asarani and Uweida families.

---

[70] "Le Mouvement de l'Unification Islamique: l'Islam au lieu de la démocratie," *L'Orient le Jour* (October 19, 1983).

[71] Interview with Ibrahim Saleh (Tawhid official in Mina), Tripoli, July 2014.

[72] Interviews with residents of Mina, Tripoli, July–August 2014. See also Abi Samra, *Trablus*, pp. 170–1.

[73] Interviews with former and current members of Tripoli's branch of the Lebanese Communist Party, Tripoli, July 2014.

338   The Illusion of Religious Violence

Crucially, this pattern trickled down to the district of Mina too, where the Communist office was headed by a member of the local Sunni upper class, Fathi Majanini, and although it counted on some working-class activists most were Christians, as the overwhelming majority of its Sunni partisans hailed from the elite.[74] As if this were not enough, the traditional strength of the Communist Party in the very neighborhood where the port was located had also allowed many already well-off members to engage militiamen to control access to the container ships, thus earning even more money. Socially the contrast between Mina's Communists and Islamists could not have been starker, and this older, simmering cleavage significantly fueled polarization between the two camps.

These sectarian and social tensions which were channeled into the Islamist–Communist ideological polarization sometimes also took on the form of intensely personalized rivalries. This, in turn, helped explain the "intimacy of violence"[75] on display in Mina, as Stathis Kalyvas called the case of killings in which the perpetrators of exactions know their victims well. The intimate nature of Tawhid's brutality in Mina stemmed from the district's social and spatial features, as seen in Chapter 5. With a population of 40,000 living in a small, confined space, Mina was one of Tripoli's most densely populated districts; one whose geographical extension was rendered impossible by seashores to its west, north and south as well as by the presence of the Rashid Karame International Fair to its east. Moreover, it had always acted as the city's westernmost enclave only connected to the rest of Tripoli by two main roads on which traffic was heavily congested, which meant that traveling outside the neighborhood was time-consuming. These two elements reinforced the sense that social life in Mina was largely self-enclosed – everyone living in close proximity, seeing their neighbors and other residents very frequently and knowing them relatively well. And this instead turned local sectarian and social tensions into at times intensely personalized rivalries. In Mina there are countless anecdotes about how many "Islamists" were subalterns living in slums at the extremities of the port district, who had since the 1970s begun engaging in a locally oriented social and political revolt through criminal and revolutionary movements. In fact, their growing involvement in contentious politics was partially what fueled the wider sense that Mina had become an "unsafe" area.[76] These local subalterns now instrumentalized Islamism's rise to become empowered

---

[74] Interviews with former and current members of the Mina section of Tripoli's branch of the Lebanese Communist Party, Tripoli, July 2014.
[75] Kalyvas, *The logic of violence*, pp. 330–63.
[76] Interviews with residents of Mina, Tripoli, July–August 2014.

Holy War or Social Jihad? 339

and, when the time came, to engage in a "social jihad" against the wealthier Communist residents who notoriously despised them.

The story of how, through "militant Islamism," Abu Ahmad channeled years of a deeply personalized breed of social resentment against Mina's upper class is most emblematic.[77] Before joining Tawhid as a street leader he had entered into a rivalry with another man in Mina who, like him, was a young Sunni, lived across the block, yet hailed from a different social world. While Abu Ahmad was a typical subaltern who had long struggled with every aspect of life, his rival seemed to have it all. He came from a locally respected upper-class family and he was so "handsome, arrogant and reckless" that he soon acquired the nickname of the "Che Guevara of Mina" after he joined the local Communist branch in his twenties. Tellingly, he was known to be especially popular with the neighborhood's often secularized Sunni upper-class women, whom he used to drive around by the seaside with a beer in hand. He had status, then, in addition to wealth, and began behaving in increasingly arrogant ways, ridiculing the neighborhood's poorer and more conservative subaltern boys in nearby slums. Abu Ahmad was reportedly the one who "envied and hated the young Communist the most." He joined Hashem Minqara as a street leader in the local Tawhid faction in Mina and, when the battle of October 1983 against the Lebanese Communist Party was launched, he finally saw the opportunity he had long been waiting for – he fought as hard as he could and, when the Communists surrendered, he spotted his rival, took him away and led him to the beach, where other Tawhid militants were reportedly covering leftists with cement in metal barrels. Even then, he took his time before killing him, first ordering the young Communist to curse leftists and leftism but, as his rival spit at his face, he took his gun and shot him on the spot. In a show of how intensely intimate his violence had been, Abu Ahmad afterward went to the extent of rushing to Mina's hospital, where the sister-in-law of the young Communist was about to give birth to a boy, and threatening to kill her baby if she dared naming him after her brother-in-law. This chilling anecdote illustrates how the exactions of that battle, although they seemed driven by "religious violence," must be primarily understood not in religious or ideological, but rather in social terms. Older, simmering social antagonisms which sometimes translated in bitter personal rivalries, underpinned by the neighborhood's social structure and combined with the chance of settling scores, explained the sheer brutality of the battle.

---

[77] I draw this anecdote about Abu Ahmad from Mohammed Abi Samra's chapter on Tawhid in his well-researched book on Tripoli's recent history. See Abi Samra, *Trablus*, p. 183.

340   The Illusion of Religious Violence

Tellingly, Tawhid's impoverished fighters then seized the houses and flats of those they had killed before looting and selling them. They also took control of the port, turning some like Hashem Minqara in millionaires. Mina's battle therefore resembled a "social jihad" more than a holy war.

One last factor rendered the battle possible and explained its timing – geopolitics. Tripoli, as we see in Chapter 7, became in November 1983 the epicenter of a bloody struggle between the Palestinian guerrilla organization Fatah and the Syrian regime. While Fatah, Chapter 7 argues, had been a staunch supporter of Tawhid from day one, the Lebanese Communist Party had grown sympathetic toward the Assad regime following the Syrian–Soviet rapprochement of the early 1980s. A 1983 Russian statement according to which Moscow considered Damascus the "vanguard of the struggle against the American-Zionist plan"[78] had cemented the alliance between Lebanon's Communists and Syria. Pushing Tawhid to crack down on the Communists in Mina, "Lebanon's Stalingrad," or standing back and watching, crucially allowed Fatah to undermine Syria's allies in Tripoli.

There is still controversy in Tripoli over the exact nature of Fatah's involvement in the battle. A statement issued by the Communist Party at the time accused Yasser Arafat of having directly "supervised and encouraged the attacks and threats that targeted the local Communists."[79] These allegations were vehemently denied by Fatah officials themselves – at the time as well as today. "We had nothing to do with Tawhid's battle and with the massacre,"[80] stated a Palestinian representative in North Lebanon. Tawhid's leaders similarly explained that Fatah, far from ordering the battle, was allegedly against it. Hashem Minqara explained having had Yasser Arafat on the phone shortly before launching the fight and recalled that Fatah's leader had expressed his disapproval – albeit in measured ways. "But I had Sha'aban's green light so I took my own decision and went ahead nonetheless."[81] Tawhid's current head, the son of Sa'id Sha'aban, similarly dismissed allegations of Palestinian involvement in the movement's battle against the Communist Party. "Fatah was officially against the battle,"[82] he noted. Tawhid's main military commander in Mina also vehemently denied ever receiving logistical support from Fatah during the battle.[83]

---

[78] "Les soviétiques réaffirment leur appui à la Syrie," *L'Orient Le Jour* (February 7, 1983).
[79] "Le PC accuse le Fatah," *L'Orient Le Jour* (October 16, 1983).
[80] Interview with Abu Marwan (Fatah's representative in North Lebanon), Beddawi refugee camp, August 2014.
[81] Interview with Hashem Minqara (head of Tawhid's faction in Mina), September 2014.
[82] Interview with Bilal Sha'aban (leader of Tawhid), Tripoli, September 2014.
[83] Interview with Abu Meriam Khassouq (military commander of Minqara's faction in Mina), Tripoli, June 2014.

Yet, for all these denials, there is little doubt that while Yasser Arafat may not have ordered the battle he at least knew what was happening – and he did not try very hard to prevent it. One Palestinian intelligence figure who was close to him testified: "He was intensely opposed to the pro-Syrian camp and saw in this incident a way to send a message to Damascus. He did not ask for the battle but let's say that he did not mind it."[84] That Tawhid's fight against Mina's pro-Syrian Communists was unfolding precisely as Yasser Arafat's relations with Hafez al-Assad were deteriorating, to the extent that clashes between pro- and anti-Syrian Palestinian factions were erupting throughout Lebanon's Palestinian camps, probably pushed Fatah's head to temporize and let Tawhid emerge as the victor. Allegations that Arafat used the Mina battle to gain leverage over Syria were confirmed by a Communist official. He explained that Monzer Abu Ghazaleh, Fatah's number one military figure in North Lebanon, was on the ground trying to "broker a truce"[85] during the battle. "However, one of the conditions he set for the fighting to cease was that the Communist Party issues a statement distancing itself from the Syrian regime – but we couldn't do that!" In sum, while Fatah may not have pushed for the battle, it did not seek to restrain Tawhid either and the timing of the Islamist movement's crackdown on the Communists coincided with its interests.

The Fatah–Syria conflict also gave a free rein to the Tawhid militants in another, less intuitive way. In retrospect, sources on both the Islamist and the Communist sides suggest that the Syrian rulers, as if playing poker, raised the stakes further by allowing the massacre to happen. The Syrian army's contingent had withdrawn from Tripoli by then, but it still had 12,000 troops stationed in the rest of North Lebanon – it could have intervened if it had been ordered to. Furthermore, some Communists today allege that Syria plotted against them. The leftist commander who was fighting in Mina argued that "Damascus manipulated us!" He went on to explain:

Before Minqara cut off the telephone lines in Mina, we called the Communist Party national headquarters in Beirut to ask officials to send reinforcements to help us in Tripoli. However, as our comrades were approaching our city a few hours later, they were stopped at a Syrian checkpoint and they were not allowed to come through and rescue us – we were betrayed![86]

---

[84] Interview with a high-ranking Palestinian intelligence officer in Fatah, Beirut, August 2014.

[85] Interview with an official in the Tripolitan branch of the Lebanese Communist Party, Tripoli, July 2014.

[86] Interview with a former commander in the Mina section of the Lebanese Communist Party, Tripoli, July 2014.

342   The Illusion of Religious Violence

One Tawhid official concurred, in hindsight, that the massacre of Communists in Mina had played into the hands of Syria.[87]

The slaughter had two positive, if indirect, medium-term repercussions for Damascus. First, it tested Tawhid's cohesion at a time when the regime was gauging if and when to enter into a battle against the Islamists to "free" Tripoli and regain military control of the city. The movement's massacre of Communists witnessed the first cracks in its foundations. Khalil Akkawi's "neighborhood Islamists," tackled in Chapter 2, had embraced Marxism in the 1970s and had a history of operating alliances across class with wealthier leftists for the sake of their district, Bab al-Tebbaneh, and their instrumentalist embrace of Islamist ideology meant that they still entertained social ties with some of these leftist figures. This faction had agreed to Tawhid's crackdown on the Iraqi Ba'ath Party and the 24 October Movement but it had reservations about the battle against the Communists and vehemently opposed any exactions. In fact, when hearing that Hashem Minqara's fighters were in the midst of carrying out a massacre of local leftists in Mina, Khalil Akkawi's men had intervened and safely escorted a dozen Sunni and Christian Communists out of their reach.[88] "It signaled the beginning of our difference with the rest of the Tawhid leadership,"[89] recalled one of the "neighborhood Islamists" who was close to Akkawi. Far from homogeneously pushing for a crackdown on all of Tripoli's leftists, then, several tendencies coexisted among the Tawhid factions and the Mina massacre initiated divisions. This internal variation in behavior underlines the heterogeneity which characterized Tawhid.

Ironically, given the plot Syria had engaged in, the brutality of Tawhid's massacre also closed the ranks of the pro-Assad camp and strengthened the Soviet–Syrian alliance. Weeks after the battle, George Hawi, the leader of Lebanon's Communist Party, thus visited Moscow and was received by a Kremlin official who asked him to "reinforce relations with Damascus"[90] in order to better counter the "Islamist threat" against the "progressive" camp. Communist fighters from all over North Lebanon would subsequently prove key to defeating Tawhid during the battle the Syrian regime eventually launched in September 1985. Geopolitical considerations alone did not fuel the massacre – but they surely contributed to it.

---

[87] Interview with a Tawhid official, Tripoli, September 2014.
[88] Interview with current and former Tawhid officials, Tripoli, August 2014 and interviews with current and former members of the Tripolitan branch of the Lebanese Communist Party, August 2014.
[89] Interview with Bilal Matar (Khalil Akkawi's political adviser), Tripoli, August 2014.
[90] "Moscou opte pour Damas," *L'Orient Le Jour* (November 28, 1983).

Unsurprisingly, however, and despite the real importance of geopolitics and of local antagonisms such as a struggle for neighborhood primacy and dynamics of "social jihad," the "master narrative" of the battle against the Communists remained a "religious struggle." The "ideological entrepreneurs" were quick to portray Tawhid's bloody victory as a divine reward for those who had killed the "hypocrites" and as evidence of Islamism's momentum. Their polarizing rhetoric seems to have been absorbed by many. One member thus claimed that the defeat of the Communists had demonstrated that "Islam is the way," while another prided himself that "Allah is with us."[91] "We eliminated the left and only Islam remained"[92] stated, in retrospect, one of Tawhid's "ideological entrepreneurs" to justify the violence.

Yet the extent to which, despite the efforts of the "ideological entrepreneurs" to construct a "master narrative" of Islamism versus leftism, the battle against the Communists in Mina was more guided by older local conflicts than by ideology fully transpired when, hours after the massacre, the battle spilled over into other districts but was much less violent. In theory, had ideology been the battle's driving motivation the slaughter in the port district should have led to an equally violent crackdown on the Communists in the rest of Tripoli. This, however, would not be the case. Although the fight did spread to the vicinity of Square of the Star near the city center, it did not feature violence to the same extent or of the same nature. There the battle against the Communists was brief and considerably less bloody, and most importantly the Islamists allowed the leftists to leave their office and escape the city (see Figure 6.2).[93] Another fight then began between Tawhid and the vehemently secular and left-wing Syrian Social Nationalist Party near New Tripoli but, while it was violent, it was rapidly contained; its members were permitted to leave the party headquarters without being butchered like in Mina.[94] Once more, the Organization of the Communist Action, which featured a secular Marxist ideology but shared Tawhid's anti-governmental political orientation, remained unharmed.[95] Figure 6.3 illustrates how the

---

[91] "A Tripoli, le Sheikh Shaaban dispense la justice par téléphone," *L'Orient Le Jour* (October 20, 1983) .

[92] Interview with a Tawhid "ideological entrepreneur" close to Abu Imara, Tripoli, June 2014.

[93] Interviews with current and former members of the Tripolitan branch of the Lebanese Communist Party, Tripoli, August 2014 and interview with Tawhid members, July–August 2014.

[94] "Tripoli: les miliciens islamiques assiègent les permanences de la gauche," *L'Orient Le Jour* (October 14, 1983) and "Tripoli: accord entre le Mouvement de l'Unification Islamique et le Parti Social Nationaliste Syrien," *L'Orient Le Jour* (October 15, 1983).

[95] Interview with Ahmed al-Amin (Organization for the Communist Action in Lebanon official), Ehden, June 2014 and interview with Gabi Sur'ur (Organization for the Communist Action in Lebanon member), Tripoli, July 2014.

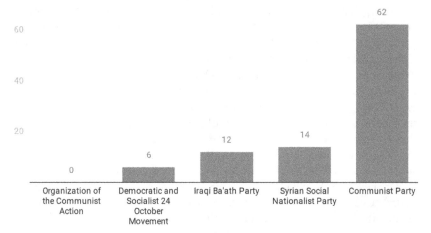

Figure 6.3 Organizational variation in Tawhid's anti-leftist violence
Note: This graph reflects the overall known death toll of Tawhid's campaign against Tripoli's leftist movements in August–October 1983.
Source: *L'Orient Le Jour, Al-Safir*

Islamist crackdown on Tripoli's leftist movements featured significant variation in its nature and extent.

The organizational and spatial variation in Tawhid's anti-leftist violence in mid-1983 casts doubt over the analytical utility of "religious violence" as a separate subcategory of political violence homogeneously driven by religion or ideology. Instead, when deconstructing "master narratives" of the battles and examining variations in Tawhid's behavior, it transpires that not one but many factors lay behind the conflicts. One of these factors was ideology. It mattered through the "ideological entrepreneurship" of some Tawhid cadres, who lobbied the leaders to undertake a crackdown on Tripoli's leftists and mobilized a radical ideological discourse that galvanized members and provoked rivals. But I also find that several other variables also affected Tawhid's decision to engage in violence and shaped the timing, extent and nature of its battles. These included considerations of a primarily political, strategic, geopolitical and social nature – and sometimes these factors had a greater causal weight on Tawhid's exercise of violence than ideology.

Variation in Tawhid's Anti-Christian Acts

Tawhid's crackdown on most of Tripoli's leftist movements in August–October 1983 paved the way for the Islamist group's nearly complete

Variation in Tawhid's Anti-Christian Acts

345

military control of the city. Only the small, gated Alawi hilltop of Jabal Mohsen, where some Syrian troops and a local pro-Assad militia were based, remained out of its hands. And, apart from two more battles, one between Syria and Fatah in November 1983 and another one building on the neighborhood rivalry between Bab al-Tebbaneh and Jabal Mohsen in July–August 1984, which are tackled in Chapters 7 and 8, Tripoli stopped witnessing large-scale violence until September 1985. "Unless Syria intervenes, no one is any longer in a position to challenge Tawhid's supremacy over the city,"[96] summed up a journalist. Yet, although by mid to late 1983 the movement had eliminated most of its ideological enemies in Tripoli, a degree of low-level violence continued gripping the city. While there might be, at first, a temptation to view this residual violence as epitomizing the sectarianism typical of militant Islamism, given that it targeted Tripoli's Christian presence, spatial variation in Tawhid's anti-Christian acts suggests that there had to be other factors beyond ideology which also fueled this tension.

Physical and symbolic sectarian violence during Tawhid's rule was certainly palpable enough that Tripoli's Christians, estimated at 20 percent of the population in the 1970s, dropped to 5–10 percent a decade later, some leaving out of "fear"[97] for their lives. Tawhid did not engage in acts of sectarian cleansing. But some of its anti-Christian acts of violence and mounting allegations in the Lebanese media that it stood behind a series of bomb attacks which targeted four Tripolitan churches in January 1985 may have pushed local Christians to leave Tripoli.[98]

Yet a preliminary note of caution on Tawhid's anti-Christian violence is in order. While Tawhid did engage in intimidation and occasional violence against Tripoli's Christians, some of the attacks against the city's churches that took place in January 1985 were fomented by the Syrian regime which, as an informed observer remarked, used to "frequently take advantage of Lebanon's sectarian politics to advance its own goals."[99] It was perhaps no coincidence that the Syrian intelligence branch in North Lebanon was led by Mohammed Sha'ar, an officer

---

[96] "Tension toujours vive à Tripoli," *L'Orient Le Jour* (October 19, 1983).

[97] Interview with Christian residents and former residents of Tripoli, July–August 2014. I draw estimates of Tripoli's Christian population from Gary C. Gambill, "Islamist groups in Lebanon," chapter 8 in Barry Rubin (ed.), *Lebanon: liberation, conflict and crisis* (New York: Palgrave Macmillan, 2009), p. 138.

[98] "Attentats contre trois églises à Tripoli," *L'Orient Le Jour* (January 9, 1985); "Les attentats contre les institutions chrétiennes se poursuivent à Tripoli," *L'Orient Le Jour* (January 10, 1985).

[99] US Central Intelligence Agency, "Lebanon: confessionalism – a potent force" (Confidential, NESA 82-10438, August 1982). It is also worth pointing out that Tawhid clearly condemned these incidents, its leader Sa'id Sha'aban even stating that

346   The Illusion of Religious Violence

who, before he took up that position and later even became Bashar al-Assad's interior minister, had served in religiously mixed areas such as Tartus, Homs and Aleppo, and was known to be skilled at using local sectarian antagonisms to benefit the Syrian regime. One figure who knew him well and had long worked on behalf of Syrian intelligence agencies in Tripoli confirmed that Damascus was engaged in disinformation operations to destabilize Tawhid. He gave the example of the bombing of Tripoli's Saint George cathedral located on Street of the Churches (*Sher'a al-Kana'es*) on January 9, 1985. "The man who set up the explosive device was anyone but an Islamist – his name was Kosti Azar and he was a Christian who worked as an agent for Fatah al-Intifada," a pro-Syrian split of the Palestinian organization Fatah, "and who was asked to create problems for Tawhid."[100] This strategy was successful as some of the Christians who began "fearing" for their lives mentioned the bombing of that cathedral as evidence of Tawhid's "anti-Christian" violence. A Christian noted in hindsight that "Syrian intelligence exploited us."[101]

There is no doubt that Tawhid did engage in symbolic and physical violence against local Christians. But, had religious and ideological considerations alone driven that violence, it would have targeted all of the Christians present in Tripoli in similar ways. Yet the bulk of Tawhid's anti-Christian violence once again notably centered on Mina. Accounts from 1983–5 as well as interviews indeed suggest that it was there, more than anywhere else in Tripoli, that Tawhid acted in especially bothersome ways against Christians. Militants desecrated and looted some of the neighborhood's seven churches, prevented bells from ringing for religious occasions, enforced a strict ban on eating food in public during Ramadan, prohibited the sale of alcohol, although in Mina many Christians used to make and sell their own *araq*, a local spirit, and forced Christian shops to close during Friday prayers.[102] There, physical violence also targeted local Christians more than in the rest of the city. One Christian woman in the neighborhood reported having been insulted and beaten because, at one point during Ramadan, Tawhid militants stopped

---

the attacks against Tripoli's churches were "shameful" and that "those behind the explosions have sold their soul to the devil" – "we consider them criminal and we will not let this happen again." See "Bayan min al-Sheikh Sa'id Sha'aban b'ad hadeth kanisat Trablus al-Maruniya" ["Statement of the cleric Sa'id Sha'aban after the incident of Tripoli's Maronite church"], *Al-Incha* (May 27, 1985).

[100] Interview with a source close to Syrian intelligence networks in Tripoli, July 2014.
[101] Interview with a Christian resident, Tripoli, August 2014.
[102] Interviews with Christian residents of the Mina neighborhood, Tripoli, July–August 2014.

her at a checkpoint and smelled her breath to ensure she had not been eating, before they realized she had been tasting apricots in a nearby cart as she bought fruits.[103] Some of the Christian shops that sold alcohol or did not respect the Friday closure were set on fire. And anecdotes abound about how some Christians were kidnapped for ransoms while others were found in the dumps of the port area with a bullet in their head, sometimes with evidence of torture.[104] Yet while, in Mina, Tawhid thus seemed bent on "terrorizing"[105] local Christians, their coreligionists who resided elsewhere in Tripoli did not report being as bothered or feeling as threatened by militants.[106]

Three possible factors can account for this spatial variation in Tawhid's sectarian violence. The first may be that, because the Christian presence was more substantial in Mina than in other Tripolitan neighborhoods, it was always bound to trigger a Sunni Islamist reaction. But this leaves unexplained the puzzle of why other heavily Christian parts of Tripoli, such as Street of the Churches, and even actual Tawhid strongholds featuring smaller Christian minorities, like the neighborhoods of Qobbe or Zehriye, in the vicinity of the Old City, witnessed comparatively very few acts of sectarian violence, physical or symbolic.

The second possible factor for the prevalence of anti-Christian acts in Mina could be that Hashem Minqara, who headed the local Tawhid faction, was initially close to the "ideological entrepreneurs" and held "Sufi jihadi" views radically hostile to Christianity. Minqara in fact used to circulate in "his" neighborhood on a white horse, a symbol of divinity, while holding a sword; something which frightened local Christians as he was known to despise them and to engage in diatribes lambasting the key tenets of Christian faith. An interview with him provided a glimpse into his views on Christianity. He first expressed his alleged "respect" for that religion, but soon noted that it was composed of "several categories" and he unambiguously stated his profound dislike for "those who think that there are three Gods on Earth – God, Jesus and the Holy Spirit." "Jesus is a messenger of God and nothing more," he maintained, "God is one and alone."[107] Minqara's ideas may be formulated peacefully now that he has lost all power, but at the time they scared Christians given his reputation

---

[103] Abi Samra, *Trablus*, pp. 181–2.
[104] Interviews with Christian residents of the Mina neighborhood, Tripoli, July–August 2014.
[105] Abi Samra, *Trablus*, p. 145.
[106] Interview with Christian residents in the districts of New Tripoli, Qobbe and Zehriye, Tripoli, August 2014.
[107] Interview with Hashem Minqara (Tawhid's Emir in Mina), September 2014.

348   The Illusion of Religious Violence

as the bloodthirsty Emir of Mina. One teacher at the Mar Elias school, a private local Christian educational institute, recalled that "fear" spread among the students after Hashem Minqara invited himself to give a lecture on religion. "His militants forced us into a room and he started telling us about faith. He had a very offensive discourse toward Christianity, equating it with polytheism, and was trying to show us that Islam is the way."[108]

Once more, however, while Minqara's views might have inspired some of his followers to take action, it does not explain why anti-Christian acts overwhelmingly focused on Mina. Far from being specific to Minqara, this sectarian discourse was espoused by other Tawhid leaders and members in Tripoli, but without being translated in violence elsewhere. Sa'id Sha'aban himself used to give speeches throughout Tripoli to assert that "we contradict Christians when they say that Jesus is the son of God as we believe that God does not have a family, Jesus is a prophet of God and that's it!"[109] And yet, despite this, the bulk of Tawhid's anti-Christian violence still seemed to disproportionately focus on Mina.

The third possible factor behind spatial variation in Tawhid's anti-Christian behavior, and which I find probably accounts for this puzzle, is that in Mina this violence was underpinned by older social and sectarian antagonisms. That local Christians dominated the district's power structures pushed Hashem Minqara's men to behave more violently there. For many Tawhid members in the port area who were in majority "subaltern Islamists," then, this was a continuation of their "social jihad" and local struggle for neighborhood primacy.

Tripoli had long been a model of peaceful Christian–Muslim relations, and the district of Mina especially was known as a beacon of coexistence before the 1975 civil war. There the indigenous inhabitants of the port neighborhood liked to see themselves as distinct from the rest of Tripoli, "more open" than the city's other inhabitants. "We respected our neighbors,"[110] recalled a Greek Orthodox Christian resident, adding: "my Muslim friends would attend Easter mass with me and I would break the fast of Ramadan with them – religious coexistence was our identity." Yet the massive wave of rural migration throughout the 1970s changed this to a degree. To begin with, it brought in new populations who were originally from those parts of the Tripolitan Sunni countryside where

---

[108] Interview with a teacher at Mina's Christian high school of Mar Elias, Tripoli, August 2014.

[109] "Ziyarat al-Sheikh Sa'id Sha'aban li-madrasa masihiya fi Trablus" ["Visit of the cleric Sa'id Sha'aban in a Christian school in Tripoli"], *Al-Incha* (April 15, 1985).

[110] Interviews with a Christian resident of the Mina district, Tripoli, July 2014.

Christians were very few, like the rural areas of Dinniye and Akkar. This not only meant that they were unfamiliar with Mina's history and the importance of "coexistence" in local identity, but that many of them were also largely unused to interacting with Christian minorities in everyday life.

The economic downturn of the 1970s worsened the difficult situation of these new Sunni residents who, impoverished and now relegated to slums at the extremities of the district, faced severe challenges trying to become integral parts of its local social fabric. Crucially, this subaltern part of Mina's population rapidly grew, due to continued rural migration and to higher fertility rates than other local Muslims and than local Christians. While in the 1960s Mina's population was split roughly equally between Sunni Muslims and Christians, by the 1980s the former had come to make up over two-thirds of the residents.[111] Yet this demographic transformation was not followed by equivalent socio-political change. Despite a declining population, local Christians could still count on controlling nearly half of the seats at Mina's city council, in addition to the post of deputy head of the municipality. Moreover, socially and culturally they continued to dominate the district. Mina's Christians often belonged to the middle and upper middle classes, were well educated and enjoyed a progressive lifestyle – one of their main hubs, Mina's old quarter, featured restaurants, cafes and shops which, before Tawhid's advent, used to sell ham and alcohol.

But the most emblematic example of continued Christian socio-cultural domination over Mina is the crucial importance played by Christian high schools in the neighborhood – and, revealingly, these local educational institutions would become a key target of Tawhid. In Mina there were seven private Christian schools, which was significant for it made up a striking half of the neighborhood's total number of high schools, the rest being public. These Christian schools were not just numerous, they were also highly reputed and they reflected the cultural, social and political preferences of the neighborhood's local Christian population. They were among the very best in Tripoli, taught in French and English and, while they were explicitly Christian or secular in character, like the *College National Orthdodoxe* or the *Mission Laïque*, they still attracted some Muslims who aspired to a quality education at a time when public schools had a bad reputation and private Muslim schools were few.[112] By the 1980s Muslims had already come to make

---

[111] Interview with Abdel Qader Alameddine (Mayor of Mina), Tripoli, July 2014.
[112] Maha Kayal, *Le système socio-vestimentaire à Tripoli (Liban) entre 1885 et 1985* (Neuchâtel: University of Neuchâtel unpublished PhD thesis, 1989), pp. 180–1.

350   The Illusion of Religious Violence

up the majority of the student body of these private Christian schools –
and, in a sign of where Mina's demographic dynamics were headed,
thirty years later Christians would merely represent one-tenth of the
students.[113] The Muslim students who wished to attend these private
high schools could not benefit from scholarship schemes reserved for
Christians and therefore had to pay high fees. This meant that most of
those who were educated in such schools hailed from the local Sunni
upper class. In other words, these private schools not only epitomized
Christian socio-cultural domination but also symbolized the symbiosis
between Mina's Sunni upper class and local Christians.

It is in this context that the symbolic violence exercised by Tawhid
against Mina's Christian high schools may be understood. "Tawhid
really bothered these schools,"[114] one of the movement's officials in
Mina acknowledged in hindsight. It did not order the closure of any of
them. But, reflecting how these local Christian schools had become a
factor in the simmering struggle for neighborhood primacy, the movement developed a discourse that targeted them harshly, and for a while it
even came to implement Islamic precepts on them. Local Tawhid officials harshly lambasted these Christian schools as "foreign" entities
plotting to carry out a "cultural invasion" and threatening them with
"severe punishments" if their teachers did not follow "the precepts of the
Quran."[115] In a twist of history, its Sunni members, who hailed from the
slums of Mina, began imposing Islamist norms in classrooms through the
"force of weapons,"[116] such as gender segregation, even introducing
Islamic education in these schools although its pupils were secular elite
Muslim and Christian kids.

Tellingly, beyond Christian schools much of Tawhid's anti-Christian
violence in Mina targeted local symbols of religious "coexistence." To
Tawhid members this concept may have been infused with social meaning given how it tended to boil down to interactions between upper-class
Sunnis and Christians in Mina's private schools, restaurants or businesses. Their willingness to assert the "Islamic" identity of Mina thus
represented as much a rejection of Christian socio-political and cultural
domination over the district as it became a way to undermine a Sunni

---

[113] Interview with the directors of two Christian schools (one secular and one religious) in
Mina, Tripoli, June 2014.
[114] Interview with Ibrahim Saleh (Tawhid cleric and a movement official from Mina),
Tripoli, August 2014.
[115] "Shaaban: 'le musulman ne peut être gouverné par un non-croyant'," *L'Orient Le Jour*
(December 1, 1984) and "Sha'aban: saper les bases de l'Etat maronite phalangiste
même si tout s'effondre avec lui," *L'Orient Le Jour* (March 9, 1985).
[116] Interview with a member of Tawhid from Mina, Tripoli, June 2014.

elite which seemed more comfortable with local Christians than with its coreligionists who had migrated to the area but without being fully integrated in its fabric. This became obvious when the local Tawhid faction in Mina explicitly targeted symbols of the neighborhood's identity which they linked to this socially loaded view of "coexistence."

Again epitomizing the importance of notions of space, and this time of "struggle for the neighborhood" rather than "for the city," as in Chapter 5, local Tawhid members gathered on one of Mina's main squares and smashed a large statue that had been built by the local municipality in honor of Ya'aqub Labban, one of the district's major notables who had been an interfaith activist some decades earlier. In its place they erected a large sign of the word God mirroring what the movement had done in Tripoli's city center, which they placed at a highly visible crossroads right at the entrance of the district.[117] The militants painted the sign in green, the color of Islam, placed it on five Roman columns, a reminder of the five pillars of Muslim faith, and surrounded it with the black flags of Tawhid. This was an overt attempt at transforming the identity and power structures of a religiously diverse local society, one dominated by upper-class Sunnis and Christians, and at turning it into an "Islamic" area now ruled by force by those Muslim subalterns who had long been relegated to its margins. Hashem Minqara who, with his faction, stood behind all these developments in Mina, justified in retrospect Tawhid's actions in the neighborhood by proudly arguing that it gave rise to a "new social order" which, allegedly, had "ensured respect for Islam."[118] This showed again how behind the strength of Tawhid in Mina lay dynamics of "social jihad."

The Spread of Islamo-Gangsterism

The "ideological entrepreneurs" may have lobbied for Tawhid's violence against Tripoli's leftists and Christians and exerted some influence on the dynamics of conflict, but the sense that the movement's behavior was driven by "religious violence" remained an illusion. The extent to which Tawhid's exercise of violence featured spatial, organizational and temporal variation indicated that other factors mattered, for example a clash over political orientation, strategic imperatives, geopolitics, dynamics of "social jihad" and myriad local antagonisms. Yet the most striking demonstration that, for all the efforts of the "ideological entrepreneurs,"

---

[117] Interview with Ibrahim Saleh (Tawhid cleric and a movement official from Mina), Tripoli, August 2014.

[118] Interview with Hashem Minqara (Tawhid's Emir in Mina), September 2014.

352   The Illusion of Religious Violence

Tawhid's engagement in "religious violence" was an illusion emerged from late 1984 until mid-1985 as it began engaging more clearly in what I call "Islamo-gangsterism" – its involvement in criminal practices prioritizing economic gain over ideological consistency. This showed how wide the movement's "spectrum of ideological commitment" was turning. And the fact that its engagement in blatantly un-Islamic activities focused in large parts on Mina, where most of the seemingly "religious violence" had taken place, confirmed that many Tawhid members in the port district had always viewed ideology instrumentally.

The development of "Islamo-gangsterism" in Tawhid takes its roots from the growth of "subaltern Islamism," a trend which I described at length in Chapter 5. As part of this phenomenon, a substantial number of urban poor had joined the Islamist movement, often with a background in revolutionary but also in criminal groups that engaged in contentious activities. While some had been attracted by the prospect of waging a "social jihad" which would act as a conduit for their locally oriented social and political revolt, others were attracted by Tawhid's willingness to channel subaltern practices, among them petty criminality. This might seem counterintuitive, but there was no necessary inconsistency at first between, on the one hand, the movement's Islamist ideology and, on the other, engagement in petty crime. Tawhid had initially been successful in blending the two well, from its rejection of the legitimacy of governmental authority and blessing of urban violence to its imposition of "religious" taxes on businesses and the wealthy and its glorification of protest masculinity.

But with time a number of contradictions emerged. There were several reasons for this. One factor was that, by late 1984, the ability of the "ideological entrepreneurs" to affect Tawhid's behavior and steer it in an ideological direction had largely declined, due to the fact that several of them were murdered after pushing the movement too close to Iran for the taste of some members, as Chapter 7 discusses. Another factor was that by then the commitment of some of Tawhid's leaders had begun to erode as well. These two factors lessened the ideological commitment of many members and empowered factions less driven by ideology, chief among them the "subaltern Islamists." Yet the trigger which led Tawhid to get involved in criminal practices to the extent that it started prioritizing economic gains over ideological consistency was its takeover of Tripoli's port in Mina. There, many "subaltern Islamists" began to engage in much more lucrative activities than before. This caught the attention of the city's most infamous gangsters, a handful of whom joined the movement as a faction. Although they were only a few dozen of these new members they rapidly grew to be influential. By 1985, what was

The Spread of Islamo-Gangsterism 353

increasingly lying behind Tawhid's "master narrative" of "religious violence" was no longer just a "social jihad" but also "Islamo-gangsterism" – the movement's behavior had been steered in a direction at odds with its professed ideology.

Tawhid's bloody victory against the Communists in Mina had paved the way for its complete control over the area in 1983 and Hashem Minqara recalled ordering its hundreds of local fighters to "continue holding weapons and take over the port of Tripoli."[119] Initially, controlling the port of Lebanon's second city seemed like a golden opportunity for the movement. It appeared to be an uncontroversial way to increase its resources at a low cost, which in turn allowed it to buy more weapons and cement its control over Tripoli. With all the money Tawhid made it also opened a radio and TV station, and was even able to engage in charity on a significant scale. The period immediately following its takeover of the port was marked by its attempt at win hearts and minds in Tripoli by spending $150,000 on the inauguration of an orphanage and several clinics and the distribution of food to the poor.[120]

If the harbor of Tripoli became the main source of Tawhid's revenues between 1983 and 1985, it was because it was the only port which was sufficiently well equipped to receive international shipping on the entire stretch of the Lebanese–Syrian coastline. This drew the interest of shipping companies ready to pay Tawhid hefty amounts to operate from there. While, to Tripoli's north, the Syrian ports of Tartus and Latakia did not yet have the infrastructure required for regional and global trade, Sidon, to its south, was under Israeli occupation. Beirut's port, for its part, had long been a key hub for transnational shipping into the Middle East, but by then it faced its own challenges. Fighting between East and West Beirut had damaged its installations and rampant insecurity meant that it had to stop functioning for long periods – on one occasion it ceased operations for a full five months. When the situation became safer, the government unveiled an ambitious plan to renovate its infrastructure, but the costs involved soon doubled. The authorities then attempted to balance their plummeting revenues by increasing taxes on shipping containers, which represented 75 percent of Beirut's maritime activities, yet this was to deliver a nearly fatal blow to the port. By 1983, taxes on imports and exports in the Beirut harbor had risen to the extent

---

[119] Interview with Hashem Minqara (Tawhid's Emir in Mina), September 2014.
[120] "Mu'tamar Jabhat al-Inqaz al-Islami fi Trablus: aktar min milioun lira lubnaniya enfaqat 'ala al-'amal al-kheiriya 'am 1984" ["Conference of the Islamic Salvation Front in Tripoli: more than a million Lebanese Pounds spent on charity work in 1984"], *Al-Incha* (August 18, 1984).

354   The Illusion of Religious Violence

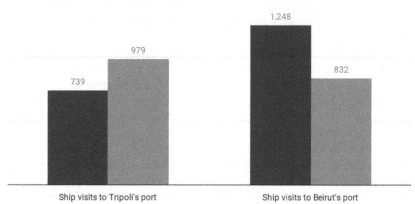

Figure 6.4 Sudden increase in Tripoli's port activities in 1984–5. Source: CIA, *L'Orient Le Jour* and interviews with a high-ranking source in Tripoli's port

that they were now 105 percent higher than the average global price, leading shipowners to complain that Beirut had turned into "the most expensive port in the world."[121] While the port of the capital had received up to 2,732 ships in 1980, the figure had dropped to 1,911 in 1982 and to as low as 1,248 in 1984.[122] These official figures could even have been artificially bolstered, for one Western intelligence assessment carried out in 1983 found Beirut's port "nearly empty."[123]

Tawhid greatly benefited from this situation. Despite its militant ideology it had much to offer shipowners. Its control of Tripoli provided relative stability in 1983–5. Given the challenges faced by Beirut's harbor, Lebanese businessmen of all religious, regional and political backgrounds began to transit merchandize through the northern port (Figure 6.4).[124] They had to pay Tawhid but this was still cheaper – and safer – than going through the capital. The port of Tripoli rapidly became "congested with ships trying to evade Lebanese customs duties."[125] A figure who was involved in facilitating Tawhid's trade

[121] "Numéro spécial maritime: le port de Beyrouth," *L'Orient Le Jour* (October 20, 1983).
[122] "Numéro special: pas de modernisation, pas de réhabilitation," *L'Orient Le Jour* (April 19, 1985).
[123] US Central Intelligence Agency, "Lebanon: decaying infrastructure" (Secret, NESA 83-10306, November 1983).
[124] Interview with a former high-ranking official in the port of Tripoli, June 2014.
[125] US Central Intelligence Agency, "Lebanon: decaying infrastructure" (Secret, NESA 83-10306, November 1983).

The Spread of Islamo-Gangsterism   355

activities recounted the way financial transactions took place. "The port of Tripoli quickly turned very busy," he observed. "We unloaded seven cargo ships a day with a queue going up to 15 boats waiting at sea." There was, he recalled, an average of 300 shipping containers per boat, and he was asked by Tawhid to tax each crate up to $5,000 before splitting the revenues between the wages of the workers and the "commissions" taken by the Islamists. He recounted meeting Hashem Minqara, in particular, on a nearly daily basis to provide accounts and hand over the money. "I used to hand him an average of $300,000 per week,"[126] he said. This was confirmed by the Emir of Mina who acknowledged having earned over $1 million a month for two years from the "religious taxes" that he imposed on ships in the port.[127]

Of course, for the sake of outside appearances Tawhid framed its control over the port by using religious and ideological arguments. To justify its imposition of taxes on the ships it lambasted the illegitimacy of governmental control, which it called the "Crusader legality," and it also grandly promised the advent of an "Islamic economy"[128] in the port. Yet the political economy of the "Islamic Emirate" ended up less *hallal* than officially certified. While Tawhid's control over the port brought massive revenues thanks to which it was able to buy weapons and engage in charity, it empowered its less ideologically committed members and pushed them to maximize profits – even at the cost of ideological consistency. The spread of "Islamo-gangsterism" in Tawhid would widen Tawhid's "spectrum of ideological commitment" even further, undermining the "ideological entrepreneurs" and steering the movement in a less ideological direction, eventually fragmenting it from within.

One of the first signs of Tawhid's "Islamo-gangsterism," as the prioritization by Tawhid of economic gain over ideological consistency, came in 1984 when the port district of Mina witnessed a counterintuitive alliance struck between Hashem Minqara, the Tawhid Emir who had been responsible for much of the seemingly "religious violence" against the Communists and Christians, and Anistaz Kouchari, one of Tripoli's most notorious gang leaders. In a show of the flagrant contradictions "Islamo-gangsterism" was beginning to give rise to, Kouchari was known as the "Christian Mafioso"[129] of Mina whose gang was involved in smuggling. He had become a prominent figure in the Tripolitan

---

[126] Interview with a former high-ranking official in the port of Tripoli, June 2014.
[127] Interview with Hashem Minqara (Tawhid's Emir in Mina), September 2014.
[128] "Iqtisad Trablus ila ayn?" ["The Tripolitan economy, where to?"], *al-Tawhid* (June 20, 1984).
[129] Interview with residents of Mina and of other neighborhoods, Tripoli, July–August 2014.

356   The Illusion of Religious Violence

underworld after befriending Sleiman Franjieh, a pro-Syria ex-Lebanese president from nearby Zghorta, who took him under his wing and whom Kouchari, harboring political ambitions, treated as a "spiritual father."[130] Their nascent "friendship," which may have also included illegal business deals, opened the doors of influential Syrian intelligence networks in North Lebanon to Kouchari. He became close to Ali Eid, the leader of Tripoli's Alawis and another figure of the local underworld, and to Syrian officers such as Mohammed Sha'ar, Ghazi Kan'an and others. "It was then that I made a deal with Tawhid," he recounted, elaborating: "I would do public relations on behalf of the movement and, in exchange, receive generous commissions."[131] Kouchari did not specify what exactly he meant by "public relations" operations. But a figure who knew him well suggested that he became involved in brokering deals between Tawhid and rogue Syrian officers involved in smuggling in 1984. In the mid-1980s a staggering half of all Syrian imports, particularly luxury items, were transiting illegally through Lebanon, and Tripoli thus came to act as "an important entry point for smuggled Syrian imports."[132] At first Kouchari was just a middleman. But after brokering several lucrative deals and earning the trust of the Islamist leaders, his gang of smugglers ultimately joined Tawhid as a faction and, in a show of the fast-growing importance it soon took through the revenues it was generating, Kouchari joined the movement's leadership. Although Kouchari insists that this did not mean that he converted to Islam, Tawhid sources recalled seeing him frequently attending Friday prayers and socializing with its leaders.[133] Even Minqara recognized his importance, acknowledging that Kouchari had been "close"[134] to him. That a movement which had implemented an "Islamic Emirate," engaged in anti-Christian acts and fought Syrian troops was, just to maximize its gains, now welcoming within its midst a man known as Tripoli's

---

[130] "A. Kouchari: the NYM, a national, non-confessional movement," *Monday Morning* (November 3, 1990).

[131] Interview with Anistaz Kouchari (Tripolitan Christian gangster close to Tawhid), September 2014.

[132] US Central Intelligence Agency, "Lebanon's ports: gateways for instability and terrorism" (Secret, G1 87-10013, February 1987).

[133] Interviews with several current and former Tawhid officials, Tripoli, July–August 2014. Note that Kouchari does not deny having headed a Tawhid faction and joined the movement's leadership for some time in late 1984 and early 1985; but justifies this by arguing that he wanted to "protect the Christians" of the port district of Mina and specifically refutes the allegation that he converted to Islam back then. Interview with Anistaz Kouchari (Tripolitan Christian gangster close to Tawhid), September 2014.

[134] Interestingly, Minqara justifies the deal he struck with Kouchari in very pragmatic, non-ideological ways, explaining that it had been a mere "business relationship." Interview with Hashem Minqara (Tawhid's Emir in Mina), September 2014.

The Spread of Islamo-Gangsterism 357

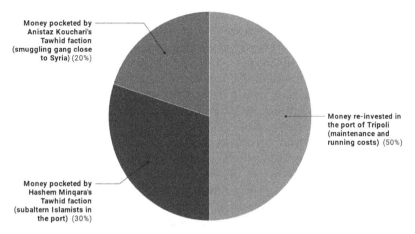

Figure 6.5 "Islamo-gangsterism": economic gains vs. ideological consistency.
Source: Interviews with Anistaz Kouchari, Hashem Minqara and a high-ranking source in the port of Tripoli

"Christian Mafioso" and as a stooge for Syrian intelligence showed the inconsistencies "Islamo-gangsterism" was beginning to give rise to – and how wide Tawhid's "spectrum of ideological commitment" was fast becoming (Figure 6.5).

Another shocking aspect of this rampant "Islamo-gangsterism," beyond Tawhid's integration of a gang as one of its factions, was the movement's readiness to actively engage in criminal activities which blatantly contradicted its ideology and attracted attention. Indeed, there is evidence to suggest that, while Tawhid had initially succeeded in blending elements of Islamism and petty crime, from late 1984 until mid-1985 it was practices typical of transnational organized crime which some of its factions and leaders started to engage in. The port neighborhood of Mina again emerged as the one space where these criminal activities took place, one Western intelligence assessment even claiming that it had turned into a regional hub for the "black market," the "export of narcotics" and "arms smuggling."[135] Of course, Tawhid's involvement in such controversial activities is hard to prove and it remains difficult, decades later, to discern myth from reality. Needless to say, movement leaders were back then as well as today adamant that none of this ever happened.[136]

---

[135] US Central Intelligence Agency, "Lebanon's ports: gateways for instability and terrorism" (Secret, G1 87–10013, February 1987).
[136] Interviews with current and former Tawhid leaders, Tripoli, July–August 2014.

358   The Illusion of Religious Violence

But the example of Tawhid's dealings with Akak Lines suggests that many members and some leaders may have blessed these transactions, even if they did not actively engage in them. Akak Lines was a shipping company owned by a Christian Maronite businessman from Mount Lebanon which was said to be involved in an international whiskey trafficking ring and, like others back then, had relocated parts of its activities away from Beirut to Tripoli. A figure close to the company recounted that Tawhid members discovered the alcohol in the first shipment and destroyed it publicly, but that in the subsequent ones the boats stopped in Cyprus where the whiskey label was replaced by a fake olive oil label.[137] Movement officials claim they were unaware of the gambit but a high-ranking source in the port of Tripoli doubted that it could ever have happened without a green light from some Tawhid leaders.[138] This was especially the case as the scale of that business was massive. Within the space of a year, Akak Lines unloaded 871 containers, most of them presumably in the port of Tripoli. These operations seem to have been profitable for Akak Lines and its "business partner," Tawhid, for the shipping company had by early 1985 become Lebanon's third wealthiest.[139]

Other anecdotes abound to suggest that, more than knowing about criminal practices that contradicted its ideology and merely allowing them to take place, Tawhid may have in fact directly engaged in some of them. One of its commanders, or lesser Emirs, Mahmud al-Aswad, was said to be involved in a drug and cigarettes trafficking ring in the port of Tripoli. This was done discreetly given that Tawhid was officially against practices such as smoking cigarettes and hashish.[140] But al-Aswad clearly benefited from important allies in Tawhid's leadership. When Lebanese customs stopped a boat that was suspected of transporting his illegal goods as it was leaving the city, Hashem Minqara, the Emir of Mina, ordered his men to take hostage the handful of customs officials who were present in the port of Tripoli, before eventually releasing them a few hours later as the ship had been allowed to depart.[141] Although it is difficult to ascertain what merchandize that boat contained, the media had days earlier reported that customs had searched a similar ship after it left the port of Tripoli and that they found over two tons of hashish

---

[137] Interview with a businessman close to Akak Lines, September 2014.
[138] Interview with a former high-ranking official in the port of Tripoli, June 2014.
[139] These figures are available in: "Numéro spécial: pas de modernisation, pas de réhabilitation," *L'Orient Le Jour* (April 19, 1985).
[140] See, for instance, "Al-mukhaddarat: zahira fattaka fi al-mujtam'a al-mu'asir" ["Drugs: a destructive phenomenon in the modern society"], *al-Tawhid* (August 2, 1984).
[141] "Episode rocambolesque au port de Tripoli," *L'Orient Le Jour* (November 21, 1984).

The Spread of Islamo-Gangsterism 359

bound for the Egyptian port of Alexandria.[142] An investigation by the CIA confirmed that Tawhid had "used the port to smuggle narcotics."[143] "Tawhid did not make a fortune out of selling Qurans!"[144] quipped a resident of Tripoli.

Anecdotes like these abound and suggest that by early to mid-1985 the spread of "Islamo-gangsterism" had become such that a growing number of members and even some leaders were using Tawhid to maximize their interests even at the detriment of its ideology. In hindsight, Tawhid officials themselves acknowledge that this period was marked by the "infiltration of criminals" and the "spread of corrupt practices"[145] in the movement. In a telling instance of the self-serving designs that Tawhid increasingly seemed to serve, Hashem Minqara, who had by then personally amassed massive revenues from his control over the port and business deals, rewarded two of his lesser Emirs or street leaders in Mina with "millions"[146] of dollars each. But while the first, Abu Heitham, pocketed the money before emigrating to Australia and living a comfortable life abroad, the second, a smuggler called Abu Fadi, was soon found shot in a flat he rented in secret in a nearby Christian town which had turned into what an observer called a "debauchery house,"[147] without elaborating further.

At times Islamist ideology was also invoked as a cover to engage in criminal violence. Calling rival gangsters "hypocrites" or "apostates" to justify their killing or issuing religious rulings (*fatwas*) to legitimize stealing became common Tawhid practices in 1985. The movement's engagement in this kind of criminal behavior became especially prevalent in Mina. The southwestern vicinity of the port neighborhood, a wasteland close to the beach, was notoriously transformed into a black site where, hidden from public view, murky deals were made, ransom money for kidnappings was paid and executions were carried out.[148] The fact that the bulk of these criminal activities and violence was at all odds with

---

[142] "Un cargo turc intercepté par la marine libanaise," *L'Orient Le Jour* (November 11, 1984).

[143] US Central Intelligence Agency, "Lebanon: Islamic fundamentalism in Tripoli" (Top Secret, NESAR 86-003JX, January 17, 1986).

[144] Interview with a resident of Tripoli, September 2014.

[145] Interview with Ibrahim Antar (Tawhid member close to the "ideological entrepreneurs"), Tripoli, August 2014.

[146] Interviews with Anistaz Kouchari (Tripolitan gangster close to Tawhid), Tripoli, September 2014 and interview with Ibrahim Saleh (Tawhid official close to Hashem Minqara), Tripoli, August 2014.

[147] Abi Samra, *Trablus*, p. 173.

[148] Interviews with residents of the Mina district, Tripoli, July–August 2014 and interviews with former members of Tawhid, Tripoli, July 2014. See also Abi Samra, *Trablus*, pp. 168–73.

360   The Illusion of Religious Violence

Islamic teachings and focused so disproportionately on this district, where Tawhid's allegedly "religious violence" had taken place, confirmed that its local base there lay with members who had instrumentalized ideology as a conduit for "social jihad" and material gains.

Although it brought Tawhid considerable revenues, "Islamo-gangsterism" eventually became a thorn in the movement's side, undermining its credentials, stretching its "spectrum of ideological commitment" to extremes and dragging it into a type of behavior which was at times in such contradiction with its ideology that factional conflicts emerged. Indeed, given the proportions it had come to assume, this phenomenon did not go unnoticed. Tawhid's most ardent rivals thus soon seized the opportunity. While the traditional clerics in Dar al-Fatwa lambasted Tawhid's "relentless pursuit of greed,"[149] opponents of all stripes were quick to denounce its engagement in "systematic theft"[150] in the port of Tripoli. The accusations that many members and some leaders were engaging in criminal dealings and activities to maximize their profits became so widespread that it even prompted the movement to issue a statement in which it clarified that its revenues were "limited" and relied on "donations."[151] This clarification, however, was not enough to prevent the development of internal conflicts.

Expectedly, the "ideological entrepreneurs" were among the first to express their disapproval of Tawhid's increasingly criminal behavior, for it stood at loggerheads with the ideologically driven direction they had long advocated for the movement to espouse. But they were soon echoed in their criticisms by other, less ideologically driven factions. Perhaps bitter to see the growing influence of Hashem Minqara's "subaltern Islamists" and Anistaz Kouchari's "Islamo-gangsters" over Tawhid's behavior, they began to also denounce activities which "cultivate relationships that are not Islamic but are rather based on personal interests, privileges and cronyism."[152] These criticisms were echoed by many members who were committed Islamists and, as a result of the spread of "Islamo-gangsterism," became somewhat demobilized. "Tawhid did not stick with its initial identity,"[153] regretted a militant who had joined the movement out of a combination of belief in Islamism and a

---

[149] Interview with Taha Sabunji (Mufti of Tripoli in the 1980s and head of Dar al-Fatwa), Tripoli, August 2014.

[150] "Violente réponse d'Amal au leader du MUI," *L'Orient Le Jour* (May 19, 1985).

[151] "Informations contradictoires sur la légalisation du port de Tripoli," *L'Orient Le Jour* (November 7, 1984).

[152] "Al-qiyada al-islamiya fi Trablus" ["The Islamic leadership in Tripoli"], *al-Taqwa* (Vol. 20, April 1985).

[153] Interview with a former member of Tawhid, Tripoli, August 2014.

The Spread of Islamo-Gangsterism 361

willingness to fight against Syrian troops. "The movement transformed into something wrong."

Interestingly enough, although "Islamo-gangsterism" was fast undermining Tawhid's cohesion and weakening its ideological credentials, its leader Sa'id Sha'aban did not do much to rein in the spread of this phenomenon. Instead, as leader he attempted to strike a middle way. On the one hand, he criticized the excesses of "Islamo-gangsterism." In one of his sermons in mid-1985 he insisted that Tawhid members had to stop issuing *fatwas* that seemed to meet no other goal than fulfilling their own "lusts and desires." "It becomes dangerous when one issues *fatwas* that permit the killing of people and stealing of property in the name of Islam." He continued by arguing that "it is a severe ideological defect and a corruption of personal behavior and demeanour for someone to issue *fatwas* by himself and for himself," going as far as warning that "there is no hope"[154] in heaven for these members. On the other hand, Sha'aban discreetly encouraged the Tawhid factions engaging in illegal dealings to continue generating revenues so that the movement could cement its control over Tripoli. In fact, far from punishing the leading figures of "Islamo-gangsterism," he promoted some of them to positions of prominence and influence in the movement.[155]

By mid-1985, therefore, it had become increasingly clear that, in spite of all the efforts and initial successes of the "ideological entrepreneurs" to steer Tawhid's behavior in an ideologically driven direction, other members were instead pushing the movement toward "Islamo-gangsterism" – even at the cost of violating basic tenets of its ideology. Far from being irrationally and homogeneously guided by beliefs, as the "religious violence" thesis suggests, Tawhid thus featured a wide "spectrum of ideological commitment." It now increasingly included members who viewed Islamism instrumentally to the extent that they were ready to sacrifice ideological consistency on the altar of material interests. That the phenomenon of "Islamo-gangsterism" primarily took root in the port area of Mina, precisely where the bulk of Tawhid's "religious violence" was alleged to have occurred, demonstrated that what had motivated the

---

[154] "Amir Harakat al-Tawhid al-Islami, fadilat al-Sheikh Sa'id Sha'aban fi Khutbat al-Jum'a: kell men y'amal al-tamziq saf al-Muslimin n'atabiru khadim lil yahud" ["The Emir of Tawhid the cleric Sa'id Sha'aban in his Friday sermon: anyone who attempts to tear the Muslims apart is a servant of the Jews"], *al-Tawhid* (September 19, 1985. This was not the first time Sha'aban had voiced concerns about the spread of gangster-like practices in Tawhid. In June 1985, he had already condemned such practices. See: "Shaaban dénonce les abus des miliciens à Tripoli," *L'Orient Le Jour* (June 22, 1985).

[155] Interview with Ibrahim Saleh (Tawhid official close to Minqara and Sha'aban), Tripoli, August 2014.

362   The Illusion of Religious Violence

anti-leftist and anti-Christian brutality of 1983 there did not fundamentally stem from locally high levels of commitment to religion or ideology. Instead, other factors had a more significant causal weight, such as dynamics of "social jihad," local antagonisms, geopolitics and growing criminality, to the point that it became hard to disentangle typically religious from social, political and criminal violence. This episode is a reminder of how "master narratives" of "religious violence" can act as illusions masking an array of more relevant explanatory factors, casting doubt on the validity of the causal linkage between religion and violence at the heart of the concept.

Theorizing Back

By unpacking what led Tawhid to engage in violence against Tripoli's leftists and Christians in mid-1983 and to get involved in criminality from late 1984 until mid-1985, this chapter draws broader theoretical implications regarding the role of ideology in contentious politics and it answers the following questions. To what extent is the concept of "religious violence" useful for understanding the effect of ideology on religiously inspired rebel and terrorist movements? And what are the exact mechanisms through which ideology affects movement behavior?

First, I build on the seemingly obvious case, at first glance, of Tawhid's involvement in ideologically driven violence to provide a critique of the "religious violence" thesis. Whereas several proponents of the concept, chief among them Mark Juergensmeyer, acknowledge that the militants who engage in "religious violence" tend to originally do so more to express deeper social and political grievances than out of inherent religious motivation, they nonetheless claim that their struggle subsequently becomes "religionized."[156] As scholar of terrorism Magnus Ranstrop put it, a "total ideological vision"[157] then disproportionately guides their actions, one in which no compromise is possible in a world divided

---

[156] Mark Juergensmeyer, "Religion as a cause of terrorism," chapter 10 in Louise Richardson (ed.), *The roots of terrorism* (London: Routledge, 2006), p. 140. See, also: David Rapoport, "Fear and trembling: terrorism in three religious traditions" *American Political Science Review* (Vol. 78, No. 3, 1983), pp. 658–77, David Rapoport, "The fourth wave: September 11 in the history of terrorism" *Current History* (Vol. 100, No. 650, December 2001), Walter Laqueur, *The new terrorism: fanaticism and the arms of mass destruction* (Oxford: Oxford University Press, 1999), Bruce Hoffman, *"Holy terror": the implications of terrorism motivated by a religious imperative* (Santa Monica: Rand Press, 1993) and Bruce Hoffman, *Inside terrorism* (New York: Columbia University Press, 2006).

[157] Magnus Ranstorp, "Terrorism in the name of religion" *Journal of International Affairs* (Vol. 50, No. 1, 1996), p. 49.

Theorizing Back 363

between good and evil and in which violence is justified, indeed inspired, by divine decree. Shaped by beliefs, so the argument goes, their behavior turns irrational and especially lethal. Yet, although the "religious violence" thesis can be credited with stimulating a lively debate on the relationship between religion or ideology and political violence, it has two main flaws. The first is that it tends to rely either on cursory accounts of a handful of religiously motivated militant groups or on analyses of cross-national instances of "religious violence." This is problematic as it overlooks sometimes stark patterns of variation in the violence of such movements as well as inconsistencies between their ideology and their actual behavior. The second flaw of the "religious violence" thesis is that it assumes that beliefs are homogeneous and cause action, without delving into whether this is the case and if so how. As a result, the body of work arguing for the classification of "religious violence" as a distinct subcategory of political violence may have had a significant echo, especially in the field of terrorism studies in which it resonates with the concept of "new terrorism" driven by religious beliefs, but it rests on empirically, theoretically and methodologically shaky ground.

This chapter contributes to that debate, providing an empirical critique of the concept of "religious violence" to complement the theoretical reservations voiced in the literature.[158] Delving into the case of Tawhid's ostensible engagement in "religious violence," I demonstrate that when looking closer, the dynamics of violence featured too much variation across time, space and organizations to be only or mostly driven by the movement's religious ideology. I also note striking instances of variation in behavior within Tawhid itself, like when a faction in the movement tried to save Communists from being slaughtered in Mina, or when many members and even some leaders engaged in criminal practices at odds with Islamist ideology. Showing variation in the movement's behavior and pointing to the heterogeneity of ideological commitments then allows me to question the strong causal linkage between ideology and movement violence which lies at the core of the notion of "religious violence."

Moreover, rather than assuming the influence of beliefs on Tawhid's violence at large, I examine the relative causal weight of ideology on subprocesses such as the decision to engage in violence, the selection of targets and the timing, nature and extent of the violence. Unsurprisingly, I find that

---

[158] Jeroen Gunning and Richard Jackson, "What's so 'religious' about religious violence?" *Critical Studies on Terrorism* (Vol. 4, No. 3, 2011), pp. 369–88 and William Cavanaugh, *The myth of religious violence* (New York, Oxford University Press, 2009). See also: Jeroen Gunning, "Critical reflections on the relationship between ideology and behaviour" in Jeevan Deol and Zaheer Kazmi (eds.), *Contextualizing jihadi thought* (London: Hurst, 2012), pp. 219–43.

364   The Illusion of Religious Violence

the movement's ideology played key roles. For instance, it pushed some committed Islamists to engage in violence when ordered to, it shaped some perceptions of who the enemy was, and in several cases it drove the rituals of violence. But I also find that other variables affected the movement's behavior as well as the timing, extent and nature of its violence. These included considerations of a primarily political, strategic, geopolitical and social nature – sometimes these factors had a greater causal weight on Tawhid's exercise of violence than ideology. Overall, the perception that Tawhid was driven by a "total ideological vision" which led it to engage in "religious violence" may have been obvious at first glance, but it revealed itself to be an illusion that overlooked striking variations and inconsistencies in its behavior and hid an array of other explanatory factors. This casts doubt on the concept's utility as a distinct subcategory of political violence.

Second, rather than assuming that beliefs shape behavior, this chapter delves into how, through one mechanism in particular, ideology affected parts of Tawhid's exercise of violence: the "ideological entrepreneurship" of highly committed Islamists who mobilized their beliefs and strove to shape the nature of activism – they translated ideology into action. One of my key findings is that even though these figures were a minority, they had by mid-1983 become prominent actors steering parts of Tawhid's behavior in an ideological direction. This resulted from the fact that they fulfilled key functions in the movement, which gave them leverage over the leadership. Chapters 2–5 laid out some of these functions, and Chapters 7 and 8 continue to do so. They comprised articulating and disseminating Tawhid's ideology, recruiting and galvanizing committed Islamists, bolstering the movement's ideological credentials to outcompete rivals, leveraging external support from like-minded foreign actors or shaping the broader ideological environment to make society more receptive to militant Islamist worldviews. It also included socializing and educating Tawhid members into ideology, which turned the instrumental embrace of beliefs into firmer commitments and cemented internal coherence. The functions fulfilled by the "ideological entrepreneurs" soon became essential for Tawhid.

Yet, beyond continuing to analyze the functions of these "ideological entrepreneurs," in this chapter I also process-trace the evolution of their influence on Tawhid, assessing whether, and to what extent, they steered its behavior in an ideologically driven direction. The significant sway this small number of cadres came to enjoy over the movement meant that they were able to impact its exercise of anti-leftist violence in mid-1983 in two crucial ways. First, through their lobbying efforts they pushed the leaders to order a crackdown on Tripoli's leftist parties – even though not all factions believed in the necessity of using violence. And, second, their mobilization of vehement ideological content galvanized some members into taking risks to fight and it also upset rivals, worsening a climate of polarization. This exacerbated ideological cleavages and created path dependencies which triggered a conflict. The "ideological entrepreneurship" of these figures was therefore a central mechanism through which ideology guided parts of Tawhid's 1983 violence and behavior in 1982–5.

In turn, the concept of "ideological entrepreneurs" makes three contributions to the study of ideology in social, rebel and terrorist movements. To begin with, it breaks with conventional views of ideology as a disembodied, abstract variable, and instead locates beliefs within human agency, contingencies and a relational context, which all have to be unpacked. This has an important implication when seeking to assess the effect of ideology in contentious politics. Rather than presuming that beliefs shape behavior one can process-trace the extent to which a movement engages in ideological behavior back to internal interactions between more or less ideologically committed factions and to the ebb and flow of the influence of the "ideological entrepreneurs" on the leaders and members. In Tawhid's case the decline in the influence of these figures from late 1984 onward allowed rival factions to steer the movement in a less ideologically driven direction, as the spread of "Islamo-gangsterism" shows. Moreover, the notion of "ideological entrepreneurs" helps to overcome the dichotomy between instrumental and sincere accounts of the role of ideology in social, rebel and terrorist movements which is prevalent in the literature. By pointing to their position at the extreme of a "spectrum of ideological commitment," this concept underlines the importance of considering the heterogeneity of commitments in movements and of grasping the role of actors bent on maximizing ideological commitment. It also highlights the fluid nature of ideological commitment, because the indoctrination activities of these actors have the potential to turn the instrumental embrace of beliefs by some members, for instance as a "protest ideology," into firmer ideological commitments. This indicates how, even when embraced instrumentally, ideology can take a life of its own. Finally, by noting that Tawhid's "ideological entrepreneurs" tended to be cadres rather than leaders, it corrects an assumption in parts of the literature that ideological commitment is pyramidal, leaders being seen alternatively either as the most or as the least committed to their movement's ideology. This suggests a need for more research into rebel and terrorist cadres, rather than just leaders or members at large, and for further studies of the functions and influence of the "ideological entrepreneurs" inside social, rebel and terrorist movements.

7 The Geopolitics of Islamism

Tawhid was a localized movement, but it drew interest from some of the most significant actors in the Middle East. And, strikingly, ideology seemed to be shaping its geopolitics. While the "secular" Syrian regime tried hard to crush it, Tawhid simultaneously received support from Syrian Islamist groups, Fatah's Islamist wing and the Islamic Republic of Iran. Sometimes it even appeared as though Tawhid's alliances with some of these ideologically like-minded foreign actors exerted a significant impact on its discourse and behavior. Iran's support seemed most emblematic of the effect which ideological alliances could have. By providing it with significant diplomatic backing but also with logistics and money, the Islamic Republic expected that Tawhid would turn from a local, spatially oriented movement into an ideologically guided terrorist group fully loyal to its "Khomeinist" breed of Islamism. It envisioned making Tawhid its "Sunni Hezbollah," its loyal Sunni Islamist ally. At first Tehran's efforts seemed about to succeed. The movement's rhetoric not only became more distinctively pro-Iran but some of its cadres also became sincerely committed to its Islamist "Khomeinist" agenda, itself made up of a mix of exporting the 1979 Islamic Revolution abroad and rolling back Western influence in the Middle East. By early to mid-1984 these figures were even recording some success in steering Tawhid's behavior in this more ideological, "Khomeinist" direction; the movement began to engage in a wave of attacks on French and American interests in North Lebanon, touted the idea of expanding from Tripoli to the rest of Lebanon and considered merging with other pro-Iranian groups. Yet there was a puzzle to Tawhid's alliances with ideologically like-minded external actors, chief among them the Islamic Republic of Iran. Despite their efforts it always remained a local Islamist movement, and when some of its pro-Tehran cadres appeared to gain too much leverage they were assassinated in what many members in retrospect called "inside jobs." There was a limit to how far Tawhid was prepared to be driven by these ideological alliances.

The Geopolitics of Islamism   367

This chapter explores the factors behind Tawhid's tensions with the
Syrian regime and the nature of its relations with Syrian Islamists, Fatah
and Iran, investigating the effect these alliances had on its behavior and
deriving broader insights on the role of ideology in the relationship
between social, rebel or terrorist movements and their foreign patrons.
On the one hand, I highlight ideology's role in Tawhid's foreign relations. After all, it was the fear that the movement would come to form a
nexus with Syria's Islamists and with Fatah's Islamist wing to topple the
regime which raised Hafez al-Assad's anxiety to the degree that he felt he
would need to crush it sooner or later, as Chapter 8 shows. A crucial
element in this perception was that Tawhid's "ideological entrepreneurs"
were close to especially influential Syrian and Palestinian Islamist "ideological entrepreneurs." This suggested that ideology might become the
cornerstone of the alliance between these actors. Had this ideologically
patterned, Lebanese–Syrian–Palestinian Islamist nexus truly seen the
light of day it would probably have been a significant thorn in Hafez al-
Assad's side. Similarly, I acknowledge the importance of ideology in
Tawhid's relationship with Iran, once again through "ideological entrepreneurs" whose preexisting social and ideational ties to the Islamic
Republic turned them into Tehran's loyal relays and pushed them to
lobby the leaders to adopt a less spatially oriented and more ideologically
driven discourse and behavior. On the other hand, I also point to the
limits of ideology's impact on the movement's foreign relations and
behavior. Although ideological solidarity mattered in Tawhid's relationship with Syrian Islamists, this alliance was primarily activated and
guided by kinship, or the longstanding cross-border ties of its
Tripolitan members to rebels in Homs and Hama. For its part, the
movement's preparedness to act on behalf of Fatah built on shared
ideology with its Islamist wing but even more importantly on the sense
that it stood to benefit immensely from this alliance at the strategic and
popular levels. Ideology played an important part in shaping these alliances, then, but other factors informed their dynamics too. Tawhid's
relation to Iran was a good case of how fluid these ideologically patterned
alliances could be. While the "ideological entrepreneurs" were sincerely
attracted by the "Iranian model" and at first sought to apply it to Tawhid,
many members as well as some leaders instrumentalized "Khomeinism"
to obtain Iran's diplomatic support and spare them from imminent war
with Syria. Internal variation in commitment to "Khomeinism" was in
fact such that, as the "ideological entrepreneurs" pushed hard to make
ideology the cornerstone of Tawhid's alliance with Iran, a heated debate
gripped the movement and even led to the assassination of some of them.
It kept its relationship with Tehran, but from then on it would be more

368   The Geopolitics of Islamism

transactional than ideological. Therefore, ideology mattered in the geopolitics of Tawhid, but most of its members were not ready to let its alliances turn it from a spatially oriented to an ideologically driven movement.

Cross-Border Ties to Syria's Islamists

One of the most important aspects of Tripolitan politics in the early to mid-1980s was the intense enmity which developed between Tawhid and the Syrian regime. As Chapter 1 tackled, Damascus had militarily intervened in the Lebanese civil war in 1976 and it came to occupy Tripoli from then until 1982, when Tawhid emerged in force. The movement began engaging in a degree of low-level, sporadic violence against Syrian troops in and around Tripoli, which pushed Damascus to fully withdraw its army from the city in 1983. Far from remaining passive, however, the Syrian regime fomented covert operations against Tawhid and it would crush it after a month-long siege of Tripoli in 1985, the topic of Chapter 8. The Syrian regime dedicated considerable military and financial resources to undermining Tawhid, and this raises the question of what motivated its obsession with the movement.

This and the next three sections tackle different but related aspects of Syria's enmity for Tawhid. Hafez al-Assad, I argue, was weaker in 1982–5 than is often acknowledged in the literature, and he especially feared that Tawhid would come to form some kind of alliance with Syria's Islamists and with Fatah's Islamist wing to topple the regime. Had this ideologically driven Lebanese–Syrian–Palestinian Islamist nexus truly seen the light of day it would have significantly undermined the Syrian president's efforts to stabilize his regime. This chapter begins by analyzing how this anxiety stemmed from the sense that Tawhid was turning the informal cross-border bonds of solidarity that linked Tripolitans to bastions of the 1980s Syrian uprising into staunch, ideologically driven support for Syria's Islamist rebels.

Interestingly, however, I find that although Tawhid and Syrian Islamist movements shared a degree of ideological affinity, their relationship originally stemmed from and remained more guided by Tripoli's cross-border solidarities with the Syrian cities of Homs and Hama than by ideology. As a result their alliance was always ad hoc, never translating in organizational unity. The next three sections then move on to explore how Assad's anxiety about Tawhid was justified to a degree, because the movement developed a strong alliance with Fatah and some of its cadres had long been particularly close to a highly influential Palestinian Islamist "ideological entrepreneur" who was sponsoring Lebanese and

Syrian anti-regime militias. This raised the specter of an ideologically patterned Islamist nexus bent on overthrowing the Syrian regime.

To outsiders, Syria gave the appearance of stability between 1982 and 1985. But, even though Hafez al-Assad appeared to be holding the country with a firm grip, Western intelligence assessed that he was actually in an increasingly "vulnerable position."[1] This was partly because of his hospitalization from a heart attack in November 1983, which brought the regime to a halt for two months. Subsequently a power struggle in early 1984 highlighted the serious factionalism plaguing his inner circle as Assad's own brother, Rif'at, launched a failed coup.

But more important was Assad's preoccupation that the Islamists still posed a threat to his rule. In retrospect this perception of a lingering Islamist threat may sound exaggerated. After all, the regime had repressed in a bloodbath the Syrian Muslim Brotherhood – the country's best organized and strongest opposition movement in 1979–82 – killing 25,000 civilians and Islamist sympathizers in Hama in February 1982 after they had risen up in a rebellion.[2] The regime's brutality had also forced the remaining Muslim Brothers to flee Syria and seek exile abroad, reinforcing the outside perception that Assad had overcome this Islamist challenge. The regime's opponents, including the Brotherhood, then teamed up within a National Alliance for the Liberation of Syria, but this remained a toothless platform that held press conferences abroad and was "unlikely to attract widespread support in Syria."[3]

Yet, for all the Syrian opposition's state of disarray, and in particular despite the Brotherhood's exile, Western intelligence agencies still continued to report that Hafez al-Assad remained deeply concerned about the Islamists, viewing them as a "significant threat" – especially as, by 1985, the Syrian Muslim Brotherhood appeared to have regained some of its strength. The Hama massacre had decimated its ranks and forced its leadership to operate remotely but it was said to "retain the capacity to conduct terrorist operations in Syria."[4] This perception became all the more prevalent after it staged a high-profile escape of some of its members from a prison in Damascus in September 1984 and began a campaign of bombings in 1985 that targeted public facilities, thus raising

---

[1] US Central Intelligence Agency, "Syria: Sunni opposition to the minority Alawite regime" (Secret, NESA 85-10102, June 1985).

[2] Raphaël Lefèvre, *Ashes of Hama, the Muslim Brotherhood in Syria* (London: Oxford University Press and Hurst, 2013).

[3] US Central Intelligence Agency, "Syria: Assad's grip on power" (Secret, NESA 83-10199, August 1983).

[4] US Central Intelligence Agency, "The Muslim Brotherhood and Arab politics" (Confidential, NESA 82-10533, October 1982).

370   The Geopolitics of Islamism

the specter of terrorism and insurrection.[5] By 1985, then, the general sense shared by Assad was that "a significant potential still exists for another Sunni opposition movement" which the Brotherhood, even from abroad, may still prove skilled at "orchestrating and exploiting" – this time "setting the stage for civil war."[6] This would eventually translate into no more than a handful of insurgent operations in the mid to late 1980s, but at the time it shaped Assad's "perception of a continuing threat from the Sunni opposition" which became a "significant element in his design of Syrian foreign policy."[7] This fear would inform to a large extent the regime's views of Tawhid and Tripoli.

At first glance, of course, it seemed obvious why the regime feared Tawhid so much. Tripoli's Islamists shared the anti-regime political orientation of the Syrian Muslim Brotherhood and its militant offshoot, the Fighting Vanguard. And, evidently, its discourse was ostensibly similar to that of Syria's Islamists as it drew heavily on their militant ideologue, Sa'id Hawwa, although as Chapter 4 argued this also fulfilled functions in Tawhid. As a result, what seemed at stake was a struggle pitting the "secular" regime against its "Islamist" opponents. Epitomizing this "master narrative," days before the regime's last-ditch battle with Tawhid in September 1985, a cell suspected of acting on behalf of Damascus bombed one of the movement's offices and released the following statement: "we want to assure the world that no Muslim fundamentalists will continue to live on Lebanese soil."[8]

Naturally, ideological polarization may have played a genuine role in exacerbating tensions between Tawhid and the regime. Some within the regime probably sincerely feared the consequences of Islamist rule in Tripoli for the Christians and Alawis. And others may have considered that the presence of an "Islamic Emirate" in Tripoli would act as a model and embolden the remaining Islamists who were still hiding in Syria. Encapsulating this mindset, one Western intelligence assessment thus pointed out that "the secular Syrian regime would be wary of any upsurge of Islamic fundamentalism in Lebanon for fear that it would encourage fundamentalist Sunni opponents of Alawi rule in Syria."[9] But, as was

---

[5] US Central Intelligence Agency, "Syria: Sunni opposition to the minority Alawite regime" (Secret, NESA 85-10102, June 1985).

[6] US Central Intelligence Agency, "Syria: scenarios of dramatic political change" (Classified, 86-20099L, July 1986).

[7] US Central Intelligence Agency, "Syria: Sunni opposition to the minority Alawite regime" (Secret, NESA 85-10102, June 1985).

[8] "44 killed by car bomb in Tripoli; militias trade fire around Beirut," *New York Times* (August 21, 1985).

[9] US Central Intelligence Agency, "Lebanon: confessionalism – a potent force" (Confidential, NESA 82-10438, August 1982).

Cross-Border Ties to Syria's Islamists   371

seen previously, although Tawhid framed its rule in Tripoli in grand ways and militant Islamist ideology played distinct roles, it often behaved as a spatially oriented movement more guided by local identities, antagonisms and grievances than by its ideology. As an occupying force in Lebanon since 1976 that had developed highly sophisticated local intelligence networks, the Syrian regime was acutely aware of Tawhid's localism. It was also conscious that, despite the ideological proximity between Tripoli's and Syria's Islamists, the former was engineering a rapprochement with the Islamic Republic of Iran while the latter was supported by Tehran's mortal enemy, Saddam Hussein's Iraq. This, it knew, significantly limited any prospect of an actual merger between Tawhid and Syria's Islamists.

The root of the Syrian regime's anxiety about Tawhid did not stem primarily from its Islamist ideology, but rather from the movement's rootedness in Tripoli. Hafez al-Assad feared that Tawhid would use the city's history of anti-regime activism, a social fabric largely hostile to his rule and its threatening proximity to the Syrian-Lebanese border in order to provide a safe haven to the Syrian opposition at a critical time and to reinvigorate it. A Syrian politician who was close to Hafez al-Assad recalled how obsessed the president was that "Tripoli's historical ties to Syria,"[10] and especially to focal points of the uprisings of 1979–82, would turn it into a safe space for the reconstitution of anti-regime networks. Assad was said to be aware that a key element of Tripolitan identity, or of the city's "global sense of place" as we saw in Chapter 1, was both attachment to the Sunni-dominated Syrian hinterland and deep-seated hostility to his regime. In fact, movements known for their virulent criticisms of the Syrian president, like the Iraqi Ba'ath Party or Fatah, had long been popular locally. As Chapter 2 pointed out, the city had even become home to Mohammed Umran, a former Syrian defense minister turned leading Alawi opponent who was assassinated there in 1972, and there are rumors that during Rif'at al-Assad's failed coup against his brother a band of Tripolitan Alawis had gone to Damascus to help him seize power.[11] Hafez al-Assad had thus long viewed Tripoli with suspicion and hostility.

After the Islamist uprising in Syria in the 1980s the president became even more concerned about Tripoli's role. Beyond its history of anti-Assad dissent, the city's physical location and social fabric made it a

---

[10] Ibid.

[11] These rumors are given credence by Hafez al-Assad's own defense minister at the time, Mustafa Tlass, who discusses them at length in his memoires. See: Mustafa Tlass, *Mirat Hayati* [*The mirror of my life*] (Vol. 4) chapter 87 (Damascus: Dar Tlass, 2004).

372   The Geopolitics of Islamism

sensitive place for the Alawi-dominated Syrian regime. The president was especially worried about Tripoli's status as an overwhelmingly Sunni city with a deep social and emotional attachment to Syria's Sunni hinterland and in particular to the major cities of Homs, Hama and Aleppo, themselves epicenters of anti-regime contention. He feared, moreover, the port's proximity to the Syrian-Lebanese border, which brought the city close to smuggling routes leading both to the strategic city of Homs to Tripoli's east and to Alawi-inhabited areas that acted as the regime's power base to its north. Finally, he was also anxious about the city's make-up of populations traditionally opposed to his rule such as Tripolitans with family from Syria's marginalized Sunni hinterland, exiled Syrians hostile to the regime and Palestinian Sunnis living in Tripoli's two refugee camps. All of these elements raised the possibility that Tripoli, under Tawhid's rule, would act as the new hub of anti-Assad forces after the Hama massacre, which would destabilize the regime once more. Western intelligence reported that the president therefore viewed Tripoli as "threatening" and that Damascus as a result developed "a strong interest in maintaining control over the area."[12]

It is true that Tawhid members who, like other Tripolitans, had deep social and emotional bonds to Syria's Sunni hinterland, provided an especially welcoming environment to the thousands of Syrian refugees and militants who escaped Hama in 1982. The distinct possibility that these particularly strong cross-border solidarities could translate in organized Tawhid support for the Syrian Islamists from the Muslim Brotherhood and its militant offshoot, the Fighting Vanguard, greatly worried Hafez al-Assad. One CIA report suggested that by June 1985 his concerns that Tripoli would act as a stronghold for the Syrian rebels were at an all-time high. It read:

Assad's determination to maintain Syrian preeminence in Lebanon almost certainly is reinforced by fear that Sunni opponents of his regime might use bases there to mount operations into Syria. [We] believe that many Sunni dissidents fled to the Tripoli area in North Lebanon after the Hama uprising in 1982.[13]

The Syrian president's worries were reinforced by the fact that, although the majority of Syrian Islamists only passed by Tripoli and used the port as a gateway to safer destinations like Europe, the Gulf, Jordan or Iraq, some of them had actually also settled there and even joined Tawhid.

[12] US Central Intelligence Agency, "National intelligence daily" (Top Secret, CPAS NID 83, January 7, 1983).
[13] US Central Intelligence Agency, "Syria: Sunni opposition to the minority Alawite regime" (Secret, NESA 85-10102, June 1985).

Estimates suggest that the Syrian Islamists from the Brotherhood and the Vanguard who joined Tawhid numbered no more than fifty but, while this may seem a relatively small figure, their role in the movement became significant and caught the regime's attention. They settled in the neighborhood of Bab al-Tebbaneh, where rents were cheap. There they interacted with other Syrians who had left the country earlier and with local Sunni residents who were deeply immersed in a violent local rivalry with Jabal Mohsen's pro-Syrian regime Alawis. Bab al-Tebbaneh rapidly became an incubator of solidarities between anti-Assad Tripolitans and Syrian Islamists. While residents of the district were not necessarily all pious, as Chapter 2 showed, they felt sympathy for these Syrian Islamists and their history of anti-Assad struggle. In fact, a couple of years earlier Bab al-Tebbaneh had even hosted for a few days the leader of the Syrian jihad, Adnan Uqla, who had been given a hero's welcome and whose tales still circulated.[14] "Our neighborhood welcomed the Syrian militants with open arms and they felt immediately comfortable with us,"[15] recalled a Tawhid fighter in Bab al-Tebbaneh proudly. These Syrian Islamists began taking part in Tawhid's sporadic fighting against the Alawis in Jabal Mohsen and Syrian troops in the vicinity of the city. They also acted as military instructors. One Tawhid commander recalled that, "they were not numerous but their role was important." In a show of how cross-border solidarities were turning into tighter networks of military support, he elaborated with pride that "they were our friends and we admired them – these militants had been fighting the regime in Hama, they represented the elite of Syria's jihadists and here they were, training us in Tripoli!"[16]

Most of these Syrian Islamists kept a low profile and escaped the city before Tawhid's 1985 battle against the Syrian regime. But at least one of them, Azzam al-Rifa'i, joined its leadership and became a Tawhid Emir. He was only sixteen years old when he reached Tripoli in 1982 but his militancy in, successively, the Fighting Vanguard and then the Syrian Muslim Brotherhood, as well as the fact that he hailed from a Sunni family in Homs with known historical ties to Tripoli, earned him the trust and sympathy of Tawhid's leaders. Azzam al-Rifa'i became a protégé of Hashem Minqara, the Emir of Mina, who then nominated him as Emir of Tal, a neighborhood close to the Old City.[17] From then on his

---

[14] Interviews with residents of Bab al-Tebbaneh, Tripoli, September–October 2014.
[15] Interview with Mazen Mohammed (former member of Tawhid from Bab al-Tebbaneh), August 2014.
[16] Interview with Hashem Yaghmur (Tawhid military commander), Tripoli, June 2014.
[17] This draws on interviews with a Tawhid figure close to Azzam al-Rifa'i in Tripoli and with his former mentor, Hashem Minqara.

374   The Geopolitics of Islamism

influence became pronounced as he emerged as one of Tawhid's key "ideological entrepreneurs," mobilizing Islamist ideology to shape the movement's behavior and pushing it to confront Syria. The military exploits of "Abu Yasser al-Suri," as he became affectively known by Tripoli's Islamists, against Syrian troops during the 1985 battle circulated widely in Tripoli and his hometown of Homs, until the regime assassinated him in August 2014 as he was reviving militant anti-Assad Islamist networks in these two cities.[18] His murder reflects the resilience of Tripoli's cross-border solidarities with Syria – and the regime's lingering fear about them.

This seemingly growing relation between Tawhid and militant Syrian Islamist movements caught the regime's attention and frightened it. One Tripolitan figure close to Syrian intelligence explained that the security services were not only worried by the presence of Syrian Islamists in Tripoli but also by the sense that, as they brought their "experience" to Tawhid, they were developing a better organized, deeper relationship.[19] This fear was reinforced by the role within Tawhid of a handful of Syrian Islamists, chief among them Azzam al-Rifa'i, something which raised the possibility that, despite different priorities, their relationship could turn more ideological. This anxiety on the part of the regime was best encapsulated by a statement from pro-Assad sources reducing Tawhid to a "bunch of Muslim Brothers who have escaped Syrian courts."[20] And, tellingly, many of the Tawhid militants who were arrested by the Syrian army in September 1985 recalled being sent to Syria's most notorious jails to be tortured, only to realize that their interrogators' questions had to do with that nexus. One fighter was sent to infamous jails such as the Palestine Branch, Mezze and Palmyra, being beaten up for days and then sent to an isolation cell. "They were obsessed by Tawhid's supposed ties to the Syrian Islamists," he recalled. "They seemed afraid that we were acting on behalf of the Syrian Muslim Brotherhood and the Fighting Vanguard."[21]

---

[18] By then, Azzam al-Rifa'i had created an Islamist rebel group in the countryside of Homs, "training hundreds" of Syrians and Tripolitans and working on consolidating the logistical and ideological relationship between Islamist movements in Homs and Tripoli. For more on Azzam al-Rifa'i's post-2011 militancy in Homs and Tripoli and his 2014 assassination, see: "Khuttat 'al-hasm': ramez wa thalatha qada" ["The 'Decisive' plan: one symbol and three leaders"], al-Akhbar (May 21, 2012); "Ikhwan Suria tan'a al-shahid al-qa'ed Azzam al-Rifa'i" ["The Syrian Muslim Brotherhood mourns the martyr and the leader Azzam al-Rifa'i"], al-Mujtam'a (August 13, 2014); and "Esteshhad qa'ed Liwa Wa'adu" ["Martyrdom of the leader of the Wa'adu Brigade"], Zaman al-Wasel (August 12, 2014).

[19] Interview with a figure close to Syrian intelligence, Tripoli, September 2014.

[20] "Calme précaire à Tripoli," L'Orient Le Jour (August 24, 1984).

[21] Interview with Abu Jandah (former Tawhid fighter), Tripoli, June 2014.

Interestingly, however, Azzam al-Rifa'i's growing role in Tawid never heralded the advent of any organizational or ideological merger between Syrian and Tripolitan Islamists. Their relationship continued functioning on the fluid, ad hoc basis of cross-border solidarities between Tripolitans and Syrians from Homs and Hama, never translating in the kind of common ideological and political vision which could have paved the way for true unity. "We certainly sympathized with the struggle of Syria's Islamists,"[22] acknowledged Hashem Minqara, who was close to Azzam al-Rifa'i and other Syrians in Tawhid. "We were not only close to their ideology but they were also our dear friends and some of us even shared relatives – my aunt, for instance, hails from Hama – but our relationship was not organized." This was confirmed through interviews with Syrian Islamists themselves. They did not view Tawhid's growing relations with Iran positively, both because Tehran was close to the Syrian regime and because their own anti-Assad struggle was backed up by Iraqi intelligence. But social ties between Homs, Hama and Tripoli had pushed individuals to "help each other."[23] A Tawhid fighter summed up the fluidity and pragmatism of these relations: "The Syrian Islamists were close to us: we shared the same enemy and sometimes we fought together but ultimately we had different ambitions,"[24] he testified, while hinting at Tawhid's much more local agenda. While, from the outside, the relationship between Syrian and Tripolitan Islamists may have appeared organizational and ideological, then, it remained driven by lingering cross-border solidarities as well as mutual interests more than by ideology per se.

In the Shadow of Fatah

What made Damascus particularly anxious that Tawhid's relations with Syria's Islamists would soon be better organized was that the movement was simultaneously developing close ties to Assad's other archenemy, Fatah. This raised the regime's fear that Tripoli might soon give birth to an ideologically driven, Islamist and anti-regime Lebanese, Syrian and Palestinian nexus – an alliance which, if it had materialized, would have truly destabilized Hafez al-Assad. In addition to making this point, the next sections also tackle the nature of Tawhid's successive alliances with

---

[22] Interview with Hashem Minqara (Tawhid's Emir in Mina and a figure close to Azzam al-Rifa'i), Tripoli, June 2014.

[23] Interview with a Syrian Muslim Brother, September 2014.

[24] Interview with Jamil Ra'ad (former member and fighter in Tawhid), Tripoli, August 2014.

376   The Geopolitics of Islamism

Fatah and Iran and, by the same token, also shed light on the dynamics of the relations between rebel movements and their foreign sponsors. While these alliances are often viewed as "proxy–patron" relations that are top-down, one-sided and complete, Tawhid's case suggests that they may be inherently fluid, dialectic and partial too. It also points to the role of nonstate external backers. During the Lebanese civil war, Fatah acted as a key sponsor of local pro-Palestinian rebel groups, including the Beirut-based Sentinels (*al-Murabitun*), the Sidon-based Popular Nasserist Organization (*Tanzim al-Sha'abi al-Naseri*) and the Tripoli-based Tawhid. The ties it developed with Tawhid were particularly profound, to the extent that between 1982 and 1983 the Islamist movement would rise as Fatah's number one Tripolitan and arguably Lebanese ally.

Ostensibly, since Tawhid had been partially created as a reaction to the Israeli invasion of Lebanon in June 1982, as we saw in Chapter 3, Fatah's support for the Islamist movement was framed as related to mutual antipathy for Israeli policies in the Middle East. But, for all of the harsh rhetoric which its "ideological entrepreneurs" deployed against the "vengeful Jewish enemy,"[25] Tawhid did not participate in any significant battles against Israel. Tawhid's only military interaction with the Israeli army was actually defensive. When Israeli gunboats approached the Tripolitan coast in June 1984 for a surveillance mission, Islamist militants manning shore-to-sea batteries opened fire on the ships. The Israeli response was fierce and effectively deterred Tawhid from further engaging in hostilities. Tel-Aviv sent warplanes to retaliate and bombed a training camp which the movement had set up on a small island off the coast of Tripoli, killing as many as nineteen local fighters.[26] A Tawhid leader recounted having ordered some of his commanders to take men, board boats and go to the island to save the dozens of wounded, only to witness Israeli fighter jets rapidly returning to sink the rescue team. "Tel-Aviv sent a message,"[27] he said. And Tawhid understood it – from then on it would stop threatening Israeli interests.

At any rate, Fatah had entirely different designs for Tawhid than fighting Israel. By mid-1982 Yasser Arafat was coming under intense internal and external pressure and was in need of all of the political and military support he could get from Lebanese militias. Israel's 1982 invasion of Lebanon and swift victory over Fatah had the effect of bringing

---

[25] *Al-khutut al-asasia li-muntalaqat wa mabade wa ahdaf Harakat al-Tawhid al-Islami* [The fundamental premises, principles and objectives of the Islamic Unification Movement] (copy given to the author, undated).

[26] "Israeli planes attack island base off North Lebanon," *Washington Post* (June 24, 1984).

[27] Interview with Ibrahim Saleh (Tawhid official from the port district of Mina), Tripoli, August 2014.

Arafat's leadership of the guerrilla organization into question – a dynamic which Damascus sought to exacerbate since it viewed him as an independent figure often acting against Syria's interests.

The Assad–Arafat relationship was characterized by what a Western intelligence cable called "longstanding animosity."[28] Already as Syrian Defense Minister in 1966, Assad had briefly imprisoned Arafat and refused to support Palestinian forces fighting in Jordan in September 1970. As president, he had then ordered a Syrian army invasion of Lebanon and an attack on Fatah's positions in Beirut and Sidon, even letting Christian militias slaughter Palestinian refugees in the Tal al-Za'atar refugee camp in the Lebanese capital in June 1976. And, although Fatah and Syrian forces fought together against the Israeli army when it invaded Lebanon in June 1982, widespread recriminations between the two effectively prevented serious cooperation and resistance. Yet it was Arafat's embrace of US President Ronald Reagan's August 1982 peace plan which dealt a fatal blow to his relationship with Assad. By embracing this roadmap he was publicly accepting the principle of a settlement with Israel. This would guarantee Fatah's safe exit from Beirut and its relocation in Tunis, away from the Syrian and Israeli spheres of influence. However, by doing this he was "weakening"[29] the Syrian president's positions. Western intelligence reports thus suggest that it was then that Assad decided that he would need to "subvert Arafat's influence."[30] Syria would do this by engaging in military hostilities against Fatah and by encouraging Fatah dissidents to create a pro-Syrian Palestinian faction.

It is against the backdrop of this geopolitical confrontation between Arafat and Assad that must be understood Fatah's support for Tawhid. One Palestinian intelligence officer who was in charge of handling the guerrilla organization's relationship to Lebanese militias, put it the following way. "Yasser Arafat needed Tripoli's Islamists on his side at a time of upheaval," he explained. The city's two large Palestinian camps of Naher al-Bared and Beddawi were Fatah's last significant Lebanese strongholds after the organization's disastrous 1982 defeat at the hands of Israel, and Arafat expected an imminent Syrian attack on them. "Tawhid was strong and its militants knew how to fight." There was "local usefulness"[31] in having the movement protect Fatah's interests in

---

[28] US Central Intelligence Agency, "Syria: Assad and the peace process" (Secret, NESA-5362, November 1988).

[29] Ibid.

[30] US Central Intelligence Agency, "The Fatah mutiny: implications for the peace process" (25X1, June 10, 1983).

[31] Interview with a high-ranking Palestinian intelligence officer, Beirut, August 2014.

378   The Geopolitics of Islamism

North Lebanon. Another Fatah figure, involved in the military training of Tawhid fighters at the time, further elaborated: "Supporting Tawhid was a way for Yasser Arafat to send a message to Hafez al-Assad that he still had enough fighting capacity to defend himself against the regime."[32] The main rational behind Fatah's backing of Tawhid was thus clearly military and political.

This Palestinian support for Tripoli's Islamists materialized in various ways. Logistically they received "full coverage" from Fatah. "We fed them and armed them," recounted a Palestinian intelligence operative back then in charge of the liaison with Tawhid. "At first, we even paid for their offices in Tripoli!"[33] Militarily, Fatah trained the Islamist militants, and some of its top commanders such as Monzer Abu Ghazaleh, in charge of Palestinian naval forces, and Mou'in al-Taher, head of an elite unit, the Jarmaq Battalion, were dispatched early on to Tripoli to coordinate relations with Tawhid and conduct joint military exercises. By October 1983 the level of military coordination between Fatah and Tawhid had become so obvious that, as Chapter 6 mentioned, when the Islamists attacked the Lebanese Communist Party in Tripoli and engaged in a massacre against members in the district of Mina the Palestinian organization was, rightly or wrongly, blamed for it. Tawhid, to outsiders, was fast becoming seen as nothing more than "Fatah's proxy."[34]

However, Fatah's influence on Tawhid was not as homogeneous, one-sided and complete as the term "proxy" suggests. The bulk of Tawhid members was sympathetic to the Palestinian issue and did not see Hafez al-Assad's attempt to subvert Yasser Arafat's leadership of Fatah in a favorable light. But this does not mean that they agreed with all the decisions of the Palestinian leader and would blindly follow every order he gave them. Instead, to ensure that Tawhid's actions on the ground matched Fatah's interests Arafat relied on particular individuals who would act as the Palestinian organization's relays within the Islamist movement. In retrospect, sources in the movement point to the role of four influential figures who toed Fatah's line in Tawhid's Consultative Council or leadership.[35] They did so for different reasons. Chapter 2

---

[32] Interview with a Fatah operative in charge of coordinating support for Tawhid, Tripoli, September 2014.

[33] Interview with Abu Marwan (Fatah's head in North Lebanon), Tripoli's Beddawi refugee camp, August 2014.

[34] Interviews with Tawhid opponents and observers of Tripolitan politics, Beirut and Tripoli, June–July 2014.

[35] This draws on interviews with former Tawhid officials Amer Arnaout, Ibrahim Saleh and Mazen Mohammed, Tripoli, June–August 2014.

tackled how one of them, Khalil Akkawi, not only had roots in Palestine but, as strongman of the "neighborhood Islamists" of Bab al-Tebbaneh, in the vicinity of the Beddawi and Naher al-Bared Palestinian refugee camps, had also developed strong social ties to local Palestinians and long benefited from Fatah's help. Chapter 3 hinted at another one, Esmat Murad, who until joining Tawhid had been the head of the Movement of Arab Lebanon, a militia loyal to Fatah and close to its military chief, Abu Jihad. Two other leaders also seemed to act as Fatah's relays in Tawhid: Kan'an Naji, Emir of Abu Samra, and Hashem Minqara, Emir of Mina, who, alongside a dozen second-rank commanders, had preexisting social and ideational ties to a prominent Palestinian Islamist "ideological entrepreneur" and were as a result deeply loyal to Fatah.

Behind them all stood another important figure in the Fatah–Tawhid relationship, a man only known by his *nom de guerre* as "Abu Mansur," who acted as Fatah's spymaster in North Lebanon. Abu Mansur's role was to ensure that, in exchange for Fatah's support to Tawhid, Tripoli's Islamists properly toed the Palestinian line and acted as the loyal "proxies" of Arafat. His influence on Tawhid was said to be highly significant, perhaps reinforced by the fact that he had long lived in Tripoli, knew the Islamists personally and had "files"[36] on some of them. The perception that he was particularly skilled at manipulating Tawhid's leaders for Fatah's benefit was best encapsulated by the persistent rumor that he had even been the one who had personally picked Sa'id Sha'aban, known for his pro-Palestinian diatribes, to become the movement's leader, while being secretly the man in charge. "Abu Mansur and, behind him, Yasser Arafat, influenced Tawhid at first,"[37] admitted a leading Islamist official. Instead of exercising its influence homogeneously, as the term of "proxy-patron" relations suggests, Fatah was able to steer Tawhid in its direction through the particular sway it came to have over a handful of movement cadres and leaders.

Even then, however, the Fatah–Tawhid relationship was never one-sided, and Tripoli's Islamists, far from remaining mere "proxies" devoid of agency, used it for their own benefit. Their alliance with Fatah had already allowed them to secure military resources. This included some armored vehicles and missile batteries as well as stockpiles of ammunition, in addition to military expertise in how to wage not just low-level insurgency warfare but also large-scale battles. But, as the months passed by and the relationship between Arafat and Assad further deteriorated,

---

[36] Interview with a former high-ranking official in Tawhid, Tripoli, September 2014.
[37] Interview with Ibrahim Saleh (Tawhid official), Tripoli, August 2014.

380   The Geopolitics of Islamism

Fatah began needing Tawhid's "protection" and "cover" in Tripoli more, which altered to a degree the power balance between the two actors and pressured the Palestinian group to provide additional benefits to the Islamists such as more heavy weapons and money.[38] This not only allowed Tawhid to secure further material benefits, it also enabled the movement to send a message to Damascus that it would not give up on its control over Tripoli so easily. "We feared that, after getting rid of Fatah, the Syrian regime would eliminate us,"[39] recounted a Tawhid official. Displaying military strength, then, was seen as a way to deter a future Syrian attack on the Islamist movement. Moreover, in addition to serving military and political purposes, Tawhid's loyalty to Fatah was also calibrated to help the movement gain legitimacy in the overwhelmingly pro-Arafat Tripolitan popular classes.[40] Local support for the Palestinian cause was, as we saw in Chapter 1, one of the significant themes running through Tripoli's collective identity and "global sense of place." This was because of the presence of the two large refugee camps of Beddawi and Naher al-Bared that had been set up in 1948, which brought residents of Tripoli into regular contact with Palestinians who settled there, and because of the story of Fawzi Qawaqji, a Tripolitan military officer who had raised an army of local volunteers to fight Jewish militias in Palestine during the first Arab–Israeli war and whose heroic tales still widely circulated.

Tawhid's loyalty for Fatah at a time when the Palestinian guerrilla organization seemed about to make its last stand reinforced the movement's aura in large sections of local society. This became all the more the case when a growing number of Fatah leaders, seeking to escape both Israeli and Syrian wrath but unwilling to exile themselves to Tunisia, trickled down to Tripoli where Tawhid took them under its wing, providing them with bodyguards, protecting the entry of their camps and defending their local presence. The first of these officials was Salah Khalaf (Abu Iyad), one of the founders and deputy chief of Fatah and the PLO's head of intelligence, who reached Tripoli in September 1982, before being joined in June 1983 by Arafat loyalists Khalil al-Wazir (Abu Jihad) and Hayel Abdel Hamid (Abu al-Hol) as well as hundreds of Palestinian rank-and-file members.[41] Finally, in September 1983,

---

[38] Interview with a former Tawhid official in charge of coordinating the relationship with Fatah, Tripoli, June 2014.

[39] Interview with Abu Meriam Khassuq (Tawhid official), Tripoli, August 2014.

[40] Interview with Aziz Allush (former Tawhid fighter close to Fatah), Tripoli, July 2014.

[41] "Il a refait surface au Liban Nord," *L'Orient Le Jour* (September 7, 1982), "Abu Ayad à Tripoli," *L'Orient Le Jour* (September 9, 1982) and "La crise du Fateh tourne au conflit militaire syro-palestinien," *L'Orient Le Jour* (June 22, 1983).

Yasser Arafat himself left his Tunisian exile to make a triumphant arrival in Tripoli, turning the northern port city into what the media referred to as the "new capital"[42] of Fatah. "The Tripolitan street loved Yasser Arafat," recalled a Tawhid fighter. "His presence in the city energized our movement – it provided us with many local recruits!"[43] This is also recognized by Tawhid's opponents who acknowledge that the Islamist movement back then became more popular in Tripoli – and that a key reason was the loyalty it displayed for Fatah. Far from being the puppet of Arafat, then, Tawhid displayed a great deal of agency in its relationship to its external backer, using it to secure military and political objectives as well as to gain popularity with the masses of Tripolitans who felt sympathetic to Fatah's plight.

Tripoli, Epicenter of the Palestinian Civil War

As the Arafat–Assad relationship fast deteriorated through 1983, the Syrian president exacerbated tensions between pro and anti-Syrian Palestinian factions inside Fatah to the point that what scholar Yezid Sayigh calls a "Palestinian civil war"[44] was about to erupt. Tripoli soon emerged as the locus of these tensions. There they crystallized as a struggle for the control of the city's two large Palestinian camps pitting Fatah against Fatah al-Intifada, with the former being backed by Tawhid while the latter was supported by the Syrian army.

The split inside Fatah which led to the birth of Fatah al-Intifada is multifaceted. Ostensibly, Fatah al-Intifada was created in May 1983 by Palestinian militants critical of Yasser Arafat's handling of the 1982 war with Israel and his subsequent endorsement of the Reagan peace plan. They began denouncing Arafat as the "Sadat of Palestine," in a reference to the Egyptian president who had years earlier made peace with Israel, criticizing the head of the Palestinian guerrilla organization for starting to show a willingness to negotiate with the "enemy," as Arafat had just done by claiming that he had "always"[45] supported compromise.

---

[42] "Tripoli, nouvelle capitale 'provisoire' de l'OLP?," *L'Orient Le Jour* (June 23, 1983).

[43] Interview with Abu Zghayar (former Tawhid military commander), Tripoli, July 2014.

[44] Yezid Sayigh, *Armed struggle and the search for state: the Palestinian national movement, 1949–1993* (Oxford: Oxford University Press, 1999).

[45] "Arafat a Moscou: 'Que Reagan et Begin comprennent que je ne suis pas Sadate'," *L'Orient Le Jour* (January 7, 1983), "Arafat: 'j'ai toujours été partisan du Plan Fahd," *L'Orient Le Jour* (September 13, 1983) and "Malaise croissant au sein de l'OLP: les initiatives d'Arafat mal accueillies par les radicaux palestiniens," *L'Orient Le Jour* (January 23, 1983).

382   The Geopolitics of Islamism

Arafat's increasingly conciliatory stance, according to intelligence reports, was fast "eroding"[46] his own position inside Fatah, and when Fatah al-Intifada emerged its leaders portrayed themselves as "hard-liners"[47] who would never compromise with Israel. "It was not the first time that there had been major disagreements within Fatah," recalled a figure in Fatah al-Intifada. "But, by saying he wanted peace, Yasser Arafat went too far."[48] Yet there were other significant issues too which exacerbated Fatah's internal tensions in 1982–3 to the point of implosion. Some of the guerrilla organization's leaders were accused of corruption. "A mafia mind-set was spreading at the leadership level," recalled a Palestinian official who joined the breakaway faction. Members of Fatah al-Intifada would use this to frame themselves as activists committed to the Palestinian cause who "never take bribes."[49] They also accused Yasser Arafat of concentrating power in the hands of a few trusted aides, many of whom belonged to an older generation born in Gaza and the West Bank, marginalizing younger activists raised in Lebanon's and Jordan's refugee camps. This generational and geographical gap was major. "The camps never had the last word,"[50] complained a militant.

Yet, if one trend only had to be singled out as leading to the split within Fatah and the rise of Fatah al-Intifada, it would have to be the combination of geopolitics and ideology. Fatah, by its 4th National Congress that took place in April 1981, was becoming irremediably divided between myriad ideological factions. Those who split to form Fatah al-Intifada, such as Mussa al-Amle (Abu Khaled al-Amle) and Nimer Saleh (Abu Saleh), were Marxist sympathizers of the USSR who felt marginalized and who did not share the animosity of its leadership for Syria, an ally of Russia, which they actually admired for being at the forefront of "socialism" and "anti-imperialism." Unsurprisingly, therefore, these figures steered Fatah al-Intifada in the direction of Moscow and Damascus. As early as in July 1983, merely two months after its creation, one of the leaders of the new Palestinian faction would go as far as bluntly stating that "our real concern" is to "protect Syria" in order to "deter the

[46] US Central Intelligence Agency, "The Fatah mutiny: implications for the peace process" (25X1, June 10, 1983).
[47] "Abu Saleh veut empêcher le chef de l'OLP de se joindre au processus de paix US," *L'Orient Le Jour* (November 22, 1983).
[48] Interview with Abu Yasser (Fatah al-Intifada's leader in North Lebanon), Tripoli's Beddawi refugee camp, August 2014.
[49] "Abu Saleh veut empêcher le chef de l'OLP de se joindre au processus de paix US," *L'Orient Le Jour* (November 22, 1983).
[50] Interview with a member of Fatah al-Intifada, Tripoli's Beddawi refugee camp, August 2014.

Tripoli, Epicenter of the Palestinian Civil War 383

enemies of the Arabs" and forge a "solid alliance"[51] with the Ba'ath Party. That relation rapidly evolved into becoming one-sided. Based in Damascus, the leaders of Fatah al-Intifada came under the wing of Ali Duba, Assad's military intelligence czar, who provided the Palestinian dissidents with cash, weapons and training. In return, the regime expected no less than Fatah al-Intifada's commitment to undermine Yasser Arafat's Fatah. One Western intelligence report thus concluded that Damascus became "the primary beneficiary of Fatah's troubles."[52]

The simmering rivalries between Fatah al-Intifada and Fatah erupted violently over the summer 1983 when the former seized the latter's positions and stockpiles of weapons across Syria and Lebanon's Beqaa Valley.[53] Within the matter of a couple of months, Yasser Arafat's loyalists became encircled in their last stronghold, Tripoli, in the vicinity of which they still controlled the two major Palestinian refugee camps of Beddawi and Naher al-Bared. Simultaneously, Tawhid's military hold over the rest of the city and its suburbs allowed them, for a time, to withstand attacks. There was little doubt that Fatah al-Intifada's offensive against Fatah was politically and militarily supported by Syria. State media in Damascus, routinely acting as a mouthpiece for the regime, had used an increasingly harsh and threatening rhetoric against the Fatah leadership throughout the first half of 1983. One regime newspaper, *Tishrin*, went as far as warning that "Syria is strong and capable of encircling the new Sadat," a reference to Yasser Arafat, and that "it would not hesitate to take whatever measure to safeguard the future [...] even if this should entail the use of unfriendly means."[54] The regime meant it. By October 1983 it had amassed 12,000 Syrian troops in North Lebanon and was ready to support Fatah al-Intifada's assault on Tripoli's Palestinian camps.

Although it is often overlooked in the scholarship, the ensuing struggle for the control of Tripoli's Palestinian camps of Beddawi and Naher al-Bared proved to be one of the bloodiest episodes of the Lebanese civil war in the north of the country. It resulted in the displacement of 30,000 residents from the two Palestinian refugee camps as well as in the killing

---

[51] "Crise au sein du Fatah," *L'Orient Le Jour* (July 4, 1983).
[52] US Central Intelligence Agency, "The Fatah mutiny: implications for the peace process" (25X1, June 10, 1983).
[53] "La crise du Fateh tourne au conflit militaire syro-palestinien," *L'Orient Le Jour* (June 22, 1983).
[54] Quoted in "Pour empêcher certains pays arabes de se joindre au processus de paix, Damas menace de recourir à des moyens 'inamicaux'," *L'Orient Le Jour* (February 27, 1983).

384   The Geopolitics of Islamism

of 428 people and the injuring of 2,059 individuals in the space of just a few weeks.[55] Hostilities started in late October and intensified in mid-November, pitting 4,000 Fatah militants alongside 3,000 Tawhid fighters against an equivalent number of pro-Assad fighters spearheaded by Fatah al-Intifada's men as well as thousands of members of the Syrian Special Forces.[56] Under the threat of constant shelling and the pressure of ever greater destruction, Yasser Arafat and his sympathizers withdrew from Naher al-Bared and, two weeks later, from Beddawi, but continued to sustain fierce resistance and to retaliate against pro-Assad forces from the vicinity of Tripoli.[57] Tawhid's participation in the battles resulted in considerably raising the stakes and enabled Fatah to withstand the offensive for another full month until a settlement between the warring factions was reached in mid-December 1983.[58]

The contribution of Tripoli's Islamists to this "Palestinian civil war" was twofold. At the military level, a Palestinian official in North Lebanon recounted that they were "very active"[59] in their support of Fatah's defense operations, mobilizing a large number of members, participating in battles, and acting as bodyguards for Fatah's top commanders. "They played a major role," admitted one of their rivals, a military leader in Fatah al-Intifada. "They were committed to defending Yasser Arafat and they were very enthusiastic about that."[60] At the political level their contribution was equally significant, since the very support of Tripoli's Islamists in his struggle for survival helped the leader of Fatah to appeal to pan-Islamic sentiment and to frame Fatah al-Intifada's attacks as an attempt to "destroy" an "Arab and Islamic city,"[61] which put the Syrian regime on the defensive. This pan-Islamic rhetoric would be key in pushing Saudi Arabia, Kuwait and Iran to pressure Syria into agreeing to a ceasefire, effectively safeguarding the Fatah leadership and ensuring

---

[55] "Le camp de Beddaoui est tombé aux mains des dissidents," L'Orient Le Jour (November 17, 1983) and "Projet d'accord syro-saoudien sur Tripoli," L'Orient Le Jour (November 24, 1983).

[56] "Tripoli au centre du cyclone – le cessez le feu n'aura vécu qu'un matin," L'Orient Le Jour (September 11, 1983) and "Tripoli: la consolidation du cessez le feu se fait attendre," L'Orient Le Jour (November 13, 1983).

[57] "Embarras de Damas qui s'attendait à une victoire rapide d'Abu Mussa sur Arafat," L'Orient Le Jour (November 20, 1983).

[58] "Tripoli: l'évacuation débutera aujourd'hui," L'Orient Le Jour (December 17, 1983).

[59] Interview with Abu Marwan (Fatah's head in North Lebanon), Tripoli's Beddawi refugee camp, August 2014.

[60] Interview with Abu Yasser (Fatah al-Intifada's leader in North Lebanon), Tripoli's Beddawi refugee camp, August 2014.

[61] In late November Yasser Arafat declared that "the goal of the Syrians is to destroy Tripoli, this Arab and Islamic city." Quoted in "Offensive contre Tripoli," L'Orient Le Jour (November 21, 1983).

its safe exit to Tunisia. Throughout this whole period, Tawhid's leaders spared no words to display their loyalty toward Yasser Arafat. Sa'id Sha'aban explicitly insisted until the eve of his departure that "you are a guest in Tripoli, we support the Palestinian revolution."[62]

Perhaps the leader of Tawhid knew that his support for Fatah would be well rewarded. As soon as Yasser Arafat departed Tripoli in mid-December 1983, he reportedly transferred $2 million to a Tawhid bank account to convey his gratitude.[63] He also left much equipment to the militants. An Islamist commander thus remembered that, before boarding for Tunisia, Palestinian officers provided Tawhid with large quantities of medium and light weapons. "They handed us so many bazookas and rifles that we no longer knew where to store all of them!"[64] This was confirmed by a report from the CIA. It explained that Arafat had "regularly funded" Tawhid, maintained a "personal relationship" with Sa'id Sha'aban and had put "a large cache of weapons at its disposal on the eve of his departure from the city in 1983."[65] Tawhid may have ostensibly served as Fatah's loyal "proxy" in Tripoli precisely when the Palestinian guerrilla organization needed its help the most during the November 1983 struggle, but it also pragmatically used this relationship for its own sake.

Palestinian, Syrian and Lebanese Islamists

One aspect of the Tawhid–Fatah relationship that frightened Damascus to the extent that it felt it would need to crush Tripoli's Islamists sooner or later was that, by then, Fatah had also developed ties to Syrian Islamists. This raised the fear that Fatah would use Tawhid to merge Palestinian, Syrian and Lebanese Islamist movements and undermine the regime. According to a source close to Syrian intelligence, Hafez al-Assad had become convinced that a key reason behind Yasser Arafat's notorious dislike of the Syrian regime was the sense that he had "Islamist sympathies."[66] Western intelligence reports suggest that Assad was

---

[62] Sa'id Sha'aban stated on the eve of Yasser Arafat's departure from Tripoli that, "You are a guest in Tripoli, we support the Palestinian revolution. You are leaving Tripoli but we will meet in Jerusalem." See "Situation à Tripoli," *L'Orient Le Jour* (December 20, 1983).

[63] Interview with several Tawhid officials, Tripoli, September 2014. *L'Orient Le Jour*'s source also mentioned that Arafat made a $2 million cheque out to Tawhid back then. "Situation à Tripoli," *L'Orient Le Jour* (December 20, 1983).

[64] Interview with Aziz Allush (former Tawhid military commander), Tripoli, July 2014.

[65] US Central Intelligence Agency, "Lebanon: Islamic fundamentalism in Tripoli" (Top Secret, NESAR 86-003JX, January 17, 1986).

[66] Interview with a figure close to Syrian intelligence, Tripoli, September 2014.

386   The Geopolitics of Islamism

anxious that Arafat "might exploit longstanding Fatah-Muslim Brotherhood links" to engineer a merger between Fatah, Tawhid and Syrian Islamists to "stir up trouble in Syria."[67]

It is true that Yasser Arafat had a conservative upbringing and Islamist sympathies. While living in Gaza and Cairo during his youth he had not been a formal member of the Egyptian Muslim Brotherhood, yet he had been given military training by its members and continued to enjoy relations with them when he later settled in Kuwait and Lebanon.[68] This, however, did not mean that his actions were guided by an Islamist ideological agenda. In fact, as head of Fatah, which regrouped several ideological tendencies united by the goal of recovering Palestine, he had to make compromises and act as a consensual leader. Today, Palestinian officials are often keen to stress that, despite his sympathy for the Islamist opposition in Syria and his dislike of Hafez al-Assad and his policies, Yasser Arafat never deliberately tried to undermine the Syrian regime.[69] But, although the scholarship overlooks the very existence of an alliance between Fatah and Syrian as well as Lebanese Islamists, there is evidence to suggest that Hafez al-Assad's fears may have been justified to a degree.[70]

Within Fatah, and under Yasser Arafat's sponsorship, there was a powerful and underground Islamist faction which supported the anti-Assad struggle of Lebanese and Syrian Islamists in the 1970s, raising the distinct possibility that a merger between Palestinian, Lebanese and Syrian Islamist movements would soon be under way and threaten the regime. This wing, embodied by a Fatah unit known as the Armed Struggle (*Kifah Mousallah*), was not represented in Fatah congresses abroad, yet it was still a major force on the ground. Officially it was only tasked with ensuring security in the camps and operating the justice, prison and police systems. But in reality this unit was more powerful than it initially appeared, for Yasser Arafat had given carte blanche to its commander, Mustafa Dib, better known as "Abu Ta'an," to train and equip anti-Assad Lebanese and Syrian Islamist militias.

---

[67] US Central Intelligence Agency, "Syria: Sunni opposition to the minority Alawite regime" (Secret, NESA 85-10102, June 1985).

[68] Interview with Ibrahim al-Masri (leader of the Islamic Group or Lebanon's Muslim Brotherhood branch), Beirut, June 2014.

[69] Interview with Fatah officials, Beirut and Tripoli, July–August 2014.

[70] An exception is Bernard Rougier, *Everyday Jihad: the rise of militant Islam among Palestinians in Lebanon* (Cambridge, MA: Harvard University Press, 2007), a book in which the author refers to the ties between Fatah and individual Lebanese and Palestinian Islamists, albeit without delving deep into the nature of these relationships.

Abu Ta'an was a Palestinian Islamist "ideological entrepreneur" who seemed to have a unique profile to trigger a merger between Palestinian, Syrian and Lebanese Islamists, underlining the importance of personal agency in ties between "patrons" and their "proxies." Born in Sheikh Daoud, Palestine, in the 1930s, he was both an ardent Palestinian nationalist and a committed Islamist. He first joined the Army of the Sacred Jihad (*Jaysh al-Jihad al-Muqadass*), an anti-Zionist and Islamic rebel group, and later became a follower of Haj Amin al-Husseini, the Grand Mufti of Jerusalem. He left Palestine in 1948 and settled in the Naher al-Bared refugee camp in Tripoli, where he built a network of social and ideational ties with Tripolitan Islamist figures and factions which would later prove invaluable. He then left Tripoli for Iraq, where he attended a military training course, before going on to join the Palestine Liberation Army (*Jaysh al-Tahrir al-Filastini*), becoming a general and, in 1972, adhering to Fatah – a movement in which he quickly rose to head the unit Armed Struggle. But, although he had by then become very close to Fatah leaders of all stripes, he had remained an Islamist and was even sometimes so guided by his ideology that he tried lobbying Yasser Arafat and other Fatah leaders into taking decisions driven by Islamism.

An interview with Abu Ta'an provided a rare glimpse of the mindset of this "ideological entrepreneur" and showed the extent to which Islamism informed his thinking and behavior. Unlike other Fatah militants he prided himself of "caring about more than just Palestine."[71] "All believers are brothers," he argued. "I feel as afflicted whether I hear a Muslim is killed in Palestine or far away." The "Islamist cause" ran through his blood. He wanted to rid Muslims of the "oppression" exercised by secular Arab dictatorships. This mindset drew him close to the ideology of the Muslim Brotherhood. "Its ideas are my ideas," he stated, while specifying that he was never a full-blown member. He did not want to forge close relations with its Lebanese chapter, the Islamic Group, which he found too institutionalized and no longer militant enough. Rather, he remained in Fatah and in the 1970s began recruiting the militant Tripolitan Islamist figures and factions that had split from the Islamic Group, as we saw in Chapter 3. They included Soldiers of God, the "Sufi jihadis" and Abu Imara, who later joined Tawhid upon its creation. "We trusted Abu Ta'an," recalled Soldiers of God's leader. "He trained us, gave us weapons and he was a real Muslim."[72] On top of

---

[71] Interview with Abu Ta'an, June and August 2014.
[72] Interview with Kan'an Naji (leader of Soldiers of God, former Tawhid Emir in Tripoli's Abu Samra district), Tripoli, August 2014.

388 The Geopolitics of Islamism

mutual interests and shared ideology, it also mattered that Abu Ta'an had long lived in Tripoli and that strong, preexisting social and ideational ties bound them.

Simultaneously, Abu Ta'an's status as an Islamist "ideological entrepreneur" who prided himself on caring about "more than just Palestine" also led him to develop hostile views of the regime and to support the Syrian Muslim Brothers and the Fighting Vanguard. "They were Sunni Muslims, Islamists and they vehemently opposed the regime – like me!"[73] Of course, Abu Ta'an's opposition to the regime was partially driven by his Palestinian origins. It originated from Hafez al-Assad's determination to shape the Palestinian militant scene according to his own interests. "He wanted the whole Palestinian file in his hands – the Syrian regime became an obstacle on our way to liberating Palestine," he stated bluntly. Yet it also seemed to be a product of sectarian animosity stemming from Sunni Islamist ideology. "I hated Hafez al-Assad because he was an Alawi," he acknowledged. He argued that "History" showed that Syria's Alawis had "always supported French and Israeli interests." His discourse was reminiscent of the ideas spread by Sa'id Hawwa, the ideologue of the radical wing of the Syrian Muslim Brotherhood. "The Alawis are outside of Islam," he stated, much like Hawwa. "Islam is the Quran and the hadith. Either you accept it or you don't. The Alawis departed from Islam and they even made a point of it." Moreover, they represented a minority, "so why," he wondered rhetorically, "should they be allowed to rule the country?"

Abu Ta'an's status as an Islamist "ideological entrepreneur" with deep-seated anti-regime views and strong ties to Tripolitan and Syrian Islamist movements made him the perfect figure to try merging anti-Assad Palestinian, Lebanese and Syrian Islamists in the 1970s. Because this was an extremely sensitive and secretive project at a time of fast-mounting tension between Yasser Arafat and Hafez al-Assad, Abu Ta'an said that the Palestinian leader never "formally" asked him what he was up to. But he asserted that Arafat naturally "knew." "He deliberately kept a distance – that's 'politics' – but he knew what he was doing when he gave me carte blanche, access to stockpiles of weapons, unlimited funds and training camps." This was confirmed by a figure who was part of Fatah's leadership and asserted that "we all knew what Abu Ta'an was up to – he had been tasked by Arafat to support the Islamists."[74]

Abu Ta'an reactivated his ties with the Tripolitan Islamists of Soldiers of God, whom he then tasked with using the smuggling routes and cross-

---

[73] Interview with Abu Ta'an, June and August 2014.
[74] Interview with a high-ranking Palestinian intelligence officer, Beirut, June 2014.

border solidarities linking them to Syrian Islamists from Homs and Hama in order to entice them to come and join the training camps he was in the midst of running in Lebanon's Palestinian camps. "Hundreds of Syrian Islamists came in secret to my military bases where my commanders trained them on several types of weapons and we smuggled them arms and money after they returned to Syria,"[75] he recalled proudly. Militant Syrian Islamist sources acknowledged his importance, pointing out that he trained such leaders of the 1979–82 insurrection as Adnan Uqla, who even fought alongside Fatah in the 1976 Tal al-Za'atar battle in Beirut. Quickly, then, Abu Ta'an's camps became privileged spaces where the socialization, indoctrination and mobilization of Palestinian, Syrian and Lebanese Islamists occurred. A militant who attended recalled how, in these camps, activists from the three nationalities created powerful bonds of solidarity with each other, acquired precious military expertise and underwent ideological training.[76] Abu Ta'an's activism raised the possibility that Palestinian, Lebanese and Syrian Islamists would merge, or at the very least effectively coordinate their anti-Assad struggle.

This underground Fatah support for Lebanon's and Syria's anti-Assad Islamists began in 1973 and went unnoticed for four years. But in 1977 a shooting accident which led to the death of a Syrian Islamist put the spotlight on Fatah's camps and Syrian intelligence learned of its role. A figure close to the Syrian security services recounted that this episode proved to be a major "irritant,"[77] to say the least, in the relationship between Yasser Arafat and Hafez al-Assad. The leader of Fatah did his best to distance himself from the "rogue" acts of Abu Ta'an. He formally denied ever being aware of Abu Ta'an's ties to anti-Assad Lebanese and Syrian Islamist movements, officially ordering the closure of his camps and going so far as to send him far away from Lebanon and Syria on a "military training course" in India for a while. Yet, as soon as the Arafat–Assad relationship deteriorated again, in mid-1982, Fatah smuggled Abu Ta'an back to Tripoli, where he was tasked with reviving the Palestinian–Syrian–Lebanese Islamist nexus and making it an integral part of Tawhid after its creation. However, he was captured there by Fatah al-Intifada during the November 1983 battle and handed over to Syria. The treatment he underwent in prison confirmed how significant the regime thought he was. Abu Ta'an spent from 1983 until 2004 in a small underground cell alone. He had nothing but a bowl in which he would

[75] Interview with Abu Ta'an, June and August 2014.
[76] Interview with a militant who attended Abu Ta'an's training camp, August 2014.
[77] Interview with a figure close to Syrian intelligence, Tripoli, September 2014.

390   The Geopolitics of Islamism

eat, drink and urinate. He was beaten so severely that he lost an eye. Unsurprisingly, the questions he was asked during the torture sessions were all about Fatah's ties to the Syrian Muslim Brotherhood and to Tawhid.[78]

A merger between the Palestinian, Syrian and Lebanese Islamists would have mounted a major challenge to the Syrian regime and considerably bolstered the opposition. And Abu Ta'an's unique combination of his access to unlimited Fatah resources, status as an Islamist "ideological entrepreneur" seeking to mold the nature of activism according to his Islamist worldviews and his ability to activate and mobilize Tripolitan and Syrian Islamist networks suggests that this ideologically patterned nexus could have seen the light of day. His 1983 capture unraveled that project prematurely. Embodying the importance of personal agency, his absence limited the prospect of a merger or even the potential for truly organized cooperation between Fatah, Tawhid and the Syrian Islamists. Yet the mere notion that such an alliance could have materialized motivated Hafez al-Assad's absolute determination to crush Tawhid as well as all forms of Sunni Islamism in Tripoli, this time once and for all.

The Genesis of the Tawhid–Iran Relationship

In this heated context, Tawhid owed its survival to its alliance with the Islamic Republic of Iran. This section tackles the genesis of the Tawhid–Iran relationship and the two following sections explore the influence which this alliance had on Tawhid's discourse, behavior and internal politics, and examine the evolution of that relationship. At first glance it appeared that a shared Islamist ideology was at the core of the Tawhid–Iran alliance, something due to the fact that "ideological entrepreneurs" on both sides initially acted as the handlers and drivers of this relationship and because Iran had begun spending considerable resources on enhancing the commitment of Tawhid members to "Khomeinism." In return Tehran expected no less than to turn Tawhid from a "spatially oriented movement" into an ideologically guided terrorist group – a "Sunni Hezbollah" which would act as its loyal proxy among Lebanese Sunnis, in a mirror of Hezbollah's role among Lebanese Shias. Yet it eventually transpired that, with a few exceptions, Tawhid's leaders had instrumentally constructed the appearance of ideological proximity with Tehran to get its support. As Iran realized that Tawhid might be a useful

[78] Interview with Abu Ta'an, June and August 2014.

The Genesis of the Tawhid–Iran Relationship 391

Sunni Islamist ally but would also remain local and never turn into its ideologically loyal proxy, their relationship turned more transactional.

If Hafez al-Assad accommodated Tehran by allowing Tawhid to keep control of Tripoli until 1985, it was because, although the Syrian–Iranian alliance was back then not as deep as it is today, it had already become such a strategic partnership that the Syrian president had every reason to tread carefully. By 1983–4 Syria and Iran, which on paper boasted diametrically opposed political ideologies – Ba'athist secularism and Khomeinist Islamism – shared similar geopolitical priorities. They were first and foremost guided by a common enmity for Iraq. Iran, as it was in the midst of a brutal war against Saddam Hussein; Syria, because the Iraqi strongman had supported the Syrian Muslim Brotherhood's uprisings in 1976–82 and was until 1985 known to provide the Islamist group with a "safe heaven," "military camps" and "weapons"[79] to continue its anti-Assad insurgency. The relationship between Iran and Syria also assumed a broader international dimension for they both belonged, alongside Libya, to a front of countries which flatly rejected the US-led Arab–Israeli peace initiatives that had led to the emergence of a Jordanian–Egyptian–Saudi axis.

It was thus as a mark of goodwill to Tehran in the context of a strengthening of the Syrian–Iranian alliance that Hafez al-Assad allowed Tawhid to continue surviving until mid-1985. Already during the regime's November 1983 struggle for Tripoli's two Palestinian camps, Damascus had let Tehran broker a settlement alongside other states wherein Fatah militiamen safely exited the city while Tawhid remained unscathed.[80] But the real sign suggesting that the Islamic Republic was prepared to throw its full diplomatic weight behind the movement surfaced in mid-1984 when the Iranian President Ali Khamane'i personally went to Damascus on his first trip abroad since taking office simply in order to mediate a truce between the Syrian regime and Tripoli's Islamists and spare the latter a war.[81] Sa'id Sha'aban displayed his gratitude, going as far as claiming that "Iran believes that Tripoli is an Islamic city and should have protection" and expressing his appreciation for the "Iranian good offices with Syria" that "helped ease pressures between Tawhid and the Syrian state."[82] In spite of Tawhid's localism,

---

[79] US Central Intelligence Agency, "Syria: Sunni opposition to the minority Alawite regime" (Secret, NESA 85-10102, June 1985).
[80] "Emissaire iranien à Tripoli," *L'Orient Le Jour* (November 27, 1983).
[81] "Le président iranien à Damas," *L'Orient Le Jour* (October 7, 1984).
[82] "Shaaban à Damas pour des entretiens avec les autorités syriennes," *L'Orient le Jour* (October 8, 1984) and "Téhéran engage une médiation pour resserrer les rangs islamiques au Liban," *L'Orient Le Jour* (October 9, 1984).

392   The Geopolitics of Islamism

then, Tehran was by 1983–4 prepared to commit significant resources to back the movement and to allow it to survive Hafez al-Assad's wrath.

The central factor which explained such a strong degree of Iranian interest for Tawhid and readiness to commit vast resources to support it was the key role played within its midst by the "ideological entrepreneurs." The Islamic Republic knew that these figures were genuinely committed to its agenda and would mobilize "Khomeinist" worldviews to push Tawhid to behave in ways consistent with or even driven by ideology. It also had strong and often preexisting social and ideational ties with some of them, which significantly bred trust. The fact that the "ideological entrepreneurs" played an influential role in Tawhid, as was seen in Chapter 6, raised Iran's hope that it would turn into its committed Sunni Islamist proxy.

The root of the Iranian interest for Tawhid particularly lay in Esmat Murad's presence in its leadership. He was known to be close to the "ideological entrepreneurs," had a history as a committed "Sunni Khomeinist" and had long acted as a loyal ally to Tehran. Chapter 3 pointed out how Esmat Murad's older connections to Iran were both social and ideational. These ties dated back to the years before the 1979 Islamic Revolution, when he was the head of a militant pro-Palestinian Maoist rebel movement in South Lebanon. There he frequently interacted with a group of Iranian volunteers also fighting Israel and he grew especially close to one of them, Jalaleddine al-Farsi, a Shia Islamist "ideological entrepreneur" who convinced him to embrace "Khomeinism" – and, while Esmat Murad initially used it instrumentally as a "protest ideology," he later became genuinely driven by it. After the 1979 Iranian Revolution, Jalaleddine al-Farsi became an influential figure of his own right in Iran, his name even being touted by the Ayatollahs as a possible president. Perhaps as a result of al-Farsi's friendship with Murad, the latter was invited to Tehran as early as January 1980 to take part in the World Congress of Liberation Movements organized by the newly established Islamic Republic with the goal of promoting its ideology. And, reflecting the strength of the social and ideational ties Murad forged with the Iranian rulers, he would be invited eight more times to Tehran within the space of the two years preceding Tawhid's advent.[83] Importantly, Murad and the small group of Tripolitan Islamist "ideological entrepreneurs" gravitating around him became personally close to what was back then called the "radical bloc" in Iran's new power galaxy. This bloc was made up of some of the Islamic

---

[83] Abi Samra, *Trablus*, p. 136.

Republic's most ardent "ideological entrepreneurs." They included Mohammed Montazeri and Mehdi Hashemi, the two successive leaders of the Office of Freedom Movements, a Revolutionary Guards unit specifically tasked with promoting "Khomeinist" ideology abroad by funding pro-Iran movements globally.[84] It is in this context that, as Murad and the circle of committed "Sunni Khomeinists" around him joined Tawhid in 1982, the Islamic Republic started developing an interest for the movement. What appealed to Tehran was that these figures were sincerely "Khomeinists," then, but also that they had pre-existing social and ideational ties to its own "ideological entrepreneurs."

The Islamic Republic began being more explicit about its willingness to back Tawhid in 1983–5 as a result of three factors. First, there was a geopolitical aspect to it. It was viewed as a good public relations move to back this pro-Palestinian Sunni Arab movement known as an ally of Fatah precisely when Saddam Hussein was painting Iran as driven by a Shia Persian agenda and was seeking to revive old rivalries between Tehran and Sunni Arabs as a way to drive a wedge between them. Indeed, publicizing its support for Tawhid and regularly inviting delegations from the movement to visit Tehran gave Sunni Arab credentials to the Islamic Republic and helped to suggest that, far from being animated by sectarian and nationalist sentiments, its foreign policy was instead truly guided by pan-Islamic solidarity. Coming within the context of the worsening of the Iraq–Iran war and of their struggle for regional primacy, Tehran's backing for Tawhid therefore had a clear geopolitical dimension.

Second, there was a domestic politics aspect to it too. Providing public support for a Lebanese Islamist movement like Tawhid which, as we saw in Chapter 4, ostensibly embraced "Khomeinist" Islamism starkly reinforced the credentials of Iran's "radical bloc" at a period of murky power struggles and violent purges in Tehran. It seemed to show the success of the enterprise of Iranian Islamist "ideological entrepreneurs" such as al-Farsi, Montazeri and Hashemi, who had spent much of their own political capital after 1979 promoting "Khomeinism" abroad through the yearly organization in Tehran of a World Congress of Liberation Movements and the dispatching of Iranian volunteers to Syria and Lebanon to fight Israel. Publicly welcoming delegations of Tawhid's "Sunni Khomeinists" to Iran suggested their efforts had not been in vain, bolstering their power in domestic politics.[85]

---

[84] Interviews with Tawhid officials close to Esmat Murad and Iran, including Ibrahim Saleh, Ghassan Ghoshe, Amer Arnaout Abu Shawqi, Nasser Murad, Selim Lababidi and Abu Meriam Khassouq, Tripoli, August 2014.

[85] Interview with Anis Naqqash (Lebanese militant close to al-Farsi, Montazeri and Hashemi), Beirut, June 2014.

394   The Geopolitics of Islamism

And, last but not least, there was a more distinctively ideological element to Iran's willingness to back Tawhid. As the Revolutionary Guards were by then in the midst of propping up Hezbollah in order to turn it into Iran's most prominent foreign ideological ally, they began touting the idea of transforming Tawhid into their other fully dedicated Lebanese ideological proxy, but this time Sunni. "They wanted to make a Sunni Hezbollah,"[86] summed up one of the officials in Tawhid who was back then in charge of liaising with Tehran. A figure close to Iranian intelligence confirmed that the Revolutionary Guards were bent on using their relation with Tawhid to turn it into "Iran's vanguard in the Sunni community,"[87] its "Sunni Khomeinist" forward arm. This prospect even rang alarm bells in Washington, DC; one report by the CIA in mid-1984 warned of the dangers to Western interests in Lebanon because, "if Iran becomes [Tawhid's] principal supporter, a relationship may develop resembling that between Tehran and [Hezbollah]."[88]

On Tawhid's side, virtually all leaders and members initially agreed on the need to forge an alliance with the Islamic Republic of Iran. But they did so for very different reasons. On the one hand, Esmat Murad and the handful of "ideological entrepreneurs" around him who had long been committed to "Khomeinism" saw in this alliance a way to steer the movement in a less spatially oriented and more ideologically guided direction. But, on the other hand, many other leaders, cadres and members viewed their alliance with Iran through a much more instrumental prism. By mid to late 1983 it had become evident to them that the financial and military support Tawhid drew from Fatah was bound to severely dwindle as the guerrilla organization's presence in Tripoli was being challenged violently. This raised the question of how, on its own and without significant external support, Tawhid would be able resist a full-blown Syrian offensive on the city.[89] Within Tawhid's Consultative Council or leadership, then, Esmat Murad and the "ideological entrepreneurs" convinced the other leaders, cadres and many members at large that forging a strong relationship with Iran was not simply a matter

---

[86] Interview with Abu Meriam Khassouq (Tawhid official in charge of coordination with Iran), Tripoli, June 2014.

[87] Interview with Anis Naqqash (Lebanese militant close to Iran's Revolutionary Guards), Beirut, June 2014.

[88] US Central Intelligence Agency, "Directory of Lebanese militias: a reference aid" (Secret, NESA 84-10171C, June 1984).

[89] Interviews with Tawhid officials who viewed Iranian backing instrumentally, including Kan'an Naji, Abu Zghayar, Aziz Allush and Abu Othman, Tripoli, June–September 2014.

of ideological consistency but also of sheer necessity. Only through Iran's backing would Syria be persuaded to leave Tawhid unscathed.

As we saw in Chapter 6, Tawhid used its exercise of seemingly "religious violence" against Tripolitan members of the Iraqi Ba'ath Party in August 1983 to send a signal to the Iranians suggesting its readiness to act on their behalf in Lebanon. And Chapter 4 showed how, when the threat of a Syrian military crackdown on Tawhid became tangible after it got drawn into a bloody struggle with pro-Assad fighters stationed on the Alawi hilltop of Jabal Mohsen in 1984, it strategically shifted the content of its ideological production in a markedly "Khomeinist" direction in order to gain the full diplomatic backing of the Islamic Republic and to spare it what would have been a devastating conflict. Although Tawhid's relationship with Iran seemed to be guided by shared ideology from the outset, mainly because some in the movement were known to be extremely committed to Tehran's ideological agenda, the alliance was from the very beginning instrumentalized in more or less subtle ways by leaders and members who were seeking to assuage tensions with Syria.

From Spatially Oriented to Ideologically Driven?

In return for its staunch backing of Tawhid, Tehran had great expectations of the movement. Reportedly aware of its spatially oriented or deeply localized nature, the Iranians wanted to transform it into an ideologically driven terrorist group. Their goal was nothing less than to turn it into a "Sunni Hezbollah" toeing their ideological line and implementing their agenda. As a result they invested massively in Tawhid. And, interestingly, for a time between early and mid-1984 it seemed as though their efforts had been successful at transforming the "neighborhood Islamism," "vernacular Islamism" or "subaltern Islamism" which characterized Tawhid into sincere commitment to their "Khomeinist" breed of Islamism.

Tawhid's discourse then not only turned more markedly pro-Iranian but a number of its cadres became sincerely convinced by the Islamic Republic's ideology, leading them to lobby for the movement to engage in anti-Western attacks, to try spreading to other Sunni-dominated parts of Lebanon and even to merge with Hezbollah in a pro-Tehran Islamist front. Tawhid seemed to be turning from a spatially oriented to an ideologically driven movement.

At the core of Iran's strategy of turning Tawhid into its "Sunni Hezbollah" lay an indoctrination campaign it carried out in late 1983 and through 1984, which aimed at socializing and educating members into "Khomeinism" in order to enhance their ideological

396   The Geopolitics of Islamism

commitment to Tehran. Interestingly this never involved any attempt at converting Tawhid's Sunni members into Shias. What Iran instead wanted was to see those members and leaders who had previously instrumentalized ideology now becoming more genuinely convinced about the need to follow Ayatollah Khomeini's leadership, roll back Western influence and set up an Islamic republic.[90] Iran's efforts materialized in various ways. For instance, it sought to create strong bonds with Tawhid's most promising cadres by instructing the movement's leadership to send two dozen of them to Baalbek, in the heart of Lebanon's Beqaa Valley. There, in a compound known as the "Sheikh Abdallah Barracks," officers of the Iranian Revolutionary Guards were in the midst of socializing and educating hundreds of Hezbollah members into "Khomeinism." "We stayed for a few days and we engaged in a dialogue with the Pasdaran," recounted a Tawhid cadre who participated in the event, using the Iranian name for the Revolutionary Guards. "We mainly talked about the benefits of the 1979 Islamic Revolution in Iran."[91] The Islamic Republic also sent its own "ideological entrepreneurs" to Tripoli to carry out proselytizing activities. Sometimes it did so through "Iranian educational delegations" which visited Tripoli to "reinforce the pedagogical relationship between Tehran and Tawhid."[92] But most often the Islamic Republic did so indirectly, by dispatching its network of non-Iranian "ideological entrepreneurs" closest to "Khomeinism" in Lebanon such as Mohammed Hussein Fadlallah, back then the most vocal proponent of the "Iranian model," or Abbas Mussawi, the leader of Hezbollah and mastermind of the group's anti-Western violence in the early 1980s.[93] Throughout 1984 all of these figures who were bent on maximizing the commitment of Tawhid members to "Khomeinism" began coming to Tripoli more frequently. They sometimes remained for prolonged stays, delivering lectures but also taking part in the activities of the movement's own "ideological entrepreneurs," like the post-Friday prayer marches they were organizing or the "summer camps" they were running.[94] This worried the CIA, which noticed with anxiety how "Hezbollah members often parade in Tripoli chanting pro-Khomeini

---

[90] Interviews with current and former Tawhid members, cadres and leaders, Tripoli, May–September 2014.

[91] Interview with Abu Meriam Khassouq (Tawhid official in charge of coordination with Iran), Tripoli, June 2014.

[92] See, for instance, "Délégation pédagogique iranienne à Tripoli," *L'Orient Le Jour* (May 19, 1985).

[93] Interviews with Tawhid officials close to Iran.

[94] Interview with several "ideological entrepreneurs" in Tawhid, Tripoli, June–September 2014.

slogans" and even wondered whether this would lead to "the establishment of a Hezbollah and Iranian foothold in Tripoli with Tawhid's complicity."[95] By committing resources to socialize and educate members into "Khomeinism," Iran hoped to give rise to a new generation of Tawhid cadres who would now be loyal to its ideology and eventually push the movement to become a "Sunni Hezbollah."

Another way through which Iran sought to transform Tawhid from a spatially oriented to an ideologically guided movement was by reinforcing its operational capacities to conduct terrorist attacks on Western targets in Lebanon, as Hezbollah was doing. The man in charge of overseeing the alliance with the movement and bolstering its capabilities was none other than Sayyed Akbar Mohtashemi, Iran's powerful minister of internal security, which showed the scale of the Islamic Republic's ambitions for Tawhid. He had also been Tehran's ambassador to Damascus and, tellingly, was widely praised in pro-Iranian circles as the "de facto founder of Hezbollah"[96] and the mastermind of the Shia group's April 1983 bombing against the American and French military barracks in Beirut. Mohtashemi, in turn, nominated three deputies to handle the practical aspects of this alliance. One of them, Issa Tabataba'i, was a militant cleric and "ideological entrepreneur" who was close to Ayatollah Khomeini and was to be the financial link between Tehran and Tawhid. The second one, Mohammed Ismael Khaliq, was an Iranian intelligence officer embedded in Hezbollah who was charged to be an intermediary helping Tawhid communicate with other pro-Iranian groups in Lebanon and the Middle East. The last one, Sayyed Mohammed Askari, was none other than the head of the Revolutionary Guards delegation in Beirut, who was tasked to equip Tawhid with sophisticated explosives and design training programs. By the account of Tawhid officials, these three figures traveled frequently to Tripoli between early and late 1984, growing close to two dozen pro-Iranian cadres as well as "ideological entrepreneurs" and supporting their efforts to push the movement to adopt a less spatially oriented and a more ideologically guided behavior, in conformity with Iran's ambitions.[97]

In turn, the central mechanism through which Iran exerted influence on Tawhid's discourse, behavior and internal politics was the

[95] US Central Intelligence Agency, "Lebanon: Islamic fundamentalism in Tripoli" (Top Secret, NESAR 86-003JX, January 17, 1986).

[96] Interview with Maher Hammud ("Sunni Khomeinist" cleric close to Tawhid and to Iran), Sidon, July 2014.

[97] Interviews with Tawhid officials close to Esmat Murad and Iran; including Ibrahim Saleh, Ghassan Ghoshe, Amer Arnaout Abu Shawqi, Nasser Murad, Selim Lababidi and Abu Meriam Khassouq, Tripoli, August 2014.

398   The Geopolitics of Islamism

"ideological entrepreneurship" of the two dozen figures who were sincerely committed to the Iranian model, mobilized "Khomeinist" worldviews and pushed the movement in a direction consistent with Tehran's interests. The Islamic Republic of Iran, aware of Tawhid's wide "spectrum of ideological commitment," did not expect it to behave in homogeneously "Khomeinist" ways. Rather, it counted on the influence in the movement of those cadres and leaders who were genuinely committed to its ideological agenda, either because they had preexisting social and ideational ties to the Islamic Republic or as they had been indoctrinated into "Khomeinism" through Iran's efforts.

Unsurprisingly, the handful of these Tawhid figures who were committed to making the movement less spatially oriented and more ideologically driven comprised Esmat Murad and the small group of pro-Iran cadres around him. As well-educated thinkers and writers, they took a lead role in Tawhid's ideological production and pushed its discourse in a more "Khomeinist" direction through 1984. But the Tawhid cadres who grew close to Iran also included others whose background would not have suggested a natural conversion to the Islamic Republic's agenda, thus showing that its indoctrination efforts had not been in vain.

The trajectory of Fu'ad al-Kurdi showed how Tehran was to an extent successful in turning the instrumental embrace of ideology by some members into sincere commitments. Tellingly, al-Kurdi had long been a part of Khalil Akkawi's faction of "neighborhood Islamists." As Chapter 2 indicated, members of this faction had embraced Islamism instrumentally as a "protest ideology" for local reasons, both to express dissent against the fast-mounting grievances of their beloved district, Bab al-Tebbaneh, and out of loyalty for their strongman, Akkawi, who joined Tawhid and thus drew them into the movement too – they were more driven by neighborhood concerns and solidarities than by ideology. Al-Kurdi turned more sincerely committed to Islamism after attending meetings of the Line of Islamic Justice. But, by all accounts, it was only through the "ideological entrepreneurs" dispatched by Tehran to Tripoli that he got socialized and educated into the "Khomeinist" breed of Islamism and that he turned into a leading pro-Iran "ideological entrepreneur" himself. From then on he was obsessed with importing the "Iranian model." He pushed Tawhid in that direction by mobilizing his worldviews to lobby the leaders and to maximize the commitment of members to "Khomeinism." He even opened a small bookshop selling copies of Khomeini's landmark treatise, *The Islamic Government*, as well as magazines featuring articles by Hezbollah ideologue Mohammed Hussein Fadlallah, and spent much of the rest of his time putting up posters of the Ayatollahs throughout Tripoli.[98] By 1984, then, the Revolutionary Guards had succeeded to turn Fu'ad al-Kurdi into one of their most ideologically committed relays in Tawhid, building a "privileged relationship" and a "direct line"[99] with him. Once guided by inherently local concerns, he was now mobilizing broader ideological goals. Through Tawhid's "ideological entrepreneurs," Iran hoped to exert influence on the movement's discourse and behavior.

Fu'ad al-Kurdi's "ideological entrepreneurship" illustrates the way ideologically patterned alliances between an external backer and a movement can impact the latter's behavior. Like Esmat Murad, al-Kurdi advocated for Tawhid's transformation into a "Sunni Hezbollah" fully committed to "Khomeinism." But, unlike him, he was not just a thinker but was also known as a "man of action" who, as a military commander, had two dozen militants at his disposal whom he would use to engage in ideologically driven violence on behalf of the movement. By all accounts, al-Kurdi was one of the best known and most feared Tawhid figures in Tripoli. This partially stemmed from his disproportionate height and muscular body – he had been a bodybuilding star during his youth, even reaching sixth and second places at the Arab and Lebanese championships of 1971. Yet it also resulted from the sense that he began often behaving in deeply ideological, Islamist ways while threatening those who did not with severe punishment.[100] After some time spent lobbying Tawhid's Consultative Council or leadership, he and his followers obtained a green light from the other leaders to engage in anti-Western operations in Tripoli in early 1984, after French warplanes retaliated against the 1983 bombing of their military barracks in Beirut by striking Hezbollah bases and Iranian outposts in the Beqaa Valley. Vowing vengeance, the leaders of the Islamic Republic had declared that "the death of one Frenchman is preferable to the death of 200 [Lebanese Christian] Phalangists,"[101] and al-Kurdi as a result supervised an unprecedented wave of anti-French attacks in Tripoli. A mere two months after the French retaliation on the Beqaa Valley, he masterminded a series of operations targeting symbols of France in North Lebanon, using Iranian logistical help to blow up Tripoli's French cultural center, set fire to the local French high school and kidnap its director as well as

---

[98] Interview with Khaled al-Kurdi (Fu'ad al-Kurdi's brother and Tawhid member close to Iran), October 2014.

[99] Interview with Selim Lababidi (former Tawhid member close to Iran), Beirut's Shatila refugee camp, May 2014.

[100] Interviews with current and former Tawhid members, Tripoli, June–August 2014.

[101] "Rafsanjani: la mort d'un français ou d'un américain est préférable à la mort de 200 Phalangistes," *L'Orient Le Jour* (January 12, 1984).

400   The Geopolitics of Islamism

destroy a local branch of the French-Lebanese bank.[102] Through the "ideological entrepreneurship" of al-Kurdi, who mobilized his world-views, lobbied for engagement in "Khomeinist" violence and personally oversaw this wave of attacks, the Iran–Tawhid alliance was affecting the latter's behavior.

Sources in Tawhid even allege that Fu'ad al-Kurdi was about to launch much more violent and spectacular, Hezbollah-style terror attacks against Western interests in Lebanon. One of his plans was to target the USS *New Jersey*, an American warship which was stationed off the shores of Shekka, a small port situated a few miles south of Tripoli. "The plan was to bomb and hijack the USS *New Jersey*,"[103] stated one of his confidants. Tawhid's Consultative Council was reportedly worried about the risk that such an operation, because of the high stakes it involved, might blow back on the movement. But, bowing to the intense lobbying efforts of both Fu'ad al-Kurdi and Esmat Murad, it approved the attack. Murad and al-Kurdi set up a special operations team in Tawhid whose members had just been trained by the Iranians and went on to coordinate with the Revolutionary Guards delegation in Beirut, which covertly provided them with a Grad rocket launcher and a speedboat.[104] The attack, however, was called off at the last minute after the USS *New Jersey*, perhaps warned of the plot, left the Lebanese coast prematurely. Fu'ad al-Kurdi was assassinated weeks later, in February 1984, in an act which was widely blamed on France's external intelligence agency, although the real identity of his killers remains a mystery today. Whoever the assassins were, the killing of Fu'ad al-Kurdi was followed by the murder of Esmat Murad months later and that of several more "ideological entrepreneurs" who were close to Iran, which by mid to late 1984 brought Tawhid's anti-Western violence to an end.

The "ideological entrepreneurship" of a handful of Tawhid cadres who were committed to and mobilized Khomeinist views had acted as the essential mechanism through which the Islamic Republic exerted influence on the movement, making its discourse and behavior less spatially oriented and more ideologically guided for a while. But, precisely because of their importance, their death would change the nature of the Tawhid–Iran alliance.

---

[102] "Sécurité renforcée autour des institutions françaises à Tripoli," *L'Orient Le Jour* (January 7, 1985); interviews with Tawhid figures close to Fu'ad al-Kurdi including Khaled al-Kurdi, Ibrahim Saleh and Abu Meriam Khassouq, Tripoli, June–September 2014.

[103] Interview with a confidant of Fu'ad al-Kurdi, Tripoli, June 2014.

[104] Interview with Selim Lababidi (former Tawhid figure close to Esmat Murad and to Iran), Beirut's Shatila refugee camp, May 2014.

Behind the Ideological Alliance, a Marriage of Convenience

This section discusses why, eventually, Iran failed to turn Tawhid from a spatially oriented into an ideologically driven movement – and how this affected their alliance. While, at first, it seemed obvious that shared ideology lay at the core of this relationship, mainly because it had been initiated and then primarily handled by "ideological entrepreneurs" on both sides who shared a similar worldview, their death gradually changed the nature of that relationship and turned it into no more than a marriage of convenience. By late 1984 and early 1985, Iran had become keenly aware that Tawhid would not turn into its "Sunni Hezbollah," fully dedicated to its ideology and designs. This resulted from three factors: sustained Syrian efforts at preventing Tawhid from spreading beyond Tripoli, a violent internal controversy over the nature of the alliance with Iran, which even led to the assassination of those "ideological entrepreneurs" who were steering the movement too much in Tehran's direction, and the lingering opportunism of Tawhid members and leaders. By 1985, then, the Tawhid–Iran relationship, which at first had seemed so unmistakably ideological, was still well and alive but had gradually turned more transactional. Once looking like an ideological alliance, it had turned into no more than a marriage of convenience.

In the southern and largely Sunni city of Sidon, Maher Hammud, a leading militant cleric who had split from the Islamic Group as he found it too institutionalized, was initially attracted by the possibility of heading a local chapter there and importing Tawhid. Hammud, by his account, had grown "fascinated by Tawhid"[105] after its alliance with Iran, rapidly becoming close to its "ideological entrepreneurs" and turning into the most prominent advocate of "Sunni Khomeinism" in South Lebanon. Yet, in order to escape the 1982 Israeli invasion and subsequent occupation of the south, he had to go into exile for two years. This, he says, limited his ability to take an active role in Tawhid's expansion in the south. And, revealingly, upon his return to Sidon after the withdrawal of Israeli troops in early 1985, he was "aggressively" told by Syrian intelligence to stay put, keep away from the movement and not to take an active role in its spread outside of Tripoli – or else face dire consequences.

In Beirut, Tawhid's main figure, Samir al-Sheikh, would be less lucky, being assassinated alongside his whole family by a member of a local pro-

---

[105] Interview with Maher Hammud ("Sunni Khomeinist" cleric close to Tawhid and to Iran), Sidon, July 2014.

402   The Geopolitics of Islamism

Assad militia, allegedly on orders from Syria.[106] By the time of his murder, al-Sheikh had become a key element in the Iranian-sponsored plans for Tawhid's expansion in the Lebanese capital. A Beiruti Sunni who was very close to Esmat Murad, he had much like him initially been an anti-imperialist Maoist activist in Fatah's Student Brigade, fought Israel in South Lebanon in 1978 and then joined the Movement of Arab Lebanon after Murad founded it. Like Murad, he drew closer to Iran in the following years, turned into a "Sunni Khomeinist" and became one of the rare non-Tripolitans to have joined Tawhid upon its formation.[107] He grew close to the "ideological entrepreneurs" and arose as an important cadre in his own right. He often traveled back and forth between Tripoli and Beirut, spending much of his time trying to recruit pro-Iran Sunni militants in the capital and leading a cell of a dozen "Sunni Khomeinists" there.[108] Al-Sheikh soon turned into one of Iran's relays in Tawhid, perhaps because he had long been close to Murad, who had the full trust of the Iranians, and as he was based in Beirut and thus met the Revolutionary Guards delegation frequently at the Iranian embassy in the capital. The strong ties he developed with the powerful Iranian figures in charge with liaising with Tawhid soon earned him the nickname "the movement's diplomat."[109] This was also due to the fact that he had graduated with an economics degree from the prestigious American University of Beirut. He was therefore better educated than the average Tawhid member and even leader, having the social codes needed to lead the high-level interactions with Iranian policymakers that took place during the movement's visits to Tehran in 1984.[110] He became one of Iran's voices in Tawhid, then, and was well placed to expand it to Beirut.

At the time of his murder, moreover, Samir al-Sheikh was said to have been preparing a merger of Tawhid and Hezbollah militants in Beirut within a pro-Iranian "Islamic Front."[111] This project would have been groundbreaking had it seen the light of the day. It aimed at bringing Beirut's Sunni and Shia Muslims together to struggle against Israel,

---

[106] Interview with Tawhid officials, Tripoli, June–July 2014.
[107] Interview with a former member of Samir al-Sheikh's Beiruti faction in Tawhid, Beirut, May 2014.
[108] Interview with Selim Lababidi (former Tawhid figure close to Esmat Murad and to Iran), Beirut's Shatila refugee camp, May 2014.
[109] Interview with Abu Shawqi (Tawhid official close to al-Sheikh and to Iran), Tripoli, August 2014.
[110] Interview with Abu Meriam Khassouq (Tawhid official in charge of coordination with Iran), Tripoli, June 2014.
[111] Interview with a former member of Samir al-Sheikh's Beiruti faction in Tawhid, Beirut, May 2014.

overthrowing the Lebanese government and replacing it with an Islamic Republic that would act as Tehran's ally. Al-Sheikh had the perfect profile to merge these two pro-Iran Sunni and Shia movements. His influential role in Tawhid meant he had obtained the movement's green light for its participation in this "Islamic Front," his strong connections to the Revolutionary Guards ensured proper funding and armament for the new body and, crucially, he had also secured the backing of Hezbollah's leaders, whom he knew well from his time fighting Israel. In a show of the trust which bound this Beiruti Sunni to Hezbollah, one of the Shia movement's leaders at the time explained that "Samir closely coordinated with us" and that his death had been a "major loss"[112] for it had killed at its inception the revolutionary attempt at merging Shia and Sunni Islamisms and, by the same token, at overcoming sectarian divisions.

The list of attendees at Samir al-Sheikh's funeral illustrates the significance that al-Sheikh and his enterprise of the creation of an "Islamic Front" had come to take in pro-Iranian Shia and Sunni circles – and it underlines the importance of his own agency in helping this plan see the light of day. No Tawhid leaders could travel from Tripoli because of security concerns. But the prominent Sidon-based "Sunni Khomeinist," Maher Hammud, as well as none other than Hezbollah's spiritual leader and ideologue, Mohammed Hussein Fadlallah and the head of the Iranian embassy in Beirut, Mohammed Nurani, were photographed paying their respects.[113] The assassination of Samir al-Sheikh, allegedly at the hands of Syria, sounded the death knell of Iran's dual attempt at helping Tawhid spread its influence outside of Tripoli and at merging the Sunni movement with its Shia counterpart, Hezbollah, within an "Islamic Front." The Syrian regime thus violently undermined Iran's "Sunni Hezbollah" project. Yet Damascus is not the only culprit to be blamed for the killing of Tawhid's pro-Iran cadres.

The second reason for the failure of Iran's attempt at making Tawhid less spatially oriented and more guided by "Khomeinist" ideology is to be found within the movement itself. By 1984 the growing influence of its most pro-Iran "ideological entrepreneurs" triggered a factional struggle which led to the murder of some of them. This also shows how, even in the case of ideologically patterned alliances, the relationship between an external sponsor or patron and local rebel or terrorist movements that

---

[112] Interview with Hani Fahs (former member of Hezbollah's leadership), Beirut, July 2014.

[113] "Fadlallah: les musulmans n'ont pas pris conscience de la réalité qu'ils vivent," *L'Orient Le Jour* (July 15, 1985).

404   The Geopolitics of Islamism

ostensibly act as its proxy is in reality less complete than is often assumed by the use of the term proxy. While Tawhid's alliance with Fatah had been relatively uncontroversial internally as the Palestinian guerrilla organization benefited from large popular support in Tripoli, its seemingly sudden transformation into a partner of Iran, a Persian Shia ally of the locally reviled Syrian regime, was not appreciated equally by all Tawhid figures. Initially, as was stated earlier, nearly all leaders and members within the movement had backed Esmat Murad's suggestion to enhance their ties with Tehran. But, with the exception of some of the movement's "ideological entrepreneurs" who were sincerely attracted by the Iranian model, most leaders and members had embraced "Khomeinism" instrumentally, within the context of Tawhid's need for Iranian diplomatic support in the face of the constant threat of a Syrian military crackdown on Tripoli after late 1983. Also, they merely envisioned a rapprochement with Tehran, certainly not a transformation into a "Sunni Hezbollah." And many were locally oriented militants with no interest in spreading to the rest of Lebanon. As Iran's influence within Tawhid gradually grew from late 1983 until mid-1984, then, the nature and extent of the movement's alliance with Iran fueled an internal controversy.[114]

The Tawhid–Iran alliance impacted the movement's internal politics in several ways. To begin with, it triggered a debate over ideology. Factions disagreed on how far Tawhid should go in toeing the Iranian line and in adopting all the tenets of the "Khomeinist" breed of Islamism. On the one hand, the handful of influential pro-Iran cadres and "ideological entrepreneurs" around Esmat Murad, Fu'ad al-Kurdi and Samir al-Sheikh all vehemently argued that the movement should make of Khomeinist ideology the cornerstone of the alliance with Iran. They systematically promoted Iran's designs for Tawhid and defended all of Tehran's positions, from domestic to foreign policy, even allegedly arguing that the movement should officially recognize the leadership of Ayatollah Khomeini, although he was a Shia and this would have been an extremely controversial move for a Sunni Islamist group. On the other hand, Tawhid's other leaders and factions had remained unaffected by the Iranian efforts at socializing and educating them into "Khomeinism." Some of them may have gone to Tehran on visits of Tawhid delegations and even kept praising the "Iranian model." But they continued to

---

[114] Interviews with Hashim Yaghmur (Tawhid military commander close to Sha'aban), Kan'an Naji (Emir of Abu Samra and member of Tawhid's Consultative Council), Ibrahim Saleh (Tawhid official close to Sha'aban) and Hashem Minqara (Emir of Mina and member of Tawhid's Consultative Council), Tripoli, August 2014.

Behind the Ideological Alliance 405

instrumentalize ideology more or less subtly and were not prepared to see their movement turn less spatially oriented and more ideologically driven.[115] In other words, the movement continued featuring a large "spectrum of ideological commitment" and heated debates on ideology thus began gripping the Consultative Council through 1984.

There were also two other controversial aspects to the Tawhid–Iran alliance beyond ideology which added fuel to the fire and enhanced the movement's internal divisions. One was that the originators and handlers of the relationship with Tehran became, through their ability to leverage Iranian support, much more powerful figures inside the movement. This was especially the case with Esmat Murad. His ability to impact the decisions taken by Tawhid's leader, Sa'id Sha'aban, became so large in early 1984 that an observer of the movement noted that he had turned into what he called "the power behind the throne."[116] This infuriated Murad's internal rivals in Tawhid's Consultative Council, who started to resent this subtle but reportedly significant shift in the balance of power within the movement after Iranian help became gradually more important in the early months of 1984.[117] This set off a conflict between factions and personalities, one which would eventually burst out violently.

The other controversial aspect of Tawhid's alliance with Iran was that it affected the movement's political orientation toward the Syrian regime. From 1984 onward, Tehran began pushing its relays within Tawhid to advocate for a more conciliatory stance toward Damascus and to focus more energy on turning the movement into a "Sunni Hezbollah." This polarized Tawhid's leadership and membership to a great extent, both because its struggle against the regime had been a key reason behind its formation, as shown in Chapter 3, and because local opposition to the Assads ran more widely through Tripoli's "global sense of place" and gave Tawhid a degree of local legitimacy.[118] Throughout this time, from early to late 1984, Sa'id Sha'aban remained uncontested as leader because he attempted to strike a middle line between the factions and figures who scrambled to steer Tawhid in a more or less "Khomeinist" direction. But, below the surface, its alliance with Iran was

---

[115] Interviews with current and former Tawhid cadres and leaders, Tripoli, June–September 2014.
[116] Interview with Amer Arnaout (former Tawhid official close to Esmat Murad and Iran), Tripoli, August 2014.
[117] Interviews with Hashem Minqara and Kan'an Naji (Tawhid's Emirs in the Mina and Abu Samra districts and members of the movement's Consultative Council or leadership in 1982–5), Tripoli, August 2014.
[118] Interviews with current and former Tawhid cadres and leaders, Tripoli, June–September 2014.

406   The Geopolitics of Islamism

triggering a bitter struggle over its leadership and its politico-ideological line.

The degree to which the nature of Tawhid's relationship with Iran had become a matter of internal division became evident in mid-1984 when Esmat Murad was assassinated.[119] The murder of this emblematic Tawhid leader was a watershed moment. It marked the loss of one of Tehran's most committed allies or relays and the subsequent decrease of the influence of the movement's "ideological entrepreneurs," to whom he had long been close. Today there is still considerable controversy in current and former Tawhid ranks over who ordered his shooting in broad daylight in Tripoli but all, whether partisans or opponents of Murad, acknowledged that it was an "inside job"[120] – the doing of one of his internal rivals. Some point the finger at Hashem Minqara. After becoming a millionaire, the Emir of Mina began harboring broader ambitions of his own, competing with Esmat Murad for influence over the rest of Tawhid's leadership and deeply resenting his growing sway over Sa'id Sha'aban. Others blame Kana'an Naji, Tawhid's Emir in Abu Samra and a figure who also sat on the movement's Consultative Council, in which he constantly toed the positions of Fatah. Alongside Minqara, Naji had long had a reputation as a loose canon and as a Machiavellian figure willing to use all necessary means to achieve his ends, including assassinating rivals. And, crucially, both of them had long been close to Abu Ta'an as well as Syria's Islamists, vehemently opposed Murad's increasingly conciliatory stance toward Syria and are said to have been bent on continuing the confrontation between Tawhid and the regime. Today both figures admit having had "disagreements" and even occasional "frictions"[121] with Murad, but they deny being responsible for his murder. Yet, whoever ordered this "inside job," Murad's killing at the hands of an internal rival encouraged further pushback against the "ideological entrepreneurs." The push and pull between factions and figures wishing to steer Tawhid in a more or less "Khomeinist" direction were beginning to violently impact its internal politics.

In a show of how polarizing Tawhid's relations with Iran had by now become, Murad's assassination was followed by the murder in late 1984 and early 1985 of another sixteen of the movement's cadres and

[119] "Assassinat d'un responsable du Mouvement de l'Unification Islamique à Tripoli," *L'Orient Le Jour* (August 5, 1984).
[120] Interviews with current and former Tawhid cadres and leaders, Tripoli, June–September 2014.
[121] Interviews with Hashem Minqara and Kan'an Naji (Tawhid's Emirs in the Mina and Abu Samra districts and members of the movement's Consultative Council or leadership in 1982–5), Tripoli, August 2014.

"ideological entrepreneurs" who were steering it in Tehran's direction.[122] Officially, "Israel" was held responsible for these killings. But all high-level interviewed sources acknowledged that they resulted from internal tensions stemming from the sense that the Tawhid–Iran relation was about to give birth to an alliance patterned and guided by ideology only. Many were not prepared to see their movement transform fully from a spatially oriented to an ideologically guided movement loyal to "Khomeinism." This also demonstrates that, beyond the seemingly obvious sense that Tawhid was becoming Iran's Sunni Islamist proxy, internal sensitivities on the topic were in fact so diverse that they had fragmented the movement from within, hampering its ability to spread outside Tripoli and preventing it from becoming Tehran's fully loyal "Sunni Hezbollah."

The third and final factor blocking the transformation of Tawhid into Iran's "Sunni Hezbollah" was the lingering opportunism of many of the movement's members and leaders, and the fundamentally instrumentalist prism through which they viewed their alliance with Tehran. Iran, indeed, may have been initially enthusiastic about the prospect of turning Tawhid into a movement more sincerely embracing its "Khomeinist" breed of Islamism. But, with the assassinations of Fu'ad al-Kurdi, Esmat Murad, Samir al-Sheikh and the dozen other influential "ideological entrepreneurs" who were close to Tehran, the Islamic Republic had by early 1985 lost its most influential and committed relays in the movement's leadership. Their death did not mean the end of the Tawhid–Iran alliance, for most of the movement's leaders and members agreed they were still in dire need of Tehran's diplomatic backing and funds; but it did signify that the relationship became less ideological and more transactional. Tawhid would be ready to act as Iran's Sunni Islamist proxy, but merely on the surface – occasionally toeing Tehran's line yet only up to a point, and in return for tangible benefits. Behind the veneer of Tawhid's grandiose statements that still glorified the "Iranian model," advocated for the establishment of an "Islamic Republic of Lebanon" and proposed to combat the "secular West," then, it had by now become clear to the Iranians that the movement they had spent a lot of resources on would not become the "Sunni Hezbollah" they had envisioned. Tawhid, they realized, would instead remain concerned with its own localized agenda, itself a mix of local solidarities and identities, as in "neighborhood Islamism" and "vernacular Islamism," socio-political grievances, like in "subaltern Islamism" or the growing search for

---

[122] Interview with Amer Arnaout (former Tawhid official close to Esmat Murad and Iran), Tripoli, August 2014.

408   The Geopolitics of Islamism

economic gain even in the cases when it contradicted ideology as in "Islamo-gangsterism." "Tawhid only cared about local issues,"[123] summarized a figure close to Iranian intelligence.

Therefore, while Iran did not suddenly lose interest for Tawhid, it did adjust the way it dealt with it. It revised the nature of its support and considerably lowered its expectations. Tehran stopped committing resources to enhance the movement's sincere adherence to "Khomeinism," as it had initially done by sending "ideological entrepreneurs" to Tripoli, organizing socialization and indoctrination events in Baalbek or by nurturing Tawhid–Hezbollah ties. It also ceased to invest in the reinforcement of the movement's paramilitary capacities. The Islamic Republic was still ready to continue providing it with some diplomatic backing and funds but, in return for this support, Tawhid leaders would from then on be expected to deliver tangible benefits to Iran too, for example by providing the Shia Persian state with Sunni Arab credentials. By early 1985, then, the Tawhid–Iran relationship which had once seemed so unmistakably driven by ideology had now by and large turned much more transactional. Even Western intelligence recognized this state of affairs, observing that for all the appearance of an ideological alliance, it had turned into a "marriage of convenience."[124]

The changing nature of the relationship between Iran and Tawhid's leader, Sa'id Sha'aban, epitomized the transactional and opportunistic character which the alliance was assuming by late 1984 and early 1985. Ostensibly, Sha'aban appeared to continue being a firm believer in the "Iranian model." Locally, in Lebanon, he toed the Iranian line. He traveled to Beirut to provide Hezbollah with Sunni Islamic blessing at a time when the struggle between the pro-Assad Shia party Amal and pro-Arafat Sunni militias in West Beirut was increasingly stirring up Sunni–Shia sectarian strife as part of the "War of the Camps."[125] He warned West Beirut's Sunnis not to fight the Party of God for there was a "unified Islamic action between all Muslims including between Tawhid and Hezbollah."[126] He often intervened in the media to defend the pro-Iran Shia militia when it came under fire, going as far as justifying its

---

[123] Interview with Selim Lababidi (Palestinian militant close to Iran's Revolutionary Guards), Beirut's Shatila refugee camp, May 2014.

[124] US Central Intelligence Agency, "Syria: scenarios of dramatic political change" (Classified, 86-20099L, July 1986).

[125] "Conférence de Shaaban au West Hall de Beyrouth sur l'unité islamique," *L'Orient Le Jour* (November 13, 1984) and "Sheikh Shaaban plaide pour la nécessité de sauvegarder l'unité des rangs islamiques," *L'Orient Le Jour* (January 26, 1985).

[126] "Sheikh Shaaban quitte brusquement Beyrouth pour Damas," *L'Orient Le Jour* (November 14, 1984).

Behind the Ideological Alliance 409

1985 hijacking of an airliner under the pretext that it had aimed to "pressure America."[127] He also invited the Islamic Republic to mediate when tensions burst out between the warring sides, acting as a channel to help Tehran bolster its regional status. In May 1985, for instance, he enquired in the media whether Iran could mediate precisely when the "War of the Camps" was intensifying in Beirut. This allowed Iran's most senior diplomat, Mohammed Hossein Lavassani, to land in the Lebanese capital a day later as a "guest"[128] to carry out negotiations, which increased Tehran's soft power in the country.

More regionally, Sa'id Sha'aban continued traveling to Iran, where he was received with honors. The support this Sunni Arab cleric voiced for the Islamic Republic became a key part of Iran's propaganda war effort, taking place within the context of its bloody conflict with Iraq. This transpired when the Iranians invited him for a high-level visit to Tehran in February 1985. Back then he was even publicly welcomed at the airport by Ayatollah Khomeini, President Khamene'i and dozens of Iranian journalists, precisely as Iran was preparing to launch a bloody offensive on Iraq, "Operation Badr," which resulted in the seizure of the Baghdad–Basra highway and in Arab fears of a Shia Persian takeover of Iraq.[129] Sha'aban, in other words, continued to display the perception of being a faithful ally of Iran.

Yet beneath the surface Tawhid's head no longer even pretended to be attracted by the "Iranian model." His relationship with other pro-Iran Lebanese figures is a case in point. Sa'id Sha'aban had long been known as an advocate of greater cooperation between Iran's allies in Lebanon. He had even taken part in the founding June 1982 conference and subsequent weekly meetings of the Gathering of Muslim Scholars (*Tajamm'u al-Ulema al-Muslimin*), a platform striving to "empower and unite"[130] local pro-Iran Sunni and Shia clerics. But his interest rapidly faded from early 1985 onward. Members of the Gathering of Muslim Scholars recall that Sha'aban began showing less commitment, ceasing to attend meetings and giving the sense to the platform's head that he no

---

[127] "Shaaban sceptique quant aux objectifs du détournement," *L'Orient Le Jour* (June 18, 1985).

[128] "Le Mouvement de l'Unification Islamique en appelle à Khomeini," *L'Orient Le Jour* (May 24, 1985).

[129] "Ziyarat al-Sheikh Sa'id Sha'aban ila Iran" ["Visit of the cleric Sa'id Sha'aban to Iran"], *Al-Incha* (February 14, 1985).

[130] Interview with Selim Lababidi (Palestinian cleric close to Iran's Revolutionary Guards and founding member of the Gathering of Muslim Scholars), Beirut's Shatila refugee camp, May 2014.

410   The Geopolitics of Islamism

longer considered himself a member.[131] Figures close to Sha'aban confirmed his loss of interest. Some attributed it to the fact that, by then, he had befriended Ayatollah Khomeini and thus could count on Iranian support irrespective of how truly dedicated he was to the promotion of "Khomeinism" as an ideology. Others suggested that, as he rose to fame, he became less inclined to share the politico-religious stage with other Lebanese clerics, even if, like him, they supported Iran's agenda. "By 1985, Sa'id Sha'aban no longer needed the Gathering of Muslim Scholars – he had become an influential personality in his own right with an aura even surpassing that of Fadlallah,"[132] claimed one of his associates proudly, referring to Hezbollah's chief ideologue. There are also those who questioned the sincerity of his commitment to Sunni–Shia "Muslim unity" in Lebanon. One of his close followers thus asserted that Sha'aban remained an orthodox Sunni Islamist throughout his life and that, in private, he often raised the theological and historical issues that pitted Sunnis against Shias.[133] In other words, it appeared that he had constructed the appearance of ideological proximity with Iran to obtain its support. This indicates how, by 1985, Tawhid's relationship with Iran had turned much more transactional.

In sum, therefore, although it may have seemed like Tawhid's foreign relations were only guided by ideology, because the movement at once drew the ire of the "secular" Syrian regime and attracted support from Syrian Islamist groups, Fatah's Islamist wing and the Islamic Republic of Iran, other factors mattered too and sometimes even more so. Ideology, of course, still played key roles in Tawhid's foreign relations, especially through "ideological entrepreneurs" who strove to make shared worldviews the cornerstone of the movement's alliances with Islamist-leaning foreign sponsors like Fatah's Abu Ta'an or Iran. Yet, tellingly, ideology ceased to shape Tawhid's relations with external backers as soon as these "ideological entrepreneurs" disappeared, whether they were imprisoned or assassinated. This occurred to the extent that, in the case of Tawhid–Iran relations, the disappearance of the "ideological entrepreneurs" rendered obvious the fact that many members and even some leaders had artificially created the appearance of ideological proximity to obtain Tehran's support. This ultimately turned what looked like an ideological alliance into a mere marriage of convenience.

---

[131] Interview with Maher Hammud ("Sunni Khomeinist" cleric close to Iran and longtime leader of the Gathering of Muslim Scholars), Sidon, July 2014.
[132] Interview with Ibrahim Saleh (Tawhid official and right-hand man to Sha'aban), Tripoli, June 2014.
[133] Interview with a former leader of Tawhid, Tripoli, July 2014.

Theorizing Back

By shedding light on the dynamics which drove Tawhid's foreign relations, this chapter also draws broader theoretical insights related to the role of ideology and answers the following questions. To what extent does ideology matter in the foreign relations of social, rebel and terrorist movements and especially in the alliances they seek to forge with external actors? And, when ideologically patterned alliances are being struck, what impact do they exert on the discourse, behavior and internal politics of movements and through which mechanisms?

Building on Tawhid's case to address these two questions, I shed light on the role of ideology in the foreign relations of movements and in their external alliances. That ideology somehow matters in the external relations of social, rebel and terrorist movements should not come as a surprise given the degree to which the alliances they strike with foreign actors often seem patterned along ideological lines. Examples abound, from the past to the present. While the Cold War featured myriad opposition groups throughout what was known as the "Third World," embracing various types of Communist ideologies and obtaining backing from the Soviet Union, China or Cuba, the past thirty years have witnessed new waves of ideological alliances, for instance "Khomeinist" and often Shia Islamist militias drawing support from Iran, Salafi terrorist groups from ideologically driven, global networks like Al-Qaeda and ISIS or alt-right social movements from Russia. But the dynamics and mechanisms of these alliances, as well as the effects they may have on the discourse, behavior and internal politics of these movements, still remain poorly understood. Of course, some conflict experts acknowledge that shared ideology increases the likelihood of external support for insurgents, but they do not explain why or how this takes place.[134] Moreover, when they delve into the reasons which push rebel groups to seek backing from ideologically sympathetic external actors, the conversation remains too often mired in the dichotomy between instrumental and sincere accounts. While, for instance, conflict scholar Barbara Walter suggests that the militant Islamist ideology of some Middle Eastern rebel groups is a form of "cheap talk"[135] instrumentally used to gain access to Al-Qaeda's "network of private Gulf funders, operational expertise and

---

[134] Idean Salehyan, Kristian Skrede Gleditsch and David E. Cunningham, "Explaining external support for insurgent groups" *International Organizations* (Vol. 65, No. 3, 2011), pp. 709–44.

[135] Barbara Walter, "The extremist's advantage in civil wars" *International Security* (Vol. 42, No. 2, 2017), p. 23.

412   The Geopolitics of Islamism

recruitment mechanisms," academics of civil wars Stathis Kalyvas and Laia Balcells on the contrary argue that sincere beliefs, or the indoctrination of "thousands of radical activists"[136] into leftism during the Cold War, was what pushed many to embrace Marxism and strike alliances with the Soviet Union. Both accounts have merits, but neither answers the questions above in fully satisfactory ways.

Deriving insights from the case of Tawhid's alliances with Syrian Islamists, Fatah's Islamist wing and Iran, I make two broad points related to the role of ideology in the external alliances of social, rebel and terrorist movements. First, like in the rest of this book, I continue to delve into the functions fulfilled by ideology. I emphasize how ideology helps these movements solicit support from like-minded actors. Engaging in a rich Islamist ideological production was indeed a central way through which Tawhid, in spite of its local nature, succeeded in attracting the interest of resource-rich, foreign Islamist actors, activating the bonds of ideological solidarity with them and securing their support. This external backing took different shapes, but it was always significant, ranging from human resources, training and diplomatic support to logistical and financial assistance. The case of its relation with Iran is the most telling example of how Tawhid instrumentalized ideology to solicit external support. Had the "Khomeinist" breed of Islamism truly guided the movement's alliance with the Islamic Republic, the dynamics of its relationship would not have varied so wildly across time. While Chapter 4 documented the striking degree of temporal variation in Tawhid's "Khomeinist" ideological production, with a peak in mid-1984 when it needed Iran's diplomatic help the most, in this chapter I trace the genesis and evolution of their relationship and show that it significantly transformed over time, gradually turning transactional as even the movement's leader showed less commitment. In other words, although from the outside Tawhid may have looked like a loyal ally of Iran, many members and leaders had in fact artificially constructed the appearance of commitment to "Khomeinism" to activate bonds of ideological solidarity and secure Tehran's support. Ideology was clearly being used to strike alliances which would benefit the movement.

Demonstrating that one of the key functions of ideology is to solicit external backing has an important implication when studying the nature of the alliances between social, rebel or terrorist movements and like-minded external actors. Indeed, instead of assuming that shared ideology

---

[136] Stathis Kalyvas and Laia Balcells, "International system and technologies of rebellion: how the end of the cold war shaped internal conflict" *American Political Science Review* (Vol. 104, No. 3, 2010), p. 420.

is the central driving element, the priority should be to assess the causal weight of ideology relative to other factors and to determine the dynamics of these alliances. This is particularly needed as the complex and fluid relations which characterize rebel and terrorist movements with like-minded foreign backers are sometimes described in the empirical litera-ture and the media as "proxy–patron" relations, the latter being so much in charge of the former that their relation is often viewed as top-down, one-sided and complete. Tawhid's case is here again instructive. The dynamics of its alliances, especially with Fatah and Iran, can be charac-terized in the following way. First of all they were fluid, or dependent on the political and geopolitical context and vulnerable to changing expect-ations on both sides; second, they were dialectic, as the proxy also greatly benefited from the relation for its own interest, profited from the changing balance of power between them and retained a degree of autonomy and; third, they were partial, for while the external backer used relays in the leadership of the proxy to enhance its influence, their defection or death negatively affected its influence, and internal disagree-ments over foreign alliances were destructive. Therefore, while shared ideology between a rebel or terrorist movement and its external backer suggests a top-down, one-sided and complete relationship between them, it may also be fluid, dialectic and partial depending on the range of factors beyond ideology which drive the dynamics of the alliance.

Second, building on the case of Tawhid's relationship with Iran which gradually turned less ideological and more transactional, I argue that the ebb and flow of ideology's effect on movement behavior can be traced back to the internal push and pull between factions and individuals committed to and therefore driven by ideology to different degrees. Showing the significance of grasping a movement's full "spectrum of ideological commitment," there were some cadres around the leaders who were sincerely attracted by "Khomeinism" and lobbied to make of shared ideology the cornerstone of the alliance with Tehran. The "ideo-logical entrepreneurship" of these vehement pro-Iranian figures acted as the key mechanism through which Iran came to back Tawhid. In turn, what explained the importance of these "ideological entrepreneurs" for Tehran was the strength of their commitment to "Khomeinism" and their preparedness to push the movement to behave in ways consistent with or even driven by the Iranian goals. It also mattered that they had strong preexisting social and ideational ties with their Iranian counter-parts, which bred trust. As a result these cadres emerged as the privileged link between Tawhid and Tehran. Importantly, acting as Iran's relays in early and mid-1984 increased their influence within the movement and this allowed them to steer its behavior and discourse in a more

414   The Geopolitics of Islamism

ideological direction. But it soon also enhanced rivalries, led to heated debates and triggered a pushback. Their influence as a result later diminished in late 1984 and through 1985, which also corresponds to the period during which Tawhid's behavior became significantly less ideological, marked by the increasingly transactional nature of its relationship to Iran and by the involvement of some of its members in gangster-like practices at odds with ideology. This not only shows that the "ideological entrepreneurs" acted as the mechanism through which seemingly ideological alliances were struck and impacted movement discourse, behavior and internal politics, but it also indicates how factions and individuals less driven by ideology forcibly pushed back against them, steering Tawhid in a less ideologically driven direction. Internal interactions between factions and figures with different levels of ideological commitment therefore greatly influence how ideological a movement's behavior can be.

8 The Downfall of Tawhid

By 1985, Tawhid was increasingly suffering under the combined weight of the spread of "Islamo-gangsterism" and the assassination of some of its "ideological entrepreneurs," which steered its behavior in a less ideological direction and significantly undermined its cohesion. So, while between 1982 and 1984 Hafez al-Assad worked hard to raise the cost of Islamist activism in Tripoli but did so covertly to avoid antagonizing his Iranian ally, by mid-1985 he saw an opportunity to crush Tawhid once and for all and ordered a crackdown on Tripoli. On Tawhid's side, it was becoming obvious that, this time, the battle would be of unprecedented proportions in its violence and that Iran would not be able to rein the Syrian president in. As the September 1985 battle was beginning to unfold, Assad committed his full weight against Tawhid. He ordered a coalition of 7,000 Syrian soldiers and Lebanese leftist militants to bomb Tripoli with thousands of shells and to try to take over the city, killing 600 people. And yet the puzzle of the September 1985 battle is that, in spite of the fast-rising cost of Islamist activism, its internal divisions and such an asymmetry of forces, Tawhid mobilized many of its 2,000–3,000 members, recruited some new members and resisted cohesively for nearly three weeks. As it was about to be bloodily crushed, Iran mediated a peace deal with Syria which allowed Tawhid to survive, although it had to relinquish control of Tripoli. This marked the effective end of the "Islamic Emirate" it had been implementing since 1982. But, even after the movement's surrender, the peace deal and the return of Syrian troops to Tripoli, a sizable proportion of members continued pouring onto the streets of the city to defy the Syrian regime. This was especially the case in Bab al-Tebbaneh, where they even launched a violent rebellion in December 1986. The Syrian army and its allies would repress it with bloodshed, slaughtering 500 residents of the district and arresting as many as 5,000. How did Tawhid succeed in mobilizing so many in these two instances of risky activism?

This chapter traces the downfall of Tawhid and analyses what pushed members to mobilize in such large numbers in "high-risk collective

416   The Downfall of Tawhid

action,"[1] when activism takes place despite grave anticipated dangers, as reflected in the movement's two doomed battles against Syria in September 1985 and December 1986. I argue that, while some fought to defend the "Islamic Emirate," many other Tawhid members put their lives on the line in order to prevent the Syrian army from returning to their city and neighborhoods – what had driven them to fight was not Islamist ideology but identification with Tripoli as a community and local solidarities. I begin this chapter by analyzing how, between 1982 and 1985, Syria strategized to raise the costs associated with Islamist activism in Tripoli and with joining Tawhid in particular. Increasingly divided and constantly on edge, the movement eventually yielded to Syrian provocations and got trapped in a spiral of violence. This allowed the regime to launch the battle which it framed as a "progressive" struggle to rid Tripoli of "fundamentalism." But, while Syria expected a quick victory, Tawhid put up what observers called a stiff resistance. Ideology explained some of the movement's ability to resist the pro-Syrian offensive. Playing the regime's game, Tawhid soon cast the battle launched by the Syrian regime and Lebanese leftist fighters as an "atheist" attack on an "Islamic city," which helped mobilize and galvanize its committed members, reinforce cohesion and recruit new Islamist militants. Tawhid also activated the ties of ideological solidarity which bound it to Islamist movements in Lebanon and to the Islamic Republic of Iran, leading them to provide it with external backing. Ideology, therefore, played important parts in the movement's stiff resistance during the September 1985 battle against Syria. But the role of beliefs in this instance of high-risk mobilization should not be overstated. In fact, Tawhid also engaged in alliances which were inconsistent with its ideology, for example when it struck a deal with Lebanese military intelligence at the height of the fighting, or when Tripolitan soldiers of the Lebanese army joined it. Moreover, it soon transpired that members on Tawhid's entire "spectrum of ideological commitment" had mobilized, including those who had always embraced militant Islamism instrumentally. What pushed them to mobilize for Tawhid and to fight the Syrian regime was not ideology but instead identification with Tripoli as a community and neighborhood solidarities, both strategically activated by the movement through its revival of local "tales of contention" and the

---

[1] See: Doug McAdam, "Recruitment to high-risk activism: the case of Freedom Summer" *American Journal of Sociology* (Vol. 92, No. 1, 1986), pp. 64–90; Sharon Nepstad and Christian Smith, "Rethinking recruitment to high-risk/cost activism: the case of Nicaragua Exchange" *Mobilization* (Vol. 4, No. 1, 1999), pp. 25–40; and Sarah Elizabeth Parkinson, "Organizing rebellion: rethinking high-risk mobilization and social networks in war" *American Political Science Review* (Vol. 107, No. 3, 2013), pp. 418–32.

enlistment of spatially rooted "champions of mobilization." The importance of local identity and solidarity would again be on display during the
December 1986 rebellion launched by former Tawhid members in Bab
al-Tebbaneh. The regime framed them as "fundamentalists" and they
did use Islamism, albeit as a "protest ideology." But they were truly
"neighborhood Islamists" driven by an inherently localized concern: a
collective thirst for revenge against the Syrian army after it murdered
Khalil Akkawi, the local "champion of mobilization," to whom they had
long been extremely loyal. The story of Tawhid's downfall had therefore
much in common with its rise in and rule over Tripoli: Islamist ideology
was always in the background, played key roles and at times affected
events, but strikingly it often acted as a vehicle for other, more
local phenomena.

Syria Raises the Cost of Islamist Activism

Between 1982 and 1985, Hafez al-Assad was becoming increasingly
concerned that, for reasons seen in Chapter 7, Tawhid's rule over
Tripoli was about to give birth to an organized Palestinian, Syrian and
Lebanese Islamist nexus which would then undermine the stability that
the regime had slowly recovered after the bloody events of Hama in 1982.
Sources with access to the regime thus asserted that "growing Tawhid
activism in Tripoli has been a thorn in the Syrian side for years" and that
"Damascus considers the growth of Tawhid's financial and military
power in Tripoli as detrimental to its long-term interests."[2] As a result,
some in Hafez al-Assad's inner circle began lobbying him to "impose a
Hama solution on Tripoli." This would involve "shelling the city into
submission"[3] just like the regime had done in 1982 when it killed 25,000
residents of Hama after they had risen up. Initially, those pushing for this
solution were overruled by the president, who knew that he had to show a
measure of restraint given the relationship that Tawhid was developing
with Iran. Rather than militarily defeating Tawhid right away, then, his
goal between 1982 and 1985 became to raise the costs of Islamist
activism to "contain" and "demoralize"[4] Tawhid members. In 1983 he
ordered a withdrawal of Syrian troops from Tripoli and their relocation
to the city's surroundings. But, behind this ostensible sign of goodwill to

---

[2] US Central Intelligence Agency, "Lebanon: Islamic fundamentalism in Tripoli" (Top
Secret, NESAR 86-003JX, January 17, 1986).

[3] US Central Intelligence Agency, "Syria: Vice President Rif'at Assad down but not out"
(NESAR86-021, September 12, 1986).

[4] US Central Intelligence Agency, "Shaykh Shaban: Lebanon's radical Sunni cleric" (Top
Secret, NESAR 85-003CX, January 18, 1985).

418   The Downfall of Tawhid

please his Iranian ally, he used all the means at his disposal to demobilize Tawhid, from adopting a posture which allowed him to divide and rule the Islamists to engaging in violent covert operations.

Tawhid, it must be pointed out, did not need Hafez al-Assad's help to become divided. The movement had been created in 1982, recruited many new members, ruled the city as part of a self-described "Islamic Emirate" and fought violent battles in 1983 against local leftists. But the brutality of the struggle against the Communists in Mina had been especially controversial and led some to begin distancing themselves from Tawhid. Moreover, although Tawhid's alliance with Iran had been beneficial because it had secured Tehran's mediation with Syria and spared the movement conflict in 1984, it violently exacerbated factional disputes to the point that some of the "ideological entrepreneurs" closest to the Islamic Republic had been murdered. Not all died then, but from late 1984 onward their influence sharply decreased. And, finally, it gradually transpired that, far from being a movement homogeneously made up of committed Islamists and only guided by ideology, as its "ideological entrepreneurs" had envisioned, Tawhid featured a wide "spectrum of ideological commitment" and its behavior was as a result also driven by dynamics unrelated to, sometimes even in contradiction with, its ideology as in "neighborhood Islamism," "subaltern Islamism" and "Islamo-gangsterism." With time these phenomena triggered enough accusations of corruption, struggles for the control of resources, turf wars between internal rivals and disagreements over politics and ideology that by late 1984 the movement had fragmented between different factions.[5] Tawhid continued to convey a sense of strength and unity because, although some of these factions on the ground had drifted away, their leaders still continued to meet and to closely coordinate with the rest of the movement within a platform they called the Islamic Gathering (al-Liqa' al-Islami) which, importantly, still recognized Sa'id Sha'aban as its head. To the media and much of the Lebanese and Tripolitan population, then, these Islamists continued to be known as "Tawhid" and their divisions remained below the surface. Yet it was fast becoming clear to the Syrian regime that one of the ways in which it could raise the cost of Islamist activism was by playing on these divisions and exacerbating them.

Damascus sought to divide and rule Tawhid by endorsing the role of what I call the "firefighter arsonist": the regime would discreetly push its local proxies to provoke the movement before it intervened as a "neutral

---

[5] Interviews with current and former Tawhid officials, Tripoli, June–July 2014.

arbiter" supposedly animated by a genuine will for stability. This would spark heated debates within Tawhid, exacerbate factional disputes and eventually raise the cost of Islamist activism to the extent that it would demobilize members.

Tripoli remained calm for eight months after the Iranians mediated a way out of the struggle for the control of its two Palestinian refugee camps that had opposed Fatah and Fatah al-Intifada in November 1983. But, by July 1984, a new round of violence erupted in the city.[6] Fighters from the Arab Democratic Party (ADP), the pro-Assad militia only made up of Tripolitan Alawis loyal to the strongman of Jabal Mohsen, Ali Eid, reactivated the old feud described in Chapter 2 which pitted them against the mostly Sunni residents of Bab al-Tebbaneh, who had joined Tawhid as part of the phenomenon of "neighborhood Islamism" in order to secure the movement's support in this very local, preexisting antagonism. The ADP, stationed on the hilltop of Jabal Mohsen, began using heavy weapons to shell Bab al-Tebbaneh, whose residents fired back, thus resuming the spatially confined but viciously violent "slum war" that the balance of terror with Tawhid had since 1982 largely put on hold. Within two months this indiscriminate mutual shelling had already cost the lives of 160 local residents and injured 479.[7] By one account as much as 80 percent of all casualties were civilians.[8]

There was little doubt that, by rekindling clashes between the rival districts, the ADP was acting on Syrian orders to provoke Tawhid and to raise the cost of Islamist activism. Indeed, originally the ADP may well have been created to address the discriminations faced by Tripoli's Alawis but it had fast turned into a vehicle for Ali Eid, who soon allied with Syria to obtain a security cover, impose his rule on Jabal Mohsen and extend his influence on the Tripolitan underworld. In exchange he would act as the regime's loyal proxy in the city. Western intelligence thus estimated that, by the early to mid-1980s, the ADP had unambiguously become a Tripolitan "front" and "cover" for the regime. The Syrian army stationed a small contingent of soldiers in Jabal Mohsen to train ADP fighters and protect them and it also equipped them with

---

[6] "Renouvellement des accrochages à Tripoli," *L'Orient Le Jour* (July 10, 1984); "Tripoli: le cycle de la violence se poursuit inlassablement," *L'Orient Le Jour* (August 5, 1984); and "Nouvelles mesures à Tripoli," *L'Orient Le Jour* (August 28, 1984).

[7] I draw these figures from my analysis of the fatalities and injuries reported in Tripolitan daily *Al-Incha*, Lebanese daily *L'Orient Le Jour* and Adib N'ame: Adib N'ame, "Al-amen fi Trablus, 1980–1985" ["The security in Tripoli, 1980–1985"], *Nada' al-Shamal* (undated, copy given to the author).

[8] This is the estimate put forward by the International Committee of the Red Cross, quoted in: "Accalmie à Tripoli," *L'Orient Le Jour* (July 27, 1984).

420   The Downfall of Tawhid

rocket launchers, artillery, mortars and assault rifles. In return the ADP would take its orders directly from "Syrian headquarters."[9] Behind the ADP's aggressiveness through the summer 1984 was thus Hafez al-Assad's hand.

Yet Syria was not just the arsonist of Tripoli – it also wished to pose as its firefighter. In a bold but highly calculated move, Hafez al-Assad invited Sa'id Sha'aban as head of a delegation of Tripoli's Islamists for a meeting to Damascus. In doing so, he hoped to exacerbate factional disputes within a movement in which all wished to avoid all-out war but disagreed on the extent of the compromises they were willing to make with the regime, their enemy. The Tripolitan cleric, at first hesitant and cautious given the vehemently anti-regime sermons he had often given throughout the city's mosques, was eventually convinced by the Iranians of the need to pacify the relationship with Damascus.[10] As a guarantee that he would return safely from the Syrian capital, the Iranian President Ali Khamene'i simultaneously traveled to Damascus while a delegation of Iranian diplomats made their way to Tripoli.[11] Sha'aban went to Syria, where he first met Ali Khamene'i, before he was joined by the leaders of the other Tawhid factions who then together met with Hafez al-Assad himself.[12]

At first, those who participated in the meeting with the Syrian president, whom they considered their mortal enemy, were positively surprised by his seemingly constructive attitude. He had also invited the head of the ADP's militia whom he pushed to meet the Islamists. They all had a "frank and sincere encounter" and agreed to "definitively solve the differences."[13] Hafez al-Assad then put Abdel Halim Khaddam, Syria's foreign minister and vice president but also the Syrian regime's most prominent Sunni figure, in charge of negotiating a deal between the Tawhid leaders, the ADP and Damascus. This was appreciated by Tripoli's Islamists, all self-described proud Tripolitan Sunnis who, as a result, began being cautiously optimistic. After days of negotiations under the aegis of Khaddam, the warring sides signed a ceasefire known as the Damascus Agreement. As part of an agreed "security plan," Tawhid would be allowed to continue ruling Tripoli but they and ADP

---

[9] US Central Intelligence Agency, "Directory of Lebanese militias: a reference aid" (Secret, NESA 84-10171C, June 1984).
[10] Interview with a figure close to Sa'id Sha'aban and to Iran's Revolutionary Guards, September 2014.
[11] "Le président iranien à Damas," *L'Orient Le Jour* (October 7, 1984).
[12] "Assad reçoit Sha'aban," *L'Orient Le Jour* (October 10, 1984).
[13] "Les troubles à Tripoli ont pris fin, annonce le leader du Mouvement de l'Unification Islamique," *L'Orient Le Jour* (October 10, 1984).

Syria Raises the Cost of Islamist Activism 421

militiamen would have to hand in some of their heavy weapons and to accept a token deployment of the Lebanese army.[14] The figure who acted as the backchannel between the Tawhid factions, the ADP and the regime recalled how, back then, he was "convinced"[15] that Syria's efforts were sincere and would result in restraining the ADP and bringing security back to Tripoli.

Yet, virtually as soon as the warring sides returned to Tripoli, a mortar shell fired from Jabal Mohsen exploded in a crowded market in Bab al-Tebbaneh, killing local Sunni residents and raising doubt about the reality of the Syrian commitment to Tripoli's stability.[16] The clashes that resumed following the mortar attack were rapidly contained, "only" causing fourteen deaths and three injuries in October, and they virtually ceased until July 1985.[17] But the very fact that Syria's Alawi proxy in Tripoli had carried out this attack so soon after the Damascus Agreement proved embarrassing for the Tawhid figures who had just publicly thanked Hafez al-Assad for hosting "constructive" talks. Expectedly, this exacerbated their divisions. The incident triggered a blame game between the factions which were vehemently opposed to the regime and advocated for more Tawhid support to the local feud fought by the "neighborhood Islamists" against those which were more willing to compromise with Syria.[18] The posture of the "firefighter arsonist," who discreetly fueled tension and then ostensibly intervened to mediate, allowed the Syrian president to divide and rule Tawhid.

Moreover, it soon became apparent that the clause within the Damascus Agreement which forced Tawhid to accept the Lebanese army's partial deployment in the city was also meant to trigger controversies within the movement. Although Sa'id Sha'aban never seriously considered handing over control of the whole city to the army, which had until then largely remained confined to its gated barracks in the neighborhood of Qobbe, he had still "reluctantly agreed" to the principle of token army units circulating in Tripoli as he needed to abide by the Damascus Agreement and did not want to see the regime become "angry."[19] Even this mostly symbolic deployment of a few dozen

---

[14] "Accord Mouvement de l'Unification Islamique/Parti Arabe Démocratique à Damas," *L'Orient Le Jour* (October 16, 1984).

[15] Interview with Abdallah Babetti (leading official in the Islamic Gathering), Tripoli, September 2013.

[16] "Reprise des combats à Tripoli," *L'Orient Le Jour* (October 16, 1984).

[17] "Vive tension à Tripoli," *L'Orient Le Jour* (October 17, 1984).

[18] Interview with Kan'an Naji (Tawhid's Emir in Abu Samra and member of the movement's Consultative Council or leadership), Tripoli, August 2014.

[19] "Sha'aban avalise le principe du déploiement de l'armée à Tripoli," *L'Orient Le Jour* (December 13, 1984).

422 The Downfall of Tawhid

Lebanese soldiers, however, felt too much for some of the "neighborhood Islamists," "subaltern Islamists," "Islamo-gangsters" and "ideological entrepreneurs" who all truly disliked, each for their reasons, the security forces. Incidents thus rapidly multiplied. As an army patrol was passing by Bab al-Tebbaneh, the "neighborhood Islamists" there attacked the truck, killing two soldiers and injuring three while another army unit transporting food and alcohol to the army barracks in Qobbe was stopped, humiliated and the bottles destroyed, and other incidents targeted patrols in Mina.[20] As a result, by the own account of the general who back then commanded the Lebanese army's detachment to Tripoli, the soldiers soon stopped patrolling the streets of the city and instead remained confined once again to their compound.[21] This created frictions with the Tawhid figures around Sha'aban who argued for a full implementation of the Damascus Agreement's "security plan," both out of Iranian pressure and an urge to avoid Syrian wrath. The regime had succeeded in bringing the movement's factional disputes to new heights.[22]

However, more than just trying to exacerbate Tawhid's own divisions, Damascus engaged in sometimes brutal covert operations to increase the costs and risks of Islamist activism. One knowledgeable observer thus noted that a strategy regularly used by Syrian officials to undermine Tawhid was to "instigate civil disorder in the city to demonstrate the need for continuing their presence in Lebanon's Tripoli and to curb anti-Syrian factions."[23] Some sources even suggest that back then the Syrian regime covertly deployed up to 150 intelligence operatives to Tripoli, whom it allegedly tasked with "infiltration" and "disinformation" operations targeting Tawhid.[24] As Chapter 6 suggested, some of these agents may have bombed a church in Mina to push Christians to rebel against the Islamist militants and to support "secular" Syrian regime rule. But these operatives also seemed to be engaged in much more bloody activities. One incident uncovered by the Lebanese media illustrates particularly well the extent to which the regime was prepared to go to foment unrest in a bid to raise the stakes and pose as the only possible "pacifier"

---

[20] "Tripoli: l'armée, enfin!" *L'Orient Le Jour* (December 21, 1984) and "Premier incident entre l'armée et le Mouvement de l'Unification Islamique," *L'Orient Le Jour* (December 25, 1984).

[21] Interview with General Jellul (Commander of the Lebanese army's Second Brigade in Tripoli in the 1980s), Tripoli, May 2014.

[22] Interview with current and former Tawhid officials, Tripoli, June–July 2014.

[23] US Central Intelligence Agency, "Lebanon-Syria: troubles in the North" (Top Secret, CPAS NID 83-006JX, January 7, 1983).

[24] "Violents accrochages à Tripoli," *L'Orient Le Jour* (June 15, 1983).

Syria Raises the Cost of Islamist Activism

of Tripoli. The media first reported that Tawhid-looking gunmen had come out of a car in the working-class neighborhood of Bahsas and indiscriminately shot at a crowd before escaping, killing fifteen civilians. Encapsulating how this was meant to negatively alter perceptions of security under Tawhid's "Islamic Emirate," one newspaper bore the headline "Tripoli, capital of violence."[25] Yet days later a journalistic investigation based on eyewitnesses and sources in Lebanese intelligence revealed that the gunmen had not been Islamists. They were Alawi militiamen from the ADP disguised as Islamists who had acted under the command of Major Hussein and Commander Hammud, officers in the Syrian intelligence branch of North Lebanon. Their goal had been to "sow confusion" and to "stir up popular anger"[26] against Tawhid.

Countless other incidents happened in Tripoli in 1982–5 and, although it remains difficult to confidently assign the blame to Syria, the regime often appears as a main suspect. A wave of bombings which were so sophisticated that only a state-run intelligence agency could have carried them out indeed targeted Tawhid training centers, offices and mosques. Shortly after the aforementioned killings in Bahsas a massive car bomb exploded at the end of Friday prayers in the main mosque of the neighborhood of Qobbe, a Tawhid stronghold. The bomb went off as the congregation was leaving, killing nineteen and injuring seventy, and the blast was so powerful that the media even reported it was heard in the mountains.[27] Another car bomb destroyed a Tawhid mosque, killing eight militants and injuring sixty-six and, days later, a new blast was aimed at one of the movement's offices, killing six and injuring twenty.[28] Even Tripoli's Great Mosque of al-Mansuri, a historical site where Sa'id Sha'aban sometimes preached, became a target, although his aides neutralized the 200 kg explosive just in time.[29] The message of these incidents was clear – joining Tawhid would end up being a risky move.

The lengths to which the Syrian regime was ready to go in order to raise the cost of Islamist activism, to such an extent that it hoped the movement would not only fragment from within but also begin losing members, fully transpired in June 1985. That was when the "Balha bombing," as it soon became known in Tripoli, took place, which

[25] "Tripoli, capitale de la violence," *L'Orient Le Jour* (June 17, 1983).
[26] "La cour de Justice saisie du massacre de Bahsas," *L'Orient Le Jour* (July 7, 1983).
[27] "La terreur frappe de nouveau au Nord," *L'Orient Le Jour* (August 6, 1983).
[28] "Tripoli: l'attentat contre la mosque a fait 8 morts et 66 blessés," *L'Orient Le Jour* (February 2, 1985); "Voiture piégée à Tripoli: 6 tués et 20 blessés," *L'Orient Le Jour* (February 11, 1985).
[29] "Découverte d'une charge de 200kg de TNT à Tripoli," *L'Orient Le Jour* (February 23, 1985).

424   The Downfall of Tawhid

targeted the eponymous ice cream concession located by the seaside in the port neighborhood of Mina with 150 kg of TNT. This was an especially vicious attack for it took place precisely at the time of year and day when the ice cream shop was most crowded with children and families – that is, during a hot evening in the middle of the religious celebrations for Eid al-Fitr, when people go out. Between fifty and a hundred civilians are reported to have died, although it remains difficult to get precise figures because the blast had been so powerful that many bodies were entirely ripped apart, some parts later discovered on the beach and even as far as on the islands off the coast.[30] Epitomizing the scale of the explosion, dozens of cars were destroyed and all windows in a 500 m radius of the Balha concession were shattered.[31] To the Islamist militants, the message of the bombing was clear. Because it targeted a part of the neighborhood near the infamous slums of Mina, where Tawhid drew hundreds of members, the "Balha bombing" was a warning of how far the regime was prepared to go to threaten them and their families.[32] No cost seemed too high to raise the stakes and intimidate members into leaving Tawhid.

The Spiral of Violence

Beyond dramatically raising the cost of activism, these covert efforts also aimed at engulfing Tawhid into a fiery spiral of violence which Syria, the firefighter, would then remedy. One indirect goal of the "Balha bombing" was thus to provoke Tawhid factions into seeking revenge, which would finally give Damascus the pretext it needed to come and "pacify" Tripoli. This strategy largely succeeded. The bombing was so shockingly brutal that it turned Hashem Minqara, the head of the Tawhid faction in Mina, from the businessman he had become through his control of the flow of money that was coming out of the port into a diehard advocate of retaliation at all costs against Damascus. "This bombing was a wake-up call," he remembered. "It showed a complete absence of willingness on the other side to stabilize the situation"[33] he said, hinting at the Syrian regime. Incidentally, the "Balha bombing" was followed, weeks later, by another massive bomb attack which targeted a Tawhid office in the residential district of Abu Samra, causing another

[30] Interview with a doctor from the Lebanese Red Cross who was on site, Tripoli, July 2014.
[31] "Tripoli fête le Fitr dans le deuil," *L'Orient Le Jour* (June 21, 1985).
[32] Interview with Tawhid members in the port district of Mina, Tripoli, June–July 2014.
[33] Interview with Hashem Minqara (Tawhid's Emir or leader in the port district of Mina), Tripoli, June 2014.

The Spiral of Violence   425

forty-eight deaths and over a hundred injuries.[34] These two bombings radicalized the views of many Tawhid members and leaders regarding the Syrian regime, leading many to argue for a quick, violent and large-scale retaliation.[35] This, however, would increase divisions and engulf the movement in a doomed spiral of violence.

At first the thirst for revenge against the Syrian regime which now animated Tawhid translated in a wave of violence targeting the handful of local pro-Assad politicians still in Tripoli. One of them was gunned down as he was leaving his home. Another was thrown in a Tawhid jail and tortured by Hashem Minqara's men, before they transported him to a nearby hospital but then riddled his body with bullets before the eyes of the doctors and nurses.[36] These brutal incidents reflected the extent of the anger at the regime simmering in Tawhid ranks. But the animosity of many members gradually morphed into a more organized and large-scale fight launched by Tawhid against the ADP's pro-Assad militiamen in Jabal Mohsen. Clashes in this area had been mostly put on a hold since the October 1984 Damascus Agreement. Yet, by rekindling them out of revenge for the two deadly bombings in Mina and Abu Samra, which they attributed to the Syrian regime, Tripoli's Islamists would trigger their own downfall for it would provide the pretext for a full-blown Syrian crackdown on the city.

Initially this new round of violence was spatially confined for it crystallized as a struggle for control of Syria Street (*Sher'a Suria*). This street, as we saw in Chapter 2, not only separated the rival neighborhoods of Jabal Mohsen and Bab al-Tebbaneh but, because of its name and location as an artery leading to the coastal road toward Syria, had also come to assume symbolic meaning as a frontier between pro- and anti-regime forces. From the outside, then, Tawhid and ADP fighters may have been largely perceived to be fighting over a street, but controlling this artery in the violently polarized context that pitted Tripoli's Islamists against pro-regime forces held major strategic and symbolic significance.

The round of violence which started on July 9, 1985 only lasted five days but it was very brutal, involving such indiscriminate shelling that

---

[34] "Voiture piégée à Tripoli: 43 morts, plus de 100 blessés," *L'Orient Le Jour* (August 21, 1985). Note that while the title of the article suggests that the car bomb killed forty-three people, a reevaluation published days later in the newspaper put the death toll at forty-eight.

[35] Interview with Bilal Diqmaq (Tawhid fighter who survived the car bomb in Abu Samra), Tripoli, June 2013; interview with Kan'an Naji (Tawhid's Emir in Abu Samra and member of the movement's Consultative Council or leadership), Tripoli, August 2014.

[36] "Sanglants règlements de comptes à Tripoli," *L'Orient Le Jour* (August 11, 1985).

426   The Downfall of Tawhid

forty-five were killed and 125 injured.[37] The use of heavy weapons meant that other areas of Tripoli than Bab al-Tebbaneh and Jabal Mohsen became affected by the fighting such as the vicinity of the Old City, Qobbe and Abu Samra neighborhoods, although it remained centered on Syria Street, 75 percent of which reportedly became destroyed.[38] The clash only stopped when Tawhid and the ADP agreed to the deployment of a Lebanese army unit on a 200 m buffer zone on Syria Street.[39]

At this stage it is worth pointing out that, while all Tawhid members and leaders deeply resented the Syrian regime's likely implication in the deadly bombings which had targeted Tripoli, far from all agreed on the need to launch the battle for Syria Street. Three Emirs or local Tawhid leaders in particular, Hashem Minqara, Kana'an Naji and Khalil Akkawi, were pushing for the movement to commit its full firepower to fighting the ADP mercilessly; the first two because they were animated by an intense, ideological dislike of the Syrian regime and its Tripolitan Alawi allies and the last because he saw once more an opportunity to leverage Tawhid's support for his district's older feud with Jabal Mohsen. But they were opposed by figures close to Sa'id Sha'aban who still privileged negotiations.[40] Sha'aban eventually failed to prevent the three factions joining forces and attacking the ADP. Yet, in a bid to avoid Syrian wrath, he still went out of his way to meet the head of Syrian intelligence in North Lebanon, praise the Syrian role in Lebanon and argue that Tawhid still abided by the Damascus Agreement. He even suggested that the battle for Syria Street had not been launched by Tawhid but by rogue factions acting as "mines planted in our midst."[41] The months of July–August 1985 were thus marked by a reactivation of internal disputes.

Syria, however, was interested in reconciliation with none of the Tawhid factions, rogue or not. The violent clash between Bab al-Tebbaneh and Jabal Mohsen which had centered so symbolically on Syria Street questioned the regime's authority in Lebanon. Crucially, this gave Damascus the pretext it had long waited for to act more aggressively toward Tawhid. From now on it would "no longer tolerate"

---

[37] "Reprise des combats à Tripoli: deux tués, sept blessés au moins," *L'Orient Le Jour* (July 9, 1985); "Les affrontements se généralisent à Tripoli," *L'Orient Le Jour* (July 10, 1985); "Situation toujours explosive à Tripoli," *L'Orient Le Jour* (July 11, 1985); and "Tripoli: échec à un nouveau cessez le feu," *L'Orient Le Jour* (July 12, 1984).

[38] "La situation à Tripoli," *L'Orient Le Jour* (July 14, 1985).

[39] "Tripoli: création d'une zone tampon," *L'Orient Le Jour* (July 18, 1985).

[40] Interview with Kan'an Naji (Tawhid's Emir in Abu Samra and member of the movement's Consultative Council or leadership), Tripoli, August 2014.

[41] "La situation à Tripoli," *L'Orient Le Jour* (July 15, 1985).

The Spiral of Violence 427

any incident, and if the Lebanese army's buffer zone failed to bring peace Syria would be "forced to take military measures."[42] Far from helping the Lebanese army fulfill its task, though, the regime once again took on the role of the "firefighter arsonist" in order to further raise the cost of Islamist activism. It tasked its proxy, the ADP, with bombing the Lebanese army barracks to undermine the ability of the soldiers to mediate, killing ten.[43] It then pushed the ADP to adopt a confrontational posture to rekindle the clashes and give Damascus the justification it needed to intervene. The ADP agreed to hold bilateral talks with Tawhid, perhaps in a bid to divide the movement even more, but included unrealistic conditions to the signing of a ceasefire agreement and then withdrew from the negotiations committee that had just been formed.[44] It then solemnly asked Syria to "cut the terrorist hand" and "find radical solutions" to put an end to "the hegemony of [Tawhid's] Emirs" and return Tripoli "to normalcy."[45] The same day it launched another round of fighting which, this time, would engulf all of the factions and crystallize as a larger-scale battle between Tawhid and the Syrian regime.[46]

Hafez al-Assad, then, had chosen September 1985 to "close the Tripolitan file,"[47] as a leading Syrian official put it back then. To Damascus the timing seemed ideal for a full-blown assault on Tawhid. From a domestic perspective the Syrian president had by then recovered from the combined effects of his heart attack and the coup staged by his brother Rif'at, but he still feared that Tripoli, under Tawhid's rule, would because of its cross-border ties to Syrian opposition bastions provide Islamist rebels with a safe haven and weapons. Geopolitically a regime crackdown on Tawhid might lead to official Iranian protests. Yet Hafez al-Assad no longer feared that it would undermine the Syria–Iran alliance, both because he framed the September 1985 battle as an answer

[42] Qassem Qassem, head of Syrian intelligence in North Lebanon, quoted in: "Les affrontements se généralisent à Tripoli," *L'Orient Le Jour* (July 10, 1985) and Brigadier Sleiman Hassan, in charge of the Syrian military contingent in North Lebanon, quoted in "Tripoli: création d'une zone tampon," *L'Orient Le Jour* (July 18, 1985).

[43] "Hécatombe dans une caserne de l'armée à Tripoli," *L'Orient Le Jour* (September 17, 1985).

[44] "Tripoli: les pro-Syriens veulent changer le statu-quo," *L'Orient Le Jour* (September 20, 1985).

[45] "Le Parti Arabe Démocratique exhorte le Président Assad à intervenir," *L'Orient Le Jour* (September 17, 1985).

[46] "Tripoli: 40 tués et 140 blessés en deux jours d'affrontements entre le Mouvement de l'Unification Islamique et le Parti Arabe Démocratique," *L'Orient Le Jour* (September 18, 1985).

[47] "Bayan Na'eb Ra'is Suria Abdel Halim Khaddam" ["Statement of the Vice President of Syria Abdel Halim Khaddam"], *Al-Incha* (August 3, 1985).

428   The Downfall of Tawhid

to the ADP's call for support and as he knew that the Tawhid–Iran relationship had by then turned into a marriage of convenience. It also helped that the Syrian president was backed by the USSR, which praised his foreign policy, and by the West which increasingly viewed him as a "Bismarck of the Middle East."[48]

From the perspective of the Syrian part in the Lebanese civil war, the battle for Tripoli came at a time when Assad was intent on showing he could single-handedly "pacify" Lebanon. The Syrian regime's mouthpiece, *Tishrin*, thus claimed in early September 1985 that the Lebanese civil war had just entered a "definitive and decisive phase" that would lead to its quick "resolution."[49] This hinted at plans by the Syrian president to gather in Damascus Walid Jumblatt, Nabih Berri and Elie Hobeiqa, all key protagonists of the Lebanese civil war and figures which he viewed as the leaders of the Druze, Shia and Christian communities.[50] Tellingly, no Sunni would be invited to these talks that aimed to put an end to the conflict, perhaps out of the regime's deep-seated fear of galvanizing a community which had by and large opposed its policies in Lebanon and Syria. It was in this framework that Damascus tightened its ties with the Lebanese Shia militia, Amal, pushing it to crack down on the Murabitun, a movement popular with Beiruti Sunnis.[51] Removing Tawhid from the political and military map in September 1985 would then allow the regime to rid Lebanon of its last significant Sunni militia. And this, in turn, would pave the way for the aforementioned talks in the Syrian capital, known as the Tripartite Agreement, to succeed. Syria thus had a very clear view of the goals it wanted to achieve by cracking down on Tawhid. And, objectively, all the ingredients appeared to be there for a swift regime victory.

A Battle between Islamism and Secularism?

Initially, to avoid any potential blowback, Syria went to great lengths to construct the "master narrative" of the September 1985 battle against Tawhid as a largely local ideological feud spearheaded by "progressive" movements bent on ridding Tripoli of "fundamentalism." And it is true

[48] "La Pravda rend hommage au rôle syrien au Liban," *L'Orient Le Jour* (July 19, 1985) and French President François Mitterrand quoted in "Mitterrand: la Syrie peut jouer un 'grand rôle' au Liban," *L'Orient Le Jour* (November 26, 1984).
[49] "*Techrine*: la phase 'définitive' de la solution a commencé," *L'Orient Le Jour* (September 9, 1985).
[50] "La Syrie veut organiser une réunion Hobeika-Berri-Jumblatt," *L'Orient Le Jour* (September 15, 1985).
[51] "Les chars syriens à Amal," *L'Orient Le Jour* (July 31, 1985).

A Battle between Islamism and Secularism?

that, on paper, those who took the lead in beginning to shell and attack the northern city belonged to the ADP, which routinely used an Arab nationalist and socialist discourse in its official propaganda, as well as to the vehemently secularist and leftist Lebanese Communist Party (LCP) and Syrian Social Nationalist Party (SSNP). On the eve of the battle the three leftist movements struck an alliance and issued a statement which was meant to articulate this "master narrative" of a local clash of ideologies between Islamism and secularism. It read that they would now break Tawhid's "monopoly" over Tripoli and that, once the ideological and physical presence of the "Islamic Emirate" was be eradicated, they would celebrate by "drinking *araq* and whiskey and Champagne there."[52]

Yet, although these leftist movements professed to be guided by the sole goal of ending Tawhid's "Islamist pressures" on Tripoli, other factors also guided their offensive. Members of the ADP in Jabal Mohsen, for instance, were impatient to finally settle scores with their longstanding neighborhood rivals of Bab al-Tebbaneh, and were also motivated by the prospect of dominating Tripoli's illicit economy alongside the regime. For their part, fighters from the LCP and SSNP were guided by revenge against those who had driven them out of the city in mid-1983. And all three, of course, were what observers called "proxy political organizations and militias"[53] whose "primary purpose" was to carry out "military operations" and serve as a "political front" on behalf of the Syrian regime in return for generous financial compensation. Syria's official press agency may have done its best to construct the "master narrative" of the September 1985 battle as a Tripolitan affair between local "Islamist militants" and "leftist fighters,"[54] but what was truly at stake was Syria's struggle to regain control of the city.

Reflecting Syria's preeminent role during the September 1985 battle, the vicinity of Tripoli witnessed the arrival of Ghazi Kana'an, the all-powerful head of Syrian intelligence in Lebanon who warned Tawhid that he had come to "neutralize the factors of troubles" and restore Syria's "control"[55] over the city. He summoned the leaders of the leftist militias to the headquarters of Syrian intelligence in Tripoli's vicinity.

---

[52] "Tripoli: les pro-syriens veulent changer le statu-quo," *L'Orient Le Jour* (September 20, 1985).

[53] US Central Intelligence Agency, "Syria's allies and assets in Lebanon" (RPM 78-10411, November 7, 1978).

[54] Statement from the Syrian Arab News Agency, quoted in: "Muslims battle leftists for Tripoli," *Associated Press* (October 1, 1985).

[55] "Tripoli, les regards se tournent vers Damas," *L'Orient Le Jour* (September 21, 1985) and "Tripoli: le point de non-retour aurait-il été atteint?" *L'Orient Le Jour* (September 22, 1985).

430   The Downfall of Tawhid

There he provided them weapons and instructed them to shell the city from the nearby hills with high-caliber cannons. He continued denying any direct Syrian involvement in the battle, pointing instead to "the role of the leftist militias" and repeatedly insisting that "they have all the weapons they need."[56] But the extent of the Syrian regime's implication had by now become evident to all observers.

Interviews with pro- and anti-Assad fighters during the battle confirmed the scale of the Syrian role. One Communist commander recognized that his militia was backed up by Syrian cannons and that, on the ground, Syrian Special Forces were fighting alongside his comrades.[57] A pro-Assad Lebanese official also confirmed that the battle against Tawhid was closely coordinated by Syrian intelligence and army officers.[58] Tawhid fighters, for their part, reported having killed not only leftist militiamen but also scores of Syrian soldiers.[59] Journalists present at the scene even witnessed a battalion of Syrian paratroopers struggling to enter Tripoli's southern suburb along with a convoy of nine Syrian T-54 tanks and artillery.[60] The media specified that by September 1985 the city was surrounded by 7,500 Syrian troops, with an extra 5,500 soldiers positioned on high alert in the rest of North Lebanon.[61] These figures, if accurate, would mean that the Syrian regime had committed half of all its troops in Lebanon, which by 1985 were estimated at 25,000, to crush Tawhid. Far from the "master narrative" of a local struggle between secularism and Islamism, then, what was really at stake was a last-ditch battle initiated by the regime to regain control of Tripoli.

What was truly puzzling about the September 1985 battle is that, in spite of such a massive amount of resources committed by the regime and its proxies to crush Tawhid once and for all, it would take them nineteen days before retaking even partial control of Tripoli. The pro-Assad camp had expected a quick and decisive victory given how far the regime had gone to raise the costs and risks associated with Islamist activism. In fact, some of its representatives had originally speculated that Tripoli would "fall within the next 48 hours."[62] According to

---

[56] "Entrenched Muslims in Tripoli beat back pro-Syrian militiamen," *Reuters* (September 30, 1985).

[57] Interview with a military commander in the Lebanese Communist Party, Tripoli, June 2014.

[58] Interview with a pro-Syrian leftist official, Tripoli, July 2014.

[59] Interview with current and former Tawhid fighters and commanders, Tripoli, June–August 2014.

[60] "Muslims battle leftists for Tripoli," *Associated Press* (October 1, 1985).

[61] "Concentration de troupes syriennes autour de Tripoli," *L'Orient Le Jour* (September 27, 1985).

[62] "Tripoli: 200,000 personnes piégées sous les obus," *L'Orient Le Jour* (September 30, 1985).

A Battle between Islamism and Secularism? 431

observers, this pro-Syrian coalition was made up of 2,500–3,000 Lebanese leftist fighters and of 4,000 Syrian Special Forces elite soldiers, who ringed the city with "troops, artillery and tanks."[63] They began bombarding Tripoli with thousands of shells and then tried to penetrate it from the east, in the neighborhood of Abu Samra, and the south, in the district of Bahsas. Yet every time they entered these areas they were violently pushed back. "Several of our attacks failed," recounted one of the officers who directed the offensive. "It was very bad, we suffered major losses and each time we had to withdraw."[64] And, when a Syrian army unit managed to enter the city after some time, it was ambushed.[65]

Two weeks into the fighting, the spokesperson for one of the leftist militias himself acknowledged that the conflict had so far been "very bitter" and had become considerably "more difficult" than anticipated. The violence was such that 600 had already perished, 1,500 were injured and the water and electricity infrastructure had been destroyed.[66] The journalists who were present in and around Tripoli described "shells and rockets exploding throughout," scenes of fighting of an "extreme violence" between the two sides, streets "strewn with corpses" and hospitals "unable to cope"[67] with the number of injured. One of them was shocked by what he saw. Tripoli, he recounted in detail, had turned into "a battlefield looking like an immense field of ruins." He reported that "all the imaginable instruments of death are being used by the warring sides," and elaborated:

Canons, Molotov cocktails, Grad missiles, mortars of all calibers, rockets of all kinds, light and heavy machine guns and even phosphorous bombs – the panoply is diverse but the result is the same, death and destruction; to the extent that no one in the memory of Tripolitans had witnessed such bloodshed.

And yet, in the face of all of this, Tawhid still opposed a "stiff resistance."[68]

---

[63] "Residents flee Tripoli as fighting rages," *New York Times* (September 30, 1985).
[64] Interview with a military commander in the Lebanese Communist Party, Tripoli, June 2014.
[65] "A Tripoli, les intégristes se battent dos à la mer," *L'Orient Le Jour* (September 29, 1985).
[66] "Tripoli: le point de non-retour aurait-il été atteint?" *L'Orient Le Jour* (September 22, 1985) and Adib N'ame, "Al-amen fi Trablus, 1980–1985" ["The security in Tripoli, 1980–1985"], *Nada' al-Shamal* (undated, copy given to the author).
[67] "Sur le terrain, les batailles ont un caractère d'extrême violence," *L'Orient Le Jour* (October 2, 1985).
[68] US Central Intelligence Agency, "Tripoli battles spawns kidnappings" (Top Secret, CPAS 86-230J3, October 2, 1985).

432   The Downfall of Tawhid

The Role of Ideology in High-Risk Activism

This and the next section assess the factors which explained Tawhid's stiff resistance and led its members to engage in what scholar Doug McAdam called "high-risk"[69] collective action, when activists mobilize even though they anticipate great dangers. While this section acknowledges and details the roles played by ideology in that risky type of mobilization, the next section will argue that its explanatory power should not be overstated. Instead of pointing to ideology, it will point to how Tawhid recruited and mobilized non-Islamist Tripolitans by activating identification with the city and neighborhood solidarities – its use of the symbolic and social dimensions of space would be central in its resistance effort.

It is remarkable how Tawhid, despite its growing divisions, the risks associated with Islamist activism in 1984–5 and the blatant asymmetry of forces with the pro-Syrian coalition, still succeeded in acting cohesively, mobilizing members and even recruiting new ones. Of course, it is difficult to gather precise data as figures vary wildly depending on sources. Whereas pro-Syrian officials recall having fought a few hundred Islamists, current and former Tawhid members for their part remember several thousand joining the battle.[70] The most neutral and reliable figures are drawn from reports by Lebanese and Western journalists present in Tripoli at the time of the fighting. They estimate that Tawhid mobilized as many as 4,000 militants, although they point out that only 900 may have played an active role in the street fighting that took place – the rest undertaking less costly, but still risky, tasks such as gathering intelligence, moving stocks of ammunition and transporting the injured.[71] Such figures, if accurate, would mean that Tawhid not only overcame the bitter divisions that were plaguing members since 1984, but that it also went on a recruitment drive shortly before or during the 1985 battle, for it was earlier estimated to have 2,000–3,000 members. And, even though they had opportunities to escape Tripoli as a series of brief lulls were enforced at the height of the fighting, most seemed

---

[69] Doug McAdam, "Recruitment to high-risk activism: the case of Freedom Summer" *American Journal of Sociology* (Vol. 92, No. 1, 1986), pp. 64–90.

[70] Interviews with members of the Lebanese Communist Party, Tripoli, June–July 2014 and interviews with current and former Tawhid fighters and commanders, Tripoli, August 2014.

[71] While *L'Orient Le Jour* mentions that the pro-Syrian offensive was opposed by "4,000 Tripolitan rebels," the *New York Times* estimates that 900 of them were "men armed with rockets and heavy machine guns." See: "A Tripoli, les intégristes se battent dos à la mer," *L'Orient Le Jour* (September 29, 1985) and "Lebanese militias attack Moslem rivals in Tripoli," *New York Times* (September 29, 1985).

The Role of Ideology in High-Risk Activism   433

prepared to keep fighting and resisting until the end. This was confirmed by a cable from the CIA which asserted that all Tawhid factions had "joined forces" to face off the Syrian and leftist attack and that membership "fluctuated considerably," with an ability to display "remarkable cohesion"[72] in this time of crisis. What, then, explained Tawhid's capacity to mobilize so many under particular duress?

I argue that ideology played a key part in Tawhid's ability to withstand the pro-Syrian offensive on Tripoli for three weeks, both through sincere beliefs and instrumental value. The mechanism through which ideology as sincerely held beliefs bolstered Tawhid's ability to mobilize so many was the "ideological entrepreneurship" of a handful of highly committed cadres. As Chapter 6 suggested, these cadres had been central to the effort of socializing and educating into Islamism those less committed members who had joined Tawhid for instrumental reasons. The spread of "Islamo-gangsterism" in late 1984 and early 1985 shed doubts on how successful their efforts had ultimately been, and the simultaneous assassination of some of them may have pushed the rest to adopt a lower profile for a while. But, as the September 1985 battle erupted, these cadres soon recovered their ability to mobilize their worldviews and to steer Tawhid's behavior in an ideological direction. By activating a radical Islamist discourse in this time of crisis, the "ideological entrepreneurs" succeeded in mobilizing and galvanizing the movement's most ideologically committed fighters and sympathizers, some of whom had become disgruntled to an extent by the development of criminal practices at odds with ideology. They also recruited new, non-Tawhid Islamists.

In the run-up to and during the September 1985 battle, the "ideological entrepreneurs" again became very active in Tripoli. Only a few actually fought, but all were omnipresent on Tawhid's radio and TV stations as well as in the city's mosques and public squares, mobilizing crowds and energizing members through a polarizing ideological discourse.[73] In the vein of the fervent and militant type of speech they had spread when Tawhid cracked down on some leftist parties in mid-1983, these figures equated the pro-Syrian offensive on Tripoli with the apocalypse, a divine struggle which every able local Muslim had to fight. Incidentally helped by the regime's "master narrative" of a struggle between Islamism and progressivism, they did not miss a chance to

---

[72] US Central Intelligence Agency, "Lebanon: Islamic fundamentalism in Tripoli" (Top Secret, NESAR 86-003JX, January 17, 1986).

[73] Interview with Salem al-Rafe'i (Tawhid cleric in the 1980s and leading "ideological entrepreneur"), Tripoli, September 2015.

434   The Downfall of Tawhid

highlight and demonize the ideological characteristics of the pro-Syrian coalition, for example when they fierily lambasted the "evil" nature of the "secular and atheist leftist parties" who "reject the rule of God on men."[74] They also emphasized the non-Sunni, Alawi composition of the ADP in Jabal Mohsen and of the Syrian Special Forces, back then led by Major General Ali Haydar, a Syrian Alawi, stoking fears that the real objective of this "evil community" was to "slaughter the Sunnis."[75] Framing the pro-Syrians as Tawhid's ideological nemesis allowed the "ideological entrepreneurs" to brand their enemies as the "servants of Satan"[76] and encourage their killing. Moreover, these figures also went to great lengths to remind their audience of the broader ideological stakes at play. Tawhid, for all its sins, had made Tripoli what they called a true "Islamic city," a "fortress of Islam."[77] It had emptied the city of leftist activists, applied Islamic law and erected the name of God on the central roundabout, which amounted to a symbolically powerful victory. It was therefore the duty of Tripoli's committed Islamists to now wage "jihad" to defend all of these ideological legacies. This, they promised, would earn them divine rewards.[78]

The "ideological entrepreneurship" of the cadres who activated such a polarizing discourse translated militant Islamist beliefs into mobilization for Tawhid in three ways: it galvanized the movement's sincerely committed militant Islamists, reinforced internal cohesion and triggered an alliance with non-Tawhid Tripolitan Islamists, who joined the fight. To begin with their discourse galvanized the Tawhid factions which had always embraced militant Islamism sincerely and had become somewhat demobilized from early 1985 onward. By all accounts, members on the sincerely Islamist side of Tawhid's "spectrum of ideological commitment" mobilized en masse. The journalists in Tripoli during the time of the battle described seeing many of those they called "diehard" Islamist militants. They wore jihadi headbands, constantly shouted

---

[74] "Tripoli: 200,000 personnes piégées sous les obus," *L'Orient Le Jour* (September 30, 1985).

[75] "Tripoli à bout de force," *L'Orient Le Jour* (September 28, 1985).

[76] "Tripoli: le MUI dénonce les forces athées soutenues par la Syrie," *L'Orient le Jour* (October 1, 1985).

[77] "Khitab min al-Muhandes Abdallah Babetti: al-tafjirat satastamiru" ["Speech by the Engineer Abdallah Babetti: the bombings will continue"], *al-Tawhid* (September 15, 1985) and Tawhid statement quoted in: "Tripoli: 200,000 personnes piégées sous les obus," *L'Orient Le Jour* (September 30, 1985).

[78] "Al-Sheikh Bader Shender fi khutbat al-jum'a: al-yum nuhajer bi tarak ma huwa sharir wa makhjul wa khata'" ["The cleric Bader Shender in his Friday sermon: today we emigrate by leaving what is evil, shameful and wrong"], *al-Tawhid* (September 19, 1985).

The Role of Ideology in High-Risk Activism 435

"God is great"[79] and promised to fight until death to resist the leftist offensive for "our dead go to heaven and theirs go to hell."[80] There is also some evidence of Tawhid's involvement in ideological behavior in the immediate run-up to and during the September 1985 battle, for example when a wave of violence targeted religious minorities or as Allah Square became the theater of a violent ambush after a column of Syrian soldiers who had been lured there was slaughtered by the militants.[81] This latter example also showed the importance of what I called "ideological artifacts" in Chapter 5: Allah Square's ideational meaning may have equally galvanized them into taking risks to fight.

The vehement Islamist discourse which Tawhid's "ideological entrepreneurs" activated and mobilized during the fight also had two other important effects: it reinforced the movement's cohesion and triggered the participation of non-Tawhid Tripolitan Islamists. By drawing the contours of the new, anti-Islamist "atheist" order which the pro-Syrians would impose on Tripoli if they were to win the conflict, which would include destroying Allah Square and drinking alcohol on its rubble, the speech of the "ideological entrepreneurs" triggered a rapprochement between all of Tripoli's sincerely committed Islamists. Competing Tawhid factions stopped quarreling and began acting cohesively once again. Many Tripolitan Islamists who had remained on the sidelines in 1982–5 also joined the movement's resistance against the pro-Syrians. This included dozens of members from the Islamic Group and from a small Salafi organization. They disagreed with aspects of Tawhid's ideology, behavior and foreign alliances, but ultimately felt they shared the same enemy.[82] Tellingly, one of them retrospectively recalled the September 1985 battle a time when "the brothers from all the [Tripolitan] Islamist movements were working together, as if they had been doing so for the past ten years." "It is Allah who brought us together,"[83] he claimed. Emphasizing the ideological stakes at play in Tawhid's struggle against the pro-regime leftists also pushed dozens of Syrian and Palestinian Islamists in Tripoli to join the fight.[84] The mechanism through which ideology, as sincere beliefs,

---

[79] "Tripoli: des cendres et des larmes, une détresse sans nom," *L'Orient Le Jour* (October 5, 1985).

[80] "Muslims battle leftists for Tripoli," *Associated Press* (October 1, 1985).

[81] "A Tripoli, les intégristes se battent dos à la mer," *L'Orient Le Jour* (September 29, 1985); "Sanglants règlements de comptes à Tripoli," *L'Orient Le Jour* (August 11, 1985) and "Les accrochages ont repris hier soir à Tripoli," *L'Orient Le Jour* (October 14, 1985).

[82] Interviews with Islamic Group members and officials as well as with Salafi activists, Tripoli, July 2014.

[83] Islamic Group member quoted in: *Harb Trablus 1985* [*The war of Tripoli in 1985*] (documentary produced by the Islamic Group, copy given to the author, 2013).

[84] Interviews with Tawhid fighters who participated in the September 1985 conflict, Tripoli, June–September 2014. The allegation that small groups of Palestinian and

436   The Downfall of Tawhid

bolstered Tawhid's capacity to resist the offensive was thus the "ideological entrepreneurship" of highly ideologized cadres who mobilized a polarizing speech which reactivated the ideological cleavage between Islamists and leftists. This galvanized ideologically committed members, reinforced internal cohesion and triggered the participation of non-Tawhid Tripolitan Islamists to the battle.

Yet ideology did not only matter because it was embraced sincerely but also as some Tawhid leaders used it instrumentally to obtain external support. Chapters 4 and 7 showed how, at strategic times, some in the movement had pushed ideological production in a "Khomeinist" direction to suggest ideational proximity with the Islamic Republic of Iran and to leverage ideological solidarity into concrete backing. During the September 1985 battle, those Tawhid figures who were known to be most skilled at instrumentalizing ideology to obtain external support, chief among them the movement's head, Sa'id Sha'aban, activated the ideological bonds which tied them to Iran and to their Lebanese Khomeinist allies by dramatizing the consequences which the downfall of Tripoli's "Islamic Emirate" would have. Sha'aban recognized that Tawhid had largely centered on one city, but he then suggested this never meant it was local, for it was just about to claim the "Islamization of the entire world."[85] Letting it be defeated by the pro-Syrian coalition would thus destroy no less than "the efforts of a century"[86] at reviving Islamic rule in the region. To help the movement make its "Islamic Emirate" more regional and global, it was the duty of "all Muslims" through the world to "take their responsibilities"[87] and to support Tawhid.

The instrumentalization by some Tawhid leaders of a discourse highlighting the broader, ideological consequences of its downfall succeeded to secure external support. This backing varied depending on the actors. Hezbollah, which was made up of Shias but shared Tawhid's "Khomeinist" ideological orientation, did not send members to fight alongside the movement in Tripoli but it gave it noticeably strong and unconditional support. The Party of God praised Tawhid's "resistance in

---

Syrian Islamists took part in the battle can also be found in the Lebanese media at the time. See, for instance, "Tripoli: la Syrie obtient gain de cause," *L'Orient Le Jour* (October 4, 1985).

[85] "Tripoli: 200,000 personnes piégées sous les obus," *L'Orient Le Jour* (September 30, 1985).

[86] "Tripoli: la détermination des syriens à l'œuvre," *L'Orient le Jour* (October 10, 1985).

[87] "Al-Shekikh Sa'id Sha'aban: nasr 'ala en yahil al-Islam mahal al-hulul al-ukhra" ["The cleric Sa'id Sha'aban: we insist that Islam should replace the other solutions"], *al-Tawhid* (September 19, 1985).

The Role of Ideology in High-Risk Activism   437

the face of Syria" and lambasted the "aggressors of Tripoli" who were "destroying the revolutionary situation"[88] there. At the height of the September 1985 battle, it even dispatched some of its top leaders to the vicinity of the city where, "under the bombs" and "out of duty toward God,"[89] they tried negotiating an end to the pro-Syrian offensive. Hezbollah's efforts did not yield any short-term results. But its rhetorical support and attempt at mediation gave Tawhid fighters a moral boost.

The external support which Tawhid instrumentally leveraged out of the bonds of ideological solidarity tying it to its Khomeinist Lebanese allies was at times more concrete. The most telling example was how one of them, a small and newly formed pro-Iran terrorist group operating out of Beirut and Sidon called the Islamic Liberation Organization (*Tanzim Tahrir al-Islami*), engaged in a wave of anti-Syrian and anti-leftist attacks of such violence that it eventually forced Hafez al-Assad to stop the offensive and strike a deal with Tawhid. The man behind the Islamic Liberation Organization was none other than Maher Hammud.[90] Chapter 7 detailed the way this deeply ideological "Sunni Khomeinist" cleric in Sidon with a significant local following had long been "fascinated" by Tawhid, to the point that he had considered opening a local chapter in the south before Syria prevented him. He was especially attracted by the vehemence of its "Khomeinist" ideology and even the CIA reported on his "deep sympathy"[91] for its pro-Iranian positions. It is likely that Tawhid's call for "all Muslims"[92] to provide support activated bonds of ideological solidarity and pushed Maher Hammud to support the movement's resistance against the pro-Syrian offensive.

As the September 1985 battle was unfolding, the Islamic Liberation Organization issued a statement which threatened the regime with "taking revenge in Beirut or Damascus" if the "atheist campaign on the Islamic city of Tripoli" was not right away "put on hold."[93] As expected the pro-Syrian offensive on Tawhid continued unabated, and a mysterious bombing campaign began targeting the regime's interests in the

---

[88] "Le Hezbollah accuse les 'services suspects'," *L'Orient Le Jour* (October 9, 1985).

[89] "Le Hezbollah réitère son appui à Shaaban," *L'Orient Le Jour* (October 7, 1985).

[90] US Central Intelligence Agency, "Lebanon: Soviet hostages" (Secret, CPAS-85239JX, October 12, 1985).

[91] US Central Intelligence Agency, "Syria: Vice President Rif'at Assad down but not out" (NESAR86-021, September 12, 1986) and interview with Maher Hammud (cleric close to Tawhid and to Iran), Sidon, July 2014.

[92] "Al-Shekikh Sa'id Sha'aban: nasr 'ala en yahil al-Islam mahal al-hulul al-ukhra" ["The cleric Sa'id Sha'aban: we insist that Islam should replace the other solutions"], *al-Tawhid* (September 19, 1985).

[93] "A Tripoli, les intégristes se battent dos à la mer," *L'Orient Le Jour* (September 29, 1985).

438   The Downfall of Tawhid

Syrian and Lebanese capitals. While a bomb exploded in a strategic location in the city center of Damascus, where two additional car bombs were discovered, days later up to five attacks targeted the Beirut office of one of the pro-Assad Lebanese leftist militias taking part in Syria's offensive on Tripoli.[94] Two high-ranking, pro-Syria, Lebanese officials in Beirut were also assassinated. Although no group officially claimed this wave of violence, the CIA suspected that the Islamic Liberation Organization, or groups similar to it, were the main culprits and may well have "used the recent bombings to pressure Damascus"[95] to stop its offensive on Tawhid. But the full extent to which, out of ideological solidarity with Tawhid, the Islamic Liberation Organization was prepared to go in order to pressure the Syrian regime into ending the battle of Tripoli, transpired when it went as far as taking four Soviet diplomats hostage in Beirut. As the terrorist group asked, but again to no avail, for the end to what it called the "genocide of Tripoli" in exchange for the release of the hostages, it gave the "divine sentence"[96] to one of them, shooting Soviet consular secretary Arkady Katkov and threatening to kill the others. This episode not only further galvanized the embattled Tawhid members, it would also eventually put a considerable degree of pressure on the USSR to lobby the Syrian regime and the Lebanese branch of the Communist Party into ceasing their offensive on Tripoli.

Finally, Tawhid leaders like Sa'id Sha'aban were also able to leverage the bonds of ideological solidarity which tied their movement to the Islamic Republic of Iran into some kind of diplomatic support. Because by mid-1985 their relationship had clearly turned into a marriage of convenience, they did not expect Iran to back them militarily. But they still hoped that the ostensibly "Khomeinist" stances they had continued espousing would push Tehran to put diplomatic pressure on Syria and find a way out of the battle. At the height of the fight, Sa'id Sha'aban even issued an "SOS" to Ayatollah Khomeini. In it he hinted at the strong degree of ideological solidarity linking his movement to the Islamic Republic, telling him that "you must understand what we have tried to achieve [in Tripoli]." Sha'aban's hope was that Khomeini would "solemnly condemn"[97] the Syrian regime's attack. And there is evidence to

---

[94] US Central Intelligence Agency, "Lebanon: wave of attacks on SSNP centres and officials" (Secret, GI TR 85-022, November 4, 1985) and US Central Intelligence Agency, "Syria: bombs linked to fighting in Lebanon" (Secret, GI TR 85-022, November 4, 1985).

[95] US Central Intelligence Agency, "Syria: bombs linked to fighting in Lebanon" (Secret, GI TR 85–022, November 4, 1985).

[96] "Les otages soviétiques," *L'Orient Le Jour* (October 2, 1985).

[97] "SOS de Shaaban à Khomeyni," *L'Orient Le Jour* (October 1, 1985).

The Role of Ideology in High-Risk Activism   439

suggest that his strategy succeeded. Days after his "SOS" none other than Ayatollah Montazeri, Khomeini's deputy, delivered a well-publicized sermon in Tehran in which he fiercely denounced "the massacre perpetrated against the innocent Muslims of Tripoli," going to the extent of wondering whether "the aggressors are thinking about saving Lebanon from Israeli evil or are rather maneuvering to keep alive the fire of the internal Lebanese war in the interest of Israel."[98] This was the prelude to a true geopolitical crisis which shook the Syrian–Iranian alliance for a few months during the summer and autumn 1985. Tehran even threatened to cut the massive flow of oil it provided to Damascus, which by then amounted to 8.7 million tons of crude a year, one million free and the rest subsidized.[99] Officially, relations between the two allies were still "excellent,"[100] in the words of Syria's foreign minister. Yet in reality all observers agreed that the pro-Syrian coalition's offensive on Tawhid, a movement notoriously close to Tehran, soon became an "important source of tension in Syrian–Iranian relations."[101] In this heated context, a delegation of Iranian diplomats traveled to the vicinity of Tripoli to demonstrate the Islamic Republic's ideological solidarity with Tawhid, which added further pressure on the Syrian regime.[102]

All in all, ideology played central roles in Tawhid's mobilization under duress and stiff resistance against the pro-Syrian coalition during the September 1985 battle. On the one hand, sincere beliefs mattered, mainly through the "ideological entrepreneurship" of a handful of highly committed cadres who, through the fiery diatribes they engaged in, mobilized and galvanized the most sincere Islamists on Tawhid's "spectrum of ideological commitment" and enlisted the support of other Islamists in Tripoli who joined its resistance. But, on the other hand, ideology was simultaneously instrumentalized by some Tawhid leaders, including its head, who strategically deployed a type of discourse which was meant to leverage the bonds of ideological solidarity with like-

---

[98] "Sermon de l'Ayatollah Montazeri, dauphin de Khomeyni, dans lequel il dénonce la 'tuerie perpétrée contre les musulmans innocents à Tripoli'," *L'Orient Le Jour* (October 2, 1985).

[99] "Le malaise s'accentue entre Damas et Téhéran," *L'Orient Le Jour* (October 26, 1985).

[100] "Khaddam remet au president iranien un message d'Assad," *L'Orient Le Jour* (September 18, 1985).

[101] US Embassy in Damascus, "Syria and Iran: almost a return to status quo ante" (No. 103, CES 143-98, December 18, 1985). See also: "Damas et Téhéran entendent 'clarifier' leurs relations," *L'Orient Le Jour* (December 2, 1985) and "Le Ministre des Gardiens de la Révolution à Damas," *L'Orient Le Jour* (December 23, 1985).

[102] "Une délégation diplomatique iranienne à Tripoli," *L'Orient Le Jour* (October 2, 1985).

440   The Downfall of Tawhid

minded external actors into support. The external backing which resulted from the activation of these bonds of ideological solidarity was significant for it ultimately contributed to Syria accepting that it had to make peace. Yet, while the sincere and instrumental embraces of Islamist beliefs thus helped explain Tawhid's stiff resistance and engagement in risky activism, ideology was only a part of the story.

The Activation of Local Identities and Solidarities

Ideological accounts of Tawhid's high-risk collective action are necessary but insufficient. In fact, the role of ideology during the September 1985 battle should not be overstated, for the movement also engaged in alliances which were in stark contradiction with its militant Islamist beliefs, for example when it struck a deal with Lebanese military intelligence at the height of the fighting, or when three dozen Tripolitan soldiers of the Lebanese army joined it. Moreover, it soon transpired that members on Tawhid's entire "spectrum of ideological commitment" had mobilized, including those who had always embraced militant Islamism instrumentally. What pushed them to join the battle against the pro-Syrian coalition in spite of the high risks was not ideology, then, but the way Tawhid had activated local identities and solidarities by casting the battle as one to defend Tripoli and to protect local communities. In other words, their mobilization was spatially oriented more than it was ideologically driven.

Strikingly, far from the official "master narrative" of a struggle between Islamism and secularism, at the height of the battle Tawhid struck a counterintuitive alliance with Lebanon's military intelligence, the Second Bureau, which provided it with support. This was done discreetly so that it would not hamper the efforts by Tawhid's leaders to bolster their ideological credentials at a time when they tried eliciting external backing. Yet the deal was sanctioned by the leadership and much of the membership was aware of it. This alliance represented a flagrant inconsistency with its ideology. As Chapter 6 indicated, while Tawhid was a militant Islamist movement, the Second Bureau was an intelligence agency in the hands of Lebanon's Christian Phalangist government and the Islamists had suspected it of supporting gangs and militias hostile to their rule, which they had then violently suppressed. That Tawhid and the Second Bureau struck a deal at the height of the September 1985 battle, although they were ideological enemies and had a history of bad blood, was a first clue that ideology alone was not a sufficient factor to explain Tawhid's engagement in risky activism.

The Activation of Local Identities and Solidarities 441

Interviews with Lebanese intelligence officers who were in post in Tripoli at the time, as well as with Tawhid members implicated in this affair, explained the rationale behind the alliance. The prevailing logic was that my enemy's enemy is my friend, even if he is an ideological foe. Intelligence officials recounted that, as a governmental agency, the Second Bureau had grown highly critical of the Syrian regime's role in Lebanon after it came under the influence of two successive directors, Johnny Abdu and Simon Qassis, who were known to be personally and politically close to Lebanese Presidents Bashir and Amine Gemayel. It was when relations severely deteriorated between the Phalange and Hafez al-Assad in the wake of Bashir Gemayel's 1982 assassination by the member of a pro-Syria militia that the Second Bureau began looking more sympathetically upon anti-Assad movements – whatever their ideology. This trend accelerated in the summer of 1985 when the regime bypassed the new Lebanese president, Amine Gemayel, and tried to turn his key rival, Elie Hobeiqa, into the representative of the Christian Maronites by inviting the latter to the tripartite talks in Damascus on how to end the Lebanese civil war. "Lebanese intelligence officers in Tripoli received their orders from Johnny Abdu and Simon Qassis who, for their part, followed the directives of Gemayel, himself at loggerheads with Syria,"[103] summarized a source who was a Second Bureau operative in Tripoli in the 1980s.

It was in this context that, as another intelligence officer confessed, the Second Bureau provided "weapons and ammunition" to Tawhid at the height of the battle and "exchanged information,"[104] with the ultimate goal of undermining Syria's position in Lebanon. Tawhid leaders and members confirmed having then developed ties to the Second Bureau. There was a temporary "alliance of interests,"[105] as the Tawhid figure who became in charge of this relationship recalled. "We passed on certain information to the Second Bureau, and in exchange we would obtain freedom of movement, intelligence and small amounts of help." Tawhid's growing relationship with the Second Bureau at the height of the September 1985 battle helped it resist the attack for a time.[106] And the fact that this alliance, despite representing a blatant ideological contradiction, had been relatively uncontroversial within the movement

[103] Interview with a former Lebanese military intelligence operative in post in Tripoli, Beirut, August 2014.
[104] Interview with a former Lebanese military intelligence officer, September 2014.
[105] Interview with Kan'an Naji (Tawhid's Emir in Abu Samra and member of the movement's Consultative Council or leadership), Tripoli, August 2014.
[106] Interview with Hashem Yaghmur (Tawhid military commander in Abu Samra), Tripoli, July 2014.

442   The Downfall of Tawhid

also showed that ideology did not lie at the core of Tawhid's risky activism.

This is further confirmed when exploring the profile of those who actively took part in Tawhid's stiff resistance against the pro-Syrians and therefore bore most of the risks. Naturally, as previously stated, they included committed Islamists. But, interestingly, they also comprised some of the less committed factions on the entire "spectrum of ideological commitment" and non-Islamist Tripolitans who joined Tawhid's side during the battle. In fact, it soon became clear to the journalists present in Tripoli during the battle that the movement's ability to withstand the pro-Syrian attack did not stem from ideology but, rather, from how "firmly entrenched"[107] it was locally. Tawhid was so rooted in Tripoli's symbolic and social fabric that it could mobilize by activating local identities and solidarities.

One mechanism through which Tawhid used the symbolic resources of space, and here more specifically channeled collective identification to Tripoli as a community into mobilization, was the movement's attempt at reviving and appropriating the "tales of contention" which associated the city to a glorified tradition of rebellion against outsiders. This was not a new practice for, as Chapter 4 showed, references to Tripolitan narratives were typical of Tawhid's "vernacular Islamism." But it reached new heights back then. In their statements on the movement's radio and TV stations or in Tripoli's mosques, Tawhid officials went to particular lengths to activate the identification of local residents to their city, which as Chapter 1 tackled had long been a key local feature. Tripoli, they insisted, was a city like no other, one where the bonds tying the residents to each other were "strong and intimate" and where even "companions of one hour"[108] had long provided mutual support. What was truly at stake in this fight was "saving Tripoli"[109] as it was submitted to the Syrian regime's "conspiracy" to "destroy the city."[110] As a result, they asked nothing less than for Tripolitans of all backgrounds "to unite as one man."[111] Together they would not just fight an ideological battle

---

[107] "Thousands of Moslem gunmen fight off waves of assault," *United Press International* (September 29, 1985).

[108] "Al-Shaykh Sa'id Sha'aban: kel min yuhawel tamziq al-Muslimin huwa khadim lil-yahud" ["The cleric Sa'id Sha'aban: anyone who attempts to tear the Muslims apart is a servant of the Jews"], *al-Tawhid* (September 18, 1985).

[109] "Tripoli: les pro-Syriens veulent changer le statu-quo," *L'Orient Le Jour* (September 20, 1985).

[110] "Kalimat al-ekh Kan'an Naji" ["Speech by the brother Kan'an Naji"], *al-Tawhid* (September 19, 1985).

[111] "Shaaban s'addresse a la Syrie," *L'Orient Le Jour* (October 1, 1985) and "La situation à Tripoli," *L'Orient Le Jour* (October 14, 1985).

The Activation of Local Identities and Solidarities   443

against leftism, but also a "historical struggle"[112] in line with the city's past, in which "the people of Tripoli" would resist "invaders." This shows how, by inscribing the Syrian regime's attempt to crush Tawhid within the local "tales of contention" which had long associated Tripoli with a glorified tradition of rebellion, the movement was seeking to activate collective identification to the city, signal belonging to the community and cast its resistance effort as a duty in line with local history. One official explicitly mobilized these "tales of contention" when he cast the battle as part of Tripoli's long and proud legacy of rebellions against the Crusaders, the French Mandate and the Lebanese government, claiming that "in the past many have tried to make Tripoli surrender – they are now trying again through terrorists and tyrants and we will not give them that chance."[113] Similarly, another Tawhid official likened the pro-Syrian offensive on the Islamist movement to "an attack on Tripoli, its people, honour and identity." He called on residents to "unite" and "defend the city," and powerfully concluded that "[the invaders] cannot stop us unless they kill us all together."[114] Reviving and appropriating Tripoli's "tales of contention" was Tawhid's strategy to channel collective identification to the city into mobilization – in other words, to use the symbolic dimension of space – in order to recruit non-Islamist Tripolitans.

There is evidence to suggest that this strategy was relatively successful. Overall, of course, the 4,000 Tripolitans who allegedly took part in Tawhid's resistance effort in September 1985 represented a very small proportion of the city's population, itself estimated at around 500,000. They also constituted a minority in comparison to the 50,000 residents who stayed during the battle but decided not to participate in the movement's high-risk activism. Yet anecdotes abound about how regular, self-described "sons of Tripoli" joined Tawhid's resistance effort, reportedly being willing to take risks and to fight on the city's most violent front lines, like in the southern suburb of Bahsas or in the eastern vicinity of Abu Samra.[115] Moreover, in a show of Tawhid's success at channeling identification to the city into active resistance, even some of the

[112] Islamic Group member quoted in: *Harb Trablus 1985* [*The war of Tripoli in 1985*] (documentary produced by the Islamic Group, copy given to the author, 2013).
[113] "Khitab min al-Muhandes Abdallah Babetti: al-tafjirat satastamiru" ["Speech by the Engineer Abdallah Babetti: the bombings will continue"], *al-Tawhid* (September 15, 1985).
[114] "Kalimat al-ekh Kan'an Naji" ["Speech by the brother Kan'an Naji"], *al-Tawhid* (September 19, 1985).
[115] Interviews with residents who participated in the September 1985 battle, Tripoli, July–August 2014.

444   The Downfall of Tawhid

movement's local ideological enemies joined its side. Three dozen Tripolitan soldiers of the Lebanese army's outpost in the district of Qobbe, who had in the past clashed with Tawhid and saw themselves as its nemesis, defected from the army with their jeeps and their weapons in order to join the battle against the pro-Syrians.[116] "Helping other Tripolitans" and "protecting the city" had enticed them into risky activism.[117] In fact, the activation of local Tripolitan identity was so central to Tawhid's successful mobilization that even some committed Islamists claimed that what led them to fight was the urge to support "the people of Tripoli" and defend the city's "pride" and "long history."[118] In an implicit recognition that Tawhid's rootedness within the city's symbolic fabric lay at the core of its success in mobilizing so many under duress, two weeks into the fighting the pro-Syrian coalition issued a statement which reminded locals that some of the leftists in its ranks were also "sons of Tripoli" and which clarified that "Syria does not wish to enter Tripoli."[119]

Another mechanism which explained Tawhid's success in recruiting beyond its ideological base at the height of the battle was its ability to tap, this time, into the social resources of space and especially into neighborhood solidarities by enlisting the support of *qabadayet* or local "champions of mobilization." These popular strongmen were often widely admired and followed in their districts and, as a result, what characterized them was their singular ability to activate neighborhood solidarities and channel them into mobilizations. Witnesses to the September 1985 battle thus remember seeing "groups of neighborhood youths" in particular in the older, popular districts of Tripoli quickly joining the resistance effort after their strongman had done so, often under the motto of "defending the quarter."[120] This was particularly striking in

---

[116] "Une trentaine de soldats déserteurs occupant pendant deux heures le sérail de Tripoli," *L'Orient Le Jour* (August 1, 1985). The trend was in fact such that even the CIA reported on "defectors from the Lebanese Army's 2nd brigade [who] have joined Tawhid against the Syrian-backed militias." See: US Central Intelligence Agency, "Lebanon: Islamic fundamentalism in Tripoli" (Top Secret, NESAR 86-003JX, January 17, 1986).

[117] Interview with a resident of Qobbe who was close to some of these soldiers, Tripoli, August 2014.

[118] Islamic Group member quoted in: *Harb Trablus 1985* [*The war of Tripoli in 1985*] (documentary produced by the Islamic Group, copy given to the author, 2013) and interviews with current and former Tawhid members, Tripoli, July–August 2014.

[119] Ghazi Kan'an, head of Syrian intelligence in Lebanon, clarified at the height of the fighting that "Syria does not wish to enter in Tripoli – we have no interest whatsoever to enter inside Tripoli." Quoted in: "Concentration de troupes syriennes autour de Tripoli," *L'Orient Le Jour* (September 27, 1985).

[120] Interviews with residents of Qobbe and Bab al-Tebbaneh, Tripoli, July–August 2014.

The Activation of Local Identities and Solidarities   445

Bab al-Tebbaneh, where Tawhid's ability to mobilize and recruit fighters was said to be by far the highest.[121] There, the movement had enlisted the support during the September 1985 battle of Khalil Akkawi who, as Chapter 2 showed, was the *qabaday* and informal leader of the neighborhood; a figure so deeply bound to his community that many local youths were prepared to take considerable risks to follow him. When Tawhid was created, Akkawi joined as one of its leaders in order to secure the movement's support in Bab al-Tebbaneh's violent neighborhood rivalry with Jabal Mohsen. Hundreds of his partisans followed through, ready to do whatever he asked of them. Akkawi's faction of "neighborhood Islamists," who were more driven by solidarity for their "champion of mobilization" and neighborhood concerns than by ideology, split from Tawhid in late 1984 as part of the growing divisions which were plaguing the movement. But Sha'aban's success in convincing Akkawi to join hands again with Tawhid to fight off the pro-Syrians triggered the mobilization of hundreds of local youths in Bab al-Tebbaneh, who followed their *qabaday* on some of the city's most violent front lines. Tawhid's enlistment of "champions of mobilization" like Akkawi channeled local solidarities into active resistance.

At the core of Tawhid's stiff resistance against the pro-Syrian offensive in September 1985 therefore lay not just the power of ideology but also its rootedness in Tripoli's symbolic meaning and social fabric. The Islamist movement was able to activate inherently local identities and solidarities through the revival and appropriation of "tales of contention" and its enlistment of "champions of mobilization," which enabled it to recruit heavily locally. The fact that many Tawhid fighters were mobilizing for the defense of Tripoli, its people and identity, then, as much as for Islamism as an ideology, largely explained why they acted so cohesively throughout the battle and were ready to take risks to prevent the Syrian victory.

One last factor which also helped Tawhid mobilize and recruit during the battle was the fear that a Syrian takeover of Tripoli would mean a return to the city's old social order. Chapter 5 explored Tawhid's base with Tripoli's subalterns, noting that many less or not ideologically committed urban poor had joined the movement in order to continue their older revolt against the Tripolitan elite and arguing that this resulted in a "social jihad." Through the imposition of religious norms by the force of weapons, the "Islamic Emirate" had overturned the city's cultural, political and social order and empowered the subalterns. But, as

[121] Interviews with current and former Tawhid members who fought in September 1985, Tripoli, June–July 2014.

446   The Downfall of Tawhid

the September 1985 battle began to unfold, Tawhid's "subaltern Islamists" started fearing that a victory of the pro-Syrians would lead to a return to Tripoli's traditional order. This sense was particularly acute as, although the pro-Syrian coalition was made up of Alawi and leftist fighters, it was also backed up by a gathering of Tripolitan Sunni notables, businessmen and intellectuals who represented the old order and deeply resented Tawhid. They released a statement explicitly calling on Hafez al-Assad to continue the battle, asking him to "shoulder Syria's historical responsibility toward Tripoli."[122] This telegram was signed by Rashid Jemali, Adnan Jisr, Ashir al-Daye and Abdel-Qader Alameddine, who represented the city's cultural, economic and political elite in charge before Tawhid's advent.

It was in this context that Tawhid's "subalterns Islamists" and many urban poor more generally participated in the September 1985 battle in order to preserve Tripoli's new order. Alongside a handful of "Islamo-gangsters," who as Chapter 6 showed were driven by material gains and had come to control Tripoli's underground economy, they mobilized and even continued resisting including after Tawhid eventually surrendered. Some of them, who had taken over the flats and houses of the leftist fighters they had evicted from Tripoli in 1983 and of the members of the upper class who had escaped the city, kept on engaging in clashes as the original owners tried returning to their homes with Syrian support.[123] In a reflection of the animosity which pitted the notables against them, a representative of the Tripolitan notability who was interviewed after the pro-Syrian coalition entered the city could not contain his joy and enthusiastically stated that "the traditional leaders are delighted that the power of Tawhid has been broken," only later regretting the "bloodshed"[124] of the battle.

Ideology, in sum, played a significant role in Tawhid's engagement in risky activism and in its especially stiff resistance against the pro-Syrians. But it was evident that other factors mattered at least as much, if not more. Indeed, members on Tawhid's entire "spectrum of ideological commitment" had mobilized and it had recruited non-Islamists too. The key to explaining this, I argue, was that many had taken up weapons in a bid to defend Tripoli, its people and identity, and to keep the material benefits they had secured since 1982.

---

[122] "Tripoli: cinq télégrammes sont envoyés à Assad pour l'exhorter à intervenir," *L'Orient Le Jour* (September 19, 1985).

[123] See, for instance: "Tripoli: la méfiance entre les intégristes et les pro-syriens demeure totale," *L'Orient Le Jour* (October 12, 1985).

[124] "Tripoli: la détermination des syriens à l'œuvre," *L'Orient Le Jour* (October 10, 1985).

The Resilience of Spatially Oriented Activism

Hafez al-Assad was eventually convinced of the need to stop his offensive on Tripoli due to a combination of several factors, including Tawhid's stiff resistance during three weeks of violent fighting, the Islamic Liberation Organization's terrorist campaign and the strong pressures exerted by the Soviet Union and the Islamic Republic of Iran on the regime. On October 8, 1985, the Syrian president ordered a lull in the battle as he invited Sa'id Sha'aban for talks in Damascus, before they both came to an agreement on ending the fight. Tawhid, in the face of the blatant asymmetry of forces which opposed it to the pro-Syrians, eventually agreed to relinquish its control of Tripoli to the Syrian army and to the Lebanese police, hand in all of its heavy weapons and accepted the return of leftist parties to the city.[125] In return for Tawhid's surrender and cooperation, the Syrian regime for its part allowed the movement to continue some of its political and religious activities, promised not to enter its strongholds and even pledged not to arrest or murder even the most ardent critics of Assad.[126] Yet, although the terms of what became known as the Second Damascus Agreement were therefore relatively favorable to Tawhid members and leaders, since it spared their lives and even enabled them to continue preaching, mass anti-regime mobilization soon returned to the city. And, strikingly, much of this anti-Syrian activism heavily centered on Bab al-Tebbaneh.

Of course, given the sheer scale of the bloodshed and destruction caused by the September 1985 battle, anti-regime sentiment was running high in many parts of Tripoli. Obviously, this was especially true with the Tripolitans who had taken part in Tawhid's resistance against pro-Syrian forces and had been ready to die in order to defend their city. They viewed the deal struck between Assad and Sha'aban as a betrayal and, although continuing to fight on their own was not an option, they remained resentful of the regime. They included some of Tawhid's own leaders who had been ardent critics of Assad, like Hashem Minqara and Kan'an Naji who as a result fully distanced themselves from Sha'aban. This represented the effective end of the movement, which had become irremediably split.[127] But even the masses of

---

[125] "Le déploiement des troupes syriennes à Tripoli," *L'Orient Le Jour* (October 7, 1985).
[126] "Les partis pro-syriens lèvent le siège de Tripoli," *L'Orient Le Jour* (October 8, 1985) and interview with Abdallah Babetti (Islamic Group official and backchannel between Tawhid and Hafez al-Assad), Tripoli, June 2014.
[127] Interviews with Hashem Minqara and Kan'an Naji (Tawhid's Emirs in the Mina and Abu Samra districts and members of the movement's Consultative Council or leadership in 1982–5), Tripoli, August 2014.

448   The Downfall of Tawhid

Tripolitans who had not taken part in the resistance against the pro-Syrian offensive became extremely critical of the regime when, as they gradually returned to their city after the deal, the scale of the damage caused by the shelling became evident. As many as 600 people had died, 700 cars had been burned and 7,000 buildings were partially or completely destroyed. The cost of the reconstruction stood at a staggering $260 million.[128] And yet, despite the existence of such a wide pool of anti-regime discontent throughout Tripoli, it only expressed itself in the neighborhood of Bab al-Tebbaneh. The district witnessed the return of mass anti-regime activism as early as three weeks after the signing of the Second Damascus Agreement. Then, thousands gathered there and violently protested against the presence of the Syrian army in Tripoli, even killing a Syrian soldier.[129] And, although the regime declared a "ban on gatherings and protests" to allow for "the city's march toward peace,"[130] demonstrations there continued unabated until February 1986.[131]

Interestingly, while the Lebanese media characterized the anti-Syrian regime protests that continued gripping Bab al-Tebbaneh as a mark of "fundamentalism,"[132] perhaps because they comprised former Tawhid members and started from the local mosque, the lingering mobilization there stemmed more from spatially oriented activism than from ideology. That is, it was more driven by local concerns, solidarities and identities than by Islamist beliefs. There were, of course, committed Islamists too who advocated for the return of Tawhid's "Islamic Emirate" and joined the protests organized in the neighborhood. This was due to the fact that they considered Bab al-Tebbaneh, much like it was described in Chapter 2, to be what Charles Tilly called a "safe space," one where dissidents could freely organize and mobilize. What attracted these Islamist figures was that, according to the terms of the Second Damascus Agreement, the neighborhood was one of the three districts

---

[128] See: "4 milliards de LL pour reconstruire Tripoli," L'Orient Le Jour (October 27, 1985); "La reconstruction de Tripoli," L'Orient Le Jour (January 11, 1986); and "Mutalabat Baladiyet Trablus bi amuel li e'adat bina' al-madina" ["Demands of the municipality of Tripoli for money to rebuild the city"], Al-Incha (December 7, 1985).

[129] "Un tué au cour d'une manifestation intégriste à Tripoli," L'Orient Le Jour (October 28, 1985).

[130] "Tripoli: manifestations et rassemblements interdits," L'Orient Le Jour (October 29, 1985).

[131] See, for instance: "Muzaharat Trablus" ["The protests of Tripoli"], Al-Incha (December 6, 1985) and "Muzahara fi Trablus" ["Protest in Tripoli"], Al-Incha (December 23, 1985).

[132] See, for instance, "Un tué au cour d'une manifestation intégriste à Tripoli," L'Orient Le Jour (October 28, 1985).

The Resilience of Spatially Oriented Activism 449

of Tripoli where Syrian troops were barred from entering, with the slums of Mina and the Old City district of Zehriye. Its layout made up of a handful of arteries connected to mazes of alleyways also rendered it a difficult place to police and to spy on, which allowed these figures to reconnect and plot in secret. Yet these Islamist figures who sporadically joined the anti-regime protests in Bab al-Tebbaneh as it was a "safe space" made up a small share of the demonstrators. Instead, the rest were simple "sons of the neighborhood" who, former Tawhid members or not, did not demand the restoration of the "Islamic Emirate" but, rather, the relocation of checkpoints of the Syrian army away from Bab al-Tebbaneh's vicinity.[133] Their activism was thus spatially grounded and oriented – and, tellingly, it had been spurred by Khalil Akkawi.

Khalil Akkawi, as Chapter 2 showed, had long played a fundamental role in spurring the engagement of Bab al-Tebbaneh's residents in spatially oriented contention. His status as *qabaday* of the neighborhood, or locally rooted "champion of mobilization" widely admired as a chivalrous strongman, meant that he embodied at once Bab al-Tebbaneh's longstanding identity as a "stronghold of contention" and especially intense local solidarities. As a result, Akkawi had shown since the mid-1970s a peculiar ability for activating the neighborhood's identity and solidarities and channeling them in mass resident mobilizations which, although they successively took up Marxism and Islamism as "protest ideologies," always remained locally grounded and oriented, Bab al-Tebbaneh being the true compass. While in 1982 he had brought hundreds of his loyal local followers into Tawhid and then took them with him again as he distanced himself from the movement in 1984, his participation in the September 1985 battle had also ensured the mobilization of many locals. Now that the Syrian regime was back in control of Tripoli, even if troops were officially barred from entering Bab al-Tebbaneh, he still feared the ultimate intentions of Damascus.

This was especially the case in the weeks following the signing of the Second Damascus Agreement. It transpired that the regime would not hesitate to violate the terms of the accord it had sponsored in order to prevent the most virulent critics of the regime from continuing to mobilize. Syrian intelligence in Tripoli began raiding Tawhid strongholds where it was barred from entering to arrest activists. It also attempted to assassinate Hashem Minqara, the leader of the Tawhid faction in Mina, who had vehemently opposed the regime. Spies riddled his body

---

[133] Interviews with residents of Bab al-Tebbaneh, Tripoli, September–October 2014.

450   The Downfall of Tawhid

with dozens of bullets, leaving him in intensive care for a full year.[134] Khalil Akkawi's bid to rally Bab al-Tebbaneh's residents in mass anti-regime protests was thus meant to display a sufficiently strong mobilizing capacity to dissuade Syrian troops from raiding his district too and from arresting the many locals who were hostile to Damascus. It was also in continuity with his neighborhood's longstanding history of enmity with the regime and the ADP, Syria's Alawi allies in Jabal Mohsen, who were his local rivals. These demonstrations represented a risky form of activism. But the very fact that he, as a locally rooted "champion of mobilization," spearheaded them was enough to make them massive.

However, it was precisely because of Khalil Akkawi's central role in the return of mass anti-regime activism in Bab al-Tebbaneh that Syria eventually ordered his assassination. In an event still remembered by local residents and told to younger generations, on February 9, 1986 Khalil Akkawi was gunned down after storming out of a meeting with Syrian officers.[135] According to a figure close to Syrian intelligence networks, Akkawi had just, for the umpteenth time, turned down a request for reconciliation and cooperation with the Syrian army and he was assassinated just minutes later on orders from Ghazi Kana'an, the head of Syrian intelligence in Lebanon, who had just arrived in Tripoli to curb anti-regime protests.[136] The murder was allegedly carried out by the associates of Tareq Fakhr al-Din, a figure of the underworld who was especially close to the Syrian intelligence networks – he had just days earlier publicly hosted a dinner in honor of Ghazi Kana'an's visit to Tripoli.[137]

The atmosphere which gripped Bab al-Tebbaneh following the assassination of Khalil Akkawi encapsulated how the beloved *qabaday* embodied more than anyone else the strong local solidarities, the neighborhood's rebel identity and his area's potential for contention. Journalists present at the scene described "a state of panic" seizing Bab al-Tebbaneh when the residents learned of his assassination, "all streets

---

[134] "Aktichaf makba' lil aslehat fi Trablus" ["Discovery of a weapons cache in Tripoli"], *Al-Incha* (October 10, 1985); "Al-Jaysh al-Suri fi Trablus yusadir al-'adid min al-asleha fi manteqat al-Madina al-Qadima" ["The Syrian army in Tripoli seizes many weapons in the area of the Old City"], *Al-Incha* (November 22, 1985); "Tripoli: la recherche des armes se poursuit," *L'Orient Le Jour* (November 30, 1985); "Mina-Tripoli: Minkara réchape a une tentative d'assassinat," *L'Orient Le Jour* (December 28, 1985); "Attentat contre un ancient responsible intégriste à Tripoli," *L'Orient Le Jour* (January 12, 1985); and "Nouvelles saisies d'armes à Tripoli," *L'Orient Le Jour* (February 9, 1985).

[135] Interviews with residents of Bab al-Tebbaneh, Tripoli, September–October 2014.

[136] "Visite de 4 jours à Tripoli pour Ghazi Kan'an," *L'Orient Le Jour* (January 31, 1985).

[137] "Ziyarat al-Lajna al-'Askariya al-Suriya ila Trablus" ["Visit of the Syrian Military Committee to Tripoli"], *Al-Incha* (January 31, 1986)].

The Return of Neighborhood Islamism

suddenly emptying and shops closing their doors right away."[138] Crowds of angry young men then gathered in the middle of the neighborhood, picked up all kinds of weapons, from stones and kitchen knives to guns, and went rioting toward the nearby checkpoints of the Syrian army, even killing two soldiers.

To these observers, it was evident that Khalil Akkawi's murder would have "particular importance" for he had had been "deeply rooted"[139] in the local social fabric. His centrality in the neighborhood's life would be on full display during his funeral. All shops closed for the occasion and estimates put the number of people who carried his body from Bab al-Tebbaneh's main mosque all the way to Tripoli's cemetery at a staggering 50,000.[140] This amounted to more than the neighborhood's population, estimated at around 40,000. Some of them may have been Tawhid sympathizers and, even more broadly speaking, anti-regime activists from throughout the city. But, by all accounts, the large majority were residents of the district who had long been deeply loyal to their "champion of mobilization." Tellingly, on its way to the cemetery the crowd engaged in acts of violence against Syrian soldiers who were posted along the road, again killing and injuring several of them.[141] Underlining the quasi-holy status that Akkawi had come to assume in Bab al-Tebbaneh, the participants in his funeral kept shouting the phrase, "the Prophet is dead but God is eternal," which was known to have been used centuries ago to announce the death of Muhammad.[142] This epitomized the rootedness of the *qabaday* of Bab al-Tebbaneh and his importance as a local "champion of mobilization" uniquely placed to spur spatially oriented contention.

The Return of Neighborhood Islamism

By murdering Khalil Akkawi, who Syria knew was central to any mobilization effort in Bab al-Tebbaneh, Damascus clearly hoped to curb lingering anti-regime activism there. In a show of the Syrian army's expectation that, with its *qabaday* eliminated, the neighborhood would return to quiescence, it made the provocative move of using Akkawi's

---

[138] "Tripoli retient son souffle," *L'Orient Le Jour* (February 10, 1986).

[139] Abi Samra, *Trablus*, p. 188.

[140] The *Associated Press* reported that "50,000 Sunni Moslems attended a funeral for Khalil Akkawi." See: "Four killed, including Syrian, in Tripoli gunfights," *Associated Press* (February 10, 1986).

[141] "Tension persistante à Tripoli après l'assassinat de Akkawi," *L'Orient Le Jour* (February 11, 1986).

[142] Interviews with partisans of Khalil Akkawi in Bab al-Tebbaneh, Tripoli, October 2014.

452   The Downfall of Tawhid

funeral, when the area's young men were carrying his body to the cemetery, to penetrate Bab al-Tebbaneh in violation of the Second Damascus Agreement and set up checkpoints, then occupying it. Shortly afterward it launched a campaign of arrests against some of the local cadres and military commanders who had long been close to Akkawi, prompting dozens of them to escape. They soon became scattered between Tripoli's northern countryside, where some hid with relatives living there, and the South Lebanon Palestinian camps of Ain al-Helwe and Mie-Mie which, after the Israeli withdrawal from Sidon in 1985, had become "safe spaces." The result was that, for ten months until December 1986, it appeared Syria's bet had succeeded. Without its "champion of mobilization" as a vehicle channeling local solidarities and identity into activism, Bab al-Tebbaneh no longer acted as Tripoli's "stronghold of contention." What Damascus had not anticipated, however, was that the loyalty many locals felt for Akkawi and for his legacy was so profound that, even dead, the "champion of mobilization" and local memories of him would still provide the basis around which collective action could occur. In late 1986, a neighborhood-wide, anti-regime rebellion which was cast as an "Islamist" one but was, in reality, considerably oriented toward Bab al-Tebbaneh, would violently challenge the Syrian army's newfound confidence and even question its local preponderance. This, in turn, would lead the regime to engage in "spatial repression" in Bab al-Tebbaneh.

In the wake of Khalil Akkawi's murder, his close aides who had become scattered and groups of Bab al-Tebbaneh's residents discreetly reconnected and formed a new movement. Three participation identities guided involvement in this new, vehemently anti-regime group. Like in the case of "neighborhood Islamism" as described in Chapter 2 and this chapter, neighborhood identity and strong local solidarities played key roles, but what now made this movement special was a third factor too – emotion, or a locally grounded thirst for revenge.

Militants explained that the goal of their new group was straightforward. They were planning a "popular armed uprising" in Bab al-Tebbaneh which would kill as many Syrian soldiers posted there as possible. This, the movement's leader recounted, would "avenge Khalil Akkawi"[143] and force the Syrian army to withdraw from the district and from Tripoli. Six interviewed rank-and-file members also cited "taking revenge" for the murder of the *qabaday* of Bab al-Tebbaneh as a key reason for joining, alongside their willingness to fight for the "honor" of

[143] Interview with Samir Hassan (leader of the 9 February movement), August 2014.

their neighborhood and to "protect" locals from the Syrian army.[144] Their group's new name, in fact, was "9 February," the date of Akkawi's murder. This underlined the extent to which, even after his death, the intense ties of loyalty which bound the *qabaday* to his partisans continued to shape their "neighborhood Islamism," as a form of Islamist mobilization more embedded within local concerns and solidarities than in ideology. In a show of how popular 9 February soon became in Bab al-Tebbaneh, sources suggest that as many as 300 residents volunteered to become a part of it, help with the coordination of members and weapons and join the rebellion when it was launched.[145] Locally rooted emotions, identities and solidarities thus explained participation in the new movement, 9 February, more than any intrinsic sense of local appeal for Islamist ideology.

And, interestingly, although this movement branded itself as an Islamist one, it used militant Islamism as a "protest ideology," in the vein of what Khalil Akkawi had long done. Members thus reconnected with two of the committed Islamist figures they used to ally with as part of Tawhid, enticing them into providing 9 February with logistical support. The first one was Hashem Minqara, Tawhid's former Emir in Mina, who was slowly recovering from the attempt on his life by Syrian intelligence from a small field hospital in the Tripolitan countryside, but still had suitcases of cash from his time in charge of the port. The other former Tawhid figure with which members of 9 February reconnected was Kan'an Naji, who was close to the Palestinian Islamists in Fatah and, due to his experience smuggling weapons to Syrian Islamist movements, could help move guns and rifles to Bab al-Tebbaneh. To these two committed Islamists, members of 9 February framed their goal of evicting the Syrian army from Bab al-Tebbaneh and Tripoli not as payback for Khalil Akkawi's murder but, instead, as the first step in a broader attempt to revive Tawhid's "Islamic Emirate." But, in reality, 9 February members who were interviewed insisted that their struggle "was never about ideology" – they had only used it to engineer a coalition with resource-rich ideological actors. After ten months spent planning as well as buying and smuggling weapons back to Bab al-Tebbaneh, members of 9 February had discreetly returned to their neighborhood and, armed to the teeth and numerous, they seemed ready to deal the

---

[144] Interviews with Abu Zghayar, Mazen Mohammed, Fahd Issa, Aziz Allush, Bilal Matar and Abed Merkabawi (former fighters for the 9 February movement), Tripoli, August–October 2014.

[145] Interviews with former members of the 9 February movement, Tripoli, August–September 2019.

454   The Downfall of Tawhid

Syrian army a violent blow. Their plan, however, would tragically fail and lead to the "massacre of Bab al-Tebbaneh."

Two reasons lay at the core of the eventual failure of 9 February to produce a sustained insurgency against Syrian troops in Tripoli. The first is that, with its "champion of mobilization" dead, the movement found it hard to provide leadership and remain cohesive. Because of his status as uncontested *qabaday* of Bab al-Tebbaneh, Khalil Akkawi had alone been the origin of all the strategic decisions of his partisans in the Popular Committees, Popular Resistance and Tawhid, from switching "protest ideologies" to engaging in risky battles. As a result, the handful of cadres long around Akkawi who were now part of 9 February lacked his legitimacy and experience to set up and sustain a movement of their own. Moreover, Akkawi had been an informal leader with such local popularity in Bab al-Tebbaneh that even the lesser strongmen who competed against each other put their differences aside and worked together for the "sake of the neighborhood." He had embodied, more than anyone else, Bab al-Tebbaneh's exceptionally strong social ties. Yet, as he had no obvious successor, 9 February soon became plagued with internal divisions. A leadership council of seven lesser neighborhood strongmen was formed and chose as their leader Samir Hassan, a militant in Bab al-Tebbaneh who had long been close to Akkawi. But, tellingly, they had selected him not because of his leadership skills but, rather, "because he was the weakest of us all" and would not become a rival to any.[146] And, indeed, the head of 9 February himself recalled how "no one followed my orders."[147] Petty disputes between various subfactions soon undermined the movement's cohesion. In one instance, it nearly split as members seemed to passionately disagree on whether the rebellion should be launched on December 31, 1986, when Syrian soldiers would be celebrating New Year's Eve, or rather on February 9, 1987, on the highly symbolic one-year anniversary of Khalil Akkawi's murder. These disagreements and overall lack of leadership did not prevent the movement from organizing the logistics of the planned uprising, like buying and smuggling weapons or recruiting locals. But it left it leaderless and ill equipped to devise a shrewd political strategy.

The second reason behind the eventual failure of 9 February was that, by structuring their goals solely around the locally grounded breed of emotion that was revenge for the murder of the *qabaday* of Bab al-Tebbaneh, members lost sight of the bigger stakes at play. Of course, making payback for Akkawi's assassination the cornerstone of their

---

[146] Interviews with Abed Merkabawi and Mazen Mohammed (members of the 9 February movement), Tripoli, August 2014.
[147] Interview with Samir Hassan (leader of the 9 February movement), August 2014.

The Return of Neighborhood Islamism 455

agenda had advantages. It allowed them to recruit 300 galvanized locals and it provided a sense of common purpose to lesser strongmen otherwise in rivalries with each other. This showed how, even after his death, loyalty for the "champion of mobilization" still allowed local activism. But emotions were a double-edged sword, for they blinded the leaders of 9 February to the fact that they were entering a much larger game when they allied with Kan'an Naji to use his connections and stockpiles of weapons, for he notoriously acted as a stooge of Fatah.

By 1986, the Palestinian guerrilla organization was once again struggling for survival. This time its fighters were being shelled by the pro-Syria Lebanese militia Amal in Beirut. A figure close to Yasser Arafat thus acknowledged that taking advantage of the thirst for revenge which animated 9 February against the Syrian army was a way for the Palestinian leader to "play his full hand"[148] and strike back at Hafez al-Assad while reducing the pressure on the camps in Beirut and the south as pro-Syrian forces would be redirected to Tripoli. This was confirmed by Western intelligence. One cable remarked how, through Naji, Arafat had given "assistance" to 9 February and encouraged its militants to "rise against the Syrians" in Tripoli to "distract Syrian forces from their increasing harassment of the Palestinian camps in Beirut," without any regard for the likely possibility it might result in a "bloody"[149] event. The survivors of 9 February are in retrospect bitter at the way they were "manipulated." "We were young and inexperienced," recognized a figure in the group. "We thought it was possible to avenge Khalil Akkawi and push Syria out of Bab al-Tebbaneh – and those who supported our plans did not discourage us,"[150] he said in a dig at Fatah, Naji and Minqara. As a result, in the run-up to the planned uprising in Bab al-Tebbaneh, 9 February may have been able to activate neighborhood solidarities to secretly hide fighters and weapons and recruit many locals, but it largely suffered under the weight of divisions and Fatah's manipulations.

The members had finally settled on the date of December 31 to launch their rebellion, but they were forced to act preemptively on 19 December after Syrian intelligence in Tripoli arrested one of the group's leaders, Samir al-Turk, and started questioning him. "We had to act then,"[151] argued a military cadre in 9 February. "Samir al-Turk was one of our key

---

[148] Interview with a high-ranking Palestinian intelligence officer, Beirut, June 2014.
[149] US Central Intelligence Agency, "Lebanon: the growing strength of the Palestinians" (Secret, NESA 87-10056, December 1987).
[150] Interview with Mazen Mohammed (member of the 9 February movement), Tripoli, August 2014.
[151] Interview with Mazen Mohammed (member of the 9 February movement), Tripoli, August 2014.

456   The Downfall of Tawhid

leaders; he knew all the details of the military plans and the names and locations of our fighters and weapons caches. His arrest marked the zero hour. Our battle had to begin." Underlining the locally bounded nature of their struggle and its lack of political sophistication, the militants in the neighborhood had not even tried to make contact with Sa'id Sha'aban. Hearing of the plot, the cleric refused to be associated with it. In a statement sounding Tawhid's death knell, he described the uprising as "sheer folly which can only bring woe and devastation" and unequivocally dismissed the fighters as "provocateurs."[152] Samir al-Turk's arrest then immediately triggered the "popular uprising" of 9 February. At 4.00 am, a local crowd led by the fighters attacked a Syrian army outpost situated close to Bab al-Tebbaneh's Harba mosque. This symbolic target galvanized the members as it had been built by Khalil Akkawi, who had often preached there and where he had spent his last night. Their rebellion seemed successful at first. They fired rockets at the outpost, took it over and then rapidly progressed to the extent that, by the afternoon, they had seized the whole neighborhood and inflicted severe damage on the Syrian army, killing sixteen and injuring thrity-five.[153]

The regime right away grasped the strategic and symbolic significance of the rebellion. One source close to Damascus argued that, if 9 February was not rapidly contained and crushed, the movement might, given its rootedness, "draw Syrian troops into a long battle and sap their military strength in Lebanon to the advantage of the guerrilla movement."[154] Yet, without significant political and military support beyond their neighborhood, the militants were not able to sustain the momentum and extend the struggle to all of Tripoli.[155] While many residents of the city shared the animosity of 9 February for the Syrian army, they also viewed it as a spatially oriented and bounded movement specific to Bab al-Tebbaneh only. Few were ready to risk bringing their city and neighborhoods back on the brink of bloodshed and destruction so soon after the high cost they had paid in mid-1985. Fatah, for its part, which had been 9 February's only significant external supporter, blamed Syria for the "military escalation" yet did not intervene further, contenting itself with vaguely

---

[152] "L'armée syrienne poursuit ses opérations de police au Liban Nord," *L'Orient Le Jour* (December 27, 1986).
[153] "Violents combats à Tripoli entre l'armée syrienne et des miliciens intégristes," *L'Orient Le Jour* (December 20, 1986).
[154] "Pro-Syrian militiamen blamed: massacre ends fundamentalist surge in Tripoli," *Los Angeles Times* (February 8, 1987).
[155] "Au lendemain des affrontements de Bab Tebbaneh, l'armée syrienne rétablit son contrôle sur Tripoli," *L'Orient Le Jour* (December 21, 1986).

"following the developments."[156] As the regime was quick to deploy considerable ground and artillery reinforcements, members and fighters of 9 February were only able to resist for two days with the help of the district's residents, before being overwhelmed by the Syrian army. This would now lead to what the inhabitants still call the "massacre of Bab al-Tebbaneh."

Spatial Repression in Bab Al-Tebbaneh

By undertaking the December 1986 "massacre of Bab al-Tebbaneh," Syria did its best to turn the neighborhood from a "safe space" for frequent mobilizations into a "repressed space." The regime was intent on using all the tools at its disposals to finally neutralize some of the unique local features identified in Chapter 2 which had long made Bab al-Tebbaneh Tripoli's "stronghold of contention" par excellence, an area frequently nurturing mobilization. In other words, Syria would engage in the strategy of what I call "spatial repression," or a deliberate attempt by the target of contention to minimize the ways in which space provides resources for activism, through physical infrastructures of support or the social and symbolic local solidarities, identities and emotions which enable mobilization.

Syria's engagement in "spatial repression" was neither specific to Bab al-Tebbaneh nor to 1986. In fact, although it is an overlooked aspect of the literature on authoritarianism in Syria, throughout its history the Syrian regime long adopted this practice to stamp out localized dissent. This strategy has taken many forms. It has involved the outright physical destruction of spaces whose layout had helped dissidents to recruit and mobilize, which is what the Syrian army did in February 1982 by razing the mazes of alleyways that had facilitated rebellion in Hama's Old City.[157] It has also included the killing of myriad spatially rooted "champions of mobilization" who, like Khalil Akkawi, were uniquely placed to channel local solidarities into activism. And it has comprised the social and symbolic engineering of spaces of contention, for example when the regime used population transfers to change the socio-demographic composition of East Aleppo in 2016, or when it renamed the Sheikh Ibrahim neighborhood, in the Damascus suburbs which it had just reconquered, as Al-Ar'in, which ostensibly means "the den" but implicitly refers to the

---

[156] Ibid.

[157] "Syria said to raze part of rebel city," *New York Times* (February 21, 1982). For more background see Raphaël Lefèvre, *Ashes of Hama: the Muslim Brotherhood in Syria* (London: Oxford University Press and Hurst, 2013).

458   The Downfall of Tawhid

regime's victory over this rebel suburb by hinting at the meaning of Assad ("lion").[158] The Syrian regime was acutely aware of how activism could be spurred by the physical, social and symbolic dimensions of space – and it had adapted its repressive practices accordingly.

The "massacre of Bab al-Tebbaneh" provides an example of how the Syrian regime engaged in "spatial repression" to disable all at once the physical, symbolic and social resources provided by space to turn the neighborhood from a safe to a "repressed space." It did so by applying the cost of contention collectively to break the neighborhood's rebel identity, undermining the strength of the local solidarities which had enabled activism and, finally, enhancing the district's isolation to prevent links between spaces of contention.

Officially, the December 1986 "massacre of Bab al-Tebbaneh" never took place. The Syrian regime's propaganda machine did recognize that a crackdown had occurred in the wake of 9 February's attempt at rebellion. But it framed it as a mere anti-terrorist operation which aimed at "hunting down" 200 of those it called "Islamist fundamentalists" in one of Tripoli's "Islamist strongholds" in order to "strike them in the cradle."[159] There is little doubt, however, that what took place was neither a targeted anti-terrorist operation nor an irrational outburst of repression, but rather a calculated attempt to prevent Bab al-Tebbaneh from continuing to act as Tripoli's anti-regime "stronghold of contention" – whatever the cost. In a show of the crucial importance of this goal for the regime, Tripoli witnessed the arrival of Syria's two highest-level security officials in the country: Ghazi Kana'an, head of Syrian intelligence in Lebanon, and Sa'id Bayrakdar, the general of the Syrian army in Lebanon.[160] The chief of Syrian intelligence in North Lebanon, Mohammed Sha'ar, also planned the crackdown and would afterward be rewarded through a series of quick promotions, until he became Bashar al-Assad's interior minister and led the repression in Syria after 2011.[161]

The first and most obvious aim of the "spatial repression" in which Syria engaged was to impose such a locally high cost for 9 February's

---

[158] See, respectively, Jihad Yazigi, *Destruct to reconstruct: how the Syrian regime capitalises on property destruction and land legislation* (Beirut: report published by the Friedrich Ebert Stiftung, 2017) and "Al-nizam yuwasil taghir ma'alem al-Ghouta al-Sharqiya" ["The regime continues to change the features of the Eastern Ghouta"], *Baladi News* (August 20, 2019).

[159] Ghazi Kan'an quoted in "Pro-Syrian militiamen blamed: massacre ends fundamentalist surge in Tripoli," *Los Angeles Times* (February 8, 1987).

[160] "Tripoli: l'ordre par les grands moyens," *L'Orient Le Jour* (December 22, 1986).

[161] "Le ministre syrien de l'intérieur accusé d'avoir ordonné la mort de centaines de personnes à Tripoli, en 1986," *L'Orient Le Jour* (December 25, 2012).

insurgency that Bab al-Tebbaneh's strong sense of community would be undermined. A blame game among residents would be triggered, internal divisions would arise and the district's rebel identity would be broken.

Years later, it remains difficult to know in detail what happened in Bab al-Tebbaneh on December 20–2, 1986. The media insisted that a "total blackout"[162] had been enforced by the Syrian army on reporting about the event. This, journalists observed, was unprecedented since the civil war's beginning. Yet interviews with survivors and doctors and reports from civil society organizations collecting testimonies shed light on the brutal and indiscriminate nature of the repression. Reflecting Syria's determination to break Bab al-Tebbaneh's neck as a "stronghold of contention," the regime ordered Syrian Special Forces to surround and fully seal that neighborhood only, preventing anyone from entering or exiting it for as long as thirty-six hours. What took place then was reported to have been sheer horror. Thousands of Bab al-Tebbaneh's residents were forcibly taken out of their homes in the middle of the night and gathered in the handful of arteries in the neighborhood. While the young men were sent in trucks to the Syrian intelligence headquarters in Tripoli to be tortured and questioned, the women, children and elderly who were gathered were summarily executed on the spot.[163]

In retrospect, survivors of the massacre and residents of Bab al-Tebbaneh at large realize that the key goal of the repression had not been to arrest or kill members of 9 February but, rather, to collectively "traumatize," "humiliate" and "defeat"[164] the neighborhood. The murders which occurred were not only brutal and indiscriminate, they are also said to have been carried out publicly and shamelessly, as if to send a message to all residents that any future involvement of locals in contention would be at the expense of the entire community. Many inhabitants of the neighborhood who were not forced out of their homes that night and were thus spared still report living with nightmares as they recollect, in particular, the screams of local women and young children as they were being brutalized and killed.

---

[162] "Tripoli: la normalisation semble pratiquement achevée," *L'Orient Le Jour* (December 24, 1986).

[163] See: *Lebanon: arbitrary arrests, "disappearances" and extra-judicial killings by Syrian troops and Syrian-backed forces in Tripoli* (Beirut: report published by Amnesty International, February 1987); "Rafles massives à Tripoli," *L'Orient Le Jour* (December 31, 1986); and interviews with survivors of the massacre of Bab al-Tebbaneh as well as with doctors from the local branch of the Lebanese Red Cross, Tripoli, September–November 2014.

[164] Interviews with residents of Bab al-Tebbaneh, Tripoli, September–October 2014.

460   The Downfall of Tawhid

When, thirty-six hours later, the doctors who had been prevented from entering Bab al-Tebbaneh by Syrian Special Forces were finally authorized to come in to collect bodies, they were shocked by what they saw. There had been no attempt to hide the extent and nature of the massacre. "We entered the neighborhood and we first noticed that the local dispensary, where we expected the dead to be, was empty. Then we continued walking and we began seeing seemingly endless piles of dead bodies scattered in the streets. These were not fighters but residents who had been executed."[165] Autopsies on their bodies back then revealed that, while some had been killed by a clean shot in the head, particularly brutal methods meant to terrorize had also been employed, such as strangulation, hanging and large-blade weapons.[166] Four entire buildings still full of residents were even filled with explosives and blown up.[167] Despite the collection of the bodies by the doctors, it remained difficult to ascertain the exact number of deaths as some corpses, after thirty-six hours, had begun rotting and decomposing, and hundreds of people had "disappeared,"[168] taken to Syria and killed or hastily buried in mass graves. The toll, as a result, varies widely depending on sources, ranging anywhere between 200 and 1,100, with the most reliable estimates putting it at around 500 with 5,000 arrests.[169] Bab al-Tebbaneh, long known for the propensity of its inhabitants to engage in contentious action, was now traumatized by the high collective cost imposed on the whole community.

The second aim of Syria's involvement in "spatial repression," in addition to trying to break the district's rebel identity, was to undermine the strong bonds of neighborhood solidarity and norms of mutual help which had frequently been channeled into mobilization. To break the

[165] Interview with a doctor from the local branch of the Lebanese Red Cross, Tripoli, September 2014.
[166] "Tripoli: le mot d'ordre est à l'apaisement," *L'Orient Le Jour* (December 23, 1986).
[167] "L'armée syrienne poursuit ses opérations de police au Liban Nord," *L'Orient Le Jour* (December 27, 1986).
[168] *Lebanon: arbitrary arrests, "disappearances" and extra-judicial killings by Syrian troops and Syrian-backed forces in Tripoli* (Beirut: report published by Amnesty International, February 1987).
[169] While most residents of Bab al-Tebbaneh mention that 1,000–1,100 locals were killed in the massacre, some residents of Tripoli who are not from that neighborhood claim that the death toll was much lower, around 200. Civil society and human rights associations such as the Union of the Residents of Tripoli, the Lebanese Muslim Students Union and the Committee on Abducted for their part advance figures of around 500–600 dead. See: "Le ministre syrien de l'intérieur accusé d'avoir ordonné la mort de centaines de personnes à Tripoli, en 1986," *L'Orient Le Jour* (December 25, 2012) and "Liban-Nord: l'armée syrienne procède à de nouvelles arrestations dans les rangs des milices intégristes," *L'Orient Le Jour* (December 31, 1986).

Spatial Repression in Bab Al-Tebbaneh

sense of community which had long characterized Bab al-Tebbaneh, the Syrian army itself did not engage in any of the killings mentioned above. Instead, it delegated them to Tareq Fakhr al-Din, a figure of the Tripolitan underworld who was himself originally from Bab al-Tebbaneh, and to the ADP, the Alawi militia in the rival district of Jabal Mohsen. That someone who hailed from a community that often prided itself in its sense of unity, and yet who was ready to engage in such a brutal and indiscriminate massacre alongside Bab al-Tebbaneh's historical rivals of the ADP, was perceived as a deep blow to the local narratives which, until then, had frequently glorified the power of neighborhood solidarity.

Tareq Fakhr al-Din was a longstanding Sunni smuggler from Bab al-Tebbaneh. He had left the neighborhood after engaging in business deals with high-ranking Syrian security officials, who would use his criminal networks to illegally import luxury items to Syria. His power subsequently increased and he arose as the leader of a large gang of criminals and mercenaries from all over Tripoli with a reputation for doing the Syrian intelligence's dirty deeds.[170] In a show of how connected he was to the Syrian army, he used to throw lavish dinner parties to demonstrate Tripoli's welcoming spirit to the Syrians during times of contention – this is what he did, for instance, shortly before Khalil Akkawi's killing.[171] In fact, Fakhr al-Din had been the one whose gang had murdered Bab al-Tebbaneh's *qabaday*. And, after 9 February's failed attempt at rebellion, his group of criminals and mercenaries would answer a request by Syria to undertake most of the "massacre of Bab al-Tebbaneh." This time, Fakhr al-Din's gang branded itself as the Tripolitan Resistance (*al-Muqawama al-Trabulsiya*) in a bid to give itself local credentials; but it remained clear to all that this remained a gathering of thugs and murderers who answered to Syrian intelligence. The only purpose which it served was to emphasize that it was not Syrian troops which would kill hundreds of civilians in Bab al-Tebbaneh but a Tripolitan militia headed by a Sunni originally from the neighborhood. A well-informed source explained that, in a reflection of the regime's gratitude for fulfilling this role and for helping to break Bab al-Tebbaneh's sense of a tight community, Fakhr al-Din was granted the rare and lucrative favor of Syrian license plates.[172] This was a reward reserved for staunch allies of

---

[170] Interviews with residents of Bab al-Tebbaneh, Tripoli, September–October 2014.

[171] "Ziyarat al-Lajna al-'Askariya al-Suriya ila Trablus" ["Visit of the Syrian Military Committee to Tripoli"], *Al-Incha* (January 31, 1986).

[172] Interview with a figure close to Syrian and Lebanese intelligence networks, Tripoli, September 2014.

462   The Downfall of Tawhid

Damascus for it allowed them to engage freely in large-scale trafficking as the army was prohibited from searching these trucks. In the process, Fakhr al-Din had "served the regime's designs,"[173] as a Lebanese intelligence officer put it. Up until today, the involvement of someone originally from the neighborhood in the killings of so many residents remains a local shame and a taboo.

It was also not neutral that Fakhr al-Din had been tasked with coordinating the "massacre of Bab al-Tebbaneh" with the neighborhood's collective rivals in Jabal Mohsen. Chapter 2 highlighted the extent to which the antagonism between Khalil Akkawi's Popular Resistance in Bab al-Tebbaneh and Ali Eid's ADP in Jabal Mohsen had turned into a "slum war" opposing residents of the two districts throughout the late 1970s and the 1980s. The ADP's involvement in the indiscriminate killing of residents of Bab al-Tebbaneh in 1986 was meant to demonstrate that there were no limits to the collective humiliation the regime would inflict on the district if it ever dared standing up again and engaging in contention. What motivated the ADP to answer the Syrian request, for its part, may have been linked to simmering Alawi–Sunni tensions between Jabal Mohsen and Bab al-Tebbaneh. But, according to the accounts of close observers, it mostly lay with Ali Eid's "thirst for revenge"[174] against the "neighborhood Islamists" who had long engaged in a rivalry against him and his movement. "Filling the district with fear and horror"[175] was his way of preventing Bab al-Tebbaneh from reorganizing and from competing again with Jabal Mohsen over the Tripolitan underworld. Tellingly, Ali Eid would, after the 1986 "massacre of Bab al-Tebbaneh," rise as one of the chiefs of the Tripolitan mafia alongside Fakhr al-Din, generating dozens of millions of dollars out of the control of the drug and oil smuggling business.[176] Neighborhood rivalries, the settling of scores and competition for the domination of the Tripolitan underworld, more than "ancient hatreds," therefore explained the ADP's own brutality. Locally, the involvement of Bab al-Tebbaneh's historical rivals in the killings of December 1986 was lived as a traumatizing collective defeat for a neighborhood long proud of its rebel spirit.[177]

Significantly, as part of the logic of "spatial repression" to break Bab al-Tebbaneh's sense of a tight community, the regime also went to great lengths to undermine local solidarities. During the massacre dozens of inhabitants were coerced into denouncing some of their neighbors close

---

[173] Interview with a Lebanese intelligence officer, Beirut, May 2014.
[174] Abi Samra, *Trablus*, pp. 188–90.   [175] Ibid.
[176] Interview with a figure close to Syrian intelligence, Tripoli, May 2014.
[177] Interviews with residents of Bab al-Tebbaneh, Tripoli, August–October 2014.

to Khalil Akkawi who might also have sympathized with 9 February. In theory, the existence in Bab al-Tebbaneh of strong solidarities and norms of mutual trust and help should have incentivized these locals not to denounce their neighbors. But, faced between saving their lives or those of other residents, many were reported to have given in. This expectedly resulted in a considerable weakening of the once strong neighborhood social ties that had enabled mobilization and in a growth of mutual mistrust and resentment. The regime even took the logic further when, after arresting most of 9 February's members and leaders, it spared the lives of a handful and even allowed some of them to return to Bab al-Tebbaneh, but only in exchange for working openly as informants and enforcers for Syria. This was at complete odds with the neighborhood's history and it meant betraying their former friends and their neighbors. Some of them now acknowledge their shame but argue that they were guided by the search for protection for themselves and their families. The regime even went as far as coercing one of Khalil Akkawi's closest associates into the provocative move of opening an ADP office in the heart of Bab al-Tebbaneh.[178] The rest of the movement became split between those who became stooges for Syria, those who were tortured and spent two decades in prison, and those who escaped to South Lebanon. Overall, the result was that the strong solidarities and norms of mutual help which had long enabled mobilization were severed, the contentious networks that had centered around Khalil Akkawi and professed to defend the district now irremediably fragmented and delegitimized.

The third and last aim of Syria's engagement in "spatial repression" was to enhance Bab al-Tebbaneh's collective sense of isolation from, even resentment toward, the rest of the city. It was perhaps hoped that, considered as Tripoli's historic "stronghold of contention" where rebels from all over the city could freely organize and mobilize, the neighborhood would interpret the lack of counter-mobilization in the wake of the massacre as a betrayal and, through this division, would in the future no longer connect with other spaces of contention. Alliances across space and class, after all, had been at the core of Khalil Akkawi's mobilization strategy and, as Chapter 2 showed, it had had bloody consequences for Syria. The complete encirclement of the neighborhood by Syrian Special Forces and the multiplication of Syrian army checkpoints throughout Tripoli for days thus ensured that even those who were prepared to risk their lives to prevent the massacre could not reach the site.

---

[178] Interview with Abu Zghayar (figure close to Akkawi who became the ADP's representative in Bab al-Tebbaneh), Tripoli, August 2014.

464   The Downfall of Tawhid

Moreover, to enhance the neighborhood's sense of isolation the regime subtly pushed its Tripolitan proxies to speak out in support of the Syrian repression. One of them, the leader of a self-styled "progressive" party, altogether dismissed rumors that a massacre had just occurred and insisted on "thanking"[179] Syria for its role in Lebanon. Even Rashid Karame who, as a prominent local notable and national politician, viewed himself as a representative of Tripoli, defended the Syrian regime's repression. He recognized that the city had just gone through "difficult circumstances" but squared the blame not on the perpetrators of the massacre but, rather, on the instigators of the rebellion, lambasting their "unjustified practices" which were bound to have "negative repercussions."[180] His reaction to the repression was in fact perceived to be so lenient toward the perpetrators of the "massacre of Bab al-Tebbaneh" that rival politicians in Beirut seized this opportunity to criticize him for being "blind about the horrible massacre."[181] Among Tripoli's public figures, only Abdel Majid al-Rifa'i, the head of the local branch of the Iraqi Ba'ath Party, denounced the killings and called on the Arab League to open an "official enquiry"[182] into it. Yet by then he was based in Baghdad and had lost some of his aura. As a result, the sense in Bab al-Tebbaneh was one of isolation from and even resentment toward the rest of Tripoli, which sharply lessened its status as a bridge between spaces of contention.

All in all, 9 February's attempt at popular insurgency in December 1986 as well as Tawhid's risky resistance in September 1985 showed how space can act as a resource for the locally rooted solidarities, emotions and identities which can spur risky mobilization, thereby also demonstrating how space is constitutive of and considerably shapes contention. The Syrian regime, it seems, had grown keenly aware of this fact. Its engagement in "spatial repression" as part of the "massacre of Bab al-Tebbaneh" was therefore a deliberate strategy to minimize the extent to which space provides physical, social and symbolic resources for the dissidents. This succeeded in turning the district from a "safe" to a "repressed space" as the neighborhood completely withdrew from activism for the twenty years that followed.

---

[179] "Les forces syriennes poursuivent la chasse à leurs adversaires intégristes au Liban-Nord," *L'Orient Le Jour* (December 28, 1986).

[180] Ibid.

[181] "L'armée syrienne poursuit ses opérations de police au Liban-Nord," *L'Orient Le Jour* (December 27, 1986).

[182] "Tripoli: la normalisation semble pratiquement achevée," *L'Orient Le Jour* (December 24, 1986).

Theorizing Back

By exploring what drove Tawhid's engagement in high-risk activism against Syrian troops in 1985 and by unpacking the dynamics of the regime's bloody crackdown on the movement and its remnants in 1985 and 1986, this chapter also draws broader theoretical insights related to the role of space and ideology in contentious politics and answers the following questions. What is the relative causal weight of ideology in high-risk activism? Through which mechanisms do space and ideology affect this type of mobilization? And what does the mechanism of "spatial repression" tell us about the role of space in hindering activism?

First, I show that ideology can play important roles in instances of high-risk collective action and that, rather than mattering only either through its instrumental use or sincere value, it may be simultaneously embraced as a deeply held belief while also being strategically utilized. In the case of Tawhid's mobilization during the September 1985 battle against the pro-Syrian coalition, ideology was important because some of the "ideological entrepreneurs" who had survived the wave of assassinations in 1984 deployed a militant Islamist discourse which galvanized members and enlisted the support of new fighters. Through interventions on Tawhid's radio and TV stations in which they warned of the dangers for Muslims if the "evil," "atheist" pro-Syrian coalition was to win the battle, the "ideological entrepreneurship" of these figures had three positive impacts which bolstered Tawhid's resistance capacity. These included enabling the mobilization of the movement's most committed Islamists, who became galvanized and engaged in instances of ideological violence against their enemies; but also the reinforcement of internal coherence and the triggering of a rapprochement with non-Tawhid Tripolitan Islamists, which allowed it to fight effectively during the battle. Yet, just as sincere beliefs mattered in the September 1985 battle, ideology was at the same time also instrumentalized. It became clear that some leaders had strategically activated the bonds of ideological solidarity which tied the movement to its Lebanese Islamist allies and to its key external backer, the Islamic Republic of Iran, in order to obtain their support. This strategy was successful as it led to a wave of anti-regime and anti-leftist violence which gripped Lebanon and Syria and put Assad under such pressure that he had to agree to a peace deal. During the September 1985 battle, then, ideology affected the course of events both because some, buoyed by the fiery diatribes of the "ideological entrepreneurs," sincerely believed in it, but also simultaneously because it was used instrumentally by others, with much success.

466   The Downfall of Tawhid

Second, beyond acknowledging and detailing ideology's role in high-risk activism, this chapter examines the other factors which enabled the mobilization by Tawhid of scores of less or not ideologically committed members during the September 1985 and December 1986 battles. I especially emphasize how the movement was able to recruit scores of Tripolitans who were not typically Islamist but felt attached to local identity and solidarities. Building on Chapters 1, 2 and 4, I point to two spatially related mechanisms which allowed Tawhid to recruit heavily in Tripoli and may apply to how social, rebel and terrorist groups can also use the symbolic and social dimension of space to root themselves locally. One way in which Tawhid was able to draw on the support of many Tripolitans was by activating identification with the city as a community through the revival of local "tales of contention." These "tales of contention" had long associated Tripoli as a rebel city with a glorified tradition of collective rebellion against outsiders, from Crusader times to the present. Reviving and appropriating locally rooted historical and cultural narratives which bound all members of the Tripolitan community together allowed Tawhid to cast the pro-Syrian coalition's attempt to crush it as an attack on Tripoli, signal rootedness in the local community and frame resistance as a duty in line with the city's rebel history and identity. This also explained why even some of Tawhid's local enemies, for example three dozen Tripolitan soldiers of the Lebanese army, joined its resistance after the regime began attacking the city.

Another way in which the movement was able to recruit fighters at the height of the battle was by enlisting the support of local "champions of mobilization," informal leaders and strongmen in Tripoli's popular neighborhoods tied to inhabitants by such strong bonds that they were uniquely placed to activate local solidarities and spearhead contention. The best known of them was Khalil Akkawi, the popular strongman or "champion of mobilization" of Bab al-Tebbaneh who had drifted away from but remained close to Tawhid. Chapter 2 showed how, by virtue of his status, Akkawi was widely admired in his neighborhood and had a significant local following. His participation in the battle against the pro-Syrian coalition triggered the mass recruitment of Bab al-Tebbaneh's youths. The full extent to which Akkawi was single-handedly able to activate strong neighborhood solidarities and channel them in high-risk mobilization further transpired in December 1986 when, even after his assassination at the hands of Syrian intelligence, the very memory of him and a collective thirst for revenge led hundreds of Bab al-Tebbaneh's residents to rebel violently. Their rebellion was cast as an "Islamist" one but it remained inherently local. The September 1985 and December

1986 battles thus showed the power of spatially related mechanisms like the revival of "tales of contention" and the activism of "champions of mobilization" in triggering and shaping episodes of high-risk activism. This also indicated how space, more than just being a resource for movements, also deeply affects mobilizations.

Third and lastly, by recounting Syria's brutal crackdown on the December 1986 rebellion in Bab al-Tebbaneh, I indicate how the regime was driven by a willingness to turn the neighborhood from the "safe space" it had long been into a "repressed space." This builds on a broader point made in Chapter 5 according to which space does not simply enhance but can also hinder mobilizations, as the "spatial constraints" showed. By overseeing the "massacre of Bab al-Tebbaneh," as it is still known today, the Syrian regime engaged in repressive practices which deliberately aimed at making local activism so costly for this tight community that it was hoped that its rebel identity would be undermined and that the local solidarities which had enabled the mobilization would be severely disrupted. Syria, in other words, activated the mechanism which I call "spatial repression" which sought to minimize the ways in which space provides resources for collective action. For nearly two decades, this "spatial repression" turned Bab al-Tebbaneh, for long Tripoli's "stronghold of contention" and a "safe space" for activism, into a "repressed space" where mobilization was made harder because local solidarities and identities had been weakened. This indicates the extent to which space can be utilized to hamper collective action.

Conclusion

Any unidimensional account of the 1982–5 "Islamic Emirate" of Tripoli is bound to fail. As I realized through the many interviews I carried out, archives I dug into, institutional records I consulted and the long ethnography I conducted, the rise of Tawhid and its rule over the city was multifaceted, at times even acting as a container for contradictory phenomena. Thirty years on, in fact, Tripolitans themselves still disagree over what Tawhid was about: an Islamist rebel and terrorist group, a local social movement opposed to the Syrian regime and the Lebanese government, a gathering of thugs and opportunists or a proxy of Fatah and Iran?

Ideology, of course, played a fundamental role in Tawhid's story. After all, it was made up of militant Islamists committed to various degrees, and Islamist ideology did shape parts of the movement's discourse, behavior, engagement in violence and internal politics. Yet many members also joined Tawhid for other motivations. These recruits were attracted by the movement's revolutionary political orientation but they instrumentalized its Islamist ideology, alternatively using it to protest against their conditions, to prevail in the city's preexisting neighborhood rivalries and social conflicts, to channel much older narratives about Tripoli as a community and a rebel city or to get involved in lucrative activities.

The deeply heterogeneous nature of their motivations had profound implications. First, it meant that, although Tawhid branded itself as a militant Islamist movement, its behavior became only partially guided by ideology, even at times in contradiction with it. Second, it also signified that, in spite of attracting the attention of the most significant geopolitical players of the Middle East in the 1980s, who were either wary of or attracted by its Islamist ideology, Tawhid remained imbued in inherently local identities, narratives and antagonisms, to the point that it never spread outside of Tripoli. And, third, the sometimes conflicting priorities and loyalties of its members and leaders triggered its fragmentation from within for, by the time of its downfall, the movement had started to split.

The Importance of Space in Contentious Politics

Far from linear, the story of the "Islamic Emirate" implemented by Tawhid was, at bottom, considerably messier and more nuanced than originally anticipated. To make sense of these arguably three most eventful years of recent Tripolitan history, then, I contextualized Tawhid in time, space and scales; from the micro level of individuals and the meso level of the movement to the macro level of wider Tripolitan, Syrian/ Lebanese and Middle Eastern trends. I also illuminated its many shades of gray, seeking to account for puzzling variations in patterns of Tawhid's discourse and behavior, confusing contradictions between its ideology and actions and the unexpected continuities with previous local movements. Crucially, unearthing this trove of local details about Tawhid then enabled me to derive broader insights into militant Islamism and to theorize back on the role of space and ideology in contentious politics.

The Importance of Space in Contentious Politics

At its core, Tawhid's success in mobilizing 2,000–3,000 members and many more sympathizers during episodes of contention in 1982–5 stemmed from its ability to root itself in Tripolitan space – the city's physical structure, social fabric and symbolic meaning. And, importantly, while space may have been originally used as a resource for the movement, it then considerably shaped its discourse and behavior, successively enhancing but also restricting the prospects of mobilization. Tawhid's case therefore shows the importance of space in spurring, hindering and significantly informing the nature of contention.

To begin with Tawhid's case confirms that space can be used as an important resource during conflictual mobilizations. This naturally includes physical space. Tawhid, indeed, proved especially skilled at using its control over Tripoli and its infrastructure to operate, fight enemies, generate revenues and project its ideology visually. Yet even more striking was its ability to use the symbolic and social dimensions of space as a resource. Aware that most Tripolitans, including ideologically driven ones like the Islamists, are characterized by a strong attachment to their city, its rich history and identity, Tawhid constructed a "vernacular ideology" that cast its Islamism against the backdrop of Tripolitan narratives. This "vernacular Islamism" mixing grand Islamist goals with the local cultural framework enabled its agenda to resonate and helped it to recruit locally. During episodes of contention, Tawhid also used two other spatially related mechanisms in order to ensure the mobilization of locals on its behalf. Through one of them, the revival and appropriation of Tripoli's "tales of contention," it cast its activism as part of the city's rich tradition of rebellions, thus framing collective action as a duty in line

470   Conclusion

with local history. Through the other one, the enlistment of "champions of mobilization" or figures who develop a large following and are uniquely placed to channel local solidarities into activism, the movement was able to ensure the mass recruitment of entire districts. These mechanisms allowed Tawhid to activate local identities and social ties to mobilize in Tripoli. That is, it succeeded in embedding itself locally by using the symbolic and social dimensions of space.

But space was more than a resource for it also shaped Tawhid's discourse and behavior. This was partially a result of its attempt to root itself locally in Tripolitan space. As part of its strategy to recruit beyond its ideological base and tap into the older and broader pool of dissent in the city, Tawhid was ready to act as a "spatially oriented movement" which would explicitly tackle local grievances and identities and seek to achieve a measure of local socio-political change. And, at first, there was no necessary contradiction for, as indicated by the examples of the transformation of Abdel Hamid Karame Square into Allah Square or the implementation of a new cultural, social and political order onto Tripoli, Tawhid was relatively successful in reconciling local issues with grander ideological concerns. But, soon enough, it became apparent that acting as a "spatially oriented movement" tackling local issues and identities was also drawing it into Tripoli's preexisting antagonisms which were unrelated to ideology. One of them was a rivalry between two Tripolitan districts. Tawhid took sides to recruit locals in one of these two areas but the new members merely instrumentalized Islamism, remaining so loyal to their district's strongman or informal leader and so driven by local concerns and solidarities that they gave rise to a "neighborhood Islamism" – they became Islamists and integrated Tawhid but kept prioritizing their district over ideology. The second older antagonism which the movement addressed was Tripoli's social tensions, which spatially materialized as a struggle between the many slums and a wealthy district. To bolster its numerical strength, Tawhid was prepared to embody "subaltern Islamism": it courted the city's urban poor by providing them with a conduit for their socio-political revolt. But, although the strategy succeeded in attracting many recruits, these members dragged Tawhid down in a "social jihad" as, if not more, driven by older social tensions than by ideology. Tawhid's immersion in these local struggles came to considerably inform its discourse and behavior, sometimes even affecting the nature of the "ideological" violence it exercised. There was also a less conscious, less deliberate aspect to the way space affected Tawhid. While the movement may have attracted no more than a minority in Tripoli, it claimed to represent and embody the city and some of its leaders and members were proud

The Importance of Space in Contentious Politics 471

Tripolitans. As a result of their local embeddedness, they internalized the historical, cultural and political narratives of Tripoli. But this "habitus of place" then affected their worldviews and discourse to the extent that, to other Islamists outside of the city, Tawhid seemed more Tripolitan than Islamist. With time it therefore transpired that the more the movement became rooted in space, the greater effect space was having on it, shaping its outlook.

Space, however, not only enhanced but at times also restricted the prospects of collective action. Conscious of this, Tawhid had developed practices and a discourse which aimed at overcoming the "spatial barriers" standing between some of its sympathizers; that is, the rivalries or conflicting priorities, traditions and identities between people sharing grievances but belonging to different spaces – even proximate ones. As a result the movement succeeded for a while in gathering constituencies belonging to different spaces. But the resilience of "neighborhood Islamism" suggests that these "spatial barriers" were never fully overcome. Yet the extent to which space could act as an impediment for collective action surfaced when "spatial repression" was undertaken in a district of Tripoli long known for its propensity to engage in heated mobilizations. It was turned from a "safe space" into a "repressed space," the local solidarities and identities that had enabled activism now broken. Although space is viewed as a resource for contention, then, it was also used for repression.

Of course, far from all social, rebel and terrorist movements are as grounded in, even oriented toward, "the local" as Tawhid was. But, arguably, all are also rooted to at least some extent in specific spaces; and the physical structure, social fabric and symbolic meaning of these spaces may impact their discourse, worldviews and behavior to varying degrees. Throughout this book I have shown that space can spur, hinder and significantly shape their mobilizations and I have identified some of its constitutive mechanisms.

Seeking to put the issue of space back on the agenda of contentious politics, I suggest two promising angles for further research to grasp how local space can affect activism. First, while the bulk of the scholarship has so far focused on how social, rebel and terrorist movements mobilize at the national level and deploy strategies to target and capture the state, I heed the wider call in social science for a "subnational turn" which, applied to the field of contentious politics, would explore the mechanisms through which movements become embedded in certain spaces and how these spaces shape parts of their agenda and behavior, pushing them to target local power structures as much if not more than central state authority. Illuminating the great deal of locally oriented contentious

472   Conclusion

politics that takes place below the level of the state has a methodological implication: it calls for data disaggregated at the subnational level, and I highlight the relevance of the city and neighborhood scales especially.

Second, I suggest a partial shift from the current focus on short-term processes of how movements mobilize to the longer-term formation of dissent in some spaces. Even before they became hotbeds of activism for social, rebel and terrorist movements, some spaces had long been "strongholds of contention" characterized by a propensity for frequent collective action. Grasping the *longue durée* of contention as well as instances of historical continuities between successive movements in some places is crucial to understanding how the physical, symbolic and social dimension of space affects activism. This has a methodological implication for it requires more ethnographies and historical analysis. These angles can help comprehend how "the local" impacts the terms on which conflictual mobilization occurs.

Ideology in Social, Rebel and Terrorist Movements

Beyond space, Tawhid's case also sheds light on the role of ideology in contentious politics. At first glance the movement seemed homogeneously driven by ideology for, while its discourse drew on the most radical strands of Islamist thinking, it also implemented an "Islamic Emirate," fought its ideological enemies and got support from like-minded allies. But, when looking closer, ideology's effect was more nuanced. In fact, Tawhid's behavior featured too much variation in its discourse, use of violence or the nature of its alliances to be only driven by its beliefs. And it even transpired that, far from all committed Islamists, many members and some leaders had engaged in practices at odds with ideology. Tawhid's case therefore shows the need to go beyond the assumption of ideology's influence over movements and, instead, to grasp the mechanisms through which it affects their behavior.

The central premise upon which I analyze the role of ideology in Tawhid is that, far from being homogeneous, the movement featured a wide "spectrum of ideological commitment." Through this term I mean to conceptualize the heterogeneity of commitments which often characterizes even the most outwardly ideological movements. Tawhid was naturally composed of many committed Islamists, a handful of whom were even extremely inspired by ideology, but also of others who instrumentalized ideology and were less or not committed. Rather than assuming that ideology guided all of Tawhid's members and leaders, then, I disaggregated ideological commitment and explored the extent to which its main factions and individuals sincerely adhered to and were driven by the movement's declaratory ideology. This analytical point about internal variation in commitment is important for it allows me to explain the ebb and flow of ideology's effect on the movement through the push and pull between factions seeking to steer its behavior in a more or less ideological direction.

A key finding is that militant Islamism was often embraced for instrumental reasons. Members had a range of self-serving, individual motivations for doing so, for example using it as a vehicle to become empowered, a cover to pursue economic gain or a weapon to settle scores. But, more frequently, the mechanism of the instrumental embrace of militant Islamism by entire factions, neighborhoods and constituencies was the way it could act as a "protest ideology." That is, many members and even some leaders were not intrinsically attracted by Islamism's deeper set of beliefs but, rather, by the contentious potential associated with its symbols, vocabulary, practices and infrastructure. This "protest Islamism" arose after the growth of the "cultural momentum" of this ideology when, through the rise of religious practice, the gradual transformation of some social views and important events, such as Iran's 1979 Islamic Revolution and the 1979–82 Syrian jihad, Islamism was made more widely available as an option in society and replaced revolutionary leftism as the quintessential rebel ideology. In fact, many of those who back then embraced Islamism as a "protest ideology" to alternatively struggle against the Lebanese government, the Syrian regime and its local allies or the Tripolitan political and economic elite had often been revolutionary Marxists or Maoists months or years earlier. And, although some later became sincerely committed to Islamism and therefore moved along Tawhid's "spectrum of ideological commitment," for most this shift from one "protest ideology" to another remained instrumental – for instance, it rarely translated into an equivalent change in their underlying practices and concerns. As a result, they pulled Tawhid toward a behavior unrelated to, at times at odds with, ideology.

Crucially, highlighting that many Tawhid members and some leaders embraced Islamism instrumentally does not dismiss in any way ideology's impact on the movement. After all, there was still a sufficient backbone of more or less committed Islamists for ideology to significantly affect parts of its discourse and behavior. Yet, in this book I especially point to the role of highly committed cadres I call "ideological entrepreneurs." By this notion I mean those actors at the extreme of a movement's "spectrum of ideological commitment," who are not just ideologically driven but also mobilize their worldviews to mold the nature of activism around them, spreading their beliefs to the members

474   Conclusion

and lobbying the leaders to take ideologically inspired decisions. Their "ideological entrepreneurship" translates beliefs into action, making movement behavior more ideological. In Tawhid's case, although they were only dozens, they became very influential. This resulted from the fact that they fulfilled important functions. These included shaping the environment in which Tawhid operated to make society receptive to Islamism, recruiting and galvanizing committed Islamists, bolstering the movement's ideological credentials to outcompete rivals, leveraging backing from ideologically like-minded external allies or socializing and educating members into ideology, which helped turn the instrumental embrace of beliefs by many into firmer commitments and also cemented internal coherence. As a result of their growing influence on the leadership and membership in 1982–4, they pushed the movement's discourse, exercise of violence and foreign alliances in an ideological direction – through their "ideological entrepreneurship," ideology was affecting Tawhid. And, tellingly, as their influence waned in 1984 and 1985 as a result of a wave of violence which targeted them, the movement then engaged in a behavior less guided by, sometimes even at odds with, its Islamist ideology. It was then that the Tawhid–Iran alliance turned more transactional, and that it also got involved in "Islamo-gangsterism," or the spread of criminal practices which systematically prioritized economic gain over ideological consistency.

This book therefore answers the puzzle of the ebb and flow of ideology's effect on Tawhid through an organizational perspective which highlights the interactions and evolving balance of power between factions and individuals guided by Islamism to various extents. Although I point to mechanisms at the micro and macro levels, such as the way individuals are socialized and educated into ideology or the broader "cultural momentum" of an ideology in society, I do emphasize in particular the importance of meso-level, organizational mechanisms like the "ideological entrepreneurship" of a few cadres in how ideology matters. The push and pull toward or away from ideology between factions on the "spectrum of ideological commitment" helped explain the ebb and flow of ideology's effect on Tawhid.

Once again, not all social, rebel and terrorist movements feature the great degree of internal variation which characterized Tawhid. But, arguably, none are ideologically fully homogeneous and all have a more or less wide "spectrum of ideological commitment" – the composition and evolution of which may explain some of the variation in their behavior. Through this book, then, I have shown that ideology matters in movements through both instrumental and sincere embraces, which can evolve, and I have identified the micro, meso and macro mechanisms through which ideology can affect contentious politics at large.

I suggest two research tracks in order to further push the boundaries of knowledge on the topic and to illuminate the processes and mechanisms through which ideology matters. First, while ideology is often treated as fixed and static and viewed through the lenses of short-term mobilizations, I propose to study more systematically the nature of and factors behind the dynamics of ideological change undergone by certain individuals and movements. This naturally includes analyzing how people are socialized and educated into new ideologies and the ways in which their initially instrumental embrace can turn into firmer commitments. But commitments can also remain mostly instrumental, and as a result the continuities between shifts from one "protest ideology" to another must be investigated. Commitments can also erode, in which case the factors behind this and its effects have to be studied too.

Second, I call for more analysis of the organizational dynamics of ideology – that is, to account for ideology's role inside and its effect upon social, rebel and terrorist movements. This implies identifying the institutions and activities in such movements which aim at socializing and educating their membership into ideology and strengthening commitment, before then investigating the extent to which they succeed and the other functions this fulfills. It also means exploring intra and inframovement dynamics and, in particular, analyzing the internal politics of how and why some factions or individuals seek to steer the movement in an ideologically driven direction, who pushes back against them and how, ultimately, these internal interactions between factions may contribute to shaping the movement's behavior. This would help break with the dominant view of ideology as a disembodied variable and, instead, locate beliefs in human agency, contingencies and a relational context. These two research tracks have methodological implications, for much more effort should be invested in disaggregating ideological commitment in movements to make sense of variation in their discourse, behavior and practices across time and space and to process-trace the influence of certain factions in particular which are bent on maximizing ideological commitment. Doing so will help to shed light on the role of ideology in social, rebel and terrorist movements.

Bibliography of Essential Sources

Key Primary Sources

Interviews with Prominent Actors

Note that due to sensitivity and the wish of some interviewees, some names do not appear.

Interviews with Current and Former Tawhid Officials
Bilal Sha'aban, Hashem Minqara, Kan'an Naji, Ibrahim Saleh, Ghassan Ghoshe, Mazen Mohammed, Abu Meriam Khassouq, Amer Arnaout, Abu Shawqi, Bilal Matar, Aziz Allush, Abu Zghayar, Fahd Issa, Samir Hassan, Abu Jandah, Jamil R'ad, Ali Agha, Abed Merkabawi, Abu Othman, Ibrahim Antar, Nasser Murad, Salem al-Rafe'i, Amir R'ad, Husam Sbat, Salem al-Rafe'i, Mohammed Imam, Hashim Yaghmur, Ahmed Harrouq, Anistaz Kouchari, Abu Bashir, Khaled al-Kurdi, Abu Riad, Bilal Diqmaq, Abu Hozeifa.

Interviews with Non-Tawhid Islamists
Mohammed Ali Dannawi, Abdallah Babetti, Fayez Iyali, Zuheir Obeidi, Ibrahim al-Masri, Azzam al-Ayubi, Hani Fahes, Maher Hammud, Bilal Hidara, Abdel Razzaq Qarhani, Iheb Naf'a, Khaled Abdelqader, Rif'at Miqati, Mohammed Ibrahim, Safwan Z'ubi, Nabil Rahim.

Interviews with Tawhid Enemies
Abdel Majid al-Rifa'i, Mahmud Shehade, Abdel Qader Alameddine, Bader Wannous, Rashid Jemali, Bassam al-Dei, Jamil Safiye, Iqbal Saba, Taha Sabunji, Bashir Mawas, Kheder Kheder, Adib Na'ame, Gabi Sur'ur, Abu Yasser, Ahmad al-Ayyoubi, Samir Khadem, Abu Ali Shawq, General Jellul.

Interviews with Tawhid Allies Close to Palestinian and Iranian Intelligence
Anis Naqqash, Abu Marwan, Selim Lababidi, Hani Fahes, Abu Ta'an, Mohammed Salim, Maher Hammud.

Bibliography of Essential Sources 477

Interviews with Close Observers

Nahla Chahal, Ahmed al-Amin, Hassan Monla, Moustafa Hajar, Elias Khlat, Maha Kayal, Faruq Uweida, Fathi el-Yafi, Hajj Nikoula, Mayez Adhami, Gabi Sur'ur, Jean Touma, Georges Droubi, Père Sarrouj, Jean Ratel, Jean Jabbour, Hares al-Sleiman, Talal Khawja, Riad al-Dada, Leila Bissar, Umar Arish, Abu Daoud.

Video Archives

Harb Trablus 1985 [*The war of Tripoli in 1985*] (documentary produced by the Islamic Group, copy given to the author, 2013).
Undated videos of sermons by Khalil Akkawi in a mosque of Bab al-Tebbaneh.
Undated videos of sermons by Tawhid clerics in mosques of Tripoli.
Undated videos of Tawhid demonstrations during the Eid religious holiday.

Miscellaneous

Al-khutut al-asasia li-muntalaqat wa mabade wa ahdaf Harakat al-Tawhid al-Islami [*The fundamental premises, principles and objectives of the Islamic Unification Movement*] (copy given to the author, undated).
"Al-qiyada al-islamiya fi Trablus" ["The Islamic leadership in Tripoli"], *Al-Taqwa* (Vol. 20, April 1985).
Lebanon: arbitrary arrests, "disappearances" and extra-judicial killings by Syrian troops and Syrian-backed forces in Tripoli (Beirut: report published by Amnesty International, February, 1987).

Institutional Records

UK Embassy in Beirut records (1944–80).
US Central Intelligence Agency records (1976–87).
US Embassy in Beirut records (1973–86).

Newspaper Archives

Al-Incha (1979–88).
Al-Safir (1982–6).
Al-Tamaddon (1974–86 and 2002–18).
Al-Taqwa (1985).
Al-Tawhid (1984–6).
L'Orient Le Jour (1971–86).
Sawt al-Shabiba al-Wataniya (1979–81).

478   Bibliography of Essential Sources

Key Secondary Sources

In Arabic

Abi Samra, Mohammed. *Trablus: Sehat Allah wa mina al-hadatha [Tripoli: Allah Square and port of modernity]* (Beirut: Dar al-Saqi, 2011).

Imad, Abdel Ghani. *Islamiyu Lubnan: al-wahda wa al-ekhtilaf 'ala 'arad al-mustahil [Islamists of Lebanon: unity and divergence in the impossible land]* (Beirut: Dar al-Saqi, 1998).

Mujtam'a Trablus fi zaman al-tahawulat al-'othmaniya [The society of Tripoli at the time of the Ottoman transformations] (Tripoli: Dar al-Insha', 1999).

Al-harakat al-Islamiya fi Lubnan: al-din wa al-siyasa fi mujtam'a mutanawe'a [The Islamist movements in Lebanon: religion and politics in a diverse society] (Beirut: Dar al-Talia, 2006).

Itani, Amal, Ali, Abdel Qadir and Manna, Mu'in. *Al-Jama'a al-Islamiya fi Lubnan mundhu al-nash'a hatta 1975 [The Islamic Group in Lebanon from the inception to 1975]* (Beirut: Markaz al-Zeytuna, 2009).

Itani, Fida'. *Al-jihadiyun fi Lubnan: min Quwwat al-Fajr ila Fatah al-Islam [The Jihadis in Lebanon: from Quwwat al-Fajr to Fatah al-Islam]* (Beirut: Dar al-Saqi, 2008).

Kayal, Maha. *Al-mai fi al-mujtam'a [Water in Society]* (Beirut: Mukhtarat, 2007).

Kayal, Maha and Atiya, Atef. *Trablus min al-dahkal [Tripoli from the inside]* (Beirut: Dar al-Mokhtarat, 2004).

Lagha, Ali. *Fathi Yakan: ra'ed al-haraka al-islamiya al mu'asira fi Lubnan [Fathi Yakan: pioneer of the Islamic movement in Lebanon]* (Beirut: Mu'assassat al-Risala, 1994).

N'ame, Adib. "Al-amen fi Trablus, 1980–1985" ["The security in Tripoli, 1980–1985"], *Nada' al-Shamal* (November 1985).

Al-Faqr fi madinat Trablus [Poverty in the city of Tripoli] (Beirut: United Nations, 2014).

Salem, Abdel Aziz. *Trablus al-Sham fi al-tarikh al-Islami [Tripoli of Syria in Islamic history]* (Alexandria: Dar al-Ma'aref, 1967).

Tadmori, Omar. *Tarikh wa athar masajed wa madares Trablus fi asar al-Mamalek [History and legacy of the mosques and the schools of Tripoli during Mamluk times]* (Tripoli: Dar al-Bilad, 1974).

Tarikh Trablus al-siessi wa al-hadari 'aber al-'asur [The political and cultural history of Tripoli through the ages] (Tripoli: Dar al-Bilad, 1978), Tomes 1, 2 and 3.

Tlass, Mustafa. *The mirror of my life [Mirat Hayati]* (Vol. 4) chapter 87 (Damascus: Dar Tlass, 2004).

Yakan, Fathi. *Al-mas'ala al-lubnaniya min manzur islami [The Lebanese question through an Islamic perspective]* (Beirut: al-Mu'assassa al-Islamiya, 1979).

Zein, Samih. *Tarikh Trablus qadiman wa hadathan [Recent and ancient history of Tripoli]* (Beirut: Dar al-Andalus, 1969).

Ziadeh, Khaled. *Al-sura al-taqlidiya li al-mujtam'a al-madani: qira' manhajiya fi sijallat mahkamat Trablus al-shara'iya [The traditional picture of civil society: methodological reading of the records of the Islamic tribunal of Tripoli]* (Tripoli: Lebanese University Press, 1983).

Yum al-Jum'a, yum al-ahad [Friday is Sunday] (Beirut: Dar al-Nahar, 1996).

In English

Atiyah, Najla Wadih. *The attitude of the Lebanese Sunnis towards the state of Lebanon* (London: University of London, unpublished PhD thesis, 1973).

Gade, Tine. *The crisis of the political-religious field in Tripoli, Lebanon (1967–2011)* (Paris: Institut d'Etudes Politiques Sciences Po Paris, unpublished PhD thesis, 2015).

"Sunni Islamists in Tripoli and the Asad regime; 1966–2014" *Syria Studies* (Vol. 7, No. 2, 2015).

Urban Sunnism and the Sunni crisis: Tripoli 1920–2020 (forthcoming monograph).

Gulick, John. "Past and present in local histories of the Ottoman period from Syria and Lebanon" *Middle Eastern Studies* (Vol. 35, No. 1, 1999).

Tripoli: a modern Arab city (Cambridge, MA: Harvard University Press, 1967).

Habibis, Daphne. *A comparative study of the workings of a branch of the Naqshbandi Sufi order in Lebanon and the UK* (London: London School of Economics and Political Science, unpublished PhD thesis, 1985).

"Millenarianism and Mahdism in Lebanon" *European Journal of Sociology* (Vol. 30, No. 2, 1989).

Ismail, Salwa. *Rethinking Islamist politics: culture, the state and Islamism* (London: I.B.Tauris, 2003).

Lawson, Fred. "Syria's intervention in the Lebanese civil war, 1976: a domestic conflict explanation" *International Organization* (Vol. 38, No. 3, 1984).

Lefèvre, Raphaël. *Ashes of Hama: the Muslim Brotherhood in Syria* (London: Oxford University Press and Hurst, 2013).

Parsons, Laila. *The Commander: Fawzi al-Qawuqji and the fight for Arab independence, 1914–1948* (New York: Hill and Wang, 2016).

Rabil, Robert. "Fathi Yakan, the pioneer of Islamic activism in Lebanon" *Levantine Review* (Vol. 2, No. 1, 2013).

Salafism in Lebanon, from apoliticism to transnational jihadism (Washington, DC: Georgetown University Press, 2014).

Reilly, James. *The Ottoman cities of Lebanon: historical legacy and identity in the Middle East* (London: I.B.Tauris, 2016).

Richard Yousaf, Timothy. *The Muslim Brotherhood in Lebanon (al-Jama'a al-Islamiya), 1948–2000* (Beirut: American University of Beirut, unpublished MPhil thesis, 2010).

Sayigh, Yezid. *Armed struggle and the search for a Palestinian state: the Palestinian national movement, 1949–1993* (Oxford: Oxford University Press, 1997).

Sing, Manfred. "Brothers in arms: how Palestinian Maoists turned Jihadists" *Die Welt des Islams* (Vol. 51, 2011).

Sluglett, Peter and Weber, Stefan (eds.), *Syria and Bilad al-Sham under Ottoman rule* (Leiden: Brill, 2010).

Weismann, Itzchak. *The Naqshbandiyya: orthodoxy and activism in a worldwide Sufi tradition* (London: Routledge, 2007).

480   Bibliography of Essential Sources

In French

Abdel Nour, Antoine. *Introduction à l'histoire urbaine de la Syrie Ottomane (16eme-18eme siècle)* (Beirut: Publication de l'Université Libanaise, 1982).

Abs, Jalal. *Etude et propositions pour une utilisation rationnelle de l'espace à Tripoli-Liban* (Paris: Université Paris VII, unpublished PhD thesis, 1981).

Al-Soufi Richard, Joumana. *Lutte populaire armée: de la désobéissance civile au combat pour Dieu* (Paris: University de La Sorbonne Nouvelle, unpublished PhD thesis, 1984).

"Le vieux Tripoli dans ses structures actuelles" *Annales de Géographie* (Vol. 2, 1981).

Bizri, Dalal. *Introduction à l'étude des mouvements islamistes sunnites au Liban* (Paris: Ecole des Hautes Etudes en Sciences Sociales, unpublished PhD thesis, 1984).

"Le mouvement Ibad al-Rahman et ses prolongements à Tripoli," chapter 4 in Olivier Carré and Paul Dumont (eds.), *Radicalismes Islamiques Tome 1: Iran Liban Turquie* (Paris, L'Harmattan, 1985).

Dewailly, Bruno. *Pouvoir et production urbaine à Tripoli al-Fayha (Liban)* (Tours: Université Francois Rabelais de Tours, unpublished PhD thesis, 2015).

"L'espace public à travers le prisme du pouvoir: quelques réflexions à partir du cas tripolitain (Liban)" *Geocarrefour* (Vol. 77, No. 33, 2002).

Dot Pouillard, Nicolas. "De Pekin à Teheran en regardant vers Jerusalem: La singulière conversion à l'islamisme des 'Maos du Fatah'" *Cahiers de l'Institut Religioscope* (No. 2, December 2008).

Douayhi, Chawqi. "Tripoli et Zgharta, deux villes en quête d'un éspace commun," chapter 3 in Eric Huybrechts and Chawqi Douayhi (eds.), *Reconstruction et réconciliation au Liban* (Beirut: Presses de l'Ifpo, 1999).

Gade, Tine. "Conflit en Syrie et dynamiques de guerre civile à Tripoli, Liban" *Maghreb-Machrek* (Vol. 218, No. 4, 2013).

Heloui, Khodr. *La rue des églises* (Paris: L'Harmattan, 2014).

Maha, Kayal. *Le système socio-vestimentaire à Tripoli (Liban) entre 1885 et 1985* (Neuchâtel: Université de Neuchâtel, unpublished PhD thesis, 1989).

Mercadier, Sylvain. *Logiques de la contestation et symbolique spatiale: l'exemple de la place Abdel el Hamid Karameh à Tripoli (Liban)* (Beirut: Université Saint Joseph, unpublished Master's thesis, 2015);.

Picaudou, Nadine. "Mutations socio-économiques du vieux Tripoli" *Annales de Géographie* (Vol. 1, 1981).

Ploteau, Loïc. *Les populations originaires du Haut-Dinniyé à Tripoli (Liban): les dynamiques de ségrégation de citadinisation* (Tours: Université de Tours, unpublished MPhil thesis, 1997).

Rajab, Mousbah. *Le vieux Tripoli (Liban), un espace historique en voie de mutation* (Paris: Université de Panthéon La Sorbonne, unpublished PhD thesis, 1993).

Rougier, Bernard. *L'Oumma en fragments: contrôler le sunnisme au Liban* (Paris: Presses Universitaires de France, 2015).

Seurat, Michel. "Le quartier de Bab Tebbane à Tripoli (Liban), étude d'une assabiya urbaine," chapter 3 in Zakaria, Mona (ed.), *Mouvements communautaires et espaces urbains au Machreq* (Beirut: Presses de l'Ifpo, 1985).

Index

9 February Movement 453–7, 458–9, 461, 463
24 October Movement 67, 72, 90, 95, 251, 253, 261, 275, 297, 310, 322–5, 329, 331, 342

Akkar 61, 90, 93, 115, 240, 270, 277, 292, 349
Akkawi, Ali 89, 96–105, 117
Akkawi, Khalil 89, 105–53, 203, 270, 342, 379, 398, 417, 426, 445, 449–57, 461–6
Aleppo 14, 42, 44–9, 74, 132, 167, 346, 372, 457
Arab Democratic Party 135, 151, 162, 190, 202, 220, 419, 135, 151, 190, 202, 220, 419
Arafat, Yasser 4, 340–1, 377–8, 380–9, 455
Assad, Hafez 4, 68–71, 119–23, 134, 192–3, 220, 290, 341, 367–72, 375, 378, 386–92, 415, 417–28, 437, 441, 446–7, 455
Assad, Rif'at 120, 123, 127, 369, 371, 427
Aswad, Mahmud 121

Daye, Ashir 253, 273, 446
defense brigades 123, 126–8, 191

education office 27, 311–21
Eid, Ali 115–29, 134–6, 141, 143, 145, 147, 151–3, 190–2, 202, 356, 419, 462
Eid, Mohsen 121, 123, 128

Farsi, Jalaleddine 176, 178, 204, 392–3
Fakhr al-Din, Tareq 450, 461–2
Fatah 17, 29, 30, 36, 68, 110–15, 117, 120–7, 141, 148, 162, 171, 173–6, 193, 196, 201, 326, 340, 345–6, 366–8, 371, 375–91, 393–4, 402, 404, 406, 410, 412, 413, 419, 453, 455–6, 464

Fighting Vanguard 132, 162, 165, 188–9, 370, 372–4, 388
Franjieh, Sleiman 83, 325, 356

Gemayel, Bashir 195
Gemayel, Amine 215–16, 298, 316, 324, 441
gathering of muslim scholars 409–10

Hama 3, 14, 20, 34, 45, 51, 64, 68, 77, 79–80, 84, 132, 152, 157, 166–8, 187–91, 193–4, 204, 213, 367–9, 372–5, 389, 417, 431, 457
Hammud, Maher 401, 403, 423, 437
Haqqani, Nazim 167, 169–70
Hawwa, Sa'id 207–14, 228, 277, 314, 370, 388
Hezbollah 20, 74, 171, 177, 195, 197, 222–5, 230, 234, 366, 390, 394–405, 407–10, 437
Holy Warriors 77, 160, 162, 218
Homs 3, 42–5, 49–51, 57, 64, 68, 76, 79–80, 132, 167, 189, 346, 367–8, 372–5, 389

Imara, Abu 169, 200, 270, 312, 387
Iraqi Baath Party 72, 90, 95, 109, 297, 302, 310, 322–9, 331, 342, 371, 395, 464
Iraqi Petroleum Company 49, 51, 62, 241
Islamic Group 74, 76–80, 157–66, 169, 183–6, 192–3, 198–9, 205, 209–11, 213–14, 217–18, 248, 311, 313, 331, 386, 387, 401, 435
Islamic Liberation Organization 437–8, 447

Jemali, Rashid 289, 291–2, 446

Kana'an, Ghazi 356, 429, 450, 458
Karame, Abdel-Hamid 3, 53, 55, 58, 238, 247–8, 269, 273, 294–6, 299, 301–4, 306, 317, 319, 470

482   Index

Karame, Rashid 58–9, 63, 159, 192, 195, 247, 273, 280, 294–9, 302, 304, 316–17, 337–8, 464
Khaddam, Abdel-Halim 191, 420
Khamene'i, Ali 220, 409, 420
Khomeini, Ruhollah 4, 175–6
Kouchari, Anistaz 27, 355–7, 360
Kurdi, Fu'ad 150, 178, 200, 270, 312, 398–400, 404, 407

Lebanese Communist Party 72, 109, 329, 332, 337, 339–40, 378, 429

Minqara, Hashem 27, 169–70, 269, 279–81, 285, 288, 291–2, 330, 332–5, 337, 339–42, 347–8, 351, 353, 355–60, 373, 375, 379, 406, 424–6, 447, 449, 453, 455
Moscow 340, 342, 382
Movement of the Alawi Youth 118, 120–7, 134
Movement of Arab Lebanon 27, 34, 156, 174–8, 180–2, 187, 192–4, 197, 204–5, 379, 402
Movement/State of the Outlaws 238, 251, 253–62, 267, 272, 275
Muqaddem, Faruq 66–8, 72, 297, 323–4, 329
Muqaddem, Rashid 296, 303
Murad, Esmat 173–82, 270, 379, 392, 394, 398–400, 402, 404–7

Naqshbandiya 157, 166–70
Nasser, Jamal Abdel 56, 67, 290
Naji, Kana'an 165, 170, 239, 270, 279, 332, 379, 406, 426, 447, 453, 455

Organization of the Communist Action 63, 72, 297, 302, 310, 324, 331, 343
Organization of Anger 89, 99–103, 106, 108–9, 113, 117, 131, 251, 253, 275

Palestine Liberation Organization 66–73, 111, 114, 171, 342, 380, 400, 456
popular committees 89, 108–13, 117, 131, 140–1, 454
popular resistance 27, 34, 88–90, 111–14, 120–4, 127, 129–37, 140–56, 162, 164, 170–1, 177, 187, 189–93, 197, 204, 275, 454, 462

Qabaday 96–9, 101–12, 114–15, 117–22, 124, 137–8, 140–1, 144–8, 150, 153–4, 255, 275, 281, 444–5, 449–54, 461

Qaddur, Ahmed 255, 257, 260–1
Qawuqji, Fawzi 65–6, 380
Qutb, Sayid 158, 183, 207, 209–14, 228, 277, 314

Rida, Rashid 75, 167
Rifa'i, Azzam 373–5
Rifa'i, Abdel Majid 63–4, 68, 72, 195, 297, 323–4, 464
Russia 49, 224, 336, 340, 382, 411

Sha'aban, Sa'id 156–7, 182–7, 193–4, 197, 200–3, 213, 216–17, 270, 272, 276–7, 278–80, 293–4, 298, 300, 312, 319–20, 326–7, 329, 332, 334–5, 340, 348, 361, 379, 385, 391, 405–6, 408, 410, 418, 420–3, 426, 436, 438, 445, 447, 456
Sha'ar, Mohammed 345, 356, 458
Shafiq, Munir 173, 175
Sidon 32, 42, 48, 53, 56–7, 62, 64, 70, 74, 78–9, 81, 203, 206, 230, 232, 253, 376–7, 401, 403, 437, 452
Soldiers of God 27, 34, 151, 153, 156, 158, 161–3, 165–6, 170, 187, 189, 191–3, 197–8, 213, 248, 279, 304, 331, 387–8
Suri, Abu Yasser 374
student brigade 171–6, 193, 402
Syrian Baath Party 68, 71–2, 119, 125, 189
Syrian Muslim Brotherhood 14, 76, 79–80, 132, 162–3, 166, 188, 210, 369–70, 374, 388, 390–1
Syrian Social Nationalist Party 63, 71, 190, 343, 429

Tartus 121, 123, 346, 353
Tehran 131, 176, 178, 183, 194, 219, 326–7, 366–7, 371, 375, 391–8, 401–9, 412–13, 418, 438–9
Tyre 42, 62, 64
Ta'an, Abu 386–90, 406, 410
Tripolitan Resistance 461

Worshippers of the Merciful 76–8, 137, 149, 168, 183

Yakan, Fathi 80, 158–60, 163, 184–6, 300

Zgharta 83, 114, 160, 162, 356

CPSIA information can be obtained
at www.ICGtesting.com
Printed in the USA
LVHW011609030821
694401LV00006B/374